NEW YORK UNIVERSITY SERIES IN SELECTED ECONOMIC WRITINGS

M. Ishaq Nadiri
Chairman, Department of Economics
and
Jay Gould Professor of Economics
New York University

•

General Editor

BOOKS IN THE SERIES

Selected Economic Writings
of William J. Baumol
Edited by Elizabeth E. Bailey

•

Selected Economic Writings
of Fritz Machlup
Edited by George Bitros

•

Selected Economic Writings
of Oskar Morgenstern
Edited by Andrew Schotter

•

**The publication of this work has been aided by a grant from the
Andrew W. Mellon Foundation**

Selected Economic Writings
of
Fritz Machlup

Edited by
George Bitros

Assistant Professor
of Economics
New York University

M. Ishaq Nadiri
General Editor

New York•New York University Press•1976

Acknowledgments

Grateful acknowledgment is made to the following for permission to use essays which appeared in their publication:

HB171
.M265

American Economic Review

Banca Nazionale del Lavoro Quarterly Review

Copenhagen Nationaløkonomisk Forening

Giornale degli Economisti

Journal of Political Economy

Quarterly Journal of Economics

Review of Economics and Statistics

Review of Economic Studies

Routledge & Kegan Paul Publishers

St. Martins Press

Southern Economic Journal

Weidenfeld and Nicolson Publishers

Weltwirtschaftliches Archiv

GENERAL EDITOR'S PREFACE

Our publication of the selected scientific writings of several eminent economists is not only a gesture of appreciation for their contribution to economic theory and policy but also a convenient means to bring their important contributions to the attention of the readers. This volume is one of three volumes pertaining to the works of Professor William J. Baumol, Fritz Machlup and Oskar Morgenstern. They bring together contributions in a wide area of econmic theory and policy. These three prolific authors have dealt with an extremely broad range of topics including fundamental methodological issues, the history of economic theory, the theory of demand, utility theory, theory of games, business decision process and pricing rules, externalities, economic dynamics, theories of inflation, unbalanced growth, monetary theory, theory of international trade and finance, sources of economic growth and economics of knowledge, mathematical and nonlinear programming and economic statistics. Each of the articles contributes to the literature and many of them were controversial at the time of their appearance. Though their styles and the problems with which they concern themselves differ considerably, they share an interest in rigorous economic theory, in the process of change, in the history of doctrine. However, the authors employ different techniques in building their models and in analyzing issues of economic policy; and in the process contribute new and important technical insights.

The editors of these volumes are not off the mark in their emphasis on the important contributions that these authors have made to economic science. They have done a very real service for the profession in providing an overview of the writings of these three distinguished authors in a one volume format.

M. Ishaq Nadiri
Jay Gould Professor of Economics
New York University

PREFACE

Fritz Machlup published his first book back in 1925. In the fifty years which have elapsed since then he has enriched the literature of the social sciences in general, and economics in particular, with an extraordinary amount of contributions. As the appended bibliography reveals, he has authored twenty-four books, co-authored another eleven, and placed in leading professional journals well over one hundred articles.[1] While students in different areas of specialization may know of him as a microeconomic theorist, a monetary economist, a specialist in international finance, an author on industrial organization, a controversial writer on issues of education at all levels, a sociologist of knowledge, a philosopher of science, a libertarian political scientist, and a champion of a variety of causes, only few will be aware of the extent and value of his scholarly endeavors in all these capacities. The primary objective here is then to present "Fritz Machlup, the Generalist."

At the same time, this anthology purports to elucidate what I feel are three of the most fundamental characteristics of Machlup's work. The first characteristic is his taxonomic method of analysis. Paper after paper, he will take the problem under consideration, break it down into its constituent parts with masterful analytic skill, and then use the concepts so derived to draw conclusions by systematically tracing out the interrelationships. His is a method where mathematics appears to be unnecessary for theoretical analysis and where, unlike mathematical model building, even the small but relevant forces of influence are given proper weight. Associated with this analytical approach is a relentless pursuit for clarity of concepts and consistency in their use, which is the second characteristic of his work. It is enjoyable to see him reveal the tricks that words can play on people and to observe his inimitable way of illuminating obscurities of thought caused by sloppy reasoning or implicit theorizing. Last, but not least, there is his pathos for individual liberties. When he is writing as an economist this pathos turns into the most eloquent defense of classical economics, and when he performs as a political scientist his appreciation of individual freedoms becomes a plea for reason. If the standards of distinction for a scholar in the social sciences are that he have a definite point of view and defend it successfully, I believe Machlup's work meets both. In an environment of integrals, complex theorems, and highly sophisticated econometric techniques, he has managed to adhere to the principles of the Austrian School and the tradition of Menger, Wieser and Böhm-Bawerk, in using, where quantitative arguments are called for, simple, numerical illustrations.

To capture the element of catholicity in Machlup's outlook, I have structured this collection of his writings so as to include material from four major areas of his work. Part I is devoted to contributions relating to the methodology of economics and the social sciences in general. Parts II to IV concentrate on his papers in economics, emphasizing specifically the fields of microeconomics, macroeconomics, and the economics of international trade and finance. His preoccupation with education and the production and distribution of knowledge finds expression in the papers presented in Part V; and finally, Part VI testifies to his interests in economic and political philosophy.

Given the range of choices for every spot of the available space, selecting the pieces to be included was not an easy task. As an indication of the difficulties I faced it suffices to mention that the essays in methodology had to be selected out of a total of twenty-three papers, and the ones in international trade and finance had to be drawn from a much larger population. In order to converge to the particular choices made for each part, some elimination rules had to be adopted. One such rule was not to include materials from his books,[2] the rationale for this being that, whenever Machlup would conceive of several related ideas and expound them in a book, in most instances the original thoughts had somehow found their way into the professional journals. Another rule was to focus on articles that appeared in major periodicals and, from among these, to consider only the ones that have received wide attention. Finally, from that semi-final pool, I chose the papers which I considered to be the most important.

In what follows, I do not intend to provide summaries of each and every selection. With as many as twenty essays included in this volume, to summarize them all would make this introduction too long. Instead, I shall focus only on the issues where Machlup has built major defenses for the classical approach to economic theorizing and I want to offer a few comments on the avenues to new knowledge which he has himself originated.

From time to time, and particularly after the introduction of new tools of analysis and testing, there arise considerable hopes among economists that a day may come at last when explanation (description, prediction) in empirical economics will be as precise or accurate as it is in, say, physics, astronomy, and applied mathematics. Yet for those who, like Machlup, have been digging deep into the methodological foundations of our discipline, such a prospect looks far removed. The first fundamental reason for this is succinctly stated in the opening essay "If Matter Could Talk." Since human actors can form and communicate constructs and theories of their own actions, Machlup suggests, the number of possible models the social investigator has to choose from in any given situation is much larger than the number of models which a natural scientist (whose subject of study is silent) faces in the ordinary course of his inquiries. As a result, the most helpful model in each case may be known less accurately in the social than in the natural sciences.

Aside from this, however, an additional source of imprecision is associated with the process of theory verification. Specifically, as argued in the essays, "Operational Concepts and Mental Constructs in Model and Theory Formation" and "The Problem of Verification in Economics," empirical testing presupposes that the investigator possesses operational counterparts for the pure constructs involved in the consequences which he deduces from his analytical apparatus. But in sciences like economics this requirement is not always met, so that the confidence in most propositions of economic theory is lower than physicists, astronomers, or applied mathematicians would consider respectable. While economists and other social scientists may expect to succeed in sharpening the accuracy of their methods over time, these three of Machlup's papers remind them of what in a mathematical context would be an impossibility theorem concerning the convergence of explanation in the social sciences to the limit of precision set by natural sciences. Part I closes with the essay "The Universal Bogey," where a strong case is made for the hypothetical nature of the Economic Man and the recognition of maximizing (utility or profit) as the fundamental principle of theoretical economics.

Leaving Machlup the ''methodologist'' and turning to Machlup the ''economic theorist'', readers will find in Part II some of his most insightful articles in microeconomics. Almost forty years before P. A. Diamond and D. McFadden showed that it is impossible to identify the elasticity of technical substitution and the form of technological change, Machlup was writing in his ''The Commonsense of the Elasticity of Substitution,'' that

> . . . in so far as the proportions of factors are different in different lines of production, indirect substitution [i.e., substitution through shifts in consumers' demand for various products] will occur together with direct (technical) substitution.

The issue was that in the economy as a whole the two kinds of substitution work simultaneously, and their empirical separation becomes impossible. But this is perhaps only a minor example of his inventive and interpretative skills.

Where we find the best of this skill is no doubt in his ''Marginal Analysis and Empirical Research.'' Challenged by the critics of ''conventional theory,'' the task he cuts for himself in this piece is to clarify what marginal theory means and state the principles which should guide its testing. To accomplish this task, Machlup starts off with the three basic premises that (a) economic theory, static as well as dynamic, is essentially a theory of adjustment to change, (b) the concept of equilibrium is a tool in this theory of change, and (c) the marginal calculus is its dominating principle. On the basis of these postulates and the realization that the relevant magnitudes involved—revenue, cost, profit—are subjective rather than objective, he proceeds to propose that what marginal analysis intends to do is to explain the effects which certain changes in conditions may have upon the actions of the imaginary decision-maker, called the firm. From this, finally, it is inferred that empirical tests should not aim at refuting the broad and formal principles of the theory, but rather concentrate on more narrowly defined hypotheses and be supplemented with a certain degree of familiarity with the technological and institutional peculiarities of the fields or cases on which the tests are undertaken. Thus, by restricting ingeniously the explanatory ambitions of marginal theory, Machlup is able to retain its most useful features and, at the same time, save it logically from the empiricists' attacks.

This is not all, however. In the course of reformulating marginal theory, Machlup opens up a whole new horizon for research in the theory of the firm. ''Producing larger production volumes, paying higher wage rates, or charging lower product prices than would be compatible with a maximum of money profits,'' he writes in this paper, ''may involve for the business man a gain in social prestige or a certain measure of inner satisfaction.'' And on the next page he will add:

> Maximization of salaries and bonuses of professional managers may constitute a standard of business conduct different from that implied in the customary marginal analysis of the firm. The extent to which the two standards would result in sharply different action under otherwise similar conditions in another open question for investigation.

Soon after these leads, we know to-day, there began to appear new theories of the firm based on principles other than profit maximization, most of which, however, employed marginal calculus as a means of obtaining a maximum. Thus, on revisiting the controversy twenty years later in the "Theories of the Firm: Marginal, Behavioral, Managerial," Machlup is able to conclude that marginalism, either in its conventional form or in its reincarnation as managerialism, is still alive and thriving.

Before I turn to the next focal area, a comment is in order relating to Part III on macroeconomics. In the appended bibliography Machlup appears to have shown only a minor interest in aggregative analyses. The lack of emphasis in this respect, I think, is not accidental. Most probably it springs from a methodological conviction, reflected in many of his works, that the foundation of all economics is microeconomic. Thus, the three papers included in Part III, which, by the way, constitute highly original contributions to dynamic analysis, may be viewed as attempts at linking certain macro-variables to the reactions of supply and demand at the micro-level rather than as exercises in pure aggregative economics.

Even if Machlup had not contributed to economic micro- and macro-analysis, he would still be considered a frontrunner of the economics profession. The influence which his writings on international trade and finance, his congressional testimonies on policy issues in this area, and his leadership in international conferences on international monetary reform, have exercised over the years, is recognized in many quarters. His scholarly writings in the area are represented in this volume by the four essays of Part IV.

In the article, "Relative Prices and Aggregate Spending in the Analysis of Devaluation," we see another example of how Machlup's insistence on exhaustive taxonomy leads him to reveal omissions and errors in other writers' reasoning. The first task undertaken by Machlup this time is to retrace Alexander's steps of analysis in an effort to identify the various effects of devaluation Alexander had recognized and to determine the directions of influence he assigned to them. Once this is accomplished, it is easily shown that the "aggregate spending" or "Keynesian" approach to the impact of devaluation, without due attention to the role of relative prices, is bound to commit several serious errors. Specifically, Alexander's analysis is found (a) to have failed to account for the fact that the transfer of resources to different uses induced by devaluation may change real national income, (b) to have attempted to deduce causal relationships from a definitional equation, and (c) to have omitted to place emphasis on certain facts which cannot be neglected without adverse repercussions on policy decisions. To avoid these analytical flaws, Machlup suggests, it is necessary that the "aggregate spending" analysis be properly supplemented by the "supply-and-demand" (or Marshallian) approach to the effects of devaluation. Thus, although challenged as inappropriate, the conventional way of thinking about the problem turns out to be complementary to Alexander's otherwise valuable contribution.

The other three selections in Part IV deal with matters relating to the central problem of international finance, i.e., the need for, and the generation processes of, monetary reserves. Among others, these papers have made three fundamental contributions. The first one has been to show that the theories which presume there is a need for a specific quantity of monetary reserves in the world are empirically unfounded. Rather, "The Need for Monetary Reserves" argues, needed is an annual increase in monetary reserves, and this not for economic or other structural reasons but for the sake of averting the imposition of restrictions by the countries in deficit. The second contribution has been the demonstration, in "The Cloakroom Rule of International Reserve Creation and Resources Transfer," that an international organization properly empowered could create reserves without implications for its liquidity and ability to pay. At the present, it is probably no exaggeration to say that Machlup's arguments in this and the previous article must have acted like catalysts in overcoming the hesitations of financial experts, because since 1970 the International Monetary Fund has been authorized to create monetary reserves in the form of Special Drawing Rights (SDR). The third contribution is the very incisive analysis Machlup offered, in "Euro-Dollar Creation: A Mystery Story," of the issues surrounding the creation of dollar deposits by European banks. Going through what appears to be an exhaustive enumeration of possible transactions, Machlup distinguishes between the transactions that generate primary deposits (and thus reserves) and those that are due to autonomous decisions of European banks to acquire earning assets, which give rise to derivative deposits (and thus new money). Then, drawing on general monetary theory, he concludes that at times the endogenous creation of dollars by European banks must have been quite significant.

Turning to the economics of knowledge and technological change, Chapter 18 presents one of Machlup's best-known essays. At the time of its appearance, "The Supply of Inventors and Inventions" was, and probably still is, the most systematic effort on record to formulate an analytical framework for explaining the flow of technical inventions. Starting from the presumption that there is a quantitative relationship between the input of inventive labor and the output of inventions, the analysis showed, among other things, that (a) as the total amount of inventive labor increases, new inventions may be produced under diminishing or even constant returns, and (b) the supply of inventive labor is subject to increasing supply prices. Thus, in essence, the paper challenged the traditional approach to looking at the flow of inventions like manna falling from heaven and proposed instead that inventive activity be viewed as a classical production process. This view has gained now wide acceptance and one may, for example, talk today about the economics of the "Invention Industry," without running the risk of being misunderstood. If this essay did not originate the shift towards an endogenous theory of inventive activity, it certainly precipitated it. Either way, then, it should be considered a pathbreaking contribution.

As Chapter 17 I have included a paper which, while highly original, has hardly been mentioned in the literature, perhaps because it has been difficult to locate. As its title reveals, "The Lag of Imitation Behind Innovation," the paper attempts to identify the factors that determine the rate of general adoption or imitation of improved technologies. Since the study of the diffusion rate of innovations is still at an infant stage, I sincerely hope that the re-appearance of the paper in this volume will attract wide attention.

Finally, Part VI features an essay bearing on a central aspect of a very old theme. The theme is the one over which Plato and Aristotle argued so lucidly 2500 years ago. It is best expressed by the following question: How can the human and economic rights of individuals or "micro-units" be preserved and still secure the ideal of a just and orderly social "total"? The aspects of it, discussed in "Liberalism and the Choice of Freedoms", center on the approaches which have been taken by the so-called "liberals" reconciling the conflicts among different freedoms and between freedoms and other social goals. After a penetrating analysis of the term, Machlup concludes that, in working out the conflicts in a way that preserves liberty, a "liberal" should never "consent to the restriction of any freedom, economic, political or intellectual, except as the price to be paid for the fuller realization of other freedoms." With this fascinating guiding principle of social conduct, I should like to conclude by considering the question: Where do Machlup's greatest achievements lie?

Reflecting my personal interests and tastes more than a systematic assessment of Machlup's bibliography, I think the choice is among three candidates: the theory of the firm; the theory of international trade and finance; and the economics of knowledge and technological change. If I had to single out the area where Machlup's work has been most fundamental, I would cast my vote for the theory of the firm. My reason for voting this way is that, among others, his essay on "Marginal Analysis and Empirical Research" contained the most path-breaking thoughts ever published on this matter. Second to the theory of the firm, I would place his work in the area of knowledge and technological change, and third his contributions to international trade and finance.

In ending, I should like to add that, while putting this anthology together, I was generously assisted by several persons. Specifically, Professors Gottfried Haberler, Harry Johnson and Robert Stern kindly gave me their expert advice as to the selections to be included in Part IV. Professors M. I. Nadiri, Elizabeth Bailey, and Andrew Schotter provided me with valuable suggestions and criticisms; and Professor Machlup himself helped me by describing to me the preference function he holds regarding his own writings, and by guiding me through his incredibly voluminous bibliography. Lastly, Messrs. Demetrius Cacnis and Pasupathy Narayanan participated in various stages of the project, and Mrs. Mary Ann Fazio did most of the necessary typing. To all these persons I express my deep gratitutde.

George Bitros
Athens 1976

1. In addition to these, Machlup's bibliography includes 61 papers in collective works, 44 articles and notes published in minor journals, 65 book reviews, 30 reports, memoranda and testimonies in public documents, and many other items in the form of discussions, abstracts, prefaces, letters to the editor, and contributions to the daily press.

2. This decision did not apply, however, to books published in joint authorship, and essays, papers and chapters contributed to collective works.

CONTENTS

PART ONE

METHODOLOGY OF ECONOMICS
AND OTHER SOCIAL SCIENCES

IF MATTER COULD TALK
Fritz Machlup

The differences between the natural and the social sciences have been both exaggerated and minimized. To some, especially Anglo-American writers, the differences have seemed so categorical that they decided to appropriate the designation "science" for the natural sciences and to deny it to the study of social phenomena. Others, especially German writers, insisted on the scientific character of the study of cultural phenomena but still he ' that natural and "cultural" sciences were so fundamentally different that they required "contrary" methodological approaches.

These extreme positions had to be countered; it was important to show that in most respects, especially regarding the logic of inquiry, cognition, generalization, verification, and application, there were no fundamental differences between natural and social sciences. Philosophers of science who applied themselves to this task have, however, in their zeal to correct the errors of the exaggerators of contrast, sometimes gone too far in minimizing genuine differences. To recognize these differences may do a great deal for the comprehension of both the unity and the departmentalization of science.

This essay is intended to present an issue which has an important bearing on the difference between the natural and the social sciences. Following my inclination to dramatize ideas when I want the reader to share my appraisal of their importance, I shall introduce the issue by means of a short story or parable.

A PARABLE

They had debated the proposal to telephone the physical laboratories at Harvard, Princeton, and Chicago and notify their counterparts in these institutions of their exciting observations; but then they felt unsure and decided to call a psychiatrist.

"Doctor, please come to the physics laboratory, Columbia University. A group of seven men—three professors and four assistants—apparently are suffering from strange hallucinations, although none of us has taken alcohol, LSD, or any other drugs. We all hear voices. They seem to come from inside our machines and apparatuses, in clear English. If we are not crazy, we are going crazy. Please come immediately."

When the psychiatrist arrived, he found the physicists engrossed in conversation, not with one another but each with some persons hidden in all sorts of containers, cabinets, and machines.

"Are you making fun of us? Is this a hoax, or what?" Professor R. spoke into an apparatus of stainless steel, cylindrical in shape.

"Nothing of the sort," a voice answered from the inside of the apparatus. "We simply have decided to end our silence and cooperate with you in your research work by telling you all we know."

The professor greeted the psychiatrist and introduced him to his colleagues and assistants. At this point he was called to the telephone. He returned after several minutes.

"The same thing happened in Princeton. Professor W. was on the phone. Apparently it started there at the same time as here. At the Forrestal Laboratory the people panicked after the stellarator started talking. . . ."

He was interrupted by a newcomer. "Someone from the *New York Times* called. He wants you to comment on a dispatch from Moscow. There are two strange headlines in *Tass*. One says: 'New Elementary Particles Are Russian'; the other says: 'Genes Pass Resolution Siding with Lysenko'."

Before Professor R. was able to answer, Dr. M., an instructor, entered. He was excited and, without waiting for his chief's nod or question, he began to report on his lab section. He had been talking to a group of undergraduates, demonstrating various cases of Brownian motion. As he spoke about the random walk of molecules and about molecular collisions at various pressures, someone shouted, "Stop that nonsense!" When he looked around to see which student had made this impertinent remark, the voice continued. It was obviously coming from the protective chamber with the suspended mirror, whose movements were being tracked by the fluctuations of a reflected light beam. This is what he heard: "It is time that you cease and desist from misleading your students. What you teach about us mole-

IF MATTER COULD TALK   287-288

cules is simply not true. This is no random walk and we are not pushing one another all over the place. We know where we are going and why. If you will listen, we shall be glad to tell you." He had not waited for more, but had rushed here to report and get Professor R. to witness the event and to hear what the molecules were about to tell.

"Oh," said Professor R., "you mean they are going to tell us what they *think* they are doing. By all means, let them go ahead."

A SKETCH OF THE HISTORY OF THE THEME

I shall resist the temptation to spin this yarn further. To do so might be fun—but each of us can do it in his spare time and make a short story long. The parable has served to pose the issue, that is, to ask what problems would arise in the natural sciences if inanimate matter began to talk. It is a fantastic idea, to be sure, but an idea worth exploring. Before I proceed, however, I shall acknowledge how it came to me.

The theme—that animals, trees, and inanimate objects could be endowed with the gift of human speech—is, of course, as old as literature. Legends, fables, and fairy tales are the best-known sources; in Homer's *Iliad* we encounter a talking horse, that of Achilles; Aesop's fables and the tales by the Grimm brothers and by Hans Christian Andersen are full of talking and chatting foxes and wolves, trees and flowers, storks and ducks, the sun and the wind, and teakettles, mirrors, and street lamps. In addition, there are the stories of Orpheus, who moved rocks and rivers by his songs; and there have been many anthropomorphic parts in epic and lyric poetry, in tragedy and in comedy.

As a youngster I delighted in reading books by Carl Ewald; among them was one with beautiful *Tales Told by Mother Nature* about talking animals and objects.[1] There was one in which earth and a comet had a discussion, joined in by the moon; another featured a chat between a spider and a mouse. A conversation between the sea and various plants and birds occurred in one tale, and another had a talk, with interesting implications of

---

1. Carl Ewald, *Mutter Natur Erzählt* (Stuttgart: Franckh, 1910); *idem, The Spider and Other Stories* (New York: Scribners, 1907); *idem, The Old Post and Other Nature Stories* (London: Dent, 1922).

conscious cooperation, between a soldier-crab and a sea-anemone. There was also a most informative debate among five germs: tuberculosis, cholera, and diptheria complaining about man's warfare against them, mold bragging about its great power, and yeast defending man as its best friend.

Much later I became acquainted with the writings of E. B. White and I fell in love with *Charlotte's Web*. But the most philosophical stories of this genre are in the poems by Christian Morgenstern. The manifesto of the "West Coasts," protesting the semantic willfulness of man and declaring their semantic independence,- belongs in the notebook of every language philosopher. But none of the human talk of these nonhuman beings and things included, to my knowledge, any allusions to the problem of scientific procedure.

In methodological and epistemological discussions of the social sciences, references to a cognate, though inverted, theme can be found: Several writers have mentioned that the natural sciences lacked two sources of information—inner experience and verbal communication—which were of essence in the social sciences. We are familiar with statements by social scientists reflecting about their advantage—in some measure compensating for several disadvantages—in having access to data of inner experience unavailable to natural sciences. Thus Friedrich von Wieser wrote: "We can observe nature from the outside only, but ourselves also from within. And since we can do it, why should we not make use of it?"[3]

The emphasis here was on the scientific observer's ignorance of how it feels to be a molecule, an electron, or a gene, contrasted with his knowledge of how it feels to be a human being, suffering pain, enjoying pleasures, and making decisions. There was little emphasis, as far as I know, on the scientific observer's inability to interrogate, and receive communications from, inanimate objects, in contrast with his ability to interrogate, and listen to verbal reports from, large samples of the members of human society.

Some philosophers of science, to be sure, have likened the controlled experiments in the physical, chemical, or biological laboratories to "inter-

2. Christian Morgenstern, "Die Westküsten," in *Galgenlieder* (Berlin: Bruno Cassirer, 1926), pp. 42–43.

3. Friedrich von Wieser, "Das Wesen und der Hauptinhalt der theoretischen Nationalökonomie: Kritische Glossen," *Jahrbuch für Gesetzgebung, Verwaltung und Volkswirtschaft im Deutschen Reich*, 35. Jahrgang (1911). p. 402.

rogations" and "cross-examinations." But, notwithstanding the cleverness of such metaphors, the observation of physical (chemical, biological) changes in response to controlled variations in conditions is essentially different from verbal replies to verbal questions. To watch the change in the speed with which molecules move as temperature is increased is not the same thing as to ask them why they are moving faster, and then to listen to the introspective explanations they might offer in reply—if they were able to talk.

Whether the fact that the natural scientist does not have to bother with verbal communications from observed objects was ever emphasized, or even mentioned, by early writers on the philosophy of science—this I must leave to the historian of ideas. I do know, however, where I encountered the idea. It came to me through Alfred Schütz,[4] who in turn gave credit to Hans Kelsen.[5]

In his theory of law, Kelsen discussed the problem of contradiction between self-interpretation and the analyst's interpretation of the written constitution of a state. What should we make of the contentions, stated in such a document, that the particular state was a federation, a democracy, a republic, if we find these contentions contradicted by our "objective" interpretation of many of its substantive provisions? Should we disbelieve and discard the self-characterization? The same problem appears frequently in connection with statutory law. Several statutes in the United States, for example, tell in their preambles that they are enacted to preserve competition and reduce monopoly, while their actual effect—intended or unwitting—is to reduce competition and increase monopoly.

It was this type of contradiction that prompted Kelsen to make a general observation about the "considerable difference between the subjects of cognition in juridical science, and indeed in all social sciences, and the subjects of cognition in the natural sciences. A rock does not say: I am an animal."[6]

---

4. Alfred Schütz, *Der sinnhafte Aufbau der sozialen Welt* (Vienna: Springer, 1st ed. 1932, 2nd ed. 1960), pp. 281–282.

5. Hans Kelsen, *Allgemeine Staatslehre* (Berlin: Springer, 1925), p. 129.

6. Kelsen, *loc. cit.* Fascinated by this story of the rock, I made the rock expand its tale: "I came here because I did not like it up there near the glaciers, where I used to live; here I like it fine, especially this nice view of the valley." Fritz Machlup, "Are the Social Sciences Really Inferior?" *Southern Economic Journal,* Vol. XXVII (January 1961), pp. 176–177; reprinted in Maurice Natanson, ed., *Philosophy of the Social Sciences* (New York: Random House, 1963), p. 166.

FRITZ MACHLUP

THE ISSUE CLEARLY POSED

The implication is clear: If a rock said of itself that it was an animal, the geologist could not be content with a statement on its chemical composition, physical form and structure, and geological origin; he would also have to explain why the rock was telling something that contradicted the geologist's finding. He would have to explain why the rock was wrong, did not know what it was talking about, or was trying to confuse those who listened to it.

It is one of the characteristics of the natural sciences that their subjects of investigation do not talk about themselves. Moreover, the

facts and events [studied by natural scientists] are neither preselected nor pre-interpreted; they do not reveal intrinsic relevance structures. ... . The facts, data, and events with which the natural scientist has to deal are just facts, data, and events within his observational field, but this field does not "mean" anything to the molecules, atoms, and electrons therein.

But the facts, events, and data before the social scientist are of an entirely different structure. His observational field, the social world, . . . has a particular meaning and relevance structure for the human beings living, thinking and acting therein. They have preselected and preinterpreted this world by a series of common-sense constructs of the reality of daily life, and it is these thought objects which determine their behavior, define the goal of their action, the means available for attaining them. . . . The thought objects constructed by the social scientists refer to and are founded upon the thought objects constructed by the common-sense thought of man living his everyday life among his fellow men. Thus, the constructs used by the social scientist are, so to speak, constructs of the second degree, namely constructs of the constructs made by the actors on the social scene whose behavior the [social] scientist observes and tries to explain in accordance with the procedural rules of his science.[7]

7. Alfred Schutz, "Common-sense and Scientific Interpretation of Human Action," *Philosophy and Phenomenological Research,* Vol. XIV (September 1953), p. 3; reprinted in Alfred Schutz, *Collected Papers,* Vol. I (The Hague: Martinus Nijhoff, 1962), pp. 5–6.

NO DIFFERENCE IN LOGIC

The inherent "meaning structure" of human action prompts Schütz, as it did Max Weber, to proclaim the postulate of subjective interpretation.[8] This postulate requires the social scientist to ask what model of an individual mind can be constructed and what typical content must be attributed to it in order to explain the observed facts as the results of the activity of such a mind in an understandable relation.[9] This does not mean that only *one* model of an individual mind would fit the observed facts. Several different models of various degrees of specificity or generality may be adequate for the explanation of the same set of observations, so that the social scientist has the same problem that the natural scientist has of choosing among alternative hypotheses. Thus, Schütz's "postulate" leaves more freedom to the social scientist than the term may suggest.

Ernest Nagel, however, remains skeptical concerning this postulate. He concedes that many social scientists seek "to explain such [i.e., social] phenomena by imputing various 'subjective' states to human agents participating in social processes"; but he questions "whether such imputations involve the use of logical canons which are different from those employed in connection with the imputation of 'objective' traits to things in other areas of inquiry."[10]

Precisely what is meant here by "different logical canons"? If Nagel means no more than that the effort "to 'understand' social phenomena in terms of 'meaningful' categories"[11] "does not annul the need for objective evidence, assessed in accordance with logical principles that are common to all controlled inquiries,"[12] he is not in any disagreement with either Weber or Schütz. Schütz, too, calls for "methodological devices for attaining ob-

---

8. The idea of subjective interpretation—*Verstehen*—was first advanced by Wilhelm Dilthey. He, however, confined it to interpretations of history and literature. Wilhelm Windelband and Heinrich Rickert extended the postulate to the social sciences, or rather "cultural" sciences, which they, however, regarded as strictly historical in character. (For citations, see footnote 30, below.) It is Max Weber to whom we owe the further extension of the principle to generalizing (and predictive) social sciences. Whether for Weber subjective interpretation was a requirement or merely an important aid in the analysis of social phenomena is still controversial.

9. Schutz, *Collected Papers*, Vol. I, p. 43.

10. Ernest Nagel, *The Structure of Science* (New York: Harcourt Brace, 1961), p. 481.

11. *Ibid.*

12. *Ibid.*, p. 485.

jective and verifiable knowledge of a subjective meaning structure"[13] and insists "that the principal differences between the social and the natural sciences do not have to be looked for in a different logic governing each branch of knowledge."[14]

THE NATURE OF THE DIFFERENCE

Nagel believes that the differences which the Weber school stresses between the explanation of social phenomena and that of natural phenomena lie chiefly in the "personal experience," "sympathetic imagination," and "empathic identification" that are possible for the social scientist and may aid him in his efforts "to *invent* suitable hypotheses."[15] But Nagel denies that these differences are essential as far as the *validity* of explanatory hypotheses is concerned. He explicates his position by the following illustration:

. . . we can *know* that a man fleeing from a pursuing crowd that is animated by hatred toward him is in a state of fear, without our having experienced such violent fears and hatred or without imaginatively recreating such emotions in ourselves—just as we can *know* that the temperature of a piece of wire is rising because the velocities of its constituent molecules are increasing, without having to imagine what it is like to be a rapidly moving molecule. In both instances "internal states" that are not directly observable are imputed to the objects mentioned in explanation of their behaviors. Accordingly, if we can rightly claim to *know* that the individuals do possess the states imputed to them and that possession of such states tends to produce the specified forms of behavior, we can do so only on the basis of evidence obtained by observations of "objective" occurrences—in one case, by observation of overt human behavior (including men's verbal responses), in the other case, by observation of purely physical changes. To be sure, there are important differences between the specific characters of the states imputed in the two cases; in the case of the human actors the states are psychological or "subjective," and the social scientist making the imputation may indeed have first-hand personal experience

13. Schutz, *op. cit.*, p. 36.
14. Alfred Schütz, "Concept and Theory Formation in the Social Sciences," in *Collected Papers*, Vol. I, p. 65.
15. Nagel, *op. cit.*, p. 484.

IF MATTER COULD TALK   291-92

of them, but in the case of the wire and other inanimate objects they are not.[16]

I should like to raise some questions about four points in Nagel's formulation:

(1) Our knowledge of the state of "fear" of the fleeing man and of the "hatred" animating his pursuers does, of course, not presuppose that we can "identify" with the people observed. It does, however, presuppose that we know what fear and hatred "really" are. We could not know what fear is if we had never felt it or at least, as some would say, if we had not been told about it by persons who had.[17] The same is true for hatred. The meaning of these words could never be grasped except on the basis of direct personal experience or perhaps (but perhaps not) on the basis of verbal communications from some who have had such experience.[18]

(2) When Nagel extends the concepts of "observation of 'objective' occurrences" and of "overt human behavior" to include "men's verbal responses," he loses the clue to the problem. That fearing and hating men can tell us about their fears and hates, whereas molecules cannot tell us about their slower or faster movements, is a difference, not only "important," as Nagel concedes, but essential enough to justify the postulate of subjective interpretation à la Weber and Schütz. For the men talking to us may deny any fears and hates that we impute to them, or claim that they are animated by feelings which we fail to impute to them in our objective interpretation of their actions. Molecules, on the other hand, never con-

---

16. *Ibid.*

17. I cannot resist recalling the operatic dialogue between young Siegfried, in Richard Wagner's music drama, and old Mime: Siegfried asking what fear is and how one could learn how to fear, and Mime first trying to teach him fear by describing his own feelings of anxiety and then, when this proves unsuccessful, promising that Siegfried would soon learn it by personal experience when he encounters Fafner, the dragon.

18. We may know what fear and hatred felt like when we felt them and how we think we acted at those times; we may also know how other people acted when they reported fearing and hating and how they described their feelings. We then try to find a correspondence or similarity—an overlap among the relevant features common to these sets of private and public observations.

tradict our hypotheses by verbal depositions—except in our parable or similar pieces of fiction.[19]

(3) Nagel's illustration contrasts a concrete observation of a particular human situation, that is, a single instance of a (poorly bounded) class of social phenomena, with a well-bound class of physical phenomena reproduced thousands of times in thousands of laboratories. We shall come back to this lack of parallelism when we discuss the difference between the constructs used in universal laws and those used in reports on particular events.

(4) The "important differences" that Nagel recognizes are those between physical and psychological states, with the possibility of "firsthand personal experience" of psychological states on the part of the social scientist. This emphasis is at the expense of even more important differences, especially that the subjects of inquiry in the social sciences can give us their opinions about our explanations of social phenomena; that their opinions may sometimes be helpful, sometimes misleading; that they may be contradictory, some saying one thing, some another; and that large portions of several social sciences have as their subject matter verbally stated theories of social "actors," or, at least, their interpretations of the actions and intentions of their "partners."

It is in reaction to this fourth point, to Nagel's emphasis on "firsthand personal experience" (and "empathic identification"), that Schütz exclaims that subjective understanding or *Verstehen* "has nothing to do with introspection."[20] What Schütz wants to say here, I suppose, is that "subjective

19. I realize that we can build instruments which tell us by means of signals in English about the physical state of matter. For example, the gauge in my automobile tells me whether the water in the radiator is "cold" or "hot." If the gauge is out of order, the "report" may be wrong. Yet, we would never say that the water was "lying" about its temperature. It is not the water that tells us about its feeling cold or hot; the gauge gives us signals by means of a mechanism which man has invented, built, and installed.

In this example, as Karl Deutsch called to my attention, there is a gap between the report by the gauge and the response by the driver. Gaps of this sort can sometimes be bridged. In the human body, signals are often coupled to a response without the intervention of consciousness, as for example by various feedback mechanisms, studied by neurophysiologists. Analogous mechanisms are designed by man: self-steering apparatuses. The difference between *automatic* and *conscious* responses in the case of human behavior is, I believe, relevant to the scientific procedures in different behavioral sciences. The "strictly behavioral" scientist studies unconscious reactions of the body; in contradistinction, the "social" scientist studies conscious reactions of man to signals received from his environment, including actions of other persons.

20. Schutz, *op. cit.*, p. 56.

understanding" goes far beyond introspection and does not always require it. It merely requires the construction of at least one model of the actor or of the type of actor, that is, an imaginative construction of perceptions, memories, and preferences that is adequate for explaining (and for predicting) the observed behavior or the observed consequences of presumed behavior.

TALES TOLD BY MOLECULES

Let us go back to the end of our parable, where the molecules, after denying the story told by the physicist, offered to tell all they knew about themselves. The lesson of the parable was not that the physicist had never been a molecule and thus had no introspective knowledge about molecules but that the tales told by the molecules would become data and problems for the physicist to deal with. The self-interpretations of the molecules and their interpretations of the actions and reactions of their fellow molecules would become integral parts of the scientists' observational field.

Whether the tales told by inanimate matter would help or hinder the scientists' work is difficult to say. New discoveries will sometimes complicate, mess up, or even destroy the nicest and most widely accepted scientific models of natural phenomena, and thus increase the "mystery" of nature for the time being. Yet, in the long run such discoveries may prove to have been significant steps in the search for "truth." On the other hand, the newly discovered facts may turn out to be errors of observation, and the scientists' efforts to accommodate them in their theoretical system may have been sheer waste. In the same sense, any verbal reports mysteriously made by inanimate matter—on the witness stand, on the psychoanalyst's couch, on questionnaires, or in informal interviews—would certainly mess up the scientists' systems of ordered knowledge; in the long run, the value of such reports may prove to be positive or negative. Undoubtedly, most scientists would prefer not to be bothered by any confessions, true or false, of their now conveniently silent subjects of observation.

The most irritating disturbances would come from contradictory communications. They would raise, among other problems, the question of who, if anyone, is right, or "more credible." Assume, for example, that some molecules explained their movements as part of a well-designed plan of action, others as emotional reactions to irritations from their fellow molecules, while a few molecules admitted that they had been pushed around in random collisions with others. The scientist would probably regard the few respondents who had the "correct" story as particularly honest and intelligent molecules. But he would still be confronted with the problem of explaining why the others were liars or, at least, confused and unreliable witnesses.[21]

TALES TOLD BY MEN

In all social sciences, theorists, empirical researchers, and practitioners are greatly hampered by (deliberately or unwittingly) false reports from men telling about their own actions. However, the question for the social scientist is not whether the reports received from human actors are helpful or unhelpful; in many instances such verbal reports are the only data at their disposal and may be the very subject matter of their investigations. (This is the case, for example, in economic inquiries about prices, which *are* reports from buyers or sellers.)

Even where the communications (from those who take actions which, or the consequences of which, the social scientist studies) are *not* the sole data for inquiry, but where the communications are data supplementary to a record about physically observable phenomena, even then the social scientist must not disregard them. He must account for them, whether they are a help or a nuisance.

Strangely enough, the discussion of these problems has often taken it for granted that the social scientists, especially those accepting the Weber position on subjective understanding, regard introspective or communicated

---

21. The first step of a scientist confronted with contradictory and dubious confessions (by hitherto silent matter) would be to ascertain how relevant the different motivations reported are for the actual movements observed. He may find that several different confessions would account for the same movements (under the same conditions). In this case he might have no *prima facie* reason for preferring one "subjective explanation" to another. The differences could become more significant as his range of experimental findings expands and yields critical data allowing or requiring him to exclude one or more of the previously eligible explanations. In any case, however, he would have to search for explanations of the contradictory "subjective" explanations. The record of the contradictory reports presents problems which call for investigation.

IF MATTER COULD TALK

insights as always helpful in their work. Thus, Nagel, questioning the superiority of "interpretative explanations" in the social sciences, asks, "Do we really understand more fully and with greater warranted certainty why an insult tends to produce anger than why a rainbow is produced when the sun's rays strike raindrops at a certain angle?"[22]

The answer probably depends on who "we" are. If we are physicists, the answer is "no"; if we are persons untrained in physics, the answer is "yes." But if we are interested in the philosophy of science, the comparison is moot. The point is that the very notions of "insult" and "anger" have no meaning outside the consciousness of those who have been insulted and angered or who have been told by some who have. At the same time, those who tell us about insults suffered and anger felt may be trying to mislead us—and perhaps themselves.

The problems of misleading tales from men engaged in all sorts of activities is well-known to social scientists. Economists have often complained about the misinformation received from persons who do the very things which economic theory tries to explain but who contest the theorists' explanations. We may recall the perpetual disagreements between practitioners and theorists of banking. David Ricardo, 150 years ago, spoke about the directors of the Bank of England who did not understand what they were doing or what they were talking about; and about dealers in foreign exchange who reported rates which could not possibly be correct. Generations of economists have written about generations of commercial bankers who failed to grasp the implications of their actions and often misinterpreted their own intentions.[23] Writers on the theory of the business

22. Nagel, *op. cit.*, p. 483.
23. That commercial banks "create" credit and money is now known to practically all sophomores studying elementary economics and is fully recognized by the official authorities reporting statistics on the supply of money. Yet, the majority of commercial bankers have stubbornly denied it in interviews, public speeches, and print. The economist can explain the failure of the bankers to form a correct image of their actions and of the consequences of their actions: The banker receives deposits from customers, which adds to his reserves; he grants loans to customers, who then draw on the bank, which will reduce his reserves; thus he cannot lend more than he has received. What the banker does not realize and cannot observe is that many of the deposits he receives are from persons who had received payments from those who had obtained loans from other banks and even from himself. Thus, the banker does not know what he really does or brings about because he cannot observe it. He may, of course, learn it from economists. But his uninstructed opinion —and frequently also his opinion unshaken by attempted instruction—contradicts the economists' theories.

firm have repeatedly been criticized by businessmen who disliked the fundamental hypotheses of the theorists and offered contradictory explanations of business conduct.[24]

SILENT NATURE VERSUS TALKING MAN: ONLY ONE OF THE DIFFERENCES

How fortunate, in contrast, are the physicists, say, those in particle theory: They do not have to put up with denials or contradictions of their propositions by verbal communications from electrons and positrons. Imagine how a physicist would react to positrons protesting that they have unjustly been called "antiparticles," or to photons denying that they were "carriers" of the electromagnetic field.

Think of the long faces of biologists if the *Tass* headline, featured in my parable, became true and genes really passed a resolution siding with Lysenko! Or if cells divided in an opinion poll about the differences between viruses and microbes. And how disturbing to microbiologists it would be if a society of cells endorsed the selection of a scientist for the Nobel Prize and cited with approval his use of an anthropomorphic analogy: ". . . a cell consists of molecules which must work in harmony. Each molecule must know what the others are doing."[25] Some microbiologists might then take heart when they learned that a minority of the cells had dissented, protesting against anthropomorphism as inappropriate in the explanation of their interactions.

To be sure, these events—the message received from particles, genes, cells, etc.—need not at all change any predicted outcomes of actual movements observed by the scientist. The trouble caused by the messages might consist only in the extension of the scientist's task: He would have to explain

24. This refers to the assumption that the firm attempts to maximize profits. At the bottom of the controversy, in which so-called business economists and professors of management science often take the side of the businessman contradicting the economic theorist, lies the confusion between the "firm" as an organization—a group of persons with a variety of objectives, somehow coordinated—and the "firm" as a pure construct in the analytical role of an intervening variable in the theory of prices, inputs, and outputs.

25. André Lwoff, "Interaction among Virus, Cell, and Organism" (Lecture delivered in Stockholm upon receiving the Nobel Prize in Physiology), *Science*, Vol. 152 (27 May 1966), p. 1216.

the processes behind the misleading messages. On the other hand, some of the messages might give clues useful in the modification of · existing theories.

Perhaps I am giving too much play to the contrast between silent nature and talking man. Claims for recognition of several other issues in the discussion of differences between natural and social sciences have been made. Without deciding the relevance and relative importance of the various issues, and fully recognizing that some of them are closely related and partly overlapping, I propose to offer a list designed to point up some notable distinctions. The list will include the question of introspection, although Schütz preferred to have it put aside. All the issues refer to the relationship of the investigator to his subject matter, that is, in the social sciences, to man, human action, or the effects of human action.

The investigator in the social sciences

(1) can feel and think like the men whose actions he investigates;
(2) can talk with other men, learn about their experiences, thoughts, or feelings, and ascertain that these are similar to his own;
(3) can listen to verbal communications, or read written communications, among persons whose actions he investigates, or among persons of the same type;
(4) can receive verbal communications, solicited or unsolicited, directly from the persons, or type of persons, whose actions he investigates;
(5) can make mental constructs and models of human thinking and acting, and can construct theoretical systems involving relationship among ideal-typical actions, counteractions, and interactions;
(6) can interpret, with the use of his abstract models and theories, particular (concrete) observations of human conduct;
(7) can interpret, with the use of his abstract models and theories, particular (concrete) data as results of certain types of action;
(8) cannot build useful constructs and theories in disregard[26] of constructs and theories formed and communicated by men of the type he observes;
(9) cannot obtain useful data (i.e., the "givens" he is supposed to ex-

---

26. While he may not completely disregard constructs and theories communicated by the subjects, he may contradict them for adequate reasons.

plain) except through verbal (and often also numerical) reports from men engaged in the activities he investigates.

Following Schütz, I regard point 8 as the most significant. But it is obviously connected with several other points, especially with point 4. Since point 4 is most easily comprehended, even by laymen and scientists with an aphilosophical or antiphilosophical orientation, I have chosen this point as the one to emphasize and dramatize.

OBSERVATION AND EXPLANATION IN ECONOMICS

My emphasis on the importance, for the invention and acceptance of theoretical models in the social sciences, of communicated interpretation of human actions by the actors themselves may give a false impression. For, alas, these "prescientific" or naïve interpretations may be very poor clues to a satisfactory theory of the network of actions, reactions, and interactions which the social scientist has to explain. This warning, however, should not support the opposite position, namely, that complete absence of verbal communications from the participants in social actions would facilitate the construction of a good theory. Indeed, certain institutions and processes could never be satisfactorily explained by observers of overt behavior exclusive of men's verbal responses.

Assume an anthropologist arrives from a populated planet (I do not know whether Mars still qualifies for this designation)—a scholar with a great gift for observation but without any knowledge of human institutions, practices, or languages. He sets himself the task of explaining the working and the function of the stock market. He might observe the traders, jobbers, messengers, brokers, and customers, their movements, their gestures, and their shouts for any length of time, but he would not even come close to a superficial description of the actual process, not to speak of the function of the institution.

Now endow him with the ability to speak and to understand the language, and permit him to interview every one of the people engaged in the activities of the stock market. He would end up with information, but he would not understand enough of what goes on to know the economic functions of the stock market, particularly its role in the utilization of investible

IF MATTER COULD TALK 297

funds and in the formation of capital. Since probably 999 out of 1000 persons working on the stock market do not really know what it does and how it does it, the most diligent observer-plus-interviewer would remain largely ignorant. Alas, economics cannot be learned either by watching or by interviewing the people engaged in economic activities. It takes a good deal of theorizing before one can grasp the complex interrelations in an economic system. And this theorizing consists mainly in constructing ideal types of motivated conduct of idealized decision-makers and combining them in abstract models of interactions.

From time to time attempts have been made, in economic literature, to do without the fundamental hypothesis of economic theory, that is, without the assumption that households and firms pursue a definite objective, such as maximization of satisfaction and profits. For example, it has been proposed "to start with complete uncertainty and nonmotivation" and rely on "the principles of biological evolution and natural selection" to explain and predict the course of economic events.[27] The principle of conscious "adaptation" by firms seeking more profits was to be replaced by a principle of "adoption" of successful firms by the environment. The survival of the "viable" firms and the elimination of the nonviable ones were supposed to be the result of "competition."

This proposal depends on the assumption of competition; but competition in markets depends on the desire of human decision-makers to make profits. Competition among hungry animals for scarce food can be understood without reference to any "thoughts" expressed by the animals. Competition among well-nourished men cannot. Of course, competition among athletes in a sport contest, competition among scholars in intellectual endeavors, and competition among businessmen in trade and industry are different matters, each presupposing different motivations. The point is that the existence of the profit motive must be presupposed to explain competition in business. If firms in particular lines of activity make good profits, the emergence of newcomers trying to get a share in the market can be expected only if one assumes that there are men who prefer more money to less and, therefore, decide to enter the industry that seems to offer

27. Armen A. Alchian, "Uncertainty, Evolution, and Economic Theory," *Journal of Political Economy*, Vol. LVII (June 1950), pp. 221 and 211.

relatively large profits.[28]

One of the most important phenomena of the social world, inaction or "negative action" ("intentional refraining from action"), necessarily escapes sensory observations,[29] other than the nonactor's verbal statement of his "reasons," that is to say, a statement of his (perhaps wrong or misleading and certainly introspective) theory about his way of thinking. Where inaction is a mass phenomenon, the construction of an ideal type of man who would "understandably" not react to a particular change in conditions is required.

UNIVERSAL AND PARTICULAR, THEORY AND HISTORY

One of the worst stumbling blocks in the methodological analysis of the social sciences was the insistence of many (chiefly German) philosophers of science on a categorical difference between natural and cultural sciences. The cultural sciences, they argued, were not "generalizing," like the natural sciences, but were, instead, "individualizing" in the sense that their only concern and interest were individual events at particular times and places.[30] For these writers, the social sciences were essentially "history." Confronted with the general theoretical system of economics, a foremost representative of this school of thought stuck to his principles and without hesitation separated economics from the other social sciences by designating it as a natural science.[31] The cultural sciences were "by definition" concerned only with historical events.

However widespread this notion was at one time, nowadays it is at best a chapter in the history of ideas. Philosophers of science, irrespective of their differences on many issues, are now fully agreed that almost all disciplines

28. Edith Penrose, "Biological Analogies in the Theory of the Firm," *American Economic Review*, Vol. XLII (Dec. 1952), pp. 804–819 (esp. pp. 809–816); *idem*, "Rejoinder," Vol. XLIII (Sept. 1953), pp. 603–609.

29. Schutz, *Collected Papers*, Vol. I, p. 54.

30. Among the major representatives of the categorical differentiation between generalizing and individualizing sciences were Wilhelm Dilthey, *Einleitung in die Geisteswissenschaften* (Leipzig: Duncker & Humblot, 1883); Wilhelm Windelband, *Präludien* (Tübingen and Leipzig: Mohr, 1903); and Heinrich Rickert, *Die Grenzen der naturwissenschaftlichen Begriffsbildung* (Tübingen Mohr, 1902, 2nd ed. 1913). See footnote 8, above.

31. Rickert, *op. cit.*, p. 224.

298-99   **IF MATTER COULD TALK**

have a core of *general* propositions, with applicability to *concrete* situations or *particular* cases. This is true of the natural and the social sciences alike. Of course, application does not mean that the propositions of the discipline will be sufficient to explain a concrete situation, change, or event (or to predict actual outcomes or to prescribe for desired outcomes). As a rule, propositions of several disciplines will have to be brought to bear on explanations (predictions, prescriptions) in particular cases. No discipline is self-sufficient when it comes to applications. Incidentally, there is much division of labor among those professing a discipline, some of them specializing in formulating, reformulating, and disseminating general propositions —theorists; others on applying them to particular cases—applied scientists and engineers (including social engineers).

Perhaps a few words should be said about one discipline which is exclusively concerned with applications of general propositions from other disciplines to particular situations and events: I refer to history. The historian is an applied sociologist, political scientist, psychologist, social psychologist, economist, anthropologist, archaeologist, military scientist, philologist, linguist, physiologist, biologist, chemist, geologist, physicist, statistician, and what not. Since he deals chiefly with human history, he is predominantly an applied social scientist and will, where propositions of natural sciences are relevant to historical research, either rely on generally known propositions (for example, that certain chemical substances are deadly poisons) or turn to specialists for advice. The historians who explain Caesar's decision to cross the Rubicon and the historians who explain Roosevelt's decision to devalue the dollar apply different mixtures of social sciences, although psychology is a strong ingredient in both.

I have said that almost all disciplines—though not history—have a core of general propositions with (usually indirect) applicability to concrete situations or particular cases, and that this is true for natural and social sciences alike. Yet, strangely enough, when we search modern treatises on the philosophy of science for illustrations in all sorts of contexts, we find a consistent inconsistency: The natural sciences are, practically without exception, illustrated by general laws or by propositions about empirical regularities, whereas the social sciences are illustrated by particular instances, singular observations, and historical events. Whatever may have been responsible for this discrimination in analysis and exposition, it cannot help being misleading. Indeed, it has, I believe, led the philosophers themselves into erroneous positions concerning the very issues we have been treating in the present essay.

To show what I have in mind I shall present and briefly examine three propositions, all in the form of questions about price increases:

(1) Why did the United States Steel Corporation raise the prices of certain steel products in April 1962 by 3½ percent?

(2) Why did prices, as measured by the cost-of-living index, rise in the United States by 7 percent from 1956 to 1958?

(3) Why will prices increase if, with a given labor force, given facilities of production, and given technological knowledge, total bank credit is expanded and aggregate spending by government and business increases?

Only the third question is a problem of economic theory. The first is chiefly a problem of business history. To answer it, many things besides economic theory have to be known; indeed, economics may be relatively irrelevant in explaining why corporate management took the particular decision. Psychology, sociology, politics, management science, industrial relations, accounting, and several other disciplines may be involved; a professional economist may, of course, know enough of all these fields to answer the question without calling in a team of experts from ten other departments. (The reader may want to be reminded that the particular price decision precipitated a row between the President of the United States and the President of the United States Steel Corporation.)

The second question is one of historical statistics. Since it involves mass conduct, that is, decisions and actions of millions of anonymous people selling and buying thousands of different things, we expect that propositions of economic theory are of paramount but not of exclusive relevance. The full explanation calls for knowledge in a variety of fields: political science, law and diplomacy, military science, logistics, technology, engineering, trade-union politics, and other arts and sciences. (The reader may have to be told that military actions in Egypt, the closing of the Suez Canal, the rerouting of oil shipments, and several other things played significant roles, besides fiscal, monetary, and labor policies.)

The third question is pure economics, and nothing but economics, because it does not refer to any particular event in time and space. It is answered by reference to general propositions in the form of "universal

300   IF MATTER COULD TALK

laws" or fundamental hypotheses. These hypotheses involve constructs of idealized human action based on (assumed) objectives to maximize profits and satisfactions. The hypothetical price increases are explained as the results of certain types of hypothetical actions which, in turn, are understood in terms of "meanings" on the part of hypothetical human actors—of homunculi made to order to suit the economist's purposes.[32]

NAGEL ON PROPOSITIONS OF SOCIAL SCIENCES

I am not sure whether Nagel sees the concepts and theories of the social sciences in this or in a very different light. For he does not choose for his illustrations general propositions of social sciences, but rather singular events involving particular persons at a specified time and place. He states this most clearly when he discusses MacIver's example of the man fleeing from a pursuing crowd and finds that it involves "an assumption, singular in form, characterizing *specified* individuals as being in certain psychological states at *indicated* times. . . ."[33]

At one point Nagel discusses a point of economic history: Southern cotton planters were "unacquainted with the laws of modern soil chemistry, and mistakenly believed that the use of animal manure would preserve indefinitely the fertility of the cotton plantation." He holds that the "social scientist's familiarity with those laws" will help him explain the gradual deterioration of the soil and the consequent need for virgin land to maintain the output of cotton.[34] I submit that it is not the "social scientist" who needs this knowledge of soil chemistry; it is the historian who, in explaining the events and changes he has selected for investigation, has to know all sorts of things, including some general laws of physics, chemistry, agronomy, and so forth. If the historian happens to have competence (or a university degree) in economics or any other social science, this does not make

32. Most economists are satisfied that *some* people—in sufficient number to be significant—really act in ways similar to the programmed decision-making by the homunculi. But there are also economists who do not care about even that much correspondence between real and imagined men, as long as the conclusions that can be derived from conjunctions between the constructed types and certain sets of specified conditions broadly correspond to the observed records of events that have actually occurred after conditions of the specified sort have actually existed.

33. Nagel, *op. cit.,* p. 482. The emphasis is mine.

34. *Ibid.,* p. 476.

physics, chemistry, or agronomy a part of social science. The exhaustion of the soil used in cotton production may be a *result* of human action (deficient fertilization), partly explained with the aid of economic theory, and in turn also a *cause* of human action (cultivation of additional land), again in part explained in terms of economics. However, this does not make the exhaustion of the soil the province of economics. Technology is not a social science, even if it plays a great role in many classes of phenomena with which social scientists have to deal. My main point is that concrete events in history, particular cases in the real world, are rarely, if ever, explained with the aid of a single discipline but require application of several fields of knowledge.

In his critical discussion of "meaningful" or "interpretative" explanation in the social sciences, Nagel tries to show that the imputation of motives or sentiments to human agents is quite unreliable.

We may identify ourselves in imagination with a trader in wheat, and conjecture what course of conduct we would adopt were we confronted with some problem requiring decisive action in a fluctuating market for that commodity. But conjecture is not fact. The sentiments or envisoned plans we may impute to the trader either may not coincide with those he actually possesses, or even if they should so coincide may eventuate in conduct on his part quite different from the course of action we had imagined would be the "reasonable" one to adopt under the assumed circumstances.[35]

We may note that in this illustration Nagel again refers to our imagined identification with a *particular* trader in wheat, even asks about "the sentiments and envisioned plans" which he *actually* possesses, and raises questions about his *actual* conduct. Since I may assume that Nagel is not alluding to the psychoanalysis of a wheat dealer of his acquaintance, but rather to the methodology of economic analysis, I take the liberty of offering an interpretation of the "actual" role which "interpretative" explanation has in economics, and I propose to do this with an illustration involving traders in wheat.

The economist is concerned with questions of the following kind: How will the price of wheat be affected by a report of a drought; by a reduction in the import quota for wheat; by a reduction in the rate of interest; by an increase in freight rates; by an announcement that the ice cover on the

35. *Ibid.*, p. 483.

301-02   IF MATTER COULD TALK

Great Lakes will delay the opening of shipping for several weeks? These questions can be answered with the aid of general propositions of economic theory. The answers do not presuppose that the economist knows any wheat dealer personally, let alone his psychological make-up. They do presuppose, however, that the economist has constructed an ideal type of dealer conduct. Its main feature is that dealers would rather make more money than less. This imputation of the profit motive to anonymous characters—"intervening variables" between, say, a newspaper report and a quotation of a higher price on the wheat exchange—is necessary for a full understanding of the causal connections.

HUNCHES

I cannot pretend to know why Nagel, like most other philosophers of science, confines himself, in illustrations from social sciences, to propositions about concrete events and particular persons. I have a hunch, however, that the explanation is related to the main issue of this essay: that human actors can talk about themselves, their actions, and the events they experience. If they could not, Nagel would not be able to question his wheat dealer in order to ascertain whether he "actually possesses" the sentiments and plans that an economist may have imputed to the dealer or, more likely, to a hypothetical dealer of a heuristic model.

Perhaps, if molecules could talk, and told about their individual sentiments and plans, the philosopher of science would be tempted to switch his attention from general to particular propositions about molecular motions. (Physicists, though, might soon learn to discount the tales told by molecules.) If genes could talk, philosophers of science would perhaps emphasize the divergences between the geneticists' readings of the hereditary code and the genes' own translations into English (even if biologists decided to disregard the confessions of the genes).

One may venture the thought that the development of the computer has opened an area in which the contrast between silent matter and talking man may vanish and the procedures of natural and social scientists converge. Assume for a moment that scientists can observe both the input and the output of a modern computer but have no access either to the information storage or to the program tape. Could they explain the behavior of the computer? This is similar to the task of explaining human behavior without knowing either the memory (information storage) or the skills and preferences (program tape) of the actors.[36]

For a primitive explanation of the computer's behavior, purely empirical methods (linking frequencies of various kinds of input and output) might suffice, though one might not have much confidence in the findings. For a more thorough and more powerful explanation, we would want to construct models of the (unknown) memory stored in the computer and of the (unknown) program tape directing its actions. If some philistines should now rebel against my assumptions and insist that we not reconstruct (imagine) but inspect (observe) the memory and the program in the computer, they would merely reestablish the contrast between natural and social sciences: After all, there is no way for the social scientist to "inspect" human memories and programs. He can introspect, he can receive and interpret verbal communications about introspections by others, and, most importantly, he can construct models of individual minds deemed adequate for the explanation and prediction of human "output."

36. I am indebted to Karl Deutsch for a stimulating discussion of these points.

[2]

OPERATIONAL CONCEPTS AND MENTAL CONSTRUCTS IN MODEL AND THEORY FORMATION

When Einstein invented the Special Theory of Relativity he developed as a by-product a new type of concept or definition. Instead of defining certain terms by stating the essential properties or qualities of the « object » to which the terms are supposed to relate, he defined them by the physical operations which an observer performs in order to ascertain the presence of the object or to measure its magnitude. His immediate concern was to make precise the meaning of the « simultaneity » of two events occurring at different places; and he demonstrated that this required *specifying the operations used by the observer.*

The physicist Bridgman generalized this procedure and proposed « operationalism » as a universal program of scientific discourse: nothing but operational definitions should be used in physics, or in any scientific discipline. This program was quickly endorsed by representatives of several fields, including philosophers. Its appeal is easily understood because it fitted perfectly the mood prevailing in many quarters: it particularly suited the radical empiricists in their insistence on factual observations, the logical positivists in their leanings toward physicalism, the behaviorists in their antagonism to non-observables.

On the other hand, the claim that concepts used for theory formation should be operationally defined was rejected by many, and most vigorously by theoretical physicists who had come to a position best described as « constructionism » (if not fictionalism). Among them was Einstein himself, who besides having proposed the *operational concept* had also emphatically endorsed the use of *purely mental constructs* in theoretical physics. In order to get the dichotomy between operational concepts and pure constructs into proper perspective, we shall have to review some of the positions taken, chiefly by physicists, on the question of the most appropriate type of concept in theory formation.

I. THE CONCEPTS OF PHYSICS

FREELY INVENTED CONCEPTS

Einstein never tired of reiterating that the basic concepts of physics were « free inventions of the human intellect » rather than « abstractions from experience »; that their « fictitious character » should be « evident » from the fact that alternative conceptual schemes can be constructed; and that the role of experience lies partly in « suggesting » some of the conceptual elements and chiefly in testing the correspondence between « separate experiences » and the « conclusions » of — that is, the « logical deductions » from — the theoretical system (1).

Einstein gave many examples of the « freely invented ideas and concepts » of physics; he mentioned « mass, force, and an inertial system » and added that « these concepts are all free inventions »; he mentioned the « ideal conductor or insulator », the « concept of a plane wave », etc., and remarked that each of these is a « fiction which can never be realized »; and he generalized: « Physical concepts are free creations of the human mind, and are not, however it may seem, uniquely determined by the external world » (2). In reply to a skeptic who was in search of the « physically real » and questioned the use of « purely fictitious concepts », Einstein wrote that « There is only one way from the data of consciousness to 'reality', to wit, the way of conscious or unconscious intellectual construction... We happen to put more trust in these constructions than in the interpretations which we are making with reference to our sensations » (3).

Bridgman was fully familiar with the role of « mental constructs » in physics, designed « to deal with physical situations which we cannot directly experience through our senses, but with which we have contact indirectly and by inference. Such constructs usually involve the element of invention to a greater or less degree » (4). But he was evidently

---

(1) ALBERT EINSTEIN, « On the Method of Theoretical Physics », *Essays in Science* (New York: Philosophical Library, 1934), pp. 12-21.

(2) ALBERT EINSTEIN and LEOPOLD INFIELD, *The Evolution of Physics* (New York: Simon and Schuster, 1938), pp. 310, 311, 75, 110, 33.

(3) Einstein's letter to Samuel, in Herbert L. Samuel, *Essays in Physics* (New York: Harcourt, Brace, 1952).

(4) PERCY W. BRIDGMAN, *The Logic of Modern Physics* (New York: Macmillan, 1927), p. 53.

dissatisfied with such arbitrary procedures. Commenting on Poincaré's dictum concerning the multiplicity of possible explanations of any phenomenon, he said: « This is very unsatisfactory. We want to be able to find the *real* mechanism » (5). But he was not equally opposed to all constructs. He regarded « body stress », although it is « forever beyond the reach of direct experience », as « a good construct » and was prepared « to ascribe physical reality to it because it is uniquely connected with other physical phenomena, independent of those which entered its definition ». He disliked the construct of the « electric field » because of the absence of « a single physical operation by which evidence of the existence of the field may be obtained independent of the operation which entered the definition ». He was quite partial to the construct of the « atom » because, although « no one has ever directly experienced an atom, and its existence is entirely inferential », so much independent new information pointing to the atom has been accumulated « until now we are as convinced of its physical reality as of our hands and feet » (6).

OPERATIONAL CONCEPTS AND « OPERATIONALISM »

But what Bridgman really was driving at was the exclusive use of operationally defined concepts: « the proper definition of a concept is not in terms of its properties but in terms of actual operations » (p. 6). « In general, we mean by any concept nothing more than a set of operations; *the concept is synonymous with the corresponding set of operations.* If the concept is physical, as of length, the operations are actual physical operations, namely, those by which length is measured » (p. 5). (At this point Bridgman makes what we shall see later was an unguarded aside, as he added: « if the concept is mental, as in mathematical continuity, the operations are mental operations »). There is « much freedom of choice in selecting the exact operations » (p. 9). « If we have more than one set of operations, we have more than one concept, and strictly there should be a separate name to correspond to each different set of operations » (p. 10, similarly p. 23).

Operationalism (or operationism, as it is called by psychologists who are probably in a hurry) as a program is then anchored to neopositivistic tenets: « If a specific question has meaning, it must be possible to find operations by which an answer may be given to it ».

(5) BRIDGMAN, *ibid.*, p. 49.
(6) *Ibid.*, pp. 54-59.

If such « operations cannot exist », the question has no meaning (p. 28). Bridgman believes « that many of the questions asked about social and philosophical subjects will be found to be meaningless when examined from the point of view of operations. It would doubtless conduce greatly to clarity of thought if the operational mode of thinking were adopted in all fields of inquiry as well as in the physical » (p. 30).

Bridgman's position and program are subject to several criticisms. It will be useful to comment here on the following six issues:

1) The type of operations - physical, statistical, or purely mental.

2) The « synonymity » between concept and operations.

3) The operation as a criterion of meaning.

4) The multiplicity of operations, meaning, and concepts.

5) The relation between operations and « real existence ».

6) The desirability of using only operational concepts in theory formation.

Criticism is directed ostensibly against Bridgman, but really against the many writers who have embraced « operationalism » as a requirement of scientific discourse. Several of Bridgman's remarks were casual, tentative, perhaps even parenthetic; why should they be subjected to detailed criticism? The answer is that some of Bridgman's followers have endorsed his methodological platform with such intransigeance that it seems best to select his statements as the target, though with apologies for any unfairness that may be involved.

TYPE OF OPERATIONS

In order to make sense of the program of operationalism it is necessary to ascertain precisely what is meant by an « operation » or a « set of operations ». Bridgman's remark about « mental operations » defining « mental concepts » elicited the following comment from Margenau:

« Originally there seemed little doubt that *experimental* operations, processes leading to measurement, were envisaged. Later, however, Bridgman has spoken of paper-and-pencil operations and even of mental operations. This seems like a retreat, for if thought were included among the operations, nobody could possibly find fault with operationalism, nor would it be saying much » (7).

Bridgman could not possibly have meant what he said about mental operations. It would have contradicted his fundamental position and repudiated his entire methodological platform. But there is a plausible interpretation of what he wanted to say. Having asserted that concepts have no meaning unless they are defined in terms of operations, he found it necessary to concede that the concepts of pure mathematics are not meaningless. He tried to accomplish this by admitting the legitimacy of « mental operations » to give meaning to purely « mental concepts » — but undoubtedly he intended to confine his approval to the mental concepts of the pure formal disciplines, not to extend it to « mental concepts » in empirical sciences. The admission ticket was good only for concepts in logic and mathematics, not for concepts in physics or other empirical subjects (and perhaps not even for « philosophical subjects »).

What kinds of operations are then approved under the program? « Physical operations » for physical concepts, to be sure; but what for biological, psychological, economic concepts? I submit that Bridgman was thinking of all sorts of *instrumental* operations and all sorts of *statistical* operations involving recorded data derived from observation. The readings of instruments and the records of other types of observation, with the workings of the instruments and the steps of the human observers fully specified, are evidently what is meant by the operations in question.

SYNONYMITY BETWEEN CONCEPT AND OPERATIONS.

I have some difficulty with the language used in this discussion. I am accustomed to distinguish the *word* by which an idea is called and the *idea* itself; to refer to the word as the « term », and to the idea as the « concept »; and to understand a definition to be a statement expressing the equivalence of the two. If the definition thus tells what is meant by a word, one should think that *a clear statement of the concept is a definition of the term which denotes it.* I cannot understand, then, why one should speak, instead, of the « definition of the concept » (as Bridgman does) and why one should avoid (as some

---

(7) HENRY MARGENAU, *The Nature of Physical Reality: A Philosophy of Modern Physics* (New York: McGraw-Hill, 1950), p. 232.

philosophers do) speaking of an « operational concept », and insist on speaking, instead, of the « operational definition of the concept » (8).

Granting now that a definition of a term may contain as an essential element a description of the operations by which one may find or measure the denoted « object ». I fail to see how one may possibly hold for all kinds of things that the set of operations should be synonymous with the definiendum. While this equivalence makes sense for such things as « distance », « time », « velocity », « weight », « temperature », and other physical quantities, it makes no sense for most other things, physical or otherwise. It becomes particularly inappropriate when taxonomic definitions are wanted. There are guide books in botany and zoology, designed to aid the student to ascertain by appropriate observations or operations the class, order, genus, species (or whatever classificatory groupings are employed) of a particular specimen. To consider the observer's operations in such a case as « synonymous » with the concept under examination would be absurd. (The operations applied to identify a particular cactus or spider can surely never become synonymous with the plant or animal in question). The demand for an operational definition would in such instances not be different from the obvious determination to employ appropriate procedures to ascertain the presence of the essential properties of the object defined, and there can be no question of a synonymity between concept and operations.

OPERATIONS AS A CRITERION OF MEANING

It is important to distinguish between three possible roles that may be assigned to the identifying or measuring operations: 1) the operations may be regarded as synonymous with the object; 2) they may be regarded as essential directions for finding the object; and 3) they may be regarded as a test or criterion of meaning. The third, in effect, implies a threat or attempted intimidation designed to obtain conformance: « If you don't prescribe physical or statistical operations, your term and concept will be declared meaningless! ».

This command under penalty of « denial of meaning » is somewhat highhanded. It goes even further than the edicts of the pragmatists

---

(8) I am aware of the distinction, made by scholastic philosophers, between the *definitio rei* and the *definitio nominis,* but I do not see that this is relevant to the quibble in the text above. To me an « operational concept » is the same as an « operationally defined term ».

and neo-positivists, who had made analogous pronouncements with regard to *propositions,* rather than mere concepts. Reichenbach, for example, had argued that « meaning » was a predicate of whole sentences, not of single words; words could have « sense » only, while « meaning » is transferred to words by the proposition in which they are employed (9). The criterion of meaning of propositions lies in their truth-value, probability-value, or verifiability; and it was not even necessary, according to Reichenbach, to insist on the « technical possibility » of verification; « physical possibility » would be sufficient, and in some cases one might generously accept merely « logical possibility » of verification — though ordinarily this would not, in his opinion, be very sound (10). The most frequently cited verdict on this issue is Wittgenstein's: « the meaning of a proposition is the method of its verification » (11).

Now, it may be held that the direct verifiability of a proposition depends on the operationality of the concepts which comprise it. The operationality of the concepts would then be a necessary condition of the verifiability of the proposition, though it would certainly not be a sufficient condition. (Indeed, a sentence may link an operationally defined subject with an operationally defined predicate and yet be patently meaningless.) This relationship between operational concepts and verifiable propositions has probably been the basis of the occasional demands for « operational propositions » (12). Unfortunately, writers on verification have all too often overlooked the important difference between the (direct) verification of a single empirical proposition and the (indirect) verification of a theoretical system consisting of several propositions, some of which need not be directly verifiable and need not be composed of operational concepts. These not directly verifiable propositions and these non-operational concepts may be perfecty meaningful.

---

(9) HANS REICHENBACH, *Experience and Prediction* (Chicago: University of Chicago Press, 1938), pp. 19-21.

(10) REICHENBACH, *ibid.,* pp. 37-46.

(11) LUDWIG WITTGENSTEIN, *Tractatus Logico-Philosophicus* (London: Routledge and Kegan Paul, 1951), p.

(12) The economist Samuelson speaks of « the derivation of operationally meaningful theorems ». PAUL A. SAMUELSON, *The Foundations of Economic Analysis* (Cambridge, Mass.: Harvard University Press, 1947), p. 3. The demand for « operational propositions » is especially insistent in DONALD F. GORDON, *Operational Propositions in Economic Theory,* « Journal of Political Economy », Vol. LXIII (1955), pp. 150-161.

All in all, the contention that concepts must be operational in order to be meaningful is untenable and has in fact been almost universally rejected. Even those who cling to the program that most of the concepts of an empirical science « ought » to be operational no longer deny that non-operational concepts may have meaning.

MULTIPLICITY OF OPERATIONS, MEANINGS, AND CONCEPTS

The insistence on the principle « different operations-différent concepts » has been criticized, chiefly because of « the consequence... that in the case of any ordinary scientific object... the multiplicity of methods of detecting its presence would result in a corresponding family of distinct meanings for the term ». This criticism was attributed to a « failure to distinguish between verification and inference » (13). If we make this distinction and realize that our experiments do not « verify » the presence of the object but merely allow us to « infer » it, then the multiplicity of alternative operations « does not give rise operationally to an embarrassing multiplicity of meanings for one and the same term. The same object can be inferred from different sets of operations... » (14).

There is no reason to be « embarassed » when a term has different meanings; indeed, we ought to get used to it and be careful to distinguish them. But it is undeniable that sometimes it is actually one object, and not a family of objects, that is identified by different sets of operations; and in these instances the rule « different operations — different concepts » would indeed be a nuisance. (For example, a salt-crystal identified by crystallographic techniques is still the same object when it is identified by chemical techiques.) The trouble, I submit, lies in the failure to distinguish metric concepts — measurable physical or statistical quantities — from concepts of sensory or imagined objects. In the case of numerically determinate quantities it is perfectly proper to insist that different metric operations yield or imply different concepts. But in all other cases different operations may point to, or identify, the same object.

The confusion has been the illegitimate extension of a principle from its proper (very narrow) area of application — measured quan-

---

(13) GEORGE BOAS and ALBERT E. BLUMBERG, *Some Remark in Defense of the Operational Theory of Meaning*, « Journal of Philosophy », Vol. 28 (1931), p. 549.

(14) *Ibid*, p. 550.

tities — to a wide area to which it does not apply. It is no surprise to find that the question of the « multiplicity of concepts » is resolved by the same clue that was previously seen to suggest the answer to the question of the « synonymity between concept and operations ».

RELATION BETWEEN OPERATIONS AND REAL EXISTENCE

In his attitude, hostile or tolerant, toward non-operational mental constructs, Bridgman, as we have seen, was guided by their more or less distant relationship to operational bases of inference. He was willing to concede that there can be « good constructs » — if they are uniquely connected with independent physical operations — and he went so far as to « ascribe physical reality » and « existence » to these constructs. Apparently there is a close connection, in the operationalist's mind, between physical operations and « real existence ».

It is rather peculiar that a physicist with a strong positivist bent should be so seriously concerned with ontological problems. One might think that a physicist, so anxious to eschew « speculation » and to trust nothing but physical observations and operations, would carefully stay away from metaphysical problems and not plunge headlong into ontology. (Or perhaps it is not so peculiar after all, since there are so many writers who first vociferously and solemnly exorcize all metaphysics as unbecoming to an earnest scientist but then keep talking about reality and real existence.)

The really strange thing in this business about the « real existence » of the objects described in mental constructs is its logical inconsistency with the pronouncements about the synonymity between concept and operations. What operationalists evidently wanted to achieve by such pronouncements was to avoid the hypostatization of an idea, to avoid the mistake of positing the independent existence of the defined thing separate from the operations by which it is defined. For Bridgman, « the union between object and means of observation or measurement is indissoluble » (15). But if the concept is nothing more than the set of operations, the concept cannot possibly at the same time be an object with an independent existence apart from the operations.

---

(15) ROBERT E. BASS, Review of Bridgman's *The Nature of Some of our Physical Concepts*, in « Philosophy and Phenomenological Research », Vol. XIV (1954). p. 416.

EXCLUSIVE USE OF OPERATIONAL CONCEPTS IN THEORY FORMATION

Even if the operationalist concedes that the physicist at present must still use some constructs of a non-operational type, his hope is that, as his science is perfected, it will use only operational concepts. This is just the opposite of the position of most philosophers of science, who stress the « symbolic aspects » of science : « We are beginning to understand how very far from being a literal generalization about observable features of observable phenomena the theories of any advanced science must be taken to be. The more advanced the science, the greater the part played in its theories by unobservables... » (16).

But physicists themselves have rejected the operationalist program in no uncertain terms. Perhaps it would be considered unfair to cite Eddington (17) or Jeans (18) as witnesses for the opposition on operationalism, because their views are often characterized as ultra-rationalistic. But one does not risk a charge of bias if one produces the testimony of Born, who went out of his way to argue against rationalism and « to offer a balanced position » on the « relationship between theory and experiment » (19). Born shows that the ultra-empiricist position taken by Heisenberg was untenable : « Heisenberg felt that quantities which had no direct relation to experiment ought to be eliminated. He wished to found the new mechanics as directly as possible on experience... But if it is taken (as many have taken it) to mean the elimination of all non-observables from theory, it leads to nonsense » (20). Born proceeds to give examples of non-observable quantities which are indipensable to physical theory.

In a more direct discussion of operational definitions, he regards them as « very useful in classical physics where one has to do with quantities accessible to direct measurements... For instance, it is reasonable to introduce temperature by describing the thermometric operations... But the operational definition is rather out of place if you wish to extend » the idea to questions involving atomic nuclei and electrons, quantum theory

---

(16) MAX BLACK, *The Definition of Scientific Method*, in « Science and Civilization » (Madison: University of Wisconsin Press, 1949), p. 90.

(17) Sir ARTHUR S. EDDINGTON, *The Nature of the Physical World* (New York: Macmillan, 1928).

(18) Sir JAMES H. JEANS, *The New Background of Science* (New York: Macmillan, 1933).

(19) MAX BORN, *Experiment and Theory in Physics* (Cambridge University Press, 1943, Dover Publications. 1956), p. 2.

(20) *Ibid.*, p. 18.

and wave mechanics. With regard to Schroedinger's « wave function » Born remarks: « there are in principle no means to observe it, hence no « operational » definition » (21).

It is clear, therefore, that the exclusive use of operational concepts in physical theory is impossible; and that a program which would restrict theory to such concepts is, and will remain, impractical. It would still be possible, however, to champion a program of giving preference to operational concepts whenever available and of admitting non-operational concepts only when no operational substitutes can be found.

EXCLUSIVE USE OF PURE CONSTRUCTS IN THEORY FORMATION

The idea that the physical theorist should build his system with a mixture of concepts, some taken over from the experimentalist — « made in the laboratory » — others freely invented — « made in the study » — is not accepted by all physicists. Even before the operationalist program was formulated, Ernst Mach (often labeled as a positivist) had stated that « All universal physical concepts and laws... are arrived at by idealization » (22). And many others, likewise, have held that even where empirical concepts are available they should be replaced by purified and idealized concepts for use in a consistent theoretical system.

While it would not be possible to find empirical (operational) counterparts to all mental constructs of physics, there is no difficulty in constructing purely abstract counterparts to all empirical concepts. This, indeed, is what theorists have done all the time, knowingly or unknowingly. This transformation of empirical concepts into pure constructs has been called the « method of successive definition » (23). Margenau likes to distinguish « epistemic definitions » (empirical, operational) and « constitutive definitions » (representing « a postulated grouping of constructs »). He holds that « without epistemic definitions science degenerates to speculation; in the absence of constitutive

---

(21) *Ibid.*, p. 39.

(22) ERNST MACH, *Erkenntnis und Irrtum* (Leipzig: J. A. Barth, 2nd ed. 1906) p. 92.

(23) « There is an abstraction of concepts from experience, the discovery of laws expressed in terms of the concepts, the definition of the original concepts to a higher order of approximation in view of the greater accuracy in the definition of conditions, the redefinition of concepts in terms of laws, the reinterpretation of original concepts in terms of the new ». V. F. LENZEN, *The Nature of Physical Theory* (New York: Wiley, 1931), pp. 274 ff.

(24) MARGENAU, *op. cit.*, pp. 232-243, esp. p. 240.

definitions it becomes a sterile record of observational facts » (25). But he makes it clear that only constitutive definitions « allow the establishment of systems » (26), and that « explanation involves a further progression into the constructional domain. We explain by going « beyond phenomena » (27).

The need for « constitutive definitions in terms of other constructs » is exemplified with regard to the concept of temperature: « Temperature, so long as it is defined operationally in terms of thermometer readings, is a rationally fruitless concept or indeed a set of different unconnected concepts. To unify them and to give them meaning, one must add that temperature is the mean kinetic energy of molecules. This is the constitutive definition which closes the ring and allows us to use the notion of temperature in calculations as well as in measurements » (28).

Thus, while operational concepts alone will allow the establishment of statistical correlations and the formulation of empirical laws (uniformities or regularities observed), pure constructs alone will allow the establishment of theoretical systems applicable to a vast range of phenomena in need of explanation.

II. EMPIRICAL LAWS AND PURE THEORY

That there is a difference between concepts used in empirical generalization and concepts used in abstract theory is not a recent discovery, nor an insight limited to physicists. Many biologists, economists and, of course, philosophers have long been fully aware of the difference, though there has been a question whether the difference is in kind or only in degree.

A DIFFERENCE IN DEGREE OR IN KIND?

It is quite understandable that some writers claim that the difference, however wide, is only one in degree because even the empirical concepts, « extracted from experience » and embodied in

---

(25) *Ibid.*, p. 243.
(26) *Ibid.*, p. 237.
(27) *Ibid.*, p. 169.
(28) MARGENAU, in a letter to the author, November 18, 1959.

experimental and observational data, presuppose mental processes including selection, abstraction, reconstruction, combination, reflection, ratiocination, and some idealization. In other words, « conceptualization » implies various thought processes which carry the objects of experience some distance away from whatever it is that supposedly is being observed. The mental construct, the concept used in abstract theory, is formed by means of more idealization, more invention, more construction, to remove it further from the domain of « phenomena » and « data » into the domain of pure « construction ». If there is no border passed on the way from concrete experience to abstract construction, one may refuse to see more than a difference in degree between the more « real » and the more « ideal » concepts.

If, however, the differences in the *formation* of concepts are considered together with the differences in the *use* of these concepts, the contrast becomes obviously categorical. Propositions which link empirical concepts in inductive generalizations are definitely *a posteriori*, dependent on experience and subject to direct verification by further experience. Propositions, on the other hand, which link mental constructs in hypothetico-deductive systems are in the nature of heuristic conventions, and therefore *a priori* — unless accompanied by a statement directing the application of the system to concrete data of experience (29).

That a theoretical system (a) whose concepts and propositions may have been suggested by experience, (b) whose purpose is to serve as explanation of experience, and (c) whose explanatory and predictive usefulness is testable by experience, should nevertheless be *a priori* has long been puzzling even to students of logic. Yet, « Logically... a proposition is *a priori* if it must be presupposed and cannot be proved or disproved within the system to which it is *a priori* » (30). The abstract theoretical propositions of science which are integral parts of a theoretical system have the character of postulates, for which no direct empirical proof is sought; only the system as a whole is tested by the correspondence between consequences deduced from the system and the data of experience which it is designed to explain

---

(29) MORRIS R. COHEN, *Reason and Nature: An Essay on the Meaning of Scientific Method* (New York: Harcourt, Brace, 1931), pp. 137-143. MILTON FRIEDMAN, *The Methodology of Positive Economics,* « Essays in Positive Economics (Chicago: University of Chicago Press, 1953), pp. 24-25.

(30) COHEN, *op. cit.,* p. 138.

or predict. It is the *a priori* character of the theoretical propositions containing the mental constructs that differentiates these propositions sharply from the empirical propositions containing empirical (operational) concepts (31).

« EMPIRICAL » OR « CONCRETE » LAWS VERSUS « EXACT » OR « ABSTRACT » LAWS

Using again physics as his example, the philosopher Morris Cohen contrasts « concrete laws » about « concrete things » with the « abstract or universal laws » of « developed sciences » which are « concerned with the relations between possible or ideal things or elements ». Of course, we « might not be interested in these ideal relations if they did not throw light... on the actual world »; but « there can be no doubt that the more developed a science is the more are its laws formulated in terms of such abstract or ideal elements » (32). « In thus deliberately sacrificing the concrete fullness of ordinary or "experiential" descriptions for the sake of abstract universality, science opens itself to the taunt that it is artificial ». But « the conceptual order which science seeks to attain » is superior in heuristic value to the « so-called perceptual order of common-sense experience »; indeed, the « most powerful organum for the apprehension and controlling of nature that man has as yet discovered is description in terms of ideal entities such as perfect levers, ideal gasses, perfectly continuous bodies, the velocity of light in an unattainable perfect vacuum, and the like » (33).

There are of course certain difficulties in applying the abstract laws and ideal concepts to uncontrolled reality since, according to Cohen, « every abstract or universal law asserts what would happen if only certain conditions prevailed and everything else remained indifferent. Prediction is possible to the extent that nature does offer us instances where the action of bodies can be accounted for by a limited number of factors, and the effects of all other influences either balance each other or are so small as to be negligible or unnoticeable. But theoretically it is true that no actual phenomenon can exclusively embody a single universal law, since in general every actual pheno-

---

(31) Margenau recognized the decisive step across the frontier from the realm of *a posteriori* to that of *a priori* when he said: « The contingency of correlation had given way to logical necessity ». *Op. cit.*, p. 28.

(32) MORRIS COHEN, *op. cit.*, pp. 100-101.

(33) *Ibid.*, pp. 104-105.

menon is the meeting place or intersection of many laws. Yet every true law is actually embodied in all instances of it, and it is that which enables us to analyze phenomena and arrange them in significant order. But while abstract laws are always necessary for the understanding of phenomena, their sufficiency varies in different fields » (34).

We might quote or cite other philosophers who presented the same ideas in slightly different language, but the formulation most interesting to economists is probably that by the economist Carl Menger. Speaking of the « types » and « typical relations » which are the elements of scientific discourse, Menger showed that they are of different degrees of « exactness » (35). Empirical-realistic research, working with « real types » — which can never be exact — attempts to formulate « empirical laws », stating « regularities — not necessities — in the succession and conjunction of phenomena » (36). Exact theoretical analysis, on the other hand, working with ideal types (« *strenge Typen* ») — which do not occur in reality — attempts to formulate « exact laws », stating the logically necessary relationships between the exact types.

The real types, the « basic forms of real phenomena », are of course also the result of abstraction, since several aspects of the phenomena observed are disregarded (37). But the abstraction does not proceed to a complete idealization, and the real type thus allows « more or less wide leeway for peculiarities ». For example, « real gold, real oxygen or hydrogen, real water » cannot be subject to « exact laws »; to arrive at « exact laws » one must construct « exact types », such as « absolutely pure gold, pure oxygen », etc., « no matter whether or not these ever exist as separate phenomena in reality, or indeed whether they can ever be produced as separate phenomena in their purity ». The exact types, which « exist only in our idea », are « prerequisites for the attainment of exact laws » (38).

Menger conceded that the findings of pure theory « look inadequate and unrealistic, in economics as well as in any other discipline. But this should be self-evident inasmuch as the results of exact

---

(34) *Ibid.,* pp. 105-106.

(35) CARL MENGER, *Untersuchungen über die Methode der Socialwissenschaften und der Politischen Oekonomie insbesondere* (Leipzig: Duncker & Humblot, 1883), p. 25.

(36) *Ibid.,* p. 36.

(37) *Ibid.,* p. 67.

(38) *Ibid.,* p. 41.

theories... are true only under definite pre-suppositions », usually under assumptions not satisfied in the real world (39). Yet, without the
« exact laws » of pure theory we could not hope to understand the
complicated relations and interdependences between phenomena of the
real world.

A LIST OF SYNONYMS AND ANTONYMS

Terminology has changed over the years, in the philosophy of
science not less than in most other areas of discussion and controversy.
The same ideas have been expressed in very different words (and sometimes the same words have been used to express different ideas).
Perhaps, to facilitate comparisons between expressions used in different
fields, for different approaches, by different writers, it may be useful
to present a tabulation of analogous or equivalent « phrases » relating
to the dichotomy between the concrete-empirical and the abstract-
-theoretical. In most of the literature these words are used to modify
the noun « laws »; some writers, however, have special tastes concerning the meaning of « law » and want to reserve this tag for only

Empirical Laws *involving operational concepts*	*Theoretical Laws* *involving mental constructs*
Empirical laws (1)	Exact laws (1)
Inductive generalizations	Deductive principles
A posteriori findings (in applied theory)	A priori postulates (in pure theory)
Material, experiential propositions	Formal, systematic propositions
Factual-observational generalizations	Hypothetico-deductive systems
Statements of regularities in data of observation (2)	Resolutions to follow analytical stipulations (2)
Generic propositions (3)	Universal propositions (3)
Concrete laws (4)	Abstract laws (4)
Empirical laws (4)	Universal laws (4)
Empirical laws (5)	Analytical laws (5)
Empirical laws (6)	Theoretical laws (6)
Synthetic universal propositions (6)	Rules of scientific procedure (6)
Strict laws (6)	Rigid laws (6)
Correlational statements (7)	Theoretical explanations (7)
Epistemic connections (7)	Constitutive connections (7)
Low-level generalizations (8)	High-level hypotheses (8)
Inductive generalizations (9)	Scientific laws (9)

Notes: Among the writers who have used these particular or very similar expressions were:
(1) Carl Menger, (2) Henry Poincaré, (3) John Dewey, (4) Morris Cohen, (5) T. W.
Hutchison, (6) Felix Kaufmann, (7) Henry Margenau, (8) Richard B. Braithwaite,
(9) E. F. Caldin.

(39) *Ibid.*, p. 54.

the one kind or only the other kind of proposition. If they feel strongly about this usage they may substitute their favorite term for what they may regard as a misnomer.

It is not claimed that the phrases collected here on the two sides of the table are perfect synonyms or antonyms, but only that they reflect the same dichotomy in concept and theory formation (40).

III. CONSTRUCT AND MODEL.

In the preceding pages the word « model » has been used sparingly. Since « model » is now being used, especially by economists, with greater frequency than any other methodological term, its place in the context of our discussion should be examined. In particular, its relation to the « construct », on the one hand, and to « theory », on the other, ought to be clarified, — though it should first be noted that there are many who have used model as a synonym of construct, and others who have used it as a synonym of theory.

« Model » as a Catch-All Word

« Model » is indeed a very handy word; it can be pressed into service as a substitute for over a dozen other words, and its convenient vagueness allows its user to avoid commitment to any strict idea. In different contexts « model » has been used in lieu of concept, mental construct, conceptual scheme, schema, ideal type, abstraction, idealization, useful fiction, fictitious construction, schematic representation, analogy, hypostasation of analogies, postulate, assumption, system of fundamental assumptions, axiomatic system, hypothesis, theory, law, system of related variables, system of equations, and probably other things. The existence of such « catch-all » words is a boon, not only for sloppy thinkers and writers, but also for thoughtful ones when they have a good reason for postponing commitment to a definite idea. Many writers, however, do not intend to be vague but wish to convey a rather definite idea when they use the word « model », and thus it might be useful to delineate a narrower meaning that places

---

(40) The dichotomy stressed by HERBERT DINGLE, *Science and Human Experience* (New York: Macmillan, 1932), between « abstractions from observation » and « elaborations of hypotheses », (p. 51), is not equivalent to the dichotomies displayed in the list, but must be regarded as a subdivision of theoretical laws.

it between « construct » and « theory », related to both but not synonymous with either.

This is not to say there is anything wrong with using « model » as a synonym of either « construct » or « theory » — as it has
often been used — but it should not be synonymous with both. Schumpeter used model and theory as equivalent terms when he stated:
« The total or ″ system ″ of our concepts and of the relations that we
establish between them is what we call a theory or a model » (41).
Others have used the word model when they referred to single constructs — such as economic man, or profit maximizer. But there is
need for a word connoting more than a contsruct and less than a complete theory; « model » can do this very well.

FORM AND COMPOSITION OF MODELS

Models may come in several forms. They may be pictorial or pla-
stic (« still models »), mechanical, hydraulic, or electro-magnetic (« mobile models »), verbal, geometric, algebraic (« symbolic models »). We
are concerned here only with the last three forms. But in all forms
the function of a model is to exhibit connections, relationships, interdependences. There would be no reason for making a model except
to show how some things « hang together » or of what « elements »
they are composed or how they « work » or are « adjusted ».

The elements of which a verbal or mathematical model is composed and whose interrelations it is designed to demonstrate are mental constructs (considered as « variables » if they are shown in functional relationships with other « magnitudes »). The logical relationship between mental constructs and mental models is quite simple:
models are made up of interrelated constructs. But, in order to be
applicable to concrete situations, should the model not be made up of
operational concepts instead?

Lest a negative answer shock those who realize that « application »
must mean reference to empirical data and, hence, to operational concepts, let us repeat that the question was inquiring into the kind of
concept of which models are « made up », composed. The answer is
that theoretical models are composed of nothing but mental constructs,
some of which, however, may have operational counterparts — and

---

(41) JOSEPH A. SCHUMPETER, *A History of Economic Analysis* (New York:
Oxford University Press, 1954), p. 562.

this is all that is needed to secure applicability of a model. In many theoretical models some of the indispensable concepts cannot be operational, and some of those that can are too inexact for use in a logically consistent system (42).

Perhaps an illustration from model construction in economics will clarify this statement. Think of the model of a competitive industry, designed to demonstrate the effects of changes in cost or in demand upon price and output. The operational concepts that we have of industry, firm, cost, demand, price, and output would obviously not do for this purpose. For example, the Census Bureau's concepts of « industry », the legal or organizational concepts of « firm », the accounting concepts of « cost », these operational concepts cannot be substituted for the idealized concepts of the model; for « demand » there is no operational concept at all; and no practically available operations can unambiguously identify one « price » and one « output » of a product in all its varieties of qualities, shapes, calipers, colors, finishes, lot sizes, delivery terms, credit terms, etc. « Price » and « output » in the theoretical model are mental constructs, and the consequences deduced from the model are « exact » in the sense that they abstract from all the complications surrounding the price and output observations of actual business. Of the « exact » (imagined) deduced consequences the « inexact » (observed) changes of magnitudes actually measured (by necessarily inaccurate statistical operations) are only very unsatisfactory *counterparts,* and the correspondence between the two cannot be anything but rough.

We shall presently furnish additional illustrations of the discrepancies between the abstract constructs employed in economic models

---

(42) This position, taken by many philosophers of science, is forcefully presented by F.S.C. Northrop He distinguishes two main classes of concept: « concepts by intuition », which include « concepts by inspection », and « concepts by postulation », which include « concepts by imagination », « concepts by intellection », and « logical concepts by intuition ». He states that « An operation in the denotatively given sense of the term is a concept by intuition »; and concludes that « in a properly constructed, deductively formulated scientific theory every concept in the theory, as deductively formulated, must be a concept by postulation. Utter confusion and nonsense enter into scientific discourse when concepts by intuition are put in the same proposition with concepts by postulation... When concepts belonging to two different worlds of discourse are treated as if they belonged to the same world of discourse, nonsense is the result ». Filmer S. C. NORTHROP, *The Logic of the Sciences and the Humanities* (New York: Macmillan, 1947), p. 128-29.

and the operational counterparts available to empirical researchers. But first we should proceed with our discussion of the relationship between construct, model, and theory.

THE MODEL AND THE THEORY

We have regarded a model as a system of interrelated constructs; and we have indicated that a theory may be more than a model. A theory may be regarded as a model plus a specification of the empirical observations to which it applies (43). The same distinction is sometimes expressed by the terms « pure » and « applied » theory (which, however, are also used with other meanings). « Model » may stand for « pure theory », working only with mental constructs; when the kinds of empirical data are specified to which the model is supposed to apply we may speak of applied theory.

This does not mean that a theory will *replace* the pure constructs of the model or models that compose it with empirical (operational) concepts. But it does mean that for *some* of the constructs empirical counterparts will have to be suggested, namely, for those variables whose changes are interpreted as the supposed « causes » and the deduced « effects » of the events simulated by the model (44). Thus, to repeat, applicable or applied theory consists of two parts: (1) a pure model and (2) a specification of the empirical facts (described, ordinarily, in term of real types or operational concepts) whose changes it will explain or predict.

This, unfortunately, is still too simple a statement since the explanatory and predictive tasks of applied theory cannot as a rule be attempted with just one model. It will usually take a combination of models (plus specifications of empirical applications) if problems arising in complex situations and complex developments are to be analyzed. Thus, applied theory ordinarily requires several models — and some of them may even be models built in different disciplines, say political science or sociology, since the models of economics alone may

---

(43) MILTON FRIEDMAN, *The Methodology of Positive Economics*, « Essays on Positive Economics » (Chicago: University of Chicago Press, 1953), pp. 24-25.

(44) For a detailed exposition of these ideas see FRITZ MACHLUP, « The Problem of Verification in Economics », *Southern Economic Journal*, Vol. XXII (1955), pp. 12-14. An Italian translation was published under the title *Il problema della verifica in economia*, « Industria » (1958, n. 3), and in the book *La verifica delle leggi economiche* by F. MACHLUP, T. W. HUTCHISON, and E. GRUNBERG, Milano 1959.

leave the analyst helpless and would need to be supplemented by relevant models borrowed from other fields of inquiry. Thus, whereas a model is a combination of constructs, applied theory may be a combination of models. This deserves to be given explicit recognition.

A few words should be added with respect to econometric models. Econometric models are applied to empirical data of the past — in order to obtain the so-called structure of the model by means of statistical estimates of the numerical values of the variables and parameters — and then tried out in predicting some empirical data of the future. The fact that the numerical values of variables and parameters are derived from statistical operations may make some of us think that the terms in the equations are not pure constructs, but operational concepts after all. This would be a mistake, as one may judge from the fact that the econometrician often examines several alternative operations for obtaining his estimates and selects what appears to him to be the closest approximations to the variables included in the model. In other words, he knows that he cannot get exactly what he wants; the constructs of the model which have *any* operational counterparts usually have *several* such counterparts, each deficient in some way, deviating from the exact (ideal) construct for which it can be only a poor analogue. It should therefore be clear that the econometric model, before numerical values have been estimated, consists of pure constructs, notwithstanding the fact that the builder of the model tries hard to design it only with constructs for which he can hope to find statistically operational counterparts. Moreover, since he immediately proceeds to apply his model to data of observation, his model is always in the nature of a theory: it specifies the empirical (operational) concepts the magnitudes of which, he hopes, it can « explain ».

MORE ILLUSTRATIONS OF OPERATIONAL COUNTERPARTS

It may be desirable to add some examples illustrating more sharply the difference between pure constructs and operational concepts in economics. Let us first elaborate on the model of the « competitive market », to which we have previously referred. Like any quantitative model, it contains two kinds of constructs: *variables* and functional *relations* between variables. The simplest market model contains only two variables — price and quantity — and two functional relations between them — supply and demand. The « simplicity » is achieved by the implicit or explicit assumptions of *ceteris paribus* and *mutatis mutandis*; that is to say, all things not included in the model but possibly suspected of having some influence upon quantities supplied or demanded are assumed either to remain unchanged or to change as they must change in logical connection with the variables officially recognized in the model. (For example, the amount of money or income buyers have left over after they make a purchase cannot be assumed to remain unchanged if the demand function is not of unit elasticity). The reference to « other things » possibly of influence implies an admission that these things are in effect part of the model, though playing silent roles, so to speak, and not listed among the cast. It would be preferable, from several points of view, to enumerate all possibly relevant variables and stipulate the silent roles they have to play in the model — such as to remain unchanged. (Stipulations regarding money incomes, real incomes, cash balances, liquidity reserves, for example, would be useful in many market models).

Every beginning student of economics is (or should be) repeatedly warned of the hypothetical nature of the functional relations between the variables. There are no « observable » supply or demand functions — unless one means merely the chalk symbols which the teacher produces on the blackboard for students to observe. All the values of the functions are imagined; the supply function assigns hypothetical quantities offered in the market to hypothetical prices paid, and the demand function assigns hypothetical quantities demanded to these prices, but since the prices and quantities are hypothetical only, they cannot be observed by anybody. (It may be said for the benefit of readers who are comforted by the thought of « conceivable operationality » that with much fantasy one may design a grand « experiment », with heroic controls of all relevant factors, to ascertatin all values of the functions. But one must add, in all honesty, that the « operations » required to establish the functions as empirical observations are not practically possible). The so-called statistical supply and demand curves have not really been « observed »; they are the result of highly imaginative computations with data recorded at different times under different conditions and manipulated on the basis of unverifiable assumptions which range from « plausible » to « contrary to fact ».

But not only the *relations* between variables in the model are constructions of our minds; the *variables* themselves are pure constructs even where several quite acceptable operational counterparts for them can be found. Think of an exceptional firm which produces only one homogeneous product, say fiberboard, only of first quality, but in different calipers; the firm measures its output by weight. The buyers of the board use it for purposes for which only square measure is significant. Perhaps a wholesaler buys it by the ton and sells it by the square foot. The recorded quantity of fiberboard sold and bought may at the same time increase in terms of tons and decrease in terms of square feet. Two different quantities would then result from our statistical inquiries. If one now thinks of the possible combinations between different sizes, different shapes, different qualities, and different products made by the same firms, one must realize that the « quantity produced » or « quantity sold » within a given period can be measured by a variety of operations, so that one must choose among a variety of operational concepts of output, none of which may be precisely the thing that fits the pure construct used in the model.

Matters are much more complicated regarding the other variable, price. What are the usual operations by which we obtain price data for an economic or econometric research problem? We may compile daily quotations from newspapers or weekly or monthly quotations from trade journals; we may send questionnaires to some or all producers, or to some or all users; we may use, or may choose to neglect (with drastic results sometimes), changes in freight costs to adjust the data for f.o.b. mill prices and delivered prices (or for changes in the « interpenetrations » of distant markets by distant producers, which may alter prices paid and net prices received in opposite directions); we may manipulate the data in order to account for some changes in the composition of output while we may choose to neglect other changes in composition where we cannot think of a « good » way of adusting the raw data; we may be able to learn of secret discounts, and may take them into account; but, on the other hand, we may not find out about such practices. The diligent researcher may end up with dozens of different series of prices for the same commodity; and he will realize that they all contain so many « impurities » that none can be said to be a very good analogue of the pure construct.

Not that our operational difficulties relate only to manufactured commodities or to personal services, where the assumption of homogeneity is so far from being fulfilled. Take a relatively homogeneous commodity, foreign exchange in the form of bank balances payable on demand by telegraphic order. The researcher looking for data — for the daily rates (bid and ask) in the important financial centers — will find his task encumbered by difficult choices. He may first turn to one of the most reliable newspapers, *The New York Times,* and copy the daily reports of the foreign-exchange markets. If he then compares his data (say, for 1947 to 1957) with the analogous data from the *Zürcher Zeitung* or the *Journal de Genève,* he will discover discrepancies. Before he gets too desperate, somebody may explain to him that the American paper has felt some (moral) inhibitions about reporting rates illegal under the laws of friendly nations, and confined itself to reports of transactions legal and authorized by the authorities in all countries involved — which under exchange restrictions may be only a small part of the actual transactions. In order to obtain complete information about the rates involved in illegal exchange transactions the researcher will have to turn to *Pick's Currency Reports,* published in New York by an expert who receives reliable reports from dealers all over the world. Now, which of these rates were *the* foreign-exchange rates to be explained, if not predicted, by our theory? The choice between these differing operational concepts of foreign-exchange rates may depend on the type of problem to be answered. But certainly one cannot say that there is an unambiguous operational concept of the price of foreign exchange that corresponds to the pure construct used in our abstract model of the exchange market.

One more illustration, also from international finance. When the trade balance of the United States turned from strongly positive to strongly negative in the years 1957 to 1959, while the balance of long-term capital movements and financial aid had not appreciably changed, accepted theory suggested that prices in the United States must have increased relative to prices in other industrial nations. Price statistics, however, did not verify this suggestion. But what did these operational price concepts really measure? Did they permit comparisons of prices of comparable qualities of comparable products with comparable delivery terms? Reconstruction and growth of European industry probably brought with it drastic improvements in the quality of engineering goods and in the terms of delivery. Assume that in the early 1950's a certain machine or machine tool was offered at similar prices in England and in America, but that delivery terms were 24 months in England and only 6 months in America; assume that in the late 1950's prices in both countries were 10 per cent higher, but English manufacturerers were now able to make prompt delivery. This would easily explain a switch of demand from American to English products, although relative prices, as recorded, were unchanged. In other words, the operation by which the statisticians establish prices and price changes fails to catch significant changes in the things for which prices are paid; and a quantification of these changes does not seem practicable, so that we cannot hope to devise more refined operations that would yield operational concepts more nearly corresponding to the pure constructs used in the model.

These illustrations may have driven home a methodological point often overlooked by positivistically inclined economists who complain about the paucity of verifications of theory. The point is that the difficulty of verification lies less in the « excessive » purity of the abstract constructs and models than in the gross impurities in the operational concepts at our disposal. Empirical tests employing inadequate operational concepts are, quite properly, not accorded much weight and, hence, the theories so tested survive any number of apparently contradictory « experience ».

DEFINITION OF « CONSTRUCT »

Not many writers have attempted to define « construct », and those who have seem to have had limited purposes in mind and thus have come up with narrow definitions. I shall try my hand at a definition which may suit the purposes of the formal sciences as well as the empirical sciences, the natural sciences as well as the social sciences. I submit this definition as a basis for discussion in the hope that it will call forth suggestions for improving it.

A mental construct is a concept designed for purposes of analytical reasoning that cannot be adequately defined or circumscribed in terms of observables or in terms of operations with recorded data derived from observation. It is the result of a mental construction, either (1) without reference to empirical data, as in the case of the constructs of pure mathematics, or (2) with some indirect reference to facts of experience but derived through idealization, heroic abstraction, or invention, as in the case of the constructs of empirical sciences. The constructs of empirical sciences may be divided into (a) constructs used as explanatory links between observable phenomena where the question of the existence of a direct « counterpart » in the real world remains problematic, as in the case of a nuclear « particle » so called; (b) constructs used for purposes of hypothetical reasoning where the existence of a « counterpart » in the real world is regarded as highly improbable, if not impossible, as in the case of imaginary « perfection » such as the physical concepts of the perfect gas, the perfectly rigid lever, perfect blackness, or the economic concepts of the economic man, perfect foresight, perfect competition; and (c) constructs which, though they have direct « counterparts » in the real world, must for purposes of hypothetical reasoning be kept free from the uncertain attributes, deviations, or associations that commonly attach to empirical concepts and would blur or vitiate the analytical (implicative) connections with other constructs of a theoretical system. Constructs in the social sciences are often in the nature of « ideal types », formed with a strong admixture of inner experience and « understanding » of the subjective meanings.

THE EMPIRICAL REFERENCE OF IDEAL TYPES AND OTHER CONSTRUCTS

Before we discuss the special kind of empirical reference which is inherent in the ideal types employed in the social sciences — a reference to inner experience — we should comment on the general kind of empirical reference that is involved in the formation of virtually *all* mental constructs. This seems advisable because some writers have made much of an apparent difference between concepts « arbitrarily constructed » and concepts « derived from experience ». The distinction is misleading since experience will necessarily affect the construction of any sort of concept, and there will be a dose of the arbitrary in the formation of any concept, however realistic (45).

The role of experience in the formation of a mental construct will be indicated, in turn, for a construct in physics and for a construct in economics. Take the « neutrino » as a relatively novel construct of physics. It got its start when experimental data failed to fit the consequences deduced from the accepted theoretical system (including the postulated law of the conservation of energy). The inclusion of a new

---

(45) "Inner experience" and "subjective meanings" are anathema to many scientists, especially to many American psychologists who have embraced "operationism" with great fervor. For example: « Since science is empirical and excluded private data, all of its concepts must be capable of operational definition ». Edwin G. BORING, *The Use of Operational Definitions in Science*, in the « Symposium on Operationism » published by the « Psychological Review », Vol. 52 (September 1945), p. 244. The editor of that Review added to the terminological confusion by speaking of « construct-terms » which could or could not be operationally defined (*loc. cit.*, p. 241). Another participant in the symposium attempted to set this straight: « A construct is something constructed. The initial data of science are not constructed. They are given ». CARROLL C. PRATT, « Operationism in Psychology », *loc. cit.*, p. 262. The term "construct" was coined in order to contrast this kind of concept with empirical concepts; to use it for any sort of concept would make it a useless term.

construct in the system seemed to be the best device for making the system yield deduced consequences that fitted the data. The new construct — the neutrino — was called a « particle » by analogy with experiences of other things. It was designed to give (in conjunction with all other variables and relations constructed for the system) results that corresponded to the experimental data; yet, it was not an object of observation or any other kind of direct experience. In other words, the reference to observed phenomena is only indirect.

Now think of the « money illusion » as a relatively novel construct of economics. It probably got its start when observations of (increased) consumer price and of (unchanged) amounts of labor available seemed to contradict deductions from a model which included labor supply as an increasing function of real-wage rates. The inclusion of a new construct seemed to be the best device for removing from the model the effect which the reduction of real-wage rates (implied in increased consumer prices) would have upon the quantity of labor supplied, and thus for allowing the deduced consequences of an increase in effective demand to fit better the acutal supposed (or hoped for) observations. The new construct — the money illusion —, since it had to offset the effects of another construct, namely, « perfect rationality », was called an « illusion » by analogy with a type of inner experience shared by many (who, though normally quite sensible, sometimes fail to wake up to certain realities). With the help of the new construct the consequences deduced from the enlarged system promised to correspond to what was thought to be the record of observation; but the construct is without direct reference to observables and no one could reasonably claim to have any direct experience of illusions suffered by other minds. The reference to observed phenomena is entirely indirect.

In many respects the empirical reference of the constructs is the *same* for natural and social sciences: (1) Inadequate correspondence between deduction (from an accepted model) and empirical observations sets off a search for new constructs. (2) The inclusion of the new constructs into the model is designed to achieve closer correspondence between deductions and observations. (3) The invention and design of the new constructs is affected by analogical reasoning based on various kinds of experience, though not necessarily related to the problem at hand. (4) The modified model is tested by the correspondence between the modified deductions and observations. A significant *difference* exists, however, in point (3), for it is a very special type of experience that affects invention and design of a new construct in the social sciences: each construct must pass the test of empathic understanding or imagined introspection; that is to say, it must satisfy the postulates of « subjective interpretation » and of « consistency with the constructs of commonsense experience » (46).

This does not mean that these ideal types are « realistic ». They are not, because the selection of the supposedly relevant trait, motive, attitude, or mode of thinking that is idealized in the construct implies the exclusion of many other traits, motives, attitudes, or modes of thinking which we all, in everyday life, know we have and which we suppose others likewise have; and this unnatural isolation of one element from all the rest makes the construct definitely unrealistic. Yet human experience is undoubtedly behind the creation of the construct, and the construct, however nonhuman in its artificial limitation dictated by the purpose of the model, must be so designed that an act performed « in the way indicated by the typical construct would be understandable » (47) by people possessing experiences of the kind involved. (Perhaps it needs to be added that an act can be « understandable » to me even if I myself were not disposed to act the same way in the same circumstances).

Experience, Realism, Relevance, and Truth

That the constructs (ideal types) of the social sciences are derived from experience and consistent with the constructs of common-sense experience does not make them « *empirical* ». Nor does it make them, or the models for which they are used, « *realistic* »; nor does it make them, or the models, « *relevant* »; nor does it make the theories for which they are used « *true* ». A few words about the widespread confusion between experience, realism, relevance, and truth may be an appropriate conclusion of this essay.

The origin or derivation of a concept has nothing to do with its logical nature. It may be « derived » from or « inspired » by experience, and yet be a « pure construct » (« ideal type »). It is empirical only to the extent that it embodies the result of observation (including experimentation), usually in the form of records of instrument readings and/or testimonies and other communications. That the records in the

---

(46) ALFRED SCHUETZ, « Common-Sense and Scientific Interpretation of Human Action », *Philosophy and Phenomenological Research*, Vol. XIV (1953), p. 34.

(47) SCHUETZ, *loc. cit.*, p. 34.

social sciences always go back to some person's interpretations of subjective meanings — such as « costs », « prices », depreciation », « profits », « purchase », « loan », « gift », « theft », « marriage », « illegitimate child » — is characteristic for the science of society (48). (This subjective interpretation is inherent in the abstract constructs as well as in the empirical concepts of the social sciences). The more manipulations (computations, corrections, adjustments) are made with the raw data contained in the record, the more refining decisions are made on the basis of preconceived theory and intelligent judgment, the further removed from the direct findings of observation and the less empirical will be the resulting figures.

The confusion between realism and relevance can best be cleared up by emphasizing the fact that they are usually opposites. To draw a picture in all « realistic » detail means to include all that hits the eye, however irrelevant it may be for a particular purpose; to draw a model with only the « relevant » features means to leave out the realistic appearances. If Johnny wants to know how a steam locomotive *looks,* we shall show him a photograph on which he will see all that is on the surface of the thing. If he wants to know how a steam locomotive *works,* we shall show him a model that includes very little of the realistic picture, but instead a few things not visible there: a schematic drawing of a cylinder, a piston, a valve, etc. An explanatory model should not be realistic; it should exhibit what are considered the relevant variables and relations.

Formal logic has taught us that a proposition is either « true » or « false ». A scientific theory, perhaps, may be true or false, but the scientist will reserve his judgment. He may be firmly convinced that his theory is « true », but he will be mindful of the fact that thousands of theories, once held to be true, have had to be rejected or modified or reformulated; hence all he will say is that his theory is the best he has got, and that it has « not yet » been disconfirmed.

Of course, this business of disconfirming has something to do with experience and with relevance. For it is by means of empirical tests,

---

(48) The « facts » of the social sciences cannot be « observed » with the five senses. If Mr. A is observed carrying an object from Mr. B's store, the observers cannot know whether he has bought it, borrowed it, stolen it, or was given it as a present. Perhaps A and B do not agree, one regarding the transaction as a gift, the other as a theft. The subjective meanings of the actors and the interpretations by record keepers and record analysts are essential.

through comparisons of the deduced consequences of the theory with empirical data recognized as their adequate counterparts, that the theory may eventually be rejected — in favor of a better one. And this will happen if the model embodied in the theory does not contain the relevant, or not all the relevant, variables for the problem at hand. Thus there is after all a connection between experience, relevance, and truth — but it certainly does not mean that the relevant concepts in a good theory must be « empirical ».

FRITZ MACHLUP

Princeton, Princeton University

TIPOGRAFIA STEFANO PINELLI - VIA FARNETI, 8 - MILANO

Reprinted from THE SOUTHERN ECONOMIC JOURNAL
Vol. XXII, No. 1, July, 1955
Printed in U.S.A.

[3]

THE PROBLEM OF VERIFICATION IN ECONOMICS*

FRITZ MACHLUP

The Johns Hopkins University

I

It will be well for us first to clear the ground lest we get lost in the rubble of past discussions. To clear the ground is, above all, to come to a decision as to what we mean by verification and what it can and cannot do for our research and analysis.

The Meaning of Verification

A good book of synonyms will have the verb "verify" associated with the more pretentious verbs "prove," "demonstrate," "establish," "ascertain," "confirm," and with the more modest verbs "check" and "test." The verbs in the former group would usually be followed by a "that"—"we shall prove that . . ."—the verbs in the latter group by a "whether"—"we shall check whether. . . ." Besides this difference between "verify that" and "verify whether," there is the difference between verification as a process and verification as an affirmative result of that process. By using *"test"* for the former and *"confirmation"* for the latter we may avoid confusion. Where the distinction is not necessary, "verification" is an appropriate weasel-word, meaning both test and confirmation.

Verification in research and analysis may refer to many things including the correctness of mathematical and logical arguments, the applicability of formulas and equations, the trustworthiness of reports, the authenticity of documents, the genuineness of artifacts or relics, the adequacy of reproductions, translations and paraphrases, the accuracy of historical and statistical accounts, the corroboration of reported events, the completeness in the enumeration of circumstances in a concrete situation, the reliability and exactness of observations, the reproducibility of experiments, the explanatory or predictive value of generalizations. For each of these pursuits, the term verification is used in various disciplines. But we intend to confine ourselves to the last one mentioned: the verification of the explanatory or predictive value of hypothetical generalizations.

Although definitions are sometimes a nuisance rather than an aid, I shall try my hand at one, and say that verification in the sense most relevant to us—the

* A paper presented at the Annual Conference of the Southern Economic Association in Biloxi, Mississippi, on November 19, 1954. The author is indebted to several of his colleagues, but chiefly to Dr. Edith Penrose, for criticism and suggestions leading to improvements of style and exposition.

1

testing of generalizations—is *a procedure designed to find out whether a set of data of observation about a class of phenomena is obtainable and can be reconciled with a particular set of hypothetical generalizations about this class of phenomena.*

Truth and Reality

I have carefully avoided the words "truth" and "reality," although the Latin *veritas* forms the root of the term defined. I eschewed references to truth and reality in order to stay out of strictly epistemological and ontological controversies. Not that such discussions would be uninteresting or unimportant; he who never studies metaphysical questions, and even prides himself on his unconcern with metaphysics, often does not know how much in fact he talks about it. To stay away from metaphysics one has to know a good bit about it.

The function of words chosen—testing, checking, confirming—is precisely to enable us to leave the concepts of truth and reality in the background. If I should slip occasionally and say that a proposition is "true" or a phenomenon is "real," this should be taken merely as an unguarded way of speaking; for I mean to say only that there seems to be considerable "support" or "evidence" for the proposition in view of a marked *correspondence* or consistency between that proposition and statements about particular observations.

Special and General Hypotheses

My definition of verification related only to hypothetical generalizations. But the status of *special hypotheses about single events or unique situations* (and their causes, effects, and interrelations) also calls for examination, for it is with these that economic history and most of applied economics are concerned. Such special hypotheses—to establish the "facts"—are of course also subject to verification, but the rules and techniques are somewhat different from those of the verification of general hypotheses.

In a murder case we ask "who done it?" and the answer requires the weighing of several alternative special hypotheses. Such special hypotheses may be mental constructions of unobserved occurrences which could have taken place in conjunction with occurrences observed or conclusively inferred. It is an accepted rule that a special hypothesis will be rejected if it is contradicted by a single inconsistency between a firmly established observation and any of the things that follow logically from the combination of the special hypothesis and the factual assumptions of the argument.

But this weighing and testing of special hypotheses in the light of the known circumstances of the case always involves numerous *general* hypotheses. For example, the generalization that "if a man is at one place he cannot at the same time be at another place" may be of utmost importance in verifying a suspicion that Mr. X was the murderer. And whenever observations have to be interpreted and special hypotheses applied to reach a conclusion about what are the "concrete facts," the argument will presuppose the acceptance of numerous general theories or hypotheses linking two or more (observed or inferred) "facts" as possible (or probable) causes and effects. This is the reason why it has to be said over and over again that most of the facts of history are based on previously formed general hypotheses or theories. Although this has been an important theme in the discussion of the relation between theory and history, and one of the central issues in the *Methodenstreit* in economics, it is not an issue in our discussion today. At the moment we are concerned with the verification of general hypotheses and theories, not of propositions concerning individual events or conditions at a particular time and place. But this much ought to be said here: to establish or verify "historical facts," we must rely on the acceptance of numerous general hypotheses (theories); and to verify general hypotheses we must rely on the acceptance of numerous data representing "facts" observed or inferred at various times and places. We always must take something for granted, no matter how averse we are to "preconceptions."

Theories, Hypotheses, Hunches, Assumptions, Postulates

No fixed lines can be drawn between theories, hypotheses, and mere hunches, the differences being at best those of degree. There are degrees of vagueness in formulation, degrees of confidence or strength of belief in what is posed or stated, degrees of acceptance among experts, and degrees of comprehensiveness or range of applicability.[1]

A hunch is usually vague, sometimes novel, original, often incompletely formulated; perhaps more tentative than a hypothesis, although the difference may lie just in the modesty of the analyst. A hypothesis may likewise be very tentative; indeed, some hypotheses are introduced only for didactic purposes, as provisional steps in an argument, in full knowledge of their inapplicability to any concrete situation and perhaps in preparation for a preferred hypothesis. Distinctions between hypotheses and theories have been suggested in terms of the strength of belief in their applicability or of the comprehensiveness (range) of their applicability.[2] But so often are the words theory and hypothesis used interchangeably that there is not much point in laboring any distinguishing criteria.

Perhaps it should be stressed that every hypothesis may have the status of an "assumption" in a logical argument. An assumption of a rather general nature which is posited as a "principle" for an argument or for a whole system

---

[1] The belief that a "hunch" is something fundamentally different from a "theory" may be responsible for certain antitheoretical positions of some historians and statisticians. Those who claimed the priority and supremacy of fact-finding over "theoretical speculation" might have accepted the contention that you cannot find facts without having some hunch. But this is practically all that the theorists meant when they claimed that theory must precede fact-finding, whether historical or statistical, and that history without theory, and measurement without theory are *impossible*. There are kinds of fact-finding which presuppose full-fledged theories; some simpler kinds may start with vague hunches.

[2] "A hypothesis is an assumption . . . tentatively suggested as an explanation of a phenomenon." Morris R. Cohen and Ernest Nagel, *An Introduction to Logic and Scientific Method* (New York: Harcourt, Brace, 1938), p. 205.—"A hypothesis . . . is . . . a theory which has, at present at least, a limited range of application. It is promoted to the status of a theory if and when its range is deemed sufficiently large to justify this more commendatory appelation." Henry Margenau, "Methodology of Modern Physics," *Philosophy of Science*, Vol. II (January 1935), p. 67.

of thought, but is neither self-evident nor proved, is often called a "postulate." Just as there may be a connotation of tentativeness in the word "hypothesis," there may be a connotation of arbitrariness in the word "postulate."[3] But since no fundamental assumption in an empirical discipline is definitive, and since all are more or less arbitrary, it is useless to insist on subtle distinctions which are (for good reasons) disregarded by most participants in the discussion.[4]

Confirmation versus Non-Disconfirmation

How is a hypothesis verified? The hypothesis is *tested* by a two-step procedure: first deducing from it and the factual assumptions with which it is combined all the conclusions that can be inferred, and second, confronting these conclusions with data obtained from observation of the phenomena concerned. The hypothesis is *confirmed* if reasonable correspondence is found between the deduced and the observed, or more correctly, if no irreconcilable contradiction is found between the deduced and the observed. Absence of contradictory evidence, a finding of non-contradiction, is really a negation of a negation: indeed, one calls a hypothesis "confirmed" when it is merely *not disconfirmed*.

Thus, the procedure of verification may yield findings compelling the rejection of the tested hypothesis, but never findings that can "prove" its correctness, adequacy or applicability.[5] As in a continuing sports championship conducted by elimination rules, where the winner stays in the game as long as he is not defeated but can always be challenged for another contest, no empirical hypothesis is safe forever; it can always be challenged for another test and may be knocked out at any time. The test results, at best, in a "confirmation till next time."

Several logicians use the word "falsification" for a finding of irreconcilable contradiction; and since a hypothesis can be definitely refuted or "falsified," but not definitely confirmed or "verified," some logicians have urged that we speak only of "falsifiable," not of verifiable propositions. Because the word "falsification" has a double meaning, I prefer to speak of refutation or disconfirmation. But the dictum is surely right: testing an empirical hypothesis results either in its disconfirmation or its non-disconfirmation, never in its definitive confirmation.

---

[3] Cf. Wayne A. Leeman, "The Status of Facts in Economic Thought," *The Journal of Philosophy*, Vol. XLVII (June 1951), p. 408.—Leeman suggests that economists prefer the term "assumption" because it "escapes . . . the undesirable connotations" of the terms "hypothesis" and "postulate."

[4] "So far as our present argument is concerned, the things (propositions) that we take for granted may be called indiscriminately either hypotheses or axioms or postulates or assumptions or even principles, and the things (propositions) that we think we have established by admissible procedure are called theorems." Joseph A. Schumpeter, *History of Economic Analysis* (New York: Oxford University Press, 1954), p. 15.

[5] There are no rules of verification "that can be relied on in the last resort. Take the most important rules of experimental verification: reproducibility of results; agreement between determinations made by different and independent methods; fulfillment of predictions. These are powerful criteria, but I could give you examples in which they were all fulfilled and yet the statement which they seemed to confirm later turned out to be false. The most striking agreement with experiment may occasionally be revealed later to be based on mere coincidence. . . ." Michael Polanyi, *Science, Faith and Society* (London: Cumberlege, 1946), p. 13.

Even if a definitive confirmation is never possible, the number of tests which a hypothesis has survived in good shape will have a bearing on the confidence people have in its "correctness." A hypothesis confirmed and re-confirmed any number of times will have a more loyal following than one only rarely exposed to the test of experience. But the strength of belief in a hypothesis depends, even more than on any direct empirical tests that it may have survived, on the place it holds within a hierarchical system of inter-related hypotheses. But this is another matter, to be discussed a little later.

Nothing that I have said thus far would, I believe, be objected to by any modern logician, philosopher of science, or scientist. While all points mentioned were once controversial, the combat has moved on to other issues, and only a few stragglers and latecomers on the battlefield of methodology mistake the rubble left from long ago for the marks of present fighting. So we shall move on to issues on which controversy continues.

II

Which kinds of propositions can be verified, and which cannot? May unverified and unverifiable propositions be legitimately retained in a scientific system? Or should all scientific propositions be verified or at least verifiable? These are among the controversial issues—though my own views are so decided that I cannot see how intelligent people can still quarrel about them, and I have come to believe that all good men think as I do, and only a few misguided creatures think otherwise. But I shall restrain my convictions for a while.

Critizing extreme positions is a safe pastime because one may be sure of the support of a majority. But it is not for this reason but for the sake of a clear exposition that I begin with the presentation of the positions which *extreme apriorism*, on the one side, and *ultra-empiricism*, on the other side, take concerning the problem of verification in economics.

Pure, Exact, and Aprioristic Economics

Writers on the one side of this issue contend that economic science is a system of *a priori* truths, a product of pure reason,[6] an exact science reaching laws as universal as those of mathematics,[7] a purely axiomatic discipline,[8] a system of pure deductions from a series of postulates,[9] not open to any verification or refutation on the ground of experience.[10]

[6] "The ultimate yardstick of an economic theorem's correctness or incorrectness is solely reason unaided by experience." Ludwig von Mises, *Human Action: A Treatise on Economics* (New Haven: Yale University Press, 1949), p. 858.

[7] "There is a science of economics, a true and even exact science, which reaches laws as universal as those of mathematics and mechanics." Frank H. Knight, "The Limitations of Scientific Method in Economics," in R. G. Tugwell, ed., *The Trend of Economics* (New York: Crofts, 1930), p. 256.

[8] "Economic theory is an axiomatic discipline. . . ." Max Weber, *On the Methodology of the Social Sciences* (Glencoe, Ill.: Free Press, 1949), p. 43.

[9] "Economic analysis . . . consists of deductions from a series of postulates. . . ." Lionel Robbins, *An Essay on the Nature and Significance of Economic Science* (London: Macmillan, 2nd ed., 1935), p. 99.

[10] "What assigns economics its peculiar and unique position in the orbit of pure knowl-

We must not attribute to all writers whose statements were here quoted or paraphrased the same epistemological views. While for Mises, for example, even the fundamental postulates are *a priori* truths, necessities of thinking,[11] for Robbins they are "assumptions involving in some way simple and indisputable facts of experience."[12] But most of the experience in point is not capable of being recorded from external (objective) observation; instead, it is immediate, inner experience. Hence, if verification is recognized only where the test involves objective sense-experience, the chief assumptions of economics, even if "empirical," are not independently verifiable propositions.

This methodological position, either asserting an *a priori* character of all propositions of economic theory or at least denying the independent objective verifiability of the fundamental assumptions, had been vigorously stated in the last century by Senior[13] and Cairnes,[14] but in essential respects it goes back to John Stuart Mill.

Mill, the great master and expositor of inductive logic, had this to say on the method of investigation in political economy:

Since . . . it is vain to hope that truth can be arrived at, either in Political Economy or in any other department of the social science, while we look at the facts in the concrete, clothed in all the complexity with which nature has surrounded them, and endeavor to elicit a general law by a process of induction from a comparison of details; there remains no other method than the *a priori* one, or that of 'abstract speculation.'[15]

By the method *a priori* we mean . . . reasoning from an assumed hypothesis; which is not a practice confined to mathematics, but is of the essence of all science which admits of general reasoning at all. To verify the hypothesis itself *a posteriori*, that is, to examine whether the facts of any actual case are in accordance with it, is no part of the business of science at all but of the *application* of science.[16]

This does not mean that Mill rejects attempts to verify the results of economic analysis; on the contrary,

We cannot . . . too carefully endeavor to verify our theory, by comparing, in the particular cases to which we have access, the results which it would have led us to predict, with the most trustworthy accounts we can obtain of those which have been actually realized.[17]

---

edge and of the practical utilization of knowledge is the fact that its particular theorems are not open to any verification or falsification on the ground of experience." Ludwig von Mises, *op. cit.*, p. 858.

[11] Ludwig von Mises, *op. cit.*, p. 33.

[12] Lionel Robbins, *op. cit.*, p. 78, also pp. 99–100.

[13] Nassau William Senior, *Political Economy* (London: Griffin, 3rd ed., 1854), pp. 5, 26–29.

[14] John E. Cairnes, *The Character and Logical Method of Political Economy* (London: Macmillan, 1875), especially pp. 74–85, 99–100.

[15] John Stuart Mill, "On the Definition of Political Economy; and on the Method of Investigation Proper to It" in *Essays on Some Unsettled Questions of Political Economy* (London, 1844, reprinted London School of Economics, 1948), pp. 148–49.

[16] *Ibid.*, p. 143.

[17] *Ibid.*, p. 154.

The point to emphasize is that Mill does not propose to put the *assumptions* of economic theory to empirical tests, but only the *predicted results that are deduced from them*. And this, I submit, is what all the proponents of pure, exact, or aprioristic economic theory had in mind, however provocative their contentions sounded.[18] Their objection was to verifying the basic assumptions in isolation.

Ultra-Empirical Economics

Opposed to these tenets are the ultra-empiricists. "Empiricist" is a word of praise to some, a word of abuse to others. This is due to the fact that there are many degrees of empiricism. Some economists regard themselves as "empiricists" merely because they oppose radical apriorism and stress the dependence of theory on experience (in the widest sense of the word); others, because they demand that the results deduced with the aid of theory be compared with observational data whenever possible; others, because they are themselves chiefly concerned with the interpretation of data, with the testing of hypotheses and with the estimates of factual relationships; others, because they are themselves engaged in the collection of data or perhaps even in "field" work designed to produce "raw" data; others, because they refuse to recognize the legitimacy of employing at any level of analysis propositions not independently verifiable. It is the last group which I call the ultra-empiricists.[19] Then there are the ultra-ultra-empiricists who go even further and insist on independent verification of all assumptions by objective data obtained through sense observation.

The ultra-empiricist position is most sharply reflected in the many attacks on the "assumptions" of economic theory. These assumptions are decried as unverified, unverifiable, imaginary, unrealistic. And the hypothetico-deductive system built upon the unrealistic or unverifiable assumptions is condemned either as deceptive or as devoid of empirical content,[20] without predictive or

---

[18] "Aprioristic reasoning is purely conceptual and deductive. It cannot produce anything else but tautologies and analytic judgments." While this sounds like an "empiricist's" criticism of the aprioristic position, it is in fact a statement by Mises. (*Op. cit.*, p. 38.) Mises emphasizes that "the end of science is to know reality," and that "in introducing assumptions into its reasoning, it satisfies itself that the treatment of the assumptions concerned can render useful services for the comprehension of reality." (*Ibid.*, pp. 65–66.) And he stresses that the choice of assumptions is directed by experience.

[19] It is in this last meaning that empiricisms has usually been discussed and criticized in philosophy. In the words of William James, radical empiricism "must neither admit into its constructions any element that is not directly experienced, nor exclude from them any element that is directly experienced. For such a philosophy, *the relations that connect experiences must themselves be experienced relations, and any kind of relation experienced must be accounted as 'real' as anything else in the system.*" William James, *Essays in Radical Empiricism* (New York: Longmans, Green, 1912), pp. 42–43.

[20] "That 'propositions of pure theory' is a name for . . . propositions not conceivably falsifiable empirically and which do not exclude . . . any conceivable occurrence, and which are therefore devoid of empirical content. . . ." T. W. Hutchison, *The Significance and Basic Postulates of Economic Theory* (London: Macmillan, 1938), p. 162.

explanatory significance,[21] without application to problems or data of the real world.[22] Why deceptive? Because from wrong assumptions only wrong conclusions follow. Why without empirical significance? Because, in the words of the logician Wittgenstein, "from a tautology only tautologies follow."[23]

If the ultra-empiricists reject the basic assumptions of economic theory because they are not independently verified, and reject any theoretical system that is built on unverified or unverifiable assumptions, what is the alternative they offer? A program that begins with facts rather than assumptions.[24] What facts? Those obtained "by statistical investigations, questionnaires to consumers and entrepreneurs, the examination of family budgets and the like."[25] It is in research of this sort that the ultra-empiricists see "the only possible scientific method open" to the economist.[26]

This, again, is the essence of the ultra-empiricist position on verification: the ultra-empiricist is so distrustful of deductive systems of thought that he is not satisfied with the indirect verification of hypotheses, that is, with tests showing that the results deduced (from these hypotheses and certain factual assumptions) are in approximate correspondence with reliable observational data; instead, he insists on the independent verification of all the assumptions, hypothetical as well as factual, perhaps even of each intermediate step in the analysis. To him "testable" means "directly testable by objective data obtained by sense observation," and propositions which are in this sense "non-testable" are detestable to him.

The Testability of Fundamental Assumptions

The error in the antitheoretical empiricist position lies in the failure to see the difference between *fundamental* (heuristic) hypotheses, which are not inde-

---

[21] ". . . that propositions of pure theory, by themselves, have no prognostic value or 'causal significance.' " T. W. Hutchison, *op. cit.*, p. 162.—The clause "by themselves" makes Hutchison's statement unassailable, because nothing at all has causal significance by itself; only in conjunction with other things can anything have causal significance. But if Hutchison's statement means anything, it means an attack against the use of empirically unverifiable propositions in economic theory, regardless of their conjunction with other propositions. Indeed, he states that "a proposition which can never *conceivably* be shown to be true or false . . . can *never* be of any use to a scientist" (*ibid.*, pp. 152–53).

[22] With regard to the "fundamental assumption" of economic theory concerning "subjectively rational" and "maximizing" behavior, Hutchison states that "the empirical content of the assumption and all the conclusions will be the same—that is, nothing." *Ibid.*, p. 116.

[23] Ludwig Wittgenstein, *Tractatus Logico-Philosophicus* (London: Routledge & Kegan Paul, 1951), p. 167.

[24] ". . . if one wants to get beyond a certain high level of abstraction one has to begin more or less from the beginning with extensive empirical investigation." T. W. Hutchison, *op. cit.*, p. 166.

[25] *Ibid.*, p. 120. This does not answer the question: "what facts?" Precisely what data should be obtained and statistically investigated? What questions asked of consumers and entrepreneurs?

[26] *Ibid.*, p. 120. I could have quoted from dozens of critics of economic theory, from adherents of the historical, institutional, quantitative schools, and these quotations might be even more aggressive. I have selected Hutchison because he is the critic best informed about logic and scientific method.

pendently testable, and *specific* (factual) assumptions, which are supposed to correspond to observed facts or conditions; or the differences between hypotheses on different levels of generality and, hence, of different degrees of testability.

The fundamental hypotheses are also called by several other names, some of which convey a better idea of their methodological status: "heuristic principles" (because they serve as useful guides in the analysis), "basic postulates" (because they are not to be challenged for the time being), "useful fictions" (because they need not conform to "facts" but only be useful in "as if" reasoning), "procedural rules" (because they are resolutions about the analytical procedure to be followed), "definitional assumptions" (because they are treated like purely analytical conventions).

A fundamental hypothesis serves to bring together under a common principle of explanation vast numbers of very diverse observations, masses of data of apparently very different sort, phenomena that would otherwise seem to have nothing in common. Problems like the explanation of the movements in wages in 13th and 14th century Europe, of the prices of spices in 16th century Venice, of the effects of the capital flows to Argentina in the 19th century, of the consequences of German reparation payments and of the devaluation of the dollar in the 1930's; problems like the prediction of effects of the new American quota on Swiss watches, of the new tax laws, of the increase in minimum wage rates, and so forth,—problems of such dissimilarity can all be tackled by the use of the same fundamental hypotheses. If these hypotheses are successful in this task and give more satisfactory results than other modes of treatment could, then we accept them and stick by them as long as there is nothing better—which may be forever.

That there is no way of subjecting fundamental assumptions to independent verification should be no cause of disturbance. It does not disturb the workers in the discipline which most social scientists so greatly respect and envy for its opportunities of verification: physical science. The whole system of physical mechanics rests on such fundamental assumptions: Newton's three laws of motion are postulates or procedural rules for which no experimental verification is possible or required; and, as Einstein put it, "No one of the assumptions can be isolated for separate testing." For, he went on to say, "physical concepts are free creations of the human mind, and are not, however it may seem, uniquely determined by the external world."[27]

Much has been written about the meaning of "explanation." Some have said that the mere *description* of regularities in the co-existence and co-variation of observed phenomena is all we can do and will be accepted as an *explanation* when we are sufficiently used to the regularities described.[28] There is something to this view; but mere resignation to the fact that "it always has been so" will not for long pass as explanation for searching minds. The feeling of relief and satisfied curiosity—often expressed in the joyous exclamation "ah haahh!"— comes to most analysts only when the observed regularities can be deduced from

---

[27] Albert Einstein and Leopold Infeld, *The Evolution of Physics* (New York: Simon and Schuster, 1938), p. 33.

[28] Cf. P. W. Bridgman, *The Logic of Modern Physics* (New York: Macmillan, 1927), p. 43.

general principles which are also the starting point—foundation or apex, as you like—of many other chains of causal derivation. This is why Margenau, another physicist, said that an explanation involves a "progression into the constructional domain. We explain by going 'beyond phenomena.' "[29] But this clearly implies that the explanatory general assumptions cannot be empirically verifiable in isolation.

Logicians and philosophers of science have long tried to make this perfectly clear. Although appeals to authority are ordinarily resorted to only where an expositor has failed to convince his audience, I cannot resist the temptation to quote two authorities on my subject. Here is how the American philosopher Josiah Royce put it:

> One often meets with the remark that a scientific hypothesis must be such as to be more or less completely capable of verification or of refutation by experience. The remark is sound. But equally sound it is to say that a hypothesis which, just as it is made, is, without further deductive reasoning, capable of receiving direct refutation or verification, *is not nearly as valuable to any science as is a hypothesis whose verifications, so far as they occur at all, are only possible indirectly, and through the mediation of a considerable deductive theory*, whereby the consequences of the hypothesis are first worked out, and then submitted to test.[30]

And here is the same idea in the words of the British philosopher of science, Richard B. Braithwaite:

> For science, as it advances, does not rest content with establishing simple generalizations from observable facts. It tries to explain these lowest-level generalization by deducing them from more general hypotheses at a higher level. . . . As the hierarchy of hypotheses of increasing generality rises, the concepts with which the hypotheses are concerned cease to be properties of things which are directly observable, and instead become 'theoretical' concepts—atoms, electrons, fields of force, genes, unconscious mental processes—which are connected to the observable facts by complicated logical relationships.[31]

And he states that "the empirical testing of the deductive system is effected by testing the lowest-level hypotheses in the system."[32]

Assumptions in Economics, Pure and Applied

Examples of *fundamental assumptions* or "high-level generalizations" in economic theory are that people act rationally, try to make the most of their opportunities, and are able to arrange their preferences in a consistent order; that entrepreneurs prefer more profit to less profit with equal risk.[33] These are

[29] Henry Margenau, *The Nature of Physical Reality* (New York: McGraw-Hill, 1950), p. 169.

[30] Josiah Royce, "The Principles of Logic," in *Logic, Encyclopaedia of the Philosophical Sciences*, Vol. I (London: Macmillan, 1913), pp. 88–89.

[31] Richard Bevan Braithwaite, *Scientific Explanation: A Study of the Function of Theory, Probability and Law in Science* (Cambridge: University Press, 1953), p. ix.

[32] *Ibid.*, p. 13.

[33] For most problems of an enterprise economy no exact specifications about "profit"

assumptions which, though empirically meaningful, require no independent empirical tests but may be significant steps in arguments reaching conclusions which are empirically testable.

Examples of *specific assumptions* are that the expenditures for table salt are a small portion of most households' annual budgets; that the member banks are holding very large excess reserves with the Federal Reserve Banks; that there is a quota for the importation of sugar which is fully utilized. Examples of *deduced "low-level hypotheses"* are that a reduction in the price of table salt will not result in a proportionate increase in salt consumption; that a reduction in the discount rates of the Federal Reserve Banks will at such times not result in an increase in the member banks' lending activities; that a reduction in sugar prices abroad will not result in a reduction of domestic sugar prices. All these and similar specific assumptions and low-level hypotheses are empirically testable.

Perhaps a few additional comments should be made concerning the fundamental assumptions, particularly the postulate of rational action, the "economic principle" of aiming at the attainment of a maximum of given ends. Any independent test of this assumption by reference to objective *sense*-experience is obviously impossible. Those who accept findings of introspection as sufficient evidence may contend that the fundamental assumption can be, and constantly is, verified. Those who accept findings of interrogation (that is, replies to questions put to large numbers of introspectors) as "objective" evidence may contend that the assumption of "maximizing behavior" is independently testable. But such a test would be gratuitous, if not misleading. For the fundamental assumption may be understood as an idealization with constructs so far removed from operational concepts that contradiction by testimony is ruled out; or even as a complete fiction with only one claim: that reasoning *as if* it were realized is helpful in the interpretation of observations.[34]

Economists who are still suspicious of non-verifiable assumptions, and worry about the legitimacy of using them, may be reassured by this admission: The fact that fundamental assumptions are not directly testable and cannot be refuted by empirical investigation does not mean that they are beyond the pale of the so-called "principle of permanent control," that is, beyond possible challenge, modification or rejection. These assumptions may well be rejected, but only together with the theoretical system of which they are a part, and only when a more satisfactory system is put in its place; in Conant's words, "a theory is only overthrown by a better theory, never merely by contradictory facts."[35]

(whose? for what period? how uncertain? etc.) will be needed. There are some special problems for which "specific assumptions" concerning profit are needed. Needless to say, the assumption about entrepreneurs will be irrelevant for problems of centrally directed economies.

[34] Or, again in a different formulation: the fundamental assumption is a resolution to proceed in the interpretation of all data of observation as if they were the result of the postulated type of behavior.

[35] James B. Conant, *On Understanding Science* (New Haven: Yale University Press, 1947), p. 36.

III

What I have said and quoted about assumptions and hypotheses on various "levels" of abstraction may itself be too abstract, too remote from our ordinary terms of discourse, to be meaningful to many of us. Perhaps it will be helpful to try a graphical presentation of a simple model of an analytical system combining assumptions of various types.

A Model of an Analytical Apparatus

The design for the model was suggested by the usual metaphors about an analytical "apparatus," "machine," or "engine of pure theory." Something goes into a machine and something comes out. In this case the input is an assumption concerning some "change" occurring and causing other things to happen, and the output is the "Deduced Change," the conclusion of the (mental) operation. The machine with all its parts furnishes the connection between the "assumed cause," the input, and the "deduced effect," the outcome. The main point of this model is that *the machine is a construction of our mind, while the assumed and deduced changes should correspond to observed phenomena, to data of observation, if the machine is to serve as an instrument of explanation or prediction*. In explanations the analytical machine helps select an adequate "cause" for an observed change; in predictions it helps find a probable "effect" of an observed change.[36]

The machine consists of many parts, all of which represent assumptions or hypotheses of different degrees of generality. The so-called *fundamental assumptions* are a fixed part of the machine; they make the machine what it is; they cannot be changed without changing the character of the entire machine. All other parts are exchangeable, like coils, relays, spools, wires, tapes, cylinders, records, or mats, something that can be selected and put in, and again taken out to be replaced by a different piece of the set. These exchangeable parts represent *assumptions about the conditions* under which the Assumed Change must operate. Some of the parts are exchanged all the time, some less frequently, some only seldom. Parts of type A, the Assumed Conditions as to "type of case," are most frequently exchanged. Parts of type B, the Assumed Conditions as to "type of setting," will stay in the machine for a longer time and there need be less variety in the set from which they are selected. Parts of type C, the Assumed Conditions as to "type of economy," are least exchangeable, and there will be only a small assortment of alternative pieces to choose from.

Now we shall leave the engineering analogies aside and discuss the status of all these assumptions regarding the operational and observational possibilities and the requirements of verification.

Verified Changes under Unverified Conditions

Both the Assumed Change and the Deduced Change should be empirically verifiable through correspondence with data of observation. At least one of the two has to be verifiable if the analysis is to be applied to concrete cases. Hence

---

[36] On the problem of prediction versus explanation see the chapter on "Economic Fact and Theory" in my book *The Political Economy of Monopoly* (Baltimore: Johns Hopkins Press, 1952), pp. 455 ff.

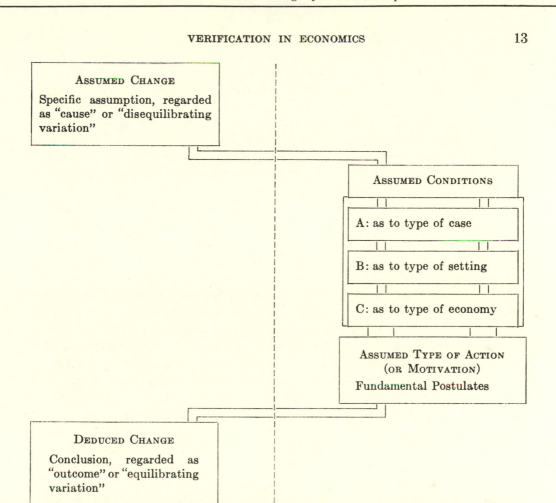

FIG. 1. A MODEL OF THE USE OF AN ANALYTICAL APPARATUS

On the right side is the "machine of pure theory," a mental *construction* for heuristic purposes; on the left side are assumptions of independent and dependent variables whose *correspondence* with data of observation may be tested.

the concepts employed to describe the changes should, if possible, be operational. This raises no difficulty in the case of most kinds of *Assumed Change* in whose effects we are interested, for example: changes in tax rates, customs duties, foreign-exchange rates, wage rates, price supports, price ceilings, discount rates, open-market policies, credit lines, government expenditures, agricultural crops— matters covered in reports and records. There are difficulties concerning some other kinds of Assumed Change, such as improvements in technology, greater optimism, changed tastes for particular goods—things for which recorded data are often unavailable. As regards the *Deduced Change* the requirement that it be operational will usually be met, because we are interested chiefly in effects upon prices, output, income, employment, etc.,—magnitudes reported in statistical series of some sort. To be sure, the figures may be unreliable and the statistical concepts may not be exact counterparts to the analytical concepts, but we cannot be too fussy and must be satisfied with what we can get.

In principle we want both Assumed Change and Deduced Change to be capable of being compared with recorded data so that the correspondence between the theory and the data can be checked. The analysis would be neither wrong nor invalid, but it would not be very useful if it were never possible to identify the concrete phenomena, events, and situations, to which it is supposed to apply. Once we have confidence in the whole theoretical system, we are willing to apply it to concrete cases even where only one of the two "changes," either the "cause" or the "effect," is identifiable in practice, rather than both. For example, we are prepared to base policy decisions on explanations or predictions where one of the phenomena cannot be isolated in observation from the complex of simultaneous variations. For purposes of verification of the entire theory, however, we shall have to identify both the phenomena represented by the Assumed Change and the Deduced Change—although such verification may be practical only on rare occasions.

We need not be particularly strict concerning the verification of the *Assumed Conditions*. Regarding them, a casual, perhaps even impressionistic empiricism will do, at least for most types of problems. The Assumed Conditions refer to personal characteristics, technological or organizational circumstances, market forms, enduring institutions—things of rather varied nature. Few of the Conditions are observable, except through communication of interpretations involving a good deal of theorizing by the parties concerned. Often the Conditions are not even specified in detail, but somehow taken for granted by analysts working in a familiar milieu. All of the Conditions are hypothetical parameters, assumed to prevail at least for the duration of the process comprising all the actions, interactions and repercussions through which the Assumed Change is supposed to cause the Deduced Change.

Assumed Conditions of Type A, that is, as to "*type of case*," refer to conditions which may vary from case to case and influence the outcome significantly, but are sufficiently common to justify the construction of "types" for theoretical analysis. Here is a list of examples: type of goods involved (durable, non-durable, perishable; inferior, non-inferior; taking up substantial or negligible parts of buyer's budget; substitutable, complementary; etc.); cost conditions (marginal cost decreasing, constant, increasing; joint costs, etc.); elasticity of supply or demand (positive, negative, relatively large, unity, less than unity); market position (perfect, imperfect polypoly; collusive, uncoordinated oligopoly; perfect, imperfect monopoly); entry (perfect, imperfect pliopoly); expectations (elastic, inelastic; bullish, bearish; certain, uncertain); consumption propensity (greater, smaller than unity); elasticity of liquidity preference (infinite, less than infinite, zero).

Assumed Conditions of Type B, that is, as to "type of setting," refer to conditions which may change over brief periods of time—say, with a change of government or of the political situation, or during the business cycle—and are apt to influence the outcome in definite directions. A list of examples will indicate what is meant by conditions prevailing under the current "setting": general business outlook (boom spirit, depression pessimism); bank credit availability (banks loaned up, large excess reserves); central bank policy (ready to monetize government securities, determined to maintain easy money policy, willing to let interest rates rise); fiscal policy (expenditures fixed, adjusted to tax revenues, geared to unemployment figures; tax rates fixed, adjusted to maintain revenue, etc.); farm program (support prices fixed, flexible within limits, etc.); antitrust policy (vigorous prosecution of cartelization, etc.); foreign aid program; stabilization fund rules; trade union policies.

Assumed Conditions of Type C, that is, as to *"type of economy,"* refer to conditions which may vary from country to country and over larger periods of time, but may be assumed to be "settled" for a sufficiently large number of cases to justify taking these conditions as constant. Examples include legal and social institutions; private property; freedom of contract; corporation law; patent system; transportation system; enforcement of contracts; ethics of law violations; social customs and usages; monetary system (gold standard, check system, cash holding habits).

Assumed Conditions are exchangeable because the effects of an Assumed Change may have to be analysed under a variety of conditions: for example, with different degrees or forms of competition, different credit policies, different tax structures, different trade union policies, etc. But it may also be expedient, depending on the problem at hand, to regard a variation of an Assumed Condition as an Assumed Change, and *vice versa*. For example, the problem may concern the effects of a wage rate increase under various market conditions or, instead, the effects of a change in market position under conditions of automatic wage escalation; the effects of a change in monetary policy with different tax structure, or the effects of a change in the tax structure under different monetary policies.

After listing the many examples of the various types of Assumed Conditions it will probably be agreed that a rigid verification requirement would be out of place. Usually the judgment of the analyst will suffice even if he cannot support it with more than the most circumstantial evidence or mere "impressions." Suppose he deals with a simple cost-price-output problem in a large industry, how will the analyst determine what "type of case" it is with regard to "market position?" Lacking the relevant information, he may first try to work with a model of perfect polypoly[37]—although he knows well that this cannot fit the real situation—and will note whether his deduced results will be far off the mark. He may find the results reasonably close to the observed data and may leave it at that. For to work with a more "realistic" assumption may call for so many additional assumptions for which no relevant information is available that it is preferable and unobjectionable to continue with a hypothesis contrary to fact. When a simpler hypothesis, though obviously unrealistic, gives consistently

[37] Under perfect polypoly the individual seller assumes that his own supply will not affect any other seller or the market as a whole and, thus, that he could easily sell more at the same price and terms. This condition was also called "pure competition," "perfect competition," or "perfect market" (although it has little to do with any effort of "competing" or with any property of the "market"). See Fritz Machlup, *The Economics of Sellers' Competition* (Baltimore: Johns Hopkins Press, 1952), pp. 85–91, and pp. 116 ff.

16   FRITZ MACHLUP

satisfactory results, one need not bother with more complicated, more realistic hypotheses.

Ideal Type of Action, Unverified but Understood

While solid empirical verification is indicated for the Assumed Change, and casual empirical judgments are indicated for the Assumed Conditions, the *Assumed Type of Action* forms the fundamental postulates of economic analysis and thus is not subject to a requirement of independent verification.

Various names have been suggested for the fundamental postulates of economic theory: "economic principle," "maximization principle," "assumption of rationality," "law of motivation," and others. And their logical nature has been characterized in various ways: they are regarded as "self-evident propositions," "axioms," "*a priori* truths," "truisms," "tautologies," "definitions," "rigid laws," "rules of procedure," "resolutions," "working hypotheses," "useful fictions," "ideal types," "heuristic mental constructs," "indisputable facts of experience," "facts of immediate experience," "data of introspective observation," "private empirical data," "typical behavior patterns," and so forth.

Some of these characterizations are equivalent to or consistent with each other, but some are not. How can a proposition be both *a priori* and empirical, both a definition and a fact of experience? While this cannot be, the distinctions in this particular instance are so fine that conflicts of interpretation seem unavoidable. Logicians have long debated the possibility of propositions being synthetic and yet *a priori*, and physicists are still not quite agreed whether the "laws" of mechanics are analytical definitions or empirical facts. The late philosopher Felix Kaufmann introduced as a middle category the so-called "rules of procedure," which are neither synthetic in the sense that they are falsifiable by contravening observations nor *a priori* in the sense that they are independent of experience;[38] they are and remain accepted as long as they have heuristic value, but will be rejected in favor of other rules (assumptions) which seem to serve their explanatory functions more successfully.

If this debate has been going on in the natural sciences, how could it be avoided in the social sciences? If issues about "self-evident," "inescapable," or "indisputable" insights arose concerning the physical world, how much more pertinent are such issues in the explanation of human action, where man is both observer and subject of observation! This, indeed, is the essential difference between the natural and the social sciences: that in the latter the facts, the data of "observation," are themselves results of interpretations of human actions by human actors.[39] And this imposes on the social sciences a requirement which does not

---

[38] Felix Kaufmann, *Methodology of the Social Sciences* (New York: Oxford University Press, 1944), pp. 77 ff, especially pp. 87–88.

[39] ". . . the object, the 'facts' of the social sciences are also opinions—not opinions of the student of the social phenomena, of course, but opinions of those whose actions produce his object. . . . They [the facts] differ from the facts of the physical sciences in being . . . beliefs which are as such our data . . . and which, moreover, we cannot directly observe in the minds of the people but recognize from what they do and say merely because we have

exist in the natural sciences: that all types of action that are used in the abstract models constructed for purposes of analysis be "understandable" to most of us in the sense that we could conceive of sensible men acting (sometimes at least) in the way postulated by the ideal type in question. This is the crux of Max Weber's methodology of the social sciences, and was recently given a refined and most convincing formulation by Alfred Schuetz.[40]

Schuetz promulgates three postulates guiding model construction in the social sciences: the postulates of "logical consistency," of "subjective interpretation," and of "adequacy." The second and third of these postulates are particularly relevant here:

> In order to explain human actions the scientist has to ask what model of an individual mind can be constructed and what typical contents must be attributed to it in order to explain the observed facts as the result of the activity of such a mind in an understandable relation. The compliance with this postulate warrants the possibility of referring all kinds of human action or their result to the subjective meaning such action or result of an action had for the actor.
>
> Each term in a scientific model of human action must be constructed in such a way that a human act performed within the life world by an individual actor in the way indicated by the typical construct would be understandable for the actor himself as well as for his fellowmen in terms of common-sense interpretation of everyday life. Compliance with this postulate warrants the consistency of the constructs of the social scientist with the constructs of common-sense experience of the social reality.[41]

Thus, the fundamental assumptions of economic theory are not subject to a requirement of independent empirical verification, but instead to a requirement of understandability in the sense in which man can understand the actions of fellowmen.[42]

IV

We are ready to summarize our conclusions concerning verification of the assumptions of economic theory. Then we shall briefly comment on the verification of particular economic theories applied to predict future events, and on the verification of strictly empirical hypotheses.

Verifying the Assumptions

First to summarize: We need not worry about independent verifications of the fundamental assumptions, the Assumed Type of Action; we need not be

---

ourselves a mind similar to theirs." F. A. v. Hayek, "Scientism and the Study of Society," *Economica, New Series*, Vol. V (August 1942), p. 279. Reprinted F. A. v. Hayek, *The Counter-Revolution of Science* (Glencoe, Ill.: Free Press, 1952).

[40] Alfred Schuetz, "Common-Sense and Scientific Interpretation of Human Action," *Philosophy and Phenomenological Research*, Vol. XIV (September 1953), pp. 1–38. *Idem.*, "Concept and Theory Formation in the Social Sciences," *The Journal of Philosophy*, Vol. LI (April 1954), pp. 257–273.

[41] Schuetz, "Common-Sense, etc.," p. 34.

[42] Disregard of this requirement is, in my view, the only serious flaw in the otherwise excellent essay on "The Methodology of Positive Economics" by Milton Friedman, *Essays in Positive Economics* (Chicago: University of Chicago Press, 1953), pp. 3–43.

very particular about the independent verifications of the other intervening assumptions, the Assumed Conditions, because judgment based on casual empiricism will suffice for them; we should insist on strict independent verifications of the assumption selected as Assumed Change and of the conclusion derived as Deduced Change; not that the theory would be wrong otherwise, but it cannot be applied unless the phenomena to which it is supposed to apply are identifiable. *Simultaneous verifications of Assumed Change and Deduced Change count as verification—in the sense of non-disconfirmation—of the theory as a whole.*

Now it is clear why some writers insisted on the *a priori* nature of the theory and at the same time on its empirical value for the area of Applied Economics; for one may, if one wishes, regard the theory, or model, as a construction *a priori*, and the directions for its use, the instructions for its applications,[43] as an empirical appendage in need of verification. Returning to the analogy of the analytical machine, one may say that the machine and its parts are always "correct," regardless of what goes on around us, whereas the *choice* of the exchangeable parts and the *identification* of the events corresponding to the Assumed and Deduced changes may be wrong.

Testing the Predictive Values of Theories

We have examined the empiricists' charges against the theorists—charges of contemptuous neglect of the requirement of verification—and have concluded that these charges must be dismissed insofar as they refer to a failure to verify all assumptions directly and in isolation from the rest of the theory. We must yet examine another count of the charge of insufficient attention to verification: an alleged failure to test the correspondence between Deduced (predicted) and Observed outcomes. These kinds of tests are obligatory.

If verification of a theory takes the form of testing whether predictions based on that theory actually come true, one might think that this can be done in economics no less than in the physical sciences. It cannot, alas, because of the non-reproducibility of the "experiments" or observed situations and courses of events in the economy. For, while certain types of events, or "changes," recur in the economy often enough, they recur rarely under the same conditions. If some significant circumstances are different whenever a phenomenon of the same class recurs, each recurrence is virtually a "single occurrence." Economic theory applied to single events, or to situations significantly different from one another, cannot be tested as conclusively as can physical theory applied to reproducible occurrences and conditions.

Not long ago I was challenged to admit that my theories, even though applied to ever-changing circumstances, could be tested provided I were prepared to make unconditional predictions which could be compared with actual outcomes. Of course, I could only dare make unconditional predictions—without hedging about probability and confidence limits—where I was absolutely certain that my diagnosis of the situation (i.e., of *all* relevant circumstances) *and* my foreknowl-

---

[43] Cf. Milton Friedman, *op. cit.*, pp. 24–25.

edge of government and power group actions *and* the theory on which the prediction rests were all perfectly correct. Suppose that I was so foolhardy as to be sure of all this and that I did make a number of unconditional predictions. Still, unless reliable checks were possible to verify separately every part of my diagnosis and of my anticipations regarding government and power group actions, my theory could not be tested. There could be lucky "hits" where wrong diagnoses would compensate for mistakes due to bad theories; there could be unlucky "misses" where wrong diagnoses spoiled the results of good theorizing. Despite a large number of good hits the theories in question could not be regarded as confirmed, even in the modest sense of not being disconfirmed, because a joint and inseparable test of diagnosis, anticipations, and theory says nothing about the theory itself.

Where the economist's prediction is *conditional*, that is, based upon specified conditions, but where it is not possible to check the fulfillment of all the conditions stipulated, the underlying theory cannot be disconfirmed whatever the outcome observed. Nor is it possible to disconfirm a theory where the prediction is made with a stated *probability* value of less than 100 percent; for if an event is predicted with, say, 70 percent probability, any kind of outcome is consistent with the prediction.[44] Only if the same "case" were to occur hundreds of times could we verify the stated probability by the frequency of "hits" and "misses."

This does not mean complete frustration of all attempts to verify our economic theories. But it does mean that the tests of most of our theories will be more nearly of the character of *illustrations* than of verifications of the kind possible in relation with repeatable controlled experiments or with recurring fully-identified situations. And this implies that our tests cannot be convincing enough to compel acceptance, even when a majority of reasonable men in the field should be prepared to accept them as conclusive, and to approve the theories so tested as "not disconfirmed," that is, as "O. K."

Strictly Empirical Hypotheses

All this seems to circumscribe rather narrowly the scope of empirical verification, if not empirical research, in economics. But to draw such a conclusion would be rash. For there is a large body of economics apart from its theoretical or "hypothetico-deductive" system: namely, the empirical relationships obtained through correlation of observations, but not derivable, or at least not yet derived, from higher-level generalizations. Every science has such a body of strictly empirical hypotheses, no matter how fully developed or undeveloped its theoretical system may be.

I define a strictly empirical hypothesis as a proposition predicating a regular relationship between two or more sets of data of observation that cannot be

---

[44] This statement, it should be noted, refers to *general* theories which are part of a hypothetico-deductive system, not to strictly empirical hypotheses obtained by statistical inference. The predictions in question can never be in precise numerical terms, because no numerical magnitudes can be deduced from the assumptions of the type used in "general theory."

deduced from the general hypotheses which control the network of interrelated inferences forming the body of theory of the discipline in question. The distinction is made in almost all disciplines; it is best known as the distinction between "empirical laws" and "theoretical laws," though several other names have been used to denote the two types of scientific propositions. The philosopher Morris Cohen spoke of "concrete laws" in contrast to "abstract laws." Felix Kaufmann, though using the terms empirical and theoretical laws, characterized the former as "strict laws," the latter as "rigid laws." The physicist Henry Margenau contrasted "epistemic" or "correlational laws" with "constitutive," "exact," or "theoretical" laws. And Carl Menger, the founder of the Austrian School and protagonist in the *Methodenstreit*, distinguished "empirical laws" from "exact laws," the latter dealing with idealized connections between pure constructs, the former with "the sequences and coexistences of real phenomena."[45]

The study of the "sequences and coexistences" of the real phenomena depicted in statistical records yields correlational and other empirical findings which have to be tested and modified whenever new data on the same class of phenomena become available. While the constructs and deductions of the theoretical systems will influence the selection, collection and organization of empirical data, the particular relationships established between these data by means of correlation analysis and other statistical techniques are not deducible from high-level assumptions and can neither confirm nor disconfirm such assumptions. But these relationships, especially the numerical estimates of parameters, coefficients, or constants, are themselves subject to verification by new observations.

Verification of Empirical Hypotheses

Every one of us has lately been so much concerned with statistical demand curves, saving and consumption functions, investment functions, import elasticities and import propensities that a description of these and similar research activities is not necessary. The trouble with the verification of the empirical hypotheses derived by means of statistical and econometric analysis is that successive estimates on the basis of new data have usually been seriously divergent. Of course, such variations over time in the numerical relationships measured are not really surprising: few of us have expected these relationships to be constant or even approximately stable. Thus when new data and new computations yield revised estimates of economic parameters, there is no way of telling whether the previous hypotheses were wrong or whether things have changed.

That the numerical relationships described by these empirical hypotheses may be subject to change—to unpredictable change—alters their character in an essential respect. Hypotheses which are strictly limited as to time and space are not "general" but "special" hypotheses, or *historical propositions*. If the relationships measured or estimated in our empirical research are not universal but historical propositions, the problem of verification is altogether different—so different that according to intentions expressed in the introduction we should

[45] Carl Menger, *Untersuchungen über die Methode der Socialwissenschaften und der Politischen Oekonomie insbesondere* (Leipzig: Duncker & Humblot, 1883), pp. 28, 36.

not be concerned with it. For we set out to discuss verification of *generalizations*, not of events or circumstances confined to particular times and places. If all propositions of economics were of this sort, the dictum of the older historical school, that economics cannot have "general laws" or a "general theory," would be fully vindicated.

If a hypothesis about the numerical relationship between two or more variables was formulated on the basis of statistical data covering a particular period, and is later compared with the data of *another period*, such a comparison would be in the nature of a verification only if the hypothesis had been asserted or expected to be a universal one, that is, if the measured or estimated relationships had been expected to be constant. In the absence of such expectations the test of a continuing "fit" (between hypothesis and new data) is just a comparison between two historical situations, an attempt to find out whether particular relationships were stable or changing. A genuine verification of a previously formulated hypothesis about a given period calls for comparisons with additional data relating to the *same period*, to check whether the previous observations and their previous numerical description had been accurate. In brief, a historical proposition can only be verified by new data about the historical situation to which it refers. This holds also for geographic propositions and comparisons between different areas.

However, although the changeable "structures"[46] estimated by statistical and econometric researchers are nothing but historical propositions, there are probably limits to their variations. For example, we may safely generalize that the marginal propensity to consume cannot in the long run be greater than unity; or that the elasticity of demand for certain types of exports of certain types of countries will not in the long run be smaller than unity. Statements about definite limits to variations of special or historical propositions are again general hypotheses; they are not strictly empirical but universal in that they are deducible from higher-level generalizations in the theoretical system of economics. The various successive estimates of changeable structures may then be regarded as verifications of general hypotheses according to which certain parameters or coefficients must fall within definite limits. Since these limits are usually rather wide, verification will of course not be the rigorous kind of thing it is in the physical sciences with its numerical constants and narrow margins of error.

But neither this nor anything else that has been said in this article should be interpreted as intending to discourage empirical testing in economics. On the contrary, awareness of the limits of verification should prevent disappointments and present challenges to the empirical worker. May he rise to these challenges and proceed with intelligence and fervor by whatever techniques he may choose.

---

[46] In the sense used by Tjallong Koopmans and other econometricians.

[4]

The Universal Bogey

Fritz Machlup

The 'bogey' to whom this essay will be devoted is Economic Man. It was Lionel Robbins who suggested that *homo oeconomicus* would probably not have become 'such a universal bogey' if those who wrote so contemptuously about him had known him better.[1] He has been quite unpopular even among some good economic theorists, who contended that they could do better without him. Others who appreciated his services, were nevertheless intimidated by the irate accusations persistently reiterated by his detractors; so they decided to avoid his name. He was admitted into most respectable company under such aliases as 'behaviour equation' or 'objective function', names by which his enemies would not recognise him.[2]

Antitheoretical economists and anti-economists in general have raged and roared with fury about that wicked and despicable Economic Man. To deal with their accusations may appear 'foolish and exasperating ... to any competent economist' but, nevertheless, Robbins thought it was 'worth some further examination.'[3] I have found it entertaining to read the angry charges against the innocent creature and I propose, before engaging in still further examinations of the nature and significance of Economic Man, to share with the reader some of the juiciest denunciations.

1.   Robbins, Lionel, *An Essay on the Nature and Significance of Economic Science*, 1935, p. 97.

2.   I do not know who was the first to use the name objective function, but he certainly had no feeling for language or he would have sensed the possibility of misunderstandings. Objective as an adjective is the antonym of subjective; as a noun it is a synonym for goal or aim; what is it if it precedes and modifies a noun? French translators have had hard times; they were prone to mistranslate objective function as *fonction objective* instead of *fonction d'objectif.* Coiners of new terms and phrases ought to feel morally obliged to test them for nonambiguity and intelligibility.

3.   Robbins, *An Essay on The Nature and Significance of Economic Science*, 1935, p. 94.

99

The Universal Bogey

A SAMPLE OF DENUNCIATIONS

What irked the critics most was that the Man's 'desire of wealth' had frequently (and unwisely) been described as a desire to acquire or possess *material* goods satisfying *physical* wants, and sometimes as a desire for *pecuniary* gains; and the goal of getting the most out of what he has had been identified with *selfishness.* Thus we read in the work of John Barton, an early and almost forgotten critic of the Ricardians, that 'a reasoner who is incapable of measuring and appreciating the higher influences, confining his views to this one sordid and narrow motive, must infallibly arrive at conclusions as false as they are grovelling.'[4]

The members of the earlier Historical School in Germany were still quite civil in their rejection of Economic Man. Opposed chiefly to the use of abstraction and the emphasis on egoism, they wanted to have 'abstract' man replaced by 'real' man, and self-interest exorcised by strong appeals to ethical values. The British branch of the Historical School, led by Leslie, was not very original. Leslie mainly commended the 'realism' of the Germans in repudiating abstract and unhistorical concepts and in deprecating the 'Love of Money'.[5] He thought he was disposing of Economic Man by reminding us that money bought not only material things but also intangibles that satisfied the finest cultural aspirations — such as cleanliness and knowledge.

The American Henry C. Carey showed some originality in the venom he directed at the Classical School and especially at Mill. He quotes Mill first on economic motives — to acquire wealth, to avert labour, and to enjoy consumption — and then on population — pressing wages down to the subsistence level — and proceeds to make the following observation regarding these two assumptions:

That having been done, we have the political-economical man, on one hand influenced solely by the thirst for wealth and on the other so entirely

4.   Barton, John, *A Statement of the Consequences Likely to Ensue from Our Growing Excess of Population if not Remedied by Colonization,* 1830, p. 47. (Reprinted in John Barton, *Economic Writings,* Regina, Sask.: Lynn Publishing Co., 1962, p. 293.)

5.   Leslie, Thomas Edward Cliffe, 'The Love of Money', in *Essays in Political Economy,* 1888, pp. 1-8. (This essay was first published in 1862.)

100

The Universal Bogey

under the control of the sexual passion as to be at all times ready to indulge it, however greatly such indulgence may tend to prevent the growth of wealth.[6]

Fascinated by Carey's angry exclamations, I cannot resist quoting him more extensively. He expects the reader of the classical writings to wonder:

He [the reader] might perhaps ask himself, has man no other qualities than those here attributed to him? Is he, like the beasts of the field, solely given to the search for food and shelter for his body? ... Has he no feelings of affections to be influenced by the care of wife and children? ... That he did possess these qualities he would find admitted, but the economist would assure him that his science was that of material wealth alone, to the entire exclusion of the wealth of affection and of intellect ... and thus would he ... discover that the subject of political economy was not really a man, but an imaginary being moved to action by the blindest passion...[7]

Again:

The British School of Economists recognizes, not the real man of society, but the artificial man of their own system. Their Theory, occupied with the lowest instincts of humanity, treats its noblest interests as mere interpolations of the System.[8]

And again:

Such is the error of modern political economy, its effects exhibiting themselves in the fact that it presents for our consideration a mere brute animal to find a name for which it desecrates the word 'man' ...[9]

To set him apart from this brute, Carey spells 'real MAN' with capital letters.

A disciple of Carey's, Robert Ellis Thompson, angry about the free-

---

6.   Carey, Henry C., *Principles of Social Science,* Vol I. 1858, p. 29. In a later book, *The Unity of Law,* 1872, p. 59, he repeats this statement almost literally, except for the insertion, after 'politico-economical man', of the words 'or monster'.

7.   Carey, *Principles,* p. 30; also *Unity,* p.61.

8.   Carey, *Principles;* p.xiii, in the table of contents describing § 5 of Ch. I.

9.   Carey, *Unity,* p. 61.

101

The Universal Bogey

traders' interest in the 'consumer' (as distinct from 'producer') and their opposition to protective tariffs, managed to combine his antagonisms against the 'consumer', against the 'economic man', and against all abstract reasoning in one statement:

> Who this consumer is, that is neither a producer as well, nor directly dependent upon the prosperity of other people who are producers, is hard to say. ... But most likely he is an innocent *ens logicum,* manufactured by the same process of abstraction by which the economists devised their economical man – 'a covetous machine inspired to action only by avarice and the desire of progress'. That is, they cut away or stole away (abstracted) the better half of the real being, and persisted in treating the remaining human fragment (if we can call it human) as a living reality.[10]

One more sample of this group of writers may be offered, John Ruskin – in my opinion, one of the most overrated writers of nineteenth-century England. He too protested vigorously against the classical economists 'considering the human being merely as a covetous machine' – although he prided himself on never having read any book on political economy except Smith's *Wealth of Nations*. This is what he had to say about the economic principle operating in exchange and commerce:

> So far as I know, there is not in history record of anything so disgraceful to the human intellect as the modern idea that the commercial text, 'Buy in the cheapest market and sell in the dearest,' represents, or under any circumstances could represent, an available principle of national economy.[12]

THE GROUNDS OF THE OPPOSITION

Some of the strictures and denunciations included in this sample can probably be best explained as the result of misunderstandings – due to ignorance or incompetence. But not all opposition to Economic Man is of this sort. The ranks of the opposition are not filled entirely with

10.   Thompson, Robert Ellis, *Social Sciences and National Economy,* 1875, p. 269.

11.   Ruskin, John, *Unto This Last,* 1901, p. 2. The four essays collected in this book were first published in 1861. The phrase 'covetous machine' was widely quoted, for example, also by Thompson, in 1875, in the passage reproduced above.

12.   Ruskin, *Unto This Last,* p. 59.

102

The Universal Bogey

anti-analysts, anti-theorists, anti-classicists, anti-liberals, and anti-economists. Some eminent economic theorists, skilled in analysis and respectful of classical economics, have also condemned the use of the concept of Economic Man. What are the grounds of their opposition?

Several such grounds should be distinguished, since different critics have different quarrels with Economic Man's nature, character, and function. One issue relates to the breaking up of Whole Man into parts and the construction of a Partial or Fragmented Man, who has only a few specific traits or objectives; there are those who object vigorously to all analytical dissection of man (as if it were physical vivisection). Other controversial questions are whether the construction of an abstract Partial Man is sound either in the sense that all disregarded traits or objectives can reasonably be dispensed with without vitiating the conclusions deduced with the help of the construct, or in the sense that the traits or objectives which are singled out for emphasis are sufficiently realistic to yield useful conclusions. Several objectors deny both propositions, some only one. There is a group of economists who are greatly worried that we may obtain only 'hypothetical' rather than incontrovertible, categorical, or 'positive' conclusions. Some object to the use of heuristic fictions and counterfactual assumptions; they hold that no worthwhile inferences can come from untrue hypotheses. The largest number of critics merely take exception to poor formulations of the behaviour equation called Economic Man.

In order to avoid the impression that the parties to this controversy can be nicely tagged and boxed, we had better go back for a bit of doctrinal history; we shall confine it, however, to a few of the main protagonists: John Stuart Mill, Nassau Senior, Walter Bagehot, James E. Cairnes and Philip H. Wicksteed.

THE HYPOTHETICAL NATURE OF SCIENTIFIC DISCOURSE

Re-reading John Stuart Mill after reading the comments and observations of his critics, one cannot help finding a strong suspicion confirmed: that many authors, even highly respected ones, read with insufficient care or poor retention. Far too many of the methodological issues raised about Mill's procedure, and about his (unnamed) Economic Man, had been anticipated and largely resolved by Mill.

103

The Universal Bogey

Mill insisted on the hypothetical nature of all science — reasoning from assumed premises — and on the especially hypothetical nature of economics (Political Economy) — presupposing 'an arbitrary definition of man'.[13] He stressed the 'uncertainty inherent in the nature of these complex phenomena [in the moral sciences in general] ... arising from the impossibility of being quite sure that all the circumstances of the particular case are known to us sufficiently in detail'.[14]

'Man..., the subject matter of all moral sciences' has to be dealt with 'under several distinct hypotheses'. The major division, in Mill's exposition, is between 'ethics' and 'social economy', and a branch of the latter was 'political economy'. 'The science of social economy embraces every part of man's nature, in so far as influencing the conduct and condition of man in society ...'. 'Political economy', in contra-distinction, 'does not treat of the whole of man's nature as modified by the social state, nor of the whole conduct of man in society. It is concerned with him solely as a being who desires to possess wealth, and who is capable of judging of the comparative efficacy of means for obtaining that end.'[15] The fundamental assumption is that man will 'prefer a greater portion of wealth to a smaller...'[16] This is, I submit, a common-sense way of formulating the postulate of maximising.

Mill makes it perfectly clear that this basic hypothesis may be contrary to fact. 'Political Economy' he states, 'reasons from *assumed* premises — from premises which might be totally without foundation in fact, and which are not pretended to be universally in accordance with it...'[17] Several times Mill points to the fictitious character of the fundamental hypothesis of economic science, in particular to the 'entire abstraction of every other human passion or motive', except 'desire of wealth', 'aversion to labour', and 'desire of the present enjoyment of costly indulgences'.[18] He cautiously warns the reader against mistaking

13.   Mill, John Stuart, 'On the Definition of Political Economy; and the Method of Investigation Proper to It' *Essays on Some Unsettled Questions of Political Economy*, p. 144.

14.   Mill, *Political Economy*, p. 150.

15.   Mill, *Political Economy*, pp.134-137. [The same sentences appear in Mill's *System of Logic*.]

16.   Mill, *Political Economy*, pp.138-139.

17.   Mill, *Essays*, p. 137.

18.   Mill, *Essays*, pp. 137-138.

The Universal Bogey

a heuristic counterfactual hypothesis for a statement of fact:

> Not that any political economist was ever so absurd as to suppose that mankind are really thus constituted ... [But] the manner in which it [Political Economy] necessarily proceeds is that of treating the main and acknowledged end as if it were the sole end; which, of all hypotheses equally simple, is the nearest to the truth... This approximation is then to be corrected by making proper allowance for the effects of any impulses of a different description, which can be shown to interfere with the result in any particular case.[19]

POSITIVE TRUTH AND MERE SUPPOSITION

Not all classical or post-classical writers were agreed on the hypothetical or postulational character of Economic Man, or of the Economic Principle. Several of them, before Mill as well as afterwards, wanted the basic assumption recognised as a factual premise, stating an unquestioned, positive truth. The most out-spoken critic of merely hypothetical economics was Senior.

Long before Mill, Senior had formulated the 'First Proposition' of Political Economy: 'That every person is desirous to obtain, with as little sacrifice as possible, as much as possible of the articles of wealth'.[20] In later reformulations he omitted the reference to 'articles' and was careful to point out that wealth included such intangibles as 'power', 'distinction', 'leisure', 'benefits for acquaintances and friends', and even contributions of 'advantage to the public'.[21] However, Senior was dissatisfied with Mill's reliance on a hypothesis which, in Mill's words, was not 'universally in accordance with fact' or was even 'totally without foundation in fact'. From mere suppositions only conclusions of uncertain truth or applicability could be inferred. Senior wanted economic science to state positive truths, not just hypotheses. 'It appears to me', he wrote in 1852, 'that if we substitute for Mr. Mill's hypothesis, that wealth and costly enjoyment are the *only* objects of human desire, the statement that they are universal and constant objects of desire, that they are desired by all men and at all times, we shall have laid an equally firm foundation for our subsequent

19. Mill, *Essays,* pp. 139-140.
20. Senior, Nassau W., *Introductory Lecture on Political Economy,* 1827, p.30. Quoted from Bowley, Marian, *Nassau Senior and Classical Economics,* 1937, p.46.
21. Senior, *An Outline of the Science of Political Economy,* 1836, 6th ed. 1872, p. 27.

105

The Universal Bogey

reasonings, and have put a truth in the place of an arbitrary assumption'.[22]

USEFUL FICTIONS

Senior's ambition for economic science — to yield absolutely true, not merely hypothetical propositions — was criticised by Walter Bagehot, who also criticised earlier classical economists for confusing useful fictions with established facts. For example, Bagehot claimed that Ricardo 'thought that he was considering actual human nature in its actual circumstances, when he was really considering a fictitious nature in fictitious circumstances'.[23]

According to Bagehot, 'English political economists are not speaking of real men, but of imaginary ones; not of men as we see them, but of men as it is convenient to us to suppose they are'.[24] The convenience lies in the simplicity of disregarding elements of lesser relevance. For this reason, 'Political Economy deals not with the entire real man as we know him in fact, but with a simpler, imaginary man..., because it is found convenient to isolate the effects of this force from all others'.[25]

Bagehot thus sided completely with Mill and against Senior, who wanted positive 'truths' in place of mere 'hypotheses'.

PREMISES AND CONCLUSIONS

James E. Cairnes defended Senior on some points and criticised him on others. He took his side on the question of fact or fiction in the assumption regarding the economic motive. The fundamental assumption of economics is, for Cairnes, not a mere supposition, let alone a counterfactual hypothesis, but a proposition which rests on well established facts of experience: 'The economist starts with a knowledge of ultimate causes.'[26] For their discovery or confirmation 'no elaborate process of induction is needed', for we have 'direct knowledge of these

22.   Senior, Nassau W., *Four Introductory Lectures on Political Economy*, 1852, p. 62. Quoted from Bowley, *Nassau Senior*, p.61.
23.   Bagehot, Walter, *Economic Studies*, 1880, p. 157.
24.   Bagehot, *Economic Studies*, p. 5.
25.   Bagehot, *Economic Studies*, p. 74.
26.   Cairnes, James E., *The Character and Logical Method of Political Economy*, 1st ed. 1858, 2nd ed. 1875, p. 87.

106

The Universal Bogey

causes in our consciousness of what passes in our own minds...' After all, 'every one who embarks on any industrial pursuit is conscious of the motives which actuate him in doing so'.[27]

However — and here Cairnes dissents from Senior's position — that the economist can start with 'facts' rather than a 'hypothesis' does not guarantee that his conclusions are anything but hypothetical. For, in Cairnes' view,

> an economist, arguing from the unquestionable facts of man's nature — the desire of wealth and the aversion to labour — and arguing with strict logical accuracy, may yet, if he omit to notice other principles also affecting the question, be landed in conclusions which have no resemblance to existing realities. But he can never be certain that he does not omit some essential circumstance, and, indeed, it is scarcely possible to include all: it is evident, therefore, that... his conclusions will correspond with facts *only in the absence of disturbing causes,* which is, in other words, to say that they represent not positive but hypothetic truth.[28]

Thus Cairnes accepts one half of Senior's and one half of Mill's position: 'the premises are not arbitrary figments of the mind', but the conclusions are hypothetical and 'may or may not correspond to the realities'.[29] He attributed Senior's dilemma, regarding the question whether economics was a positive or a hypothetical science, to 'an ambiguity of language'. If the two adjectives are used 'with reference to the character of [the] premises' of a science, they may point to a genuine difference: the 'positive' premises of the physical sciences, dictated by 'the existing facts of nature', can be contrasted with the 'hypothetical' premises of the science of mathematics, which are 'arbitrary conceptions framed by the mind'.[30] If, however, the two adjectives are used 'with reference to the conclusions of a science', the advanced physical and other empirical sciences may be regarded as both positive and hypothetical: positive in the sense that there is a probability that the conclusions deduced from the premises 'represent positive realities', and hypothetical in the sense that these conclusions can be true only 'on the hypothesis that the premises include all the

27.   Cairnes, *Character and Logical Method,* p. 88.

28.   Cairnes, *Character and Logical Method,* pp. 63-64. (Emphasis in the original.)

29.   Cairnes, *Character and Logical Method,* p. 62.

30.   Cairnes, *Character and Logical Method,* pp. 60-61.

107

The Universal Bogey

causes affecting the result', of which we 'can never be sure'.[31]

Cairnes' view, in a nutshell, is that 'it is surely possible that the premises should be true and yet incomplete — true so far as the facts which they assert go, and yet not including all the conditions which affect the actual course of events'.[32]

EGOISM, TUISM, AND SIMPLIFIED PSYCHOLOGY

Cairnes' disquisitions were lost on Philip Wicksteed, who embraced Senior's position on several issues. Like Senior, Wicksteed (quite rightly) insisted on keeping maximising behaviour apart from egoism and from the desire to possess material goods; like Senior, Wicksteed rejected mere suppositions as the basis of economic deductions; and like Senior, Wicksteed was not satisfied with a merely 'hypothetical science'.

Wicksteed was well advised in restating the irrelevance of material possessions and of self-interest, simply because so many exponents of economic theory continued to advertise these false criteria of economic conduct. But the issues had been fully discussed and understood by many. If wealth was defined as material goods, this was partly a device to eschew problems of statistical estimation, which were especially difficult with regard to intangible values. This, at least, was Malthus' explanation, back in 1812. The issue as to whether the scope of egoism had to be narrowed to the fulfilment of bodily desires or could be extended to include 'higher' impulses had already been discussed by Hobbes,[33] back in 1651. Why then, in the opinion of so many eminent writers, the desire to attain with given means a maximum of ends (objectives, satisfaction, utility) had to be identified with egoism or self-interest is nowadays difficult to understand. Senior was one of the few who recognised that the economic motive could accomodate altruism along with any other preferences of the acting individuals. Yet we find reversions at much later, more enlightened times. Edgeworth, for example, in 1912 stuck to the old, unreconstructed view according to which 'the first principle of pure economics' was 'the prevalence of self-interest'.[34]

31.   Cairnes, *Character and Logical Method,* p. 61.
32.   Cairnes, *Character and Logical Method,* p. 68.
33.   Hobbes, Thomas, *Leviathan,* 1651.

108

The Universal Bogey

Wicksteed offered the most patient exposition of the egoism-altruism issue. He has no difficulty demonstrating that it is quite irrelevant whether a decision-maker acts on the basis of a preference system that includes only his personal interests or also those of his family, his friends, his clients, his compatriots, or any *alteri*.[35] In any case the principle of 'true economy', that is, of 'making the best of existing conditions',[36] yields the same results, regardless of whether the 'maximum advantage'[37] is desired only for the decision-maker himself or for other beneficiaries.

Wicksteed makes one exception to the possible inclusion of other persons' interests among the aims of a decision-maker: the interests of a trading partner must not actuate his behaviour. If I bargain with you, I, *ego*, may think of my own interests or of the interests of others, *alteri*, but I must not think of you, *tu,* and of your interests. Hence, egoism and altruism are both all right, but 'tuism' must be ruled out. 'It is only when tuism to some degree actuates my conduct that it ceases to be wholly economic'.[38] Thus, 'The specific characteristic of an economic relation is not its "egoism", but its "non-tuism" '.[39]

Wicksteed, although he could accommodate altruism along with egoism, thought that he had to exclude tuism, probably because otherwise the terms of an exchange between two transactors would be indeterminate. He evidently overlooked that an isolated exchange, outside a competitive market, would be indeterminate in any case, with or without tuism. On the other hand, if the market is competitive, a trader may wish to give his trading partner a 'break', and thus include the partner's interests in his own considerations, without any harm to the determinateness of the market price; the 'rebate' in the case of the 'tuistic' trader would be an understandable deviation.

Wicksteed rejected the construction of Economic Man, less because of the awkward traits of materialism and egoism with which some

34. Edgeworth, Francis Y., 'Contributions to the Theory of Railway Rates, III', *Economic Journal,* Vol. XXII, 1912, p. 199. Reprinted in *Papers Relating to Political Economy,* Royal Economic Society, 1925, Vol. I, p. 173.
35. Wicksteed, Philip H., *The Common Sense of Political Economy* 1910, pp. 170-183.
36. Wicksteed, *Political Economy,* p. 94.
37. Wicksteed, *Political Economy,* p. 70.
38. Wicksteed, *Political Economy,* p. 181.
39. Wicksteed, *Political Economy,* p. 180.

109

The Universal Bogey

model-makers had endowed him than because of the other two limitations: the 'artificial simplification' through isolation of selected motives and abstraction from all others, and the restriction to 'hypothetical' conclusions which is involved in the reliance on unrealistic assumptions. In his arguments against these limitations Wicksteed engages in a great deal of verbal hair-splitting, particularly when he tries to do away with an 'economic motive' and replaces it by an 'economic relation'.

Wicksteed's stance in his opposition to an abstract construct of man resembles that of the anti-analytic, anti-vivisectionist holists: he rejects 'the hypothetically simplified psychology of the Economic Man' and the convention of 'imagining man to be actuated by only a few simple motives; and he proposes that we 'take him as we find him... under the stress of all his complicated impulses and desires'.[40] Many of Wicksteed's observations are perfectly sound, for example, when he states that

> a man may be just as strenuous in the pursuit of knowledge or of fame, or in his obedience to an artistic impulse, as in the pursuit of wealth... The demands of vanity may be as imperious as those of hunger, so that all the motives and passions that actuate the human breast may either stimulate or restrain the desire to possess wealth. How, then, can we isolate that desire as a 'motive'?[41]

And in a similar vein:

> There is no occasion to define the economic motive, or the psychology of the economic man, for economics study a type of relation, not a type of motive, and the psychological law that dominates economics dominates life. We may either ignore all motives or admit all to our consideration, as occasion demands, but there is no rhyme or reason in selecting certain motives that shall and certain others that shall not be recognised by the economist.[42]

We shall later justify how we can reasonably regard these observations as sound and yet irrelevant. The apparent contradiction has to do with the distinction between (spontaneous) action and (induced) reaction, and with the differences in complexity in explaining the two types of decision-making. Wicksteed was one of many who failed to

40. Wicksteed, *Political Economy*, p. 4.
41. Wicksteed, *Political Economy*, p. 164.
42. Wicksteed, Philip H., 'The Scope and Method of Political Economy in the Light of the "Marginal" Theory of Value and Distribution', *Economic Journal*, Vol. XXIV, March 1914, p. 9.

110

The Universal Bogey

recognise these differences. His opposition to the basic simplifying assumption was based on a methodological tenet:

> We have now to ask further, are these psychological data, whether facts or principles, to include all the psychological considerations that actually bear upon the production, distribution, etc. of wealth, or are we artificially to simplify our psychology and deal only with the motives supposed to actuate the hypothetical 'economic man'? In the latter case political economy will be a hypothetical science. In the former it will aim at positivity.[43]

Here we meet again the objection Senior had raised against Mill's 'hypothetical science'. The ambition for something 'more positive', which would assure *true* deductions from *true* assumptions rather than merely valid deductions from fundamental postulates, moved Wicksteed, as it had moved Senior, to oppose the construction of a simplified model in favor of a supposedly complete one. This ambition reached its extreme in Ludwig von Mises' praxeology, the all-embracing theory of human action, in which economic action, rational action, and action of any kind become one and the same.[44]

THE OBJECTIVES OF ECONOMIC MAN

From the sample of quotations offered here it should be clear that the exact content of the 'fundamental hypothesis' embodied in the construction of *homo oeconomicus* has changed from one economic treatise to another. Many critics have suffered from a tendency to interpret the descriptions of Economic Man too narrowly and too literally. The differences in the scope of Economic Man's aspirations can perhaps be visualised in the following schema: Economic Man is assumed to seek (A) more wealth with given sacrifices of other advantages, (B) the largest gains in exchange and trade, (C) greatest pleasure with given pain, (D) highest returns from given resources, (E) highest pecuniary and nonpecuniary benefits from business, or (F) maximum utility from given means.

In some of the constructions proposed, Economic Man was only a

43. Wicksteed, Philip H. 'Political Economy and Psychology', *Palgrave's Dictionary of Political Economy*, 1926, Vol. III, p. 142.
44. von Mises, Ludwig, *Nationalökonomie: Theorie des Handelns und Wirtschaftens*, 1940, also English edition, *Human Action: A Treatise on Economics*, 1949.

The Universal Bogey

consumer, only a trader, only a producer, only an investor, only a businessman. Some writers insisted that the construct could never fit some of these roles, whereas others were convinced that it fitted them all, indeed, a few were even prepared to extend it to other roles, such as the politician, the government, or society as a collective decision-maker.

Within each of the constructs several further variations can be found. The wealth which the first Economic Man sought to maximise was thought of as a stock by some, as a flow by others; as consisting of material consumer goods, of material assets of any sort, of tangibles and also intangible goods and services, or of money or general purchasing power. The failure to distinguish between a stock and a flow of 'wealth' has trapped a good many, friends and foes of Economic Man. Smith said 'wealth' but explained that he meant 'the necessaries and conveniences of life', hence, a stream of income. Mill said 'necessaries, conveniences, and luxuries', but at the same time spoke of the desire to 'possess' wealth. No wonder that critics with literal minds found these descriptions wanting and thought the whole conception useless.

The idea of confining wealth to material goods was supposed to serve statistical convenience, to ease quantitative estimation. But, surely, where no statistical operations were intended or needed, it was supererogatory to subject the construct to an operational constraint. The distinction between physical wants 'of a low order' (Jevons) and gratification of higher values was entirely uncalled for. The substitution of money or general purchasing power for goods and services of any sort was all right, but of course not with the disparaging connotation of a miser's 'love of money', avarice and cupidity. The difference between selfish and nonegoistic desire of wealth is understandable in the light of the discussions of utilitarian philosophy, but proved irrelevant to the maximisation postulate. In the same context, emphasis on the 'calculus of pleasure and pain' and the conception of Economic Man as a 'pleasure machine' (Edgeworth) were instances of misplaced hedonism and made it harder for the student of economics to arrive at an understanding of 'utility maximisation'.

The Economic Man in business was also having serious problems of a schizophrenic nature: was he a pure maximiser of money profits or did he have also other objectives, was he subject to various pulls and pressures of conflicting obligations, responsibilities, loyalties, and preferences? The problems of the multi-goal firm in business have been

112

The Universal Bogey

much discussed in the last thirty years and perhaps we should only remind the reader that most of these problems are serious only as far as spontaneous business action is concerned, but quite innocuous with regard to reactions and responses to changes in the conditions confronting the firm.[45]

THE LOGICAL NATURE OF ECONOMIC MAN

Homo oeconomicus is the metaphoric or figurative expression for a proposition used as a premise in the hypothetico-deductive system of economic theory. This settles, however, only the question of the logical *status,* not of the logical *nature* of the proposition, especially regarding its derivation, evidence or truth value.

Alas, this question has remained as controversial as it ever was. We have sampled some of the methodological positions defended in the older literature and have seen that Mill, Senior, Cairnes, Bagehot and Wicksteed had rather different views on the subject. We have not quoted any of the pronouncements of Mises, Knight, Robbins, Samuelson or Friedman — to name only a few of the major living disputants on economic methodology — chiefly because their views are more widely known, and known to contradict one another. The fundamental assumptions of economic theory — the 'economic principle', 'the postulate of rationality', the 'assumption of maximisation', or whatever they have been called — have been characterised in so many different ways that an enumeration must suffice:

> ... they are regarded as "self-evident propositions", "axioms", "*a priori* truths", "truisms", "tautologies", "definitions", "rigid laws", "rules of procedure", "resolutions", "working hypotheses", "useful fictions", "ideal types", "heuristic mental constructs", "indisputable facts of experience", "facts of immediate experience", "data of introspective observation", "private empirical data", "typical behaviour patterns", and so forth.[46]

Going from *a priori* statements and axioms, via rules of procedure, useful fictions and ideal types all the way to empirical data, the spectrum of logical possibilities seems to be complete. Since there is no

45.   Machlup, Fritz, 'Theories of the Firm: Marginalist, Behavioral, Managerial', *American Economic Review,* Vol. LVII, March 1967, pp. 1-33; and 'Corporate Management, National Interest, and Behavioral Theory', *Journal of Political Economy,* Vol. 75, October 1967, pp. 772-774.

113

The Universal Bogey

way to settle conflicts of methodological taste, we shall refrain from attempting arbitration.

One suggestion, however, may be permissible and, indeed, may stand a good chance of being acceptable to the representatives of the most divergent views. It is probably agreed that *homo oeconomicus* is not supposed to be a real man, but rather a man-made man, an artificial device for use in economic theorizing. Thus, he is not a *homo* but a *homunculus*. It is *homunculus oeconomicus* we have been talking about all along.

THE FUNCTION OF ECONOMIC MAN

Economic Man, I repeat, is a figurative expression for a proposition which serves as a premise in the theoretical system of economics. To ask for the function of the construct Economic Man is, in effect, to question the need for that premise. To put it bluntly: is the behaviour equation expressed by that construct really necessary — necessary, that is, for the theoretical system in which it is employed?

I shall try to answer this question in the form of an argument that focuses on the most important tasks of economic theory, namely, the explanation of changes in output and changes in price (exchange value). Illustrations will help illuminate the argument.

Changes in output.   The output of any product never, or hardly ever, increases unless some producers allocate additional productive services to the particular activities or improve the techniques of production. The output of any product never, or hardly ever, decreases unless some producers reduce the quantities of productive services allocated to the particular activities. Hence, changes in output can be satisfactorily explained only by stating (a) the conditions under which producers are likely to take any of these actions, and (b) the general motive or objective that is likely to induce them to respond in the specified way to the stated changes in conditions.

Changes in price.   Prices of anything sold, bought, or exchanged never rise unless some suppliers ask for higher prices and buyers are

46.   Machlup, Fritz 'The Problem of Verification in Economics', *Southern Economic Journal*, Vol. XXII, July 1955, p. 16.

114

The Universal Bogey

willing to pay them, or some buyers bid higher prices and suppliers are willing to accept them. Prices of anything sold, bought, or exchanged never fall unless some suppliers offer to sell for reduced prices and buyers are willing to pay less, or some buyers bid lower prices and suppliers are willing to accept less. Hence, changes in prices can be satisfactorily explained only by stating (a) the conditions under which suppliers and buyers are likely to take such decisions, and (b) the general motive or objective that is likely to induce them to respond in the specified way to the particular changes in conditions.

A universal principle.   There are obviously many different changes in conditions that could have the results mentioned and, likewise, one could think of a variety of motives or objectives that would induce the stated responses. No theoretical system, however, can be built if *all* premises vary from case to case; at least *one* premise must be found that can serve to deduce applicable conclusions in a very large number of cases. If no such universal premise could be found, but all assumptions had to be chosen from a large variety of possibilities, it would be impossible ever to predict the outcome of any change in conditions with any degree of confidence. A fundamental postulate acceptable as universal premise of at least approximate universal relevance is needed, and it stands to reason that an assumption of a pervasive and invariant objective or behaviour equation can serve in this capacity. Three examples shall be given in order to clarify the meaning of uniformity or universality in the basic hypothesis.

First example: more research..   We do not doubt that many a person may, as Wicksteed reminded us, 'be just as strenuous in the pursuit of knowledge' as in the desire for more wealth. Would it then be wise if we tried to explain the large increase in the number of persons devoting their time to research and development, say, for space ships and moon shots, as a result of their thirst for knowledge? Or are we not better advised to point to the improved job opportunities and pay levels offered these persons in the research and development activities financed by government and industry — conditions of which they were glad to take advantage?

Second example: more music.   Undoubtedly many persons 'may be just as strenuous in the obedience to an artistic impulse' as in the desire for more wealth. Should this lead us to attribute the increase in the

115

The Universal Bogey

number of professional musicians solely to heightened obedience to their artistic impulses? Or had we not better look for the cause in such pecuniary factors as the offer of more positions in more symphony orchestras thanks to larger appropriations of funds to musical organisations, out of increased tax revenues due to higher national incomes?

Third example: vanity and sloth.   No one in his right mind has any doubt that 'vanity' and 'love of ease' are strong motives of human action. But are there many changes in quantities produced or in prices paid and received that would be most credibly explained by changes in the love of ease or by changes in the degree of vanity? To be sure, an increase in incomes or earnings opportunities may affect prices and production in ways that could be explained by reference to given degrees of desires of leisure or prestige, but the substantive change is then on the pecuniary side, not in the system of subjective valuations.

Action and reaction.   The preceding three examples should have illuminated the clue for solving the issue: the economist's chief task is not to explain or predict human action of every sort, or even all human action related to business, finance, or production, but instead only certain kinds of people's reactions (responses) to specified changes in the conditions facing them. For this task a *homunculus oeconomicus,* that is, a postulated (constructed, ideal) universal type of human reactor to stated stimuli, is an indispensable device for a necessary purpose.

Example of an exception: We must not be dogmatic and exclude exceptions to the rule. For we cannot always find the explanations in economic reactions or adjustments to changes in opportunities that present themselves in changes of prices or incomes. Consider the following case: All during the 1950s and later, there was a substantial flow of Austrian maids and waitresses to England, where they could earn much better wages than at home. In the 1960s, however, there began a movement of English girls to Austria, where their wages were lower. Needless to say, wage differentials can explain why Austrian girls go to England, but not why English girls go to Austria to work in hotels and pensions. What hypotheses could be adduced? We may have two plausible explanations: one, the English girls' newly discovered love for learning – learning to speak German, to ski, to have fun –; the other, newly obtained information about these existing opportunities. The

116

The Universal Bogey

first explanation posits a change in *preferences,* perhaps a fashion, the second a change in the availability of *information,* perhaps furnished by employment agents or by travel agents. These hypotheses are, of course, not inconsistent with the economic principle (utility maximisation), but if the bulk of all cases were of this kind, the usefulness of our theoretical system would be much reduced. For most of our explanatory and predictive assignments we need to assume given preferences and given information.

No quantitative predictions.   The conclusions deduceable from the theoretical system with its objective function as fundamental assumption will, by and large, be only qualitative, that is, they will indicate only the direction of change to be expected from certain changes in conditions. No exact quantitative predictions can be derived from the system, although it may be possible to give plausible limits for the deduced changes. For example, the imposition of an excise tax on the product of an oligopolistic industry will be most unlikely to result in a price reduction, but similarly unlikely to result in a price increase by several times the amount of the tax. The increase will most probably be greater than zero and not much greater than the tax. If this appears 'plausible', it is so only from the conjunction of the maximisation assumption with several assumptions concerning cost and demand conditions, possibly also managerial ambitions, political considerations, and institutional constraints. There are other instances in which quantitative estimates may be possible, for example, in macroeconomic problems, but there the estimates are usually derived from correlational regularities (empirical laws), which themselves are not deduceable from any general hypotheses and for which no claims of universality can be made. On the other hand, these empirical laws will not have any great standing — apart from their place in economic history — if they are not at least understandable by reference to individual reactions consistent with the economic principle.

Conclusion.   I move the following resolution: The fundamental assumption — whether it be regarded as a conventional postulate, a useful fiction, or a well-known fact of experience — of maximising behaviour, that is, of utility-maximising reactions of households and firms, is recognised as a useful and probably indispensable part of the theoretical system of economics. This assumption has frequently been hypostasised into the symbolic figure or 'personal ideal type', the Economic Man.

117

PART TWO

MICROECONOMICS

[5]

PROFESSOR HICKS' *REVISION OF DEMAND THEORY*

A Review Article

By FRITZ MACHLUP*

The "demand theory" which Hicks is revising in his new book[1] is that of the first three chapters of his *Value and Capital*,[2] published in 1939. The original version was 42 pages long, the revision covers 194 pages. The new version goes deeper into the "foundations" and is more than patient in its "elaborations."

Among the chief reasons for undertaking the revision are the ascendancy of Samuelson's "revealed preference" approach (about which Hicks is sceptical), certain developments in the mathematical set theory of "strong" and "weak ordering" (of which Hicks gives a presentation which avoids mathematics), the discovery of a more closely reasoned derivation of the law of demand from a few simple propositions of logic, and the realization of some mistakes in his earlier treatment of consumer's surplus and complementarity.

The book falls into three parts: I. "Foundations"; II. "The Demand for a Single Commodity"; III. "The General Theory of Demand." There is no treatment of the "welfare side" of demand theory, nor of its empirical-statistical side, the book being confined to the deductive aspects of what Hicks calls "Plain Economics." He promises to present us with a statement of welfare economics at some later time. But empirical demand analysis, being "concerned with the statistical application of the theory rather than with the theory itself," is regarded by Hicks as outside his field (pp. vi–vii). Yet, "econometric application" is to him an important test, for "a theory which can be used by econometrists is to that extent a better theory than one which cannot" (p. 3).

A brief chapter is devoted to the rejection of (even hypothetically) measurable utility. Hicks holds that in the more elementary parts of the theory the assumption of cardinal utility neither helps nor hinders, but "in the more difficult branches cardinal utility becomes a nuisance" (p. 9). If one rejects, as one probably is forced to by rather simple reflection, the hypothesis of independent utilities, and if one grants the usefulness and possibility of dividing the effects of price changes into those of substitution and of changes in income, one has in effect eliminated cardinalism from the argument (pp. 11–15). Perhaps Hicks wanted to go further, for he elimi-

---

* The author is professor of political economy at the Johns Hopkins University.

[1] J. R. Hicks, *A Revision of Demand Theory* (Oxford: Clarendon Press. 1956. Pp. vii, 196. $3.75.)

[2] J. R. Hicks, *Value and Capital* (Oxford, 1939).

nated even the word "utility" from most of the rest of the book. But is this more than a terminological gesture? The pages are full of "levels of indifference," which after all are not really different from levels of satisfaction or utility; several times the term "real income" is used as an equivalent (*e.g.*, p. 80); and finally there is much discussion of "the consumer's valuation" of units of goods, "average valuation" as well as "marginal valuation," of the practical unimportance of "cases of increasing marginal valuation," of the position of equilibrium where the consumer's marginal valuation of a good is equal to its price (pp. 89–90), of the theorem of the "Additivity of Marginal Valuations" and the "generalized law of Diminishing Marginal Valuation" (p. 153). I cite this list without any critical intent; on the contrary, I approve the introduction of new terms where it is desired to avoid some of the connotations associated with old terms. But the old-fashioned utility theorists, cardinal, semicardinal, as well as ordinal, may note with a sense of satisfaction that the "newfangled" techniques are not so very far removed from their good old ways.

The methodological position underlying Hicks' approach is eminently sound. He is free from positivist-behavioristic restrictions on the study of consumers' behavior, and he also avoids contentions about the supposedly empirical assumptions regarding rational action. Instead, he starts from a fundamental postulate, the "preference hypothesis." Faced with factual data about quantities of commodities purchased and with the task of explaining changes in these quantities, the economist has at least three possibilities: explanations in terms of nonprice data, explanations in terms of effects of current price changes, and explanations in terms of lagged effects of price changes. No matter which of the explanations seems most pertinent, one "needs a technique for separating out the current-price effects from the others," and for this purpose one needs a theory "which will tell us something about the ways in which consumers would be likely to react if variations in current prices and incomes were the only causes of changes in consumption." Thus we must proceed "by postulating an *ideal consumer*, who by definition is only affected by current market conditions. . . . The assumption of behaviour according to a scale of preferences comes in here as the simplest hypothesis . . . " (p. 17). No direct test of the preference hypothesis is practically possible (pp. 17 and 58). It is a postulate accepted because of its fertility in deduced "consequences that can be empirically applied" in the sense that they are successful in aiding "the arrangement of empirical data in meaningful ways" (pp. 17–18).

I. *The Logic of Weak Ordering and the Elementary Law of Demand*

Since the "demand theory, which is based upon the preference hypothesis, turns out to be nothing else but an economic application of the logical theory of ordering" (p. 19), the reader will first have to take the lesson Hicks offers on the "logic of order." He must learn the difference between *strong* ordering, where each item has a place of its own in the order, and *weak* ordering, where some items may be clustered in a group within which none can legitimately be put ahead of the others. (The indifference curve, he is told, implies weak ordering inasmuch as all the points on that curve are *equally* desirable, whereas the "revealed preference" approach implies to Hicks that the positions between which choice is actually made can be strongly ordered.) Hicks teaches this lesson in logic in a relatively painless way, using chiefly examples involving the consistency and transitivity of propositions about the spatial positions of certain things to the left or right of one another. Without graphical support, his examples of "items left of P" and "items right of P" (pp. 26–35) may trouble readers who are alert to the possibility that Q may be left or right of P depending on the position of the observer or on the direction in which P or Q is facing. Forgetting this relativity of right and left, readers may learn, as Hicks wants them to, the distinctions between, and applications of, "two-term consistency conditions" and "transitivity conditions." And the most flexible, studious and docile of the readers may actually keep these conditions in mind ready to be produced to demonstrate certain theorems of demand theory. Older teachers of theory, including the present reviewer, will probably forget enough of these lessons to force them to stick with their accustomed didactic techniques.

In the explanation of the consumer's choice between two goods which are available only in discrete units, the theory of strong ordering seems superior. But where the choice is between any good which may be imperfectly divisible and money which is finely divisible, the possibility of equally desired combinations must be accepted and "strong ordering has to be given up" (p. 41). Weak ordering implies that rejected positions need not be inferior to a position actually chosen, but may have been indifferent; hence, actual choice fails to reveal definite preference. But, adopting the weak-ordering approach, committing ourselves to some degree of continuity (justified by the divisibility of money or general buying power), we must make two additional basic assumptions "to get any farther": that the consumer will always prefer a larger amount of money to a smaller amount and that his preference order is transitive. Hicks has no objections to these assumptions, and I have none either.

From the logic of weak ordering and the two additional assumptions just stated all major propositions of the theory of consumer's demand can be deduced. Hicks proceeds to do this first for the demand for a single commodity, that is, for the behavior of a consumer "confronted with a market in which the price of no more than one good is liable to change" (p. 47). The primary task is to derive the law of demand, that is, "the principle that the demand curve for a commodity is downward sloping" (p. 59). The technique chosen is that "of dividing the effects of a price-change into two parts": income effect and substitution effect. The latter "can be deduced from consistency theory." The income effect, according to Hicks, rests on observation; but he might just as well have said that it rests on the definitions of "normal" and "inferior" goods. (Observation comes in only to support the proposition that the income-elasticities of demand are nonzero for most goods, and positive if the goods are broadly defined.) The substitution effect, as Hicks demonstrates, tends to increase the consumption of a good at a reduced price. The income effect will do the same, except for inferior goods. Hence, an exception to the law of demand—the Giffen case—can occur only when the good is inferior ("with a negative income-elasticity of significant size"), the substitution effect is small, and the proportion of income spent upon the inferior good is large (pp. 66–67).

II. *A Family of Hypothetical Income Variations*

The division of the effects of a price-change into substitution and income effects is arbitrary to the extent that the income effect is the hypothetical effect of a hypothetical change in income by an amount deemed commensurate to the price change. For separating out the two effects Hicks presents two alternative methods, neither of which corresponds to the one he presented in his earlier book. Since, to follow him, we have to manipulate three different income effects and two related concepts of consumer's surplus, a catalogue of the alternative concepts of relevant income variations and a graph showing the relevant indifference curves and budget lines will be useful. (Figure 1 uses indifference curves, which Hicks avoids in his book. There are no indifference curves in any of his 22 graphs, though there are points that are defined as representing "indifferent positions.") Since the relative magnitudes of the various hypothetical variations of income depend on whether the good whose price is reduced or increased is a normal or an inferior one, we must state what we assume: we assume the good to be normal.

Alternative Concepts of Income Variations Measuring Some Relevant Effects of Price Changes upon the Consumer

Pertaining to Price Reductions

The *cost difference L* [for Laspeyre] (shown as *FG* in Figure 1) equals the amount of a lump-sum *tax* which the consumer, following a reduction in the price of *X*, would have to pay in order to be able to purchase just the same quantities, and no more, of *X* and of all other goods that he purchased before the price reduction.

The *compensating income variation* (shown as *FH* in Figure 1) equals the amount of a lump-sum *tax* which the consumer, after a reduction in the price of *X* has caused him to purchase a larger quantity of *X* at the lower price, would have to pay in order to be pushed back to the same indifference level that he had attained when he purchased a smaller quantity of *X* at the higher price—provided that he is permitted after paying the tax to adjust again (reduce by *B'C'*) the quantity of *X* purchased.

Pertaining to Price Increases

The *cost difference P* [for Paasche] (shown as *FJ* in Figure 1) equals the amount of a lump-sum *subsidy* which the consumer, following an increase in the price of *X*, would have to receive in order to be able to purchase just the same quantities, and no less, of *X* and of all other goods that he purchased before the price increase.

The *compensating income variation* (shown as *FI* in Figure 1) equals the amount of a lump-sum *subsidy* which the consumer, after an increase in the price of *X* has caused him to purchase a smaller quantity of *X* at the higher price, would have to receive in order to be lifted back to the same indifference level that he had attained when he purchased a larger quantity of *X* at the lower price—provided that he is permitted after receiving the subsidy to adjust again (increase by *A'E'*) the quantity of *X* purchased.

The *compensating consumer's surplus* (shown as *FS* in Figure 1) equals the amount of a lump-sum *tax* which the consumer, after a reduction in the price of X has caused him to purchase a larger quantity of X at the lower price, would have to pay in order to be pushed back to the same indifference level that he had attained when he purchased a smaller quantity of X at the higher price—provided that he is *not* permitted after paying the tax to adjust again (reduce) the quantity (OB') of X purchased.

The *compensating consumer's surplus* (shown as *FT* in Figure 1) equals the amount of a lump-sum *subsidy* which the consumer, after an increase in the price of X has caused him to purchase a smaller quantity of X at the higher price, would have to receive in order to be lifted back to the same indifference level that he had attained when he purchased a larger quantity of X at the lower price—provided that he is *not* permitted after receiving the subsidy to adjust again (increase) the quantity (OA') of X purchased

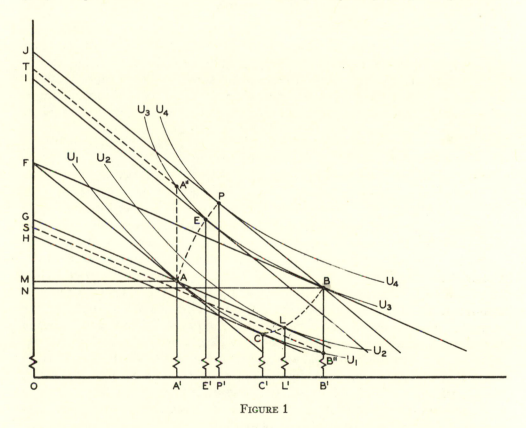

FIGURE 1

The *equivalent income variation* (shown as *FI* in Figure 1) equals the amount of a lump-sum *subsidy* which the consumer, after purchasing a certain quantity of X at a given price, would have to receive in order to be lifted up to the same indifference level that he would attain if a reduction in the price of X caused him to purchase a larger quantity of X at the lower price—provided that he is permitted after receiving the subsidy to adjust (increase by $A'E'$) the quantity of X purchased.

The *equivalent income variation* (shown as *FH* in Figure 1) equals the amount of a lump-sum *tax* which the consumer, after purchasing a certain quantity of X at a given price, would have to pay in order to be pushed down to the same indifference level that he would attain if an increase in the price of X caused him to purchase a smaller quantity of X at the higher price—provided that he is permitted after paying the tax to adjust (reduce by $B'C'$) the quantity of X purchased.

The *equivalent consumer's surplus* (shown as *FT* in Figure 1) equals the amount of a lump-sum *subsidy* which the consumer, after purchasing a certain quantity of *X* at a given price, would have to receive in order to be lifted up to the same indifference level that he would attain if a reduction in the price of *X* caused him to purchase a larger quantity of *X* at the lower price—provided that he is *not* permitted after receiving the subsidy to adjust (increase) the quantity (*OA'*) of *X* purchased.

The *equivalent consumer's surplus* (shown as *FS* in Figure 1) equals the amount of a lump-sum *tax* which the consumer, after purchasing a certain quantity of *X* at a given price, would have to pay in order to be pushed down to the same indifference level that he would attain if an increase in the price of *X* caused him to purchase a smaller quantity of *X* at the higher price—provided that he is *not* permitted after paying the tax to adjust (reduce) the quantity (*OB'*) of *X* purchased.

We have here five different income variations relevant to price reductions, and five relevant to price increases; since four of the latter have counterparts among the former of equal size (though of opposite signs) we have six different magnitudes. Let us defer the discussion of the four consumer's surpluses—of two sizes—and deal first with the three pairs of income variations called "cost differences," "compensating variations," and "equivalent variations." (All these terms are of Hicksian coinage.)

A. *The Three Pairs of Income Effects and Substitution Effects*

First of all, why, for the case of a price reduction, are two of the income variations visualized as taxes and one as a subsidy? The point is that the imaginary subsidy is to be given *instead* of the price reduction—hence, an "*equivalent* variation of income." The two imaginary taxes, on the other hand, are to be imposed, *after* the price reduction becomes effective, in order to undo some of the effects of that reduction, the one by taking away enought to offset the gain in total utility obtained through the price reduction—hence, a "*compensating* variation of income"—the other to take away enough to offset the money saving made in buying the old quantity at the reduced price—hence a "*cost difference à la Laspeyre*."[3] The relative sizes of the three income variations should now be clear (for the case of a price reduction of a normal good). The cost difference is the smallest; the compensating variation must be bigger in order to offset the gain the consumer could make through adjusting his purchases after paying the cost-difference tax; the equivalent variation must be bigger still because no price reduction and no substitution have yet taken place.

The income effect of a price reduction of a "normal" good is, of course, positive. How then can imaginary taxes, or income reductions, describe it? The trick is that the imaginary taxes are to be thought of as immediately followed by imaginary tax refunds, and these refunds are regarded as the income effect. First we tax the consumer (thus eliminating the income

[3] Since the latter tax would seize only what the consumer could save if he purchased the old collection of goods, and would thus leave it open to him still to improve his position (by substituting more of the cheapened good for other goods), it was once referred to as an "*undercompensating* variation of income." See P. A. Samuelson, "Consumption Theorems in Terms of Overcompensation rather than Indifference Comparisons," *Economica*, Feb. 1953, N.S. XX, 1–9.—Samuelson discussed a price increase and, hence, an "overcompensating" variation of income, since the Paasche cost difference would be larger than the compensating variation.

effect) and see how he would adjust his purchases to the price reduction—the substitution effect in isolation—and then we refund the tax to see how he would spend this increase in income. The order is reversed when the equivalent variation is used: we first eliminate the substitution effect and, by giving the consumer a subsidy and watching him adjust his consumption to it, we isolate the income effect; then we take the difference between this subsidized consumption level and the one induced by the uncompensated price reduction as the substitution effect.[4]

The three methods trace three different paths from position A to position B (see Figure 1). The equivalent variation sends us *via E*, the compensating variation *via C*, and the cost difference *via L*. Students of Hicks' *Value and Capital* may remember that they were told to take the E-route.[5] In my review article of 1940 I proposed the L-route.[6] Strangely enough, Hicks forgot both my directions and his own. He now (p. 61) attributes the L-route to a 1953 article by Samuelson,[7] and states that he himself had adopted the C-route.[8] He recommends the C and L routes as alternatives, though he finds the C-route less convenient in relation to the income effect and more convenient in relation to the substitution effect (p. 69). The E-route, once the only one described in this context, he now finds least convenient (p. 80).

The effect of the price reduction upon the consumption of X is invariably $A'B'$, but with the different imaginary intermediate points the substitution effects are $A'C'$, $A'L'$, or $E'B'$, respectively, and the respective income effects are $C'B'$, $L'B'$, or $A'E'$. If we reverse the direction of change and describe the effects of a price increase, we see that the equivalent variation will be found through C as the intermediary point, and the compensating variation through E, while the cost difference, now *à la Paasche*, will have a new point, P, as a half-way place. The relative sizes of the income variations are rather different from what they were before: the equivalent variation is now the smallest, the compensating variation is bigger, and the cost difference is the biggest (this time deserving the Samuelson designation as "overcompensating" variation). The substitution effects upon the consumption of X will now be $B'E'$, $B'P'$, or $C'A'$, the income effects $E'A'$, $P'A'$, or $B'C'$.

[4] This asymmetry in procedure is apt to cause confusion regarding the signs of the income effects. It is already a little strange that we, following Hicks, speak of a positive income effect when a negative change of price causes a positive change in the consumer's real income. It may be confusion worse confounded if we, departing from Hicks but following common sense, mark imaginary taxes with negative signs, and imaginary subsidies with positive signs, and yet use both in the explanation of a "positive" income effect. Consistency is hard to restore in this matter and I can do no better than warn the reader about the deceptive signs.

[5] *Op. cit.*, p. 31.

[6] Fritz Machlup, "Professor Hicks' Statics," *Quart. Jour. Econ.*, Feb. 1940, LIV, 280–82.

[7] See footnote 3, above. Samuelson informs me that the method was already used in Slutsky's article, "Sulla teoria del bilancio del consumatore," *Giorn. d. Econ.*, July 1915, LI, 1–26, was then repeatedly described in the index-number literature, and was alluded to by Hicks himself in the Mathematical Appendix to *Value and Capital*, p. 309. An English translation of Slutsky's article is available in *Readings in Price Theory*, G. J. Stigler and K. E. Boulding, ed. (Homewood, 1952).

[8] Hicks probably thinks of his exposition of consumer's surplus, for which he had used the C-method.

B. *The Four Consumer's Surpluses*

In *Value and Capital* the compensating variation in income figured as the consumer's surplus. "But this was a mistake," which Hicks corrected in his article on "The Four Consumer's Surpluses"[9] and corrects now again (p. 96). The "mistake" is easy to make and hard to clear up. There are, as Hicks now takes pains to explain, two angles from which demand theory can be viewed: one may ask either what quantities would be consumed at certain prices, or what maximum prices would be paid for certain quantities. Hicks accordingly distinguishes "price-into-quantity analysis" and "quantity-into-price analysis" (p. 83). The former is best understood by visualizing the consumer as a pure competitor in the market, free to purchase at a given price any quantity he chooses. For the other approach we have to imagine the consumer in a market where goods are rationed out to him, where he may have to pay discriminatory prices for every unit or at least for additional units of the commodity, or where he may be compelled to take certain quantities. The question what is the maximum amount of money the consumer might be willing to pay for a certain quantity can be answered only if we do not permit him to take less than that quantity at that price, as he would if he had his choice. Since consumer's surplus is the excess of this maximum over the actual price paid, its definitions have to provide for some such restraint concerning quantity purchased.

These restraining provisions were made in the descriptions of the four concepts of consumer's surplus included in our catalogue of alternative concepts. And these restraints account also for the size relations between the various income measures. The definition of the compensating consumer's surplus fixes the quantity that was chosen at the changed price and does not permit it to be adjusted when a compensating tax or subsidy reduces or raises the consumer back to the indifference level he had attained before the price change. The definition of the equivalent consumer's surplus freezes the quantity that was chosen before the price change and does not permit it to be adjusted when an equivalent subsidy or tax lifts or depresses the consumer to the indifference level he would attain as a result of the price change. Hence, in the case of a price reduction, the compensating consumer's surplus must be smaller than the compensating variation because a tax in the amount of the latter, with no quantity readjustment permitted, would reduce the consumer below the initial indifference level. (In Figure 1, if the consumer were assessed a tax of FH and were compelled to take the quantity OB', he would be worse off than initially. If he is to stay on the initial indifference level, U_1, he cannot pay more than $BB'' = FS$ as a compensating-surplus tax.) Similarly, the equivalent consumer's surplus must be larger than the equivalent variation because a subsidy in the amount of the latter, with no quantity adjustment permitted, would fail to lift the consumer to the indifference level that the price reduction would afford him.

[9] J. R. Hicks, "The Four Consumer's Surpluses," *Rev. Econ. Stud.*, 1943–44, XI, 31–41. Hicks gives due credit for "discovering" the mistake to A. M. Henderson, "Consumer's Surplus and the Compensating Variation in Income," *Rev. Econ. Stud.*, 1940–41, VIII, 117–21.

(In Figure 1, if the consumer were given a subsidy of only FI and were held to a quantity of OA', he would not reach the indifference level U_3; it would take a subsidy in the amount of $AA'' = FT$ to get him there.)

C. *Arithmetic and Graphical Illustrations*

The quantitative relationships expressed here in written language and shown geometrically in an indifference graph may be profitably reviewed by an arithmetic illustration—although to admit the usefulness of such simple devices takes courage in these days of high-powered mathematical techniques. Let us then assume a simple demand schedule with just two prices of a normal good; let us calculate the cost-differences L and P, and let us assign arbitrary but plausible values to the other income variations relevant to movements between these two points of the demand schedule. The demand schedule is reversible and, depending on the direction of the change, each price-quantity pair will in turn constitute the "initial position."

DEMAND SCHEDULE FOR GOOD X

Price	Quantity	Amount Paid
10¢	1000	$100.00
9¢	1150	103.50

Relevant Variations	As Price Is Reduced		As Price Is Increased	
	Dollar Amount	Fig. 1	Dollar Amount	Fig. 1
Change in expenditure for X	+3.50	MN	−3.50	MN
Cost difference of initial quantity	−10.00	FG	+11.50	FJ
Compensating income variation	−10.50	FH	+11.00	FI
Equivalent income variation	+11.00	FI	−10.50	FH
Compensating consumer's surplus	−10.25	FS	+11.25	FT
Equivalent consumer's surplus	+11.25	FT	−10.25	FS

Note: The inconsistencies in the signs are discussed on p. 125 above. The graph (Figure 1). is not drawn to correspond to the dollar amounts used in this illustration.

Yet another device will aid in exhibiting the income effects and the substitution effects "operating" upon the quantity of X consumed as a result of the reduction or increase in price. We may draw for the two prices a family of "uncompensated" demand curves, each with income as a parameter. Disregarding the four consumer's surpluses (because they are less helpful in "price-into-quantity analysis") we shall need four demand curves besides the one for the initial income Y: two for incomes after taxes, (Y − 10.00) and (Y − 10.50) and two for incomes after subsidies, (Y + 11.00) and (Y + 11.50), as shown in Figure 2. Using the above demand schedule for income Y and connecting the initial positions A (for the price reduction) and B (for the price increase) with the relevant points on the other demand curves, we can identify AC and AL as the two "compensated demand curves" for the price reduction, one after the tax to offset the utility gain,

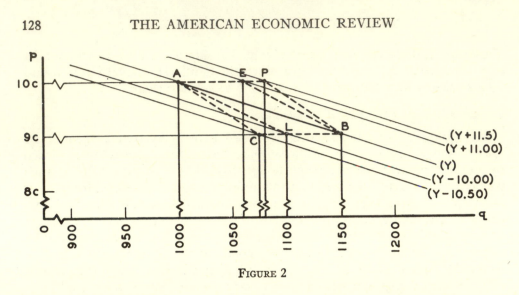

FIGURE 2

the other after the tax to offset the cost difference; and *BE* and *BP* as the two "compensated demand curves" for the price increase, one after the subsidy to offset the utility loss, the other after the subsidy to offset the cost difference.

We can again trace the effects of the price changes along alternative routes: *ACB*, *ALB*, and *AEB* for the price reduction, *BEA*, *BPA* and *BCA* for the price increase. The alternative substitution and income effects upon the consumption of *X* can be read off the graph as follows:

Cause	Route	Substitution Effect	Income Effect	Total
Price reduction from 10¢ to 9¢	*ACB*	*AC* = 75 units	*CB* = 75 units	*AB* = 150 units
	ALB	*AL* = 100 units	*LB* = 50 units	*AB* = 150 units
	AEB	*EB* = 90 units	*AE* = 60 units	*AB* = 150 units
Price increase from 9¢ to 10¢	*BEA*	*BE* = −90 units	*EA* = −60 units	*BA* = −150 units
	BPA	*BP* = −70 units	*PA* = −80 units	*BA* = −150 units
	BCA	*CA* = −75 units	*BC* = −75 units	*BA* = −150 units

D. *Marginal Valuation*

For the "quantity-into-price" approach we must become better acquainted with "marginal valuation" and the "compensated marginal valuation curve." Hicks had introduced this ingenious device in his 1944 article under the name of "marginal indifference curve." (At that time he used the term "marginal valuation curve" for a curve which is now stowed away in the attic with other old gadgets.) The new marginal valuation curve is presented together with a corresponding average valuation curve. (These curves look exactly like the well-known marginal and average product curves, with which they in fact have much in common.) The compensated marginal valuation curve is designed to show "the amounts of money which the consumer is willing to pay for successive units of the commodity *X*" provided that he "pays the full marginal valuation of each unit before making his valuation of the next" (p. 86).

What is the difference between the compensated marginal valuation curve and the compensated demand curve? The latter shows the quantities consumed at each price "under the assumption that income is continuously adjusted so as to maintain indifference of the successive positions" (p. 76). The difference is, essentially, that a marginal valuation curve may go up before it goes down, whereas the compensated demand curve can only go down. Any rising part of the marginal valuation curve will not, however, be of practical interest if the consumer can purchase as much as he wants. His demand will be "zero until price falls to his maximum average valuation" (p. 88), and at lower prices the quantities taken will be such as to secure equality between marginal valuation and price.[10]

III. *The General Theory of Demand*

After graduating from the study of "elementary" theory of demand—"in which the price of no more than one good is liable to change" (p. 47)—we advance to the study of the "general" theory—in which "more than one price-ratio is allowed to vary" (p. 107). At the outset Hicks makes us exercise with a "Second Consistency Test," only to conclude that this approach "is not promising" (p. 112). Instead, he puts us to work with so-called "indifference tests." (His penchant for giving a new name to every step in the argument leads to a bewildering proliferation of terms, which few will care to remember even if they should be able to do so.) The "first indifference test" says no more than "that as between two indifferent positions, the compensating variation C is less or equal to the cost-difference P," the Paasche cost-difference; "the second indifference test is expressed by saying that when we are comparing two indifferent positions, C must be greater or equal to L," the Laspeyre cost-difference (p. 116). These are merely new names for old ideas (which I had expressed in my 1940 article). But from these "tests" Hicks is able to deduce that the substitution effect of a price reduction must be positive (or zero, at worst). For, without income effects $P - L = S$, that is, the positive substitution effect is implied in the excess of the Paasche cost-difference over the Laspeyre cost-difference.

---

[10] I must briefly report on Hicks' reflections concerning the Giffen case and his discovery of an "anti-Giffen case" (p. 92). Just as the Giffen possibility rests on exceptionally strong income effects upon the *consumption* of exceptionally "strongly inferior" goods, the anti-Giffen possibility rests on exceptionally strong income effects upon the marginal *valuation* of "strongly normal" goods, possibly causing the marginal valuation curve to slope upward for another stretch. But the possibility is only of theoretical interest and of little, if any practical importance. The probability of sufficiently strong income effects is negligible, especially since what counts in practice are not single consumers, but large groups of consumers heterogeneous in tastes as well as incomes (pp. 67–68). But in addition Hicks shows that stretches of Giffen slopes would not provide equilibrium positions and would be quickly passed in swift movements of prices (or of quantities, in the anti-Giffen case). Thus, even if these unlikely situations should exist, they "would not show up," for "All that would be seen . . . would be a fall in price," and "We should not be able to tell that the law of demand was failing to operate, for the effects of that condition would be indistinguishable from the effects of a demand that was extremely inelastic" (p. 94); or especially elastic in the anti-Giffen case.

Where two or more prices change at the same time, the "Total Substitution Effect" is the sum "of the differences in quantity consumed of each good, each being valued at the corresponding difference in price" (p. 117). If price reductions are "reckoned as positive," and price increases as negative, "the total substitution effect of any price-change, however complex" must always be positive (or zero). This is christened "the First Substitution Theorem"; it contains "the downward slope of the compensated demand curve as a special case" (p. 117). To put it differently, when a compensating variation in income has made two constellations of prices and quantities equally desirable, the price reduction of X times the quantity increase of X, plus the price reduction of Y times the quantity increase of Y, plus etc., can never be negative.

From the "transitivity of indifference" follows "the additivity of compensating variations," as Hicks demonstrates in easy steps. Soon thereafter he makes the nonmathematical readers feel happy by assuring them that they have just been introduced to a statement, in economic terms, of "the fundamental theorem of Riemann integration" (p. 123). Their confidence thus being bolstered up, the readers, determined to hang on for another ride, will be glad to accept the assumption that compensated demand curves can be treated as straight lines, since "any continuous curve, over a sufficiently short stretch, is indistinguishable from a straight line (p. 125). This will take them to another vista, named "the Reciprocity Theorem."

This theorem, good for comparing three or more price-quantity constellations (with small price differences only) which are made indifferent through compensating income variations, tells us that "the sum of the quantity-changes from (0) to (1) each being valued by the price-change of the same commodity from (0) to (2), equals the sum of the quantity-changes from (0) to (2) each being valued at the corresponding price-change from (0) to (1)" (p. 126). A simple but useful implication of this theorem is that "the cross-effects of price-changes . . . are equal" (p. 127) and hence, "the relation of substitution (and complementarity) is reciprocal" (p. 128). Incidentally, discussions of complementarity are beyond the scope of elementary theory of demand because "in the two-goods case, the relation between the two goods must be that of substitution. . . . Complementarity can only occur when there are other goods outside the group of complements at whose expense the substitution in favour of the group of complements can take place" (p. 129).

Since the designation of the "first" substitution theorem has indicated that there must be more in store, my conscience forbids me to skip the "second substitution theorem." But I shall mention merely that it is chiefly concerned with a "limit on the size of the cross-effect," and provides formal support to the intuitively obvious fact that "X and Y cannot be highly substitutable for one another unless each has a demand which is highly elastic with respect to its own price." As another boon to the nonmathematical reader, I may quote an aside of the author to the effect that he finds in connection with this theorem an "example of the way in which a blind adherence to standard mathematical methods sometimes produces nonsense results" (p. 134).

While we are on the subject of the cross-effects, it may be worth stressing that all references up to this point have been only to the "cross-substitution effects," isolated by means of compensating income variations. If income is not tampered with, "the equality between the cross-substitution effects may well be masked by inequality between the cross-income effects on income-elasticities" (p. 147). This was clearly set forth by Hicks in his *Value and Capital*.

A. *Exceptions to the Law of Demand*

Some other consequences of the income effect, however, are either demonstrated in novel ways or newly discovered. The chief question is whether the "Total Income Effect," which is "a combination of the separate income-effects on the separate commodities," may modify the "generalized law of demand." Hicks sees "three possible sorts of exceptions" to the law: "those due to inferior goods, to commodity asymmetry, and to asymmetrical effects of redistribution" (p. 146). The first of these exceptions is of course the "generalization of the Giffen case," in which all or most of the "price-changing goods" are inferior. Since "the share in consumer's expenditure going upon all inferior goods taken together may be much larger than that going upon any particular inferior good," a large negative income effect has a somewhat better chance of being realized where many prices may change than where only one price changes (p. 139). But it would be a very odd thing indeed if price changes in the same direction happened to be concentrated in the group of inferior goods.

The second exception is "perhaps more interesting." It is conceivable that the income-elasticities of demand for the goods that rise in price are very different from those that fall in price. Imagine sharp price reductions for a group of "necessaries (with income-elasticity zero), and a rise in the prices of a group of luxuries (with high income-elasticity)," with the gains from the price reductions exceeding the losses from the price increases. The freed income would go after the luxuries; if there is no third group of goods, and if the price ratios within the two groups have not changed, the quantities of luxuries consumed may rise despite their higher prices (p. 142). We need not expect this often, if ever, to happen in reality, but it is fun to think about it.[11]

The third exception relates not to the demand of an individual consumer but only to the market demand. In general the "probability of exceptional cases is diminished when we take a large group of heterogeneous consumers together" (p. 144). But there is the possibility of a changed distribution of a constant total income where the gainers and the losers have very different

[11] If the luxuries did not rise in price, the demand for them would surely increase by more. Thus the price increases operate in the expected, not exceptional, manner: they reduce the quantities demanded below those that would result from the price fall in necessaries. (This comment is the result of a discussion with William Fellner.)

income-elasticities of demand. Thus there is the chance of a "redistribution income-effect," and Hicks can state: "If the price of X falls (other prices constant), while the total income of consumers remains constant, it is always possible that the consumption of X may fall, if income is redistributed from X-likers to X-dislikers" (p. 145). I cannot persuade myself to see this case as an "exception" to the law of demand; the peculiar change in the distribution of income is in no way connected with the change in prices, but is just one of those things that by some queer coincidence may happen and prevent a result of another change that has occurred from being realized. The first two exceptions are due to given conditions and may occur while other things remain unchanged. The "third exception" abrogates the *ceteris paribus* clause and invokes a fortuitous change of other things.

B. *Substitutes and Complements*

The inversion of "price-into-quantity theory" to "quantity-into-price" theory, which was profitably carried out in "elementary theory," affords no less valuable insights in the general theory. What we have just learned to call the "first substitution theorem" becomes now the "generalized law of Diminishing Marginal Valuation" (p. 153). The main additions to the set of previously formulated propositions on marginal valuation concern the relationships of substitutability and complementarity, and it is on these issues that Hicks proposes some of the most significant revisions of his earlier theory. In part they represent developments of suggestions made since 1939 by Lange, Mosak, and Ichimura.

The most basic revision lies in the recognition of two alternative definitions of substitutability (complementarity), one looking toward the effect of price changes upon quantity with other prices unchanged, the other toward the effect of quantity changes upon valuation with other quantities unchanged. In order to distinguish between the two definitions, Hicks speaks of goods as "p-substitutes," "q-substitutes," "p-complements," and "q-complements." Thus, "X and Y are p-substitutes when . . . a fall in the price of X [diminishes] the demand for Y, when all *prices* save that of X are fixed, and income is adjusted so as to maintain indifference." And "X and Y are q-substitutes when a rise in the quantity of X diminishes the marginal valuation of Y (or the price at which a fixed quantity of Y would be purchased) when the *quantities* of all other commodities than X are fixed, saving the quantity of money, which is adjusted so as to maintain indifference" (p. 156).

Only in the simplest case will p-substitutability and q-substitutability be exactly equivalent, namely, in the case in which the prices of all other goods than X and Y are fixed. If other prices, say the price of Z, can vary as a result of a price change of X, there may be cross-effects upon the demand for Y which may offset the initial effect of the price change of X; indeed, the cross effect (Z upon Y) may wipe out the initial effect (X upon Y) so that "X and Y would be q-substitutes, even though they are p-complements" (p. 157). Because of such reactions through third goods the distinction between the two meanings of the relationship is necessary, although the "reciprocity theorem holds for each of the two meanings" (p. 158).

The discussion of related goods in terms of the effects only of price changes had left a bad gap—noted in my 1940 article, identified by Lange,[12] and provisionally filled by Ichimura[13]—in that the effects of other changes, including changes in the system of wants, could not be analyzed with the tools at hand. The "sympathetic" changes in demand of which Lange had spoken in cases of what Hicks now calls "intrinsic complementarity" (p. 162) can be explained by means of the new set of concepts. It turns out that the marginal valuations of complementary goods may move in different directions while their quantities move together; and that the marginal valuations of close substitutes will move together while their quantities do not. This fits in perfectly with the old insight that "perfect substitutes tend to have constant price-ratios, perfect complements constant quantity-ratios" (p. 165).

Some of the problems of consumer's choice have been unnecessarily clouded by the practice of regarding substitutability (or complementarity) between consumer's goods always as a matter of wants or tastes even when it is a matter of technology. Hicks reminds us of Menger's distinction between "objectives" and "means of reaching" them (p. 166). Consumers may make technical decisions about alternative means of reaching their given objectives. Hence, technical substitutability (or complementarity) is relevant not only in production but also in consumption; not only in the theory of the firm but also in the theory of the household. The brief remarks which Hicks makes on this point may open up good opportunities for enterprising economists, theoretical or empirical, in search of subjects in which to invest their analytical talents.

IV. *The Importance of All That*

Many of the relationships which Hicks "discovers" or elaborates in this book are fascinating to a seasoned teacher of abstract economic theory. Does this make the book and its discoveries "important"? When I tried out some of its arguments on a more worldly economist, his reaction was "So what?". By pragmatic tests, I must admit, we shall hardly be able to claim any importance for Hicks' discoveries. They will in no way affect any recommendations of economic policy, any predictions of future events, any explanations of the past. None of our actions will be different from what it would be if this book had never been written—except perhaps the teaching of some fine points in university courses on pure economic theory (and even here most students may fail to notice the difference).

But is it fair to apply such crudely pragmatic criteria? Judged by such tests most works of art would lack importance, and so would most works in philosophy and logic. Indeed, most improvements of theoretical systems in the empirical sciences would be "unimportant," for as a rule they do not

[12] Oskar Lange, "Complementarity and Inter-relations of Shifts in Demand," *Rev. Econ. Stud.*, Oct. 1940, VIII, 58–63.

[13] S. Ichimura, "A Critical Note on the Definition of Related Goods," *Rev. Econ. Stud.*, 1950–51, XVIII, 179–83.

affect the conclusions but merely reduce the number of assumptions from which the results are deduced. The conventions of scientific methodology are quite clear on recognizing the "importance" of reconstructions in which some of the old pillars of a theoretical framework are razed.

I can understand, however, that some discontent with the rule of Occam's Razor may arise if it shaves away some very familiar assumptions and forces us to engage in brain-racking logical exercises in order to deduce our familiar conclusions from fewer (or weaker) hypotheses. This is precisely what Hicks' Revision of Demand Theory does or claims to do. Some very well-known empirical propositions (such as the law of demand) are here deduced, without the use of some very familiar assumptions (such as given systems of utility or indifference), from a smaller number of hypotheses or from less restrictive ones; and this involves heavy demands on the syllogistic agility of the readers. I can hear them say: "Why should we work so hard to obtain our results from three assumptions if we can get them with so much less effort from four or five? After all, hypotheses come quite cheap; why skimp?"

I take it that we must not give in to such lowbrow laziness. Much as we may prefer to economize in mental effort, as gentlemen and scholars we are obliged to economize in hypotheses. "A body of propositions, such as those of pure mathematics or theoretical physics [or, let us add, theoretical economics], can be deduced from a certain apparatus of initial assumptions concerning initial undefined terms. Any reduction in the number of undefined terms and unproved premises is an improvement since it diminishes the range of possible error and provides a smaller assemblage of hostages for the truth of the whole system." This, in Bertrand Russell's words,[14] is the maxim we obey; and under this maxim one may give recognition to the importance of Hicks' work even if one should not be satisfied with the contributions it makes through the theorems which are discussed in the foregoing pages. Whether Hicks' approach is an improvement not only on his earlier presentation but also on the revealed preference approach will probably be debated. The latter uses still fewer assumptions, but Hicks' assumptions are weaker (less restrictive). On different grounds some may claim that revealed preference is superior because of the "empirical meaning" of the fundamental hypothesis. For me it is sufficient that such a hypothesis be "understandable" in the light of my inner experience casually checked against like experiences of others.[15] I find superfluous the polite bows to neopositivism which the revealed preference theorists make. Whether their theory yields conclusions which Hicks' theory cannot yield is another matter, but this is not examined here.

An important book is sometimes enjoyable to read. Unfortunately this cannot be said about this book. Not that higher mathematics or complicated graphs stop the reader's progress. The exposition is nonmathematical; if there are equations and mathematical symbols on many pages of Part III,

[14] Bertrand Russell, "Philosophical Analysis," *Hibbert Jour.*, July, 1956, LIV, 321.

[15] See Fritz Machlup, "The Problem of Verification in Economics," *South. Econ. Jour.*, July 1955, XXII, 1–21, esp. pp. 16–17.

they are merely abbreviations and are not subjected to algebraic manipulations.[16] Of course, the formally literary exposition is still mathematical in the sense in which all logical reasoning is mathematical. Since the entire book is a tightly knit logical argument, it is not possible for the reader to skim the book with much chance of success; if he attempts to skip a few pages or even paragraphs he is likely to get lost. Indeed, a reader who pauses too long between chapters may have to go back and re-read lest he miss his connections. All this may explain why the book is a difficult one; but it does not explain why it gives little reading pleasure. Does perhaps Hicks' style of writing account for that? It is interesting to speculate how a master of literary exposition—rare indeed among present-day economists—might mould Hicks' material into graceful, enjoyable prose. Hicks is a very serious man and he takes his work very seriously. But could he not, metaphorically speaking, indulge in a smile once in a while? On the rare occasions when he attempts a somewhat humorous touch, the result is not always felicitous. For example, when he announces "there is a dragon waiting at the door who must first be cleared out of the way. It is the old crux of the measurability of utility" (p. 7). To be sure, we have heard of all sorts of creatures being transformed into dragons; but a dragon who is an old crux is even more forbidding than Cardinal Utility.

[16] It is disturbing, though, that Hicks uses dots where in usual practice we would find parentheses; he writes consistently $(p_0 - p_1 \cdot q_1)$ instead of $(p_0 - p_1) q_1$.

202

[6]

FRITZ MACHLUP
The Commonsense of the Elasticity
of Substitution

THE discussion of the "elasticity of substitution" is conspicuous for its unintelligibility. To say this is not at all to belittle the pioneering work of the "tool-makers", J. R. Hicks[1] and Joan Robinson[2]. Scientific discussion, undoubtedly, becomes more confusing the more similar the things denoted by one and the same name. The concepts discussed by the two authors are so much alike as to be mistaken for one another. In an early comment[3] it was asserted: "Dr. Hicks' elasticity of substitution is exactly the same as Mrs. Robinson's elasticity of substitution". As the discussion went on, slight differences were discovered. Dr. Hicks was even accused[4] of having introduced a "loose form of the concept of elasticity of substitution", though he was the first author who ever had used it. More and more mathematics entered into the discussion to make things more precise—and less intelligible for the average reader, not to speak of the marginal reader. At the risk of being despised as a "popularizer" of high science I undertake this commentary as a contribution to simpler economics.

I. THE RELATIVE SHARE IN THE NATIONAL DIVIDEND

"An increase in the supply of any factor will increase its relative share (i.e., its proportion of the National Dividend) if its 'elasticity of substitution' is greater than unity."[5]

"The case where the elasticity of substitution is unity can . . . be defined . . . by saying that in this case (initially, before any consequential changes in the supply of other factors takes place) the increase in one factor will raise the marginal product of all other factors taken together in the same proportion as the total product is raised."[6]

These statements of Dr. Hicks' invite us to reflect upon the absolute and relative incomes of the factors of production. We can visualize the portions of the factors most clearly by simple diagrams.[7] Figure I shows the products due to additional increments of labour applied with a given (constant) quantity of other factors (denoted by "capital"). It is assumed that labour gets an income equal to its marginal product times quantity of labour employed. The total product is distributed among the two groups of factors in such a way that the shaded area

---

[1] J. R. Hicks, *The Theory of Wages*. London, 1932.
[2] Joan Robinson, *The Economics of Imperfect Competition*. London, 1933.
[3] R. F. Kahn, Notes on the Elasticity of Substitution, REVIEW OF ECONOMIC STUDIES. Vol. I, p. 72.
[4] A. P. Lerner, Notes on the Elasticity of Substitution, REVIEW OF ECONOMIC STUDIES, vol. I. p. 148.
[5] Hicks, *loc. cit.,* p. 117.
[6] Hicks, *loc. cit.,* p. 117.
[7] I am much indebted to Prof. B. F. Haley, Stanford University.

represents the income of all labour (the total wage-bill), the unshaded area the income of all "capital."

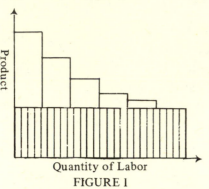

FIGURE 1

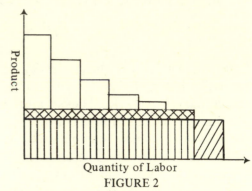

FIGURE 2

A further unit of labour enters now into the picture (Figure 2). The increment to total product due to this last unit of labour added is shown by diagonal shading. The new total labour income (the decreased wage-rate times increased quantity of labour) can be smaller or larger than, or equal to,

the former total labour income. It is equal if the increment ⬜ is equal

to the decrement ▨▨▨▨▨. The increment divided by the decrement is, if both are of the same magnitude, equal to one.

$$\frac{⬜}{▨▨▨▨▨} = |$$ This case is called "unit elasticity of demand."

The proportion of the increment to the decrement is (with due qualifications regarding the discontinuity of the curve) the elasticity of demand for labour (which later will be denoted by η).

If the increment to labour income exceeds the decrement, the absolute change in labour income is shown by the difference. The absolute change in the labour

income ⬜ — ▨▨▨▨▨ may be set in relation to the former

total labour income. By such division, $\dfrac{⬜ - ▨▨▨▨▨}{\text{▥▥▥▥▥}}$, we obtain the relative change in labour income. How does this relative change compare with the relative change in National Income? The National Income (all areas together) has been absolutely increased by the marginal product 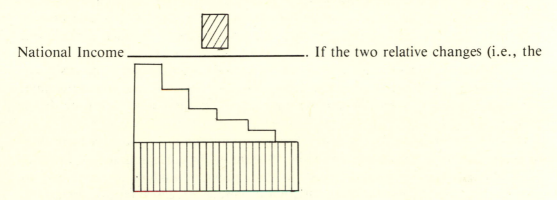. The relative change in National Income is the absolute increase divided by the former

National Income ⎯⎯⎯⎯⎯⎯⎯⎯⎯⎯⎯⎯⎯⎯⎯⎯. If the two relative changes (i.e., the

relative change in labour income and the relative change in National Income) are equal, a division of the one by the other,

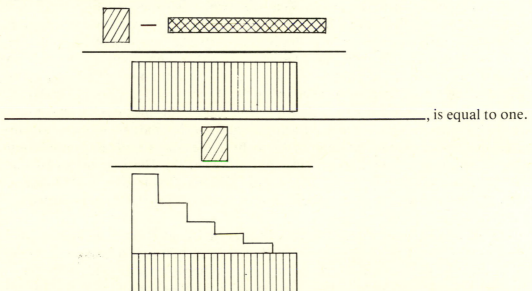

, is equal to one.

This case is called (in the given quotation) "unit elasticity of substitution". If the elasticity of substitution is smaller or greater than unity, the relative increase in total labour income is smaller or greater than the relative increase in National Income. (The elasticity of substitution will later be denoted by σ.)

II. A FUNCTIONAL CONNECTION BETWEEN THE ELASTICITY OF SUBSTITUTION AND THE ELASTICITY OF DEMAND

The elasticity of demand (η) and the elasticity of substitution (σ) are implicitly connected in a certain way. Let us see in what way.

If the National Income increases and the labour income remains unchanged, the relative share of labour in the National Income is decreased. An elasticity of demand for labour of unity $(\eta=1)$ means that, as the amount of labour increases and the wage-rate decreases, the total wage-bill, i.e., total labour income, remains unchanged. The National Income is increased by the employment of more labour, otherwise the marginal productivity of labour would have been zero. The absolutely unchanged labour income $(\eta=1)$ represents, consequently, a decreased relative share for labour in the National Income. This means an elasticity of substitution of less than one $(\sigma<1)$.

On the other hand, if the elasticity of substitution is unity $(\sigma=1)$ the relative share of labour in the national income remains constant by the given definition. Hence the total labour income has to increase at the same rate as the national income. An increase of the total wage-sum, as the amount of labour increases, means an elasticity of demand for labour greater than unity $(\eta>1)$. A unit elasticity of substitution means therefore an elasticity of demand greater than unity.

This functional connection between the two elasticities (if $\eta=1, \sigma<1$; if $\sigma=1, \eta>1$) is implicit in the statement quoted from Dr. Hicks. It may be sharply contrasted with a statement of Mrs. Robinson's[1]: "It can be seen that, when the conditions are such that the aggregate amount of capital remains contant, the elasticity of demand for labour is equal to the elasticity of substitution." The condition of constant amount of capital was assumed in Dr. Hicks' analysis also. If Dr. Hicks' implicit conclusion $(\eta>\sigma)$ as well as Mrs. Robinson's conclusion $(\eta=\sigma)$ have been correctly inferred from the outset, it becomes obvious that the two authors have different concepts in mind. The difference may be in the concepts of substitution or in other assumptions. It lies, in fact, in both. Anyway, Dr. Hicks' elasticity of substitution, determining the factors' share in the National Dividend, is not the same as Mrs. Robinson's elasticity of substitution. The nature of the divergence will be shown in a later section.

This is, however, the place to refer to Professor Douglas' production function.[2] His formula tells us that labour has contributed a constant portion of 75 per cent to the production of the National Income in U.S.A. It implies that changes in the quantity of labour do not change this relative share; it implies therefore an elasticity of substitution of unity and, according to the proportion of the shares, an elasticity of demand for labour of 4.[3] This makes it still more peculiar that Professor Douglas seems to dislike and to disregard the new concept.

[1] Robinson, *loc. cit.,* p. 260.
[2] Paul H. Douglas, *Theory of Wages,* New York, 1934, p. 133.
[3] It depends on the definition whether we have to write $\eta = 4$ or $\eta = -4$.

III. THE CAUSAL CONNECTION BETWEEN SUBSTITUTABILITY AND THE ELASTICITY OF DEMAND

Professor Douglas argued against the significance of the elasticity of substitution as follows[1]: ". . . the question as to the effect which the increase of a factor will have upon its unit, its aggregate, and its relative return . . . will not depend solely or perhaps even primarily upon the relative elasticities of substitution. On the contrary the elasticities of the curves of the diminishing incremental product . . . would seem to be the more decisive influences."

The curve of the diminishing incremental product constitutes, for Douglas as well as for Hicks (with some qualifications), the demand curve for the factor. When Professor Douglas upholds the influence of the shape of the demand curve while he rejects the influence of the substitutability, he must have, of course, overlooked the functional connection between the "two" influences. But it is more than that. One may ask why the decrease in marginal product is relatively smaller than the increase in quantity of labour, or in terms of market analysis, why the decrease in wage rates is relatively smaller than the increase in quantity of labour. If one answers "because of the elasticity of the productivity curve, or respectively, demand curve," one has to bear in mind that this is a definition rather than an explanation. One *calls* a curve which shows the given qualities a curve with an elasticity greater than unity. We should not explain something by the "decisive influence" of the definition.

If we now ask why the demand curve has the shape that it has, we come to the decisive influence of substitutability. "The demand for anything is likely to be more elastic the more readily substitutes for that thing can be obtained," says Pigou,[2] reformulating Marshall's statement. Certain conditions which make for a certain rate of decrease in marginal productivity and, consequently, for a certain rate at which the demand price decreases, as the quantity of a factor increases, are conveniently expressed by the "ease of substitution" or the "degree of substitutability." The higher the elasticity of substitution the higher the elasticity of demand.

IV.   SUBSTITUTION VERSUS INCREASE

We wish to place chief emphasis on the statement that it is the increase (or decrease) in the quantity of factors which is the point of the whole argument. The question is what effect on prices of the factors results from an increase in one factor if substitution for the others is easy or hard to arrange.

Imagine the existence of many units of two factors *A* and *B*. They are combined in many groups in different proportions. There are production-groups with 5*A*'s and 5*B*'s, others with 5*A*'s and 4*B*'s, others with 5*A*'s and 3*B*'s, and so on and so forth, groups with almost all various combinations of the two factors. With given resour-

[1] Douglas, *loc. cit.*, p. 59
[2] Pigou, *Economics of Welfare*, Bk. IV, Chap. V

ces, given technical conditions and given consumer demand schedules, these combinations are "optimum-combinations." That means that no change in combination (no substitution of a unit of *A* for a unit of *B*, and *vice versa*) would be preferred. Now, one or two newcomers of the sort *A* appear and wish to be taken in by any group. If no group can take them in, they would do by themselves a very poor job and pull down, by competition with their "brothers," the price of the *A's* very sharply. If they are permitted to join one or the other group, the incremental product for these groups is likely to be pretty small so that, by competition among the *A's*, the price and share of *A's* might be considerably lowered. But perhaps one of the modest newcomers might be invited by a group to displace one of the *B*-fellows. This *B*-fellow is dismissed and has to look for a corner to crawl into. He might find it convenient to form a new group together with the other new *A*-fellow. Or some other changes in the group-teams might be arranged. At any rate, the possibility of displacing one of the *B's* is good for the case of the *A's*. The ease of substituting one of the increased factors for one of the other sort helps the *A's* to avoid too great a fall in their price. If no substitution is possible they can compete only with their own comrades for the collaboration with the complementary fellows. "Substitution is possible" means that the newcomers compete also with the fellows of the other sort so that the gain of the latter is not so great. The increase in the quantity of factor *A* is partly completing and partly competing with the factor *B* if substitution is possible. The greater the substitutability the stronger the competing element within the complementarity.

Our primitive image helps us to understand a feature which has been almost universally misunderstood. The increase in quantity of the one factor brings with it a rearrangement of the combinations in the various groups. The substitution takes place in certain groups, i.e., in certain industries. In such industries more factors of the one kind and less factors of the other kind might be employed. But while such *substitution* of one factor for another occurs in single industries, it remains for the community as a whole an *increase* in the quantity of one factor with an unchanged quantity of the other. In the community as a whole, there is not a displacement but only a rearrangement of the factors if the one is increased.

The failure to grasp this idea of "substitution within increase" has been responsible for much confusion. Some commentators plainly thought that substitution of labour for capital means that, in the community as a whole, labour is employed instead of capital, and capital is, therefore, thrown away or left unemployed[1]. The sharp line which it has been suggested be drawn between substitution and increase (by Mr. Lerner) might make readers forget that it is the increase which causes the substitution and that it is the substitution which shapes the effects of the increase.

The term "substitution" gives, of course, the impression of mere displacement. But the displacement in single industries is not only compatible with but even necessary for the whole absorption of more factors into the productive system as a

---

[1] If capital were disposed of, as labour is increased, then Professor Douglas would be right in saying that with unit elasticity of substitution labour gets a constant absolute return, which is also a constant relative share, since "the total produce remained constant." *Loc., cit.,* p. 58.

whole. An increase in quantity of a factor brings with it a rearrangement of combinations of factors: the substitution within single industries. We are interested in the ease of substitution because it determines the form of the influence upon the prices of the factors as their quantity increases.

V. PARTIAL EQUILIBRIUM VERSUS GENERAL EQUILIBRIUM

The substitutability among factors in a single industry is one thing, the substitutability in the system as a whole is another; that the former is contained in the latter seems, however, indisputable. Mrs. Robinson gives us a theory of substitutability in single industries. So does Hicks in the Appendix of his book, while in the text he argues in terms of the system as a whole. He states once in a note[1] that Mrs. Robinson's and his own expression for the elasticity of substitution "become equal" if "constant returns"—a linear and homogeneous production function—are assumed. When he made this statement he was obviously thinking only of the Appendix and forgot his theory of the "relative share in the National Dividend."

The partial equilibrium analysis, i.e., the analysis of the equilibrium of the single firm or of the single industry assumes that (under perfect competition) the various factors are employed by the productive units, in such proportion as to make their respective marginal product equal to their price. A change in the price relation of the factors results, consequently, in a change in the proportion in which the factors are employed in the firm or industry under consideration. "The proportionate change in the ratio of the amount of factors employed divided by the proportionate change in the ratio of their prices to which it is due"[2] is the elasticity of substitution in the single industry. It "is determined by the technical conditions of production."[3]

If we know the elasticity of technical substitution in an industry we do not know yet the changes in its demand for the factors (due to a certain change in their relative prices). Our knowledge is still so incomplete because the elasticity of technical substitution informs us only about the changes in proportion of the factors employed in the production of a "fixed product" at "given prices of the product." The change in the relative prices of the factors will, however, result also in a change in the quantities produced at given prices of the product," and, after all, also in a change in the prices of the product. Hence we have to know the elasticity of demand for the product. The changes in the amount of commodities produced change, of course, the amount of all factors demanded by the industry. This change in demand for factors might meet various conditions of supply, so that the elasticity of supply of all the factors comes into the picture. In order to know how many more units of a factor will be employed by a single industry as its price decreases, that is, in order to know the elasticity of demand for a factor, in a single industry, four conditions have to be known[4]: (1) the proportion in which the factors were employed before the change

---

[1] Hicks, Notes on the Elasticity of Substitution, REVIEW OF ECONOMIC STUDIES, Vol. I, p. 78.
[2] Robinson, *loc. cit.,* p. 256.
[3] *Ibid.*, p. 256.
[4] Hicks, *Theory of Wages*, p. 242, Robinson, *loc. cit.*, p. 260, *et seq.*

occurred, (2) the elasticity of substitution, (3) the elasticity of supply of the other factors, and (4) the elasticity of demand for the commodity produced.

elasticity of substitution, (3) the elasticity of supply of the other factors, and (4) the elasticity of demand for the commodity produced.

This is the role of the elasticity of substitution in the partial equilibrium analysis of demand for a factor. An attempt at a simple translation from terms of partial equilibrium into terms of general equilibrium would look like this: The elasticity of demand for all commodities together, if hoarding and dishoarding of money is ruled out, is unity; the elasticity of supply of all other factors might, for certain purposes, conveniently be considered zero, or in other words, the quantity of all other factors supplied might be assumed constant. Thus the conditions (3) and (4) from the above set are reduced to universally applicable assumptions and the changes in demand for a factor in the community as a whole would be determined solely by the elasticity of technical substitution. This is simple, but, unfortunately, wrong.

The elasticity of demand for the product, which is so important for the single industry analysis, is not reduced to simple "unit elasticity of demand for the total National product" if we switch to a total-system analysis.[1] The place of the elasticity of demand for the commodity produced, in partial equilibrium analysis, is taken by the elasticity of substitution between the commodities produced, in general equilibrium analysis. Substitution of one commodity for another, on the part of consumers, influences the demand for the producers. As the prices of factors vary, the prices of products vary in the sense that the commodities which "contain" more of the increased factor become relatively cheaper. Commodities which have become relatively cheaper are substituted for commodities which have become relatively dearer. The elasticity of consumers' substitution combines with the elasticity of producers' substitution in determining the ease of substitution of one factor for another.

VI. TECHNICAL SUBSTITUTION VERSUS COMMODITY SUBSTITUTION

The term "elasticity of substitution" was introduced by Hicks in dealing with the factors' relative shares in the National Dividend. It is now, I think, absolutely clear that a definite statement about the factors' relative share could never be solely read off from the elasticity of technical substitution. If the elasticity-expression is to be relevant for the theory of distribution it has to be the aggregate measure of the elasticities of technical substitution and of commodity substitution.

This line between the two elasticities would, however, be rather arbitrary. The distinction between producers' substitution and consumers' substitution depends on whether we call commodities of different qualities *one* or *different* commodities. If we speak of bread as of one commodity, wheat, corn, and rye will be substitutes in

---

[1] It should be noted that unit elasticity refers to money demand. Dr. Hicks (*loc. cit.*, Appendix, p. 246) assumed "real demand" of elasticity, which is no more correct.

the production of bread. If we call wheat-bread, corn-bread, and rye-bread different commodities the substitutability between these commodities lies in the sphere of consumption. Are houses of cement, brick, wood, stone, houses with different kinds of roofs, etc., etc., one commodity or different commodities? Are hand-made shoes and manufactured shoes one or different commodities?

There are, of course, many cases in which purely technical substitution between factors of production does not affect the perfect homogeneity of the product. In such cases the direct substitution, by producers, can be neatly separated from the indirect substitution which takes place when consumers rearrange the distribution of their expenditure. But always, in so far as the proportions of factors are different in different lines of production, indirect substitution will occur together with direct (technical) substitution. Since for the community as a whole both kinds of substitution are merged into one aggregate measure, the location of the dividing line between producers' and consumers' substitution is of no particular importance.

Let us follow up once more, in order to make it unmistakably clear, the process of absorption into the productive system as a whole of an additional supply of a factor. Let labour be the factor the supply of which is increased. The price of labour tends to go down. Technical substitution of labour for other factors ensues. Products which are made from relatively more labour are supplied relatively more cheaply than products made from relatively less labour. Consumers' substitution of "more-labour-products" for "less-labour-products" ensues. The absorption of the new units of labour will finally have taken place with lesser reductions in wage-rates the more easily the technical substitution and the consumers' substitution is brought about. The elasticity of total substitution determines the change in labour's relative share in the National product.

VII.   SYMMETRY IN SUBSTITUTABILITY

"The elasticity of substitution of labour for capital is the same as the elasticity of substitution of capital for labour."[1]

According to this statement of Dr. Hicks, the change in the ratio of the prices of the factors which is necessary to change the ratio of their amounts employed so as to absorb additional units of a factor is the same, though in opposite direction, whether capital or labour is to be absorbed. The conditions of absorbing more labour or more capital would be "symmetrical."

The arguments pro and contra this symmetry run mostly in terms of geometrical curves. The technical substitutability is derived from "isoquants" or fixed-product curves.[2] The substitutability of commodities is derived from indifference curves.[3] Elasticity of a curve, at a point, refers to movements in either of the

---

[1] Hicks, *loc., cit.,* p. 119.

[2] Lerner, *loc., cit.,* p. 68.

[3] J. R. Hicks and R. G. D. Allen, *A Reconsideration of the Theory of Value,* Part I. *Economica, New Series,* No. I, p. 58.

two directions. Against the validity of such reasoning it is said that an increase in the quantity of factors employed means increase in the product and therefore necessarily movement away from a fixed-product curve. According to which one of the factors is increased, one departs from the old isoquant in different directions. What is true for movements in either of the two directions *along* one curve cannot be true for movements *away* from the curve.

It is convenient to think it over in terms of economics. If technical substitution were not possible, the return to a factor the amount of which is increased would be considerably reduced. And there would be no reason whatsoever to think that the effect upon price of an increase in one factor would be the same as the effect upon price of an increase in another factor. But the situation is not so if technical substitution is possible. The new unit of a factor does not have to open up an entirely new job but only to drive out of its job a unit of another factor (which has to seek other employment). This displacement or substitution takes place with a certain ease, which is determined, at first, by technical conditions. The ease of managing the displacement the other way round, i.e., if the other factor had increased in amount and has to drive out its rival, is, surely, the same since it is determined by the same technical conditions. This sounds reasonable; it is, however, subject to certain qualifications.

Suppose that factor A is used for making the commodities R and S, while factor B is used for making the commodities S and T. There is, at first, substitutability between A and B in the production of S. If the supply of B increases, and its price falls, more B's are substituted for A's in the production of S. Moreover, as the price of S falls, more S's are substituted, by consumers, for other commodities. There might come a point at which all S's are made from B. If the amount of B increases further, the substitutability of B for A is confined to consumers' substitution, the opportunities of technical substitution being exhausted. But if, instead, the amount of A increases, a wide range of opportunities for technical substitution is available. The elasticity of total substitution of A for B is at this point indeed greater than the elasticity of total substitution of B for A. (In a graphical illustration one would have to show that the fixed product curves hit the coordinate representing B, the amount of A used being zero. To move from this point along the curves is possible in only one direction.[1] Similarly no symmetry of the elasticity is to be expected where the curves from which we derive it are not continuous. "Kinks" or corners in the curves would make impossible "symmetrical elasticity" at the points concerned. The whole discontinuity argument is, however, not very important.)

Another example made me first suspicious of the symmetry in total substitutability because of a seeming asymmetry in certain assumptions concerning

---

[1] Asymmetrical substitutability of this sort has been, for many years, an argument in the theory of capital and interest. Some writers used to hold that, if the supply of capital becomes more and more plentiful, there must come a point at which technical substitution of capital for labour would no longer be possible. At such a point, however, technical substitution of labour for capital, being a mere reverse movement, would be easily arranged. (That substitution of capital for labour could go on by way of commodity substitution and the interest rate, therefore, remain positive has been overlooked in the whole argument.)

circumstances in commodity substitution. Suppose (as before) *A* and *B* being technical substitutes (rivals) in the production of commodity *S*, factor *A* engaged also in the production of *R* unrivalled by factor *B*, and *B* engaged also in the production of *T* unrivalled by factor *A*. The technical substitutability of *A* for *B* and *B* for *A* is symmetrical in the production of *S*. As to the consumers' choices we now assume that commodities *R* and *S* are substitutes for each other, while the commodity *T* is no rival of *R* nor of *S*. If the amount of *B* increases, and its price falls, more *B's* are substituted for *A's* in the production of *S*. As the price of *S* falls, more *S's* are substituted by consumers for other commodities inclusive of commodity *R*. Factor *B* is rival to factor *A* once in the field of production, by way of substitution in producing *S*, and again in the field of consumption, by way of substitution of *S* for *R*.

If the amount of factor *A* increases, rather than the amount of *B*, the situation is, it might seem on the surface, somewhat different. In the field of production the substitution is symmetrical. But in the field of consumption, is factor *A's* substitutability for factor *B* equal to factor *B's* substitutability for factor *A* although the product *T* is unrivalled by the products in which *A* is engaged? Does symmetry in the substitutability between consumers' goods involve symmetry in the "derived substitutability" between factors of production? I first was inclined to answer in the negative. Dr. Hicks warned me against it.[1] The competition of factor *A* against factor *B* in the consumers' choice by way of substitution of commodity *R* for commodity *S* is not less efficient than the competition of *B* against *A* by substitution of *S* for *R*. One more point can be made for the assertion of symmetry of derived substitutability. If the existence of other factors, besides *A* and *B*, and the existence of other commodities, besides *R*, *S*, and *T*, is assumed, mediate rivalry through other commodities is to be considered. Though *T* is not rivalled by *R* and *S*, it might be rivalled by U and *V*, which, for their part, might be rivalled by *R* and *S*.

On the other hand, if many factors and many commodities are assumed, the rearrangement, due to the increase in one factor, will face different conditions of supply of the other factors. (Even if their total supply is assumed to be fixed, rearrangement involves mobility and faces thereby different conditions of supply for particular industries.) Under such circumstances no symmetry in substitutability would seem to be tenable.[2]

VIII. SUBSTITUTABILITY AS A FUNCTION OF TIME

Substitution is consumers' and producers' reaction to changes in relative prices. Such reactions are not "timeless," of course. It seems appropriate to discuss the time-element in the problem of the ease and degree of substitution.

The rearrangement of consumers' expenditures that results from a change in relative prices of commodities might vary in degree according to the length of time allowed for the changes to work themselves out. (Some of the theorems of the

[1] In private correspondence.
[2] A. C. Pigou, The Elasticity of Substitution, *Economic Journal*, Vol. XLIV.

"long-run demand curve" which have been recently suggested are interesting but too vague to be fruitful. After all, no definitive statement can be made about "induced changes in consumers' preferences").

The rearrangement of producers' plans is perhaps still more time-conditioned. Even if one disregards such long-run changes in productive technique as may result from "induced inventions," the adaptation of the production structure to altered relative prices of factors is substantially different in the short run and in the long run. The main source of the dependence upon time of productive adaptation is the "fixity" and "specificity" of capital invested in durable equipment.

The substitution of capital for labour and of labour for capital in the short run and in the long run is so fundamentally different that it might be better to work with different concepts of capital in the two kinds of analysis. In the short run, the existing equipment, more or less specialized plants, structures, machines, tools, materials, and so on, will have to be looked upon in examining substitutability. In the long run, "liquid capital", disinvested from old equipment and transformable at command into any desired form, is the more adequate concept. It goes without saying that the short-run substitutability between the thousands and thousands of heterogeneous factors "capital" and the numerous factors "labour" (heterogeneous by location and quality) is much less than the long-run substitutability between capital and labour.

This is, however, not the place to expatiate on these problems. It would not be possible to do so without lingering in the fields of capital theory. All that is necessary for this commentary is to express the idea that the elasticity of substitution is obviously an increasing function of time. Hence we may infer that the elasticity of demand for a factor will be greater the more time is allowed for the changes to work themselves out.

IX. RESUME

It may be desirable to give a short summary of my own commentary. We have found that the term "elasticity of substitution" is used, in Mrs. Robinson's book as well as in the *Appendix* of Dr. Hicks' book, for denoting a concept of *partial* equilibrium analysis. In Dr. Hicks' *text* it is used for denoting a concept of *general* equilibrium analysis. The "elasticity of technical substitution" is not sufficient to determine the factors' relative share in the total product. For this purpose it is necessary to consider "elasticity of total substitution," which comprises technical substitution as well as consumers' substitution. The elasticity of total substitution is the essential element by which the elasticity of demand for a factor of production is determined.

A unit elasticity of total substitution makes the elasticity of demand for a factor necessarily greater than unity. It does not seem that there is an *a priori* reason why the elasticity of total substitution should be of the same magnitude for all factors. (The problem of the "symmetry" of the substitutability of the factors needs further scrutiny. Our answer to this question is to be considered as merely tentative). The elasticity of total substitution is, undoubtedly, greater the more time is allowed. This is, therefore, true also for the elasticity of demand for factors.

Cambridge, Mass.—Vienna,   FRITZ MACHLUP

[7]
MARGINAL ANALYSIS AND EMPIRICAL RESEARCH
By FRITZ MACHLUP*

Certain critics of "conventional" economic theory from time to time voice surprise at the general acceptance of marginalism and at "the confidence of the textbook writers in the validity of the marginal analysis."[1] They disapprove of allowing the principle of marginalism to play the rôle of a fundamental postulate in the teaching of economics.

Marginalism Implied in the Economic Principle

These critics would probably revolt against all those definitions of economics which contain marginalism as an implicit criterion. Marginalism, as the logical process of "finding a maximum," is clearly implied in the so-called *economic principle*—striving to achieve with given means a maximum of ends.

Economics in a narrow sense is confined to such aspects of conduct as can be explained with reference to the principles of maximizing satisfaction, income, or profit. Under definitions of this sort any deviations from the marginal principle would be extra-economic. Yet, to refuse to deal with any type of business conduct that cannot qualify by the strict standards of marginalism may justly be regarded as a lazy man's excuse. If certain types of business conduct can be found in reality with regularity and consistency, it is undoubtedly desirable to analyze them regardless of their "economic rationale."[2] And if some of these allegedly "non-economic" aspects of conduct can be explained within the conceptual framework of economics, one may prefer definitions which admit behavior types not strictly subject to marginal analysis among the proper subject matter of economic theory.

Interpretation of Business Behavior

To recognize the study of certain types of merely "traditional" conduct as legitimately within the province of economic theory is one thing; it is another to accept as correct the interpretations of business behavior offered by the critics of marginal analysis. Unable to see how marginal analysis can be applied to their material, these critics have concluded that marginalism should be discarded. It can be shown, however, that

---

* The author is professor of economics at the University of Buffalo.

[1] Richard A. Lester, "Shortcomings of Marginal Analysis for Wage-Employment Problems," *Am. Econ. Rev.*, Vol. XXXVI, No. 1 (Mar., 1946), p. 63.

[2] *Cf.* the admonition that "if an economist finds a procedure widely established in fact, he ought to regard it with more respect than he would be inclined to give in the light of his own analytic method." R. F. Harrod, "Price and Cost in Entrepreneurs' Policy," *Oxford Economic Papers*, No. 2 (1939), p. 7.

the alleged "inapplicability" of marginal analysis is often due to a failure to understand it, to faulty research techniques, or to mistaken interpretations of "findings."

This is not to deny that a goodly portion of all business behavior may be non-rational, thoughtless, blindly repetitive, deliberately traditional, or motivated by extra-economic objectives. But the material thus far presented as the result of empirical research has not proved what the analysts intended to prove. In some instances their findings were the result of careful research, based on a thorough knowledge of economic theory, but their interpretations were still questionable. In other instances the whole approach of the research project was so faulty that the findings as well as the interpretations are all but worthless except as targets for critical discussion.

I. Marginal Analysis of the Single Firm

Any attempt to "test" marginalist theory through empirical research presupposes full understanding of the theory. It is necessary to know precisely what the theory says, what it implies, and what it intends to do. Since it has been developed gradually over a period of more than a century,[3] it will not suffice to take any particular writer as one's authority or any particular exposition as one's text. Earlier versions lack the necessary refinements and methodological foundations; later formulations often take for granted necessary assumptions or qualifications made in previous expositions. To criticize the theory because of the errors and omissions in any treatise, however representative, is unfair.

The following statement of essential elements in the marginalist analysis of the single business firm attempts merely to give major emphasis to points often overlooked or misunderstood.

The Determination of Output and Employment

The theory of the "equilibrium of the single firm" is not as ambitious as is often believed. It does not attempt to give all the reasons why a given firm makes the type or quality of product which it makes; why it produces the output that it produces; why it employs the workers that it employs; or why it charges the prices that it charges. It is probably an understatement of the importance of the historical situation when Hall and Hitch modestly remark: "There is usually some element in the prices ruling at any time which can only be explained in the light of the history of the industry."[4] The phrase "usually some element" does

---

[3] Cournot was among the earlier expositors of marginal analysis of the single firm.

[4] R. L. Hall and C. J. Hitch, "Price Theory and Business Behavior," *Oxford Economic Papers*, No. 2 (1939), p. 33.

not do justice to the part played by historical antecedents in the determination of product, output, employment, and prices. The rôle of the past in shaping the actual conditions under which the firm operates, in developing the routine of its responses to changes in conditions, and in impressing it with experiences which have taught it to size up and anticipate these changes as the basis for its decisions—this rôle is by no means denied by marginal analysis. The rôle of the past in the process of adjusting the present to the anticipated future is essential in all theory of human conduct. It is implied in the very attempt of constructing a pattern of behavior of the single firm.

Instead of giving a complete explanation of the "determination" of output, prices, and employment by the firm, marginal analysis really intends to explain the effects which certain *changes* in conditions may have upon the actions of the firm. What kind of changes may cause the firm to raise prices? to increase output? to reduce employment? What conditions may influence the firm to continue with the same prices, output, employment, in the face of actual or anticipated changes? Economic theory, static as well as dynamic, is essentially a theory of adjustment to change. The concept of equilibrium is a tool in this theory of change; the marginal calculus is its dominating principle.

A. *Marginal Revenue and Cost of Output*

Subjectivity of Cost and Revenue

The proposition that the firm will attempt to equate marginal cost and marginal revenue is logically implied in the assumption that the firm will attempt to maximize its profit (or minimize its losses). It should hardly be necessary to mention that all the relevant magnitudes involved—cost, revenue, profit—are subjective—that is, perceived or fancied by the men whose decisions or actions are to be explained (the business men)—rather than "objective"—that is, calculated by disinterested men who are observing these actions from the outside and are explaining them (statisticians and economists as theorists—not as consultants).

The marginal cost that guides the producer is the addition to his total cost which he expects would be caused by added production. An outside observer, if he had expert knowledge of the production techniques and full insight into the cost situation of the producing firm, might arrive at a different, "objective" figure of the firm's marginal cost; but what the observer thinks is not necessarily the same as what the producer thinks. The producer's actual decision is based on what he himself thinks; it is based on "subjective" cost expectations.

One may perhaps assume that the producer is intensely interested in knowing his cost and that, in general, he has the experience which enables him to know it. Yet, one must not assume that all producers "really" know their cost in the sense in which an efficiency expert would determine it; several of them may lack the interest or experience; they may not find it worth their while to dig too deeply into the mysteries of their business. (After all, we know that there are good business men and bad, and that the majority is somewhere between good and bad.) But this does not invalidate the proposition that the producer is guided by marginal cost.[5]

The same thing is true with regard to price expectations and sales expectations. It is the "demand as seen by the seller" from which his revenue expectations stem. The increase in demand which is relevant in the analysis of the firm need not be "the real thing"; it may precede an "actual" increase in demand, lag behind it, or be entirely imaginary. The business man does what he does on the basis of what *he* thinks, regardless of whether you agree with him or not.

Marginal analysis of the firm should not be understood to imply anything but subjective estimates, guesses and hunches.

The Range of Price and Output Variations

Beginning students of economics who watch their instructor draw demand and cost curves covering half the blackboard may be misled into believing that the business man is supposed to visualize the possibilities of producing and selling amounts of output ranging from almost zero up to two or three times the amounts that he is currently producing and selling; that the business man is supposed to figure out how much he might be able to sell at prices several times as high as the current price, and how much at prices only one-half or one-third as high. The curve draftsman, indeed, seems to ascribe extraordinary powers of imagination to the business wizards.

Misunderstandings of this sort, and erroneous criticisms of marginal analysis, could be avoided if it were made clear to the students that the length of the curves, *i.e.*, the wide range they cover, was chiefly designed to enable those in the back rows of the class room to make out what goes on on the blackboard; and to permit them to practice curve analysis without using magnifying glasses. The range of possibilities—prices, sales, outputs—which a business man may have in mind is probably quite narrow. Rarely will a business man bother pondering the probable effects of a price increase or cut by 50 per cent; but he may easily think about what a 10 or 15 per cent price change might do to his sales; or what discount it might take to land some additional orders.

The principles of analysis are not altered by the realization that the

---

[5] One may wish, of course, to qualify any social implications of the proposition once the subjective character of the relevant cost data is recognized.

alternatives which business men weigh concerning prices or production volumes cover a much more moderate range than the curves which teachers of economics draw to depict the pattern of marginal calculus.

The Time-Range of Anticipations

In view of the known attempts to derive statistical cost curves from accounting data—which of necessity refer to conditions of the past—it is important to mention that the marginal cost and marginal revenue concepts in the analysis of the equilibrium of the firm refer to expectations of future conditions. To be sure, past experience is always in the background of anticipations of the future, and past accounting records may form a firm point of departure for evaluating prospective and hypothetical cost and revenue figures. But anticipations alone are the relevant variables in the marginal calculus of the firm.

What is the time-range of the significant anticipations? How far into the future do they reach, and what period, if any, is given special emphasis? Is tomorrow more important than next year or several years hence? Is it the "short run" or the "long run" which controls current action?

When a firm wishes to increase production, it usually has a choice of expanding the equipment and productive capacity of its plant or of stepping up the output of the existing plant with unchanged equipment. If productive capacity is already well utilized, the marginal cost of producing larger outputs will be higher in the existing establishment with unchanged equipment than in an establishment with adjusted, increased equipment. If several degrees of adjustment in the productive equipment are possible, several marginal cost functions will be "given" and several different outputs will be "the equilibrium output" under given sales expectations.

To cope with these problems economists have made the distinction between the "short period," assuming no adaptation of equipment, and the "long period," assuming complete adaptation of equipment. Students often believe that the latter period is called "long" because it takes a long time to expand the plant. This need not be the case. A better understanding of the concepts might be achieved by associating the degree of planned plant adjustment with the length of time for which the changed production volume is expected to be maintained. If an increased demand is expected to prevail for a short period only, it will not pay to invest in plant expansion, and "short-run cost" will determine output. On the other hand, if demand is expected to continue at the higher level for a sufficiently long period, an expansion of the establishment will be considered a profitable investment, and "long-run cost" will determine output. Needless to say, many intermediate periods, that is, several degrees of plant adjustment with different marginal cost conditions, may exist.

On the basis of this reasoning one will recognize it as a misunderstanding to argue that short-run cost is of controlling influence on the ground that we always live and work in the short period. The duration for which demand conditions are expected to prevail will determine the relevant "period" of cost anticipations. Of course, this relevance is again subjectively determined, not by the "objective" judgment of the economist.

The time-range of the anticipations with regard to the demand and selling outlook is subject to similar considerations. It is a mistake to think that the relevant "period" for demand and marginal revenue expectations is determined by the length of time it takes for today's production to reach the market.[6] If a price reduction is apt to spoil the market for a long time to come, or a price increase to harm customer loyalty, the effects on future profits will hardly be neglected in considering current actions. If a firm were to regard a certain price change as a desirable step for the time being, but feared that a later reversal might be difficult or costly, it would weigh this anticipated future cost or loss against the short-run benefit.

Anticipations of this sort, complementary or competing with one another, are not exceptions to marginal analysis but are part and parcel of it. To be sure, when an instructor teaches graphical analysis, he will do well to abstract from complicated cost and revenue anticipations and to concentrate on those that can be neatly packed away in geometric curves.

The Numerical Definiteness of the Estimates

The geometric curves and arithmetic schedules by which the instructor presents marginal cost and marginal revenue of the firm seem to leave no room for doubt that these anticipations take the form of estimates of definite numerical values. While this may be necessary for teaching purposes, it should not mislead the student into believing that every action of the business man is in fact the result of a conscious decision, made after careful calculations of differential revenue and cost.

Business men do not always "calculate" before they make decisions, and they do not always "decide" before they act. For they think that they know their business well enough without having to make repeated calculations; and their actions are frequently routine.[7] But routine is based on principles which were once considered and decided upon and have then been frequently applied with decreasing need for conscious

---

[6] Richard A. Lester, *Economics of Labor* (New York, 1941), p. 181.

[7] See George Katona, "Psychological Analysis of Business Decisions and Expectations," *Am. Econ. Rev.*, Vol. XXXVI, No. 1 (Mar., 1946), p. 53.

choices.[8] The feeling that calculations are not always necessary is usually based upon an ability to size up a situation without reducing its dimensions to definite numerical values.[9]

The business man who is persuaded to accept a large order with a price discount or some other concession usually weighs the probability that he will have to make the same concession to his other customers. This is one of the business man's considerations included in the "calculation" of marginal revenue. In order to explain this to the student, or to reduce it to curves and schedules, the economics teacher makes "exact" calculations; in order to make up his mind whether to take or reject the order, the business man ordinarily needs no arithmetic, mental or written, and indeed needs no concrete figures. Yet his reasoning or his routine behavior is most conveniently analyzed in terms of marginal revenue.

Where the marginal revenue is negative, that is to say, where gross receipts after accepting the additional order (with the price concession) would be smaller than without it, no further consideration is necessary. But if the dollar volume of sales can be increased by accepting the order (taking full account of all repercussions on future marketing possibilities), the business man must take another step in his reasoning: will it pay to make more sales in view of the additional cost of producing the larger output? If conditions have not changed, he will not have to make new calculations; if changes have occurred or are expected, some figuring may be required. But it is a type of figuring for which usually no accounting records are consulted, no memoranda prepared and of which no records are made. Often the business man can do this "figuring" in his head; if not, he may take a piece of scrap paper, jot down a few round numbers, reach his conclusion, and throw the paper in the waste basket.

The theorist's contention that such reasoning is typically based either on additional cost or on total cost—and hence most conveniently described in terms of marginal cost—is contradicted by certain empirical researchers who claim that most business men calculate on the basis of average cost even if they lose money by doing so. With this contradiction we shall deal later.

Non-Pecuniary Considerations

Marginal analysis of the equilibrium of the single firm rests on the assumption that the business firm attempts to maximize its profits. To

[8] Discussing the difference between "routine behavior" and "genuine decisions," Dr. Katona explains with regard to routine actions that "principles, well understood in their original context, tend to be carried over from one situation to another." *Ibid.*, p. 49. Genuine decisions are made when expectations "change radically." *Ibid.*, p. 53.

[9] Although I do not know either the width or length of my automobile, I am quite capable of making adequate comparisons between these magnitudes and the space between two parked cars, which I estimate again without thinking of feet, inches, or any numbers.

make this assumption is not to deny that the men who run a business may be motivated also by other considerations.

That a business man is motivated by considerations other than the maximization of money profits does not necessarily make his conduct "uneconomic." The economic theorist finds no difficulty in fitting into the pattern of "economic" conduct (that is, into the conceptual scheme of consistent maximization of satisfaction within a given preference system) the householder and consumer who makes donations to friends or the church; or the seller of labor services who chooses a badly-paying but less strenuous job in preference to one that pays more but calls for more exertion. Likewise, there is nothing essentially "uneconomic" in the conduct of a business man who chooses to pay higher prices for raw material purchased from a fraternity brother, or to sell at a special discount to members of his church, or who refrains from embarking on a promising expansion of his business because he prefers an easier life.

There are economic theorists who would include considerations of this sort among the data for the marginal calculus of the firm. The satisfaction from favoring his friends through higher purchase prices or lower selling prices is a special reward or "revenue" to the business man; he may ask himself how much it is worth to him, and we may conceivably add it to his revenue curve. To give up an easier life, expend greater efforts and increase his worries are among the business man's "costs" when he considers an expansion of his business; we may conceivably add it to his "cost" curve. Any number and type of non-pecuniary sacrifices and rewards could thus be included, at some sort of "money equivalent," among the costs and revenues that make up the profits of the firm: the marginal calculus of the firm would become all-inclusive.

It seems to be methodologically sounder if we do not reduce the non-pecuniary satisfactions and dissatisfactions (utilities and disutilities) of the business man to money terms and do not try to make them part of the profit maximization scheme of the firm. If *whatever* a business man does is explained by the principle of profit maximization—because he does what he likes to do, and he likes to do what maximizes the sum of his pecuniary and non-pecuniary profits—the analysis acquires the character of a system of definitions and tautologies, and loses much of its value as an explanation of reality. It is preferable to separate the non-pecuniary factors of business conduct from those which are regular items in the formation of money profits.

This methodological controversy is not too important. Not much depends on whether non-pecuniary considerations of the business man are translated into money terms or, instead, treated as exceptions and qualifications in the explanation of typical business conduct. The purpose of the analysis of the firm is not to explain all actions of each and every firm in existence; we are satisfied if we can explain certain strong tendencies in a representative sector of business. The chief aim of the analysis, moreover, is to show the probable effects of certain changes; if the direction in which output or price is likely to move as a result of a certain change in "data" is not affected by the existence and strength of non-pecuniary factors in business conduct, their inclusion in or exclusion from the marginal analysis of the firm is not a crucial matter.

As a matter of fact, the nature, strength and effects of non-pecuniary considerations in business behavior are problems that need to be investigated. One may presume that producing larger production volumes, paying higher wage rates, or charging lower product prices than would be compatible with a maximum of money profits may involve for the business man a gain in social prestige or a certain measure of inner satisfaction.[10] It is not impossible that considerations of this sort substantially weaken the forces believed to be at work on the basis of a strictly pecuniary marginal calculus.

During the war we were able to observe that patriotism was a strong force in the production policy of American business. There can be no doubt that many firms produced far beyond the point of highest money profits. To be sure, they made large profits, but in many instances they could have made still more money without the last, particularly expensive, portions of output. Their conduct was not defined by the principle of maximization of money profits.[11]

Another of the possibly important qualifications in the analysis of the firm refers to the conflict of interests between the hired managers and the owners of the business. The interest of the former in inordinately large outlays or investments may be capable of description in terms of a

---

[10] A gain in social prestige may sometimes increase the good will of a firm on which it expects to cash in later. If such a gain is an aim of the firm's policy, it should be treated as a part of its pecuniary considerations. For example, a firm may grant extraordinarily high wage rates as a part of its selling and advertising expense; that is to say, it may hope that its "generous labor policy" will make its products more popular. A portion of current labor cost of the firm would then properly be allocated to future rather than current output.

[11] Observance of laws and regulations presents a special problem for the analysis of business conduct. It will depend on business morals whether prohibited, unlawful alternatives may be regarded as definitely excluded and therefore non-existent; or whether they may be considered as possibilities subject only to certain peculiar risks. Assume, for example, that a price ceiling is fixed for the sale of a product, and fines are provided for violations. To the business man who is unconditionally law-abiding the ceiling price is the only possible price, regardless of how insistently some of his customers may tempt him with higher bids. To the business man, however, who abides by the law only because of the risk of being found out and fined, "demand prices" above the ceiling are real possibilities and the risks of penalties are additions to cost or deductions from revenue. If the sanctions for violations include jail sentences, the risk becomes largely non-pecuniary and it is up to the potential violator, or to the theorizing economist, whether or not that risk will be "converted" into money terms. Black-market prices are in part the result of such risk conversions.

pecuniary calculus, but it is not maximization of the firm's profits which serves here as the standard of conduct. Maximization of salaries and bonuses of professional managers may constitute a standard of business conduct different from that implied in the customary marginal analysis of the firm. The extent to which the two standards would result in sharply different action under otherwise similar conditions is another open question in need of investigation. At this juncture we know only that a qualification must be made. How much it may modify the results of marginal analysis of the single firm we do not know.

B. *Marginal Productivity and Cost of Input*

The Firm, the Industry, the Economy

Marginal productivity has different meanings in the equilibrium theories of the single firm, the industry, and the whole economy. In the theories of demand for particular "factors of production" (productive services) by the industry or economy as a whole marginal productivity analysis is of another methodological character than in the theory of factor employment by the individual firm: the level of abstraction and the frame of reference are different.

In this article we are concerned only with the analysis of the single firm. Like marginal product cost and marginal revenue in the theory of the firm's output, marginal factor cost and marginal productivity are the variables in the theory of the firm's input.

Determination of Input and Output

In a sense, the determination of input on the basis of factor cost and factor product is merely the reverse side of the determination of output on the basis of product cost and revenue. In the former, the cost of and revenue from employing additional factors are balanced; in the latter, the cost of and revenue from producing additional product are balanced. Before we draw curves for the cost of production of a good, we must assume that the supply curves of the factors of production are known, because the buying prices of factors are among the things that make up production cost. Before we draw curves for the revenue productivity of a factor we must assume that the demand curves for the products made with the help of this factor are known, because the selling prices of products are among the things that make up factor productivity. Hence, in each pair of curves one of the curves comprises the data shown in one curve of the other pair.

The interrelationship between the four curves (or functions) can be shown schematically as follows:

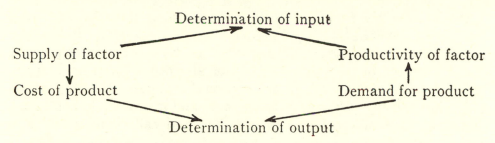

A fifth set of data, the production function, showing the technological transformation of factors into products, is implied in both pairs of curves: in the analysis of output it is among the data determining the cost of production; in the analysis of input it is among the data determining the productivity of the factor.[12]

These remarks should make it clear that neither of the two analyses is prior to the other. They are of strictly equal rank, merely two ways of looking at the same thing, namely, the conduct of a single firm maximizing its profits. The only difference is that the significant magnitudes of the analysis are, on the one side, units of factors (such as labor hours) and, on the other side, units of product.

Marginal Net Revenue Productivity

When we speak in the analysis of the firm of "marginal productivity" of a factor, this is an abbreviation for longer but synonymous expressions such as "marginal value productivity" or "marginal net revenue productivity."

The following steps are pedagogically expedient in explaining the concept of marginal net revenue productivity:

(1) Determine by how much a given physical volume of production, X, is increased if the employment of a particular factor is increased slightly (*e.g.*, by one unit), and call the output increase the factor's "marginal physical product," MPP.

(2) Determine the selling price, P, at which MPP can be sold.

(3) Multiply MPP by P in order to obtain the "value of the marginal physical product," $VMPP$.

(4) Determine whether X, because of the sale of MPP, has to be sold at a price lower than it would sell if MPP were not sold; if so, multiply this price reduction, ΔP, by X, and obtain the "revenue loss on sales because of price cut," $X \Delta P$.

[12] This shows that the customary analysis lacks elegance. Production cost and factor productivity are "derived" rather than "original" data. One could do more elegantly with only three sets of data: (a) the possibilities of buying productive services (the factor supply function), (b) the possibilities of transforming them into products (the production function), and (c) the possibilities of selling the products (the product demand function).

(5) Deduct $X \Delta P$ from $VMPP$ in order to obtain the "marginal gross revenue product," $MGRP$.

(6) Determine whether the production of MPP was connected with increased or decreased outlays for any other complementary or substitutable means of production (materials, fuel, lubricants, labor of any sort, capital funds, wear and tear of equipment, etc.), exclusive of the factor in question, and call them (positive or negative) "incidental expenses," ΔC.

(7) Deduct ΔC from $MGRP$ in order to obtain the "marginal net revenue product," $MNRP$.

The use of the word "revenue" as an adjectival modifier is preferred by many writers in order to stress (a) the distinction between physical product and money product, and (b) the fact that marginal revenue is less than selling price if it takes a price cut to dispose of additional output. The use of the word "net" is preferred in order to stress the fact that additional output will rarely be produced efficiently by increasing the employment of one particular factor while leaving all other outlays unchanged; as a rule, some other adjustments will be appropriate. That "marginal productivity" refers regularly to a net revenue product has been clear to economic theorists for over fifty years.[13]

Technology, Market and Supply Conditions

The marginal net revenue product of a factor, at some level of employment, becomes zero or negative. This may be due to technological difficulties—shown in step (1) of the above scheme—or to difficulties in marketing—shown in step (4)—or to difficulties with other supplies and expenses—shown in step (6).

On the other hand, it is possible that both the marginal physical product and the marginal gross revenue product are zero and, nevertheless, the marginal net revenue product is positive. This will be the case if additional units of factor are used only to secure "incidental reductions in expenses" for other means of production (*i.e.*, substitution) rather than an increased production volume. For example, an additional unskilled laborer may be employed as another watchman to reduce the "use" of certain materials which are in heavy demand outside of the plant. Or he may be employed to dust or cleanse certain valuable equipment and thus reduce outlays for repairs or replacements. Substitution

---

[13] *E.g.*, "the net product . . . is the net increase in the money value of . . . total output after allowing for incidental expenses." (Alfred Marshall, *Principles of Economics*, 8th Edition, p. 521.) For a more detailed discussion of the concept, see my essay, "On the Meaning of the Marginal Product," *Explorations in Economics*, Contributed in Honor of F. W. Taussig (New York and London, 1936), pp. 250–63.

of this sort is nearly always possible[14] and will usually make for positive marginal net revenue productivities even where marginal gross revenue productivities are negative because of limitations in the demand for the product.

Marginal productivity reflects all sorts of technological possibilities. An increased amount of the factor may be used (a) for reducing other expenses without increasing total output (substitution in the narrow sense), (b) for increasing total output with no or few adjustments in the use of other factors (substitution in a wider sense), and (c) for increasing total output with corresponding increases in the use of other factors (inclusive of long-run adjustments, possibly without any substitution). In the last case the incidental expenses will certainly absorb the major portion of the marginal gross revenue product.

Marginal productivity reflects also all possible situations in the demand for the product. If demand is completely inelastic beyond a certain volume, that is, if additional output is not saleable at all, the effect upon marginal productivity is not any worse than if larger outputs can be marketed at severely reduced prices. For whenever the elasticity of demand is less than unity, gross revenue from larger outputs would be lower than from smaller outputs. Hence, the marginal gross revenue product of the factor would become negative. Possibilities of landing additional orders at a price discount but without affecting the rest of the business (that is, possibilities of price discrimination) would show in the fact that no deduction for revenue loss would have to be made from the value of the marginal physical product. Whatever views the firm may have concerning the market for its product are fully reflected in the marginal productivity of the factors employed.

Marginal productivity, finally, reflects all possible conditions of supply of complementary and substitutable factors. Extreme scarcity of a complementary factor may cause a most rapid decline in marginal productivity. Increased supply of a substitutable factor may drastically reduce the whole marginal productivity schedule.

While the conditions of supply of complementary and substitutable factors are among the data determining the marginal productivity of a particular factor of production, the conditions of its own supply are regarded as a separate matter. The "incidental expenses" of increased

[14] The assumption of fixed coefficients of production sometimes affords convenient and permissible simplifications of analysis. But in actual fact, substitution is a practical possibility in almost any production. Beginners sometimes think that substitution of labor for capital must mean the scrapping of machines and shifting of their functions to hand labor. Better care or maintenance work for equipment, postponing the need for replacement, constitutes a clear case of substitution of labor for capital. Increased utilization of plant capacity with increased employment and output also raises the ratio of labor to capital and is another form of substitution.

employment of the factor do not include any of the cost of that factor. The cost of the factor itself is not a part of its marginal net productivity but, instead, is the counterpart with which a balance is sought.

Marginal Factor Cost

Where the supply of the factor is perfectly elastic at a given point, that is, where the firm may be able to employ an additional amount without having to pay for it a higher price per unit, the "marginal factor cost" is equal to the price of the factor (wage rate). If, however, by purchasing or employing more of a factor the firm bids up the price not only of the additional units of the factor but also of the units previously employed, this increase in outlay is a part of the cost of the additional employment. The additionally employed factors would cost the firm not only what they themselves are paid but also the incidental increase in the pay of their fellow factors.

Marginal factor cost, in other words, is the total increase in payment for the particular type of productive service: it consists of (1) the price (wage) paid to the additionally employed, and (2) the price increase (wage increase) paid for the amount of services employed before the addition. In the case of labor, these increases may be due to union action anticipated because of the increased demand for labor, or to the impossibility of discriminating against older employees when new ones can be attracted only at higher rates of pay.

In considering any increase in employment the employer will ask himself whether the additional services will "pay for themselves," that is, what they will cost him and what they will be worth to him. This is all that the economist means when he says that the employer, maximizing his profits, equates marginal factor cost with marginal productivity.

Monopoly, Monopsony, Discontinuities

Neither the existence of monopoly nor of monopsony need invalidate the proposition that the firm will equate marginal productivity and marginal cost of input. For any degree of monopoly is fully reflected in marginal net revenue productivity, and any degree of monopsony is fully reflected in marginal factor cost.[15]

---

[15] To be sure, there may be a large difference between the price of the factor and the value of its marginal physical product. This difference is due to (a) the reduction in product price that the firm must grant to its customers in order to dispose of an increased output and (b) the increase in factor price that the firm must grant to its suppliers or employees in order to acquire an increased input. These two parts of the spread between the price of the factor and the value of its marginal physical product have been called (a) "monopolistic exploitation" and (b) "monopsonistic exploitation" of the factor. These terms, misleading in several respects, are merely to remind the student of the fact that the spread would not exist if the firm were (a) selling its products under pure competition and (b) buying its factors under pure competition.

Discontinuity of the marginal productivity and marginal factor cost curves, however, may make it impossible for the two magnitudes to be equal. If marginal factor cost at a certain level of employment is below marginal productivity but would be above it at the next higher possible level of employment, the firm will stop short of the latter. Moderate jerks from "marginal cost below revenue" to "marginal cost above revenue" are nothing unusual in arithmetic illustrations; in geometric curves they occur only under special assumptions.

For example, marginal net revenue productivity may precipitously drop at a given employment if the product is sold under certain oligopoly conditions (involving high elasticity of demand in the case of a price increase and low elasticity in the case of a price reduction[16]) and if the factor is not easily substitutable for other factors. The marginal factor cost curve might intersect this marginal productivity curve in its vertical portion. Likewise, marginal factor cost may precipitously rise at a given employment if the factor is bought or hired under certain oligopsony conditions (involving high elasticity of supply in the case of a reduction in the factor price and low elasticity in the case of a raise.[17]) The marginal productivity curve might intersect this marginal factor cost curve in its vertical portion. Under such circumstances the firm would be in equilibrium, with its profits maximized, at a volume of input (employment) at which marginal factor cost is below marginal productivity.

Subjectivity, Range, Concreteness

Almost everything that has been said in earlier sections concerning the meaning of marginal revenue and marginal cost of output holds true, *mutatis mutandis*, in regard of the meaning of marginal productivity and marginal cost of input. More specifically, we should emphasize that

(1) the concepts are to be understood as referring to subjective estimates and conjectures;

(2) the range of imagined variations of the magnitudes in question may be rather narrow;

(3) the time-range of the relevant anticipations will depend on the cirumstances of each case and will rarely be confined to the short run;

(4) the estimates need not be reduced to definite numerical values;

(5) non-pecuniary considerations may effectively compete with those pertaining to the maximization of money profits.

It is probably unnecessary to expatiate again on these points in connection with marginal productivity analysis. Only on the subject of

---

[16] Under such oligopoly conditions the firm will maximize profits at a volume of output at which marginal revenue is above marginal cost.

[17] Oligopsony in the labor market is probably not as frequent as oligopoly in the product marker.

numerical definiteness does further discussion seem advisable, especially in view of what was said above about the concept of marginal net revenue productivity. The process by which this magnitude may be derived, involving seven separate "steps" and at least as many variables, is rather formidable. If this analytical pattern were taken as a realistic description in photographic likeness of the actual reasoning of the typical employer, the employer would have to be endowed with talents which only few possess in reality.

An analogy may explain the apparent contradiction.

The "Extreme Difficulty of Calculating"

What sort of considerations are behind the routine decision of the driver of an automobile to overtake a truck proceeding ahead of him at slower speed? What factors influence his decision? Assume that he is faced with the alternative of either slowing down and staying behind the truck or of passing it before a car which is approaching from the opposite direction will have reached the spot. As an experienced driver he somehow takes into account (a) the speed at which the truck is going, (b) the remaining distance between himself and the truck, (c) the speed at which he is proceeding, (d) the possible acceleration of his speed, (e) the distance between him and the car approaching from the opposite direction, (f) the speed at which that car is approaching; and probably also the condition of the road (concrete or dirt, wet or dry, straight or winding, level or uphill), the degree of visibility (light or dark, clear or foggy), the condition of the tires and brakes of his car, and—let us hope—his own condition (fresh or tired, sober or alcoholized) permitting him to judge the enumerated factors.

Clearly, the driver of the automobile will not "measure" the variables; he will not "calculate" the time needed for the vehicles to cover the estimated distances at the estimated rates of speed; and, of course, none of the "estimates" will be expressed in numerical values. Even so, without measurements, numerical estimates or calculations, he will in a routine way do the indicated "sizing-up" of the total situation. He will not break it down into its elements. Yet a "theory of overtaking" would have to include all these elements (and perhaps others besides) and would have to state how changes in any of the factors were likely to affect the decisions or actions of the driver.[18] The "extreme difficulty of calculating,"[19] the fact that "it would be utterly impractical"[20] to attempt to work out and ascertain the exact magnitudes of the

[18] Very cautious drivers are apt to work with so wide safety margins that small changes in the "variables" may not affect the actions. Timid souls may refuse to pass at all when another car is in sight.

[19] Lester, *Am. Econ. Rev.*, Vol. XXXVI, No. 1, p. 72.

[20] Lester, *ibid.*, p. 75.

variables which the theorist alleges to be significant, show merely that the *explanation* of an action must often include steps of reasoning which the acting individual himself does not *consciously* perform (because the action has become routine) and which perhaps he would never be *able* to perform in scientific exactness (because such exactness is not necessary in everyday life). To call, on these grounds, the theory "invalid," "unrealistic" or "inapplicable" is to reveal failure to understand the basic methodological constitution of most social sciences.

Imagine an empirical researcher attempting to test by a naïve questionnaire method the "theory of overtaking," questioning hundreds of drivers about their ability to estimate distances and speed, and to calculate the relevant time intervals and the degrees in which a small change in any one of the variables affected the result. Would he not obtain the most hopeless assortment of answers? Would not these answers support the conclusion that the assumptions of the theorists had been wrong and that one must look for other explanations? Yet I can hardly believe that any sensible person would deny the relevance of the enumerated variables and would contend, for example, that speed and distance of the approaching automobile could not have been taken into account by the driver passing the truck, because he was not good in mathematics.[21]

The Analysis of Change Needs No Exactness

The business man who equates marginal net revenue productivity and marginal factor cost when he decides how many to employ need not engage in higher mathematics, geometry, or clairvoyance. Ordinarily he would not even consult with his accountant or efficiency expert in order to arrive at his decision; he would not make any tests or formal calculations; he would simply rely on his sense or his "feel" of the situation. There is nothing very exact about this sort of estimate. On the basis of hundreds of previous experiences of a similar nature the business man would "just know," in a vague and rough way, whether or not it would pay him to hire more men.

The subjectivity of his judgments is obvious. Just as different drivers may reach different conclusions about the advisability of passing another car under given "objective" conditions, different business men will have different "hunches" in a given situation. The subordinates or partners of the man who makes a decision may sharply disagree with him; they may see the situation quite differently. They may be more optimistic about the possibilities of obtaining more orders with only

---

[21] Driving at night, when he has nothing to go by except the size and brilliance of the headlights of the approaching cars, the experienced driver becomes conscious of the fact that in daytime he has better ways of sizing up their speed and distance. With reduced visibility he will "calculate" with greater safety margins.

slight price concessions or through increased sales efforts (which would raise both the marginal revenue and marginal productivity curves drawn by the theorist to characterize their considerations). Or they may be more certain about the technical possibility of achieving a larger output by certain production methods (which would lower the marginal cost curve, and could raise or lower the marginal productivity curves). Some decision, usually a routine decision without debate, is made, or at least some action is taken; and the decision or action is necessarily affected by the business man's conjectures concerning sales possibilities and production possibilities.

The way in which changes in the essential variables will affect the probable decisions and actions of the business man is not much different if the curves which the theorist draws to depict their conjectures are a little higher or lower, steeper or flatter. These curves are helpful to the student of economics in figuring out the probable effects of change — in learning in what direction output, prices and employment are likely to be altered, and under what circumstances increases or decreases are likely to be drastic or negligible. Better markets or higher costs are likely to affect business men of different vision or daring in rather similar ways; and any differences can be conveniently "typed" in terms of shapes, positions and shifts of the curves into which the theorist condenses the business men's conjectures.

Equipped with this understanding of the meaning and purposes of marginal analysis, we may proceed to a discussion of the findings of empirical research which purportedly failed to verify it — or by which it was deemed to be contradicted and disproved.

II. EMPIRICAL RESEARCH ON THE SINGLE FIRM

There is not as yet available any large amount of material derived from systematic empirical research on the business conduct of the single firm. But almost everybody interested in these questions has had occasional conversations with business men, and the impressions gained from such inquiries into the business men's experiences often form an empirical basis for the doubts which so-called "realistic" critics entertain of "theoretical" analysis.

I submit that the few systematic and the many casual researchers have often been misled by pitfalls of semantics and terminology and by a naïve acceptance of rationalizations in lieu of genuine explanations of actions.

Economists' Vocabulary and Business Language

The vast majority of business men have never heard of expressions such as elasticity of demand or supply, sloping demand curves, marginal revenue, marginal cost. If they do not know the words or the concepts, how can they be supposed to think in these terms? A scattered few of the men may have been exposed to such words and ideas in half-forgotten college courses, but they have found in practice they had no use for a vocabulary unknown to their associates, superiors, subordinates, and fellow business men. Thus the most essential terms in which economists explain business conduct do not exist in the business man's vocabulary. Does this not prove that the explanations are unrealistic or definitely false?

Only an inexperienced researcher could draw such a conclusion. The technical terms used in the explanation of an action need not have any part in the thinking of the acting individual. A mental process in everyday life may often be most conveniently described for scientific purposes in a language which is quite foreign to the process itself.

To ask a business man about the "elasticity of demand" for his product is just as helpful as inquiring into the customs of an indigenous Fiji Islander by interviewing him in the King's English. But with a little ingenuity it is possible to translate ideas from the business man's language into that of the economist, and *vice versa*. Questions such as " Do you think you might sell more of this product if you cut the price by 10 per cent?" or "How much business do you think you would lose if you raised your price by 10 per cent?" will evoke intelligent answers in most cases provided the questions are readily reformulated and adapted to the peculiarities of the particular man and his business. Often it will be necessary to know a good deal of the technology, customs and jargon of the trade, and even of the personal idiosyncrasies of the men, before one can ask the right questions. A set formulation of questions will hardly fit any large number of business men in different fields and, hence, questionnaires to be filled out by them will rarely yield useful results.

Rationalizations of Decisions or Actions

Psychologists will readily confirm that statements by interviewed individuals about the motives and reasons for their actions are unreliable or at least incomplete. Even if a person tries to reconstruct for himself in his memory the motives and reasons for one of his past actions, he will usually end up with a rationalization full of afterthoughts that may make his actions appear more plausible to himself. Explanations given to an interviewer or investigator are still more likely to be rationalizations in terms that may make the particular actions appear plausible and justified to the inquirer. In order to be understood (and respected) the interviewed person will often choose for his "explanations" patterns of reasoning which he believes to be recognized as "sound" and "fair" by others. Most of these rationalizations may be subjectively honest and truthful. It takes an experienced analyst to disentangle actual from imaginary reasons, and to separate relevant from irrelevant data, and essential from decorative bits of the information furnished. Written replies to questionnaires are hopelessly inadequate for such purposes.[22]

Questions of business policy are particularly difficult objects of inquiry because the business man usually is anxious to show by his answers that he is intelligent, well informed, and fair. The standards of fairness and business ethics to which he wishes to conform are often those which he believes are accepted by his lawyers, accountants, customers, competitors, fellow citizens, economists and whatnot. Only through detailed discussions of different situations and decisions, actual as well as hypothetical, will an investigator succeed in bringing out true patterns of conduct of the individual business man.[23]

A. *Average Cost and Price*

One of the conclusions of casual or systematic empirical research on the business firm is that business men do not pursue a policy of maximizing profits, and of pricing according to the marginal cost and marginal revenue principle, but instead follow rules of pricing on the basis of average cost calculations even where this is inconsistent with profit maximization.

We shall attempt to reinterpret the findings of systematic research along these lines. For this purpose we must first clear up some misunderstandings which appear to have contributed to the support for the average-cost theory of pricing.[24]

Averaging Fluctuating Costs and Prices

In discussions with business men I have found that two different types

---

[22] *Cf.* George Katona, *Price Control and Business* (Bloomington, Ind., 1945), p. 210. He states that "only detailed interviews can probe into the motives behind business decisions."

[23] For further comments on the difficulties of good empirical research on business conduct, see my paper "Evaluation of the Practical Significance of the Theory of Monopolistic Competition," *Am. Econ. Rev.*, Vol. XXIX (1939), p. 233. After discussing the policies of my former business partners I concluded (p. 234): "An investigator who would have based his findings on their answers to questionnaires or even on personal interviews, would have come to erroneous results. An investigator who could have seen all the actually or potentially available statistics would have come to no results at all. The only possibility for a fruitful empirical inquiry into these problems lies, I think, in the more subtle technique of analyzing a series of single business decisions through close personal contact with those responsible for the decisions."

[24] According to modern theory price equals average cost (inclusive of normal profit) chiefly under the pressure of competition. The individual firm will charge a price above or below average cost depending on the situation and in line with the marginal calculus. However, when price has risen above average cost, other firms will expand production and new firms will enter the industry and their competition tends to reduce price to the average cost level. Thus it is not the price policy of the individual firm but the pressure of actual or potential competition which makes prices equal to average cost. In contrast with this, the theory advanced by the critics of marginal analysis asserts that firms set their prices according to average cost regardless of the state of competition and regardless of the market situation.

of averages must be distinguished: averages over time and averages as a function of the volume of output.

Selling prices frequently fluctuate over time, not only cyclically and seasonally but during the week or the day. In calculations for investment, cyclical price fluctuations will be taken into account and average prices will be estimated. In planning the production of seasonally demanded goods—summer dresses, swimming suits, winter sport clothes, Christmas toys—price discounts for off-season sales will be counted into the average selling price. Hotels in resorts may charge preferential rates for guests arriving on Tuesdays and leaving on Thursdays; wholesale grocers will dispose of over-ripe fruit and vegetables at reduced prices; public utilities may charge lower rates to industrial off-peak customers; in all these cases the firms will have to figure out their average revenue or average price.

Costs may show similar fluctuations over time. Raw materials and fuel prices may vary cyclically and seasonally, electric power rates even over different hours of the day. Seasonal changes of the weather may cause cost differences in several technical processes—natural instead of artificial heat for drying when wind, temperature and humidity are favorable; hydroelectric instead of steam-generated power when rivers carry sufficient water; and so on. These and hundreds of other reasons call for calculations of average costs by the affected business firms.

The average revenues and average costs which must be calculated to take care of such variations over time are not in the least inconsistent with the marginal revenue and marginal cost principles. Indeed, if increases in output are under consideration, the marginal changes of revenue and cost as functions of output will have to comprise any changes over time that will affect revenue or cost. That the firm figures with these averages over time does not mean that it makes its decisions concerning price policies on the basis of an average-cost rule rather than the maximum-profit rule.

Actual versus *Potential Average Costs*

The absence of the expressions "marginal cost" and "marginal revenue" from the business man's vocabulary and the fact that he usually explains his price policy in terms of "average cost" account for a good part of the skepticism of the empiricists. Yet, the words used are not indicative of the lines of thinking; the marginal calculus may be followed without pronouncing or knowing any of the terms in question.

In the economist's jargon, the business man who considers taking more business is supposed to say to himself: "At the increased volume of output, marginal cost will be this much and marginal revenue that much." (Statement I.) In a literal translation into everyday language, he would say, "The increase in production will cost me this much and will bring in that much." (Statement II.) He could say it also in a different version: "The increase in business will raise total costs from this to this much, and total receipts from that to that much." (Statement III.) These statements are absolutely equivalent, all expressing the marginal calculus of variations.

The same thing can also be expressed in a fourth, much more complicated way: "The increase in business will change average cost from this to this much, and average price from that to that much; it will, therefore, change profits by changing the margin of so and so much, times an output of this much, to a margin of so and so much, times an output of that much." (Statement IV.) With all its complications the statement is still equivalent to the former ones. It is a bit foolish to divide total costs and receipts by the output figures just in order to multiply afterwards the differences again by the output figures; but it is not incorrect. The average cost figures as such are, of course, irrelevant in the calculation.[25]

The average cost figures, in spite of their prominent place in our business man's complicated statement, had no place in his actual decision. The decision was based on the profitableness of the added business. When not only the current but also the potential average cost—that is, the average cost at a different production volume—and also the change in total receipts are considered, then the reasoning is true marginal calculus, not average-cost reasoning as some mistakenly believe.

Average-Cost Pricing as the Lawyer's Ideal

Generations of lawyers have accepted and proclaimed the fairness of the average-cost standard of pricing. Decades of regulatory experiments and arguments, and a long history of court decisions, have emphasized the average-cost principle as the just basis of pricing. Is it then surprising that business men try to explain their pricing methods by average-cost considerations?

---

[25] This can be easily illustrated by assuming any set of figures. Assume that the firm considers taking new orders for 1,000 tons of product, reducing its average price. Statement IV might read: "The increase in business from 10,000 tons to 11,000 tons will raise total cost from $80,000 to $86,900 and, hence, will reduce average cost from $8.00 to $7.90; it will raise total receipts from $99,500 to $107,800 and, hence, will reduce average price from $9.95 to $9.80; it will, therefore, raise profits by changing a margin of $1.95, times an amount of 10,000, *i.e.*, $19,500, to a margin of $1.90, times an amount of 11,000, *i.e.*, $20,900. Let's take the business."

Statement III would read under the same circumstances: "The increase in business will raise total costs from $80,000 to $86,900, that is by $6,900, and will raise total receipts from $99,500 to $107,800, that is by $8,300. Let's take the business."

Statement II on the same situation would read: "The increase in production will cost me $6,900 and will bring in $8,300. Let's take the business."

Statement I, finally, would read: "At the increased volume of output, marginal cost will be $6.90 and marginal revenue $8.30. Go ahead."

Corporations in regulated industries are sometimes caught in their official price justifications: a change in the market situation may make it wise and profitable to change the selling price, but that price has been anchored to an average-cost calculation which it is now difficult to disavow. The companies cannot very well submit to their regulatory commissions revised average-cost calculations every time market conditions change. They have to put up with relatively inflexible prices which, were it not for the regulatory authorities, might be as much against their own interests as against those of the consumers.

More often, however, the business man is not conscious of the fact that he uses average-cost considerations merely as rationalizations or justifications. Selling with high profit margins might indicate monopoly and "squeezing of the consumer"; selling below cost might indicate unfair competition and "cutting the throat of the competitor." As a good citizen the business man wishes to avoid both these wicked practices. As long as he can justify his prices as covering "average cost plus a fair profit margin" he can say, to others as well as to himself, that he is living up to the accepted standards of law and decency. If this "fair profit margin" is at times a bit generous and at other times rather thin, he can still justify his price. (That such variations betray his "explanation" of this pricing method as incomplete or untenable may escape his attention as well as that of his inquirers.)

Average-Cost Pricing as the Accountant's Ideal

Selling price must cover average cost inclusive of overhead and fair profit margin if the business enterprise is to live and to prosper. A good accountant regards it as his duty to watch over the soundness of the firm's pricing methods and to warn against prices below full cost.

Practical and academic accountants have sometimes attacked the marginal-cost principle as a fallacy conducive to practices that are liable to result in business losses. They have reasoned that a general application of differential cost considerations might mean that firms forget that they ought to recover their overhead in *some* part of their business.

Reasoning of this sort reveals a twofold misunderstanding of the marginal principle. (a) That marginal cost does not "include" fixed overhead charges need not mean that it will always be below average total cost; indeed, marginal cost may equal or exceed average cost. (This will always be true for volumes of output at or beyond "optimum capacity" of the firm.) (b) To use marginal cost as a pricing factor need not mean that price will be set at the marginal cost level. Indeed, this will never be done. In the exceptional case of pure competition, price cannot be "set" at all but is "given" to the firm and beyond its control; and marginal cost will be equal to price not because of any price policy but only because of adjustments in the firm's production volume. In the normal case of monopolistic competition, the firm will never charge a price as low as marginal cost; it will charge a price at which marginal revenue is equal to marginal cost, and this price must therefore be above both.

It is a stupid misunderstanding to believe that the use of marginal cost in the business man's pricing technique implies an advice that selling price should be set at the marginal cost level. Marginal cost and marginal revenue considerations mean nothing else but what a business man means when he asks himself: "Could I get some more business and would I want it under the conditions under which I could get it"?

The idea, held by some accountants, that pricing on the basis of the marginal principle would sacrifice profits is the opposite of the truth—except in one very special sense: where the average-cost rule has been used as a monopolistic device, resort to the marginal principle might be taken to mean abandonment of a cartel arrangement in the industry and "outbreak" of unrestricted competition.

Average-Cost Pricing as a Cartel Device

In times of depression business men often discover that it is wiser to lose only a part rather than all of their overhead cost; that it is better to sell at prices below full cost than to stick to prices which would cover all costs but at which they cannot sell. They usually deplore these deviations from the full-cost principle of pricing and argue that nobody would *have* to sell below cost if nobody *did* sell below cost.

Price fixing among producers or official price codes may in such situations succeed in the maintenance of a monopolistic level of price in spite of strong temptations for competitive price cutting. Tacit understandings about the observation of average-cost rules of pricing sometimes constitute an alternative way of achieving price maintenance in a declining market. Moral suasion in the direction of "good accounting" and of "sound pricing" on the basis of "full cost" may be an effective device of domestic price cartels (through trade associations or in the form of tacit understandings).

Outright price fixing, just as any other cartel agreement, is a device to affect the estimates of demand conditions for the products of the individual firms. Only if demand as seen by the individual seller is effectively changed through his anticipations of serious reactions on the part of his competitors and fellow cartel members will he find it advantageous to restrict his output to the extent necessary for the maintenance of the agreed price. The essential effect of the agreement is upon the elasticity of the expected demand. As a rule, elasticity becomes absolutely zero (that is, the demand curve breaks off abruptly) at the largest volume of output which the individual cartel member thinks he can sell at the fixed price. If he considers price cutting in contravention of the agreement as a practical alternative, the demand curve will not break off but continue downward with reduced elasticity—reduced because of the risk of penalizing or retaliatory actions.

The general adoption of an average cost rule is in effect a price agreement among the members of the particular industry. Where a trade association announces a representative "average cost," the announced value need not tally at all with the average cost of an individual firm. Where cost conditions are believed to be very similar throughout the industry, the understanding may be informal and tacit. It may be made entirely a matter of "business ethics" not to sell below average cost plus fair profit margin. For the firm which strictly observes this ethical code the demand curve breaks off abruptly at the output it can sell at that price. The average cost calculation of that firm takes the place of the fixed cartel price and is the essential determinant of its demand and marginal revenue considerations.

If a business man believes that the best policy for him in the long run is to stick to the cartel, this does not mean that he disregards the marginal principle. On the contrary, the feared consequences of breaking away from the cartel, its probable effects upon long-run demand and revenue, dictate his continued adherence. Likewise, if violations of the ethical code of average-cost pricing are feared to have adverse consequences, continued membership in this "ethical cartel" is not a departure from the marginal principle. The average-cost rule and the sanctions for violating it have the same sort of effects upon demand elasticity and marginal revenue which other types of price agreements have been shown to have.

Average Cost as a Clue to Demand Elasticity

Even without any ethical or unethical code prescribing an average-cost rule of pricing, average cost may be the most important datum for the estimate of demand elasticity. The elasticity of demand for any particular product is determined by the availability of substitutes. In order to estimate how much business a firm may lose if it raises its price, it will consider whether existing or potential competitors can supply competing products at the particular price. The elasticity of supply from competing sources determines the elasticity of demand for the firm's product. The supply from competing sources will depend on their actual or potential cost of production. And usually the best clue that a firm has to the production cost of competitors is its own production cost, corrected for any known differences of conditions.

Assuming that competitors have the same access to production factors, materials and technology, their production cost can not be much different from that of a particular producer who may just be weighing the chances of a price increase. In the absence of any cartel arrangements he will have to count on his competitors to expand their business at his expense if he ventures to raise his selling price above average cost. Where he need not fear the capacity of existing competitors, but entry into the industry is relatively easy, he will have to reckon with newcomers' competition if he makes the business too attractive by allowing himself too generous a profit margin above average cost. Under such circumstances he will know that he stands to lose too much business and had better stick fairly closely to a price based on average cost.

Notwithstanding any rationalizations of this price policy, the reasons for it lie in the competitiveness of the industry resulting in a high elasticity of demand visualized by individual sellers.[26] To "explain" this price by reference to some emotional attachment to the average cost principle is to miss the mark. The rôle of average cost in the firm's pricing process in this case is to aid in gauging the elasticity of the long-run demand for its product.

Reasons and Variables

Seeing how many different rôles average cost may play in the pricing process without in the least contradicting the statement that marginal cost and marginal revenue determine output and price, one should realize the dangers of attempts to use utterances of business men as evidence against the correctness of marginal analysis.

Business men's answers to direct questions about the reasons for charging the prices they are charging are almost certainly worthless. Every single fact or act has probably hundreds of "reasons"; the selection of a few of them for presentation to the inquirer is influenced by the prejudices or old theories which the informant had impressed upon him by school, radio, newspapers, etc.

Except in the case of a genuine decision leading to a recent change of policy, one may say that an approach much more fruitful than that of asking about reasons *for* some policy is to ask about reasons *against* its alternatives. Instead of asking for explanations of the price actually charged or the output volume actually produced, questions about "why not more" and "why not less" are likely to yield more revealing results. But even these answers must be checked and double-checked through a network of cross-examination, segregating and isolating certain variables in a manner familiar to the scientist working with the calculus of variations and with the determination of partial derivatives.

[26] Where the average-cost rule is a cartel device, the elasticity of demand will be small or zero from the actually realized point on *downward*. When average cost is a clue to size up potential competition, the elasticity of demand will be high from the actually realized point on *upward*. The former prevents price reductions, the latter price increases.

Research on Actual Pricing Methods

On the basis of marginal analysis of the firm and the industry, we should expect for most industries that price in the long run would not deviate too much from average cost, yet that the firm would attempt to get better prices when it could safely get them and would not refrain from cutting prices when it believed that this would increase its profits or reduce its losses.

Now let us compare with this the findings of one of the empirical research undertakings which shook the researchers' confidence in the marginal principle and convinced them that business men followed the "full-cost principle" of pricing regardless of profit maximization. Inquiry was made through interview of 38 entrepreneurs.[27] "A large majority" of them explained that they charged the "full cost" price. Some, however, admitted "that they might charge more in periods of exceptionally high demand"; and a greater number reported "that they might charge less in periods of exceptionally depressed demand."[28] Competition seemed to induce "firms to modify the margin for profits which could be added to direct costs and overheads."[29] Moreover, "the conventional addition for profit varies from firm to firm and even within firms for different products."[30]

This is precisely what one should have expected to hear. Do these findings support the theory of the average-cost principle of pricing? I submit that they give little or no support to it. The margins above average cost are different from firm to firm and, within firms, from period to period and from product to product. These differences and variations strongly suggest that the firms consult other data besides or instead of their average costs. And, as a matter of fact, the reported findings include some that indicate what other considerations were pertinent to the price determinations by the questioned business men.

Of 24 firms which gave reasons for not charging higher prices, 17 were tabulated as admitting that it was "fear of competitors or potential competitors" and a "belief that others would not follow an increase." Another two stated that "they prefer a large turnover."[31] To me the 19 answers indicate that these business men were estimating the risk of losing business if they raised prices or, in other words, that they were concerned about the elasticity of demand.

Of 35 firms which gave reasons for not charging lower prices, 4 firms explained that they were members of price-fixing combinations; 2 stated

---

[27] R. L. Hall and C. J. Hitch, *op. cit.*, p. 12.

[28] *Ibid.*, p. 19.

[29] *Loc. cit.*

[30] R. L. Hall and C. J. Hitch, *op. cit.*, p. 20.

[31] *Ibid.*, p. 21.

that it was "difficult to raise prices once lowered"; and 21 referred directly or implicitly to their estimates of demand elasticity. (Nine firms: "Demand unresponsive to price"; one firm: "Price cuts not passed on by retailers"; eleven firms: "Competitors would follow cuts.") Only 8 firms gave reasons other than monopolistic price fixing or monopolistic elasticity considerations; these 8 were listed as having "quasi-moral objections to selling below cost."[32] Unfortunately the interviewers did not find out what these conscientious objectors to price cutting thought about the responsiveness of demand; and whether they would remain adamant if they were sure that a small price concession would produce a large increase in sales. I suspect that a cross-examination would have brought out the fact that the moral or quasi-moral views on price maintenance were regularly coupled with a very strong opinion that a price reduction would not produce sufficiently more business and, thus, would constitute useless sacrifice of profits.

In any event, there is little or nothing in the findings of this inquiry that would indicate that the business men observed an average-cost rule of pricing when such observance was inconsistent with the maximum-profit principle. On the other hand, there is plenty of evidence in the findings that the business men paid much attention to demand elasticities — which to the economist is equivalent to marginal revenue considerations.

The Absence of Numerically Expressed Estimates

Why should others in the face of this evidence have come to the conclusion that the marginal principle was not applied and profit maximization not attempted by the group of business men studied? How could others have failed to be impressed by the facts just recited?

It seems that their confidence in the conventional analysis was lost when they found to their surprise that the business man had no definite numerical estimates of the magnitudes relevant to the application of the marginal principle. They had assumed that a business man should "know" the elasticity of demand for his product, and now they were shocked to find "that the great majority of entrepreneurs were in profound ignorance with regard to its value."[33] A student who had expected to find exact estimates must indeed have been disappointed when most of his informants "were vague about anything so precise as elasticity."[34]

The inquirers found the same vagueness with regard to marginal cost estimates. While the entrepreneurs usually computed direct cost and

---

[32] *Loc. cit.*

[33] R. F. Harrod, *op. cit.*, p. 4. Concerning this discovery Mr. Harrod remarks emphatically: "This, indeed, must be regarded as one notable result of our inquiry."

[34] R. L. Hall and C. J. Hitch, *op. cit.*, p. 18.

total overheads "with some pains at accuracy,"[35] they could not furnish any data on marginal cost. He who expected that marginal cost and marginal revenue were equated on the basis of precise calculations must feel stultified. The student who had to do homework computing marginal cost and revenue figures to the second or third decimal point may feel befooled when he learns that the business man does not do anything of the sort. But to conclude from the absence of definite numerical estimates that the magnitudes in question were irrelevant in the conduct of the firms is a *non sequitur*. On the basis of the previous discussion of this subject (see above pp. 534 *ff.*) we should understand that the construction of a pattern for the analytical description of a process is not the same thing as the actual process in everyday life; and we should not expect to find in everyday life the definite numerical estimates that are part of the scientific pattern.

Apart from the absence of numerical estimates of marginal revenue and marginal cost it is difficult to see what other findings of the inquiry could have persuaded the researchers that they had disproved the theory of marginalism in the conduct of the firm. There is not a single proposition in the tabulated results of the inquiry that can not be fully harmonized with marginal analysis. The "Analysis of Replies to Questionnaire on Costs and Prices," which the researchers presented as an appendix to their report,[36] contains a wealth of illustrative material—illustrative, as I see it, of the application of the marginal principle to business decisions of the single firm.

B. *Marginal Productivity and Wage*

Empirical research designed to verify or disprove marginal productivity theory in the analysis of input of the individual firm is beset with difficulties. Few systematic endeavors have been made and none has led to any suggestion, however vague or tentative, of an alternative theory. Whereas in certain price research projects those who felt compelled to reject the marginal theory have advanced the average-cost theory of pricing as a substitute, no substitute theory has been forthcoming from those who decried marginal productivity theory.

Statistical Research

Empirical research on cost, price and output of the individual firm has resulted in several interesting attempts to derive marginal cost functions from statistical data; and also in one or two attempts to derive price elasticities of demand for a firm's products. But nobody, to my knowledge, has ever undertaken to construct from actual data a

---

[35] R. F. Harrod, *op. cit.*, p. 4.
[36] R. L. Hall and C. J. Hitch, *op. cit.*, pp. 33–45.

marginal net revenue productivity curve for a given type of labor employed by a firm. The difficulties are formidable and, since the raw material for the calculations could not come from any records or documents but merely from respondent's guesses of a purely hypothetical nature, the results might not be much more "authentic" than the schedules made up by textbook writers for arithmetical illustrations.

Statistical studies of the relationship between wage rates and employment in large samples of individual firms or industries would be nearly useless because we have no way of eliminating the simultaneous effects of several other significant variables, especially those of a psychological nature. An increase in wage rates may have very different effects depending on whether the employer (1) (a) has foreseen it, (b) is surprised by it; (2) (a) reacts quickly to it, (b) reacts slowly to it; (3) (a) expects it to be reversed soon, (b) expects it to be maintained, (c) expects it to be followed by further increases; (4) (a) assumes it to be confined to his firm, (b) assumes it to affect also his competitors, (c) believes it to be part of a nation-wide trend; (5) connects it with an inflationary development; or is influenced by any other sort and number of anticipations. Most of these moods and anticipations can be translated by the economist into certain shapes or shifts of the marginal productivity functions of the firms; but since the researchers cannot ascertain or evaluate these conjectural "data" for the large number of firms contained in a representative sample, statistical investigations of the wage-employment relation of individual firms are not likely to yield useful results.

Questionnaire on Employment

It has been pointed out above (p. 538) why the method of mailed questionnaires without supporting interviews is hopelessly inadequate for empirical studies of business conduct. Even the most intelligently devised set of questions would not assure reliable and significant answers. Questions designed to achieve the necessary separation of variables would be so complicated and call for so high a degree of "abstract thinking" on the part of the questioned business men that questionnaires of this sort would be too much of an imposition, and coöperation would be too small. Although the questions in Professor Lester's research project on employment did not even approach these standards, he received only 56 usable replies from 430 manufacturers whom he had asked to fill out his questionnaires.[37]

Professor Lester's questionnaires suffered not merely from the inherent weaknesses of the method but also from defects in formulation. These defects were so serious that even the most complete, reliable and intelligent

[37] R. A. Lester, *Am. Econ. Rev.*, Vol. XXXVI, No. 1, pp. 64–65.

answers could not have yielded significant findings. The business men were asked to rate the "importance" of several factors determining the volume of employment in their firms. No explanation was given whether this importance of a variable—that is, I presume, its responsibility for changes in the employment volume—should refer to (a) the frequency of its variations, (b) the extent of its variations, or (c) the effects of its variations. Surely, the variable rated as least important—perhaps because it varied less frequently than the others—may be just as strategic as any of those with higher importance ratings. What we really need to know, however, is not the *comparative* importance of several factors but rather the effects of variations of each factor separately while the others remain unchanged.

If I want to know by how much an increase in the price of spinach may affect its consumption in an individual household, I shall not get very far by asking the householders to give a percentage rating to each of several listed factors that are believed to be "important" influences on spinach consumption. If it were tried, we should not be surprised to find changes in family income, the number of children and guests at dinner, and the notoriety of Popeye the Sailor's gusto for spinach, receiving much higher percentage ratings than changes in the price of spinach. (In a number of households price may not be a factor at all.) Nobody, I hope, would conclude from such a poll that price is an unimportant factor in the consumption of spinach.

Yet Professor Lester followed just this procedure when he wanted to find out how important wage rates were in determining the volume of employment in the individual firm. He asked the executives of the companies to "rate" the following factors "in terms of the percentage of importance of each":

a. Present and prospective market demand (sales for your products, including seasonal fluctuations in demand).
b. The level of wage rates or changes in the level of wages.
c. The level of material costs and other non-wage costs and changes in the level of such non-labor costs.
d. Variations in profits or losses of the firm.
e. New techniques, equipment, and production methods.
f. Other factors (please specify).

Of these items the first unquestionably excels all others in frequency and extent of variations. That it won first prize in Professor Lester's importance contest is therefore not surprising. If several respondents gave ratings to item d (variations in profits or losses) and at the same time also to other items, they obviously did not realize that this variable comprised all the others. Professor Lester does not explain why he listed it when he knew that it was not "completely independent" and that "for example, wages affect profits."[38] Nor does he state whether the 43 firms which failed to mention changes in wage rates as an important factor meant that they would continue in business and continue to employ the same number of workers regardless of any degree of wage increase. If this is what they meant, they can hardly be taken seriously. If they meant something else, then it is not clear just what the replies should indicate about the probable effects of wage increases upon employment.

The strangest thing about Professor Lester's list of possibly important variables is that all—except f, the unspecified, and d, the all-inclusive profit-and-loss item—are essential variables of the very analysis which he means to disprove. The prize-winning item, a, the demand for the product, is certainly a most crucial determinant of marginal productivity. (See above pp. 529 and 531.) Items c, non-labor cost, and e, production techniques, are two other determinants of marginal productivity. How Professor Lester came to think that the results of this poll would in any sense disprove or shake marginal productivity analysis remains a mystery.

Questionnaire on Variable Cost

Professor Lester asked his business men also some questions on unit variable costs and profits at various rates of output. The information obtained in answer to these questions might have been useful had it not been based on an undefined concept of "plant capacity." Unfortunately, it must be suspected that not all firms meant the same thing when they referred to "100 per cent of capacity."

Economic theorists use different definitions of capacity. One widely-used definition marks as 100 per cent of capacity that volume of output at which short-run total cost per unit is a minimum; another definition fixes the 100 per cent mark at the output at which variable cost per unit is a minimum. The former definition implies decreasing average total cost, the latter decreasing average variable cost, up to "100 per cent capacity." Professor Lester after painstaking empirical research arrives at the following finding:

The significant conclusion from the data in this section is that most of the manufacturing firms in the industries covered by this survey apparently have decreasing unit variable costs within the range of 70 to 100 per cent of capacity production. . . . [39]

Has Professor Lester asked himself whether this is not merely a self-evident conclusion implied in the definition of capacity used by his respondents?

[38] *Ibid.*, p. 66.
[39] *Ibid.*, p. 71.

The steepness of the reported decline in unit variable cost, however, would be an interesting observation—if the data were reliable. (Few of Professor Lester's firms had "constant unit variable costs," or anything approaching this situation, over a considerable range of output.[40]) It is rather peculiar that unit variable costs should decrease steeply (at an increasing rate!) down to a certain point and then abruptly start rising —as one must infer from the term "100 per cent capacity." Where equipment is not utilized for 24 hours a day, the steep decline and abrupt rise of the unit cost is somewhat questionable.

Professor Lester, nevertheless, has sufficient confidence in his findings to draw conclusions—conclusions, moreover, which could not even be supported if the findings were of unquestionable validity. He states:

> If company output and employment policies are based on the assumption of decreasing marginal variable cost up to full capacity operations, much of the economic reasoning on company employment adjustments to increases and decreases in wage rates is invalid, and a new theory of wage-employment relationships for the individual firm must be developed.[41]

This deduction simply does not follow from the premises. There is no reason why decreasing marginal costs should invalidate the conventional propositions on factor cost and input. Professor Lester could have found dozens of textbook examples demonstrating the firm's reactions under conditions of decreasing marginal cost.

Professor Lester may have been deluded by a rather common confusion between related concepts: from decreasing marginal cost he may have jumped to the assumption of increasing labor returns,[42] and from increasing physical returns he may have jumped to the assumption of increasing marginal productivity of labor. Both these jumps are serious mistakes. For instance, the very conditions which may cause a firm to restrict the employment of labor to a volume still within the phase of increasing physical productivity per unit of labor are likely to result in decreasing marginal net revenue productivity of labor. These conditions are:

(a) an indivisibility of the firm's physical plant facilities,[43] combined with either (or both),

(b) a low elasticity of the demand for the firm's products[44] or (and)

[40] *Ibid.*, p. 70.

[41] *Ibid.*, p. 71.

[42] *Ibid.*, p. 68.

[43] *I.e.*, the firm cannot adjust the number of machines or production units to smaller production volumes but must instead produce small outputs with an inefficiently large productive apparatus.

[44] *I.e.*, the firm realizes that it can charge much higher prices for smaller outputs or cannot dispose of larger outputs except with substantial price reductions.

(c) a low elasticity of the supply of labor to the firm.[45]

The first condition, (a), makes a phase of increasing physical productivity of labor in the firm a practical possibility; the other conditions, (b) or (c), make that phase relevant for actual operations by providing the pecuniary incentive to operate the plant inefficiently. Condition (b), the low elasticity of demand for the product, will cause marginal net revenue productivity of labor to be diminishing in a range of employment in which average or even marginal physical productivity of labor are still increasing.

It is not possible from Professor Lester's exposition to find out whether his failure to see these relationships was at the bottom of his faulty theorizing on this point. In any event, his findings on variable costs contain nothing that would even vaguely bear on the validity of marginal analysis.

Questionnaire on Adjustments

Professor Lester's fact-finding and theorizing on substitution between labor and capital and on other adjustments of the firm to changes in wage rates are also marred by inconsistencies and misunderstandings.

After trying to make the most of increasing returns to labor and only a few lines after referring to "unused plant capacity," Professor Lester asserts that "most industrial plants are designed and equipped for a certain output, requiring a certain work force. Often effective operation of the plant involves a work force of a given size."[46] To operate within the phase of increasing returns is to operate inefficiently, that is, with an employment of less labor with a given plant than would be compatible with efficient operations. (Because an increase in employment would raise output more than proportionately.) "Effective operation," on the other hand, logically implies employment at or beyond the point where diminishing returns set in. Professor Lester does not seem to be clear which way he wants to argue.[47]

Professor Lester seems to think that substitution between capital and labor can occur only in the form of installation of new or scrapping of existing machinery[48] and that it is supposed to occur "readily" and would, therefore, be "timed" with the wage changes.[49] These are rather common but nevertheless mistaken views.

[45] *I.e.*, the firm realizes that it can enjoy much lower wage rates at lower employment levels or cannot obtain more labor except with substantial wage increases.

[46] *Amer. Econ. Rev.*, Vol. XXXVI, No. 1, p. 72.

[47] Absolutely fixed proportions between factors of production would imply that short-run marginal productivity of labor drops precipitously to zero at the full capacity level of employment.

[48] *Am. Econ. Rev.*, Vol. XXXVI, No. 1, p. 73. See my comments, above, pp. 530–31.

[49] *Ibid.*, pp. 73 and 74.

Professor Lester does not discuss a glaring contradiction in his findings: On the basis of replies to one questionnaire he states that his data indicate "that industry does not adapt its plant and processes to varying wage rates in the manner assumed by marginalists."[50] But on the basis of another questionnaire about adjustments to increases in relative wages, he reports that the introduction of "labor-saving machinery" was given the highest rating in relative importance by the questioned firms whose labor costs were more than 29 per cent of total cost.[51]

The last-mentioned questionnaire apparently was designed to show that wage increases had no important effects upon employment. Six alternative adjustments to increases in relative wages were listed and manufacturers had to give percentage ratings for relative importance. In this popularity contest an item called "deliberate curtailment of output" got the booby prize. Quite apart from the fact that the words were loaded against this item, the result is not in the least surprising. For it is a well-known fact that where competition is not pure (as it rarely is in industrial products), output adjustments to higher production costs take place by way of changes in selling price. Price and product adjustments were another of the alternative items and scored rather well in the poll. If all employment-reducing adjustments—labor-saving machinery, price increases, and deliberate output curtailment—are taken together, they clearly dominate in the importance ratings by the firms.[52] This, or anything else, may not mean much in such an "opinion poll," but it certainly does not prove what Professor Lester wanted to prove. Nevertheless, he contends that "it is especially noteworthy that deliberate curtailment of output, an adjustment stressed by conventional marginal theory, is mentioned by only four of the 43 firms."[53] And he concludes that marginal analysis is all but done for, that "there can be little doubt about the correctness of the general results" of his tests[54], and that "a new direction for investigations of employment relationships and equilibrating adjustments in individual firms" is indicated.[55]

C. *Conclusions*

I conclude that the marginal theory of business conduct of the firm has not been shaken, discredited or disproved by the empirical tests discussed in this paper. I conclude, furthermore, that empirical research on business policies cannot assure useful results if it employs the method

[50] *Ibid.*, p. 73.
[51] *Ibid.*, p. 78.
[52] *Ibid.*, p. 78.
[53] *Ibid.*, p. 79.
[54] *Ibid.*, p. 81.
[55] *Ibid.*, p. 82.

of mailed questionnaires, if it is confined to direct questions without carefully devised checks, and if it aims at testing too broad and formal principles rather than more narrowly defined hypotheses.

The critical tone of my comments on the research projects discussed in this paper may give the impression of a hostile attitude towards empirical research as such. I wish to guard against such an impression. There should be no doubt that empirical research on the economics of the single firm is badly needed, no less than in many other fields. The correctness, applicability and relevance of economic theory constantly need testing through empirical research; such research may yield results of great significance.

Sharp criticism of bad research can be constructive in two respects: it may save some of the waste of time which the published research findings are apt to cause if they remain undisputed and are allowed to confuse hosts of students of economics; and it may contribute to the improvement of research. The chief condition for improved research is a thorough understanding of the theories to be tested. Supplementary conditions are a certain degree of familiarity with the technological and institutional peculiarities of the fields or cases on which the research is undertaken and a grasp of the research techniques employed.

[8]

REJOINDER TO AN ANTIMARGINALIST

BY

FRITZ MACHLUP

Reprinted from
AMERICAN ECONOMIC REVIEW
Volume XXXVII, No. 1, March, 1947

Rejoinder to an Antimarginalist

In his note[1] Professor Lester replies to certain critical comments which I made in a recent article[2] on antimarginalist prejudices and misunderstandings of the type exhibited by him.[3] I avail myself of the traditional right of rejoinder.

I begin with a concession. I readily concede to Professor Lester that I did not know whether he had asked his questions of Southern industrialists on one sheet of paper or on separate sheets; at one time or at different times. Thus I spoke of each of three sets of questions as a "questionnaire." Now I learn that they were "parts of one questionnaire" (although there had been

---

[1] "Marginalism, Minimum Wages, and Labor Markets," pp. 135–48 above. Cited hereafter as "Marginalism."

[2] "Marginal Analysis and Empirical Research," *Amer. Econ. Rev.*, Vol. XXXVI (Sept., 1946), pp. 519–554.

[3] "Shortcomings of Marginal Analysis for Wage-Employment Problems," *Amer. Econ. Rev.* Vol. XXXVI (Mar., 1946), pp. 63–82. Cited hereafter as "Shortcomings."

"two questionnaires").[4] I wonder what difference that makes. The inconsistencies between the answers to Professor Lester's questions on employment and adjustments are neither eliminated nor explained but rather emphasized by the fact that they were given in response to "one" questionnaire.[5]

I am sorry that with all the expository efforts invested in my article I did not succeed in making clear to Professor Lester what marginal analysis means and what it does not mean. Had I succeeded, he could not have reiterated several statements of his earlier article.

It would be wasteful of time and space if I countered reiteration with reiteration. It may be desirable, however, to restate the issues concisely in the order of the "tentative conclusions' 'which Professor Lester enumerated at the end of his earlier article.

1. *"Market demand is far more important than wage rates in determining a firm's volume of employment."*[6] If "important" means that market demand is a more *variable* variable than wage rates in the determination of employment, Professor Lester is absolutely right and I know of no one who has ever said anything to the contrary.[7] Economists cannot but be aware of the fact that market demand (orders, sales, sales expectations) is subject to seasonal and cyclical variations while wage rates are usually settled by contract for specific periods such as a year; and that market demand may be halved or doubled in these fluctuations while wage rate variations of as much as 20 per cent in one year are an extraordinary occurrence (except in countries with heavy inflation). Hence, there is absolutely no argument about the fact that "variations in the total volume of employment in a modern manufacturing plant already constructed are primarily the result of actual and anticipated changes in the volume of sales or orders for the products of the plant."[8] Professor Lester makes it appear as if this were *his* "position" and as if it were inconsistent with marginal productivity theory. In fact, sales expectations are an integral part of marginal productivity, as I explained patiently in my article.

2. *"Most manufacturing concerns apparently are considered by their execuiives to be operating at decreasing unit variable costs all along the scale between 70 and 100 per cent of plant capacity. Consequently, it is seldom practical for a firm to curtail output (and, therefore, employment) simply in response to an increase in wage rates."*[9] Decreasing unit variable costs have always been

---

[4] Marginalism," p. 137.

[5] "Marginalism," p. 137. On the basis of one set of questions Professor Lester had concluded that substitution between labor and machinery is rare; on the other set of questions he had reported that in firms with high labor costs the introduction of labor-saving machinery was the most important form of adjustment to increased wage rates. Instead of explaining the contradiction, Professor Lester now declares that my mistake of thinking of separate questionnaires instead of only one "may help to explain why so much of [my] criticism miscarries."

[6] "Shortcomings," p. 81.

[7] If "important" should mean that demand is in some sense a more fundamental variable, the statement would be meaningless. The significance of the concept of demand for the product of a single firm lies in the juxtaposition to costs.

[8] "Marginalism," p. 138.

[9] "Shortcomings," p. 81.

included among the possible assumptions for marginal analysis; their effects neither contradict nor qualify any of the general propositions of marginal productivity theory. That certain manufacturing industries operate under decreasing unit variable costs has been assumed in conventional theory. Professor Lester states that "consequently" output reductions in response to wage rate increases are "seldom practical." This is a *non-sequitur*, and no amount of reiteration can make it a correct inference. To be sure, manufacturing firms may not "curtail output" in *direct* response to wage increases; they are more likely to raise selling prices, which in a given market situation will reduce sales—so that it would be the sales volume rather than the wage level that appears as the "direct" cause of any output reductions. (In this case the reduced sales volume is, of course, not a reduced demand in the sense of conventional terminology.)

3. *"In modern manufacturing, a firm's level of costs per unit of product is influenced considerably by its scale of output; the reverse, as assumed by conventional marginalism, is not generally true."*[10] "Costs" may mean either a series of points on a curve or the level of the whole curve. It is not clear which "cost" Professor Lester has in mind when he says that the "reverse" —that is, output influenced by cost—is not generally true. His statement may mean at least three things. If it is to mean that the volume of output produced by the firm is usually not influenced by the shape of the cost curve, it is clearly incorrect, or producers would in good times produce far above "capacity" and might in slack times curtail output even more than they do. If it is to mean that there are situations in which a change in the level of the cost curve need not result in a change in output, it is a correct statement; indeed such situations, far from being inconsistent with marginal analysis, can be most conveniently described by it. If, finally, it is to mean that changes in the cost level will *usually* be without influence upon output, then the statement is not supported by any evidence and should be considered as false until such evidence is furnished.

4. *"For many manufacturing concerns it is not feasible, or would prove too costly, to shift the proportion of productive factors in response to current changes in wages, in the manner suggested by marginal analysis."*[11] If "current" is to suggest "immediacy," there is nothing wrong with this statement, except the last clause. Marginal analysis of the general equilibrium has often assumed absence of substitutability between factors in a given plant. This assumption of fixed coefficients of production was made for the sake of simplicity. In reality the elasticity of technical substitution is probably much greater than most "marginalists" have assumed. To be sure, a continuous, gradually sloping, short-run marginal productivity curve for a productive factor employed in a single firm implies a considerable elasticity of substitution between factors, but not a greater one than that which Professor Lester confirms as existing when he permits variations in the utilization of plant capacity between 70 and 100 per cent. Substitution between

---

[10] *Loc. cit.*
[11] "Shortcomings," p. 82.

capital and labor does not have to take the form of changes in the machinery of the plant; marginal productivity curves may be relatively elastic over certain ranges without any such variability of equipment. It goes without saying that there is much more substitution in the long run than in the short run.

5. *"The practical problems involved in applying marginal analysis to the multi-process operations of a modern plant seem insuperable, and business executives rightly consider marginalism impractical as an operating principle in such manufacturing establishments."*[12] This is a misunderstanding of the meaning of marginalism. Professor Lester relied on the ability of his industrialists to know their "unit variable cost" at various scales of output. Yet, calculations of unit costs, in a single-process plant as well as in a multi-process plant, are much more complicated than estimates of marginal cost. Incremental costs and revenues can be known without any knowledge of average costs and revenues; the reverse is not true. (For example, one may know the *additional* expenses caused by increases in output without bothering to allocate and calculate the *total* expenses before or after the increase. Those totals are needed for a calculation of averages; of course, whenever the totals are known the differences between the totals are given implicitly. In cases of joint products—multi-product plants—incremental (marginal) cost is the only cost that is separable and determinate.)

6. *"Of the three adjustments stressed by business executives to meet a rise in wages relative to those paid by competitors, two—better management practices and increased sales efforts—are neglected by conventional marginalism; whereas the adjustment stressed by marginalism—curtailment of output—is considered so unimportant and exceptional as to be mentioned in only one out of every 11 replies."*[13] Professor Lester refers here to an item in his questionnaire in which the respondent business man should state that he would "reduce production by deliberately curtailing output." Such wicked conduct Professor Lester represents as the one "adjustment stressed by marginalism." As if marginalist theorists had never said anything about adjustments through higher selling price, greater selling efforts, changes in quality and type of product, different production methods, substitution between factors, etc. Professor Lester, however, adds this to his last conclusion: *"Indeed, experience seems to indicate that, on an individual-firm basis, the adjustments considered important by the business executives may, at times, even result in larger firm employment at a higher wage level."*[14] No marginalist theorist will deny that this ("at times") is a *possibility.* But in order to justify putting it as the final proposition in a set of conclusions supposedly "drawn from the data contained" in his study, Professor Lester should have offered some support for the *probability* of the occurrence. Yet, he has furnished not even the thinnest scrap of evidence, not the vaguest suggestion of plausible reasons in support of the proposition.

[12] *Loc. cit.*
[13] *Loc. cit.*
[14] *Loc. cit.*

I have the impression that Professor Lester is fighting against marginal productivity theory chiefly because it appears to establish a presumption that changes of wage rates result in inverse changes of employment in the single firm. I must say that there is nowhere an explicit statement to that effect, neither in his earlier article nor in his present communication, and I must beg his pardon if my impression is incorrect. But Professor Lester repeatedly refers to "cases" in which increased wage rates need not result in reduced employment and may result or did result in increased employment. (Unfortunately, he does not bother to say whether the demand for the product was unchanged in these cases. But he does not hesitate to refer to experiences between 1939 and 1941—defense boom!—to support his argument.) If my impression about the chief aim of the attack is correct, Professor Lester could have served his purpose by showing under what conditions the presumption would not hold and by proving that such conditions actually prevail in a number of industries. Instead, he set out to fight against "marginal analysis" in general and to prove *its* "shortcomings." Yet, of his six "tentative conclusions" the first four are perfectly consistent with marginal analysis, and the sixth—at least in the cautious way in which it is formulated—is not inconsistent with it. Only the fifth proposition—that marginalism is "impractical"—would, if true, contradict marginalist theory of business conduct (or at least one of its interpretations).

What is Professor Lester's alternative theory of business conduct and employment? I take it that Professor Lester does not accept the anti-marginalist "full-cost" theory of pricing which was advanced by Hall and Hitch.[15] This theory would suit the purpose of proving insensitiveness of the firm's output to wage increases much worse than marginal analysis; it holds that wage increases as a rule are shifted forward in full to the consumer—which would reduce output by more than the marginal principle usually calls for.

According to marginal productivity theory employment depends on several variables: anticipated selling prices and sales quantities with their potential variations; technological possibilities; conditions of supply of complementary and substitutable factors; and conditions of supply of the factor in question. Is it perhaps Professor Lester's theory of employment in the individual firm that of the several variables considered by marginal productivity theory only one counts, namely, the demand for the product? This interpretation is suggested by the fact that his proposition on the importance of market demand is reiterated several times in his foregoing note. He varies the formulation of the proposition by the use of the modifiers "primarily," "generally," "simply," "independently." Thus, after having emphasized the primacy of selling possibilities in the determination of employment—see the sentence quoted above with Professor Lester's first conclusion—and after minimizing the importance of the principle of maximizing business profits, he says that "*on the contrary*, the volume of output and employment in the individual firm *generally* varies *simply* and directly with

[15] R. L. Hall and C. J. Hitch, "Price Theory and Business Behavior," *Oxford Econ. Papers*, Vol. 2 (1939).

the volume of present and prospective demand for products of the plant."[16] And again: "The existing and expected volume of product sales appears to be a factor in firm employment that operates *independent* of the principle of equating its marginal net revenue productivity and marginal labor cost."[17] If this were all, the difference between Professor Lester and the marginal productivity theorists would boil down to the question whether or not it is true that employers take account of anything besides the selling possibilities for their wares. Professor Lester, guarded by a few adverbs, denies it. Marginal productivity theorists believe that other variables count too, although in certain well-defined situations one or another variable may be neutralized.

Professor Lester tries to show why these other variables are of no importance. His favorite point, that conditions of "declining unit variable costs up to 100 per cent capacity"[18] somehow interfere with the operation of the marginal principle, is untenable. Another of his points concerns cases where "product prices and demand elasticities remain unchanged with variations in actual or anticipated demand."[19] We know several cases in the theory of imperfect competition in which selling prices remain unchanged in spite of changes in demand. Perhaps Professor Lester thinks of the case of tacitly fixed prices under oligopoly in which the sales curve breaks off at the volume of sales expected at the given price. (Since under the oligopolistic conditions price reductions are regarded as impractical, there is no practical possibility of expanding sales.) We all have learned that in such a case the marginal revenue curve exhibits a vertical drop. If there should also be no possibility of technical substitution for labor, the marginal productivity curve will, of course, reflect that condition and have the vertical range over which changes in wage rates (or marginal labor cost) are without any effect upon employment in the firm. This is nothing new to the marginalist. Does Professor Lester wish to regard it as the "general theory" of employment in the firm? To me it is a special case.[20]

Other points brought up by Professor Lester refer to the cost of changing the size of the work force. To reduce employment may be costly for several reasons: deteriorated "morale of the remaining workers"; possible slowdowns; increased "employer's tax rate under experience rating in unem-

[16] "Marginalism," p. 138. Emphasis supplied.

[17] "Marginalism," p. 148. Emphasis supplied.

[18] "Marginalism," p. 138.

[19] *Loc. cit.*

[20] The vertical range in the marginal productivity curve of labor employed in the firm will make the firm insensitive to changes in the wage rate *only if these changes are confined to that firm.* If the competitors of the firm must pay the same or similar wage increases, the situation is altogether different: the oligopolistic sales curves will shift because each producer is apt to expect his competitors to follow suit when he raises his selling price in line with the increased production cost; hence, the "break" of the "imagined demand curve" will occur at a higher price; but at this increased price the physical sales volume will be smaller, and employment will have to be reduced. Propositions about oligopoly situations making selling prices inflexible and employment in the firm insensitive to increased cost must not be generalized: they are not likely to hold when the costs of competing producers are also increased.

ployment compensation," etc. Every "marginalist" will agree with Professor Lester that "such factors . . . must be taken into account in discussing employment adjustments to wage changes."[21] (Are there, after all, "employment adjustments to wage changes"? Does then employment vary also on account of other things than demand? If Professor Lester grants all this, what is left of his case against marginal productivity theory?) Professor Lester is mistaken in thinking that to take account of such matters is "troublesome to a marginalist." No trouble at all. The cost of changing the work force is one of the causes—besides the smaller elasticity of the short-run sales curve and the difficulties of certain types of technical substitution —why marginal productivity curves are less elastic in the short run than in the long run. (Or, if one prefers to look at change-over costs of this sort as part of the conditions of labor supply, they will make the marginal factor cost curve less elastic in the short run than in the long run.) The "mental ruts of the marginalists"[22] are equipped to take care of all the economic considerations which Professor Lester has mentioned as factors in business decisions. This makes marginal analysis less simple but more revealing than a theory which tries to explain the volume of employment in the firm solely with reference to its sales possibilities.

FRITZ MACHLUP*

[21] "Marginalism," p. 147.
[22] "Marginalism," p. 148.
* The author is professor of economics at the University of Buffalo.

[9]

CORPORATE MANAGEMENT, NATIONAL INTEREST, AND BEHAVIORAL THEORY

THERE was a time when most business managers owned the businesses they managed. Hence, there was no conflict between the managers' interests and those of the owners. At the same time, the best economists proclaimed that the interests of society would be served best if businessmen competed with one another, each trying to maximize his own profit. Thus, no conflict was seen to exist between the managers' interests and those of society.

This is different from what we hear today. Managers are told, and tell one another and everybody who is willing to listen, that their social responsibilities override most of their other objectives. The story is one of divided loyalty and split personality.

In order to be able to "look the facts straight in the eye," I have prepared the minutes of a management meeting of the famous XYZ Corporation. I submit that the minutes will speak for themselves.

MINUTES OF THE MANAGEMENT MEETING OF THE XYZ CORPORATION

Chairman: Gentlemen, I am glad to report that the remarkable record of our firm last year is being surpassed by the figures for the current year. Our sales for the first six months of this year are 18 per cent above those of the same period last year and the backlog of orders is even higher. The cash flow is accordingly enlarged, and we have to decide on the best use of the new funds generated, whether they are regarded as net income or as means to defray additional expenses.

We must make our decision in full consciousness of our responsibilities. These responsibilities are not only to the owners of the firm and its creditors, but equally to our employees, suppliers, and, of course, our customers—and, last but not least, to society at large. The national interest, indeed, must be served by anything we do.

May I now entertain your views and suggestions regarding the use of a large part of the incremental funds generated by our business this year.

Mr. A: Mr. Chairman, let me emphasize that we are operating at full capacity, that our delivery terms are getting longer, that improved equipment has become available. I conclude that we must use our increased profits for *investment in plant expansion.* This will enable us to produce a larger output more economically. I need hardly stress that such investment in increased productivity contributes to growth and is clearly in the national interest.

Mr. B: Mr. Chairman, as comptroller of this company I consider it my duty to speak up for financial prudence, in the interest of both our company and the nation. The economy has been overheating, and total investment must be reduced if inflationary pressures are to be abated. When Congress, at the request of the administration, suspended the tax credits for investment, it was a clear declaration that the national interest called for a cutback in private investment. I propose that we use the increase in profits for *debt retirement.* This will also reduce our interest burden and improve our current position.

Mr. C: Mr. Chairman, let me raise a voice on behalf of the owners of this company. Dividend payments to our stockholders have remained unchanged, although our earnings have greatly increased. Not all stockholders are satisfied with a growth stock that never pays increased dividends. Such neglect of the stockholders' interests will sooner or later be reflected in a reduced price-earnings ratio and, in turn, in increased capital cost to the company when

772

it decides to raise additional equity capital. Moreover, I submit that the national interest calls for increases in taxable income, and to this we can contribute by using our increased profits for *paying increased dividends*.

Mr. D: Mr. Chairman, I cannot accept this reasoning at all. It is neither in the national interest nor in the interest of the company that we dissipate funds by larger distributions to stockholders. The stockholders themselves may prefer to see the funds used in ways that would not increase their heavy burden of double taxation. Let me speak of an important asset of the company that does not show up in the books of the firm: customer loyalty. Investments in customer loyalty can be expensed, so that neither corporate nor individual income taxes are paid on funds put to this use. Our budget for *advertising and public relations* has been starved. I submit that our additional funds should be used to strengthen our promotional efforts.

Mr. E: Mr. Chairman, I agree with the VP in charge of promotion that we should not label the additional cash generated this year as profits but, rather, use it for outlays that can be expensed. But I see better ways of spending money than for advertising. Let me propose *increased development expenditures* for the improvement of our products. This would be at least as efficient as advertising in gaining customer loyalty, and much more efficient as a contribution to the standard of living of our people. The public image of a company nowadays is a function of its R & D expenditures, and the national interest is clearly served by greater developmental efforts.

Mr. F: Mr. Chairman, let me support this plea for an increased budget for R & D. But I should like to shift the emphasis away from D and toward R. Business has often been criticized for taking too short a view, for thinking only of immediate applications of technological progress. Basic research has largely been left to the universities and the government. I do not think this socialization of research is in the national interest.

Private enterprise must be more active in basic research. Enlightened self-interest demands that we do our share in promoting pure science. I propose that we appropriate a good part of the new funds to *basic research*.

Mr. G: Mr. Chairman, I share this civic-minded attitude, but I doubt our capability of doing a really good job in basic research. Our universities are better equipped to do this, and we ought to help the universities. This help, however, should not be confined to aid in their research activities. The chief emphasis should be on their educational work. This is where our future management, our future scientists, engineers, technicians, and inventors are being trained. Investment in human resources is the No. 1 requirement of our nation. I propose that we make large *educational contributions*, in the form of gifts to our private universities and fellowships to graduate students.

Mr. H: Mr. Chairman, I support the view that investment in human resources should be the most urgent concern of our company. However, I submit that the greatest shortage is in managerial talent, in executive ability. Enough money is available for training young men, but the trouble is that we cannot attract them into business careers. We must try to attract the most capable men coming out of the colleges and universities, and this means increasing the pecuniary rewards to people in management. This is not a self-seeking proposal to line my own pocket but, rather, a plea to improve management morale and the attractiveness of the managerial career by using large parts of our increased earnings to increase the *bonuses and other payments to management*.

Mr. I: Mr. Chairman, I recognize that this proposal is well-meant and is in the national interest. But we must be realistic and think of the effects on labor relations. Let me propose an investment in industrial peace by offering a *profit-sharing* plan to all our employees besides *increased wage rates and fringe benefits*. Our contract with the union still has a year to run. Let us gain the good will of our labor force by volunteering higher pay and benefits at this time, and avoid strikes that may otherwise come in years ahead.

Mr. J: Mr. Chairman, I am opposed to wage increases at this time. When the boom subsides, we may regret having increased our labor costs. But, before all, such wage increases are inflationary and violate the guide posts urged upon us by the government. Let me make a proposal which makes several contributions to the welfare of the nation as well as this company, an action that would enhance customer loyalty, be appreciated by the workers, raise the standard of living, and combat inflation: Let us *reduce the prices of our products.*

Chairman: Gentlemen, it is time for a coffee break.

CONCLUDING OBSERVATIONS

Permit me to join in the coffee-break conversation. I know I intended to let the facts tell their own story. On second thought, however, I remember that most people are hard of hearing, and most facts are poor expositors of their meaning.

Those who proclaim, as a tenet of normative economics, that businessmen ought to meet their "responsibilities" to society have not been sufficiently explicit on just what this means. If it is not enough that businessmen observe the law, should they obey all the exhortations of government officials and editorial writers? Or should they seek their own interpretations of the national interest? How should conflicts of evaluation be resolved (say, among the ten vice-presidents of XYZ Corporation, every one of whom argued for a different policy as securing the greatest good for society)? If compromises are required, to what extent should the interests of the owners of the business be sacrificed for the sake of some of the favored national goals?

Economists who are skeptical (regarding both the competence of corporate managers to decide what is best for society and the possibility of safe guidance becoming available) prefer to reduce the leeway that corporate managers have for decisions of this sort. Effective competition from existing producers, domestic and foreign, and from firms newly entering the industry relieves managers of all worry about the social-bliss function and forces them to strive continuously to improve their products and the efficiency of production. This effort demands their full attention, and, with the highest attainable profits just high enough for survival, the managers cannot indulge any alternative objectives.

Leaving normative economics aside, we may ask whether the recorded minutes of the management meeting reinforce any lessons in positive economics. Perhaps they illustrate the enormous difficulties of "behavioral theories": ten participants in corporate decision making propose ten different courses of action, and there is no warrant for any generalization as to what they are likely to decide after the coffee break. If the firm were under heavy competitive pressure, which it apparently is not, one might entertain some hunches concerning its reactions to *some* kinds of environmental changes (though these hunches would still be extremely unreliable, since economic theory is really adapted only to deal with the consequences of mass reactions, not the actual behavior of particular firms or individuals). The change to which the management of the XYZ Corporation is invited to react is an increase in sales, profit opportunities, and cash flow, but we are not told whether this is partly the pay-off of past efforts of the firm to gain business from other firms and industries or only the reflection of general boom conditions. Perhaps the story illustrates the trivial generalization that increased affluence and increased liquidity are likely to lead to increased expenditures for all sorts of good things. This generalization can be derived from the most abstract theorems of utility maximization as well as from the most empirical researches of observed behavior.

FRITZ MACHLUP

Princeton University

[10]

The American Economic Review

Volume LVII   MARCH 1967   Number 1

THEORIES OF THE FIRM: MARGINALIST, BEHAVIORAL, MANAGERIAL*

By FRITZ MACHLUP

Last year, when it was my task to plan the program for the annual meeting of our association, a friend suggested that, with twenty years having passed since the outbreak of the "marginalism controversy," it was appropriate to review what has since happened to the embattled theory of the firm. The topic did not fit the general theme I had chosen for the 1965 meeting, but I reasoned that 1966 would give me a good opportunity to undertake the review myself.

The Battlefield Revisited

So let us recall that literary feud and the warriors, and let us revisit the battlefield. The major battlefield was the *American Economic Review,* with six articles and communications between March 1946 and March 1947 [16] [43] [21] [17] [22] [44]. There had been earlier gunfire elsewhere, chiefly in the *Oxford Economic Papers* in 1939 [14]. But, since the shooting then was not returned and it takes at least two opponents to join battle, it must be agreed that the real hostilities were the exchanges in the *AER*.

The fight was spirited, even fierce. Thousands of students of economics, voluntary or involuntary readers, have been either shocked or entertained by the violence of some of the blows exchanged and may have thought that the opponents must have become mortal enemies forever. These readers would have been wrong. Even before we came out for the last round of the fight, we exchanged friendly letters (December 1946) assuring each other that we would bear no grudges.

We have remained the best of friends; for several years now Richard Lester and I have been colleagues in the same department; and, as a token of our friendship, he has generously accepted my invitation to share this platform with me today as chairman of the session. Thus the veterans of both sides of the War of 1946 are now joined in revisiting

---

* Presidential address delivered, in a shorter version, at the Seventy-ninth Annual Meeting of the American Economic Association, San Francisco, December 28, 1966.

the battlefield. This, incidentally, does not mean that either of us has succeeded in converting the other to the "true faith."

What was the outcome of the controversy? Who won? We could not possibly say if we have not first agreed on precisely what the shooting was about. I have heard it said that Machlup won the battle but Lester won the war. What this means, however, cannot be known unless we know what the issues and objectives of the war had been. Was it merely to make economics safe for or from marginalism? Were there not several other issues being fought over?

Some of the Major Issues

There were no doubt a good many contentions of all sorts—major, minor, essential, incidental, interpretative, factual, methodological, substantive, and all the rest. To present a complete catalogue of the issues involved would be too ambitious a task for this occasion, but a partial listing might be helpful.

The chief issue, of course, was whether marginal analysis was invalid and ought to be discarded, especially as far as the theory of prices, cost, wages, and employment in manufacturing industry is concerned. This issue, however, implied the question of the correct interpretation of marginal analysis, including the tenets of the marginal-productivity principle. In this connection, differences in the models of the firm customarily used in different kinds of analysis became relevant. Involved here was the question of whether the postulate of maximizing money profits led to conclusions very different from those derivable from assumptions of conduct guided by a variety of largely nonpecuniary considerations.

Underlying all these questions were some issues of general scientific methodology: the legitimacy and usefulness of abstract theorizing on the basis of unrealistic assumptions, or perhaps on the basis of assumptions regarded as "reasonable" thought not "universally true." These issues, in particular, were whether an assumption of profit maximization as the effective objective of the firm in the theoretical model may be accepted as a tenable hypothesis only if it can be verified that all or a majority of those who actually run business firms in the real world agree that this is their only or major objective, that they are capable of obtaining all the information and of performing all the calculations needed for the realization of that objective, and are really carrying out the actions found to be optimal in this fashion; or, alternatively, whether all these tests may be dispensed with and the assumption of profit maximization nevertheless accepted as a fruitful postulate from which conclusions can be derived which correspond with what can be observed in the records of prices and quantities.

Concerning the empirical testing of theoretical conclusions, there were issues of the validity of surveys through mailed questionnaires and of the proper interpretation of responses to various types of questions about managerial judgment. In the background of the whole controversy, but undoubtedly of pervasive significance, was the comparative acceptability of empirical findings to the effect that the elasticity of demand for labor was virtually zero and of the conventional theoretical inference that the elasticity was normally above zero.

Realizing how manifold were the issues of the controversy, one can appreciate that no clear decision can be made about its outcome. Some of the issues had been raised decades or centuries before 1946 and were not decided in this confrontation one way or the other. Attacks on the assumption of maximizing behavior and on the lack of realism in price theory have occurred with great regularity ever since "economic man" and similar postulates were introduced. The running battles between the classical and the historical schools were largely on these points. The *Methodenstreit* of 1883-84 dealt essentially with the same issues. And in the United States, institutionalism may be seen as a movement animated by the same spirit of protest against abstract theory.

However, the particular form of explicit marginalism (under the name of "theory of the firm") which became the target of the attacks of 1939 and 1946 had only come into being in the 1930's—if one suppresses the memory of the great master of 1838 [9]. Ironically, some interpreter of recent history of economic thought—I have forgotten who it was—regarded the 1933-34 versions of the theory of the firm [8] [32] [41] as the theorists' concession to institutionalism, as attempts to supplement the neoclassical model of the firm under atomistic competition with some "more realistic" models allowing for a greater variety of conditions. It was this theory of the profit-maximizing firm in all sorts of market positions, in monopolistic and oligopolistic competition as well as in pure and perfect competition, that was attacked by the researchers in Oxford; and it was the marginal-productivity principle in the explanation of the demand for labor on the part of the individual firm that was the prime target of the attack of 1946.

If the chief aim of the attack was to force the abandonment or subversion of marginalism, and if the chief aim of the defense was to turn back the subversive forces and secure the reign of marginalism once and for all, then, to be sure, the war of 1946 ended in a draw. Look at the textbooks and you will find that marginalism has continued to dominate the teaching of microeconomics, perhaps though with occasional reservations and references to current attempts at greater realism. But look at the journals and monographs and you find that research on alternative approaches to the theory of the firm is regularly reported with the implication that a superior theory may eventually replace marginalism. This replacement, however, according to the proponents of the best-known alternatives to marginalism, is expected chiefly with regard to industries where firms are few and competition is ineffective. The marginalist solution of price determination under conditions of heavy competition is not seriously contested.

In pointing this out, I am not trying to claim that marginal analysis is invincible and forever irreplaceable. If I follow the philosophy of science which, instead of pronouncing theories "false" or "true," distinguishes only between those "rejected" and those "still open to criticism" [30, pp. 246-48], the only victory that can be claimed for the cause of marginalism is that it is still open to criticism. I must go beyond this and concede that some anti-marginalist suggestions have led in recent years to a number of revisions in the marginal analysis of the firm which amount to the incorporation of other goals besides money profits into expanded marginalist objective functions.

The Alternative Approaches

In their arguments against the profit-maximization model the various alternative approaches to the theory of the firm are very much alike; only their positive programs can distinguish them.

The program of behaviorism is to reject preconceptions and assumptions and to rely only on observation of overt behavior. Thus, behaviorism rejects the assumption of marginal analysis that economic action is directed by the objective to maximize the attainment of ends with given means, and that business action can be deduced from a postulate that firms attempt to maximize money profits. Instead, we are directed to *observe* how businessmen really act and by what processes they reach decisions.

Perhaps it is not entirely fair to suggest here an association between "behaviorism" and the working program of the proponents of a "behavioral theory of the firm" [10]. In any case, behavioral research proposes to observe and study the "real processes," in the sense of a "well-defined sequence of behaviors" by which decisions are reached in "actual business organizations." The hope—faithfully inductive—is to develop a theory "with generality beyond the specific firms studied" [10, p. 2]. Such a theory will be based on "four major sub-theories" regarding "organizational *goals,* organizational *expectations,* organizational *choice,* and organizational *control*" [10, p. 21]. It is assumed that five organizational goals—a production goal, an inventory goal, a sales goal, a market-share goal, and the profit goal—become the subject of bargaining among the various members of the "coalition" which make up the business organization but that the goals are continually adapted and are being pressed with varying force [10, pp. 40-43]. The behavior theory of the firm, with regard to the determination of prices and outputs, will run in terms of a "quasi resolution of conflict" within the organization, of an "adaptively rational, multiple-objective process" with responses to "short-run feedback on performance" and with continuing "organizational learning" [10, pp. 269-70].

This behavioral approach has been characterized as striving for "realism in process," in contrast to approaches aiming at more "realism in motivation" [48, p. 11]. Such realism in motivation is felt to be needed chiefly because of the separation of ownership and control in the modern corporation, whose managements have great power and wide discretion.

In principle, I could expect three different views to be taken regarding the relative independence of corporation management: (1) Whereas owners would run their business chiefly with a view to a maximum of money profits, managers run it with several supplementary and partly competing goals in mind. (2) Whereas owners, especially wealthy ones, would often allow nonprofit considerations to enter their decision-making, managers have a sense of dedication and identification with the business that makes them the more single-minded seekers of profits. (3) Even if managers are inclined to indulge in seeking other goals as long as profits look satisfactory, they are as professionals, trained in the art and science of management, able to make better profits than the owners could ever hope to make running their own show.

What consequences can be drawn from this? One attitude would be to stick with the assumption of profit maximization because it is the simplest and is applicable with much less detailed information to the largest field.[1] Another attitude would be to insist on starkest realism with a complete catalogue of goals and indices of their effectiveness in each firm. A third attitude would be to select two or three of the most

---

[1] "To use marginalism in the theory of the firm it is not necessary to assert that firms attempt to maximize money profits only nor to deny that a goodly portion of all business behavior may be nonrational, thoughtless, blindly repetitive, deliberately traditional, or motivated by extra-economic objectives. It merely presupposes that the 'rational-economic' portion of business conduct is by and large sufficiently important to affect what is going on in the world to an extent large enough to warrant analysis; and that the substitution of money profits for a composite of pecuniary and nonpecuniary rewards simplifies the analysis so much that the gain in expediency far exceeds the loss in applicability" [23 pp. 30-31]. A similar view is expressed by Scitovsky: "Empirical studies of businessmen's behavior suggest the need for modifying or qualifying the assumption of profit maximization here and there, rather than scrapping it altogether. Accordingly, . . . we shall retain the assumption that the firm aims at maximizing its profit. But we shall regard this assumption as a working hypothesis rather than as a universal rule" [37, p. 111].

important managerial objectives of a type that can be reduced to quantitative analysis and to combine them in a single manageable "objective function." This third approach merges marginalism with managerialism in that it integrates money profits with other managerial goals within one formula of "maximizing behavior."

The question is whether managerial marginalism is prescribed for general application or only for so-called noncompetitive cases. Its most prominent proponents prefer to use the old formula, based on profit maximization, in situations where competition is effective and managerial discretion therefore narrowly circumscribed. In the next sections we shall discuss matters that at first blush may seem unrelated to this issue but on reflection can shed indirect light on it.

The Analogy of the Theoretical Automobile Driver

One of the best remembered points in my exposition was the use of an analogy designed to warn against mistaking theoretical variables and their links for realistic descriptions of observable processes. This was the analogy of the "theory of overtaking" automobiles on the highways [21, pp. 534-35].

Analogies are often misleading, but in this particular case it served its main purpose: to show that the theoretical variables need not be estimated and the theoretical equations need not be solved through actual calculation by the actors in the real world whose idealized types are supposed to perform these difficult operations in the models constructed for the explanation of recorded observations.[2] The critics of marginal analysis believed they had refuted it if they could show that the exact numerical calculations of marginal magnitudes—cost, revenue, productivity—were difficult or impossible to perform by real decision-makers.

Yet, my analogy was only partially successful. An implication which should have been obvious has been widely overlooked: that the type of action assumed to be taken by the theoretical actor in the model under specified conditions need not be expected and cannot be predicted actually to be taken by any particular real actor. The empiricist's inclination is to verify the theoretically deduced action by testing individual behavior, although the theory serves only to explain and predict effects of mass behavior.

We may illustrate this again by means of the same analogy, the theory of overtaking. Assume a change of driving conditions occurs, say, that the roads have become wet and slippery and fog has reduced visi-

[2] The theoretical automobile driver had to estimate, among other things, the speeds of three vehicles and the distances between them, and to perform calculations involving potential acceleration and a few other things, before he could decide to overtake the truck ahead of him. An actual driver simply "sizes up" the situation and goes ahead.

bility. Theory enables us to predict that traffic will be slower and accidents more frequent, but it does not enable us to predict that any particular driver will drive more slowly or have an accident. The model of the reactions of the individual driver was not designed to explain the actual driving of any particular operator but only to explain the observable consequences of the observed change of conditions by deducing from the model the theoretical reactions of a hypothetical driver.

Our analogy can also show us the limitations of the model: the prediction will hold only if there is a large number of automobiles on the road. If only a very few cars are around, there may be no accident and there need not be a reduction in their speed. Conceivably, the operators may all be good and self-confident drivers. Marginal analysis of hypothetical driver reaction will suffice for explaining and predicting the consequences of a change in driving conditions if the number of automobiles on the highways is large. If the number is small, behavioral research will be needed, though it may or may not be worth the cost.

Still another use can be made of our analogy: to show the vast differences in the scope of questions to which answers can or cannot be expected with the aid of a given theory, for example, from the theory of overtaking as sketched in my article. Compare the following four questions: (1) How fast will traffic move? (2) How fast will the automobile driven by Mr. X move? (3) How will the speed of traffic be affected by fog? (4) How will the speed of Mr. X's driving be affected by fog?

The theory sketched by me offers no answer to the first question, because each of the variables specified may have very different values for different cars and drivers; it has no answer to the second question, and only a suggestion, a rebuttable presumption, for answering the fourth question, because the theory is not really concerned with particular persons or their actions and reactions. The theory is equipped only to answer the third question, regarding the effects of a change in driving conditions on automobile traffic in general, and even this answer will be qualitative only, without good clues to numerical results. It may be interesting to get answers to all four questions, but since Question 3 can be answered with a fraction of the information that would be needed to answer the other questions, it would be foolish to burden the models designed for Question 3 with irrelevant matters, or to reject such models because they cannot do what they are not designed to do.[3]

[3] A behavioral theory of automobile driving would probably study the process by which the decision to pass a truck is arrived at in a sequence of bickering among the members of the family: Mama and Sis trying to argue against taking an unnecessary risk, Sonny egging on his Dad to speed up and pass the truck "crawling" ahead of them. Moreover, the theory would not be satisfied with "explaining" the decision to overtake but it would

Confusion of Purposes

The same sort of confusion about the scope of problems and models for their solution has been fostered in recent writings on the theory of the firm: models have been condemned or rejected because they could not be used for purposes for which they had not been designed, and significant differences in the questions to be answered have been obscured or underemphasized.

Let us again pose four typical questions and see which of them we might expect to answer with the aid of "price theory." (1) What will be the prices of cotton textiles? (2) What prices will the X Corporation charge? (3) How will the prices of cotton textiles be affected by an increase in wage rates? (4) How will the X Corporation change its prices when wage rates are increased?

Conventional price theory is not equipped to answer any but the third question; it may perhaps also suggest a rebuttable answer to the fourth question. But Questions 1 and 2 are out of reach. We could not obtain all the information that would be required for their answers and there is, therefore, no use burdening the models with variables remaining silent and inactive throughout the show.

We ought to guard against an easy misunderstanding of our denial that conventional price theory can predict actual prices of specified goods. Prediction of future prices of a particular commodity may in fact be quite manageable if we know its present price. It should be obvious, however, that this is Question 3, not Question 1. Or, one may be able to predict prices on the basis of good information on production cost. But this presupposes that we know the demand for the commodity and assume it will remain unchanged; which again comes down essentially to evaluations of changes of some variables with others held constant, that is, to Question 3.

If the number of firms producing cotton textiles is large and the X Corporation does not supply a very large part of the aggregate output of the industry, price theory may suggest an answer to Question 4, although this is not the purpose of the theory and there may be a considerable chance for the suggested answer to be wrong. The point is that a model of a theoretical firm in an industry consisting of a large number of firms can do with a much smaller number of assumptions, provided the model is used to predict, not the actual reactions of any one particular firm, but only the effects of the hypothetical reactions of numerous anonymous "reactors" (symbolic firms). If it were to be applied to predictions of reactions of a particular firm, the model would have to

---

also wish to determine the speed of driving, the frequency and length of stops at roadside stands, and all the rest.

be much more richly endowed with variables and functions for which information could be obtained only at considerable effort and with results that may or may not be worth the cost of the required research.

My charge that there is widespread confusion regarding the purposes of the "theory of the firm" as used in traditional price theory refers to this: The model of the firm in that theory is not, as so many writers believe, designed to serve to explain and predict the behavior of real firms; instead, it is designed to explain and predict changes in observed prices (quoted, paid, received) as effects of particular changes in conditions (wage rates, interest rates, import duties, excise taxes, technology, etc.). In this causal connection the firm is only a theoretical link, a mental construct helping to explain how one gets from the cause to the effect.[4] This is altogether different from explaining the behavior of a firm. As the philosopher of science warns, we ought not to confuse the *explanans* with the *explanandum*.

Misplaced Concreteness

To confuse the firm as a theoretical construct with the firm as an empirical concept, that is, to confuse a heuristic fiction with a real organization like General Motors or Atlantic & Pacific, is to commit the "fallacy of misplaced concreteness." This fallacy consists in using theoretic symbols as though they had a direct, observable, concrete meaning.

In some fields, investigators are protected from committing the fallacy, at least with regard to some of their problems, by the fact that a search for any empirical counterpart to the theoretical construct seems hopeless. Thus, some physicists working on particle theory were able

[4] The same statement can be made about the household. The "household" in price theory is not an object of study; it serves only as a theoretical link between changes in prices and changes in labor services supplied and in consumer goods demanded. The hypothetical reactions of an imaginary decision-maker on the basis of assumed, internally consistent preference functions serve as the simplest and heuristically satisfactory explanation of empirical relationships between changes in prices and changes in quantities. In other words, the household in price theory is not an object of study.

Behavioral studies of real households are something entirely different. A realistic, behavioral theory of the household might conceivably distinguish the large, children-dominated household from a simpler, father-dominated one. The decisions in the children-dominated household, where mother frequently and father occasionally try to exercise some influence, are probably not consistent, since different preference systems are made explicit at various times, with varying decibels and gestures deployed to make them prevail over the preferences of other members of the family.

One can imagine studies on the behavior of particular households selected at random or in structured samples. If the researcher learns that a spoiled brat in a family wants to eat nothing but beef and throws a tantrum every time his mother tries to feed him other kinds of meat, a reduction in the price of chicken will probably not substantially increase the consumption of chicken in this family. Thus, the weight of the child's taste in the decision process of the family can explain a low elasticity of its demand for chicken. But none of this has much bearing on general price theory.

to answer the question "Does the Neutrino Really Exist?" [11, pp. 139-41] laconically with "Who cares?" and to explain that any belief in the "real existence" of atoms, electrons, neutrinos, and all the rest, would hold up the progress of our knowledge. Some biologists working in genetics warned, after empirical genes were discovered, that these "operational genes" should not be confused with the "hypothetical genes," which had been useful constructs in explanatory models before the discovery of any empirical referents [42, p. 814]. Economists, however, know for sure that firms exist as empirical entities and, hence, they have a hard time keeping the theoretical firm and the empirical firm apart.

For certain economic problems the existence of the firm is of the essence. For example, if we study the size distribution of firms or the growth of the firm, the organization and some of its properties and processes are the very objects of the investigation. In such studies we insist on a high degree of correspondence between the model (the thought-object) and the observed object. For other problems, however, as for problems of competitive-price theory, any likeness between the theoretical construct of the firm and the empirical firm is purely coincidental.

Economists trained in scientific methodology understand this clearly. I might quote a dozen or more writers, but will confine myself to one quotation, which states that "in economic analysis, the business firm is a postulate in a web of logical connections" [15, p. 196]. Let me add the statement of another writer, who however was plaintiff rather than advocate when he wrote that "It is a fascinating paradox that the received theory of the firm, by and large, assumes that the firm does not exist" [45, p. 249].

Here is what I wrote on one of the several occasions when I have discussed this problem:

> . . . the firm in the model world of economic micro-theory ought not to call forth any irrelevant associations with firms in the real world. We know, of course, that there are firms in reality and that they have boards of directors and senior and junior executives, who do, with reference to hundreds of different products, a great many things—which are entirely irrelevant for the microtheoretical model. The fictitious firm of the model is a "uni-brain," an individual decision-unit that has nothing to do but adjust the output and the prices of one or two imaginary products to very simple imagined changes in data [26, p. 133].

I went on, of course, to say that this purely fictitious single-minded firm, helpful as it is in competitive-price theory, will not do so much for us in the theory of monopoly and oligopoly. To explain and predict price reactions under monopoly and oligopoly we need more than the construct of a profit-maximizing reactor.[5] I shall come back to this after discussing the demands for "more realistic" assumptions where they are plainly irrelevant and therefore out of place.

Realistic Models of the Firm under Competition

Many of the proponents and protagonists of a more realistic theory of the firm are quite aware of the fact that the managerial extension and enrichment of the concept of the firm was not needed except where firms in the industry were large and few, and not under the pressure of competition. There are many very quotable statements to this effect.[6]

Too many students, however, want a realistic model of the firm for all purposes. They forget the maxim of Occam's Razor that unnecessary terms in a theory be kept out (or shaved off). These students seem to miss in a simplified model the realistic trimmings of the observable world; they distrust such a model because it is obviously

---

[5] You may wonder whether I have changed my mind on these matters. Incidentally, I hold that it is important for scholars and scientists to have an open mind, and the only evidence showing that they do are instances in which they have actually changed their minds. On this particular issue, however, I cannot oblige. Whether I am right or wrong, I have been consistent regarding these points. Let me quote from an article I wrote 28 years ago: "The problem of oligopoly is by definition the problem of the effects of the actions of few, giving a greater importance to the behavior of each member of the group. . . . The theory of the oligopoly price involves an interpretation of the significant motives behind the actions of a small number of people. . . . Even the most superficial theory will have to include many more ideal types of behavior in order to handle the problem of *few* sellers than it takes to handle the problem of a *mass* of competitive sellers" [20, p. 235].

On the other hand, I must plead guilty to a charge of the same error of misplaced concreteness against which I have just warned. It occurred in a sentence in which I spoke of various magnitudes (subjectively) "perceived or fancied by the men whose decisions or actions are to be explained (the business men) . . ." [21, p. 521]. If this sentence referred only to oligopolistic or monopolistic behavior, it would not be so bad, for, as I said above, the theoretical constructs of decision-makers in this case have a closer correspondence to real businessmen than the constructs in the theory of competitive prices. But the sentence was supposed to apply to the constructs of the firm in any position whatever. Hence it was a misleading sentence in that (1) it gave the impression that the decision-makers in question were *real* men (real businessmen, whom you could interview) and (2) it said that the actions of these men were to be explained, whereas the purpose of the theory was not to explain observed actions but only observable *results* of imtgined (postulated) reactions to observable events.

I apologize for this error. Not that I do not approve of a busy shuttle-traffic between the domain of theoretical construction and the domain of empirical observation, but we must never fail to specify the side of the frontier on which we happen to be. The theoretical terms may have empirical referents (counterparts), but to believe, or allow an impression of belief, that the two are identical is a methodological fallacy.

[6] "When the conditions of competition are relaxed . . . the opportunity set of the firm is expanded. In this case, the behavior of the firm as a distinct operating unit is of separate interest. Both for purposes of interpreting particular behavior within the firm as well as for predicting responses of the industry aggregate, it may be necessary to identify the factors that influence the firm's choices within this expanded opportunity set and embed these in a formal model" [48, pp. 2-3].

"descriptively false." In view of this sentimental hankering for realism, it may be helpful to survey some of the inclusions which various writers have proposed in order to meet the demands for greater realism in the "theory of the firm," and to examine their relevance to the theory of competitive price. The following considerations are supposed to supplement, qualify, restrict, or replace the objective of maximizing money profits.

(1) Entrepreneurs and managers cannot be expected to have an inelastic demand for leisure; indeed, one must assume that this demand is income-elastic so that higher profit expectations will cause them to sacrifice some income for the sake of more leisure [36, p. 356]. (2) Managers are anxious to avoid resentment on the part of their colleagues and subordinates and will, therefore, not enforce their orders with the sternness required for maximization of profits; similarly, minor functionaries do not want to disturb the routines of their superiors and, hence, they often abstain from suggesting improvements which would maximize profits [31, p. 452]. (3) Managers are more interested in their own salaries, bonuses, and other emoluments, than in the profits of the firm or the income of its owners [27, pp. 226-27]. (4) The realization of certain asset preferences (for example, liquidity as against inventories and fixed assets) may be in conflict with profit maximization [5, p. 99]. (5) The flow and biased screening of information through the various levels of management may cause systematic misinformation resulting in earnings far below the maximum obtainable [27, p. 229]. (6) The objective of maintaining control in the hands of the present control group may require a sacrifice of profit opportunities [31, p. 455]. (7) The preference for security may be so strong that even relatively conservative ways of making higher profits are eschewed [12, pp. 270-71]. (8) The striving for status, power, and prestige may be such that it results in conduct not consistent with a maximum of profit [1, p. 145] [28, p. 207] [13, p. xii] [27, p. 227]. (9) The wish to serve society, be a benefactor, or soothe one's social conscience, may militate against actions or policies that would maximize profits [7, pp. 16-17] [13, pp. 339-40]. (10) The instinct of workmanship [46, p. 187], a desire to show professional excellence [1, p. 146], a pervasive interest in feats of engineering, may lead to performance in conflict with highest possible profits. (11) Compromises among the different goals of executives with different interests—production, sales, personnel relations, finance, research and development, public relations, etc.—are sure to "compromise" the objective of maximum profits [10, p. 29]. (12) A variety of influences may be exerted on management decisions, perhaps pulling in different directions and possibly away from maximum profits, as for example influences from labor organizations, suppliers of materials,

customers, bankers, government agencies [13, p. 340] [12, p. 270] [28, pp. 195-205].

I shall not prolong this catalogue even if it is far from complete. Let us admit that each of the possible deviations from maximum profit may be "real" in some circumstances. But how effective and significant are they? If the industry is effectively competitive—and it does not have to be "purely" competitive or "perfectly" competitive—is there much of a chance that the direction in which firms react, through their decisions regarding prices, inputs and output, to a change in conditions would be turned around by any of the "forces" listed? Before we say apodictically no, we should examine a few of the reservations.

Security and Managerial Coordination

Let us single out two items which have been given especially wide play: the "objective of security" and the question of "managerial coordination."

The demand for the recognition of a separate "security motive" conflicting with the profit motive deserves a good discussion. But when I prepared for it, I reread what I had written on this subject and found that I could not improve on it. Will you do me the favor of reading it [23, pp. 51-53 and 424-28] and, if you like it, make your students read it?

That there are no business profits without risks and that there is not much point in treating the two quite separately; that it would be silly to call a decision one of profit-maximizing if it increased risk and uncertainty so much as to reduce the chance of survival; that the notion of long-run profits comprises all considerations of risks of loss; that, in terms of my automobile-driving analogies, only a fool would assume that maximization of speed means driving 120 miles an hour regardless of curves and bumps; these are some of the things that have to be said in this connection. But the most essential point to be made is that in the economics of *adjustment to change* the issues of security, survival, and maximum profit are merged. How primitive again to confuse new ventures and daring moves with mere responses to stimuli, obvious reactions to change. If a change in conditions calls for a certain reaction in the name of maximum profits, the very same reaction is called for also in the name of security of survival.

The other matter is of a more "behavioral" nature: the coordination of different goals and judgments on the part of different members of the management and the deviations from profit maximization that may be involved in the process. Frankly, I cannot quite see what great difference organizational matters are supposed to make in the firm's price reactions to changes in conditions. Assume, for example, the import duties on foreign products competing with the products of domestic industry are raised, with a resulting increase in the demand for the products of the firm. Why should the clashes and compromises of divergent opinions reverse the direction of the change that would be "dictated" by the simple rule of profit maximization? Perhaps one vice president wants to raise prices without increasing output, while another wants to increase output without (at least at the moment) raising prices. No matter what their compromise will be, it is likely to conform with what the simple rule suggests. But if not, so what? Remember we are talking about industries with more than a few firms and with free entry.[7]

Other Qualifications to Competitive Price Theory

Substitution between income and leisure looks like the strongest reason for a qualification in cases in which the change in conditions is such that not only the locus of maximum profits is shifted but also the amount of profit obtainable is changed. Take again the example of a tariff increase shutting out foreign competition. The firms in the industry will find that given outputs will now fetch higher prices and that increased outputs can be sold at prices higher than those prevailing before tariffs were raised. And profits will be higher in any case, so that managers—even owner-managers—will be inclined to relax their efforts. Yet would anybody seriously argue that the substitution of leisure (coffee breaks, cocktail parties, golf) for potential profits would be such that total output would be reduced instead of increased? It is not a likely story, and where the industry consists of several or many firms, the small probability vanishes quickly. What remains of the argument is that total output would increase, in reaction to the tariff increase, somewhat less than it would if the managers were eager beavers and did not relax in their efforts when profits increased. Thus, the elasticity of supply of the products in question is a little smaller. But since we do not know how much it would be anyhow, the unknown substraction from an unknown number should not cause the economic theorist any serious anxieties. (And if the politicians who push for the tariff increase decide to push less hard if we tell them that their friends in the industry will enjoy some of the added protection in the form of more leisure and recreation, we would not really mind.)

Even if formal accuracy demanded that we accept the maximization of the decision-maker's total utility as the basic assumption, simplicity and fruitfulness speak for sticking with the postulate of maximization of money profits for situations in which competition is effective. The question is not whether the firms of the real world will *really* max-

[7] A great champion of more realistic theories of the firm summed up his reflections on their implications for general economics with this statement: "We shall not be far wrong in concluding . . . that the impact of more realistic theories of the firm on static price analysis is likely to be small" [6, p. 42].

imize money profits, or whether they even *strive* to maximize their money profits, but rather whether the *assumption* that this is the objective of the theoretical firms in the artificial world of our construction will lead to conclusions—"inferred outcomes"—very different from those derived from admittedly more realistic assumptions.

The second qualification in my list—regarding bosses, colleagues and subordinates—is quite irrelevant, except perhaps for questions of welfare economics, where it matters whether firms "really" do all they can to maximize efficiency. For theories concerned with *changes* in prices, inputs, and outputs in response to *changes* to conditions (of production, resource availability, and product demand) the strictness with which efficiency is watched in the firm does not matter. The effects of the tariff increase in our illustration, or the effects of changes in wage rates, interest rates, tax rates, and so forth, are if there is effective competition, essentially independent of the relations among the various levels in the managerial hierarchy of the firm.

It would take too much time here to go through our entire list of reservations. Anybody who makes the effort will find that some of the "realistic assumptions" proposed for inclusion in the theory can affect (by an unknown amount) the magnitude but not the direction of any change that is likely to result from a specified change in conditions; and that other assumptions will not even do that much. In short, they are all irrelevant for purposes of competitive price theory.

Oligopoly, Monopoly, and Managerial Discretion

I repeat: In the theory of competitive price the "real existence" of firms is irrelevant; imaginary (postulated) agents pursuing a simple (postulated) goal react to assumed changes in conditions and thereby produce (or allow us to infer) changes in prices, inputs, and outputs [24, pp. 13-14]. The correspondence between these inferences (deduced changes) and actual observations (observed changes in prices, inputs, and outputs, following observed changes in conditions) is close for two reasons: (1) The number of firms in the real world is so large that it suffices if some of them react as posited by the theory; and (2) the profits of firms are only about "normal," that is, excess profits are about zero, because of competitive pressures from newcomers (pliopolistic pressures [23, pp. 211-23]), so that profits below the maximum obtainable would in fact be net losses in an economic sense.

These two reasons do not hold in the theories of oligopoly and monopoly price.[8] For these theories the real existence of firms (that is, an

---

[8] The idea that profit maximization is the appropriate hypothesis for the theory of competitive price but not necessarily for the theory of monopoly or oligopoly price has been expressed repeatedly over the last century.

Pareto, for example, said that "pure economics" cannot tell us anything about the con-

empirical counterpart to the theoretical construct) is required, because the explanation of changes in prices, inputs, and outputs is at the same time an explanation of decisions of some particular firms, in the sense of organizations of men acting in particular, sometimes unpredictable, ways. Various attempts have been made to develop patterns of oligopolistic and monopolistic conduct and to correlate these patterns with types of organization or with types of personalities exercising ultimate decision-making power. The success has thus far been small; even if the decision-making (say, pricing) in a particular firm was sometimes satisfactorily modeled (for example, in a simulated computer program), the model has usually not been transferable to other cases, to predict decisions in other firms. I do not recall, moreover, that the behavior patterns in these cases were shown to be inconsistent with the postulate of profit maximization.

Under these circumstances, retreat to simpler, less realistic models of firms in oligopoly and monopoly positions is indicated. The first approach is to apply the polypolistic model, in full awareness that the actual facts are entirely different. In many instances the use of the polypolistic model for situations which in our judgment would merit to be labeled as oligopolistic will still yield satisfactory explanations and predictions. Where this is not so, the analyst will resort to the use of models of oligopolistic or monopolistic firms, postulating the simplest possible pattern of action and reaction, dispensing with all peculiar attitudes and "special" strategies. Only where these simple models of oligopolistic and monopolistic firms yield quite unsatisfactory predictions will the analyst need to go further, to more special types of behavior, provided he finds it worth while. It depends on the research interests and on the problems under examination how much effort one wishes to invest in behavioral research where the findings hold little promise of yielding generalizations of wide applicability.

There are, however, some simple models of oligopolistic behavior

---

tinuing shifts of position of competing oligopolists, and we have to turn to "the observation of facts," which would show us the variety of possibilities [29, pp. 601-2].

Schumpeter, in 1928, had this to say about the dichotomy: "We have much less reason to expect that monopolists will . . . charge an equilibrium price than we have in the case of perfect competition; for competing producers *must* charge it as a rule under penalty of economic death, whilst monopolists, although having a *motive* to charge the monopolistic equilibrium price, are not forced to do so, but may be prevented from doing so by other motives" [33, p. 371].

Finally, Scitovsky in 1951 stated that "not only does the monopolist's secure market position enable him to relax his efforts of maximizing profit, but his very position may prevent his aiming at maximum profit. He may regard his immunity from competition as precarious or be afraid of unfavorable publicity and public censure; and for either reason, he may judge it wiser to refrain from making full use of his monopoly position. We conclude, therefore, that although in some cases the monopolist will aim at maximizing his profit . . . in other cases—which may well be the important ones—he will refrain from maximizing profit" [37, p. 377].

which seem to be of sufficiently wide applicability. A model that equips the oligopolistic decision-maker not under heavy competitive pressure with an objective of gross-revenue ("sales") maximization, subject to the constraint of satisfactory net-revenue ("profit") [2, p. 49], succeeds in explaining the lack of response to some cost-increasing events observed in several instances. There are other simple models explaining the same phenomenon, and one may think of good reasons for finding one model or another more satisfactory. If the sales-maximization hypothesis can explain a greater variety of observed responses or nonresponses than other hypotheses can, and if it seems to correspond better with self-interpretations offered by interviewed businessmen, it merits acceptance, at least for the time being.

An alternative to the maximization of sales is the maximization of the growth rate of sales [3, p. 1086]. This hypothesis is especially interesting because it involves an endogenous relation with profits: while some of the growth of gross revenue may encroach on profits, it does so with an automatic limit in that profits are needed to finance the investment required for the growth of sales.

Another extension of the objective function proposed on the basis of behavioral research combines two managerial preferences for specific expenses of the firm with the usual profit motive. The two additional motives are expenditures for staff personnel and expenditures for managerial emoluments; both figure prominently in the utility functions of executives of companies which, sheltered from competitive pressures, make enough profits to allow management to indulge in these personal desires [48, pp. 38-60].

All these "managerial-discretion models" are simple and sufficiently general to allow relatively wide application. We shall have more to say about them later.

Effective Competition and Managerial Discretion

In mapping out the area of applicability for theories of managerial discretion, we have spoken of "oligopoly," "monopoly," and of "firms not under heavy competitive pressure." These are rather vague guideposts, but unfortunately the literature has not been very helpful in ascertaining precisely what it is that allows or restricts the exercise of wide managerial discretion.

Some writers stress the size of the firm, suggesting that it is only in the *large* firm that management can exercise discretion. Others stress the condition of *diffused ownership* as the one that affords management the opportunity of pursuing objectives other than maximization of profits. Those who stress oligopoly as the domain for which objective functions richer than profit maximization are needed are usually not quite specific as to their criterion of an oligopoly position: it may be *fewness of firms* active in the same industry, or the subjective state of awareness of the *interdependence of price making* often characterized as "conjectural variation," or simply the *absence of aggressive competition for increasing shares in the market*. Others again stress *closed entry,* or absence of newcomers' competition, as the essential condition for a profit level sufficiently comfortable to allow managers to indulge in the satisfaction of objectives other than maximization of profits.

To combine all these conditions would probably be far too restrictive; it would confine the application of managerial-discretion models to large firms with diffused ownership, few competitors, full awareness of interdependence in pricing, absence of agressive efforts by existing competitors to increase their market shares, and little danger of new competitors entering the field. The size of the firm may actually not be relevant, and diffused ownership may not be a necessary condition for some deviations from profit maximization to occur, say, in the interest of larger sales or larger expenditures for staff. Fewness of competitors may be more significant, chiefly because the danger of newcomers' competition is likely to be small where the number of firms has been few and continues to be few; partly also because the few competitors may have learnt that aggressive price competition does not pay. The essential conditions, it seems to me, are these two: that no newcomers are likely to invade the field of the existing firms, and that none of the existing firms tries to expand its sales at such a fast rate that it could succeed only by encroaching on the business of its competitors.

Competition from newcomers, from aggressive expansionists, or from importers is sometimes called "heavy," "vigorous," or "effective." The simplest meaning of these adjectival modifiers is this: a firm is exposed to heavy, vigorous, or effective competition if it is kept under continuing pressure to do something about its sales and its profits position. Under this "competitive pressure" the firm is constantly compelled to react to actual or potential losses in sales and/or reductions in profits, so much so that the firm will not be able to pursue any objectives other than the maximization of profits—for the simple reason that anything less than the highest obtainable profits would be below the rate of return regarded as normal at the time.

I am aware of a defect in this definition: its criterion is lodged in the effect rather than in an independently ascertainable condition. Perhaps, though, "effective" is quite properly defined in this fashion, namely, by whether certain effects are realized: competition is effective if it continually depresses profits to the level regarded as the minimum tolerable. What makes it effective is not part of the definition, but has to be explained by the conditions of entry, aggressive attitudes on the part of existing firms, or imports from abroad.

If my reasoning is accepted, several formulations proposed in the literature will have to be amended. Managerial discretion will be a function, not of the independence of the management from the control of the owners, but chiefly of the independence of the management from urgent worries about the sufficiency of earnings. If one insists, one may still say that all managers are primarily interested in their own incomes. But, since it is clear that their long-term incomes are jeopardized if profits go below the acceptable rate of return, maximization of managerial incomes and maximization of profits come to to the same thing if competition is effective.[9]

There can be no doubt about the fact that competition is not effective in many industries and that many, very many, firms are not exposed to vigorous competition. It follows that managerial discretion can have its way in a large enough number of firms to secure wide applicability of well-designed managerial-discretion models—or to invite the use of managerial total-utility models.

I was fully aware, when I wrote my 1946 article, that there were many qualifications and exceptions to the principle of profit maximization.[10] But I considered it hopeless for predictive purposes to work with total-utility maximization and I did not see the possibility of combining a few selected managerial goals with the profit motive.

Marginalism Extended: Total Utility

In order to show how hopeless it is to construct a comprehensive total-utility model and obtain from it definite predictions of the effects of changes in conditions upon the dispositions of the managers, one merely has to visualize the large variety of possible "satisfactions" and the still larger variety of things that may contribute to their attain-

[9] For competition to be effective it is not necessary that competition is either pure or perfect or that all or any of the markets in which the firm buys or sells are perfect.

[10] Several of my statements, if I presented them without source reference, might well be mistaken for quotations from critics of marginalism, including behavioralists and managerialists. Here are samples [21]: ". . . a business man is motivated by considerations other than the maximization of money profits"; "it is preferable to separate the nonpecuniary factors of business conduct from those which are regular items in the formation of money profits" (p. 526); "one may presume that producing larger production volumes [or] paying higher wage rates . . . than would be compatible with a maximum of money profits may involve for the business man a gain in social prestige or a certain measure of inner satisfaction"; "it is not impossible that considerations of this sort substantially weaken the forces believed to be at work on the basis of a strictly pecuniary marginal calculus"; for patriotic reasons during the war "many firms produced far beyond the point of highest money profits"; "the conflict of interests between the hired managers and the owners of the business" may call for "important qualifications" (p. 527); "the interest of the former in inordinately large outlays or investments may be capable of descriptions in terms of a pecuniary calculus, but it is not maximization of the firm's profits which serves here as the standard of conduct" (pp. 527-28); "maximization of salaries and bonuses of professional managers may constitute a standard of business conduct different from that implied in the customary marginal analysis of the firm"; and "the extent to which the two standards would result in sharply different action under otherwise similar conditions is another open question in need of investigation" (p. 528).

ment. The satisfactions consist not only in receiving money incomes, immediate or deferred, and various incomes in kind, but also in distributing incomes to others and in gaining prestige, power, self-esteem, as well as in enjoying a good conscience and other pleasurable feelings.

What makes things really complicated is that the creation of these satisfactions is related to very different flows of funds into and out of the firm: some to gross revenue (sales volume), others to net revenue; some to profits distributed, others to profits retained; some to investment outlays, others to company expenses. The managers' immediate money incomes and some of the emoluments received in kind are partly at the expense of profits, partly at the expense of corporate income taxes (and every change in tax rates changes the trade-off ratios.) The same is true of several other company expenses which add to the prestige, power, and self-esteem of the managers. Special mention may be made of the provision of stock options for managers, which are either at the expense of the owners' equity (through watering down their stock) or at the expense of potential capital gains on treasury stock earmarked for such stock options, but which, on the other hand, may be a powerful force aligning the managers' personal interests with the goal of maximizing the net profits of the firm.

The point of it all is that the total utility of managers can be increased by decisions which increase expenses at the expense of profits. (Of course, this is confined to situations where profits are high enough to stand encroachments by avoidable expenses—to situations, that is, where the firm is not hard-pressed by competition.) The question is how various changes in conditions will affect managerial decisions on inputs, outputs, and prices if the objectives of management include the gratification of preferences for certain expenses of the firm that compete with the maximization of profits.[11]

---

[11] Instead of cataloguing the various contributions to the "utility" of the management and their relationships to the sources and uses of the firm's funds, one may wish to classify the expenses of the firm with reference to "discretionary" decisions of the management influenced by the decision-makers' preferences. Here is a tentative classification of this sort:

1. Expenses required for the production of (*a*) current output of unchanged size, (*b*) additional current output, with marginal cost not exceeding marginal revenue (hence, contributing to higher profits), and (*c*) additional current output, with marginal cost exceeding marginal revenue (hence, reducing profits).

2. Expenses not required for the production of current output, but increasing the productive capacity or efficiency of the firm for future production.

3. Expenses for managerial personnel in the form of (*a*) salaries and bonuses, and (*b*) services rendered to them for their convenience and pleasure.

4. Expenses not required for either current or future production, but (*a*) expected of a profitable firm as a social service, and only slightly promoting the public image of management, (*b*) widely recognized as contributing to the social or national benefit and as indicative of the public spirit of the management, (*c*) contributing chiefly to the gratification of personal desires of supervisory and managerial personnel, and (*d*) largely

For purposes of illustration let us reproduce in a literary form the utility function of a management (perhaps of its "peak coordinator" [28, pp. 190-91]) in full control and confident that stockholders will not make any fuss as long as the firm makes a "normal" profit and pays out a fair share of it in dividends. Total utility, which the manager by his decisions will try to maximize, will be a function of a large number of variables, by virtue of the contributions they make to his pride, prestige, self-esteem, conscience, comfort, feeling of accomplishment, material consumption, and anticipations of future benefits and pleasures. Among the variables may be total profits of the firm, growth rate of profits, rate of profits to investment, total sales, growth rate of sales, increase in market share, dividends paid out, retained earnings, increase in market value of stock, price-earnings ratio of stock, investment outlay, salary and bonus received, stock options received (capital gains), expense accounts (consumption at company expense), services received (automobile, chauffeur, lovely secretary, theatre tickets, conferences at resorts), size of staff, expenses for public relations and advertising, expenses for research and development, technological and other innovations, leadership in wage increases and good industrial relations, expenses for public or private education and health, other contributions to public interest and patriotic causes, free time for leisure and recreation, and indications of influence over government, industry, and society. This list of variables is, of course, only representative, not exhaustive.[12]

Now what can one do with a utility function of this sort? Will it be of much use in telling us what the firm will do with its freedom of action if it has to respond to a change in conditions?

The answer will depend partly on a simple condition, namely, whether the acceptable trade-off ratios between all the factors contributing to total utility remain unchanged, or approximately the same, if any one of them, say, total profit, increases. If this were the case, we could shout hurrah or sigh a sigh of relief (depending on our temperament). For, if the marginal rates of substitution among all the various "utilifactors" are constant, the distribution of funds among them will remain unchanged with changes in conditions that increase or decrease the total of funds available. Only if the cost of any of the factors

wasteful, that is, contributing nothing, and economizing nothing but managerial effort or capability.

This list may be suggestive of the actions that may have to be taken when, after years of ease and growth, the firm finds its profits declining or disappearing.

[12] Perhaps there ought to be a place on the list for some gratifications that are more stable, less subject to quantitative variation, such as the pleasure of being known for honesty and fairness, on the one hand, and for sharpness and shrewdness, on the other, or at least the pleasure of being convinced of having and exercising these qualities. And last, though not least, there is the general feeling of gratification from "running" a large, well-known profitable, widely respected firm with growing assets and employment.

changed, say, the cost of staff personnel and, hence, the cost of prestige and other benefits that accrue from having a sizable staff, would the marginal rates of substitution be adapted to the new cost relation. In such a case we might also perhaps be able to tell the kind of response of the decision-makers.

Alas, the condition that the marginal rates of substitution are independent of the total funds available is not likely to be satisfied; in addition, certain types of change in conditions have the bad habit of affecting at the same time funds available and relative costs of utilifactors. For example, an increase in the corporate income tax will change the trade-off ratio between expensable outlays and profits in favor of avoidable expenses.

Marginalism Extended: Choice of Maximanda

If we were interested only in a formal solution, and perhaps in a proof of "existence" of an equilibrium position, we might be satisfied with the maximization of total utility by those who effectively run the firm. If, however, we want to predict the direction of the changes which a given change in conditions is likely to bring about, then mere formalism will not be enough. For predictive purposes we need *more* to go by with the help of *fewer* variables. Maximization of money profits is certainly the simplest "objective function," but it works only in the case of firms exposed to vigorous competition. The management of a firm that makes more than enough money need not go all out to maximize profits; it can afford to do a few other things that it likes, such as serving what by its own lights it regards as the national interest or indulging in other luxuries.

Would this imply "giving up" the principle of marginalism in the theory of the profitable firm? This is chiefly a semantic question. I have been inclined to use a more extended definition. In 1946, I called marginalism "the logical process of finding a maximum" [21, p. 519]. I did not say that it had to be maximization of money profits— though I struggled hard to justify the use of profit maximization in all cases. In the meantime several writers have shown that profit maximization may not be a completely unambiguous objective, even where it is used in splendid isolation from all competing goals, in that it may refuse to yield unambiguous conclusions regarding the effects of certain changes, such as the effects of changes in profit taxes. In addition, it has been shown that several workable "objective functions" can be developed that give plausible results with a few relatively simple terms added. Any of these functions that can be maximized, with or without specific constraints, would still be a part of marginal analysis.

The choice of the *maximandum* is of course a pragmatic matter: we should prefer one that yields sufficiently good approximations to what we consider reasonable on the basis of empirical research, with wide applicability and fruitfulness and with great simplicity. The compromise among these goals that we accept is, admittedly, a somewhat "subjective" standard of selection, but perfectly in line with the standard accepted in all scientific fields. Concessions to any one of these desiderata must be at the expense of the others.

Let us list some of the alternative *maximanda* that have been suggested and are available for our choice: Total quasi-rents over a short period of time (But how short? This is good only for a freshman course); total quasi-rents during the service-life of existing fixed assets (But is a replaceable part of a machine a fixed asset? This works only for a one-hoss shay); present value of all profits (after taxes) expected in the future, discounted at a "normal" or "competitive" rate; internal rate of return to equity; equity of controlling stockholders; present values of retained earnings; growth rate of equity; gross rate of total assets; growth rate of gross revenue (sales); gross revenue (sales), if net revenues (profits) are satisfactory (over what period of time?); salaries, bonuses, and other accruals (including services in kind) to management, over their entire lives; all accruals to management plus expenditure for staff personnel, compatible with minimum profits; all accruals to management, consistent with satisfactory profits and gradually rising prices of corporate stock; and, of course, the present values of the various combinations of flows mentioned.

Surely a much longer list could be prepared, but there is no use to this. The point should be clear: profit maximization proper may mean a variety of things—several entries apply to money profits—and in addition there are a few other *maximanda* of possible relevance. Incidentally, if profits or accruals to stockholders are not explicitly included in some of the entries, let no one believe that they are really out of the picture. No management could try to maximize its own accruals in the long run if it completely disregarded the interests of the stockholders. Hence, all *maximanda* are subject to the constraint of some minimum benefits to the owners of the business in the form of dividends, capital gains, or both.[18]

Subjective Information and the Charge of Tautology

I have a few remaining tasks, and one of them is to lay a ghost, one that has long played tricks on economists and led them astray. He has

[18] The four "managerial" variables included in the list—sales, growth of sales, expenses for staff, and emoluments to the management—may well be the most important deviations from profit maximization, although I may easily be persuaded of the existence of other "extravagances" of management. Among the managements of our large corporations there are so many civic-minded men, bursting with social responsibility and cocksure of their ability to know what is in the national interest, that I incline to the thought that rather serious deviations from the profit motive occur in the area of virtuous striving for the so-called

done this in their discussions of the subject of information, its availability, its uncertainty, and its subjectivity. I mean, of course, information available to the "firm," and this raises the question whether we mean the firm as a purely theoretical construct or the firm as an organization of real people or anything else.

The firm as a theoretical construct has exactly the kind of information the theorist chooses to endow it with in order to design a good, useful theory. The firm as an organization of real people has the information system that it actually happens to have and which, in some instances, the management scientists (operations researchers) have succeeded in developing. For purposes of competitive price and allocation theory, it does not make much difference whether the information which we assume the firm to have concerning the conditions of supply, production, and demand under which it works is correct or incorrect, as long as we may safely assume that any *change* in these conditions is registered correctly. If we want to inquire into the effects of a change in wage rates or tax rates or something of this sort, we must of course take it for granted that the decision-makers who supposedly react to the change have taken notice of it. But whether their "previous" store of information—from which they started when the change occurred—was accurate or not will only in exceptional instances make a qualitative difference to the reactions.

This important difference between information about conditions and information about changes in conditions has eluded several writers, who shouted "tautology" when they confronted my statements about the subjectivity of information. They reasoned like this: If firms act on the basis of information which is entirely subjective, then *anything* they do may be said to follow from whatever they believe they know: hence, the assumption of subjectivism defeats any explanatory purposes. This is a sad confusion. In teaching elementary economics we ought to be able to make our students grasp the difference between the shape and position of a curve, on the one hand, and the shift of a curve, on the other. The direction of the effects which we derive from the shift is usually, though not always, independent of the shape and position of the original curve. We need not fuss about the curve reflecting "accurate information" if we only want to see what happens when the curve shifts in a certain direction.

---

common good. I hope I am not excessively naive if I believe that the excess profits secured through restrictions on competition are to no small extent used for what the discretionary managers believe to be worthy causes. But I see no way of formulating any hypotheses that would enable us to predict either just what the firms' outlays in the public interest will be or how they will affect total output in the long run. I suppose that Boulding's witty question, "do we maximize profit subject to the constraints of morality or do we maximize virtue subject to the constraints of satisfactory profits? [7, p. 17] was not intended to suggest an answer with empirically fertile conclusions.

Since ghosts are hardy creatures, the laying of this one will probably not constitute a once-and-for-all execution. We shall probably see him again thumbing his nose at us in the next textbook or in the next issue of one of our journals.

Imperfect Information and the Question of "Satisficing" Behavior

The same confusion sometimes encumbers the discussions about the alleged "imperfection" of knowledge available to firms for their rational decision-making [39, pp. xxiv-xxvi, 40-41, 81-83, 241-42] and the screens and blockages in "the flow of information through the hierarchies of the organization" [27, pp. 228-29]. But what can be "imperfect" about the information on, say, a tax increase? Why should it take special theories of bureaucracy to explain how the news of a wage increase "flows" through various hierarchical levels up or down or across? Yet this, and this alone, is the information that is essentially involved in the theory of prices and allocation, since it is the *adjustment to such changes* in conditions for which the postulate of maximizing behavior is employed.

One can understand, of course, how the confusion arose. The proponents of managerial analysis have the creditable ambition to reorganize firms in such a way that their managements can really, as a matter of actual fact, maximize the results of their performance, not only in adjusting to changes in conditions, but also in making the most rational arrangements on the basis of the *complete environment* in which they operate.[14] Incidentally, not only "normative micro-economics," as management science has been called [40, p. 279], has this ambition; many propositions of welfare economics are also based on such presuppositions.

As a matter of fact, the interesting distinction made between "satisficing" and "maximizing" or "optimizing" behavior [39, pp. xxiv-xxvi] [40, pp. 262-65] had its origin in precisely the same issue; management, realizing the complexity of the calculations and the imperfection of the data that would have to be employed in any determination of "optimal" decisions, cannot help being satisfied with something less: its behavior will be only "satisficing." What behavior? The mere adjustment to a simple change or the coordinated, integrated whole of its activities? Evidently, only the latter is the overly ambi-

---

[14] "Economic man deals with the 'real world' in all its complexity," says Herbert Simon [39, p. xxv]. The *homo oeconomicus* I have encountered in the literature was not such a perfectionist. Incidentally, even Simon's "economic man," two years before the ambitious one just quoted, did not have "absolutely complete," but only "impressively clear and voluminous" knowledge of the "relevant aspects of his environment" [38, p. 99]. My point is that we ought to distinguish perfect or imperfect knowledge of (a) the entire environment, (b) the relevant aspects of the entire environment, (c) the relevant changes in environmental conditions.

tious aim. The theory of prices and allocation, viewed as a theory of adjustment to change, does not call for impossible performances.[15] I ask you to remember what I spelled out, twenty years ago, about the difference between exact estimates and calculations, on the one hand, and "sizing up" in nonnumerical terms, on the other [21, pp. 524-25, 534-35]. And I ask you to realize how many more good predictions can be made on the basis of the assumption that firms try to maximize their profits than on the basis of the assumption that they want no more than satisfactory profits. Take one illustration: if an easy-money policy is introduced, we expect that some firms will increase their borrowings, some firms will increase their purchases, some firms will sell at higher prices, and some firms will increase their output. But if everybody was satisfied before the change, we cannot infer any of these things. On the other hand, if we assume that firms prefer a larger profit to a smaller one, all the mentioned consequences follow from the simple model.

The Twenty-one Concepts of the Firm

Several times in this paper I have spoken of the fallacy of misplaced concreteness, committed by mistaking a thought-object for an object of sense perception, that is, for anything in the real, empirical world. My warnings might have given rise to another confusion, namely, that there are only two concepts of the firm. There are many more, and I do not wish to suppress altogether my strong taxonomic propensities. I shall offer a list of ten different contexts calling for even more different concepts, some theoretical, some more empirical.

One of my favorite philosophers, who was a past-master of the art of making fine distinctions, enumerated 13 concepts of "pragmatism" [18], 66 concepts of "nature" [19, pp. 447-56], and "a great number" of concepts of "God."[16] I am sure there are at least 21 concepts of the firm employed in the literature of business and economics,

---

[15] Suppose the government imposes a 15 per cent surcharge on all import duties. The theory of the profit-maximizing firm will without hesitation tell us that imports will decline. What will the theory of the satisficing firm tell us? "Models of satisficing behavior are richer than models of maximizing behavior, because they treat not only of equilibrium but of the method of reaching it as well. Psychological studies of the formation and change of aspiration levels support propositions of the following kinds. (a) When performance falls short of the level of aspiration, search behavior (particularly search for new alternatives of action) is induced. (b) At the same time, the level of aspiration begins to adjust itself downward until goals reach levels that are practically attainable. (c) If the two mechanisms just listed operate too slowly to adapt aspirations to performance, emotional behavior—apathy or aggression, for example—will replace rational adaptive behavior" [40, p. 263]. I admit that this is an unfair use of the theory of satisficing, but I wanted to show that everything has its place and no theory can be suitable to all problems. I suspect, however, that Simon's theory of satisficing behavior will yield neither quantitative nor qualitative predictions.

[16] Lovejoy Denied Approval by Senate Group," *The Baltimore Sun*, April 1, 1951.

but I shall exercise great forbearance and confine myself to a selection. Everyone may join in the game and fill in what I leave out. I shall first state the context, then delimit the concept, and finally add a few words of explanation.

1. In the theory of competitive prices and allocation, the firm is *an imaginary reactor to environmental changes*. By "imaginary" I mean to stress that this a pure construct for which there need not exist an empirical counterpart. By "reactor" I mean to deny that this robot or puppet can ever have a will of his own: he is the theorist's creature, programmed to respond in the predetermined way.

2. In the theory of innovation and growth, the firm is *an imaginary or a typical reactor or initiator*. Depending on which theory one has in mind, we see that several combinations are possible. In the theory of "entrepreneurial innovation" by men of very special qualities [34, pp. 78-94] the entrepreneur is neither imaginary nor a mere reactor; he is a typical initiator. By "typical" I do not refer to the ideal type of German sociology [47, p. 44] [35, pp. 20-63, 81] [25, pp. 21-57], but rather to the common-sense kind of person that many of us have met in person or, at least, have heard about. On the other hand, there are also theories of "induced invention"—assuming latent inventiveness (though an invention can never be a mere reaction)—and theories of "induced growth," employing the construct of the imaginary reactor.

3. In welfare economics, the firm is *an imaginary or a typical reactor or initiator with accurate knowledge of his opportunities*. Depending on the proposition in question, all combinations are again possible, but in any case a new requirement is introduced: accurate knowledge of the environmental conditions on the part of all reactors and initiators. For, in contrast to the theory of price and allocation, the welfare theorist wants to ascertain, not only in which direction price, input, and output will move in response to a change, but also whether this move will increase or reduce welfare. For such an exercise it is no longer irrelevant whether the subjective information of the firms is correct or false.

4. In the theory of oligopoly and monopoly, the firm is *a typical reactor and initiator in a small (or zero) interacting group*. I have explained earlier why a theory of oligopoly with nothing but imaginary reactors may not be widely applicable.

5. In the theory of organization (or bureaucracy), the firm is *a typical cooperative system with authoritative coordination*. I have accepted this formulation from one of the authorities [28, p. 187] and thus may disclaim responsibility for it.

6. In management science (or the art of business management), the firm is *a functional information system and decision-making system*

for typical business operations. The normative nature of management science should be stressed. Several management scientists include operations research among the agenda of management science. I take this to mean that the principal techniques of operations research of such matters as inventory problems, replacement problems, search problems, queueing problems, and routing problems have to be mastered by the management scientist. He should, however, make a distinction between the science and its application: the science deals with typical systems, but is applied to particular cases.

7. In operations research and consultation, the firm is *an actual or potential client for advice on optimal performance*. In this context the reference is not to the techniques and principles of operations research but rather to the particular projects planned or undertaken.

8. In accounting theory, the firm is *a collection of assets and liabilities*. It should be clear how different this concept is from most of the others.

9. In legal theory and practice, the firm is *a juridical person with property, claims, and obligations*. This may be a very deficient formulation; I defer to the experts, who will surely correct it.

10. In statistical description (such as the Census of Manufactures) the firm is *a business organization under a single management or a self-employed person with one or more employees or with an established place of business*. I have adopted here the definition used by the U.S. Census.

This exercise should have succeeded in showing how ludicrous the efforts of some writers are to attempt *one* definition of *the* firm as used in economic analysis, or to make statements supposedly true of "the" firm, or of "its" behavior, or what not. Scholars ought to be aware of equivocations and should not be snared by them.

A Sense of Proportion

I hope there will be no argument about which concept of the firm is the most important or the most useful. Since they serve different purposes, such an argument would be pointless. It would degenerate into childish claims about one area of study being more useful than another.

I also hope the specialist who uses one concept of the firm will desist from trying to persuade others to accept his own tried and trusted concept for entirely different purposes. The concept of the firm in organization theory, for example, need not at all be suitable for accounting theory or legal theory; and I know it is not suitable for either competitive price theory or for oligopoly theory.

Most of the controversies about the "firm" have been due to misunderstandings about what the other specialist was doing. Many people cannot understand that others may be talking about altogether different things when they use the same words.

I am not happy about the practice of calling any study just because it deals with or employs a concept of the firm "economics" or "microeconomics." But we cannot issue licenses for the use of such terms and, hence, must put up with their rather free use. My own prejudices balk at designating organization theory as economics—but other people's prejudices are probably different from mine, and we gain little or nothing from arguing about the correct scope of our field.

Now what conclusions from all our reviewing may we draw on the conflicts between marginal analysis, behavioral theory, and managerial theory of the firm? Fortunately, not much time is being wasted on descriptive studies of a narrowly behaviorist kind, in the sense of recording observed behavior without any prior theoretical design. Most proponents of behavioral studies of the firm are too competent theorists for that. As far as the proponents of managerial theories are concerned, they have never claimed to be anything but marginalists, and the behavior goals they have selected as worthy for incorporation into behavior equations, along with the goal of making profits, were given a differentiable form so that they could become part of marginal analysis.[17] Thus, instead of a heated contest between marginalism and managerialism in the theory of the firm, a marriage between the two has come about.

Not all marriages, these days, are permanent; divorces are frequent. Whether this marriage will last or end in divorce will depend chiefly on what offspring it will produce. If the match of the profit hypothesis with the various managerial hypotheses proves fertile of sufficiently interesting deductions, the prospects of a lasting marriage are good.

It is not easy to judge the future sterility or fertility of this marriage between marginalism and managerialism, because most of us are inclined to underrate the kinds of problem on which we have never

---

[17] While under profit maximization $MR - MC = 0$, sales maximization requires that $MR = 0$; hence, for some of the output sold marginal revenue is less than marginal cost, which cuts into profits. A minimum-profit constraint sets a limit to this.

In the case of maximization of the growth rate of sales the limit on nonremunerative selling is built into the objective itself because a growth of productive assets is required to support the growth of sales, and the acquisition of these assets presupposes a sufficiency of profits, either for internal financing or as a basis for outside finance [3, pp. 1086-87]. If at any time sales were pushed too hard at the expense of profits, there would arise a shortage of funds for acquiring the productive assets needed for producing more output. Thus no separate minimum-profit constraint has to be imposed, since it is inherent in the objective of maximization of the growth of sales. It should be understood, however, that the growth rate of assets under this objective is still less than it could be under straight profit maximization. (This shows why we should never speak of the "growth of the firm" without specifying by what criterion we measure it.)

worked: we have a bias in favor of our own research experience. Most of the researchers on behavioral versions of the theory of the firm look for their problems to the records of selected large corporations. They take it for granted that their theory must be designed to explain and predict the behavior of these firms. This, however, is less so in the case of economists engaged in the analysis of relative prices, inputs, and outputs. They look for their problems to the records of entire industries or industrial sectors. To be sure, some industries are dominated by large corporations, yet the accent of the analysis is not on the behavior of these firms but at best on some of the results of that behavior. Where the focus is not on the behavior of the firm, a theory that requires information on particular firms to be "plugged in" seems to them less serviceable than a more general theory, at least as long as only qualitative, not numerical, results are sought. Hence, even if the "partial-equilibrium analyst" knows full well that the actual situation is not a really competitive one, he probably will still make a first try using the competitive model with good old-fashioned profit maximization. And if the results appear too odd, appropriate qualifications may still be able to take care of them more simply than if he had started with a cumbersome managerial model. (In saying this, I am showing my bias.)

It is revealing to ask what kind of theory we would apply, at least in a first approximation, if we were called upon to predict the results of various kinds of public-policy measures. For questions regarding short-run effects of changes in the corporation income tax (or an excess-profits tax) I believe a strong case can be made in favor of a model of the firm with some managerial variables. If the problem is whether an increase in cigarette taxes is likely to be fully shifted onto the consumer or what portion of it may be absorbed by the producers, I may feel safer with a model that includes managerial objectives. If, however, the problem is what qualitative effects an increase in the import duty on a material used in several industries will have on its imports and on the prices and outputs of the various products of the industries in question, I would be inclined to work with the simple hypothesis of profit maximization. I would find it far too cumbersome in this case to go down to the level of the "real" firms; I could probably not obtain the necessary data and, even if I did, I might not be able to rely on the composite results obtained from a firm-by-firm analysis. The old theory of the firm, where all firms are pure fictions, may give me—in this case—most of the answers, in a rough and ready way, not with any numerical precision, but with sufficient reliability regarding the directions of change.

I conclude that the choice of the theory has to depend on the problem we have to solve.[18] Three conditions seem to be decisive in assigning the type of approach to the type of problem. The simple marginal formula based on profit maximization is suitable where (1) *large groups* of firms are involved and nothing has to be predicted about particular firms, (2) the effects of a *specified change* in conditions upon prices, inputs, and outputs are to be explained or predicted rather than the values of these magnitudes before or after the change, and nothing has to be said about the "total situation" or general developments, and (3) only *qualitative answers*, that is, answers about directions of change, are sought rather than precise numerical results. Managerial marginalism is more suitable to problems concerning particular firms and calling for numerical answers. And, I am sure, there are also some problems to which behavioral theory may be the most helpful approach. My impression is that it will be entirely concerned with particular firms and perhaps designed to give answers of a normative, that is, advisory nature.

It looks as if I had prepared the ground for a love feast: I have made polite bows in all directions and have tuned up for a hymn in praise of peaceful coexistence of allegedly antagonistic positions. But I cannot help raising a question which may tear open some of the wounds of the battle of 1946. The question is whether the effects of an effective increase in minimum wages upon the employment of labor of low productivity can, at our present state of knowledge, be fruitfully analyzed with any other model than that of simple marginalism based on unadulterated profit maximization.

If I answer in the negative, does this mean that we are back at the old quarrel and have not learned anything? It does not mean this. Deficiencies in marginal analysis have been shown and recognized; and a great deal of good empirical as well as theoretical work has been accomplished. But the deficiencies dealt with were not just those which the critics twenty years ago attacked. That attack questioned the applicability of marginal analysis to the employment effects of wage increases in industries with many firms presumably under heavy competition [16, pp. 64, 75-77]. In such circumstances the managerial theories of the firm, according to their proponents, do not apply. On this narrow issue, therefore, the old-type marginalist cannot retreat.

[18] As a matter of fact, it will also depend on the research techniques which the appointed analyst has learned to master; we can eliminate this bias by assuming an ideal analyst equally adept in all techniques.

REFERENCES

1. C. I. BARNARD, *Functions of the Executive*. Cambridge, Mass. 1938.
2. W. J. BAUMOL, *Business Behavior, Value and Growth*. New York 1959.

3. ———, "On the Theory of the Expansion of the Firm," *Am. Econ. Rev.*, Dec. 1962, *52*, 1078-87.

4. ———, *Economic Theory and Operations Analysis*, 2nd ed. Englewood Cliffs, N.J. 1965.

5. K. E. BOULDING, *A Reconstruction of Economics*. New York 1950.

6. ———, "Implications for General Economics of More Realistic Theories of the Firm," *Am. Econ. Rev.*, Proc., May 1952, *42*, 35-44.

7. ———, "Present Position of the Theory of the Firm," in K. E. Boulding and W. A. Spivey, *Linear Programming and the Theory of the Firm*, New York 1960, pp. 1-17.

8. E. H. CHAMBERLIN, *The Theory of Monopolistic Competition; A Reorientation of the Theory of Value*. Cambridge, Mass. 1933.

9. A. A. COURNOT, *Recherches sur les principes mathématiques de la théorie des richesses*, Paris 1838. English transl. by N. T. Bacon under the title *Researches into the Mathematical Principles of the Theory of Wealth*, New York 1897, reprinted 1927.

10. R. M. CYERT AND J. G. MARCH, *Behavioral Theory of the Firm*. Englewood Cliffs, N.J. 1963.

11. S. M. DANCOFF, "Does the Neutrino Really Exist?" *Bull. Atomic Scientists*, June 1952, *8*, 139-41.

12. R. A. GORDON, "Short-Period Price Determination in Theory and Practice," *Am. Econ. Rev.*, June 1948, *38*, 265-88.

13. ———, *Business Leadership in the Large Corporation*, 2nd ed. with a new preface, Berkeley 1961.

14. R. L. HALL AND C. J. HITCH, "Price Theory and Business Behaviour," *Oxford Econ. Papers*, May 1939, *2*, 12-45. Reprinted in T. Wilson, ed., *Oxford Studies in the Price Mechanism*, Oxford 1951, pp. 107-38.

15. S. R. KRUPP, "Theoretical Explanation and the Nature of the Firm," *Western Econ. Jour.*, Summer 1963, *1*, 191-204.

16. R. A. LESTER, "Shortcomings of Marginal Analysis for Wage-Employment Problems," *Am. Econ. Rev.*, March 1946, *36*, 63-82.

17. ———, "Marginalism, Minimum Wages, and Labor Markets," *Am. Econ. Rev.*, March 1947, *37*, 135-48.

18. A. O. LOVEJOY, "The Thirteen Pragmatisms," *Jour. Philosophy*, Jan. 2, 1908, *8*, 5-12, 29-39. Reprinted in *The Thirteen Pragmatisms and Other Essays*, Baltimore 1963.

19. A. O. LOVEJOY AND G. BOAS, *Primitivism and Related Ideas in Antiquity*. Baltimore 1935.

20. F. MACHLUP, "Evaluation of the Practical Significance of the Theory of Monopolistic Competition," *Am. Econ. Rev.*, June 1939, *29*, 277-36.

21. ———, "Marginal Analysis and Empirical Research," *Am. Econ. Rev.*, Sept. 1946, *36*, 519-54.

22. ———, "Rejoinder to an Antimarginalist," *Am. Econ. Rev.*, March 1947, *37*, 148-54.

23. ———, *The Economics of Sellers' Competition*. Baltimore 1952.

24. ———, "The Problem of Verification in Economics," *So. Econ. Jour.*, July 1955, *22*, 1-21.

25. ———, "Idealtypus, Wirklichkeit, und Konstruktion," *Ordo,* 1960-1961, 21-57.
26. ———, *Essays on Economic Semantics.* Englewood Cliffs, N.J. 1963.
27. R. J. MONSEN AND A. DOWNS, "A Theory of Large Managerial Firms," *Jour. Pol. Econ.,* June 1965, *73,* 221-36.
28. A. G. PAPANDREOU, "Some Basic Problems in the Theory of the Firm," in B. F. Haley, ed., *A Survey of Contemporary Economics,* Vol. II, Homewood, Ill. 1952, pp. 183-219.
29. V. PARETO, *Manuel d'économie politique,* 2nd ed. Paris 1927.
30. K. R. POPPER, *Conjectures and refutations.* New York and London 1962.
31. M. REDER, "A Reconsideration of the Marginal Productivity Theory," *Jour. Pol. Econ.,* Oct. 1947, *55,* 450-58.
32. J. ROBINSON, *The Economics of Imperfect Competition.* London 1933.
33. J. A. SCHUMPETER, "The Instability of Capitalism," *Econ. Jour.,* Sept. 1928, *38,* 361-86.
34. ———, *The Theory of Economic Development.* Cambridge, Mass. 1934.
35. A. SCHUTZ, *Collected Papers,* Vol. II. The Hague 1964.
36. T. SCITOVSKY, "A Note on Profit Maximisation and its Implications," *Rev. Econ. Stud.,* Winter 1943, *11,* 57-60. Reprinted in AEA, *Readings in Price Theory,* Homewood, Ill. 1952, pp. 352-58.
37. ———, *Welfare and Competition.* Chicago 1951.
38. H. A. SIMON, "A Behavioral Model of Rational Choice," *Quart. Jour. Econ.,* Feb. 1955, *69,* 99-118.
39. ———, *Administrative Behavior,* 2nd ed. New York 1957.
40. ———, "Theories of Decision-Making in Economics and Behavioral Science," *Am. Econ. Rev.,* June 1959, *49,* 253-83.
41. H. VON STACKELBERG, *Marktform und Gleichgewicht.* Vienna 1934.
42. L. J. STADLER, "The Gene," *Science,* Nov. 19, 1954, *120,* 811-19.
43. G. J. STIGLER, "The Economics of Minimum Wage Legislation," *Am. Econ. Rev.,* June 1946, *36,* 358-65.
44. ———, "Professor Lester and the Marginalists," *Am. Econ. Rev.,* March 1947, *37,* 154-57.
45. H. B. THORELLI, "The Political Economy of the Firm: Basis for a New Theory of Competition?" *Schweiz Zeitschr. Volkswirtschaft und Stat.,* 1965, *101,* 248-62.
46. T. VEBLEN, *The Instinct of Workmanship and the State of the Industrial Arts.* New York 1914.
47. M. WEBER, *On the Methodology of the Social Sciences,* transl. and ed. by E. A. Shils and H. A. Finch, Glencoe, Ill. 1949.
48. O. E. WILLIAMSON, *Economics of Discretionary Behavior: Managerial Objectives in a Theory of the Firm.* Englewood Cliffs, N.J. 1964.

PART THREE

MACROECONOMICS

[16]

THE JOURNAL OF
POLITICAL ECONOMY

Volume 43	**OCTOBER 1935**	*Number 5*

PROFESSOR KNIGHT AND THE "PERIOD OF PRODUCTION"

FRITZ MACHLUP
University of Buffalo

THE past few years have been prolific of contributions about "capital and the period of production."[1] Any increase in the output of such contributions certainly takes place under increasing cost (because it is necessary for the writer to study all his predecessors' products), and, probably, under decreasing return. Nevertheless, there seems to be good reason for submit-

[1] Frank H. Knight, "Capitalistic Production, Time, and the Rate of Return," *Economic Essays in Honour of Gustav Cassel* (London, 1933); "Capital, Time, and the Interest Rate," *Economica*, August, 1934; "Professor Hayek and the Theory of Investment," *Economic Journal*, March, 1935; F. A. von Hayek, "Capital and Industrial Fluctuations," *Econometrica*, April, 1934; "On the Relationship between Investment and Output," *Economic Journal*, June, 1934; Martin Hill, "The Period of Production and Industrial Fluctuations," *ibid.*, December, 1933; C. H. P. Gifford, "The Concept of the Length of the Period of Production," *ibid.;* "The Period of Production under Continuous Input and Point Output in an Unprogressive Community," *Econometrica*, April, 1935; J. Marschak, "A Note on the Period of Production," *Economic Journal*, March, 1934; K. E. Boulding, "The Application of the Pure Theory of Population Change to the Theory of Capital," *Quarterly Journal of Economics*, August, 1934; Wassily Leontief, "Interest on Capital and Distribution: A Problem in the Theory of Marginal Productivity," *Quarterly Journal of Economics*, November, 1934; R. F. Fowler, *The Depreciation of Capital, Analytically Considered* (London, 1934); Erich Schiff, *Kapitalbildung und Kapitalaufzehrung im Konjunkturverlauf* (Vienna, 1933); Richard von Strigl, "Lohnfonds und Geldkapital," *Zeitschrift für Nationalökonomie*, January, 1934; *Kapital und Produktion* (Vienna, 1934); Walter Eucken, *Kapitaltheoretische Untersuchungen* (Jena, 1934); Karl H. Stephans,

577

ting another unit of product. In a series of ingenious articles[2] Professor Knight has proposed to discard as worthless some tools of economic analysis which I consider indispensable for successful handling of certain problems. The tools he wants to scrap are those concepts which have been used in capital theory under different names, such as "length of the production process," "roundaboutness of production," "period of waiting," "period of production," "period of investment," "time structure of production," "period of maturing," and similar terms. Professor Knight's opinion has great weight with every serious student of economics; if the disputed concepts are to be rehabilitated, Professor Knight's criticism must be answered. This will be attempted here, partly with explicit reference to the contentions of Professor Knight, partly by way of general discussion of the concepts and the problems involved. An effort will be made, upon this occasion, to clear up a number of obscurities and ambiguities connected with the theory of capital "promulgated by Böhm-Bawerk and his followers and generally accepted and taught in the past generation."[3]

I. IS CAPITAL PERPETUAL?

1. *Stationary, growing, or retrograde economy.*—The usefulness, or even necessity, for economic theory of the conception of a "stationary economy" cannot be seriously questioned. This concep-

---

"Zur neueren Kapitaltheorie," *Weltwirtschaftliches Archiv*, January, 1935. The following articles come to my attention too late to be taken account of in the present analysis: Howard S. Ellis, "Die Bedeutung der Produktionsperiode für die Krisentheorie," *Zeitschrift für Nationalökonomie*, June, 1935; M. Joseph and K. Bode, "Bemerkungen zur Kapital- und Zinstheorie," *Zeitschrift für Nationalökonomie*, June, 1935; Oskar Morgenstern, "Zur Theorie der Produktionsperiode," *Zeitschrift für Nationalökonomie*, June, 1935; Richard von Strigl, "Zeit und Produktion," *Zeitschrift für Nationalökonomie*, June, 1935; Ragnar Nurkse, "The Schematic Representation of the Structure of Production," *Review of Economic Studies*, June, 1935. Besides the published material, manuscripts by F. A. von Hayek and an unpublished discussion in correspondence between G. von Haberler, F. A. von Hayek, J. Marschak, L. von Mises, and myself were drawn upon in writing this article.

[2] Besides the three articles by Professor Knight listed in the last footnote, see also his paper, "The Ricardian Theory of Production and Distribution," in the *Canadian Journal of Economics and Political Science*, February, 1935.

[3] Knight, *Economic Journal*, XLV (March, 1935), 79.

THE "PERIOD OF PRODUCTION"   579

tion is inseparably bound up with the application of the method of variation in economics. One cannot arrive at any conclusion about the effects of any change if the "other" (independent) things (or conditions) are not set "invariant" or assumed to be unchanged. Thus, in a discussion of the effects of a certain "shift in demand," or of a changed supply of money, or of better crops, or of any other "substantive" change, one conveniently starts out with the assumption that the supply of "capital" does not change independently at the same time. One of the greatest difficulties in our theory, the problem of "maintaining capital intact," is, of course, evaded by assuming a stationary economy, but this can be considered permissible for certain problems. There is, however, one problem in the discussion of which the simple assumption of the stationary state is not permissible, namely, the problem of the capital stock or capital structure itself. To assume perfect maintenance of capital where one should discuss the conditions of such maintenance is a case of begging the question, or, at least, of avoiding the problem which is to be solved.

A statement such as "all capital is inherently perpetual"[4] is of doubtful value. If it is limited to the case of an economy which is assumed to maintain, or to add to, its capital, it is but a repetition of the assumption. If it is stated as a fact, it is wrong. If we define a stationary economy as one which (perhaps among other things) maintains its capital, and if we call capital "perpetual" when it is (at least) maintained, then the assertion that for a stationary economy all capital is inherently perpetual obviously means no more than that an economy which maintains its capital maintains its capital. Much more important is the question whether economies always maintain their capital, and under what conditions they do so.

Professor Knight thinks he is warranted in asserting "the *fact* of perpetuity."[5] He adds, however: "Unless society as a whole becomes decadent with respect to its stock of capital, no increment of capital viewed as a quantity ever is disinvested."[6] This "un-

---

[4] Knight, *Economica*, August, 1934, p. 264.

[5] *Canadian Journal*, February, 1935, p. 15 (italics are his).

[6] *Ibid.*, p. 15.

less" qualification reduces the "fact" again to tautology. (Unless society acts differently it acts in the asserted way.) In other places the "fact of perpetuity" is stated in a less safe—because less tautological—formulation.[7] There was and is always the choice between maintaining, increasing, or consuming capital. And past and "present" experience tells us that the decision in favor of consumption of capital is far from being impossible or improbable.[8] Capital is not necessarily perpetual.

2. *Individual disinvestment, social disinvestment.*—In a "capitalistic society," in which property is owned privately, the process of capital disinvestment is the result of action or inaction of individuals, under the influence of their personal preferences or of certain institutional forces or of state interference.[9] It must be clear that at any moment of time the alternatives are open to change in either direction, or to leave unchanged the relation between the current stream of consumption income and the future stream of consumption income, the latter partly being represented in the existing capital (which is the "capitalized" value of future income). The conditions under which such alternatives can be realized are dependent on the given production structure of the whole community and on the simultaneous choices on the part of the other individuals within the community. Dissaving and disinvesting by one individual can be offset by saving and investing by another individual, in which case the individual disinvestment does not become social disinvestment. That "in a stationary or growing society disinvestment by an individual owner in no wise involves actual reconversion of 'capital' into income"[10] is again nothing but a tautology. It is just the relation of the total amounts of capital individually disinvested to the total amounts

[7] "Capital is perpetual in so far as economic principles obtain and economic reasoning is applicable" (*Economica*, August, 1934, p. 277); or, "in a society which is not planning for the end of all things, all property income is perpetual" (*ibid.*, p. 268). Neither of the two contentions seems to be correct. Economic reasoning can be perfectly well applied to an economy which consumes parts of its capital. Nor is it necessary that such a society plan for "the end of the world."

[8] For an illustration of a case of capital consumption see my article, "The Consumption of Capital in Austria," *Review of Economic Statistics*, January, 1935.

[9] *Ibid.*   [10] Knight, *Economica*, August, 1934, p. 273.

of capital individually invested at any moment of time which makes society stationary, growing, or retrograde.

The problem of social "net" investment or "net" disinvestment is important, and its discussion calls for consideration of certain "time relations." Since investment is a conversion of present income into future income (i.e., capital) by abstaining "for a certain interval" from a "strip" of the present consumption stream; and since disinvestment is a "reconversion of 'capital,' i.e., of [future] income, into income for a short period at a correspondingly higher time rate,"[11] it is an economic problem of major importance to find out about the time distance between those present and future incomes, about the mentioned "interval," and about the mentioned "period." These "periods" are important for the main problems of capital theory which is the theory of actual or potential changes in the quantity relationship between present and future services—or, in other words, the theory of distribution of services over time.

3. *Are production and consumption simultaneous?*—The assertion that all capital (in terms of value of anticipated future income) is always maintained and, therefore, "perpetual" was made to support the view that the notion of a period between production and consumption is meaningless. The assertion to the contrary that capital need not, and, in fact, is not, always maintained ought to support the view that the notion of the mentioned period has meaning and significance. Professor Knight is prepared to admit that "the notion of a lapse of time between production and consumption has practical meaning where society has to meet *unanticipated* changes in conditions."[12] Apart from the theoretical and practical importance of unanticipated changes in conditions —it is not far from correct to call reality a continuous series of unanticipated changes—it is clear to me and many others that the "potentiality" of change is always present and that the choice between alternatives (only one of which is to abstain from changing, and hence to repeat, former choices) is a category in economics.

For the picture of a stationary state, from which change is ab-

---

[11] *Ibid.* In the original, "perpetual" income stands for "future" income.

[12] *Ibid.*, p. 276.

sent, simultaneity of production and consumption can be a useful fiction. With the aid of a "cross-section" view of production and with the element of time abstracted, certain relations in the economic system become more readily perceptible. Hence, propositions such as "production and consumption are simultaneous,"[13] or "the production period for consumed services . . . . is zero,"[14] are useful and admissible (fictitious) assumptions for the discussion of certain problems of the stationary economy. But the "as if" character of such heuristic suppositions must never be forgotten. And for discussion of problems other than those of an absolutely stationary state, especially of problems of capital, of investment,[15] of changes in demand, and similar ones, the assumption of "simultaneity of production and consumption" is misleading and inadmissible and has to be dropped. Only for problems of the first type may maintenance of capital, including replacement of particular items of "plant," be conceived as a part of the production of the output consumed at the same time.[16] But any theory of economic change and any theory of capital has to regard the time element as its integrant part. The production of a definite quantity of output can be done with or without full maintenance of the instruments necessary for its production. Therefore, the output of consumable services is not dependent upon the simultaneous input of productive services used for maintenance or replacement of plant; the productive services used for maintenance or replacement of plant are not a part of the production of services consumable at the same time, but at later moments of time; there is a time interval between the input of services and the "dependent" output of services,[17] and this

[13] *Ibid.*, p. 275.

[14] Knight, *Economic Journal*, March, 1935, p. 88.

[15] Note the following concession of Professor Knight's: "In the act of growth, 'waiting' can be said to be involved, both during the interval of construction itself and at least for such time thereafter as is required for the new capital to yield a total of consumption equal to that which was sacrificed in creating it" (*Economic Essays in Honour of Gustav Cassel*, p. 339).

[16] Knight, *Economic Journal*, March, 1935, pp. 84–85.

[17] It is absolutely incomprehensible to me that Professor Knight, as one of the rare economists who understands, holds, and teaches "the only theory which makes

interval may conveniently be called "period of production" or "period of investment."

4. *Capitalization of perpetual or of time-limited income.*—That the cost of production of any "capital good" is equal to its capitalized future return is a well-established condition of equilibrium. How the rate of interest enters into both sides of the equation was shown by Professor Knight with utmost clarity.[18] On the cost-of-production side of the equation interest is calculated (as "carrying charges") on the services successively invested during the "period of construction." On the capitalized-income side of the equation interest is calculated on the series of future yields to reduce it to the "present value." There are two methods of capitalization. The one simply capitalizes the series of gross returns expected during the service life of the capital good; the other method reduces first the time-limited series of gross returns by way of deducting all maintenance and replacement costs to a perpetual series of net returns and then capitalizes this perpetual series. However, "it happens to be somewhat simpler algebraically not to make this conversion formally, but to express the present worth of the time-limited income stream directly."[19]

In practical life capitalization of a limited series of returns is more usual than that of an infinite series, not only on account of mathematical simplicity but on account of the character of the capital items. Cases of perpetual annuities are rare. The valuation of plants, buildings, machines, etc., fixes attention upon a limited service life of the particular object valued. The valuation of bonds takes into account the maturity of all payments for interest as well as for the "principal." How complicated capitalization would be if the "perpetual income method" were to be used

---

sense at all" (*ibid.*, p. 82), namely, the theory which explains "cost" as "displaced alternative," should not see this point. Consumable services available at different, more or less distant, future points of time are the "alternative" uses of the productive services available at any one moment of time. The simultaneous output is not—or only for an infinitesimally small part—among the alternatives.

[18] *Economica*, August, 1934, pp. 265–66; *Canadian Journal*, February, 1935, pp. 14–15.

[19] *Canadian Journal*, February, 1935, p. 14.

is easily seen when one again faces the fact that we live in a changing world. With "bygones forever bygones," the cost of production of existing items does not count for their valuation. There is now no "actual" capital value to start with, and replacement quotas could be known only with respect to the "historical value" but not to the "present value." With replacement quotas unknown there is no way of knowing the net yield. There is, then, nothing but a limited series of gross returns, and this is what is capitalized. Only afterward, when the calculation of the present value has been finished, could a "perpetual-income series" be constructed. Take the case of finding the capital value of a plant in an industry which is experiencing bad times. Maintenance of the plant[20] would mean negative net returns. But this does not at all mean that the value of the plant is negative. If there are positive gross returns, for a limited period of time, of course, there will be a positive capital value.

These few illustrations, I hope, make it sufficiently clear that practice does not make things obscure by supposing "perpetuity" of income or of capital. Theory should not do so either.

II. THE LENGTH OF THE PRODUCTION PERIOD

5. *The concept and its name.*—It has been stated, in the preceding discussion, that the time interval between the input of (productive) services and the "dependent" output of (consumable) services is significant for a number of economic problems. This time interval was called, by Böhm-Bawerk, the "degree of roundaboutness of production," or the "length of the production process," or the "period of production." The last two names, which Böhm and most of his followers continued to use in spite of the protests of Wicksell and others, contributed much to the confusion about the concept. The words convey a meaning which is not that of the concept: one thinks of the duration of the process of production proper, which is by some writers called "*direct* production period" (as distinguished from the duration of *indirect*

---

[20] It is fair to note that Professor Knight does not assume maintenance of particular capital items, but only of their actual value.

production) and by others "duration of the technical process" (as distinguished from direct and indirect *durability*).

A number of different sorts of durations or periods are embraced by Böhm's concept. If one had to find out what time would elapse from the moments at which certain services, say a number of labor hours employed in a machine shop, are being "put in" (invested) until the moments at which the dependent consumable services mature, the following durations would have to be considered: (*a*) the duration of producing the machine; (*b*) the duration of the production of the goods made with the help of the machine, and the duration of the production of the succeeding products made with the help of the mentioned goods, etc., all the way up to the final stage; (*c*) the durability of the machine, (*d*) the durability of the goods made with the help of the machine, and the durability of the products made with the help of the mentioned goods, etc., all the way up to the final services which are to be had. All these four sorts of durations have to be considered, but this does not at all mean that they have to be added. We shall speak about this presently. First it should frankly be stated that all objections to "period of production" as a name for that composite period meant by Böhm's concept are fully justified. Terminological magnanimity may tolerantly pass over the misnomer and continue to use it. But it certainly would be better to return, according to Professor Hayek's recent suggestion, to Jevons' and Wicksell's practice and speak of the "period of investment."[21]

6. *Absolute versus average length of the period.*—We warned against the fallacy of adding up all the "durations" of direct and indirect production and direct and indirect service life. It is easily understood that, under the technique of our times, such adding-up would arrive at an infinite period. Production is continuous— not only in the sense that at any moment of time "past services" are consumed and "future services" provided, but also in the

---

[21] Professor Eucken, in his *Kapitaltheoretische Untersuchungen*, coined the word *Ausreifungszeit*, i.e., "period of maturing." The choice of the name is, however, a matter of indifference compared with the importance of using the concept in an appropriate way. In the rest of the discussion the terms period of production and period of investment will be used interchangeably.

sense that durable instruments constructed in the past are used in the construction of durable instruments for future use. In this sense "the production period has no beginning and no end unless . . . . the date of the end of the world is known from the beginning."[22] Or, more correctly, only "the beginning and end of social economic life"[23] would mark the boundaries of that "period of production." And "it would never be possible to give any sensible answer to the question" when (to repeat Professor Knight's examples) the production of a certain glass of milk "began," or when the process of consuming the result of productive activity such as feeding a cow would "end."[24]

Has the *naïveté* or absurdity of the whole conception employed by Böhm-Bawerk now been revealed and sufficiently ridiculed? Let Böhm himself give the answer:

> Where I have spoken [above] of extension or prolongation of the roundabout process of production . . . . I must be understood in the sense [just] explained. The length or the shortness of the process, its extension or its curtailment, is not measured by the absolute duration of the period that lies between the expenditure of the first atom of labor and the last—otherwise the cracking of nuts with a hammer which might chance to be made of iron brought from a mine opened by the Romans would perhaps be the most "capitalistic" kind of production.[25]

Can one warn more expressly against the pitfall of taking the absolute period of production for the significant time interval? Böhm's concept was "the *average* period which lies between the successive expenditure in labor and uses of land and the obtaining of the final good."[26] The fact that some of the services reach into the indefinite future represents no difficulty for averaging the time dimensions. The bulk of the services mature in the near future and fewer in the more distant future, while the number of services maturing after infinite intervals is infinitesimally small.

In the well-known diagrams used by Jevons, Böhm, Hayek, and others—be it the ring diagram or the triangle diagram—the ab-

[22] Knight, *Economic Essays in Honour of Gustav Cassel*, p. 338.

[23] Knight, *Economica*, August, 1934, p. 275.

[24] *Ibid.*

[25] *The Positive Theory of Capital* (London, 1891), p. 90.

[26] *Ibid.* On the limitation to "labor" and "land," see below (sec. 14).

solute period of investment is assumed to be finite. This assumption would imply that there is one stage of production at which no tools and no instruments, but only the "original" services of land and labor, are employed. If to this entirely unrealistic assumption another one is added, namely, that the further input of "original" services takes place continuously at a uniform rate during the whole absolute period, then the average period of investment is half of the absolute.[27] The fiction of a finite absolute production period facilitates the exposition of certain relations but has to be dropped in the course of any further analysis. It is to be regretted that it has contributed to so many serious misunderstandings.

7. *Average period versus shape of the investment function.*—It might be well to familiarize ourselves somewhat further with the meaning of the average investment period, before we deal with a more complicated concept. Imagine for a moment that labor is the only kind of productive service and is homogeneous in quality. At any point of time all labor being invested at that instant is planned and expected to yield (to contribute to) consumable services at some future time. (Most of the input of labor of that instant is planned to be combined with additional labor which is to be invested at successive moments of time, and the final product will be, of course, a joint product of services invested at different points of time.) The labor invested today includes a certain amount which is to yield services consumable today, another amount which is to yield services consumable tomorrow, another the day after tomorrow, etc. Smaller amounts of labor invested today in some durable instrument of production will get very high "futurity indices" and an infinitesimal amount will get the futurity-index (or time-dimension) infinity. The average of all these indices, weighted according to the respective number of labor units, is the average period of investment.

[27] There is another concept which is sometimes confused with the average period of production, namely, the "average period of waiting," which is dependent, apart from the other time dimensions, upon whether production is arranged in simultaneously operating stages, i.e., upon whether output becomes available continuously or with intervals (e.g., crop output). See Böhm-Bawerk, *op. cit.*, pp. 327–28. The subsistence-fund theory refers directly to the "waiting period" and through it to the production period.

The "average period" as an expression for the distribution of services over time is serviceable only for certain purposes and only if this distribution scheme is rather simple. Imagine changing our plans, one day, simply by switching some units of labor to activities of later maturing yield. This switching may be expressed by saying that the average period of investment has been lengthened. But take another type of rearrangement, where some productive services are transferred from uses with quick maturity to uses with later maturity, but also some other productive services are transferred from uses with very late maturity to uses with medium-high futurity indices.[28] Such a change in the distribution of services over time would be possible without any change in the "average." This shows that not only the average of all time dimensions but also their dispersion may be significant. The "shape of the investment function" would tell what the simple "average investment period" conceals.

There are other reasons for not accepting the "average period of investment" as an adequate expression for, or measure of, the time structure of investment. Professor Hayek reminds us that the time intervals of waiting are, as to their economic significance, not homogeneous magnitudes which can be averaged.[29] Another argument advanced by Professor Hayek is concerned with the relationship between the interest rate and the investment function. The investment function, he explains, is rather complicated because of the "investment in compound interest"; this makes it not only impracticable to represent it in terms of averages but also to represent it in one-dimensional diagrams.[30] But this need not

[28] Changes of this type play a rôle in the business-cycle analysis of Professor Strigl (see *Kapital und Produktion* [Vienna, 1934], pp. 192–95).

[29] Hayek, unpublished manuscript.

[30] Hayek, "On the Relationship between Investment and Output," *Economic Journal*, June, 1934, p. 217. Three principal kinds of investment functions should be distinguished. The most usual may be called the "cumulative investment function." It represents either the cumulative amount of services applied at any successive moment of time in the course of the process of producing the output finished at one moment of time or the cumulative amount of services (simultaneously) applied at successive stages (i.e., consumption distances) of production up to the final output. A second kind may be called the "service-application function," since it shows the application of services in the process of production at successive moments of

frighten us too much. For most analytical purposes it will be quite sufficient to bear in mind that one cannot do everything with the average period without reference to the "shape of the investment function." But one can use it for first approximations to the solution of a number of important problems in the theory of capital and, I believe, in the theory of fluctuations.

8. *"Time" per unit of output versus "time" per unit of input.*— Two more sources of confusion must be disclosed and blocked. The one originated from a careless use of the word "time" to measure both the input of productive services (labor hours, service hours, land-use years) and the interval elapsing between input and the dependent final output. The second confusion came from erroneous averaging of those intervals per unit of output rather than per unit of input.

A simple numerical example (Table I) will illustrate clearly this type of error. Under unchanged technical knowledge, unchanged length of the working day, homogeneous labor, and homogeneous product, three cases will be considered in one of which the average period of investment will be lengthened (Case II), and in another the number of workers will be increased (Case III). Both variations (support of workers through longer period, and support of more workers through unchanged period, respectively) are assumed to be rendered possible through the provisions of more "subsistence fund."

Comparing Case I with Case II we see that the increase in

time or successive stages of production. It is simply the slope (first derivative) of the cumulative investment function. The third kind, investment function proper, represents the distribution of all productive services rendered at a moment (small interval) of time among the uses of different consumption distances. It is but the inverted service-application function. Services applied to the earliest stage of production are, for the inverted figure, services applied for uses of greatest consumption distance. Services applied to latest stages of production are, for the inverted figure, services applied for uses of smallest consumption distances.

Professor Hayek drew a figure of the cumulative investment function and inverted it instead of its first derivative (*ibid.*, p. 210). Unfortunately, he interpreted the inverted figure as though it were the inverted service-application function. I am afraid that this error may have confused some readers. It should be noted that for changing conditions only the third sort of investment function is significant, though it is for certain purposes too sensitive with regard to discontinuous outputs.

length of the investment period leads to a less than proportional increase in output per labor hour. Now "critics" would say: "The production of one unit of output needs in Case II not more but less time than in Case I; namely, one-eleventh rather than one-tenth hour." The "time" of which they speak obviously means "labor," which is, of course, measured by time. The saving of "time" in this sense, i.e., the saving of labor services per unit of

TABLE I

	Case I	Case II (Labor Constant; Subsistence Fund Increased)	Case III (Labor Increased; Subsistence Fund Increased Proportionately)
Number of workers.........	100 men	100 men	120 men
Length of working day......	10 hours	10 hours	10 hours
Average period of invest-ment*..................	100 days	120 days	100 days
Labor input during this period	100,000 hours	120,000 hours	120,000 hours
Output during this period...	1,000,000 units	1,320,000 units†	1,200,000 units
Labor input per day........	1,000 hours	1,000 hours	1,200 hours
Output per day............	10,000 units	11,000 units	12,000 units
Output per hour...........	1,000 units	1,100 units	1,200 units
Output per man hour (i.e., per unit of labor input).......	10 units	11 units	10 units
Labor input per unit of output	$\frac{1}{10}$ hour	$\frac{1}{11}$ hour	$\frac{1}{10}$ hour

* The length of the investment period is assumed (not calculated from the other data). In Case II production is assumed to be more roundabout through the use of an intermediate tool which is entirely used up at the end of the 120 days. In Case III the same production method as in Case I is applied.

† This figure does not show increasing returns. It has to be more than in proportion to the increase of the average period of investment, i.e., 100:120, even to show decreasing returns. A figure of less than 1,200,000 units of output over the longer period would imply negative return to the added 20 days of investment. The total "waiting" is increased not simply by the lapse of time, but by time multiplied by the amount invested at any moment.

output, is the very objective of the lengthening of the investment period. The increment in product per labor hour constitutes the "productivity" of the extension of the investment period. The measurement of the amount of services invested in terms of time units must not be confused with the "time dimension" of the investment in the sense of its "time distance" from consumption.

But other "critics" would say: "Not only 'labor time' but also 'waiting time' per unit of output is less in Case II. In Case I we had to wait 100 days for 1,000,000 units of output; in Case II we have to wait 120 days for 1,320,000 units of output. Therefore, average unit waiting time in Case I was one-ten-thousandth of a day; in Case II only one-eleven-thousandth of a day." This "waiting time per unit of output" is an embarrassing confusion. The 100 and 120 days, respectively, were already averages per unit of labor input, and there is absolutely no sense in dividing these figures by the amount of output. That it does not make sense is shown by a comparison between Cases I and III, both of which include an equal and unchanged production period. In Case III, 1,200,000 units are produced in 100 days. The absolute increase in output, due to the increase in men and the proportional increase in "subsistence fund," with the unchanged period of production would give a shorter "period of production per unit of output"[31] if this had any meaning. The production period is the average number of waiting hours applied to the labor hour; it is an average period only in terms of input (of services other than waiting). If the average investment period is to be set in relation to output, not the absolute amount of output but average output per unit of labor input is the adequate magnitude for comparison. An "average period in terms of total output" is meaningless.

9. *Construction period and utilization period.*—The misconceptions dealt with in the last sections are of very old acquaintance— Böhm-Bawerk himself was concerned with them in his "excursus."[32] A novel method of arriving at erroneous averages is applied by Professor Knight. He divides the sum of the periods of construction and utilization of different plants by the number or value of plants, and states then, correctly of course, that an addition to the existing equipment may well "involve an increase in

---

[31] The erroneous reasoning would be: "We have to wait 100 days for 1,200,000 units; average waiting time per unit of output is therefore one-twelve-thousandth of a day; this is less than the one-ten-thousandth in Case 1." It should be noted that in Case III more workers are employed in an unchanged production period, hence with a constant amount of "capital per head." This will be discussed later. It was on purpose that I assumed here the subsistence fund to be increased proportionately with the number of men at work, in order to avoid the complications of shortening the investment period necessary when less "capital per head" is available. This is also reserved for later discussion.

[32] See the third or fourth German edition of his *Positive Theorie des Kapitales*.

the capital, while *shortening* the average cycle."[33] He thinks of the replacement cycle of durable capital goods. This cycle consists of the period of construction of the equipment plus its durability. Imagine that there are three plants, one with a period of construction plus utilization of 5 years, another with such a period of 10 years, and a third with one of 15 years. Now, additional investment is made by creating a fourth plant with a 6-year period. (The productive services engaged in constructing and maintaining the fourth plant must have been employed formerly in other lines, say, in farming.) In the case of three plants Professor Knight's "average period" was 10 years (5+10+15 divided by 3), while in the case of four plants (more capital!) the "average period" is only 9 years (5+6+10+15 divided by 4). This "average per unit of plant," or, weighted with the value of plant, the "average per capital invested," he erroneously took as the average investment period and, of course, found that it did not bear the well-known relation to the quantity of capital, viz., that it failed to increase with the increase in investment. The "average period of construction" plus the "average period of utilization" (both averages per unit of plant value) is by no means equal to the average period of investment (which is an average per unit of productive service inclusive of those not engaged in the construction and replacement of durable goods).

Making goods which need a longer time of construction and making goods which last longer are perhaps only "two details which are of the same significance as any of an infinity of other details," and are certainly only two "among an infinite number"[34] of ways of investing more capital. But "the two together" do certainly not constitute, as Professor Knight so strongly believes,[35] Böhm-Bawerk's period of production. It is inexplicable how Professor Knight could arrive at such an extremely narrow definition of the production period. Böhm-Bawerk, who is now accused of "simply selecting these two details" and giving them "the false

---

[33] *Economic Journal*, March, 1935, p. 81 (italics are his).

[34] Knight, *Economica*, August, 1934, p. 268.

[35] *Ibid.*, pp. 268–70; *Economic Journal*, March, 1935, pp. 78, 81, 88, etc.

designation of length of the production process,"[36] wrote the following sentence about investment in increased durability:

It represents but one of the many special forms of using labor for obtaining consumption goods by those roundabout processes which make it possible to get out more goods per unit of original factors of production but at points of time which on the average are more remote from the time of input of those factors.[37]

Hence there is no conflict of opinion between the critic and the criticized that "average durability of the goods" and, similarly, the "average construction period for such goods"[38] need not be increased if total investment increases.

10. *Average durability.*—In spite of the fact that it was quite foreign to the theorists who reason in terms of investment periods to identify this concept with average construction periods plus average durability of goods, it should be noted that the relationship between "average durability" and "capital supply" is much closer than Professor Knight seems to allow for. An increase in "capital supply," in a money-enterprise economy, leads to increased investment through a lower rate of interest. (The supply of other services is assumed to be unchanged.) A reduction of the interest rate decreases construction cost as far as "carrying charges" are concerned and increases the present value of durable goods because of the lower discount of future returns. The latter phenomenon is of major significance. The increase in present value is the stronger the more durable the instruments are.

Let us compare this effect on the value of instruments of different durability. An instrument with a service life of one year and a gross return of $1,000 would have a present value of $940, if the interest rate is 6 per cent, and a present value of $970 if the interest rate is only 3 per cent. An instrument with a service life of two years and a gross return of $1,000 in each year would have under simple interest of 6 per cent a present value of $(940+880=)$ $1,820, and under simple interest[39] of 3 per cent a present value of

---

[36] Knight, *Economica*, August, 1934, p. 268.

[37] *Op. cit.* (3d ed., 1909), p. 170; *ibid.* (4th ed., 1921), p. 127.

[38] Knight, *Economic Journal*, p. 78.

[39] A simple example was preferred here. Compound interest should be calculated for almost all practical (and theoretically important) cases.

(970+940=) \$1,910. A fall of the interest rate from 6 to 3 per cent raises the value of the short-lived instrument from \$940 to \$970, i.e., by 3.2 per cent, while it raises the value of the long-lived instrument from \$1,820 to \$1,910, i.e., by 4.9 per cent. Cost of construction (aside from interest) being unchanged—the case is still stronger if the more durable instrument requires a longer time for construction and, hence, becomes now relatively cheaper in construction—it will be much more profitable to construct the more durable instrument.

The differences in the price increases of goods of different durability become the sharper the greater the expected service life is. Let the rate of interest drop only from 5 to 4 per cent and there results an increase in present value of a good with ten years' service life by about 5 per cent whereas the increase is more than 9 per cent for a good with twenty years' service life. (Compound interest was calculated here.)

There is, hence, a very strong presumption for the belief that increased supply of liquid capital leads to increased investment in durability, even in the sense of "average durability of goods," the concept emphasized by Professor Knight.

11. *"More durable" goods versus more "durable goods."*—In his criticism of the production period Professor Knight concentrates his forces against the alleged increase in the durability of goods. Again and again he asserts that increased investment need not involve increased durability and "therefore" need not involve increased "time between production and consumption,"[40] i.e., a longer investment period. The crux of the whole argument is the idea that making goods "more durable" is, but making more "durable goods" need not be, a lengthening of the investment period, according to Professor Knight's interpretation of the "Austrian" theory of capital.

Investment means, for the "Austrians" at least, using productive services for future consumable services. Increased investment means using the productive services on the average for consumable outputs in a more remote future. This lengthening of the period of maturing can be done in many ways, one of which is

[40] *Economica*, August, 1934, p. 269.

the making of goods and instruments of higher durability, another is the making of a greater amount of durable goods and instruments. If the primitive inhabitants of the famous isolated island, where fishing is the only line of production, and nets are the only type of durable instruments, abstain temporarily from some portions of consumption and add one more net to their stock, they certainly lengthen their investment period. (Labor is withdrawn from fishing and employed for making the net. Total labor supply remains constant, of course.) "Average durability" per unit of stock, per net, would remain equal. But even if they make the new net of lower durability, and decrease thereby the "average durability" of nets, the investment period would still be lengthened. Or if our good old Robinson Crusoe adds to his stock of tools, which last "on the average" one year, a new knife which lasts only two weeks, he still lengthens his production period. By refraining from direct consumptive use of some labor hours and using them for making the knife (and, later on, for maintaining or replacing the knife), he changes the average time distance between input and dependent output.

That, with a given amount of productive services employed, the making of a greater amount of durable goods per se would not involve any greater length of the investment period is a unique interpretation of the concept. The emphasis placed on this point by Professor Knight is striking. "More goods of the same kind," he says, "would mean no permanent change in either investment function or output function, as defined by Professor Hayek."[41] This should be contrasted with Professor Hayek's statement about the possibility of "changing the investment function for industry in general without changing it for any one industry."[42] The proportions *within* any one industry may be rigid and remain unchanged (the durability of their equipment, of course, too), but the proportions *between* industries may change. The investment function of society as a whole changes not only if goods are made "more or less durable" but also if more or less "durable goods" are made.

[41] *Economic Journal*, March, 1935, p. 78.

[42] "The Relationship between Investment and Output," *ibid.*, June, 1934, p. 224.

III. DIFFICULTIES AND COMPLICATIONS

12. *The view backward and the view forward.*—In the few places where we, thus far, had to define the production period we tried to avoid one dilemma which probably has not been seen clearly by Böhm and some of his immediate followers. The question how far into the future the output that depends on present activities is expected to reach, on the average, is different from the question how far back into the past reach, on the average, the activities on which the present output depends.[43] Under the assumption of a stationary economy in an unchanging world, the "historical" production period and the "anticipated" production period may be equal. But how are the two "production periods" related to each other in a changing world with changing men of changing mood? If people decide to change the time distribution of their current service input, how does this affect the "age distribution" of the output of today, tomorrow, and the immediate future? Is there not a considerable lag of the "real" time structure of production behind the "anticipated" one? And if the "anticipated" period undergoes heavy fluctuations, is it likely or possible that the "real" production structure varies concomitantly? And if this is found to be impossible, is it then not illicit to theorize about fluctuations in the production structure in the short run?

When Mr. Hill raised all these doubts he did not suggest the scrapping of the concepts altogether but a reconsideration, or the discontinuance, of their use in business cycle theory. The reconsideration may lead to a number of distinctions, refinements, qualifications of the concept, and what has been stated about it. So much seems to be clear: (1) that the significant hypotheses about the investment period and its changes refer exclusively to the so-called anticipated period, i.e., to the time distribution of the current input of services; (2) that the "historical"[44] produc-

---

[43] Hill, "The Period of Production and Industrial Fluctuations," *ibid.*, December, 1933, p. 601. In drawing the distinction Hill followed F. Burkhart, "Die Schemata des stationären Kreislaufs bei Böhm-Bawerk und Marx," *Weltwirtschaftliches Archiv*, Vol. XXXIV (1931).

[44] Mr. Hill speaks (*op. cit.*, p. 603) of the "completed" period rather than of a "historical." It is better to reserve the term "completed" for the discussion of other phenomena in the process of lengthening or shortening the period.

tion structure undoubtedly offers resistance to quick changes or even to fluctuations, a resistance which is the very substance of the explanation of cyclical and other disturbances; (3) that a production period between past input and present output[45] seems to be of no heuristic value for economic theory other than as a historical account of some "given data."

The "view forward" determines the employment of services available. That "it is by its nature hypothetical, representing an average of anticipations which may not be realized"[46] is not in contradiction with the fact that it is very real in its effects on what is being done at any one moment of time.

13. *Current investment versus total investment.*—The clean distinction between the "anticipated" investment period and the "historical" period is more or less the distinction between an economic problem and the data given for its solution. The economic problem is the problem of choice, in this case the problem of distributing the available productive services among purposes of different time index. The data include the total equipment available which is the result of history. The historical time distributions are materialized in the stock of "capital goods," the quantity, composition, and quality (including durability) of which are, of course, of influence upon the present choices as to the distribution of services over time. In other words, "past" investment, through the man-made equipment available "at present," influences (together with other factors) the "present" or current investment for "future" output. The investment function (the only significant one as an economic problem) refers wholly to the current investment. Hence it does not contain what one could call "total investment," i.e., the current investment plus the existing capital

[45] Mr. Hill writes (*op. cit.*, p. 605): "Owing to the existence of fixed capital the structure of production will not contract as rapidly as the anticipated production period. The average time in which existing specific capital-goods . . . . pass into consumers' goods is not likely to change appreciably over a short period." One should not forget that the fact that less or no services are currently employed to construct or reconstruct such fixed capital is quite an "appreciable change," even in the shortest run. Moreover, the "contraction" of the structure of production may be very rapid indeed, if value changes rather than physical changes are considered.

[46] *Ibid.*, p. 610.

goods (durable and non-durable), which are the result of past investments.[47] To mix existing capital goods with current investment and to make out of both one investment function is to mix historical data with economic problems. Past investments, so far as they are materialized in existing equipment (capital goods), certainly influence the shape of the current investment function (the investment period), but they are not contained in it with respect to the productive services which they will yield in the future. Only the productive services rendered at the moment of investment[48] constitute (with their consumption distances) the investment function.

14. *Investment of services of "original" factors versus services in general.*—At this point in the present discussion it is high time to dispense with the idea that only "original" factors of production should be considered. It was undoubtedly a mistake to look only at the services of "labor" and "land," as Böhm-Bawerk did throughout his discussion. Whether it was an inappropriate use of the stationary-state fiction, or whether it was the fear of reasoning in a circle, which led to the exclusion of the services of existing equipment from the investment account, it was a mistake to assume that the services which can be had from capital goods are, apart from their history, different in principle from the services of land and labor. (That there is no homogeneity within these categories should be clear.)[49] At any moment of time the services available from any sources of any kind—"free gifts" of nature as well as human labor-capacity as well as the results of past investment—are "given" for the economic choice. Labor services, land services, machine services, are institutionally, biologically, and

[47] It should be noted that this does not fit into Jevons' terminology. Our "total investment" would correspond to his "amount of capital invested" but not to his "amount of investment of capital." See his *Theory of Political Economy*, chap. vii (esp. p. 229 in the 4th ed.).

[48] To make it indubitably clear: The durability of existing equipment influences the current decisions about current investment and through it the investment period, but it does not enter as an item into the investment function.

[49] See Knight, *Economica*, August, 1934, p. 279. Professor Knight forcefully criticizes the fallacy of distinguishing "primary" from "produced" factors. I also owe much to an unpublished manuscript by Professor Hayek.

historically different, but there is no difference with regard to their economic position in the time structure of investment.

The resources that yield the productive services may be permanent or durable or perishable. The services are perishable altogether because they are related to the single moment of time. The labor hours, land-use hours, machine hours, become, in being employed, the items which constitute the current investment.

15. *The "unit" of investment.*—Labor is not homogeneous in kind, in quality, in efficiency; nor is land or capital goods. There is not much more sense in trying to compare in "physical units" the floor-space hour in a factory with the water-power hour from a river (both in some way related to "nature" or "land") than in comparing them with the labor hour of a bricklayer, or with that of a stockbroker, or with the hourly service from a steel hammer or that from a paper machine. And yet, should all of those services and their time dimensions be "averaged" in an investment period or, at least, brought into one investment function? (An additional complication consists in the circumstance that the special form of employment of transferable and versatile factors sometimes depends on the length of the investment period.)[50]

Is there a way out of the dilemma? Is it fair to "assume" homogeneity of services, to theorize on that basis, and be satisfied with conclusions *per analogiam?* Or is it better to take "value" as the only possible *tertium comparationis?* There may be an impenetrable series of implications in adopting value as the "unit" of input. If it is done, the time dimensions of the productive services being invested at a moment of time would have to be weighted with the values of these services.[51]

16. *Investment period and the amount of capital goods.*—The correlation between the investment period and the amount of capital

[50] Much emphasis was placed on this point by Franz X. Weiss, "Produktionsumwege und Kapitalzins," *Zeitschrift für Volkswirtschaft und Sozialpolitik*, N.F., I (1921), 568–72.

[51] This raises a number of the most serious theoretical problems. The value of productive services is dependent on the value of their future consumable services. Both are dependent on the length of the investment period, since an increase in that period yields an increase in future output. It is not only a matter of space when I abstain from entering into so trying a discussion. I may recall to the reader that

goods has sometimes been held to be true "by definition," sometimes rejected as meaningless or wrong. The customary proofs for the existence of the correlation run again in terms of a stationary state. The assumption of the stationary state implies that the investment function does not change but remains the same through time. The investment function of "today" would look exactly like that of any time in the past, and exactly like that of any time in the future. In this case the amount of capital goods in existence at any moment of time would be a certain function[52] of the investment function. It goes without saying, then, that the investment function and the amount of capital goods in existence are correlative.

Imagine now a change in the system; people start saving and investing; this involves a change in the investment function through a switch of services from lower to higher consumption distances. Assume, furthermore, that the new investment function is being maintained from then on and that the mobility and transformability of capital goods was sufficient to make the change take place without any losses. The changed investment function would tell that the physical quantity of capital goods of any type

---

Pigou withdrew the "Pound Sterling worth of resources" from his last editions of the *Economics of Welfare* and substituted physical units for it. The issue was a different one but similar considerations are likely to be relevant in our problem. (Cf. the recent remarks by Howard S. Ellis, *Zeitschrift für Nationalökonomie*, June, 1935, pp. 158–59.)

[52] The investment function, as we defined it, represents the distribution of all services invested at a moment (small interval) of time among uses of different consumption distance. If such an investment function is (for a stationary state) drawn only for the services of original factors, then inverted and transformed to a cumulative function (now looking like Hayek's Fig. 1*b*, in his article in *Economic Journal*, June, 1934, p. 210), then the area under the cumulative investment function represents the stock of produced production goods. (About the simple and the cumulative investment function see also *supra*, p. 588, n. 30.) The statement in the text about the constancy through time of the investment function must be qualified by the further assumption that output is continuous. While cumulative investment functions are insensitive to discontinuities of output, and are therefore constant for a stationary state, the investment function as we defined it would vary according to the crop-distance. This is a technical defect. Better technicians may find an improved mode of expressing the investment function.

will be greater in the future than it is at the moment of change.[53] One could hold, however, that, although the physical quantity of capital goods is still unchanged at the very moment of the change of the investment function, there may be an immediate increase in stock value because of the lower capitalization rate of future income. In other words, the same "causes" which change the investment function change at once the rate of capitalization and, therefore, the value of existing equipment.

Another approach seems to be better adapted to the concepts as we have used them in this discussion. The relationship between the amount of capital goods and the investment period shows itself in both directions. First, the greater the amount of serviceable capital goods in existence, the greater is the part of the current productive services from resources of any kind which can be invested for a more distant future. Thus, the amount of capital goods in existence represents, so to speak, a potentiality of investing more for longer periods. It is a potentiality which has not necessarily to be made use of. (And, indeed, capital goods may lose in value if and when, through a change in time preferences, given "specific" equipment cannot be utilized fully.) But, generally speaking, the investment period tends to be longer the greater the amount of capital goods in existence. Second, if we use an increased part of the given productive services for things of greater time distance, the amount of capital goods in existence will increase. This means that, other things remaining equal, a lengthening of the investment period gradually increases the amount of capital goods in existence.

17. *Investment period and the supply of free capital disposal.*— In a single-plan economy, from the simple economy of the Crusoe type up to a communistic economy, the change in time preference

---

[53] If all productive services are consumed simultaneously, no "intermediate good" can exist. If production takes time, goods in process, and perhaps tools, are likely to be on the "inventory" at any moment of time. If production is arranged in stages which work continuously, the more goods must be on the inventory the longer the production period which is chosen. With a given input (per time) of productive services the inventory, at any moment of time, must be greater the greater the average time interval is until output is consumed.

(in the plan-makers' taste) and the change in the investment function are analytically the same. The time preference expresses itself in the distribution over time of the use which is made of the productive services currently available.

In an exchange-enterprise economy the time distribution of productive services is not *uno actu* changed with the time preferences on the part of certain individuals. Individuals who save transfer their disposal over services to other individuals who invest. Increased supply of "free capital disposal"[54] tends to reduce the exchange ratio of present to future income, which in turn leads to increased investment of productive services for longer periods. Individuals who disinvest, so far as they cannot draw upon the disposal over services released from individuals who save, withdraw the disposal over services from entrepreneurs. Decreased supply of "free capital disposal" tends to increase the exchange ratio of present to future income, which in turn leads to decreased investment of productive services for longer periods.

In a money-enterprise economy "free capital disposal" is supplied and demanded in the form of "money capital." Insight into the functioning of this system is much impeded by the fact that goods in process are passed over from firm to firm by way of exchange against money, whereby money appears to be free capital disposal for the individual without being so for the community as a whole. This is why the unreal assumption of production vertically integrated in a single firm is so convenient; and why under more realistic assumptions problems of great complexity emerge from monetary changes. So much seems to be clear that an increase in the supply of money capital tends (other things, including the amount of services, being equal) to lengthen the investment period; and, vice versa, a decrease in the supply of money capital tends to shorten the investment period. And this is so, whether disposal over services really is released by savers or withdrawn by dissavers, respectively, or whether only the "elasticity"

---

[54] I follow Cassel in using the term "capital disposal." It is better to avoid the term "capital" *simpliciter*. The terms "capital goods," "capital disposal," "capital value," "money capital," convey more definite meaning than the ambiguous word "capital."

of the money system does the trick. Thus changes in the investment structure are inseparably linked with the credit cycle.

18. *"At" a point of time versus "within" a period of time versus "for" a period of time.*—Discussions of "capital" and "investment" suffer not only from ambiguous meanings of these terms but also from confusion with respect to their time quality. The terms suggested by Jevons were not striking enough to be accepted by later writers. The "amount of investment of capital" was to mean something different from the "amount of capital invested,"[55] but neither of them was the "amount of capital being invested." The first was to be a product of a multiplication (more correctly, integration) of the amount that has been invested by the time for which it has been invested. The second, the "capital invested," was the amount that has been (and continues to be) invested up to a certain point of time, but without consideration of "the length of time during which it remains invested."[56] In other words, it was the inventory at a point of time. The third is the amount that is being invested within a (very small) interval of time.

"Capital invested" in the sense of capital that has been invested can, in a changing world, apart from setting up a profit-and-loss account, be significantly expressed, not in terms of its (historical) cost—i.e., in terms of the value it had at the time when the investments were made—but only in terms of the present value of the goods or resources which exist as result of those past investments. The present value is, of course, the capitalized income which is expected to accrue from the services from these goods or resources. Since the present value of these goods or resources has not much to do with the historical amounts invested, the term "capital invested" had better not be used for them. "Capital equipment" or "capital goods" are adequate terms.

"Capital invested" in the sense of capital that is being invested within a small interval of time can be expressed in terms of cost or value, both being the same under the assumptions of equilibrium theory. Can this "capital being currently invested" be expressed without time dimension? It certainly needs a reference to

[55] Jevons, *op. cit.* (4th ed.), p. 229.   [56] *Ibid.*

the unit of time chosen, since it is a time rate (such as per hour, per day, per week). Is it necessary to add to the time within which it is being invested, also the time for which the investment is to be? The answer to this becomes clear if we recall what is being invested. If we think of capital disposal or of money capital, it can be expressed as a mere quantity without reference to the duration of investment. But if we think of the "real" investment, of productive services, we immediately see that the time dimensions become necessary because almost all productive services employed —except the personal services of servants, actors, etc.—are "invested" and the question is only one of their distribution over time. Under full employment no increase in investment would be conceivable if it were not for the investment of services for periods longer than those for which they were hitherto invested.

This circumstance is, I think, rather significant. The money capital which is being invested need not, and cannot, be assigned to any certain period of investment. Even if the individuals who supply it were quite determined as to the length of time for which they would like to tie it up, or even if the individuals were determined to invest it for eternity, the services which are invested by means of the money capital are invested for a period which is independent of the will of the particular saver. And the single new investment makes, *ceteris paribus* (hence, with the amount of services unchanged), the average period of investment just a little longer than it was before. If there is full employment, the increase in the amount of money capital being invested per unit of time increases the period for which the services are being invested on the average.

19. *Capital per capita.*—Productive services are distributed among uses of different consumption distance. To distribute a given amount of services is one problem. To distribute the services from a given amount of resources and men is another problem, because the capacity of resources and men may not be utilized fully. To distribute the services from a changing amount of resources and men is a third problem. It goes without saying that these distinctions are highly relevant for the problem of the average period of investment or, more correctly, for the problem of comparing investment structures.

A greater amount of services distributed over time (over consumption distances) in the same proportions as a smaller amount of services means, of course, an unchanged average period. Should there be an increase in the number of men employed, the amount of other resources would have to increase too, if a change in time distribution is to be avoided. This is often expressed by saying that changes in the average period of investment can be seen by changes in the amount of "capital per head." If population grows more quickly than capital equipment, with the result that less "capital per head" is available, shorter periods of investment become necessary. On the other hand, increased investment permits lengthened investment periods only so far as it is not accompanied by a proportional increase in men.

This interrelation (which I chose to formulate as a statement of tendencies) is sometimes suggested in the form of an analytical statement. If a cumulative investment function is drawn in the customary way (representing cumulatively the amounts of services applied at successive moments of time in the course of one process of producing the output finished at one moment of time),[57] the area under this investment curve is defined as capital (more correctly, capital goods in terms of incorporated services). The average period of investment is measured by dividing the area under the curve by the final output (i.e., by the income measured in terms of input or incorporated services.) This division represents, by definition, the ratio between capital and income.[58] If only labor income, rather than total income, is considered, and if it is (according to the ordinates of these diagrams) expressed in terms of service input, the analogous division gives the ratio between capital and labor services, or, if labor hours per laborer are fixed, capital per head.[59]

[57] See, among recent publications, the diagram in Marschak's article, *Economic Journal*, March, 1934, p. 147, or Fig. 1a in Hayek's article, *ibid.*, June, 1934, p. 210. For a short explanation see above, p. 588, n. 30.

[58] Professor Knight (*Economic Journal*, p. 88) considers this ratio "one of the least meaningful."

[59] Which of the two ratios is more significant for capital theory is still an open question. The discussion in the following paragraph places more emphasis on the second ratio. I owe much to Dr. Marschak's previously cited article and to his unpublished contribution to our private "round-letter" discussion.

An increased supply of money capital with unemployed labor services available would lead to an absorption into the production process of more labor services rather than—or in addition to—a redistribution over longer investment periods of the hitherto employed services. (Without increase in the supply of money capital, such absorption would be practicable only by a shortening of the investment period with lower returns to labor services). There would, however, be a different sequence of events if the additional money capital is supplied by an expansion of bank credit from what it would be if it were supplied by voluntary saving, i.e., under voluntary abstinence from consumption.

20. *The proportion between the factors employed.*—The reflections upon "capital per head" above suggest the coherence between the concepts of the "investment period" and the "proportion between the factors employed." So far as changes in the investment period are connected with changes in methods of production within single industries or even single firms, reasoning in terms of proportion between factors becomes necessary. A single firm which, under the influence of lower interest rates, buys new machines to substitute them for less efficient ones or for labor services, certainly does not calculate investment periods. The firm makes cost comparisons, and the elasticity of substitution[60] will, among other conditions, be decisive for the firm's choice. The result is, for the particular section of the economic system, to be stated only in terms of the proportions in which the factors are employed by the single firm or industry.

An average investment period or a certain investment function becomes significant only for the community as a whole. In a total system analysis it will sometimes be more convenient to theorize in terms of the proportion between the factors employed, sometimes in terms of the investment period. The use of the latter conception recommends itself in all problems where explanations of changes through time are essential. The "analytical correlation,"

[60] See J. R. Hicks, *The Theory of Wages* (London, 1932), p. 117; Joan Robinson, *The Economics of Imperfect Competition* (London, 1933), pp. 256–60; C. H. P. Gifford, *Econometrica*, April, 1935, pp. 208–10; Fritz Machlup, "The Commonsense of the Elasticity of Substitution," *Review of Economic Studies*, Vol. II (June, 1935).

mentioned in the preceding paragraph, is, of course, without significance for causal relations. What are really significant are questions as to the probable effect upon the investment period of an increased supply of money capital, and as to the effect upon the quantity of capital goods (producers' goods) of a lengthening of the investment period. Lags and friction in the realization of such sequences are not unimportant; the appreciation (increase in present value) of the bulk of existing capital goods in the case of a lengthening is not less relevant than the differentials for longer-lived and shorter-lived goods and (in the case of a sudden increase in voluntary saving) the depreciation of some specific instruments adapted for the production of consumers' goods.

The chances for a statistical measurement of the investment period are not too good,[61] for reasons which have been sufficiently indicated in the discussion of the difficulties and complications. Of these difficulties the greatest is the problem of comparability—which is present throughout the field of economic statistics and is comprehensible to anybody who has a clear understanding of subjective value theory. The chief working hypothesis of every statistical attempt at measuring the investment period seems to be its approximate correlation with the proportions in which the factors are employed.[62]

IV. SPECIAL PROBLEMS

21. *Width of income stream versus length of investment period.*—A great many economists substitute for the concept of the "length of the investment period" the concept of the "width of the income stream." The latter concept does not encounter so many complications as the former and has the advantage of not only suggesting a picture readily grasped but also of easily fitting into any analysis of economic dynamics, i.e., of fluctuating, progressive, or declining

[61] See Marschak, "Economic Parameters in a Stationary Society with Monetary Circulation," *Econometrica*, January, 1934; and Gifford, *Econometrica*, April, 1935.

[62] Lack of statistical "verification," or even theoretical impossibility of measurement, is no evidence whatsoever against the usefulness of a concept. As Professor Knight has said, absolutely to the point, clear and indispensable notions often "cannot be given exact definition; but this limitation applies to all quantitative analysis in economics" (*Economic Journal*, March, 1935, p. 90 n.).

608   FRITZ MACHLUP

economies. Saving is pictured as a narrowing of the income
stream, which later becomes wider again, wider than it was before
the narrowing; dissaving is pictured as a widening of the stream,
which later becomes narrower again, narrower that it was before
the widening. There are possibilities of continuous and of discontinuous changes in the width—in short, the concept is useful
and adaptable.

Yet, it is a mistake to believe that one could dispose of the investment-period concept without disposing of one of its most significant purposes: to solve the time problem. Of course the "income stream" is a function of time, but one which remains unknown as long as the "investment period" is not introduced. It is
certainly true that the income stream becomes wider again after
having been narrowed by voluntary saving—but only after a
while. After how long a while? How long a time does it take before the widening of the income stream occurs, and how long before the "abstinence" is fully offset? The answer may be sought
by using a concept like the "investment period," or it may not be
sought at all. What relates the changes in width of the income
stream with one another is the investment period which has been
thought to have been thrown overboard. That these intervals
have meaning and significance is admitted by almost every economist—even by Professor Knight.[63]

22. *Investment period and the "stages of production."*—In discussions of the length of the investment period one ordinarily
meets also propositions about the "stages of production." It
would, however, be too optimistic to believe that these terms have
a clear and unambiguous meaning. Although there is much over-

[63] See *Economica*, August, 1934, p. 273: "In reality most investments not only
begin *at a fairly early date* to yield their income in consumable services . . . . but in
addition they begin *fairly soon* to yield more than interest on cost in this form, and
entirely liquidate themselves *in a moderate period of time*" (italics are mine). Or, on
p. 278: "Any net saving and investment naturally means reduction in consumption somewhere and subsequent increase somewhere, raising the total rate of consumption in the system above that obtaining before saving started, the increase
measuring the rate of return. In terms of *income* sacrificed for an interval and ultimately more than made up, the notions of roundaboutness and waiting have some
meaning . . . ." (italics are Professor Knight's). Any investment is displaced earlier
consumption income; this is the very point of the theory of the investment period.

lapping, one can distinguish "stages" of production in terms of (a) units of technical acts or divisions of the process (different acts), (b) locational units (different plants, buildings), (c) vocational units (different crafts, professions), (d) financial units (different firms), (e) time units (different consumption distances). Only the last of these concepts is inherently connected with the concept of the investment period, while the others are sometimes merely phases of the underlying technical conditions, sometimes among the more or less probable accompanying phenomena, but sometimes entirely unconnected.

In the attempt at illustrating an abstract exposition by concrete examples many authors pictured the lengthening of the investment period by pointing to the introduction of certain technical or financial stages of production. Readers—indeed, sometimes the authors themselves—then took the technical or financial properties of the process for the essential factors. In the discussion of production processes without durable instruments, the divergence of the technical stages from those in terms of "time distance from consumption" is not too disturbing; but when durable instruments are introduced into the scheme, the divergence between the two concepts becomes considerable. The steel plant and the machine shop, two definitive stages, of course, in the technical process, represent by no means two stages in the sense of consumption distance but an infinite number of such stages. One has to keep in mind that services employed for the making of a machine are, as to their consumption distances, distributed over a great range of time. Unless one goes through the procedure of averaging these time distributions for any single unit of equipment, or unit of plant—which is neither necessary nor possible—one must not consider a certain technical stage of production as a certain time stage of production.

The divergence between financial stages and time stages is not much less remarkable. This was not made clear enough by Professor Hayek in his *Prices and Production*, and led to much confusion. His diagrams are devised to show the money stream between the financial units engaged in the production process. That the lengthening of the investment period (i.e., the increase in the time stages of production) would involve an increase in money transactions to be performed because of an increase in the number of financial stages of production was an assumption of Professor Hayek's which he certainly did not state clearly enough and which was justly criticized by Professor Ellis.[64] In anticipation of the confusion, Böhm-Bawerk had expressly given warning that the length "of the process, its extension or its curtailment . . . . is not measured by the number of independent intermediate members which the production process embraces."[65]

23. *The investment period during new capital construction.*—"In a sense, *all* work done in a stationary society is replacement work."[66] This mode of approach has perhaps much more justification than the crude division of the production system into producers' goods and consumers' goods production, whereby the "early stages" of production are assumed to be engaged in the one, the "later stages" in the other part of that process. According to this last view, the number or the work of the earlier stages is imagined to be increased if society becomes progressive. The question then arises whether lengthening of the investment period is not confined to the period of capital accumulation, while shortening occurs when the process of accumulation comes to an end and a stationary state sets in.

This is Professor Knight's view. If more capital goods are constructed, he says, "there will be, *temporarily* (while the expansion is taking place, but not after it is completed), a slight increase in the proportion of goods in the earlier stages of processing operations, in comparison with later stages."[67] It will be shown, nevertheless, that a society which stops constructing new capital and confines itself to maintaining capital does stop lengthening its investment period; it need not shorten it if the transition is not too sudden.

[64] Howard S. Ellis, *German Monetary Theory, 1905–1933*, ("Harvard Economic Studies," Vol. XLIV), p. 354. "A given increment of capital has nothing to do with the number of independent productive stages through which the intermediate products pass."

[65] *Positive Theory*, p. 91.

[66] Marschak, *Economic Journal*, March, 1934, p. 151.

[67] Knight, *Economic Journal*, March, 1935, p. 78 (italics are his).

The essential point in the argument is the gradual transition from a state of new capital formation to a state of pure capital maintenance. It is easy to see that there is a rate at which new saving and investing may slow down, and finally dwindle, without necessitating a shortening of the investment period (and difficulties in the construction-goods industry). Any increment of capital involves an increment in replacement funds necessary for full maintenance. If society is "progressive" but at a decreasing rate, the funds supplied for maintenance still continue to increase. The decrease in the supply of new savings may, therefore, be compensated by the increase in the supply of replacement fund, so that the total supply of free capital disposal remains equal.[68] In other words, the increase in construction of equipment for replacement purposes may offset the decrease in construction of new capital equipment. If the rate at which saving and investing falls off does not surpass these limits,[69] no shortening of the investment period need ensue.

On the other hand, it should be noted that if the increase in capital takes place within too short an interval, it will not be sufficient to maintain the lengthened investment period. If in an economy which has been stationary hitherto one single investment is made and not followed by any further complementary investments, the single investment is, generally, bound to be wasted.[70] The lengthening of the production process is itself a process which needs time to be completed and, hence, to become definitive. But if after a sufficiently long phase of capital formation the transition from this phase to a phase of pure maintenance of capital is gradual enough to "permit the processes which have already been

[68] Suppose a current replacement fund of 300 units and new capital formation of 40. In the next interval the replacement fund will have to be (if the replacement quota is 10 per cent) 304 so that new capital formation can fall to 36 without causing a reduction in the supply of capital disposal (see Fritz Machlup, *Börsenkredit, Industriekredit und Kapitalbildung* [Vienna, 1931], p. 106).

[69] These limits are determined, as shown by Fowler (*The Depreciation of Capital* [London, 1934], pp. 36–54), by the average durability and its relation to the average construction period of capital goods. Here is the place where these concepts used by Professor Knight (see above, sec. 9) adequately come in.

[70] For detailed explanations, see my book, *op. cit.*, pp. 103–11; and Hayek, *Econometrica*, April, 1934, pp. 153–58.

started to be completed,"[71] the lengthening of the investment period will have been not temporary but definitive.

24. *Changes in demand.*—Changes in the investment period are not always caused by changes in time preferences. Purely qualitative changes in demand of intentionally equal time index may cause changes in the investment function. For a single-plan economy, however, this is not true, since the omniscient plan-makers will see whether or not the changed tastes can be satisfied without any different, or more or less, equipment and, hence, without any changes in the time distribution of services. If changed tastes could be satisfied only by a changed time structure of production, the plan-makers would immediately have to balance the displaced alternatives, which in this case would be alternatives of different time index. In a money-enterprise economy the situation is different, because of the lag of cost reactions behind consumers' choices. The prices of consumers' goods between which the individuals choose may be, at the time of the choice, different from what they would be after all rearrangements of productive services necessary for the provision of the goods demanded had been performed or calculated. The change in investment periods comes about by way of interactions of entrepreneurs, and it is only through consecutive changes in prices that consumers find their changed tastes to be incompatible with unchanged time preferences.

Using less abstract language, we may say that the consumers' choices between goods made from different materials or made in different types might cause major adaptations in the productive equipment. If the specificity of equipment does not permit technical adaptation, the change can be made only out of replacement funds. The quasi-rent in the still underequipped line of production becomes apparent in higher rates of interest offered for free capital disposal. In this way replacement funds not only from the overequipped line of production (overequipped relative to the changed demand) but also from quite different industries are attracted by the more profitable production. Resulting price increases in other products force the consumer to reconsider the

[71] Hayek, *ibid.*, p. 157.

distribution of his budget. (This redistribution may include the item "saving" because it is not only prices of commodities but also the rate of interest which undergo change.)

The adaptation in the productive apparatus to a change in demand may lead either to merely temporary or to definitive changes in the investment structure. This depends on two circumstances: first, a change in demand so sudden and sharp that the producers of the product that fell into disfavor cannot earn any replacement quotas (definitive loss of the sunk investment) will tend to definitive shortening of the investment period; second, the quasi-rents of the producers of the favored product, if saved and invested, might counteract the first tendency.

There is another point calling for attention. Apart from the losses and gains of transition, differences in the "capital intensity" of the goods between which the demand has shifted may be important. The favored product may not only need different equipment but more or less equipment than the product in disfavor has needed for its production. The shift in demand may, for instance, finally be "capital saving." (Crude examples: Tents preferred to houses; services of stage actors preferred to services of automobiles.) Whether or not such changes lead to shorter investment periods depends on many questions, e.g., whether consumers use all the money diverted from capital-intensive products for purchases of less capital-needing products (or what else they use it for); whether the sunk capital can be extracted from the industries in disfavor; whether the capital extracted from these industries is used for reinvestment elsewhere (probably under reduced interest rates), etc.

In an economy in which new savings are continually forthcoming, a part of the new savings will be used for financing the adaptations of equipment to changed demand. Since the presumption that net losses of capital are connected with these adaptations is very great, it is fair to assume that an economy can be stationary in respect to its capital base only if it provides new savings to rebuild its equipment needed for changed tastes. An economy which is stationary in terms of new savings (i.e., savings are zero) is declining in respect to its capital base, if changes in demand occur. Or, to put it in another way, "quick change in the objects of consumption without the emergence of new savings is itself a form of consuming capital."[72] Changes in demand represent, therefore, one of the qualifications of the proposition that any increase in the supply of capital disposal leads to a lengthening of the investment period. Changes in demand represent, furthermore, one of the important, but neglected, points in the theory of the natural rate of interest. Changes in demand tend to raise the equilibrium rate of interest[73] and may involve a sufficient impulse for an (inflationary) expansion of bank credit.

25. *Changes in technical knowledge (inventions).*—The invention case was the basis of the very first critical discussions following publication of Böhm-Bawerk's *Positive Theory.* The greatest part of these discussions was occupied by repetitions of simple misunderstandings. The misnomer "period of production" led critics to look at the duration of the direct technical production process proper, and then to believe that almost all inventions shorten this period. Sewing by hand is a much slower method of making dresses than sewing by machine. Hence, thought the critics, the production period was shortened by the invention of the sewing machine. Böhm-Bawerk had a hard time to explain that sewing of the dress was only the last part of the process, while in the process as a whole services were invested in iron production and machine shops and in the sewing machine and only finally in the dressmaking.[74]

In his ardor to refute the assertion that the production period is shortened by such inventions, Böhm went so far as to assure us

[72] Machlup, "The Consumption of Capital in Austria," *Review of Economic Statistics*, XVII (January, 1935), 14.

[73] The effect upon the equilibrium rate of interest of changes in demand can be the result of several opportunities of investment, e.g.: (*a*) financing technical adaptations; (*b*) financing quick construction of the *different* equipment needed for the newly favored product; (*c*) financing construction of the *increased* equipment if the newly favored product is capital-intensive; (*d*) financing construction of different and increased equipment which was, due to lumpiness, hitherto not to be used profitably but becomes so if the demand for the newly favored product reaches a certain minimum.

[74] See especially Böhm-Bawerk's "Exkurse," e.g., "Exkurs II," in *Positive Theorie des Kapitales*, II (4th ed.), 44.

of the contrary, which is not true either. The invention neither shortens nor lengthens the investment period. All it does is to make investment opportunities more or less profitable. If and when new capital disposal is supplied (e.g., by new savings), then the investment period can be lengthened. But if these new savings would have come forth in any case, then the investment period would have been lengthened in any case. The new invention, if it was of the mentioned type, merely made the interest rate higher than it would have been otherwise.

If there is no increase in the supply of money capital above the current supply of replacement funds, then there is generally no possibility of a lengthening of the investment period. But if the new invention is connected with some especially durable instruments, will not substitution of new instruments of itself involve a lengthening of the investment period? If exploitation of the invention appears to be profitable in spite of its taking so much capital away from other industries (under a sharp rise of the interest rate), so many other investments which would otherwise have been made are omitted that the investment period is left unchanged. The high rate of interest might, of course, induce people to save or to dissave, and in this way lead to a change in the investment period.

New inventions may suggest new sorts of equipment which compete with, and render obsolete, existing equipment. This may cause major losses of sunk investment; the investment period may be shortened (in case replacement funds have to be attracted from other industries) or may be left unchanged (in case new savings are just sufficient to finance the new investment) or lengthened in a smaller degree than would otherwise have been possible. But it would be quite unwarranted to consider this a social loss. If an undiminished or even increased product can be provided with less capital or in a shorter investment period, there is no reason for resenting such a development. (Of course, if the inventions had been known many years earlier, many past investments would have been made differently and their obsolescence saved.) Obsolescence occurs if the new equipment is relatively more efficient or if it is cheaper. The latter is a case of a "capital-saving" invention. The old equipment is depreciated to the lower value of the new, because the price of the products of this equipment would no longer cover replacement of the former value. What the consumer had to contribute to this replacement now becomes his increased purchasing power, which may be spent for increased consumption or which may be saved. The capital loss through obsolescence is capital consumption in the sense that it is accompanied by increased consumption, but it is not capital consumption in the sense that it renders impossible permanent maintenance of consumption on the higher level.

In substance, the effect of inventions, capital-needing or capital-saving, upon the investment period is per se neither lengthening nor shortening; their indirect effects depend on the incidental losses of transition and on the incidental changes in saving and dissaving.

26. *Investment period and disinvestment period.*—Changes in technique, it has just been shown, need not involve changes in the investment period. But neither need changes in the investment period involve changes in the technical methods employed. In an economy where no durable goods exist and where no technical substitutability exists, so that the proportions between the factors in the production of any one product are fixed, shortening of the investment period would be possible through changes in the relative proportions of different industries. There are two ways of shortening the investment period without changing the technique of production in an economy which employs durable goods. One way is changing the proportions between industries; the other is neglecting temporarily the replacement of durable goods. To say this is not to assert that these are the only or the most likely procedures in disinvesting societies; but it is necessary to warn against the belief that an unchanged technique of production offers any evidence for an unchanged investment structure.

Consideration of the "disinvestment period" is necessary for the analysis of a number of problems connected with capital disinvestment either as a phase of the business cycle or as a general trend,[75] as well as of problems connected with the adaptation of

---

[75] See Machlup, "The Consumption of Capital in Austria," *Review of Economic Statistics*, XVII (January, 1935).

specific capital equipments to changing conditions. It is nevertheless not true that immobility or specificity of equipment are the only factors that matter. Even if every good were perfectly transformable into any other good, if we, therefore, could eat up machines and buildings directly rather than through a lengthy process of undermaintenance, even then the disinvestment period would remain significant for the questions how long "overconsumption" can be continued, and after what interval the consecutive shrinkage in width of the consumption stream will come about.

The statement that "in equilibrium the period of investment for the total volume of capital . . . . is equal to the period of disinvestment"[76] is liable to misinterpretation. Within what time the total capital of society can be disinvested is not the point in question. The notion of the investment period, being an "average" of an infinite number of time indices, would not help to answer such a question. To put the question for the length of the disinvestment period in terms of an individual investment would be still less sensible. The individual investor can exchange his property rights against present consumption income (of course not at a fixed ratio) at any time, whether they are taken over out of new savings or, in want of new savings, out of some replacement funds. And the marginal investment at one moment of time will hardly concern the same lines of production as the marginal disinvestment at another moment.

The use of replacement funds for "taking over" property rights of disinvesting individuals, hence the use of replacement funds for the disinvestors' consumption,[77] is the essential point. The speed or rate of supply of replacement funds, on the one hand, the consequences of withdrawing parts of them from reinvestment, on the other hand, are dependent on the time structure of investment. The average time interval from investment to consumption is also the average time interval from investment to the forthcoming of the capital disposal free for reinvestment, because it is the receipts

[76] Fowler, *The Depreciation of Capital*, p. 35.

[77] Not necessarily the disinvestors' personal consumption; if they disinvest, say, in order to pay taxes, state employees might be the persons who do the consuming. Disinvestment for the sake of financial liquidity is to be discussed later.

from the sales of the consumption goods which provide the replacement quotas for all the earlier stages of production.[78]

Imagine a barter-enterprise economy with vertically integrated production. The entrepreneur exchanges the final products of his production, or other consumption goods which he received in exchange for his, against productive services, if he wants to continue the enterprise, i.e., if he wants to reinvest. But he eats them himself if he does not want to reinvest. In a money-enterprise economy the money receipts for the final consumption goods are the funds available for reinvestment or disinvestment. The industry where a disinvestment takes place—i.e., where reinvestment is omitted—need by no means be the same as, or be closely connected with, the industry which received for its products the money that "financed" the disinvestment, first, because replacement, though continuous in the economy as a whole, is not continuous in single lines of production; second, because the money capital circulating in an economy with vertically differentiated production (i.e., not integrated in one firm) is a multiple of the "real" replacement funds. This monetary phenomenon is partly responsible for the difficulties, in practice as well as in theory, which result from the fact that the money capital *de facto* available for disinvestment exceeds in so large a degree the money capital "genuinely" released from production through the final sale of consumption goods. The meaning of these phrases is more readily apparent if one imagines the money funds which would be available for reinvestment or disinvestment in an economy with vertically integrated production.

V. THE CREDIT CYCLE

27. Credit expansion and investment period.—Analysis of the consequences of an increase in the amount of money capital given to entrepreneurs has to cover a number of possibilities. Apart from an increase in the holdings of cash reserves (hoarding), and from an increase in the money work to be done on account of a possible increase in "interfirm transactions," the incre-

[78] On this point see my *Börsenkredit, Industriekredit und Kapitalbildung*, pp. 15–16; and Strigl, *Kapital und Produktion*, pp. 30–37.

ment in money capital may be used (1) for employing a given amount of services for other work than that for which they were hitherto employed; (2) for paying higher rates per unit of service; (3) for employing a greater amount of services from the factors hitherto employed (longer labor week); (4) for employing a greater amount of services from factors hitherto unemployed.

An analysis that begins with full employment and given supply of services has to take into consideration only the possibilities (1) and (2). But these two will have to go together under almost all assumptions. If the increase in the amount of money capital given to producers is due to voluntary saving, hence to a decrease in the amount of money spent directly on consumers' goods, the tendency toward a rise in the prices of productive services will be smallest. But there will still be a tendency for such a rise, because marginal-value productivity of labor services should be assumed to rise in those employments which are made profitable by the interest-rate reduction that accompanies the increased supply of money capital. The rise in wage rates will, of course, be sharper if not voluntary saving (abstinence from consumption), but credit expansion is the source of the increased supply of money capital. But in both cases the first of the mentioned possibilities is rather certain to come true, and, according to what has been said above (see especially secs. 17 and 18), the work that will be favored at the expense of some other work will be of a type that yields consumable services at, on the average, more distant points of time.

The sequences of events characterized as lengthening of the investment period have mostly been described for the case of a fixed supply of productive services. Increased employment of services —i.e., the possibilities (3) and (4) above—have been ruled out. This was correct as a first approximation, but a further step is to analyze the sequences without the assumption of fixed supply of productive services.

The inclusion of the possibility (3)—i.e., of employing more services from an unchanged number of men—is theoretically fascinating (because of the interesting complications in assuming various shapes of labor supply curves), but it has less practical significance than the possibility (4)—i.e., employing formerly unemployed factors of production. The absorption into the productive process of unemployed factors has been regarded by many writers as the realistic case where the irrelevance of an investment-period theory for the analysis of credit expansion would become apparent. And this for two reasons: first, it has been said that if sufficient productive capacity is available no services have to be withdrawn from consumption-goods industries as, owing to an expansion of credit, the production of investment-goods industries is extended; second, the amount of service input being increased, the increased investment need not involve any lengthening of the investment period. There is more investment, but there are also more productive services, hence no change in proportion and no "distortion of the investment structure" will ensue.

The correctness of this view and the applicability of an investment-cycle theory are not incompatible. One has to bear in mind that, according to the capital theory under consideration, an increased amount of services can be employed, without additional voluntary abstinence from consumption, only if the investment period is shortened[79] and the earnings per unit of service are reduced. By employing more services, through credit expansion, at unreduced rates of earnings without voluntary saving, the investment period, absolutely unchanged, becomes longer than it would be without credit expansion.

The case of credit expansion with full employment and that without full employment are, therefore, equivalent in respect to the fact that the investment period becomes longer than it would

[79] Less capital per head is available. See above, p. 590, and also p. 605. It need not be explained that the return to labor is smaller the shorter the period of investment. In terms of cost theory one would speak of decreasing returns of increased application of labor, or of increasing marginal cost of production. A qualification should be made with reference to the unused capacity argument. If unused capacity of equipment of all sorts is available in all stages of production, and if materials, goods in process, and finished goods of all kinds are on stock in sufficient quantities, synchronized production (and consumption) could set in at a stroke all at once. No additional waiting for intermediate or finished goods would be needed. (Why there should be unemployment, under such circumstances, is, however, hardly intelligible.)

be if the supply of money capital were confined to its "natural"[80] sources: namely, replacement funds and voluntary savings.

28. *Investment period and inevitableness of the breakdown.*—Absolute or relative overlengthening of the investment period is the probable result of expansion of producers' credit. The length is excessive in the sense that without any "outside" influences (without change in data) internal forces will lead to a reshortening of the investment period, sooner or later. The "internal forces" consist in a divergence between the individual time preferences (as expressed in the proportions in which the money incomes are saved and invested or spent for consumers' goods) and the time structure of production. The divergence is concealed so long as the credit system continues to subsidize successfully the employment of productive services for work of great consumption distance—work which would not be done if the voluntary distribution of the existing money funds alone were decisive for production.

A discussion of the details of business-cycle theory and monetary management cannot be embarked upon here. But all that is needed here is to point to the essential connection between investment period and credit cycle. While some writers find the causes of the breakdown of prosperity in the imperfections of monetary institutions or in lack of skill of monetary authorities, the investment-cycle theory suggests that there is no money system and no credit management conceivable which could permanently maintain a production structure (i.e., time distribution of productive services) which does not correspond to the structure of expenditures (i.e., time distribution of purchasing power). Though monetary forces help to bring about "prosperity," and lead to the excessive length of the investment period, monetary forces do not seem to be capable of maintaining it permanently.

Why the boom is doomed is explained by the investment-cycle

[80] No value judgment is implied in using the word "natural" as distinguished from "artificial." The "natural" sources refer to the concept of the "natural" rate of interest, which is simply that rate which equalizes the demand for money capital to the amount supplied out of replacement funds and voluntary savings.

theory. This theory does not make the pretense of being the only explanation of all cycles and crises that have ever occurred, nor does it pretend that it states unconditional necessities. The gist of the theory is that there is a high chance that increased bank credit,[81] unless offset by hoarding or similar phenomena, makes for investment periods different from what they would be otherwise; that there is, furthermore, almost no chance that the distribution of expenditures in consecutive phases will adapt itself to the investment structure;[82] and that, therefore, the investment structure will be forced to undergo a process of readjustment.

29. *Liquidation for consumption versus liquidation for liquidity.* —The "liquidation mania" commonly observed during crises and depression, the urgent attempts to exchange capital goods and property rights for liquid funds, are not motivated by the wish to use the liquid funds for buying consumption goods but by the wish to keep the liquid funds on reserve. These rather obvious facts are taken by some writers for the whole substance behind the notion of depression. The struggle for liquidity alone is held to account for the disinvestment after prosperity. Hence, the breakdown is considered either as the result of psychic (or psychopathic) phenomena or as the result of the failure of the credit system to supply the money necessary to satisfy this increased demand for liquidity.

Nobody can seriously question the fact or the significance of this "liquidation for liquidity." But this clearly visible fact should not lead us to forget that it is as a rule preceded and, in a sense, "caused" by "liquidation for consumption." This "liquidation for consumption" is the discontinuance of activities of great consumption distance forced upon, or suggested to, the entrepreneurs through lack of capital disposal or through cost increases which are but the expression of the comparatively more urgent demand

[81] Increased utilization of bank balances may take the place of increased amounts of bank balances. (Increase in V' rather than increase in M', i.e., "dishoarding.")

[82] The adaptation of the expenditure distribution to an excessive period of investment would consist in providing increased savings to take the place of infusions of new bank credit.

for consumption goods. That the use of productive services ceases to be profitable for a certain kind of work is the expression of the buyers' preference for other products, e.g., for "present" consumption goods. The first attempts at disinvesting—i.e., the failure to reinvest in work of great consumption distance—may easily, and actually did mostly, start a general flight from investment into greater holdings of cash. Although in reality the two types of liquidation are ordinarily combined, they should be distinguished in theoretical analysis. Complete absence of the liquidity rush would not imply elimination of the business cycle or of depression; only the depth of the trough, the amplitude of the cycle, would be much smaller.

30. *Deflation and shortening of the investment period.*—How much of the difficulties and frictions would be taken away from society if deflationary liquidation did not accompany and aggravate consumptive liquidation cannot be known. But that the shortening of the investment period is connected with difficulties and frictions of its own seems to be certain. They may result from several circumstances: (1) Many capital goods are specific, i.e., not capable of being used for other purposes than those they were originally planned for; major losses follow then from the change in production structure. (2) Capital values in general—i.e., anticipated values of future income—are reduced by higher rates of capitalization; the owners of capital goods and property rights experience, therefore, serious losses. (3) Specific capital goods serviceable as "complementary" equipment for those lines of production which would correspond to the consumers' demand are probably not ready; employment in these lines is, therefore, smaller than it could be otherwise. (4) Marginal-value productivity of labor in shorter investment periods is lower; wage rates are, therefore, depressed. (5) Under inflexible wage rates unemployment ensues from the decreased demand prices for labor.

That capital loss, wage cuts, and unemployment can be explained apart from any deflation does not mean that in reality they are not entangled with deflation. We said before, and repeat here, that deflation, though sometimes "caused" by the process of shortening the investment period, aggravates this process considerably.[83]

31. *Immobility of factors and rigidity of costs.*—The immobility and specificity of capital goods—strengthening the resistance to adaptation and adjustment—has something to do with the durability of instruments and thereby with the investment period. But, as Professor Knight points out correctly, there is no definite relation between durability and the lack of adaptability.[84] And there is certainly not the least economic connection between investment period and the main force of resistance to adjustment: cost rigidity. Hence, with immobility of factors (human and produced) and rigidity of costs (labor and material) as the essential factors of the trouble, the period of investment would have no place in the analysis of depression.

If capital goods were mobile and perfectly adaptable there would be no unused plant capacity. And "if labor were mobile and wages flexible, no fixity in the capital structure would give rise to unemployment."[85] And yet, to explain unemployment (through wage stickiness) is one thing; to explain the business cycle is another. If wages were perfectly flexible there would perhaps be no sharp fluctuations in employment, but there would be fluctuations in wage rates instead. Why the perfectly flexible wage rates go up through some length of time and why they fall most heavily through some succeeding length of time—in other words, why there is boom and depression, and whether and why depression must follow the boom—would still remain open questions. For a theory of the business cycle, with no unemployment but wage fluctuations instead, the concept of the investment period would be as valuable a tool as it is for the theory of the business cycle with little wage flexibility and unemployment.

[83] To state this is by no means to advocate reflationary measures. Although they may offset hoarding and mitigate the difficulties connected with it, they may also interfere with, and actually delay, the necessary adaptations in the production structure.

[84] *Economic Journal*, March, 1935, p. 93; *Canadian Journal*, February, 1935, p. 21.

[85] Knight, *Economic Journal*, March, 1935, p. 94.

[12]

REPRINTED FROM
QUARTERLY JOURNAL OF ECONOMICS
NOVEMBER, 1939

PERIOD ANALYSIS AND MULTIPLIER THEORY

SUMMARY

Significant periods: transaction periods, 2; income periods, 3; plan adjustment periods, 5; equilibrium adjustment periods, 6.—The relevant income period, 7.— The length of the adjustment period, 11.— Marginal propensity to consume treated as a psychological factor, 13.— The lag of cumulative income, 16.— Schematic illustration, 17.—Analysis of the leakages, 17.— The leakage through imports, 21.— Dropping some assumptions: effective demand, 23; the state of confidence, 24; cost of production, 24; interest rates, 25.— Unpredictability of idle balances, 26.— Conclusion, 27.

This article is not an exegesis of the theory of the Multiplier; nor is it a critique; it attempts merely to be an analysis of some essentials of that theory. I intend to place much emphasis on points which have received little emphasis, if any, by the founders of the Multiplier theory, Messrs. Kahn and Keynes; and I shall employ a terminology of which they disapprove. Not that I wish to criticize them for their distribution of emphasis or for their use of terms. I have found, however, in countless discussions that the choice of terminology is not always quite disassociated from the importance which one wishes to assign to various problems. For a discussion of time lags, transition phases, and other intertemporal relationships, Keynesian terminology is not well suited. The time element in the theory of the Multiplier is, I submit, of great importance. Hence the use of concepts more appropriate for "period analysis" — such as the concepts employed by D. H. Robertson — recommends itself.[1]

1. The main difference concerns the concepts of "income" and "saving." While Keynesian concepts compare rates of flow at simultaneous instants of time, we shall employ Robertsonian terminology, for which saving is the difference between "today's" consumption and "yesterday's" income. The meanings of "today" and "yesterday" will occupy us presently.

1

2   QUARTERLY JOURNAL OF ECONOMICS

Significant "Periods"

The meaning of "period analysis" is ambiguous, and recent discussion has suffered from a confusion of various sorts of "periods." Especially these four groups of periods are often confused with one another: transaction periods, income periods, plan adjustment periods, and equilibrium adjustment periods. They all have their place in economic analysis. The following digression on economic periods has, of course, wider application than merely to the theory of the Multiplier, and it is for that reason more detailed than would be necessary for an understanding of Multiplier theory.[2]

The concept of a "transaction period" is useful in order to take account of the facts that dates of receipts and outlays are usually fixed, and that nobody can spend any part of his receipts (gross or net income) before he receives it. (That one can borrow in addition to ordinary receipts, or spend out of a balance carried over from the past, are obviously important matters which no period-analyst neglects.) For some persons the (individual) transaction periods may be more significantly determined by fixed dates of heavy expenditures, or, more correctly, by the intervals between these dates, than by dates of receipts. (Example: the weekly or bi-weekly pay rolls of firms whose wage payments constitute a considerable part of their total money transactions.) For other persons fixed intervals between the dates on which they receive the largest payments affect their individual transaction periods. There are at least three different transaction periods which ought to be distinguished.

Transaction period A is the length of the cycle of ebb and flow in the balances of the individual cash holder; or, in other words, the time interval between the peaks (or normally recurring troughs) in his cash balances.[3] This period does not reflect either large or small amounts held permanently idle (i.e., throughout the period under consideration), or long or short average intervals between receipt and outlay. (If a firm pays wages every Friday, its transaction period A may be a week, whether the bulk of receipts come in earlier or later in the week or at an even rate.)

Transaction period B is the time interval during which money, both the currently received funds and the funds carried as more

2. I am indebted to Mr. Abba P. Lerner for suggestions which helped me to improve an earlier formulation of these passages.

3. "Money" or "cash balance" include both currency and check deposits.

permanent reserve, can be said to rest, on the average, in the cash balances of the individual cash holder; or, in other words, the ratio of average cash balance to total of outlays; or, again in other words, the period of time for which total outlays are equal to the average cash balance. This period can be calculated for individual persons (accounts) or for groups of persons. For the whole economy it is the reciprocal of the transaction velocity of circulation. For individual accounts transaction period B will be shorter than transaction period A, if the individual holds only negligible minimum balances; it will be longer, if minimum balances are considerable. For the economy as a whole transaction period B is almost certain to be longer than average transaction period A.

Transaction period C is the time interval during which currently received money amounts can be said to rest, on the average, in the cash balances of the individual cash holder, neglecting those amounts which are carried as a minimum balance; it is, in other words, the ratio of average minus minimum balance to the total of outlays; or, again in other words, the period of time for which total outlays are equal to the active part of the average cash balance; i.e., to the excess of the average over the minimum cash balance. Transaction period C is shorter than transaction period B, because it neglects the inactive part of the cash balance; it is also shorter than transaction period A, because the average interval between receipt and outlay is shorter than the interval between consecutive dates of periodic receipts or periodic outlays. For a person whose receipts come periodically while his outlays take place at an even rate (or *vice versa*), transaction period C will be half of transaction period A; if the same person carries no minimum balances, i.e., if he exhausts his balances completely, so that the lows are zero balances, transaction periods B and C will be the same.

For persons whose receipts constitute their net income, the transaction period is an "income period." There are at least five different "income periods" which ought to be distinguished. The first three are analogous to the three transaction periods.

Income period A is the length of the cycle of ebb and flow in the cash balance of the individual income recipient; or, in other words, the time interval between the consecutive peaks (or troughs) in his cash holdings. For the wage earner paid weekly, income period A is a week; for the recipient of a monthly salary, income period A is a month.

Income period B is the time interval during which money, both the currently received funds and the funds carried as more permanent reserve, can be said to rest, on the average, in the cash balances of the individual income recipient; or the ratio of his average cash balance to his total outlays; or the period of time for which his total outlays are equal to his average cash balance.[4] Income period B for the whole economy is not the reciprocal of the income velocity of circulation. Applied only to check payments, it is the reciprocal of the velocity of circulation of income deposits (see Keynes' Treatise on Money); applied to all sorts of money, it is the reciprocal of the velocity of circulation of the money balances carried by income recipients. Income period B is greater or smaller than income period A, according as minimum balances are large or small.

Income period C is the time interval during which currently received money incomes can be said to rest, on the average, in the cash balances of the individual income recipient, neglecting the amounts carried as minimum balance; or, in other words, the ratio of average minus minimum balances carried by the income recipient to his total outlays; or the period of time for which his total outlays are equal to the active part of his average cash balance.[5] The average income period C for the whole economy is a much less significant factor than the differences between the income periods C of different classes of people. These differences are relevant for discussions of problems connected with the income distribution between "fast spenders" and "slow spenders."

Income period D is the length of time which it takes for money, both active and inactive funds, to complete a circuit flow from income recipient to income recipient; or, more exactly, it is the ratio of the existing money volume (i.e., average total cash balances) to the sum total of money net incomes; or, again in other words, the period of time for which the sum total of net incomes is equal to the existing money stock.[6] Income period D is not meaningful with respect to individual accounts; it is a concept which relates only to the whole economy or to a group of individuals in a

4. Further modifications of this concept result, if "net income" or, on the other hand, "outlay for consumers' goods" is substituted for "outlay."

5. See preceding footnote.

6. Further modifications of this concept result if "income recipients' total outlays" or, again, "total outlays for consumer's goods" is substituted for "total net income."

certain region. Income period D is the reciprocal of the income velocity of circulation, or the period of time for which the income velocity of circulation is equal to one. It is obvious that income period D is longer than any of the other income periods, because it relates not only to the balances of income recipients but to all balances in existence. It includes, therefore, the sum of all non-income transaction periods which lie between the receipts of consecutive incomes.

Income period E is the length of time which it takes for the money in active circulation to complete a circuit flow from income recipient to income recipient; or, more exactly, it is the ratio of the active part of all cash balances (average total cash balances minus total of minimum balances) to the total of money net incomes; or, again in other words, the period of time for which the sum total of net incomes is equal to the total of active money balances.[7] Income period E is, of course, shorter than income period D, but considerably longer than A, B or C. Since it refers to the flow of money as it creates the incomes of consecutive recipients, income period E might be called the "income propagation period."

None of the transaction or income periods implies any assumptions regarding fixed plans or fixed propensities on the part of the persons involved. Transaction period A and income period A may be quite influential in shaping the normal planning periods, especially as to budgeting and expenditure planning. But normal planning periods are less significant than *plan adjustment periods*. The concept of a plan adjustment period rests on the fact that plans remain unchanged over a certain time interval, even if conditions change. In most cases plans may be easily changed within an income period (in all senses), whereas in some cases plans may be fixed over more than an income period. The length of the plan adjustment periods of various persons is a function of their speed of reaction, which is, in turn, the result of psychological, institutional and technical conditions.[8] The first change usually will not be the final plan adjustment; the final adjustment may come about as the result of a succession of little adjustments; the time it takes to initiate the adjustment may affect seriously the path toward a

7. See preceding footnote.
8. Since writing this article I discover that Professor Hicks employs an almost identical concept in his Value and Capital, pp. 123 and 247. There he speaks of "the length of time necessary for entrepreneurs (and others) to wake up and change their plans."

new equilibrium and, indeed, the position of the new equilibrium.

The direction of the change of plans is determined by a "given" state of tastes and propensities. There is sense in talking about propensities in this connection only if we may assume these propensities and preferences to be stable in relation to the length of adjustment periods (or, at least, to change only in a predictable manner). The adjustment of plans to changes in data is supposed to take place according to given propensities. Little can be said about any adjustment or equilibrium of any sort, if we may not assume that the propensities and preferences will be constant over the adjustment period. The constancy of a state of propensity may be safely assumed for the initial plan adjustments; whether it may be assumed also for long-run equilibrium adjustments has to be seriously considered.[9]

The *equilibrium adjustment period* is the time interval during which certain (predicted) adaptations to certain changes in data are expected to work themselves out, either completely or so far that further repercussions may be neglected. One may limit the analysis of certain problems to a certain degree of adjustment or to certain types of adjustment, ruling out a number of repercussions which are expected to take place in an adjustment period of different length. Marshallian period analysis is a case in point. The final adjustment (final in the sense that further repercussions are neglected) will mostly be reached by a succession of little steps, but it is a quite legitimate methodological procedure to skip intermediate phases of transition, and try to confine the hypothetical prediction to the ultimate outcome. It is imperative, however, for many practical problems to form an estimate as to the actual length of the equilibrium adjustment period, and to ascertain whether or not one may safely assume all "other circumstances" which have a bearing on the outcome to be invariant over that whole period.

All four groups of period concepts have their role in a period analysis of the theory of the Multiplier. Some of the periods may be needed as tools of reasoning, others may be needed only to aid in estimating the length of the periods which are themselves inherent parts of the theory. For an elementary understanding of the underlying monetary mechanism, that is, of the money flow which

9.   Some propensities, on the other hand, may be fairly stable only in the long run, while wide fluctuations are likely during short periods.

"multiplies" an initial outlay up to a higher level of income, an income period concept is fundamental.[1]   Which of the various income periods is relevant, and how long is it in terms of clock-time?

The Relevant Income Period

Let us try to make up a little story of a money flow that is started by an outlay of "new money," say, for building a road.[2]

At the moment when that increase in investment takes place and the outlay of the new money is made, a money income of exactly the same amount is received by somebody, to wit, by the workers employed on the investment project. We assume, as is proper for such stories, that nothing else has changed. Thus there is at that moment (or short interval) an increase in income which equals the increase in investment; that is, the instantaneous Multiplier is one.

The recipients of the income thus created, our road workers, are likely to turn around and spend the greatest part of the income for their consumption. In our story they take advantage of a cheap sale and buy new boots. This expenditure implies, of course, the receipt of the money by the shoe dealer. It happens, however, that the latter, who sold the boots out of his stock, regards no part of the proceeds as his net income. Strictly speaking, such a liquidation of inventory should be called a disinvestment, but we shall quickly repair this damage to the simplicity of our story by having the shoe dealer re-stock with little delay. The money goes to a wholesaler and from him, *via* a collecting agency, to a shoe factory which increases its production in order to fill the increased orders. New workers are employed by the shoe factory, and they receive the money as their net income. The money spent by our first income recipients, the road workers, has now reached second income recipients, the shoe factory workers. If our road workers have remained at their employment (i.e., if the rate of investment is continued at the increased level), they may receive another pay

1. All problems which are relevant for the "Investment-Multiplier," i.e. the ratio of total income increase to primary investment, are a fortiori relevant also for the "Employment-Multiplier," i.e. the ratio of total employment increase to primary employment.

2. There are those who feel that primitive stories are unworthy of being embodied in a scientific article. I believe, however, that if more such stories were employed by writers when they develop their arguments, they might avoid a good many pitfalls, or their critics, at least, might discover them more quickly.

envelope at just the same time that their former expenditure reaches the shoe factory workers, our second income recipients. The total increase in the flow of income above its size before the increase in investment exceeds the investment of the moment (or short interval) by the income of the second income recipients; the Multiplier at the particular moment is, therefore, greater than one.

The time interval between the first and the second increase in income was determined by the number of persons through whose hands the money had to pass, and by their particular transaction periods C, in addition to the income period C of our road workers. We should also point out (and hope that we do not thereby confuse the issue) that the length of some plan adjustment periods was involved too; the store keeper and the wholesaler had to increase their orders, and the shoe manufacturer had to increase his output. We may, however, assume here for the sake of simplicity that the reactions of all the persons involved were so fast that we need not reckon with any longer intervals than those which result from the circuit flow of money. Simplicity commands that we also neglect at this point another problem which is often connected with the emergence of increased demand: the problem of windfall profits on the part of the sellers.

On the other hand, we seem now to be ready for other, unexpurgated, versions of our story to the effect that the time interval between first and second income recipient will be replaced by a series of intervals of different length. Our shoe dealer, in this version, regards a part of his gross receipts as net income; the wholesaler, the collecting agent, and the shoe manufacturer do likewise; the second income is, therefore, split among all these people together with the shoe factory workers, leather dealers, leather dressers, tanners, etc. The average interval between the income receipt by our road workers and the income receipts by all these people who receive income out of the road workers' purchases is not something easily measured. Moreover, if our road workers did not spend all their money on boots but on a number of different things, then the "second income recipient" is a composite of several hundred different persons who receive their income at very different moments of time.

Our composite "second income recipient" will again spend a part of "his" increased income on consumption. We know already that the second receipt took place at very different moments of time. The expenditure, in turn, will take place after very different intervals, depending on so many individual income periods C, and gradually a third income receipt will arise. The "recipient" this time is a composite of tens of thousands of different persons; they will receive the income increases after intervals which include a varied number of transaction periods of varied length. It is easily conceivable that a fraction of the primary outlay will arrive at a "sixth" income recipient when another fraction is just arriving at a "second" income recipient. It is clearly imperative to simplify the analysis by thinking in terms of an average income period.

This average income period cannot be any of our periods A, B or C, because it has become apparent from our story that intermediate non-income transactions are a part of the intervals between the income receipts. Should income period D, the reciprocal of the income velocity of circulation, be the relevant interval? The income velocity of circulation for the United States has frequently been estimated at approximately 2 per year; Professor Angell estimated it at approximately 1.6 per year as a long time normal,[3] and Professor Clark arrived at a velocity figure of less than 1.1 for the depression year 1932.[4] These figures correspond to income periods D of 6 months, 7½ months, and 11 months duration respectively. These periods are clearly much longer than the income period germane to our story of the money flow.

Income period D is of so long a duration because it refers to both active and inactive money balances. The income period relevant for our purposes refers to active balances only. The income period relevant for the circuit flow of newly created or newly activated funds must neglect the existence of balances with zero velocity of circulation. The possibility that splinters of the new money flow may come to rest through hoarding on the part of successive income recipients is accounted for, in the theory of the Multiplier, by the assumption of a dwindling series of derivative incomes; it must not be counted a second time by applying the low income velocity figure. The long income period D is not relevant for our purpose.

Income period E refers only to the active, or circulating, part

3. James W. Angell, "Money, Prices and Production," *Quarterly Journal of Economics*, November, 1933, p. 75; also *The Behavior of Money*.
4. John M. Clark, *Economics of Planning Public Works*, Washington, D. C., p. 88.

of money balances; the inactive minimum balances are deducted. Income period E, the period in which total incomes are equal to the total of active balances, is much shorter than income period D. Unfortunately we have no information concerning the actual sizes of the active and of the inactive portion of our monetary stock. Information might be obtained at not too great expense. For a representative sample of accounts, minimum balances, average balances, and debits could be obtained, and transaction periods B and C calculated. Since the difference between transaction periods B and C hinges on the same distribution between active and minimum balances which is responsible for the difference between income periods D and E; since, furthermore, transaction period B and income period D are known for the economy as a whole, income period E could be deduced from the rest.

So long as we have no information, we must have recourse to guesswork. If we assume that between 50 and 60 per cent of all balances are minimum balances (with zero velocity of circulation), an income velocity of circulation of between 1.6 and 2 per year for all balances would correspond to an income velocity of 4 per year for active balances only. This would mean that income period E, or, as we called it, the income propagation period, had a duration of three months.

This does not settle the issue. The "marginal" income propagation period might be shorter than the average income propagation period. To use a metaphor, a new tributary to the existing money flow might cause some swifter currents within the flow.[5] Increased incomes (and increased gross receipts) may be passed on faster than the average of previous incomes (and gross receipts). However, the opposite is just as easily conceivable. Although the presumption seems to be more in favor of a shortened income propagation period, we shall assume for the further analysis that the marginal propagation period is the same as that of the (guessed) average period, i.e., of three months duration.[6]

5. This does not mean (abandoning the metaphor again) that formerly inactive funds are activated. Induced dishoarding is a separate problem. Here we speak only of the accretion to the money flow that started directly from the primary investment.

6. John M. Clark, op. cit., p. 87, estimated the relevant period at two months. He based his estimate more on income periods *A* and *C*, thus neglecting intermediate non-income transactions.

Another question was raised by Professor Alvin H. Hansen in private discussion: Is the income propagation period, which refers to new additions to

Two more points should be mentioned before we proceed. The pure theory of the Multiplier usually abstracts from induced changes in liquidity preference and investment propensities, hence from induced dishoarding and hoarding. Through the medium of induced dishoarding on the part of business firms the actual propagation of incomes may be much faster than that which is possible on the basis of the circuit flow of money. For the present, however, we shall rule out induced dishoarding, as it has been ruled out by most writers on the subject.

The second point is an anticipated qualification of several propositions in our further analysis. The length of the income period will be found to be an important factor in the determination of the length of the adjustment period. Yet there is nothing which assures that the income period shall not vary during transition phases. We do not refer here to the shortening of the income period D through activation of idle funds (dishoarding). Income period E is independent of this. What changes income period E is the emergence of new, or elimination of old, intermediate (non-income) transactions. An increase in transactions arising from the transfer of assets might lengthen the income period; an increase in the use of money substitutes and of clearing arrangements might shorten the income period. The effects on the propagation speed of the new income flow may be considerable.

The Length of the Adjustment Period

The statement that an increase in the rate of investment will raise the rate of income by an amount which is a certain multiple of the amount of the additional investment can be true only after the lapse of a certain period of adjustment. One factor which affects the length of the adjustment period is the length of the

the money flow, not altogether different from the regular income period *E*? Was the latter not defined as the period which elapses until a receipt of, say, $100 income of one person becomes again $100 income of other persons — while we are now satisfied with the arrival of $60 or $80 at other income recipients in case the first income recipient withholds $40 or $20 from consumption? There is, as far as I can see, no essential difference between the two income periods. In the "stationary" income propagation period $100 become again $100 income, while in the "dynamic" income propagation period $100 may become only $60 or $80 income; but, for that, the latter need not be different in length from the former. What is withheld from expenditure will not arrive at another recipient; but what is spent need not arrive there any faster.

income period.[7] Another major factor is, as will be shown presently, the actual value of the Multiplier, the length of the adjustment period varying directly with the value of the Multiplier.

With the Multiplier equal to one, the final rate of income is, of course, reached simultaneously with the increased rate of investment, or without any time lag. The Multiplier is equal to one, if there is no secondary income, that is, if the primary income recipient uses no part of it for consumption expenditures. (If the reader finds it hard to assume such a thing, let him imagine that the income recipient has had pressing bank debts which he repays or reduces with the increment to his income.)

With the Multiplier equal to infinity the "final" rate of income would be reached only after a time lag of infinite length. Table I may illustrate this case, which is hardly possible, because the duration of fixed propensities (to consume, to save, to invest, to be liquid, etc.) will be shorter than the adjustment period: the propensities that would make for the infinite increase in income are likely to change after a finite time interval.

The assumptions which underlie the figures of Table I—some of which are likely to be somewhat offensive to common sense — are these: (1) An additional investment at a rate of $100 per period is undertaken by the Public Works Authority and financed through the issue of securities which are bought by the Central Bank. (2) Every income recipient spends all of his income received on consumption goods.[8] (3) In spite of increased incomes, people do not wish to augment or reduce the absolute amount of their inactive money balances (i.e., their liquidity for speculative or precautionary purposes). (4) In spite of the increase in the public debt and in the monetary circulation, no change in "confidence" takes place, so that private investment incentives as well as speculative liquidity-preferences are unaffected by this influence. (5) In spite of the financing of the additional investment, interest rates and the availability of money capital remain unchanged, so that other investment activities are not affected by this influence. (6) In spite of increased incomes and increased demand, no increase in derived investment takes place, so that the extra-investment by the PWA

7. By "income period" we mean here and in the rest of the article the period relevant for the propagation of income.

8. We might say "domestic consumption goods." Foreign trade will be discussed in a later section.

TABLE I

					Income Receipt								Total Increase of Income
Period	I	II	III	IV	V	VI	VII	VIII	IX	X	XI	XII	
1	100												100
2	100	100											200
3	100	100	100										300
4	100	100	100	100									400
5	100	100	100	100	100								500
6	100	100	100	100	100	100							600
7	100	100	100	100	100	100	100						700
8	100	100	100	100	100	100	100	100					800
9	100	100	100	100	100	100	100	100	100				900
10	100	100	100	100	100	100	100	100	100	100			1,000
11	100	100	100	100	100	100	100	100	100	100	100		1,100
12	100	100	100	100	100	100	100	100	100	100	100	100	1,200

is not followed by any other investment increases. (This is really an impossible assumption, because there must be, at least for a time, increased investment in working capital.) (7) In spite of the increased demand for productive resources on the part of the PWA, cost of production remains unchanged, so that the extra investment by the PWA does not on this account change the rate of private investment.

These assumptions have merely the purpose of ruling out, for the time being, a number of problems which we prefer to deal with at a later stage of the exposition; problems which are usually hidden under two short-cut assumptions, viz., that the marginal propensity to consume is equal to one, and that there is a net increase in the rate of investment of $100.

It can easily be seen that, under these assumptions, the total increase in the rate of income rises in every income period. If marginal propensity to consume is to refer to the behavior of consumers, it makes no sense to state that with a marginal propensity to consume of unity the Multiplier is infinity: what is true only after a time lag of infinite length is not true in our world. If the length of the income period is three months, the Multiplier which corresponds to a propensity to consume of unity becomes 3 after half a year, 5 after a year, 9 after two years, 13 after three years, and so on.

We should point out, however, that we have here used the concept marginal propensity to consume in a sense in which it has been used by Keynes only in a few places in his General Theory, viz. as a psychological factor determining the behavior of consumers. Another definition is used when the relationship between the marginal propensity to consume and the Multiplier is said to be reducible to an algebraic expression between simultaneous rates of investment and rates of income. That an empirical phenomenon and an analytical (tautological) ratio cannot be one and the same thing is obvious. Professor Haberler has shown the difference in the logical nature of the two concepts of the marginal propensity to consume.[9] If one wished to apply the tautological concept of the marginal propensity to consume to the case of the gradual rise in the rates of income, one would have to state that the "marginal propensity to consume" is rising gradually from zero to unity — in spite of the fact that *every* successive income recipient spends *all* of his income on consumption, that is to say, in spite of the fact that the "psychological propensity to consume" is unity throughout the transition period. It is, of course, the psychological propensity which will be referred to throughout the argument.

The thought that an infinite income corresponded to a propensity to consume of one prevented most writers from seeing that the marginal propensity to consume can be greater than one.[1] After all, the Multiplier cannot be greater than infinity! Yet the Multiplier can easily be greater than 3 after half a year, or 5 after

---

9. Gottfried Haberler, "Mr. Keynes' Theory of the 'Multiplier': A Methodological Criticism," Zeitschrift für Nationalökonomie, Vol. VII, 1936, pp. 299–305.

1. That the increase in consumption is absolutely greater than the increase in income, i.e. that $\frac{\Delta C}{\Delta Y} > 1$, refers to consumption compared with *received* income, hence to $\frac{\Delta C_t}{\Delta Y_{t-1}}$. If one applied Keynes' Multiplier formula of $K = \frac{1}{1 - \frac{\Delta C}{\Delta Y}}$ to the case of $\frac{\Delta C}{\Delta Y} > 1$, the Multiplier would be a *negative* value and the whole matter would refer to a diminished rate of investment (because if $\Delta C > \Delta Y$, then ΔI would be negative) instead of an increased rate of investment. The confusion arises from the fact that any increased consumption would, in turn, involve increased income, increased income again increased consumption — until the system would "explode." The crux is that it is not of much value to speak of simultaneous rates which are applicable to "any instant of time" and yet include all effects which take place only through time. In any finite period the Multiplier would, of course, be less than infinity, and the "tautological marginal propensity to consume," therefore, would be less than unity.

a year, in spite of a three-month income-period — and it will be so if the marginal propensity to consume is greater than one. It is easily conceivable that income recipients increase their consumption by an amount which exceeds the rise of their received income. They can do this by borrowing or by dishoarding. Indeed, investigations in installment buying seem to indicate that increases of consumption in excess of increases in received incomes are actual occurrences.

If the marginal propensities to consume are between zero and unity, it is interesting to know the eventual Multiplier that would be approached after "full" adjustment.[2] But since the adjustment period may exceed the calendar periods with which the Treasury and other authorities must deal, and, moreover, since we must not calculate with "given conditions" for too long a period, it is more important to know the Multiplier that may be expected to be reached after half a year, after a year, etc.

For small marginal propensities to consume, and hence small values of the Multiplier, the adjustment periods are short enough to be of practical significance. If the marginal propensity to consume were $\frac{1}{2}$ and the "full" Multiplier, therefore, equal to 2, the increased rate of income would come within 10 per cent of the full multiple after a lapse of only three income periods. $(100+50+25+12.50=187.50.)$ This would mean that with an average income period of three months, the approximate adjustment period would be some nine months.

For a marginal propensity to consume of $\frac{2}{3}$, and a full Multiplier of 3, an increased income flow of 10 per cent below the full multiple of the extra investment would be reached after five income periods, or, according to our previous assumption, after fifteen months. $(100 + 66.67 + 44.44 + 29.63 + 19.75 + 13.17 = 273.66.)$ The Multiplier after a quarter of a year would be only $1\frac{2}{3}$, the Multiplier after a year would be $2\frac{49}{81}$. Had the PWA, the Treasury, or the Banking authorities reckoned with the "long-run Multiplier," they would be considerably off the expected figures — even if all the other assumptions were less "incredible" than they unfortunately are.

2. We speak of "full" adjustment when further repercussions become so slight that they may be neglected.

THE LAG OF CUMULATIVE INCOME

For many problems the current rate of income is the significant factor. For other problems cumulative figures which include the changing rates of income over a transition period are more significant. For an estimate of the income-tax proceeds for the next year or two, neither the full (long-run) Multiplier nor the value that the Multiplier may reach after certain dates is relevant. Since the rate of income rises gradually, a period of a year includes the low income figures which belong to the early phases of the adjustment period. The sum total of income increase of the first year after the beginning of the investment program bears to the sum total of additional investment a ratio which falls short of the ratio which the increase in the income *flow* bears to the *rate* of additional investment at the end of the year.

Let us assume, for example, a net increase in investment of $100 per income period and a marginal propensity to consume of $2/3$. The long-run Multiplier is 3; that is, the eventual increase in the rate of income would be $300. The Multiplier after one year would have reached, according to the above reasoning, $2\frac{49}{81}$, that is, the rate of income per period would have increased by about $260. The total income for the year would show a still more modest increase in relation to the total extra investment. With a total extra investment of $100 per income period, hence $400 for the whole year, the total increase of income would be $718.52 for the whole year $(100+166.67+211.11+240.74=718.52)^3$; this is only a little more than $1\frac{3}{4}$ times the total investment increase.

The greater the long-run Multiplier, the more disappointing (relatively, of course) will be the short-run effects. A long-run Multiplier of 5, which would correspond to a marginal propensity to consume of four-fifths, would take an adjustment period of the length of 10 income periods in order to be approximated by a 10 per cent margin. (The income increase would reach $457 in the 11th period. See Table II.) If the income period is three months, the adjustment period would be two and a half years. After a year and a quarter, i.e., in the sixth income period, the increase in the income flow would be about $3\frac{2}{3}$ times the rate of additional investment; and the total increase in income since the beginning of the

3. The income level reached after the lapse of the fourth income period would not be included in the incomes realized during the first year.

investment program would be about 2½ times the total additional investment. These figures compare rather poorly with the full-fledged Multiplier of 5, yet they are, no doubt, the ones which have to enter into a realistic account.

If, therefore, the adjustment periods are longer as the Multiplier is higher, or, in other words, if high Multiplier values are not realized in short calendar periods, the short-run effects of public works will not differ so much as one might think for higher and lower marginal propensities to consume.

A Schematic Illustration

Some of the points discussed so far, and a few others to be dealt with presently, can be made much clearer with the help of a table showing the successive income payments. Table II assumes a marginal propensity to consume of four-fifths. We shall make again our whole series of assumptions, with the promise to drop most of them later. The second assumption (see above, p. 12) now reads thus: Every income recipient spends 80 per cent of his received income on consumption goods. Assumptions (3) to (7), which all had the purpose of ruling out any induced changes in private investment, may be retained here, except that assumption (3) should now read: In spite of the increased "savings" on the part of the individual income recipients, interest rates and the availability of money capital remain unchanged, so that other investment activities are not affected by this influence. If the marginal propensity to consume is defined in terms of wage units, we might add, for the sake of the simplicity of dealing in dollar figures, another assumption (8) to the effect that wage rates remain unchanged throughout the upswing of income which is created by the public investment program.

What Are the Leakages?

The marginal propensity to consume is, of course, not the same for all individuals; the value of the marginal propensity to consume for society as a whole will, therefore, depend on the distribution of the income flow among different individuals. We chose to conceal this problem — which is of importance because of the changes in income distribution resulting from the income change — by making the assumption that *all* individual marginal propensities to consume are four-fifths, so that each income recipient

TABLE II[1]

	I	II	III	IV	V	VI	VII	VIII	IX	X	XI	XII	XIII	XIV	XV	XVI	XVII	XVIII	XIX	XX	XXI	XXII
Sum Total of Extra-Investment since the beginning	100.00	200.00	300.00	400.00	500.00	600.00	700.00	800.00	900.00	1000.00	1100.00	1200.00	1300.00	1400.00	1500.00	1600.00	1700.00	1800.00	1900.00	2000.00	2100.00	2200.00
Sum Total of Increase of Income since the beginning of extra-investment	—	20.00	56.00	104.80	163.84	231.07	304.86	383.89	467.11	553.69	642.95	734.35	827.47	921.97	1017.57	1114.05	1211.23	1308.97	1407.16	1505.71	1604.55	1703.62
Sum Total of Increase of Saving since the beginning of extra-investment	100.00	280.00	524.00	819.20	1155.36	1524.29	1919.43	2335.54	2768.43	3214.74	3671.79	4137.44	4609.97	5088.00	5570.43	6056.38	6545.15	7036.18	7529.02	8023.31	8518.76	9015.14
Total Contribution to Saving of the period	—	20.00	36.00	48.80	59.04	67.23	73.79	79.03	83.22	86.58	89.26	91.40	93.12	94.50	95.60	96.48	97.18	97.74	98.19	98.55	98.84	99.07
Total Contribution to Income of the period	100.00	180.00	244.00	295.20	336.16	368.93	395.14	416.11	432.89	446.31	457.05	465.65	472.53	478.03	482.43	485.95	488.77	491.03	492.84	494.29	495.45	496.38

Income Recipient / Period (Income and Saving per recipient, diagonal pattern repeating across periods):

Period	Income	Saving
1	100	
2	80.00	20.00
3	64.00	16.00
4	51.20	12.80
5	40.96	10.24
6	32.77	8.19
7	26.21	6.56
8	20.97	5.24
9	16.78	4.19
10	13.42	3.36
11	10.74	2.68
12	8.60	2.14
13	6.88	1.72
14	5.50	1.38
15	4.40	1.10
16	3.52	0.88
17	2.82	0.70
18	2.26	0.56
19	1.81	0.45
20	1.45	0.36
21	1.16	0.29
22	0.93	0.23

1. It should be kept in mind that in the table "income period" stands for "income propagation period," and not, as one might think, for the individual income periods "A" of the first income recipients. If the income propagation period were twelve weeks, but the primary investment were paid out in weekly periods, $100 per income period would mean $8.33 per week. (It would, of course, be possible to construct a table with weekly payments which reach the next income recipient after so many weeks as correspond to the income propagation period. The intermediate non-income payments might be entered in such a table. The gain for "realism" would be a loss for "simplicity.")

saved twenty cents out of each dollar received. These twenty cents represent the famous "leakage."[4]

Many of the critics of Multiplier theory were not able to interpret the leakage as anything but "hoarding." Accumulation of idle cash balances (and cancellation of bank deposits through debt repayment) was the only answer which these critics had for their query as to the nature of the leakages. This identification of the leakages with hoarding is liable to make full-blooded Keynesians furious. They usually react to it with an explanation of the meaninglessness of the concept of hoarding — in the Keynesian language — but they do not tell their misinterpreters "what happens to the leaked-out funds." They confine themselves to the contention that all that matters is the fact that these amounts are not spent on consumption. This answer, in turn, is apt to make their opponents furious.

As a matter of fact, it *is* irrelevant for the immediate effect what the nature of the leakage really is. It *is* true that it does not make any immediate difference "what happens to the leaked-out funds." But the critics have nevertheless a perfect right to know what happens if the funds are not "hoarded." Additional curiosity does more good than harm; and incidentally what happens to the leaked-out funds has its indirect bearing through its effects on liquidity, interest rates, debt structure, and other matters.

That the savings of individual income recipients may be used for debt cancellation, or for accumulating inactive savings deposits, or for piling up idle demand deposits are, of course, possibilities. If the banking system creates $100 in demand deposits by its acquisition of the securities which finance the PWA investment, and if (e.g.)the $36 which are "saved" in the third income period (Table II) are used for bank debt repayments, the *net* increase in active balances in this period will be only $64. Exactly the same will be true if the $36 are employed to purchase securities from the banking system. And again the same will be true if the $36 are used to buy a part of the newly issued securities which finance the PWA investment. For if $36 of the new security issue is bought "out of current savings," only $64 will flow from new bank credit as a "contribution to income." The critics were not able to see that the $36 would constitute a leakage, even if they were "invested,"

4. The problem of "leakages due to imports" will be discussed separately.

because they overlooked the fact that it had been *assumed* that no additional investment over and above the $100 PWA investment was being made. Hence, if the $36 were not hoarded but "invested," they simply alleviated the demands on the banking system. As to the effects upon secondary income, it did not matter what happened to the saved funds, as long as the assumption was maintained that the total net increase of the rate of investment was no more and no less than $100.

The secondary saving, as the voluntary saving out of the secondary incomes may be called, increases with the secondary income from period to period. If the rate of total investment remains constant, as has been assumed, an increasing part of the public investment outlay will be financed out of voluntary saving, or, at least, offset by voluntary saving. The continuing PWA investment will, therefore, make smaller and smaller net contributions toward further increases in income. In the 12th income period, for example (to illustrate again with our Table II), secondary saving is $91.40, so that only $8.60 of the public investment during that period is of expansionary character. Income in this period rises, accordingly, only by $8.60 above the income of the preceding period. In the 15th period more than 95 per cent of the public investment can be financed out of voluntary savings. The income flow approaches a new equilibrium level as the amount of voluntary additional saving approaches the amount of additional investment. When almost the entire outlay for the public investment can be financed directly or indirectly by voluntary saving, the continued investment outlay will not result in any further increase in income.

It will be noted that the rate of income reaches practically its new equilibrium level (the famous multiple of the rate of investment) at the time when the rate of investment no longer exceeds the rate of voluntary saving. This is a remarkable meeting of the timeless and the period analyses of Saving and Investment: the Multiplier principle will have worked itself out when saving out of received income becomes equal to investment. The emergence of a new equality of saving and investment (in the Robertsonian sense) marks the end of the adjustment period for the (Keynesian) Multiplier principle.

THE LEAKAGE THROUGH IMPORTS

The leakages in the income stream which were attributed to various forms of saving are totally different in nature from the leakages attributed to imports. In a superficial account, however, they look much alike. The part of income, for example, which is applied to the repayment of a bank loan will cause a reduction of bank assets ("loans and discounts") and an equal reduction of bank deposits. The part of income which buys imports will likewise cause a reduction of bank deposits and of bank assets (the reduced assets being "due from foreign banks" or "reserve with central bank," directly, and "gold," indirectly). Indeed, were the whole Multiplier theory not based on the condition of an elastic credit supply, one might enlarge upon the more stringent effects which the increased imports are likely to have owing to the loss of bank reserves.

The error in this type of reasoning lies in the neglect of the increase in foreign incomes derived from the increased domestic incomes. If it is assumed that a certain part of any domestic income increase will be used for purchasing not domestic but foreign consumers' goods, then we must go the whole length and assume that a certain part of any foreign income increase will be used for purchasing imports and will thus create, through "our" increased exports, a further domestic income increase. If the foreign country does not itself pursue expansionary policies, so that the increase in "our" imports is the only contribution to the foreign income increase, then we must, of course, not expect that our increased imports will bring forth an equal increase in exports; but they will bring forth some increase in exports. It is likely that the income propagation period becomes longer because of a time lag of exports behind imports, although the opposite result is also conceivable. If the foreign countries happen to engage in the same expansionary policies, the increase in exports might equal the increase in imports, and the "leakage" through imports would then be absolutely zero.

One might hold that the increased imports which result from the increase in income constitute "leakages for the time being," and that an eventual increase in exports should be treated as a separate, new impulse. Such a procedure would be most arbitrary; it would involve coupling a timeless Multiplier theory with a time-conscious foreign trade theory. Consistent timeless analysis would have to include the increased exports no less than any other derived purchases in the aggregate income increase. If period analysis is applied, it becomes obvious that the increase in exports is likely to come about within the adjustment period and, therefore, that imports must not be treated as definite leakages. Only when the country is very small in comparison with the rest of the world is the error involved in neglecting induced exports slight. In this case the full "leakage through imports" may be accepted as a sufficient approximation.[5]

DROPPING SOME ASSUMPTIONS

Any statement which "predicts" a certain income increase as the result of a certain amount of public works and of a given propensity of consumers to use a certain portion of their income increase for increased consumption is based on a fundamental assumption: viz. that the identical amounts which are spent by consumers are eventually received by income recipients. This implies that business firms expend no less and no more than they receive, which will be true only (1) if they do not increase or decrease their investments, and (2) if they do not change the minimum cash balances which they carry. These two conditions were the gist of those contained in the list of assumptions which we put as preamble to Tables I and II. The probability that these conditions will be fulfilled is almost nil.

Equilibrium analysis is generally not vitiated by the discovery that things which in theory are assumed to be unchanged are likely to change in reality, if only these changes are either independent of the analyzed causal relationship or if their influence upon the outcome is negligible. That conditions *may* change is no argument against assuming them to remain unchanged. But conditions which *must* significantly change, or are most likely to change when a certain event occurs, should not be treated as unchanged in an applicable theory of the effects of that same event.

Several of the assumptions made in the theory of the multiplying effects of public works involve conditions which are liable to change, not only independently but as direct or indirect effects of the additional investment and the increased income. There is,

5. It ought to be mentioned at this point that other factors which are sometimes treated as leakages, such as "saving on the dole" or displacement of private investment, should be dealt with as factors influencing the rate of investment increase, not as leakages from the income flow.

first of all, the inducement to invest which is affected by the "primary investment," that is, in our case, by the outlays on public works. Private investment will be affected on four counts: first, because of the change in effective demand; second, because of changes in the state of confidence; third, because of changed production costs; fourth, because of changes in interest rates and in the availability of capital. All of these may affect private investment in either direction, the net resultant being determined by the relative importance of the component forces.

Effective demand. The income flow which is created by the public works may decrease private investment by facilitating disinvestment. In the early phases of a public works program, especially if it is started before the downswing has reached its bottom, private disinvestment may easily be the concomitant of public investment: firms sell out of inventories which they do not replace at the time; the new money flow then disappears immediately through the leak of liquidation (unless dividend payments are increased).

In a later phase of a public works program, when disinvestable inventories are exhausted, a tendency toward increasing the marginal efficiency of private investment seems to be obvious. To satisfy the increased consumers' demand through increased production of consumers' goods implies increased investment in *working* capital. Any appreciable increase in employment above the public works employment will clearly bring with it increased outlays for building up inventories: the principle of acceleration is set in operation with respect to working capital both more certainly and much earlier than with respect to durable equipment.

In a third phase increased investment in *durable* equipment will be induced by the continued rise in effective demand, unless such inducement is offset by opposite forces. The neglect of opposite forces and, therefore, the active interplay between Multiplier and Acceleration principle was perhaps the substance behind the pump-priming theories of recent years.

The assumption that private investment remains unchanged, and hence the theory that the income increase will tend toward its multiple of the public investment, would fit in our world only the conditions prevailing at the transition stage between the first and second phase, when disinvestment through inventory liquidation and induced investment in inventory accumulation just balance each other. A justification of the assumption of unchanged private investment might, however, also be found in the idea that the building up of inventories would merely be a temporary adjustment whose effects would not change that long-run equilibrium level of income which corresponds to a permanent rate of public investment.

For an analysis of aggregate income and aggregate spending it seems to be a rather arbitrary procedure to single out the marginal propensity to consume and to shove aside the marginal propensity to invest. A rise of a craftsman's income, for example, may induce him to buy a new hammer just as it may induce him to buy new boots. To include the boot purchase (through the assumption of increased consumption), but to exclude the hammer purchase (through the assumption of unchanged investment opportunities), has the sure advantage of making possible a theory with simpler formulæ but the disadvantage of making that theory less applicable.

The state of confidence. Prejudice more than experience and common sense often make for certain changes in the state of confidence, which may either reinforce or offset the effects of the public works outlays. "Confidence" is an aggregate of vague ideas about general prospects of profits or losses, influenced mostly by expectations as to general price movements, taxes, restrictions, and the like. Unbalanced budgets and a rising public debt, both involved in a public investment program, may easily affect the state of confidence and, thereby, the inducements for private investment. While the fear of an immediately imminent inflation might lead to a wave of heavy private investment, vague uneasiness and uncertainty might lead to a decline in investment offsetting the effects of the public outlays.

"Confidence" not only affects investment directly as a part of the investor's expectations (i.e. as a part of the marginal efficiency of capital); it enters in a second time through its influence upon lenders, the resulting effects upon interest rates and the availability of capital.

Cost of production. Both primary public investment and secondary consumers' demand are likely to raise the prices of some factors of production. Higher cost tends to reduce the marginal efficiency of investment. While the expectation of quickly rising costs may temporarily increase private investment, the persistent effect of increased costs of production is certainly toward a diminution of private investment. The level of production cost may indeed be the critical factor in the whole question of private investment and employment. A mere sign-post must suffice here; a discussion of the point would go much beyond the scope of this article.

Interest rates. It is conceivable that interest rates may remain unchanged in spite of the additional investment and its results; but this is not likely to be the case. The ways of financing the extra investment, on the one hand, and changes in liquidity-preference, on the other, would not be without influence. Higher interest rates would restrict, lower interest rates would enhance private investment activities. Of importance also, in a world of credit rationing, is the fact that the "internal rates of interest" of individual business firms may be higher than the rates at which they actually borrow. If, because of narrow lines of credit, firms cannot borrow as much as they would like to, the marginal efficiencies of the funds which are available to them constitute their internal interest rates. It has been mentioned above that changes in effective demand are likely to change the schedules of marginal efficiencies of investment. No matter whether and in what direction such changes occur, the internal interest rates of firms may be automatically diminished (along the revised schedules) when, through increased demand, increased proceeds (profits) make more funds available to the firms. The public investment may have been financed by a banking system with large excess reserves and, hence, perfectly elastic credit supply — in other words, under unchanged market rates of interest; yet internal interest rates to secondary money recipients may be reduced. Even a slight rise in the market rate of interest may be compatible with a reduction of many an internal interest rate, if the funds of the "primary" borrower — the PWA — reach secondary recipients who had been able to borrow only less than they demanded. It should be repeated that the "external" rates of interest charged to particular firms may also be changed simply as a result of changed risk estimates.

Ordinarily, however, the fact that the banking system may be able to finance the additional investment only under rising interest rates would imply — unless the marginal efficiency of capital had already risen — that private investment is encroached upon by the public investment. If the capacity of the banking system to create credit was small — as was the case in many Central European countries — public loan expenditures would be almost completely at the expense of private investment; and the Multiplier theory of public works would be of little use. To be more exact, one should state that, in a system incapable of creating money, the funds for public investment may be drawn, through increased interest rates, from three sources: (*a*) from the investment funds of private industry; (*b*) from dishoarded idle balances; (*c*) from increased voluntary saving. Only source (*b*) would have any multiplying effects upon income. The theory that the interest rate cannot rise unless "liquidity-preference" rises has no explanatory value. Those who hold this theory would readily admit that the funds drawn from inactive balances will be "held" in (consecutive) cash balances for transactions purposes, and will become available for inactive reserves only very slowly and to the extent that secondary savings are brought forth. If an increased income level is to be supported by a fixed quantity of money, with unchanged preference to be liquid for speculative purposes, the interest rate would have to remain at an increased level, and public investment would *for the larger part* be permanently at the expense of private investment.

If the banking system is capable of creating credit, and if a part of the public investment is directly or indirectly financed by the central bank, the liquidity of the member banks and, as secondary savings come forth, the liquidity of individuals and firms will be increased. A fall in interest rates will most likely ensue; and private investment may, therefore, become more attractive. There is another reason why interest rates may fall (or money capital become more easily available to potential investors). The increase in effective demand, which is the very essence of Multiplier theory, may lead to a fall in the liquidity-preference for speculative purposes. This would probably occur if price increases resulted from the increased demand and were expected to continue. Unfortunately, exactly the contrary development is not impossible either; "confidence" may change for the worse, and liquidity-preference may increase.

The complete unpredictability of changes with respect to idle balances deprives any statement about the multiplying effects of public works of most of its predictive value. And, incidentally, there are many cases for which the tools "liquidity-preference" and "marginal propensity to consume" fit only under strain. Take the case of business corporations which make increased profits from their sales of consumers' goods and retain a part of these profits in the form of idle cash and PWA-financing securities. Must we then speak of a decreased marginal propensity to consume (although corporations can never be said to consume at all, but merely to influence their stockholders' consuming power by greater or smaller profit distributions) and, at the same time, of an increased liquidity-preference (although the relative distribution of wealth between cash and other assets may not have changed)? Anyway, in whatever terms we put it, the fact would remain that the money spent on consumption by one income recipient would not reach the next income recipient to the full amount; and the Multiplier would be less than the "psychological marginal propensity to consume" would lead us to expect.[6]

Every proposition can be made "true under all circumstances," if it is reduced to an empty tautology. This can be easily done with the theory of the Multiplier. Instead of speaking of a certain amount of public works, one can speak of a certain net increase in the rate of aggregate investment. And instead of speaking of a certain psychological propensity to consume, one can speak (see above, p. 13) of a ratio between investment and total income. But it should be clear that the theory of the Multiplier is then of no use. It would not refer to the possible effects of public works, because public works are not likely to be identical with the "net increase in the rate of aggregate investment." And it would not refer to the typical behavior of consumers, but rather to an infinite number of possible events whose composite but wholly unpredictable effect is expressed by a term confusingly named "propensity to consume."

The theory of the Multiplier, if it is to be of use to those who wish to know the possible and the probable effects of public works, must renounce the attractive appearance of neatness and preciseness. The two variables which seem to play the main parts in the play of the Multiplier must be decomposed into the all too large number of variables which play the important rôles in the real world.

Fritz Machlup.

The University of Buffalo

6. That business firms retain part of their profits and hold them in cash or securities can, after all, not be said to be a function of an increase in real income and of the propensity to consume a certain part of it.

[13]

The Review *of* Economics *and* Statistics

VOLUME XLII   MAY 1960   NUMBER 2

ANOTHER VIEW OF COST-PUSH AND DEMAND-PULL INFLATION

Fritz Machlup

IT is with some hesitation that I join the discussion and thus contribute to the galloping inflation of the literature on the creeping inflation of prices. My excuse is probably the same as that of most of my fellow writers: dissatisfied with much of what others have written, I have, perhaps presumptuously, decided that my way of thinking would be more successful. Hence, I am presenting another view of cost-push and demand-pull inflation.

The Current Debate

Before I set forth the controversial issue and the most widely held views, I shall indulge in a few preliminaries by referring briefly to the old squabble about what should be meant by inflation.

Inflation of What?

Some people regard "inflation" as a *cause* (explanation) of a general rise in prices (and of some other things too), while others use the word as a *synonym* (equivalent) for a general rise in prices. In times when governments undertake to control prices by prohibitions with threats of sanctions against unauthorized price raising, many writers realize how awkward it is to use the term inflation to signify price increase, because then they want to discuss the "latent" or "repressed" inflation — one that does not show up in a general price index, or does not show up adequately. Also when one talks about inflation and deflation as apparent opposites, a definition in terms of general prices is quite inconvenient, inasmuch as the problem of deflation is so serious largely because it shows up in falling volumes of production and employment instead of falling prices.

One solution would be to use the word infla-

tion always with a modifying word that tells exactly *what* is blown up: currency, credit, spending, demand, wages, prices, etc. This would be a great help; indeed some controversial problems would disappear, because the disputants would find out that they were talking about different things, and other problems would be greatly clarified. The most lively issue of our times, whether "our" inflation in the last four years has been due to a demand-pull or to a cost-push, would lose some of its muddiness if the analysts had to qualify all their pronouncements with regard to the inflation of credit, spending, demand, wholesale prices, consumer prices, and so forth.

A search of the learned literature would yield scores of definitions of inflation, differing from one another in essentials or in nuances. A search of the popular literature, however, reveals no realization of the differences in the meanings experts give to the term. The differences apparently have been reserved for the treatises and the quarterlies; the daily papers and the weeklies were not to be encumbered with "technicalities." Now that inflation has become such a widely debated topic, with many scholars participating in the debates, the popular meaning of inflation, denoting an increase in the consumer price index, has been increasingly adopted by the professional economists. Although this is probably bad for analysis, we may have to accept it. But at the risk of appearing pedantic I shall continue to speak of various kinds of inflation and to specify which I happen to be speaking about.

The Controversial Issue

Opinion is divided on whether consumer prices in recent years have increased chiefly (1)

[125]

because industry has invested too much and government has spent too much (relative to the nation's thrift) or (2) because big business has raised material prices and/or big labor has raised wage rates too high (relative to the nation's increase in productivity). The issue is partly who is to be "blamed" for the past rise in consumer prices, and partly what policies should be pursued to avoid a continued increase.

If demand-pull inflation is the correct diagnosis, the Treasury is to be blamed for spending too much and taxing too little, and the Federal Reserve Banks are to be blamed for keeping interest rates too low and for creating or tolerating too large a volume of free reserves, which enable member banks to extend too much credit.

If cost-push inflation is the correct diagnosis, trade unions are to be blamed for demanding excessive wage increases, and industry is to be blamed for granting them, big business may be blamed for raising "administered prices" of materials and other producers goods to yield ever-increasing profit rates, and government may be assigned the task of persuading or forcing labor unions and industry to abstain from attempts to raise their incomes, or at least to be more moderate.

Not everybody draws the appropriate conclusions from the theory which he espouses. And not everybody is willing to adopt policies to correct the undesirable situation. (Nor does everybody find the situation sufficiently undesirable to get seriously worried.)[1] The ambivalent position of many partisans of labor unions is noteworthy. They reject the wage-push diagnosis because, understandably, they do not wish to take the blame for the inflation. But they also reject the demand-pull diagnosis, because this diagnosis would militate against the use of fiscal and monetary policies to bolster employment. They want effective demand to be increased at a rate fast enough to permit full employment at rapidly increasing wage rates; but they do not want to attribute increasing prices either to the increase in demand or to the increase in wage rates. The only way out of this logical squeeze

is to blame the consumer-price increase on prices "administered" by big business; but in order to support this hypothesis one would have to prove that the profit margins and profit rates of the industries in question have been rising year after year — which they have not.[2] But we shall see later that matters are not quite so simple and cannot be analyzed exclusively in these terms.

Our first task is to deal with the contention that the distinction between cost-push and demand-pull inflation is unworkable, irrelevant, or even meaningless.

"Cost-Push No Cause of Inflation"

There is a group of outstanding economists contending that there cannot be such a thing as a cost-push inflation because, without an increase in purchasing power and demand, cost increases would lead to unemployment and depression, not to inflation.

On their own terms, these economists are correct. The rules of inductive logic say that if A and B together cause M; and if A without B cannot cause M, whereas B without A can cause M; then B, and not A, should be called the cause of M. Make A the wage-raising power of the unions and the price-raising power of the corporations; make B the credit-creating and money-creating power of the monetary system; make M the successive price increases. It should be quite clear that without the creation of new purchasing power a continuing price increase would be impossible. Hold the amount of money and bank credit constant (relative to real national product) and all that the most powerful unions and corporations can do is to price themselves out of the market.

Having admitted all this to the economists who reject the possibility of cost-push inflation, we can shift the weight of the argument to the question whether, given the power of the monetary system to create money and credit, this

[1] Cf. "Argument for Creeping Inflation," *New York Times*, March 3, 1959; "Slow Inflation: An Inescapable Cost of Maximum Growth Rate," *Commercial and Financial Chronicle*, March 26, 1959; "Inflation — A Problem of Shrinking Importance," *Commercial and Financial Chronicle*, April 23, 1959 — all by Sumner H. Slichter.

[2] "The period 1947 to 1958 was a time of decreasing profit margins. This fact is important because it shows that the initiative in raising prices was not being taken by employers. In the four years 1947 to 1950 inclusive the net income of non-financial corporations after taxes per dollar of sales averaged 4.45 cents. In the next four years the average net income was 4.10 [cents] per dollar of sales; and in the three years 1955 to 1957 inclusive, it was about 3.3 cents per dollar of sales." Slichter, *Commercial and Financial Chronicle*, April 23, 1959.

COST-PUSH AND DEMAND-PULL INFLATION

power would be exercised to the same extent if strong trade unions and strong corporations desisted from raising wages and prices as it actually is exercised when wages and prices are being pushed up. There would probably be quick agreement that, given our present system, the exercise of the wage-raising power of strong unions and the price-raising power of strong corporations induces, or adds impetus to, the exercise of the ability of the banking system to create purchasing power.

The point then is that an increase in effective demand is a necessary condition for a continuing increase in general prices, but that a cost-push under present conditions will regularly lead to an expansion of credit and to that increase in effective demand which will permit the increase in consumer prices.

There remains, however, an important question of fact. Assume it is decided not to exercise the power to create money and credit — more than is needed to maintain a constant ratio to real national product — even at the risk of severe unemployment that might result if wages and prices increased; would we then have to expect that the strong unions and corporations would continue to make use of their wage-raising and price-raising powers? Some economists are convinced that unions and business firms would adopt much more moderate policies if they had to fear that any lack of moderation would lead to unemployment and stagnation. This does not mean that a considerable level of unemployment would be required to impress industry and unions with the desirability of moderation. Industrial firms would know that, under an unyielding monetary policy, they could not hope to pass increases in labor cost on to consumers and they would therefore refuse to yield to union pressure. Unions, in turn, would not strike for higher wages if they were sure that industry could not afford to give in. Hence, no cost-push and no extra unemployment.

Acceptance of this view by any number of economists would not yet make it a practicable policy. It could not work unless the monetary authorities embraced it without reservation, since any indication of a lack of faith and determination on the part of the authorities would remove the premise: unions could hope that industries would hope that an eventual relaxation of the monetary brake would "bail them out" and by means of an expansion of demand avert the business losses and the unemployment that would threaten to arise in consequence of wage and price increases.

"Demand-Pull No Cause of Inflation"

Having shown that there is a sense in which the contention is correct that "cost-push is no cause of inflation, it takes a demand-pull to produce it," we shall now attempt to show that the opposite contention may likewise be correct. There are indeed assumptions for which it would be appropriate to say that "demand-pull is no cause of inflation, it takes a cost-push to produce it." What are these assumptions and how do they differ from those of the traditional model?

In the traditional model, prices rise or fall under the impact of anonymous market forces. They rise when at their existing level the quantity of goods demanded exceeds the quantity supplied. Not that producers, noticing the increased demand, would decide that they could do better if they "charged" more; rather the mechanism of a "perfect market" would automatically lift prices to the level where the consumers would not want to purchase any more than was supplied. Sellers, in this model, don't ask higher prices, they just get them. The same thing happens in the model of the perfect labor market. When the demand for labor increases, workers don't ask for higher wages, they just get them as a result of competition.

In a large part of our present economy, prices and wages do not "rise" as if lifted by the invisible hand, but are "raised" by formal and explicit managerial decisions. Assume now that prices and wage rates are administered everywhere in the economy in such a way that changes in demand are not taken into account; instead, they are set in accordance with some "rules of thumb." Prices and wages may then be so high (relative to demand) that inventories accumulate, production is cut, and labor is unemployed; or they may be so low (relative to demand) that inventories are depleted, production is raised, customers must patiently wait for delivery or their orders are rejected, and there are plenty of vacancies, but no workers to fill them. If the rules of thumb are universally observed by producers, distributors, and labor unions and take full account of increased cost of production and increased cost of living, but disregard all changes in demand, then there can be no demand-pull upon prices. In such circumstances an increase in effective demand leads to unfilled orders and unfilled vacancies, but not to higher prices.[3]

One may object, of course, that such a model cannot possibly apply to all markets; that there exist numerous competitive markets in which no producer has enough power to "set" or "charge" a price; that in many markets in which prices are administered the would-be buyers, in periods of increased demand, offer higher prices in order to be served and sellers are glad to accept them even though they exceed their list prices; and that this regularly happens when the demand for labor is brisk, so that wages paid can be higher than the rates agreed in collective bargaining. Thus, demand-pull is likely to work despite the existence of administered prices and wages.

Although the objection may be sustained on practical grounds, this does not destroy the value of the model. If there are, in actual fact, *many* industries where backlogs of orders accumulate while prices fail to rise and where job vacancies grow in number while wages fail to rise, then the model has some relevance, and it is legitimate to speculate about the functioning of an economic system in which *all* prices and wages are administered on the basis of cost calculations and held at the set levels even in the face of excess demand. It is not easy to decide whether on balance the institutions in our economy are such that a model featuring "market-clearing prices" or a model featuring "cost-plus prices" fits better the purposes of speculating about the over-all performance of the entire economy.

In any case, the contention must be granted that there may be conditions under which "effective demand" is not effective and won't pull up prices, and when it takes a cost-push to

produce price inflation. But this position disregards an important distinction, namely, whether the cost-push is "equilibrating" in the sense that it "absorbs" a previously existing excess demand or whether it is "disequilibrating" in the sense that it creates an excess supply (of labor and productive capacity) that will have to be prevented or removed by an increase in effective demand. Thus we are back at the crucial issue; a "monistic" interpretation cannot do justice to it.

Statistical Tests

It is possible to grant the usefulness of the distinction between cost-push and demand-pull in building theoretical models for speculative reasoning, and yet to deny its usefulness in identifying the causes of general price increases in concrete situations. It may be that the concepts are not operational, that statistical tests are either unavailable or unreliable.

Some have proposed to answer the question, whether wage-push or demand-pull had "initiated" the upward movement of prices, by looking to see which has *increased first*, prices or wages. But "first" since what time? If prices and wages have risen in turn, in successive steps, the choice of a base period is quite arbitrary, and a conclusion assigning the leading or initiating role to one factor or the other would be equally arbitrary. (This is especially so if our statistical information is limited to annual data.)

Not much better is the idea of looking to see which of the two, money-wage rates or consumer prices, has *increased more*. The arbitrary choice of the base period for this comparison is again a serious difficulty. But even more important is the fact that the annual rise in productivity (output per labor hour) normally secures increases in real wages over the years. Hence it is to be expected that wage rates increase relative to consumer prices regardless of whether there is inflation, and regardless of whether prices are pulled up by demand or pushed up by wages.

Even some highly-seasoned economists have fallen victim to another logical snare: that any increase in money-wage rates that *exceeded the increase in labor productivity* was a sure sign of a wage-push. Yet, even if there were no labor union in the country and no worker ever asked

---

[3] ". . . if all prices were administered on the basis of markup over direct cost — then excess demand might exist in all markets, yet without effect on the price level." Gardner Ackley, "Administered Prices and the Inflationary Process," *American Economic Review*, Papers and Proceedings, XLIX (May 1959), 421.

for higher wages, a demand-pull inflation would eventually pull up the wage level; and if the demand-pull were such that prices and wages rose by any percentage above two or three a year — and it may well be five or ten or twenty per cent — money-wage rates would be up by more than the rate of increase in productivity. This, then, would have been the result of demand-pull only, without any wage-push at all. Hence the proposed statistical test is completely inconclusive.

A test which is based on a fundamentally correct chain of reasoning would compare profit rates with wage rates, and diagnose demand-pull when *profit rates increase faster than wage rates*. A slight variant of this test uses the relative shares of profits and wages in national income. The theory behind these tests is simply this: when an expansion of effective demand — without a wage-push — pulls up product prices, an increase in profits and profit rates would result until wage rates are pulled up by the derived demand for labor. On this theory, an increase in consumer prices associated with increased profit rates, but with wage rates lagging, would reliably indicate the existence of a demand-pull inflation. The operational difficulties with a test based on this theory are the same as those connected with other statistical tests: the arbitrary selection of the time periods. The theory, moreover, applies to an economy in which most prices are the result of anonymous market forces, not of administrative decisions. If most prices were administered and the price setters decided to raise their "profit targets" (perhaps at the same time that trade unions were out to engineer a wage boost, but a little faster or by a bigger jump) we could find — given the present monetary regime guided by the high-level-employment goal — that prices and profit rates increase ahead of wage rates even though the movement was not started by an autonomous expansion of demand. Hence, the lead of profit rates is not a reliable indication of demand-pull; it may occur also in conjunction with a cost-push in which price setters take a leading part.

Widely accepted as reliable symptoms of demand-pull inflation are over-employment and over-time payments. The statistical operations proposed to establish these symptoms are, for over-employment, to see whether *job vacancies exceed job applications* and, for over-time pay, to see whether *average hourly earnings have increased faster than wage rates*. Some critics rightly point out that the presence of these symptoms does not rule out that some cost-push has contributed to the inflation of prices. Indeed it would have been possible that a cost-push actually initiated the process and that the compensatory monetary injection, expanding demand to avoid the threatening unemployment, turned out to be heavier than necessary. Thus while these tests can verify the existence of an inflation of demand, they cannot prove that it was excess demand that precipitated the inflation of consumer prices.

Proposed Concepts and Distinctions

The diversity of expert opinion and the absence of any good statistical tests to support a diagnosis may in part be due to the lack of precise definitions. It is clear that an inflation of effective demand is a necessary condition not only for a demand-pull inflation of consumer prices but also for a cost-push inflation. Without an expansion of demand the cost boost would result in less production and less employment, not in a continuing rise of the level of consumer prices. Should one then speak of a demand-pull inflation only when the expansion in demand is clearly the initiating factor and any administrative cost increases are clearly induced? Or should one also speak of a demand-pull inflation if administrative wage and material-price increases start and lead the procession of events, but are then joined and overtaken by induced or compensatory expansions of demand?

Autonomous, Induced, and Supportive Demand Inflation

It is useful to distinguish autonomous from induced and supportive expansions of demand. *Autonomous* would be expansions which are not linked to previous or to expected cost increases; hence, disbursements which would also occur if no cost increases had been experienced or anticipated. *Induced* expansions of demand are direct consequences of a cost increase, in that those who receive the increased cost-prices or those who pay them will make larger disbursements than they would have made otherwise. For example, the industrial firms yielding to union pressure for a wage increase may borrow from banks (or dig into cash reserves) in order to pay the higher wage bill; or the recipients of higher wages may increase installment purchases and induce an expansion of consumer credit. *Supportive* (compensatory) expansions of demand would be those which are engineered by monetary or fiscal policy designed to reduce the unemployment arising, or threatening to arise, from cost increases. For example, the monetary authorities may reduce reserve requirements or create reserves in order to allow banks to extend loans, or the fiscal authorities may increase government expenditures in an attempt to expand effective demand and employment.

Without wishing to restrict the freedom of choice of those who formulate definitions, I submit that the choice should be appropriate to the purposes for which the concept is used. If the concept of a demand-induced inflation, or demand-pull inflation, is to serve for diagnostic and prognostic purposes in the development of economic policies, it would seem preferable to confine it to autonomous expansions of demand. This would not obstruct but rather aid the analysis of instances in which cost-induced expansions or supportive expansions of demand should turn out to be excessive in the sense that they create more employment opportunities than are destroyed by the cost increases, and hence give rise to some of the symptoms of a demand-induced inflation.

Aggressive, Defensive, and Responsive Cost Inflation

Similar obscurities due to a lack of essential distinctions surround the concept of the cost-induced inflation. Perhaps so much is clear that the term refers to increases in consumer prices that are the (direct or indirect) result of cost increases — labor cost, material cost, or any other cost. But it is not clear whether these cost increases have to be *autonomous* in the sense that they would not have come about in the absence of any monopoly power (price-making power), merely as a result of competitive demand. For it is quite possible that formal administrative decisions are behind cost increases

which, however, do not go beyond what would have occurred without such decisions. For example, a trade union may achieve a "victory" in its negotiations with an employer group, bringing home the same raise in pay which the individual employers would have offered (without collective bargaining) in trying to get or keep the labor force they want. Let us decide to call these cost increases *responsive* (or competitive) to distinguish them from those that could *not* be obtained in a purely competitive market.

It would be misleading to denote all non-responsive (non-competitive) price or wage increases as "autonomous," since they may well be "induced" by some changes in the economic situation. (And the adjectives "autonomous" and "induced" are usually used as opposites.) A wage-rate increase, for example, is not responsive unless it is in response to an excess demand (short supply) in the particular labor market; but an increase which is not "demand-induced" (and which therefore presupposes some "autonomy" with respect to competitive market forces) may yet be induced by (a) an increase in the employer's profits, (b) an increase in wage rates obtained by other labor groups, or (c) an increase in the cost of living. I propose to call (a) a "profit-induced" wage increase, (b) an "imitative" (or "spill-over") wage increase, and (c) a "defensive" wage increase. Any one of these increases may act as either an "impulse" or a "propagation" factor in the inflationary process.

Profit-induced and imitative increases as well as spontaneous increases may be called *aggressive* because they are designed to achieve a net advance in the real wage rate. A *defensive* increase merely restores real earnings which the group in question has long been enjoying; an aggressive increase raises real earnings above that level. The specification of a time interval is necessary in the definition so that one avoids calling "defensive" what really is a battle to defend the ground just gained in an aggressive action. For example, an aggressive wage-rate increase of ten per cent is likely to be partially eroded within less than a year through the resulting cost-push inflation (aided by induced and supportive expansions of demand). If the same trade unions then demand "cost-of-living raises" to restore their real wages, it would be somewhat ironic to call these new wage adjustments "defensive." But there will always be a wide range in which cost increases may as legitimately be considered defensive as aggressive, especially since trade unions take turns in their actions, each defending the real earnings of its own members that have suffered in consequence of the aggressive actions of other unions, and at the same time attempting to obtain a net improvement.

Administrative price increases by industries producing materials and other producers goods which enter as significant cost items into the prices of many other products can likewise be characterized as responsive (competitive), defensive, or aggressive. Purely responsive increases cannot occur in an industry with much unused productive capacity; only when plants are working at capacity and orders are piling up can administrative price increases be merely responsive; in such circumstances it is economically irrelevant that these prices are administered. Defensive increases leave real profit rates substantially unchanged; these increases take account of increased production cost and no more. Needless to say, the rates of return must be calculated on the basis of the reproduction cost of the required capacity; that is to say, the book values of the fixed capital may be too low if reproduction cost of buildings and equipment is higher than at the time of their acquisition, or too high if assets are included which are not required for current production. Thus, price increases designed to defend, in periods of falling production, a profit rate that is calculated on the basis of the value of assets inclusive of unused capacity are really aggressive; and price increases designed to raise the money rate of return on capital just enough to take care of increased replacement costs are really defensive.

Should all kinds of wage increase and price increase be included in the concept of a cost-push inflation whenever they are collectively negotiated, unilaterally announced, or otherwise the result of administrative action? I submit that increases which are merely responsive (competitive) do not belong there at all. Defensive increases do of course play an important role in the process of price inflation and the economist will surely not leave them out of his analysis.

But in an explanation of an inflationary process going on year-in year-out the aggressive increases have a more substantive role to play than defensive increases; and when it comes to assign "blame" for an inflation of consumer prices, the aggressive cost boosts will obviously be the more eligible candidates.

The Basic Model Sequences

With the help of the proposed concepts the two basic model sequences of consumer-price inflation can be easily described.

(A)	*Demand-pull inflation:*	Autonomous expansions of demand (government spending, business spending, consumer spending) are followed by responsive (competitive) price and wage increases.
(B)	*Cost-push inflation:*	Aggressive increases of wage rates and/or material prices are followed by induced and/or supportive (compensatory) demand expansions.

Cost-push models are relatively simple as long as they contain only a single impulse — either wage or price increases — with all sequential changes in the nature of adjustments.

(B-1)	*"Pure" wage-push inflation:*	Aggressive increases of wage rates are followed by induced and/or supportive demand expansions, and by responsive increases of material prices and other wage rates.
(B-2)	*"Pure" price-push inflation:*	Aggressive increases of material prices are followed by induced and/or supportive demand expansions, and by responsive increases of other material prices and wage rates.

Models become more complicated as more discretionary actions are included in the sequence of events, especially imitative and defensive increases of cost elements, or even aggressive increases, requiring further adjustments. For example, an autonomous demand expansion may be followed by administered wage and price increases more drastic than merely competitive increases would be; thus, the increases would be partly responsive and partly aggressive, requiring further demand expansions, induced or supportive, if unemployment is to be avoided. Or, aggressive wage and price increases may be followed by excessive demand expansions, perhaps because a nervous government rushes in with overdoses of supportive injections of buying power; some of the effective demand thus created would then be in the nature of an autonomous expansion, resulting in further (responsive) upward adjustments of costs.

Attempted Application

Even the most complicated model sequence will probably still be much simpler than the actual course of events as reflected in the data at our disposal. Since reality is so messy that no neat and simple model will fit at all closely, whereas various complex models will fit approximately, it is not surprising that even impartial analysts arrive at divergent interpretations of the so-called facts.

The Postwar Inflation

In the narrow scope of this article no attempt can be made to sift the data, to assess the comparative applicability of the various models, and to award first prize to the best-fitting model. But I shall not dodge this question and shall indicate briefly what impressions I have derived from the data presented by governmental and private researchers.

I believe that for an explanation of the consumer-price inflation from 1945 to 1948, and from 1950 to 1952, the basic model of the demand-pull inflation does as well as, or better than, any of the other models, simple or complicated. On the other hand, for the period 1955–59 several cost-push models appear to do better, and I am prepared to regard the consumer-price increases of these four years as a result of a cost-push inflation.

The choice among the various cost-push models is a hard one, especially in view of the controversy about the behavior of administered material prices. The periodic increases in steel prices have sometimes been regarded as the most strategic impulse factor in the inflationary process. A special theory of "profit-target pricing" assuming "periodic raising of the target" has been devised in support of this diagnosis and an array of empirical material has been added in its support.

Wage or Profit Push?

Neither this theory nor the statistical data seem to me to make the model of the "material-price-push inflation" a plausible explanation of the period in question. While many of the administered price increases may have hampered the performance of our economy and accelerated the inflationary process, I doubt that all or most of them have been "aggressive" in the sense defined. The reported data on profit rates and profit margins do not, in my judgment, indicate that the price increases were aggressive. Of course, few, if any, of the increases since 1955 have been in the nature of responsive adjustments to excess demand—but probably most of them were defensive in nature, taking account of cost increases without raising real profit rates. I cannot verify this impression of mine to everybody's satisfaction, and perhaps not even to my own. But my impression is strengthened by the deduced consequences of certain assumptions, which I consider plausible, concerning the policies and objectives of business managers.

There is, in my opinion, nothing invidious in contending that there are essential differences between most wage increases obtained by strong labor unions and most increases of material prices announced by strong corporations. Nor is it meant to be critical of union policies or uncritical of business policies if many wage increases are held to be aggressive, and many administered price increases defensive. The point is that the situation of most businesses is such that a series of aggressive price increases would be either injurious to them in the long run or downright impossible. A series of aggressive wage increases, on the other hand, may be both possible and beneficial to the labor groups concerned.

To hold that most administered price increases have been defensive rather than aggressive, does not mean (a) that the prices in question were not too high — they probably were, (b) that the increases did not speed up the inflationary process — they certainly did, or (c) that they were "justified" — which they were not if a competitive market model is used as the standard. But if the question is only whether these price increases were the "impulse factors," the "initiating forces" of the price inflation, then I believe the answer is negative.

Wage Increases and Productivity

I do not expect serious exception to the proposition that most of the wage increases obtained by strong trade unions in the last four years, whether spontaneous or profit-induced or imitative, have been aggressive in the sense defined. (This is in contrast to most wage increases between 1945 and 1952, which were responsive.) We must now inquire whether aggressive wage increases are inflationary if they do not exceed the relative rate at which productivity increases.

Aggressive Wage Increases to Capture Average Productivity Gains

According to accepted doctrine, the consumer price level can be held approximately stable, and full employment maintained, if the average increase in money-wage rates does not exceed the average increase in productivity in the economy as a whole. Some of the necessary qualifications to this proposition are not relevant to the issues under discussion. For interested readers they are presented in a footnote.[4] One

qualification, however, that may matter here to some extent concerns the additional profits needed as returns on the additional investments required for the increase in national product. It is sometimes possible for total product per worker to increase thanks to a progress of technology, organization, or skills, without any increase in capital investment. More often, however, it takes some additional investment to achieve an increase in productivity. If such investments were not allowed to earn a return, progress might be stopped short; but if they are to earn a return, total profits must increase lest the rates of return on capital are cut, which could lead to reduced investment and employment. Hence, as a rule, wage increases must not absorb the entire increase in output. And if the additional investment were so large that capital per worker has increased at a percentage rate greater than that of output per worker, wage rates cannot even increase by as much as output per worker and still allow price stability with full employment.[5]

The following formulation will steer clear of such technicalities and express the essential points. Apart from a few modifying influences, such as a squeezing of quasi-rents in stagnant industries, a whittling down of the real claims of recipients of contractual incomes, or a lucky improvement in the terms of foreign trade, real wages per worker cannot increase faster than product per worker. If *money*-wage rates are raised faster than productivity, and the monetary authorities supply the money needed to pay the increased wages without unemployment, prices will rise enough to keep *real*-wage rates from rising faster than productivity. To say

[4] There is first the qualification for the sacrifice of fixed-income recipients. The existence of contractual payments in fixed money amounts makes it possible for wage rates to increase a little more than productivity. Assume, for the sake of a simple arithmetical illustration, that of a national product of $1000 a share of $700 is distributed in the form of wages, $100 in the form of profits, and $200 in the form of fixed interest, rent, and pension payments. If now net national product rises by $20 (or 2 per cent) and the recipients of fixed money incomes get no share in the increased product (because prices are held stable), 20 per cent of the increased product, i.e., $4, becomes available as a possible bonus for labor in addition to their 70 per cent share or $14. Total wage payments can thus increase by $18 or 2.57 per cent.

A second qualification relates to possible improvements in the terms of trade. Assume that the price of imports (relative to the price of exports) falls by 2 per cent and that imports had amounted to 10 per cent of the net national product, or $100. If the entire gain of $2 is seized as another bonus for labor, wages can rise by $20 or 2.86 per cent.

A third qualification concerns the possible effects of increased tax revenues. Assume that the effective tax rate on profits (distributed plus undistributed) is 50 per cent while the marginal tax rate on wages is 20 per cent. The additional profits are (10 per cent of $20=) $2 and the taxes on this are $1. The taxes on additional wages are (20 per cent of $20=) $4. If the government kept expenditures constant despite increased revenues, another bonus of $5 could be distributed in the form of wages, bringing the total addition to $25 before taxes, or more than the entire increase in net national product. (We neglect now the tax on the third bonus.) Wages before taxes could with all three bonuses be increased by 3.57 per cent, compared with a 2 per cent increase in national income.

The second and third bonuses, however, cannot be counted upon; the second bonus may just as likely be negative

since the terms of trade may deteriorate rather than improve. Even the first bonus is likely to disappear in an economy with perpetual inflation, because contractual incomes might gradually be made subject to automatic cost-of-living adjustments. All three qualifications are probably less important than the one presented in the text and this one works in the opposite direction.

This exposition has been freely adapted from Friedrich A. Lutz, "Cost- and Demand-Induced Inflation," *Banca Nazionale del Lavoro*, No. 44 (March 1958), 9–10. The adaptations were necessary because I believe Lutz's argument to be partly erroneous.

[5] If wage rates were to increase as much as output per worker while prices were kept from rising, total output would not be large enough to allow any return to be earned by the new capital; employers, then, might not want to maintain the level of investment and employment. See Lutz, *loc. cit.*, 4.

that the price inflation has the "function" of keeping the increase in real wages down to the rate at which productivity increases may help some to understand the mechanism. But it is not really an appropriate expression, for nothing has to "function" to "prevent from occurring" what cannot occur anyway. Either prices rise (with the help of supportive expansion of demand) to cut the real wage rates to the level made possible by the productivity increase, or unemployment occurs (if demand expansion is prevented or restrained) and cuts total real wages even lower.

If money wages were not increased at all and all increments to the net national product that are due to technological progress were distributed to consumers in the form of lower prices, *all* income recipients — wage earners, owners of businesses, and fixed-income recipients — would share in the increased product. If money wages all over the economy are increased approximately by the rate at which average productivity has increased, prices on the average will neither fall nor rise and hence the fixed-income recipients (bondholders, landlords, pensioners, perhaps also civil servants, teachers, etc.) will be cut out of their share in the increment. Thus, aggressive money wage increases which, on the average, equal the average increase in productivity in the economy will improve the relative income share of labor at the expense of the receivers of contractual income.

Aggressive Wage Increases to Capture Individual Productivity Gains

The "rule" that price stability and full employment can be maintained if all money wage rates are increased by the same percentage by which average productivity has increased in the economy as a whole is frequently misunderstood and mistakenly applied to advocate increases in money-wage rates in individual firms or industries by the same percentage by which productivity has increased in these firms or industries. In other words, the rule is perverted to the proposal that the benefits of advancing productivity should accrue to the workers in the industries in which the advances take place. It is twisted into a proposition justifying

. . . union demands in those industries, which, because of

improved technology and consequent cost reductions, can afford to pay higher wages without charging higher prices for their products. This proposition is thoroughly unsound. It misses completely the economic function of prices and wages; its realization would sabotage the economic allocation of resources without serving any purpose that could be justified from any ethical or political point of view.[6]

A sensible allocation of resources requires that the same factors of production are offered at the same prices to all industries. It causes misallocations if industries in which technology has improved are forced to pay higher wages for the same type of labor that gets lower pay in industries where technology has not changed. Wage rates should be temporarily higher in fields into which labor is to be attracted, not in fields where labor is released by labor-saving techniques. It is economic nonsense to advocate that wage rates should be forced up precisely where labor becomes relatively abundant.

One might accept an economically unsound arrangement if it were ethically much superior. But no one could claim that the proposition in question satisfied any ethical norm. If five industries, let us call them A, B, C, D, and E, employ the same type of labor; if any of them, say Industry A, develops a new production process and is now able to make the same product as before with half the amount of labor; then this Industry A could afford to raise its wage rates without raising its selling prices. Should now workers in Industry A get a wage increase of 100 per cent while their fellow workers in Industries B, C, D, and E get nothing? Should the coincidence that the technological advance took place in A give the workers there the windfall of the entire benefit, raising them above the rest of the people? I can see no ethical argument that could be made in favor of such a scheme.

But as a matter of practical fact, apart from economics and ethics, the scheme could never be consistently applied, because the workers in other industries would not stand for it, . . . similar wage increases would have to be given in all . . . firms and industries regardless of their ability to pay, regardless of whether their selling prices would remain stable or go up slightly or a great deal. It simply would not be fair if a favored group were to be the sole beneficiary of progress while the rest of the population would have to sit back and wait for better luck.[7]

No fair-minded person would ask them to sit back and wait; every labor union with any power at all would press the claims of its mem-

[6] Fritz Machlup, *The Political Economy of Monopoly* (Baltimore, 1952), 403.
[7] *Ibid.*, 404–405.

bers, and where no unions existed workers would eventually appeal to their employers and to the public to end the injustice. Yet, any "equalizing" wage increases would be clearly of the cost-push type and would, if unemployment is prevented, lead to consumer price increases which take away from the originally privileged worker groups some of the real gains they were first awarded (with the approval of short-sighted commentators and politicians).

This spill-over of money-wage increases and the cost-push inflation which it produces (with the help of a supportive demand inflation) serve to redistribute some of the productivity gains first captured by the workers in the industries where the gains occurred. This redistribution by means of consumer-price inflation cuts back the real wages of the first-successful labor groups, whose unions will then complain about the erosion of their incomes and will call for seemingly defensive wage increases to regain the ground lost through inflation (though they rarely lose all of their gain in real income and often keep a large part of it).

In short, a policy that condones wage increases in industries which, because of increased productivity, can afford to pay increased wages without charging increased prices, is actually a policy that accepts a rising cost-price spiral without end.

Price Reductions Essential for Stability

A wage increase obtained by a particular labor group may initiate an inflationary process, but the speed of this process will depend largely on the incidence of defensive price increases and of imitative and defensive wage increases. If nothing but responsive (competitive) price and wage increases were to occur, the rate of inflation initiated by an isolated wage boost would be very small, perhaps negligible. It is, nevertheless, interesting to examine models of price inflation that include neither defensive nor imitative increases.

Inflation Without Spill-Over Wage-Push

In the inflationary process described in the last section, the industries that were forced to pay the increased wages (out of the economies provided by improved techniques) were as-

sumed for the sake of the argument not to increase their selling prices. The price inflation was chiefly the work of a spill-over of the wage increases into fields where productivity had increased less or not at all. But even in the absence of any spill-over, even if no worker in the country were to receive a raise that did not come from economies in production, some degree of consumer-price inflation would be inevitable in an economy in which (a) wage rates are never reduced in any sector, even in the face of unemployment, (b) wage rates are increased to capture productivity gains entirely in the industries where they accrue, and (c) full employment is secured, if necessary, through expansion of effective demand. Now when workers are released in the industries where productivity increases, but production, with unchanged prices and unchanged demand, is not increased, it will take an inflation of demand to create employment for the workers set free by the advance of technology. In other words, the "technological unemployment" will have to be cured by an expansion of demand, which in turn will cause a rise in consumer prices.

Does not this argument overlook the increase in demand on the part of workers who receive wage increases? It does not. Since the wage increases were granted just to offset the cost reduction made possible by the increase in output per worker, the workers who stay employed receive their raise out of funds no longer paid out as wages to the workers who lost their jobs. A little arithmetic may clarify this point. If 90 workers can now produce the output previously produced by 100, and are now paid the total wage that was previously paid to 100, the total purchasing power in the hands of the workers stays the same. The 10 workers who were released get nothing, and what was saved on them is being paid to the "more productive" 90. The firm, paying the same wage bill (though to fewer workers), finds its costs neither increased nor reduced and keeps its selling prices unchanged. Since at these prices demand is the same as before, the firm has no use for the 10 workers; nor has anybody else if wages rates are nowhere reduced. If the authorities want them reemployed, a demand inflation has to be engineered. True, the 10 workers will produce something once they are employed, but only after increased prices have created incentives for employers to use more labor; or they will have to be employed (and paid for with new money) in the production of public services not sold in the market.

The assumptions built into the model underlying this chain of reasoning have excluded growth (of labor force and capital stock) and excess capacity. If there were adequate excess capacity in each and every line of production, the demand created (in order to re-employ the labor released by the more productive industries) could be satisfied without price increases anywhere. But no inflation model can reasonably include the assumption of ubiquitous excess capacity; limited facilities (bottlenecks) are implied in any explanation of inflation. Thus, no exception should be taken to the assumption that the new wages paid to the re-employed workers will not all be spent for their own products, but largely for other things, and that prices will be bid up in the process.

The exclusion of a growing labor force and a growing capital stock have served merely to simplify the reasoning. When inputs and outputs are increasing, a certain increase in the money supply and in aggregate spending will be required to manage the increase in output and trade at given prices. An expansion of money demand to effect a re-absorption of technological unemployment would be over and above the money demand required to take care of the growth in labor force and capital stock. To combine the analyses of such growth and of technological unemployment would be an unnecessary complication; the other growth factors can be disregarded without vitiating the conclusions derived in an isolated treatment of technological unemployment.

The price inflation to be expected from a demand inflation engineered to absorb "technological unemployment" will of course be quite moderate in this case, where all the spill-over wage increases are ruled out. Here is a type of inflation that cannot be characterized as a cost-push inflation, and not as a demand-pull inflation either, if that term is reserved for autonomous expansions of demand. To be sure, aggressive wage increases are involved in the process, but these increases, merely offsetting the growth of productivity, will push up only the cost per labor hour, not the cost per unit of output, and thus no price increases can be said to result from cost increases.

Inflation Without Any Wage Increases

One may easily jump to the conclusion that technological unemployment, and the need to resort to demand inflation as its only cure, is entirely due to the aggressive wage increases, giving to the workers in the technically advancing industries the entire benefit of the productivity gain. This conclusion would be wrong. The consequences will be the same if in the absence of any wage increase the firms in question find their profits increased but for some reason fail to let consumers benefit in the form of lower selling prices.

Does this argument rely on lower marginal propensities to spend, or on insufficient investment opportunities, or on excessive liquidity preferences? It does not. Even if it is assumed that corporations spend all of their retained profits and stockholders spend all their dividends — just as the workers would have spent their wages — the workers released in the industries where technology has advanced will not be re-employed without the help of demand inflation unless prices to consumers are lowered. The case is almost the same as that in which the workers captured the productivity gain, except that now the corporations and their owners pocket the entire benefit.

Why "almost" the same, why not exactly the same? Because there is the possibility that an increase in retained earnings, as an increase in capital supply, raises the marginal productivity of labor and thus the demand for labor at given wage rates. But it would be absurd to expect that this would suffice to re-employ all the released labor. Assume that the entire amount saved on the wage bill is spent on new machinery; this new demand for machinery (and indirectly for the labor that goes into its manufacture) merely takes the place of the former workers' demand for consumer goods (and indirectly for the labor that went into their production). Thus the spending of the retained profits — earned by reducing the wage bill — constitutes no increased demand for labor. Only the resulting increase in productive facilities may eventually help the demand for labor to the extent of a small fraction of the technological unemployment created by the (labor-saving) increase in productivity. Hence the conclusion is the same as it was in the case of wage increase: only if consumers get a chance through lower prices to buy more product with their given money incomes will the released workers get a chance to find jobs in the absence of demand inflation.[8]

But why should firms refuse to lower their prices when production costs fall? The well-known theoretical models of a monopolist responding to a lowering of his cost curve show with no reasonable exceptions that he would reduce his selling price and increase his output. If firms can be observed acting otherwise, what is wrong with the model or what is wrong with the firms? One possible hypothesis would be that the firms of the real world had been in "disequilibrium," charging less than profit-maximizing monopoly prices and waiting for a good occasion to adjust their position. If now their costs are reduced, inaction, failure to reduce their prices, may be an easy way to adjust. Another hypothesis would be that the firms of the real world are in positions of not firmly coordinated oligopoly, where the safest rule is always "not to rock the boat," that is, never to reduce prices lest a rival mistake it for an outbreak of price competition. A third hypothesis would be that the "administered" prices in modern business cannot be explained by any models based on intelligent considerations, but are set by some fixed rules of thumb, and that one of these rules is never to reduce a price. There are perhaps still other hypotheses to explain the fact of "downward inflexibility" of prices — if indeed it is a fact. But no matter which hypothesis is accepted, the conclusion remains valid that if prices are not reduced when productivity has increased, technological unemployment arises and cannot be absorbed ex-

[8] This does not mean that the entire increase in productivity must be passed on to consumers in the form of reduced prices. Technological unemployment will neither be perpetuated nor require a price-inflating demand expansion for its cure if wage rates are raised by the national average increase in productivity. This will still permit price reductions in the industries where productivity has increased. The money the consumers save in buying these products at reduced prices will be spent on other goods and will drive up some other prices, without however raising consumer prices on the average.

cept through demand inflation and consequent consumer-price inflation.

Stabilization of Individual Prices Necessitates Inflation

The argument of the preceding pages was designed to demonstrate that the failure to reduce prices in industries where productivity has increased will result in an inflationary increase of general prices, which

(a) will be most rapid if the productivity gains are captured by the workers of these industries by way of wage rate increases — because of the practically inevitable spill-over of the wage increases to other worker groups; but

(b) will also occur, though much more slowly, in the absence of such spill-over, because it will take a demand expansion to re-employ the workers released when the wage bill of the progressive industries is distributed over fewer workers; and

(c) will not be avoided even in the absence of any wage increases, because a demand expansion will be required to re-employ the workers released when the entire part of the wage bill that is saved through the technological advance is transformed into profits without giving consumers a chance to buy more product.

An economist willing to rely on the most abstract and general principles of economic theory can derive this "inevitability" of inflation from a simple set of theorems. He can deduce from the equilibrium conditions in a system of general equilibrium that general prices must rise if individual prices are maintained in industries where productivity increases. For a fall of production cost in one industry will call forth a reduction of the price of its product relative to the prices of all other products; this adjustment of relative prices will, in a money economy, proceed either through a fall in the money price of the product that now requires less labor per unit than before or through an increase in all other money prices (or through a combination of both); hence, stabilization of the money price of the more economically produced product implies that equilibrium will be restored through a general increase in money prices.

I do not propose to use this technical way of reasoning to convince trade union leaders, business executives, or members of Congress. But the previous argument was, I trust, understandable before I added the sophisticated demonstration of its conclusion.

The O'Mahoney Plan to Check Inflation

It should now be clear that the only way to prevent inflation of consumer prices, and prevent unemployment too, is to make prices more flexible in the downward direction and, in particular, to encourage price reductions in industries where productivity has increased. Senator O'Mahoney's plan, partly incorporated in Senate Bill 215 of April 1959, and receiving serious consideration by several members of Congress, would achieve exactly the opposite. According to the preamble of the Bill, its author believes that "inflation will be checked if the pricing policies of these [dominant] corporations are publicly reviewed before increased prices may be made effective." On this theory the Bill provides for public hearings and investigations of large corporations whenever they want to raise prices. But the harder it is made for firms to raise prices the more surely will they avoid ever reducing their prices.

If a nation is committed to a full-employment policy, that is, to a policy of using demand inflation to create employment, it can avoid inflation only by avoiding anything that may create unemployment. Since economic growth proceeds chiefly through technological progress, and technological unemployment can only be avoided through price reductions, the prime requirement of a non-inflationary full-employment policy is to prevent the workers, owners, and managers of the progressing industries from capturing all the productivity gains accruing in these industries in the form of increased money wages and increased profits, respectively, and to encourage the dispersion of most of these gains to consumers in the form of reduced prices.

The O'Mahoney policy in effect encourages the trade unions in the industries in question to get out and capture the entire productivity gains for their workers. It does so implicitly because, if the firms are prevented from raising prices after the aggressive wage increases have absorbed "only" the new economies, the labor unions will no longer be blamed by the public for causing or precipitating higher prices. The "visible link" between these wage increases and price inflation is removed, and the union leaders will have even less compunction in pressing for these supposedly non-inflationary wage increases. The firms, losing all or most of the productivity gains to their workers, will hardly be eager to reduce prices. But even if they should, by means of tough bargaining, succeed in keeping a good deal of the gains, they will surely not dream of sharing any part of them with the consumers, because they would consider it foolish to reduce prices that cannot be raised again except after expensive, cumbersome, and perhaps embarrassing public inquisitions.

The O'Mahoney plan to check inflation would actually tend to make inflation perennial and perpetual. The only thing that can be said for the proposed policy is that it might in the short run, perhaps for a couple of years, slow down the progress of the price inflation. But even this is doubtful since, apart from encouraging trade unions to fight for the productivity gains accruing in their industries, it does nothing to check the spill-over wage increases, which in genuine cost-push fashion engender many chains of defensive, "approvable" price increases and necessitate continual resort to supportive demand inflation.

Conclusion

It was not the purpose of this article to lead up to a critique of a proposed policy; this was a mere by-product. The intention was to examine the conceptual framework employed in recent discussions and, in view of its inadequacies, to propose some improved theoretical tools that may serve better in the analysis of the inflationary process of our time.

Analysis requires the following distinctions: an administered cost increase may be "equilibrating" in the sense that it merely "absorbs" a previously existing excess demand, or it may be "disequilibrating" in the sense that it creates an excess supply that may be prevented or removed only by an expansion of demand. To facilitate the analysis, three kinds of demand expansion are distinguished: *autonomous, induced,* and *supportive.* Likewise three kinds of cost increase are distinguished: *responsive, de-*

fensive, and *aggressive.* Any one of these cost increases may be 'administered"; but the responsive ones would also occur in a fully competitive market. Neither defensive nor aggressive increases are in response to excess demand, and both therefore presuppose monopolistic power; defensive increases, however, attempt merely to restore previous real earnings of the group concerned, while aggressive increases raise real earnings above previous levels.

With the aid of these new concepts one can construct models of the inflationary process of various degrees of complexity. It may be possible to develop empirical tests for the choice of the model that fits best the recorded data of particular periods. The author believes that the price inflations of the periods 1945–48 and 1950–52 were of the demand-pull type, but that for 1955–59 a cost-push model would fit better.

He tentatively suggests that wage-push was more effective than profit-push.

Finally the relation of inflation to increases in productivity was examined. The popular idea of a "non-inflationary" distribution of productivity gains by way of wage increases to the workers employed in the industries in which technology has advanced was found to be untenable. Imitative wage increases would lead to a brisk inflation. But some degree of inflation would occur even without such "spill-over" wage increases, because the distribution of the productivity gains to the workers or owners in the progressing industries would result in technological unemployment, and remedial full-employment measures would inflate the price level. The only way of avoiding inflation is through price reductions in industries where productivity has improved.

PART FOUR

INTERNATIONAL TRADE AND FINANCE

[14]

The American Economic Review

VOLUME XLV　　　　　JUNE, 1955　　　　　NUMBER THREE

RELATIVE PRICES AND AGGREGATE SPENDING IN THE ANALYSIS OF DEVALUATION

By Fritz Machlup*

Two approaches to the question of the effects of devaluation have been presented as alternatives, and one of them has been treated as inferior, if not absolutely inappropriate.[1] The purpose of this article is to examine the supposedly superior approach and to give a comparative evaluation of both.

The problem is how to analyze the probable effectiveness of a devaluation undertaken to remove or reduce an existing excess demand for foreign exchange without the use of direct controls, when money incomes have been stable, and when no autonomous capital movements take place either before or after the devaluation. These restricting conditions serve to present the problem in splendid isolation from certain very realistic conditions—such as the presence of direct controls or of autonomous capital movements—from which abstraction must initially be made in a clean analysis.

We are not concerned here with the question whether devaluation is the "most appropriate" policy under given circumstances, or under what circumstances devaluation would be "more appropriate" than other policies. Our question is merely this: what is the best way of finding out whether devaluation will reduce the trade deficit, or what per cent of devaluation would eliminate a given trade deficit, or what size of a deficit would be eliminated by a given per cent of devaluation?

I refer to the two ways of analyzing the problem as the *relative-prices* approach and the *aggregate-spending* approach. Alexander called them the "elasticities approach" and the "income-absorption ap-

---

* The author is professor of political economy at the Johns Hopkins University.

[1] S. S. Alexander, "Effects of a Devaluation on a Trade Balance," Internat. Mon. Fund *Staff Papers,* Apr. 1952, II, 263-78.

255

proach."[2] There are other possible names: the "supply-and-demand approach" and the "income-and-outlay approach"; or, with an allusion to doctrinal history, the "Marshallian approach" and the "Keynesian approach" to the problem.

I. *Deficiencies of the Relative-Prices Approach*

The most widely used version of the relative-prices approach works with supply and demand curves for foreign exchange. The positions and shapes of these curves, and thus their elasticities at various points, are "deduced" from the supply and demand for exports and from the supply and demand for imports; and all these, in turn, are "deduced" from the supply conditions and demand conditions in all foreign and domestic markets, because every supply in foreign trade is an excess supply over domestic demand, and every demand in foreign trade is an excess demand over domestic supply.

Now the question has been raised whether one can take the shape of any of these curves as given; whether one can regard their elasticities as predetermined and use them in the solution of foreign-exchange problems. I had thought it useful to assume so,[3] and so had many others.

Given and Unchanged Cost Conditions

We said, for example, that the supply of exports would depend in part on "cost-conditions"—as if cost conditions were something definite. But is this defensible? The cost of *one* product can be shown in a curve, other things being given and unchanged; but if other things change, the cost curve no longer stays put; if the production of many goods is to change at the same time, we cannot easily know what the cost curve for any one of them will do.[4]

In the production of a certain good, productive resources are needed; for the production of more of that good, more resources are needed. If not much is happening elsewhere, one may foretell at what prices additional resources may be available, and one may, on the basis of technological knowledge, foretell what the cost of additional output will be. But for the prices of additional resources it will make a great difference whether at the same time these resources are being released by other industries or are being demanded by them in increased amounts.

[2] Alexander obviously means price elasticities by the first name, since income elasticity of demand plays a main part in the second approach.

[3] Fritz Machlup, "The Theory of Foreign Exchange," *Economica*, Nov. 1939, VI, 375-97, and Feb. 1940, VII, 23-49. Reprinted in *Readings in the Theory of International Trade* (Philadelphia, 1949), pp. 104-158.

[4] For an excellent exposition of the general problem of cost and supply curves, see Joan Robinson, "Rising Supply Price," *Economica*, Feb. 1941, VIII, 1-8. Reprinted in G. J. Stigler and K. E. Boulding, ed., *Readings in Price Theory* (Chicago, 1952), pp. 233-41.

It is possible that, when the production of a certain product rises, say in order to provide increased exports under the stimulus of a devaluation, the production of other goods may be cut and productive services released to the expanding export industry. But it is also possible that some other industries will increase their output under the stimulus of the same devaluation, and that they also will require more of the same productive factors; and if several industries simultaneously demand these factors, their prices will rise. Where then are our "given" cost conditions?

Given and Unchanged Incomes

A second argument against the relative-prices approach is the possibility of changes in incomes. The devaluation itself may have income effects: incomes may rise or fall as a result of the devaluation. But the supply and demand curves are drawn, of course, on the basis of a given buying power, a given income. Thus, these curves will not help much if we know that incomes must have changed; we have to know how income has changed and how the new curves look.

Even if we did not allow total money income to change (and we shall return to this point), there is still the possibility of significant changes in income distribution. After all, devaluation will raise the domestic prices of imported goods which may be important in the budgets of certain groups; this would alter the distribution of real income. But if income distribution changes, demand is likely to change and our curves again may shift considerably.

That these arguments make it necessary to qualify and supplement the "simple" elasticity analysis had been clear to many.[5] But what Alexander suggests amounts to a repudiation of the relative-prices approach.[6] His arguments are persuasive and, with our confidence in

---

[5] The income effects of devaluation have often been discussed. I wrote: "If depreciation through its effects upon the volume of exports or upon the balance or the terms of trade should raise or lower total income, it would probably also raise or lower the demand for imports. These income effects of depreciation may be negligible in the beginning, but in the course of time, as the 'multiplier mechanism' becomes operative, they may become strong enough substantially to weaken or reinforce the price effects of depreciation." "Elasticity Pessimism in International Trade," *Econ. Internaz.*, Feb. 1950, III, 11. See also, J. J. Polak, "Discussion," *Am. Econ. Rev.*, Proceedings, May, 1952, XLII, 180-81; A. C. Harberger, "Currency Depreciation, Income, and the Balance of Trade," *Jour. Pol. Econ.*, Feb. 1950, LVIII, 47-60; T. Balogh and P. P. Streeten, "The Inappropriateness of Simple 'Elasticity' Concepts in the Analysis of International Trade," and "Exchange Rates and National Income," *Bull. Oxford Univ. Inst. Stat.*, Mar. and Apr. 1951, XIII, 65-77, 101-08.

[6] ". . . the total elasticities appropriate for the analysis of the effects of a devaluation depend on the behavior of the whole economic system, and the statement that the effect of a devaluation depends on the elasticities boils down to the statement that it depends on how the economic system behaves." ". . . it is suggested that a more fruitful line of

the criticized approach shaken or destroyed, we are eager to examine the novel approach that is offered as a superior substitute.

II. *Alexander's Aggregate-Spending Approach*

The new approach to the problem of the effect of devaluation is the aggregate-spending approach, or "income-absorption" approach. While following Alexander's exposition, I shall slightly change the notations.

The Fundamental Equation

The *total income* of a nation can be divided or classified into *consumption* plus *investment* plus *government contribution*[7] plus *exports* minus *imports;* or

$$Y \equiv C + I + G + X - M.$$

This identity is used as the fundamental equation; it can be shortened by merging the first three terms on the right side, that is by calling C plus I plus G by the name "absorption,"[8] or A. (The expenditures of households and business and governments are the part of the national income that is being "absorbed.") The two remaining terms of the identity, X minus M, the difference between exports and imports, constitute the trade balance, signified by B. Thus, what we now have is that the *national income* is the sum of the *absorption* by the nation plus its *trade balance;* or

$$Y \equiv A + B.$$

It follows that the trade balance must always be the difference between income and absorption:

$$B \equiv Y - A.$$

The trade balance is negative when the nation absorbs more than its income. The trade balance can improve if income increases while absorption increases less or stays unchanged or falls; or if absorption decreases while income decreases less or stays unchanged.

Devaluation Effects on Income and Spending

The question we now have to ask is to what extent devaluation can

---

approach can be based on a concentration on the relationships of real expenditure to real income and on the relationships of both of these to the price levels, rather than on the more traditional supply and demand analysis." Alexander, *op. cit.*, pp. 264, 263.

Balogh and Streeten also rejected the "elasticities approach": ". . . we shall contend that this approach to the problem is erroneous" (*op. cit.*, p. 65). But they did not suggest an alternative one: "It is regrettable but inevitable that no single new method of analysis can be put into the place of the old approach" (*ibid.*, p. 66).

[7] This term was not included in Alexander's exposition.

[8] This term was first used by K. E. Boulding, *Economic Analysis* (New York, rev. ed., 1948), pp. 402-8.

affect *B*, that is, the difference between income and absorption. Alexander breaks this down into three questions:[9] (1) How does devaluation affect income (*Y*)? (2) How does a change in income (ΔY) affect absorption (*A*)? (3) How does devaluation directly (that is, not via income) affect absorption (*A*)?

The change of the trade balance is the change in income minus the change in absorption; or

$$\Delta B \equiv \Delta Y - \Delta A.$$

The effect of devaluation upon income will show in ΔY; the effect of the change in income upon absorption, and the direct effect of devaluation upon absorption, will both show in ΔA. In other words, there will be an income-induced change in *A* and a nonincome-induced, or directly effected, change in *A*. The direct effect of the devaluation upon absorption can be expressed by δA. The income-induced change in absorption can be expressed by $\alpha \Delta Y$, where α is the "marginal propensity to absorb income" (which of course will be the sum of the marginal propensities to consume, to invest and to spend public funds).

The new symbols help to merge the devaluation effect upon income, ΔY, and the income effect upon absorption $\alpha \Delta Y$, into a single expression $(1 - \alpha) \Delta Y$, which stands for the nonabsorbed change in income. Thus,

$$\Delta B = (1 - \alpha) \Delta Y - \delta A.$$

Assume, for a moment, that income will increase as a result of devaluation. This devaluation effect upon income and the consequent income effect upon absorption will improve the trade balance only if α is smaller than unity. But, while the marginal propensity to consume is usually smaller than unity, α, the combined marginal propensity to consume, invest, and spend publicly, may well be greater than unity. If so, $(1 - \alpha) \Delta Y$, the nonabsorbed change in income, will be negative and the trade balance will deteriorate, rather than improve, on this score. Only the direct effect on absorption can then still help matters.

Alexander states that the analysis on the basis of his model will hold in real terms as well as in money terms; he then proceeds in the belief that he talks about real income, real absorption, and real trade balance throughout.

Following the clue from the last equation, Alexander divides the further discussion into two parts: the effects upon and via incomes—

[9] *Op. cit.*, p. 266.

$(1 - \alpha)\ \Delta Y$—and the direct effects upon absorption—δA. He recognizes the following effects:

Effects upon and via Income $[(1-\alpha)\Delta Y]$	Direct Effects on Absorption $[\delta A]$
Idle-resources effect Terms-of-trade effect	Cash-balance effect Income-redistribution effect Money-illusion effect Three other direct absorption effects

The Idle-Resources Effect

If the devaluing country has idle resources, their employment can be increased by additional consumption, investment, government expenditures, or exports. Since C and I (and tacitly, G) are assumed by Alexander to be functions of income, additional exports are the strategic factor; and additional exports are the very thing that one should expect to result from devaluation.

The increased value of foreign moneys in terms of domestic money stimulates the production of export goods; if idle resources are available, employment will increase in the export industries; as the recipients of the income increment spend it for consumption, further employment may be created in the consumers-goods industries. This process is the familiar operation of the "foreign trade multiplier." But while the multiplier, in the customary exposition, includes only induced consumption, Alexander's employment effect comprises induced spending of all kinds.

Alexander inclines to the belief that α is greater than unity, that $(1 - \alpha)$ therefore is negative, and consequently that the trade balance will become worse as a result of the income increase due to the idle-resources effect of the devaluation. If improving the trade balance is the policy objective, it would follow that the devaluing country must hope either that there will be no increase in its income and employment, or that the propensity to absorb income is less than unity—or at least that the other effects of devaluation will be in the right direction and stronger than the idle-resources effect.

The Terms-of-Trade Effect

Alexander joins the majority of economists in the belief that devaluation will deteriorate the terms of trade of the devaluing country. He thinks that this is so because "a country's exports are usually more specialized than its imports."[10]

[10] *Ibid.*, p. 268.

If devaluation affects the terms of trade, the change in the terms of trade will affect national income and absorption. Alexander divides the terms-of-trade effects of devaluation on the balance of trade into an initial effect through price changes and a secondary effect through income-induced changes in absorption. He holds that "the normal result of a devaluation will be such deterioration of the terms of trade of the devaluing country as to" cause an initial deterioration of its balance of payments equal to "the reduction of the country's real income associated with the deterioration of the terms of trade."[11] In other words, the initial effect will normally be an equal and simultaneous reduction (deterioration) of the trade balance and of real national income. The secondary terms-of-trade effects of devaluation upon the balance of trade—the income-induced changes in spending—will depend on the marginal propensity to absorb income. The income-induced changes in absorption may either reinforce or attenuate the initial terms-of-trade effect on the balance of trade, or may turn it in the opposite direction.

Alexander, having concluded that the *initial* terms-of-trade effects upon trade balance and upon real income are (normally) equal in direction and in amount—he uses one symbol, t, for both—believes that he can find the ultimate terms-of-trade effect upon the trade balance by multiplying the initial effect by the marginal propensity not-to-absorb. Hence, the ultimate terms-of-trade effect upon the balance of trade would be $(1 - \alpha)t$, and thus could be positive (*i.e.*, improving the balance) only if (since t is assumed to be negative) $1 - \alpha$ is negative, that is, if α is greater than unity.

The Income Effects Combined

Alexander combines the two "income effects of devaluation" which he recognizes—the idle-resources effect and the terms-of-trade effect—in one expression equivalent to $(1 - \alpha) \Delta Y$. This presupposes that a change in the terms of trade resulting from devaluation will affect the balance of trade only through the change in real income, and to an extent commensurate with it.

Either or both of the income effects of devaluation may be zero. The idle-resources effect—"presumably positive," according to Alexander—can be positive only if there are unemployed resources and if their employment is not obstructed by bottlenecks (lack of complementary factors or lack of finance). The terms-of-trade effect may be zero if devaluation does not change the terms of trade, or if the "initial" effects on the trade balance as well as the "secondary" effects

[11] *Ibid.*, p. 269.

through income-induced changes in spending are checked or counteracted by monetary policy.

Direct Effects on Absorption

Effects of devaluation upon the balance of trade which are not associated with changes in income but only with changes in the absorption of a given income, are called "direct effects on absorption." If there is no change in income, the trade balance can be increased only through a reduction in the domestic absorption of income, C, I, or G, and an equal increase in exports or reduction in imports. Such a switch from A to B, from domestic absorption to foreign-trade balance, can possibly be accomplished without transfer of productive resources or changes in production if the reduction in domestic absorption relates to imported goods or to exportable goods. Otherwise it will require a shift of production from goods and services hitherto used for C, I, or G to goods and services for X, or to goods and services substituted for M. This will involve not only adaptations in production plans but ordinarily also a transfer of productive resources between plants, firms, industries, and locations. The question is, what mechanisms are set in motion by devaluation to induce these adaptations and transfers, and what obstacles have to be overcome in the process?

A reduction in consumption and investment can, in general, lead to a reduction in employment and income just as easily as to an increase in the trade balance.[12] Whether the productive resources released from domestic C and I industries will remain idle or will be transferred to industries producing X and substitutes for M, will depend chiefly on how the economy responds to price incentives; this need not involve price reductions, because the release of the resources will have been preceded by an increase in prices of export goods and of substitutes for import goods. Moreover, the reduction in spending for C and I will have been offset by an increase in receipts for X. But the chief object in Alexander's discussion of the "direct effects on absorption" is to examine whether and how devaluation may bring about the reduction in domestic spending.

The Cash-Balance Effect

Devaluation raises the domestic prices of imports and of exports; and it will tend to raise the prices of import substitutes, of potential exports, and of intermediate goods required for their production. Thus, unless the monetary authorities restrict credit in order to force price reductions in other sectors of the economy, the price level will be somewhat increased as a result of the devaluation.

[12] *Ibid.*, p. 272.

If the monetary authorities do not create more money than may be needed to purchase the foreign exchange forthcoming as a result of positive devaluation effects on the trade balance, the elevated price level will imply a reduction in the real value of total cash balances. Households and firms will attempt to build up their cash balances to the relative size they have found appropriate. They will try to do this by buying less and by selling assets and securities (debts).

Buying less in order to accumulate cash balances implies "a reduction in their real expenditures relative to their real incomes,"[13] that is, a foregoing of consumption and investment. Selling assets and debts securities will depress their prices or, which is the same thing, increase interest rates. The offer of assets and debt securities at reduced prices would attract foreign buyers—which would greatly help matters—but we have excluded any autonomous capital movements from our analysis. With foreigners ruled out as buyers—because we wish to abstract from capital inflows in order to concentrate on the trade balance— and with banks ruled out as buyers— because we have excluded additional credit creation—there are only nonbank residents left as buyers, and they will overcome their liquidity preference only if the prices of securities are so attractive that it pays them to defer real investment, reduce consumption, and part with liquidity. The increased interest rates will have the effect of cutting down investment expenditures of business and consumption expenditures of households.

The Income-Redistribution Effect

The lift in the price level that is associated with devaluation may also reduce aggregate spending from a given income by redistributing it from groups with higher to groups with lower marginal propensities to spend. Alexander mentions three such shifts of real income: from fixed-income recipients "to the rest of the economy,"[14] from wage recipients to profit recipients, and from taxpayers to government.

A loss of real income which the recipients of fixed income suffer through increased prices will result in a reduction of aggregate absorption if the corresponding gain in real income accrues largely to people richer and thriftier than rentiers, fixed-salary workers, and pensioners —which is not unlikely.

A shift of real income away from wage earners will occur when wage goods are among those whose prices are raised through devaluation— which is rather common. If the shift of real income is towards profit recipients, their investment incentives may be increased by more than

[13] *Ibid.,* p. 271.
[14] *Ibid.,* p. 273.

the consumption demand of the real-income losers is reduced. And if investment outlays increase accordingly, total absorption of income may be increased rather than reduced.

A shift from taxpayers to government would most effectively cut down aggregate spending where government expenditures are not dependent on tax revenues but are fixed in an inflexible budget not to be stepped up with a larger flow of tax receipts. Income-tax receipts would be increased where an income redistribution takes place in favor of richer people and tax rates are progressive. And income tax receipts would also be increased where total money income is allowed to increase in consequence of devaluation.[15]

The Money-Illusion Effect

This is what Alexander has to say on the money-illusion effect:

> The money illusion may contribute a favorable effect to a devaluation if it actually leads people to pay more attention to money prices than to money incomes. If at higher prices people choose to buy and consume less *even though their money income has increased in proportion,* over and above what can be attributed to the cash balance effect, the result on the balance of payments will be favorable. But *rising money incomes and rising prices may actually operate in the opposite manner;* for example, annual savings may be calculated in money terms and may fail to rise in proportion to money incomes and prices.[16]

It should be noted that Alexander speaks here, in the italicized clauses, not of higher prices of foreign-trade-connected goods, but of rising prices and of money incomes rising in proportion.

Other Direct Absorption Effects

Three other direct effects of devaluation upon absorption, and thus upon the trade balance, are mentioned by Alexander. One of them, which we may call the "price-expectations effect," may unfavorably affect the trade balance by increasing absorption: people expecting prices to rise following the devaluation may rush out to increase their inventories.

The other two are favorable influences on the trade balance. What may be called the "high-cost-of-investment effect" consists in the discouragement which increased cost of imported investment goods may cause to investors. Investment that requires foreign equipment, to be

---

[15] On the other hand, the revenues from specific import duties may be reduced rather than increased, and in many countries import duties are a significant portion of the budget.

[16] *Loc. cit.* Emphasis supplied.

imported at increased domestic prices, may be less attractive than it was before the devaluation and may be cut out altogether.[17]

The third effect generalizes the principle involved in the second effect to all kinds of imports: when certain goods, previously imported, become very expensive, some of the domestic buyers may give up buying these goods and may buy nothing instead. Alexander mentions this merely as a "theoretical possibility."

III. *Some Consequences of Neglecting Relative Prices*

My exposition of Alexander's analysis is, I hope, fair and accurate. In the first part of my critique I shall—without questioning the validity of the framework of the analysis or the merits of the procedure employed—point to some omissions and errors of reasoning which I believe can be attributed to Alexander's concentration on aggregate magnitudes and his neglect of relative prices. Although Alexander does not explicitly state that his enumeration of "income effects" and "direct absorption effects" is exhaustive, an impression is conveyed that, if not all, at least the more important ones have been covered. This, however, is not the case; we can find omissions in both categories.

The Resource-Reallocation Effect

There are three ways in which an increase in real national income can be achieved: through fuller employment of the available productive resources; through their better utilization and more economic allocation; and through more favorable terms of trade. Only two of these possibilities are recognized in Alexander's analysis: changes in the volume of employment and in the terms of trade. Transfer of resources to different uses does play a considerable role in his analysis, but only in connection with the direct absorption effects of devaluation. That such transfer may change real national income is not mentioned and has evidently been overlooked.

In the long run, greater economy and efficiency in the use of resources has been the most important factor in the increase in the living standards of the nations. In the short run, changes in the volume of employment and in the terms of trade may overshadow the effects of changed resources-use upon real income; but there is no presumption for one or the other to be more important. All three kinds of changes may be effected by devaluation (and each of them may be positive or negative).

---

[17] This seems to have been of considerable practical importance in several countries: Investment in imported labor-saving machinery, very profitable at predevaluation exchange rates, turned out to be too expensive relative to domestic labor once the exchange rates were corrected.

The "resource-reallocation effect" of devaluation may be especially significant when the "idle-resources effect" is negligible or zero; total employment may remain practically unchanged while the output produced may increase through a more economic or more efficient use of the resources employed. But it is also possible that both effects operate at the same time; more or fewer resources may be employed in a more or less economic way.

There are problems involved in measuring increases in real income when there are changes in the composition of output. Where the reallocation of resources implies a shift to "more valuable" products, with reductions in the output of "less valuable" products, the gain in real income can be measured only by means of a welfare index (based on market prices combined with other criteria). Even so, the principle that a reallocation of resources may increase the value of real output cannot reasonably be questioned. And where trade and production have been conducted on the basis of "unrealistic" exchange rates (overvaluing the currency) it is quite plausible that devaluation may effect a more economic use of resources with a consequent increase in real income.[18]

Substitution Effects

The resource-reallocation effect has been named here as another income effect of devaluation, although in Alexander's analysis resource reallocation is treated only in connection with direct absorption effects. But all of the direct absorption effects discussed by Alexander have to do with aggregate spending, with changes in the outlay of money; if they "work" to reduce total absorption they do so owing to the failure of some income recipients to spend all of their receipts or to make all the money expenditures they would otherwise have made.[19] Perhaps the most important absorption effects are thereby disregarded: the effects of shifts in relative prices and the effects of price increases which reduce real absorption even if absorption in money terms should be unchanged or slightly increased. This reduction in real absorption

[18] Besides the more economic resource allocation achieved through changes in relative prices, there may be two incidental resource-economizing effects of devaluation in systems operating with direct controls: one is the saving of administrative cost by government and by business when devaluation permits some controls to be removed and others to be improved; the second is the improved efficiency under the pressure of revived competition as the industry quota arrangements implied in the bureaucratic allocation of foreign exchange and imported materials are dropped when devaluation reinstates prices in the function of resource allocation.

[19] For example, in connection with the third of the three "miscellaneous direct absorption effects" Alexander says that "when the domestic prices [of imported goods] rise, the domestic purchasers cut their expenditures on these goods but save or hoard the difference, rather than shift the expenditures to other goods." *Op. cit.*, p. 274.

may be additional to that induced by a reduction in real income, although the increased prices may reflect such a real-income reduction.

Assume, for example (in order to isolate the outcome examined here from any terms-of-trade effects), that devaluation leaves the terms of trade unchanged, lifting the domestic prices of exports and of imports by the same percentage. As imported goods are now relatively higher in price than domestic goods, substitution in consumers' plans seems inevitable; and as exportable goods are now relatively higher in price than domestic goods, substitution in producers' plans seems inevitable; transfers of productive resources will ensue. And the increased demand for import-substitutes together with the reduced supply of domestic goods from the production of which resources have been diverted cannot but cause relative price movements which are apt to reduce the real value of aggregate absorption even if total money expenditures should be somewhat higher than before.

This reduction in real absorption will be additional to that induced by a reduction in real income if some among the substitutions induced take the form of shifts between consumption and asset holding (or indebtedness) or between investment and liquidity. Let us not forget that an import surplus implies an increase in indebtedness or decrease in the holdings of securities or other liquid assets on the part of some who absorb (consume or invest). Changes in relative prices may affect the willingness of "absorbers" to run up their debts or run down their liquid asset holdings. Substitution effects may significantly influence the absorption of real income and the physical volumes of imports and exports; these are price-induced changes in absorption, not predicated on any given "propensity to absorb" or on any general price level increase.

In all four kinds of direct effects on absorption discussed by Alexander, price movements play some role. But Alexander relies little on changes in *relative* prices to bring about the required adaptations and transfers.[20] Most of the time he looks to increased or rising price *levels* to do the trick. No wonder that he is disappointed in the performance.

The Terms-of-Trade Effect Amended

The neglect of the substitution effects impairs some of Alexander's analysis of the terms-of-trade effect of devaluation. It can be shown—although only in a lengthier exposition than we can here afford—that Alexander is in error when he holds that the initial effect—before any income-induced changes in absorption take place—will "normally" be an equal and simultaneous reduction (deterioration) of the trade

---

[20] Except in connection with the high-cost-of-investment effect.

balance and of real national income. To be sure, these two reductions can be made equal by definition, but it would be a rather useless definition; otherwise there is nothing that would cause the initial changes in trade balance and real income to be normally equal in amount or even in direction.

The source of Alexander's error in reasoning about the terms-of-trade effect lies in the conceptual decision to treat all effects of devaluation either as effects upon and via income or as direct effects upon absorption. Since a change in the terms of trade will affect income, Alexander at once puts the terms-of-trade effects under the first heading, and fails to notice that a change in the terms of trade will also affect absorption directly, through relative-price effects.

A change in the terms of trade may be viewed as a change in the ratio of an index of export prices to an index of import prices. The effects of relative price changes are customarily (following Hicks) divided into simultaneous income effects and substitution effects. By assuming that a change in the terms of trade will "initially" affect only income but not absorption, Alexander loses sight of the substitution effect. Absorption will actually be affected through both the substitution effects and the income effects of the change in the terms of trade. Thus, Alexander's conclusion that the ultimate terms-of-trade effect upon the balance of trade would be $(1 - \alpha)t$, or equal to the income effect times the marginal propensity not-to-absorb, is wrong.[21]

IV. *Reasoning from Definitional Equations*

The argument underlying the aggregate-spending approach has been developed from a "fundamental equation" which represents mere definitions. Such equations usually serve a useful purpose in aiding the organization of the analysis. But they may easily tempt an analyst into "implicit theorizing," illegitimately deducing causal relationships, and overlooking the shifting meanings of terms in different contexts. These temptations have not been successfully resisted in this instance.

Income and Output, Money Terms and Real Terms

As Alexander interprets the fundamental equation (or identity), "real income . . . is equal to the output of goods and services," and the relationships expressed "hold, of course, both in real and in money terms."[22] While this makes good sense for a closed system, it does not

---

[21] A clear exposition of the rather complicated relationships involved requires considerably more space, particularly because some fundamental questions concerning the use of terms-of-trade analysis ought to be explored at the same time. I reserve these tasks for a separate article.

[22] *Op. cit.*, p. 266.

for an open one, especially when the balance of trade plays a major role.

Even in a closed system there may be difficulties—due to problems of depreciation and depletion—in equating real income and output; but these difficulties can be defined away. In an open system where some output is produced for export, and imports contribute to consumption and domestic investment, output produced is not the same as real income. In order to relate output and income one would have to take account of changes in foreign assets and debts, as well as of unilateral transfers—items for which no provision is made in the equation. It is possible for employment, production, consumption, domestic investment, exports and imports, all to remain absolutely unchanged in physical terms, and for real national income nevertheless to be changed by some of the exports being sold at increased or reduced prices or given away free, or by some of the imports being bought at increased or reduced prices or received as gifts.

The conceptual difficulties implied in the possible deviations between changes in national product and national income[23] may have a significant bearing on the analysis of the effects of devaluation, especially in connection with changes in the terms of trade. What, for example, is the relevance of a "given" marginal propensity to absorb, when output and employment are affected one way, but income (with changes in foreign debts or assets) in another way? Will changes in absorption be induced by changes in employment and production or rather by changes in income that are partly due to changes in the foreign exchange reserves?

The supposed equivalence between relationships in money and in real terms is sometimes troublesome, occasionally even meaningless. Alexander intends to "deal only with real quantities, not with money values."[24] But what is a "real" trade balance? When a country has to pay increased prices for its imports and buys a slightly reduced physical quantity of imports, what is the meaning of an improved "real" trade balance if at the same time the balance in money terms has deteriorated? Or, should, perhaps, a trade balance in terms of money be translated into one in real terms by deflating the contracted foreign claims or debts by a price index? To treat exports and imports as "real quantities" makes sense; but can the difference between the two be meaningfully treated as a real (physical) quantity?[25] Can what is

---

[23] More correctly, possible deviations between changes in the total production of goods and services and in the total amount of income earned by the members of the economy. We are not concerned here with the difference between national income and disposable income.

[24] *Op. cit.*, p. 266.

[25] While horses and apples cannot be added, apples can be added *to* horses, but never subtracted *from* horses.

essentially an increase or decrease in foreign claims or debts be regarded as anything but a money value, however deflated?

Trade Balance in Foreign or in Domestic Money

But this is not all. Even if the concept of a trade balance in real terms is given up, the fact remains that, as a result of devaluation, an import surplus may increase in terms of domestic money and decrease in terms of foreign money. Indeed, this is a rather probable outcome.[26] But the ΔB in the equation $\Delta B \equiv \Delta Y - \Delta A$ is expressed either as a domestic money value or as the "real" equivalent of a domestic money value. This ΔB may be negative, so that a negative B may become even more negative, while the trade balance in terms of foreign money actually improves.

If one realizes that the whole purpose of the analysis is to find out what will happen to the trade balance of a country resorting to devaluation because of a shortage of foreign currency, one may be quite disappointed about the wrong result obtained. But, serious though it may sound, the damage is easily repaired by dividing $B + \Delta B$ by the increased exchange rate of the foreign currency: the deterioration of the balance in terms of domestic money may then show an improvement in terms of foreign money. It remains true, however, that $\Delta Y - \Delta A$ will not directly give the right answer.

Causal versus Ex Post Relations

The fundamental equation in the analysis, in the form $Y \equiv C + I + G + X - M$, is helpful in organizing an examination of the relationship between the components of aggregate spending and the foreign balance, but misleading if it is deemed to show causal *(ex ante)* rather than classificatory *(ex post)* relationships. For example, an increase in consumption expenditures may result in an increase in Y (if employment rises) or a decrease in I (if inventory is depleted) or a decrease in X (if exportable goods are domestically used) or an increase in M (if imports are purchased) or no real change at all (if prices of consumption goods rise); and there are many other more indirect possibilities and combinations—the study of which may be underemphasized by overconfident reliance on the "insight" afforded by the equation.

As a matter of fact, the equation gives very little insight into causal relationships. The merging of planned investment and unintentional inventory accumulation into one term, I, which in turn is part of A, is an example of an actually misleading "clue" suggested by the equation. Reduced consumption and reduced planned investment may some-

[26] See Machlup, "Theory of Foreign Exchange," *op. cit.*, VI, pp. 375 ff. and *Readings*, pp. 104 ff.

times be offset by increased unintended inventory accumulation (due to the unexpected decline in sales). This latter part of ΔA is inversely related to ΔY as far as causal relationship is concerned; and, incidentally, the effects of devaluation upon planned inventory holdings may causally be more important than any positive relation between income and inventory investment.

The difference between causal and mere *ex post* relationships can perhaps be made clearer by asking for the meaning of the equation $\Delta Y \equiv \Delta A + \Delta B$. Obviously, if any two of these terms are given, the third can be calculated. But this is not to say that ΔB "depends" on $\Delta Y - \Delta A$ in any causal sense. To say this has no more merit than to say that ΔA "depends" on $\Delta Y - \Delta B$, or that ΔY "depends" on $\Delta A + \Delta B$.

Yet the "income-absorption" approach does rest on such "dependence" if it proposes that an investigation of the effect of devaluation upon the trade balance should proceed by analyzing the "basic questions" how devaluation affects both income and absorption.[27] With the same justification—or lack of justification—one might investigate the effect of devaluation upon national income by analyzing the "basic questions" how devaluation affects both absorption and the trade balance. And an analogous procedure might be proposed for an investigation of the effects of devaluation upon consumption and investment. Such an analytical merry-go-round is entirely "in character" whenever definitional equations furnish the sole basis for inquiry into presumably causal relationships.

Reversing the Direction of Causation

The income-absorption approach of analyzing the effect of devaluation upon B assumes that causation goes this way: devaluation affects Y; Y affects A; devaluation affects A directly; the net changes of Y and A determine the change of B.

At one point, however, the question of a reversible process is openly raised: if devaluation affects A directly, cannot A affect Y? No doubt, it can. If absorption is reduced as a direct result of devaluation, this may cause unemployment, partly or fully offsetting a positive idle-resources effect (due to increased activity in export industries) or even resulting in a net decline in employment and output.

In the event and to the extent that the directly effected reduction in absorption causes a net decline in employment (instead of the desired transfer of resources), a sequence of secondary nonspending will cut down consumption and investment even further, depending on the propensity to absorb; and if the transfer of resources should

---

[27] Alexander, *op. cit.*, p. 266.

still fail to take place, at least the purchase of imports will be reduced, with a definitely positive effect on the trade balance. Needless to say, no government would want to have the improvement of the trade balance take this form, but it is only fair to mention that it can happen. Analysts, however, may exclude this sequence of events by assuming that the government, pursuing a policy of full or high-level employment, will succeed in preventing a decline in employment.

V. *Implicit Shifts of Emphasis*

The income-absorption approach and the fundamental truism on which it rests may be helpful for the purpose of impressing the responsible leaders of the state as well as their economic advisers with the need "to recognize that, if the foreign balance is to be improved, the community as a whole must reduce its absorption of goods and services relative to its income."[28] At the same time the approach may be misleading in that it conceals the dependence of B (or of $Y - A$) on some key facts which can only be neglected at the risk of perilously obfuscating the policy problem.

The Role of Gold and Exchange Reserves

If no loans, investments, or repayments are received from abroad, there cannot be any negative B unless someone in the country is willing to give up foreign balances or other foreign assets. Ordinarily, the monetary authorities are the only willing sellers of foreign balances (or gold). If they do not sell, or have none to sell, the import surplus no longer exists; the real problem is not how to improve the trade balance, but whether to avoid its "automatic" improvement by the operation of "cruel" market forces—and how to make the unavoidable correction of the trade balance least painful or least harmful to the economy.

In a free market for foreign exchange—with no rate-pegging, rate-fixing, or rationing controls—there would surely evolve exchange rates at which all excess demand for imports is eliminated. One may ask *how*—by what forces and strains and stresses—this depreciation of the currency would succeed in balancing trade, but one cannot doubt that it would. A continuing import surplus, in the absence of autonomous capital imports, presupposes a policy of pegging the exchange rate by selling gold or foreign exchange; it disappears when that policy is discontinued.

The Role of Credit Creation

If no loans, investments, or repayments are received from abroad,

[28] *Ibid.*, p. 275.

there cannot be any negative B unless someone in the country is using previously inactive domestic cash balances (which is not likely to go on for very long), or new currency is printed, or the banking system, with the active support of the monetary authorities, engages in a continuing expansion of its loans-and-securities portfolio. If this continuing supply of domestic funds is not explained, one cannot understand how "propensities to absorb" can ever lead to absorption in excess of income.

The continuing supply of new bank credit need not be a continuing net increase in the supply of money. When the monetary authorities sell foreign exchange from their reserves, the domestic money (bank deposits) that is paid for it is canceled. The expansion of the loans-and-securities portfolio of the banks merely recreates the bank deposits canceled by the purchases of foreign balances from official reserves. To put it differently, the current credit expansion finances the current "excess absorption" by consumers and investors as well as the purchase of the foreign exchange that it requires.

Without continuing dishoarding or bank credit expansion, the negative trade balance could not continue. Every day of excess imports would bring a further reduction in the money supply of the people and, inevitably, a decline in absorption. A persistent import surplus, in the absence of autonomous capital imports, presupposes a policy of enabling the banking system to expand credit; it disappears when that policy is discontinued.

The possibility of credit expansion, incidentally, besides being a prerequisite of the maintenance of a negative trade balance and of any deterioration of the trade balance, is also essential in other phases of the operation of Alexander's model. In particular, the working of the idle-resources effect may depend on it. While some increase in employment can usually be financed by hitherto inactive liquid funds, by and large it takes new bank money to do this job.[29]

Assumptions about the Supply of Money

Nothing can be said about the effects of a devaluation unless exact specifications are made regarding the supply of money and credit and

---

[29] Alexander's attempt to combine his two income effects of devaluation in one expression and to treat them alike suffers not only from the defect that the terms-of-trade effect on the trade balance does not operate solely via income, but also that "finance" is no prerequisite for it. An increase in real income produced by the idle-resources effect must be accompanied by an increase in money income and money flow; on the other hand, a change in real income produced by the terms-of-trade effect may be merely a matter of relative prices and need not be reflected in a change in money income and circulation. This difference, neglected by Alexander, may be significant and has even its policy aspects, because inelasticity of the supply of money may be part of the monetary policy of a country or a built-in feature of its currency system, which would largely inhibit the operation of the idle-resources effect.

the fiscal policy of the government. There seems to be a tendency in the "New Economics" tacitly to regard the supply of money as a dependent variable rather than as a policy variable. In the "very old economics," where models of an unmanaged gold standard still had some applicability, the supply of money could be treated as a dependent variable. But when everybody has views on how the supply of money "ought" to be managed, and when in fact almost every government in the world does manage the supply of money, one may reasonably expect economic analysts to be explicit on this point and to state what happens under the various monetary policies which a government may choose to pursue.

On some occasions Alexander follows this good practice; for example, in discussing the cash-balance effect he first stipulates that "the money supply is inflexible." But in many places he fails to make such stipulations.[30] Indeed, he later returns to the cash-balance effect and calls it transitory because "the money supply may *respond* to the increased demand for cash balances."[31] As economists we should, I submit, make a clear distinction between a "response" explainable in economic terms (such as an increase in quantities of product supplied in consequence of increased effective demand reflected in higher prices and in greater profitability of an increased output) and a "response" explainable in political terms (such as an increase in the quantity of money—associated with increased government expenditures, reduced reserve requirements, increased open-market purchases by the central bank, etc.—either in consequence of political pressures or in anticipation of economic, social and political repercussions considered to be undesirable by the political powers). An economic response will be treated as a dependent variable; a political response should be treated as a policy variable and enumerated among the "special assumptions."

To assume tacitly, as is often done, that the money supply will "respond" to an increased demand for credit (to finance increased wage payments and increased foreign payments) may deprive an analysis, such as that of the effects of devaluation, of much of its meaning. To be sure, where the purpose of devaluation is to stimulate employment through the stimulation of exports, it will be the policy of the authorities to help supply the additional credits that are demanded. Even in this case the analyst should state what policy is assumed. But where the purpose of devaluation is to reduce or remove an excess demand for foreign money (that is, with regard to the external balance, an excess supply of domestic money), a policy of supplying the credit demanded

---

[30] *Op. cit.*, pp. 270, 273, although he speaks there repeatedly of "rising money incomes and rising prices."

[31] *Ibid.*, p. 274. Emphasis supplied.

to replace the excess demand that was squeezed out by the devaluation is not very consistent—even if it should be politically unavoidable.[32]

VI. *Comparing the Two Approaches*

Given and Unchanged Parameters

The reason given for advancing the aggregate-spending approach was that its predecessor the relative-prices approach suffered from incurable deficiencies. The basic trouble of the latter is that it works with price elasticities which presumably are given and knowable, but actually are neither —and are even changed as a result of the very devaluation effects which they are supposed to determine.

The new approach assigns strategic importance to spending propensities. Since these spending propensities are supposed to determine the effects of devaluation upon the trade balance, the impression is created that α, the marginal propensity to absorb, is both given and knowable. Actually it is neither; indeed, we have every reason to believe that α is not stable over time and that it may change not only with the mood of the time but also momentarily according to the circumstances of the situation. Although called a "propensity" to absorb income, it contains both intentional and unintentional reactions, including unintended investment or disinvestment in inventories, which sometimes may offset the effects of intentional reactions; it comprises government expenditure (inclusive of public capital expenditure), which is not a function of income but an independent variable that can be administered in a direction opposite to that of changes in income; even in so far as it refers to private actions, it may be significantly influenced by monetary and fiscal policy; and, finally, it may be substantially changed as a result of the very devaluation the effects of which it supposedly determines.

Hence, what was said about the "elasticities approach," namely, that "the statement that the effect of a devaluation depends on the elasticities boils down to the statement that it depends on how the economic system behaves,"[33] may with equal justification be said about the income-absorption relation. For, after all, the devaluation effects upon income and absorption, including the supposedly given "propensities to absorb," depend "on how the economic system behaves"—and, we may add, on how it is made to behave by monetary and fiscal policies.

From the point of view of stability over time it is hard to say which of the parameters are less reliable as indicators of the effects of devalua-

---

[32] Even in this case a policy of devaluation may be adopted with the idea of taking advantage of lags and of gaining a breathing spell between devaluation and re-inflation.

[33] *Op. cit.*, p. 264.

tion on the trade balance—the price elasticities or the spending propensities. From the point of view of changeability in the very process the outcome of which they help determine, the spending propensities are probably less reliable than the price elasticities. And from the point of view of malleability through public policy, one probably should regard the price elasticities as the tougher factors to deal with, and the spending propensities more subject to the influence of (monetary and fiscal) policy—which means that in the last analysis not given propensities but chosen policies will determine the outcome.

Foreign Supply and Demand Conditions

An explanation of the volume, composition, terms, and balance of trade between nations can hardly be regarded as fully convincing if it takes account of the conditions in only one of the nations concerned instead of considering all parties involved. The relative-prices approach attempts to satisfy this precept by including the supply and demand conditions in foreign markets among the determining factors. In particular the elasticities of foreign demand for the exports and of foreign supply of the imports of the devaluing country are assigned important roles.

The aggregate-spending approach makes no such provision, at least not explicitly. It attempts to deduce the devaluation effects on the trade balance solely from the effects upon national income and absorption in the devaluing country. Since the "resulting" change in the trade balance is necessarily also a change, by the same amount though with opposite sign, in the trade balance of the trading partner—perhaps the rest of the world—one wonders how this change is imposed, so to speak, on the latter, regardless of the magnitudes of their spending propensities, etc. If only the ΔY and ΔA of the devaluing country were to determine the outcome, would this not imply that in the other countries changes in income and absorption would be "dictated" by a change in the trade balance, instead of the other way around?

Alexander's analysis is silent on this point. An enterprising builder of aggregative models might set out to construct a two-country model embodying the income-absorption relations based on the spending propensities in both countries affected by the change in foreign exchange rates. But I am not convinced that this would be a worth-while undertaking. It is probably more expedient to assume that "the foreign country" is the rest of the world, that the world-wide income and absorption effects of the devaluation of the one currency are so widely dispersed as to be negligible, and that therefore the elasticities of foreign demand and foreign supply are not sufficiently altered to lose their determining force on the outcome.[34] But this solution would obviously restore the elasticities approach to at least half its former role in the analysis of devaluation.

Price Elasticities in the Spending Approach

As a matter of fact, this restoration of relative prices and price elasticities to a strategic position in the model is not left to its reconstruction by future renovators; price elasticities have been allowed to continue all along, though inconspicuously, to do their job under the new regime. Supposedly banished under the aggregate-spending approach, they have in fact played important roles in Alexander's analysis.

At some points the elasticities work behind the scene. For example, whether there can be an idle-resources effect of devaluation depends on whether the production and sale of export goods can be expanded, hence, on elasticities of domestic supply and of foreign demand; but this is not explicitly said. At other points the elasticities are clearly visible on the stage. For example, whether a direct devaluation-effect upon absorption will result in a transfer of resources or in unemployment, depends on "how the economy responds to price incentives,"[35] or on the "price differential between the foreign and the domestic markets" and on "the substitutability of domestic goods for imports in consumption, and of resources as between the production of domestic goods and exports."[36] At one point at least, the role of price elasticities is dominant: in the terms-of-trade effect. For it is impossible to come to any conclusion concerning the effects of devaluation upon the terms of trade except on the basis of an examination of the relevant elasticities of supply and demand.

Alexander would probably deny none of this. For, although he regards aggregative analysis as "a more fruitful line of approach," to be adopted in lieu of "the more traditional supply and demand analysis,"[37] he concedes that "supply and demand conditions, in the sense of partial elasticities, may be useful tools in this [income-absorption] analysis."[38] His objection is to discussions in terms of "total elasticities" and he believes that it is "total elasticities for which the conventional formulas alone are valid."[39]

[34] This suggestion was made by Michael Michaely, *Devaluation and Dual Markets under Inflation with Direct Controls*, a doctoral dissertation submitted to Johns Hopkins University, January, 1955.

[35] See above, p. 262.

[36] Alexander, *op. cit.*, pp. 270, 271.

[37] *Ibid.*, p. 263.

[38] *Ibid.*, p. 275.

[39] *Ibid.*, p. 275. These "formulas," as I have understood them, had no other purpose than to suggest qualitative (directional) relationships and quantitative possibilities. Alex-

Conclusion

The upshot of all this is that relative prices and elasticities were not really discarded in the analysis of devaluation effects; and that aggregate spending and propensities by themselves cannot possibly do the explanatory job that was assigned to them. Neither of the two "alternative" sets of tools can be spared; both are needed.

Alexander, I am afraid, has confused his readers by presenting the new approach as a substitute for the old. If clearly presented as complementary to the old, and properly amended, the new analysis can be helpful. The new tools fashioned by Alexander cannot replace the old tools of "conventional analysis"; but they can, after some substantial reshaping, increase the usefulness of the latter.

It is the habit of innovators to disparage the old ways of doing things; it is the duty of critics to appreciate the value of the new without depreciating the value of the old. In trying to pare down the exaggerated claims of the innovator they are sometimes overly critical of the new ideas. Lest I have erred in this direction, I should like to end by paying my respect to Alexander's innovating enterprise and to his contribution to the development of international trade theory. A contribution it is, and an especially meritorious one where it gives scope to the roles of both aggregate spending and relative prices.

---

ander must have mistaken them for operational devices or for mere *ex post* relationships. If he means *"ex post* elasticities" when he says "total elasticities," he surely misunderstands most of those who have argued in terms of price elasticities. I, for one, have always had *ex ante* elasticities in mind.

[15]

The Need for Monetary Reserves

This article will address itself to the question whether it is possible to find any objective criteria for the need of monetary reserves, either for individual countries or for the world at large.

Although questions of terminology are uninteresting to some readers, I find it worth while to explain first why I speak of the " need for monetary reserves " and not, as so many others, of the " demand for international liquidity ".

Liquidity Is More Than Reserves

It is not easy to have a clear idea of what is meant by international liquidity or liquidity of the international payments system. Most people seem to mean by it the liquidity of all national monetary authorities taken together, although this leaves the important question of the distribution of a given total among the individual countries out of consideration.

By liquidity of a monetary authority one means its capacity to make payments to other countries if its foreign receipts were to drop or stop. For such payments, that is, to cover a deficit in foreign payments, it can use its own reserves or outside finance. The latter consists of borrowing facilities (including " drawing rights ") and facilities to liquidate assets other than monetary reserves.

Measurements of outside-financing facilities are not quite meaningful. Both the liquidity of assets (other than the perfectly liquid assets counted as monetary reserve) and the availability of credit for any one country depend on the simultaneous demand for liquid funds by others. For example, while every one of many central banks may have potential borrowing power of a certain amount if it *alone* asks for credit, it would not make sense to add these amounts as a measure of *aggregate* borrowing facilities: they would in fact not be available to all at the same time. This is different only with regard to unconditional drawing rights. They are available no matter how many countries wish to draw on the International Monetary Fund (I.M.F.) at the same time. It has, therefore,

175

FRITZ MACHLUP

become accepted practice to add such unconditional rights to the gross reserves of the countries.

That most statistical tables of international liquidity report *gross* reserves, rather than net reserves, is fully consistent with the principles of the gold-exchange standard. Calculating the total of *net* reserves raises hard questions, for it is not clear just what kinds of foreign liabilities should be deducted from the total reserve assets of a country. There are 1) official liabilities to official foreign creditors (such as debts of the central bank to other central banks, or Treasury securities held by foreign monetary authorities); 2) private liabilities to official foreign creditors (such as deposit liabilities of commercial banks to foreign monetary authorities; 3) official liabilities to private foreign creditors (such as Treasury notes held by foreign banks); and 4) private liabilities to private foreign creditors (such as deposit liabilities of commercial banks to foreign private banks). Should only the first kind of liabilities be dedeucted from the gross reserves of a country, or the first two, or the first and the third, or the first three, or all four? It may be worth pointing out that, by the second method of computation (that is, deducting all current liabilities to official creditors) the net reserves of the United Kingdom are minus $4,700 million and those of the United States are minus $650 million.

The practice of looking at gross reserves, rather than net reserves, if global figures are wanted, corresponds also to the practice used in statistics of the total money supply in a national economy. When one talks about the total money supply, or stock of money, in any country, one does not deduct from anybody's cash balances his current liabilities to anybody, official or private. The total stock of money is equal to the sum of the cash holdings of all individual and corporate persons in the economy.

One may, however, point to another analogy in national statistics, that of commercial-bank reserves. Some banking specialists prefer to make two distinctions: one between required and excess reserves, and another between borrowed and free reserves. The first distinction is quite sound, because excess reserves are a basis for measurements of the unused lending capacity of the banking system. The second distinction, however, relies on theories which I do not regard as sound, and it happens that the notion of *free* reserves of the commercial banks in a national economy is in many respects similar to the concept of net reserves in the international economy.

176

THE NEED FOR MONETARY RESERVES

All these statistics — of the total money supply and aggregate commercial-bank reserves in a country, and of total official reserves in the free world — disregard the distribution of the totals among cash holders or reserve holders. This is a serious limitation. Since the propensities to spend, lend, and invest differ among the holders of cash balances and among the holders of reserves, the same total may mean very different rates of spending, lending, and investing, depending on its distribution. A redistribution from more liquid to less liquid holders of cash or of reserves would quickly increase aggregate spending and, hence, the velocity of circulation of the money supply or of the total of reserves. No one, to my knowledge, has shown how to present statistics giving totals with some index of their distribution. But for certain simplified and accelerated trains of reasoning one may neglect the problem of distribution and confine oneself to totals.

It has become fashionable to speak condescendingly, if not contemptuously, of the quantity of money and of the total of international reserves. A group of monetary theorists have decreed that liquidity in the national economy comprises more than money (and even more than " money plus quasi-money "), and that liquidity in the international economy comprises more than official reserves. This is correct, but not very helpful if we have no statistical data measuring the " supplementary liquidity ". We lack such data both for national and for international liquidity.

On the level of international financial statistics we have one set of data which we can add to those of total reserves: the unconditional drawing rights provided by the I.M.F. Any other borrowing facilities and liquidating facilities have to be left aside. Under these circumstances we decide to remain old-fashioned and to stick with those parts of liquidity that are definite and measurable, that is, official gross reserves plus unconditional drawing rights.

Need Is Not the Same As Demand

It may be a little tedious if I point here to the popular confusion among three words: need, desire, and demand. I have done it before, but find it important enough to repeat (1).

---

(1) Fritz Machlup, *International Payments, Debts, and Gold* (New York: Scribner's, 1964) or *International Monetary Economics* (London: Allen and Unwin, 1966), Chapter 13.

177

FRITZ MACHLUP

Demand implies an offer of something in exchange for the object demanded; hence, it involves an exchange ratio or price; it states the quantities of the object that are demanded at various prices.

Desire is a psychological concept indicating a feeling, usually connected with an anticipation or imagination of its satisfaction; it implies neither a willingness to offer anything in exchange for the object desired nor a specification of any consequences of its nonfulfillment.

Need implies that certain, usually undesirable, consequences will arise if the needed object is not obtained in due time. In case of a personal need, the object may also be desired; this is not always so, for example, if the person does not know his need; if a person has a need and desire for an object and has possessions he could give up, he will also demand the object. But need does not always refer to persons, and may therefore be unrelated to demand or desire. It may be an objective statement of the consequences to be expected if what is " needed " does not actually occur. That a plant needs water and sunshine means that it will wilt without them; a sailboat needs wind if it is to move without any other force; a child needs vitamins in order to stay healthy and avoid rickets. A growing economy needs an increase in the stock of money if a decline in the level of wage rates and prices or a decline in the rate of employment are to be avoided.

The last example is of an objectively stated need of an economy: it specifies the consequences of a failure to provide an increase in money supply when the labor force increases. It is in precisely this sense that one may speak of the need for additions to total reserves of the monetary authorities in the countries that form the international economy (in the non-communist world).

Just what these consequences are, why they would occur, and on what grounds they are regarded as " bad " and " to be avoided ", these are questions which this paper will attempt to answer.

Alternative Quantitative Measures

We shall not propose our answers before examining some of the answers that have been advanced by others. Strictly speaking, most of them have not been explicit. For example, when certain groups of experts offered a quantitative measure of "world liquidity"

178

THE NEED FOR MONETARY RESERVES

by compiling statistics of official reserves and of world trade and then computing the ratios of reserves to trade for a long series of years, they did not really say that a particular ratio of reserves to trade was " needed ". They did not indicate what would happen if it fell below any particular level, nor why anything should happen in this case, nor why it ought to be avoided.

Some of these thoughts, however, are implied. It would make no sense to compute these ratios if one did not assume that they mattered. In other words, those who directed or executed the research ascertaining these ratios must have had a hypothesis or theory in mind. The researchers did not, after all, look into the ratios of reserves to total ton-miles of freight shipments, to the total amount of rainfall in the country, or to the total number of windows in the central-bank building. When they selected foreign trade as a relevant denominator they must have seen a connection between foreign reserves and foreign trade. The theory of this connection will have to be formulated and examined.

Ratios of reserves to several other magnitudes have sometimes been considered. Some have been discussed in the literature, others suggest themselves as improvements of those discussed. In each case the ratios may be regarded either as relevant for individual countries (as terms in " behavior equations " indicating the decisions of the authorities) or as relevant for a group of countries representing a large part of world trade (as terms in some " aggregative equations " in a causally interrelated system).

We shall look into the relations between official reserves and 1) imports, 2) seasonal and cyclical variations in foreign trade, 3) imports and capital outflows, 4) past deficits in the balance of payments, 5) domestic money supply and domestic money plus quasi-money, and 6) current domestic or total liabilities of the central bank or current foreign liabilities of the entire banking system.

To the extent that data are available, we shall present them for the 14 " industrialized countries " listed in *International Financial Statistics* (I.F.S.), published monthly by the I.M.F. The 14 countries are those commonly called the Group of Ten, plus Australia, Austria, Ireland, and Switzerland. Each statistical presentation will be accompanied by a critical discussion of the underlying theory. Where no adequate statistical data are available, we shall confine ourselves to brief theoretical observations.

179

FRITZ MACHLUP

The theory of the relevance of the ratio of foreign reserves to imports rests chiefly on the analogy with the theory of the demand for cash balances on the part of the individual household. The money transactions of the household which determine its "transactions demand" for cash balances are its income and what it purchases with it (hence, its real income). These purchases are the "imports" of the household. By analogy, the imports of the nation are supposed to determine its "demand" for foreign balances to pay for them. The two conceptual jumps from demand to need and from household to nation have often been thoughtlessly accepted.

If a household is said to hold enough cash to pay for, say, four months' purchases, the ratio of its average cash balance to annual purchases is one-third, or 33 1/3 per cent. There is nothing wrong in expressing the ratios of a nation's foreign reserves to its annual imports in the same way: a ratio of 50 per cent pays for six months imports, 33 1/3 per cent for four months, 25 per cent for three months, 12 1/2 per cent for 6 weeks. To describe the size of the foreign reserve in this way is one thing; it is another, however, to explain it or to attribute to it any particular consequences.

In the Appendix, Table A-I presents the relevant statistical series for 1949 to 1965 for the 14 industrial countries (to the extent that they are given in *I.F.S.*). It shows the size of official reserves at the end of each year. These may be accepted in lieu of the unavailable averages for each year. (I have compared some end-of-year figures with the averages of the end-of-quarter figures in years for which the latter were available; I found the differences insignificant, which indicates that the substitution of end-of-year figures is not too unreasonable. I might have taken averages of the reserves at the beginning and the end of each year, but have not considered this exercise worth its cost.) The table shows, secondly, the annual imports for each year. Both the reserves and the imports are given in US dollars. The third column gives the ratio of reserves to imports.

A selection of a few of the data of Table A-I and computations made with the data for recent years will facilitate comparisons. Table 1 shows for each of the 14 countries first the highest ratio, in any year between 1949 and 1965, of its reserves to imports, then

180

THE NEED FOR MONETARY RESERVES

the lowest ratio in the same period, and finally the average ratio of reserves to imports during the five-year period 1961-1965.

TABLE I

RATIOS OF RESERVES TO IMPORTS IN 14 INDUSTRIAL COUNTRIES:
Highest and Lowest Ratios from 1949 to 1965 and Mean Ratios for 1961-1965

	Highest Ratio		Lowest Ratio		Mean Ratio	
	Year	%	Year	%	Years	%
Australia	1953	92.6	1960	33.8	1961-65	55.8
Austria	1963	73.4	1949	15.5	»	66.6
Belgium-Luxembourg . . .	1949	54.2	1957	33.3	»	38.3
Canada	1950	59.0	1957	31.1	»	37.8
France	1965	61.3	1957	10.5	»	57.0
Germany a	1958	77.6	1950	7.0	»	55.4
Ireland	1950	87.7	1965	39.4	»	45.3
Italy b	1959	90.7	1952	29.8	»	58.7
Japan c	1952	54.3	1957	19.3	»	29.4
The Netherlands	1953	51.9	1951	21.7	»	35.2
Sweden	1953	35.3	1960	18.2	»	24.1
Switzerland	1949	191.8	1964	86.5	»	93.2
United Kingdom	1950	46.8	1964	15.0	»	22.1
United States	1949	345.0	1965	66.6	»	90.6

a Data for imports in 1949 not available.

b Data for reserves in 1949 not available.

c Data for reserves in 1949, 1950, and 1951 not available.

The highest ratio of reserves to imports, in all 14 countries during the 17 years under observation, was that of the United States in 1949 — that is, before its long series of deficits began. The ratio was 345 per cent, which is enough to pay for almost 3 1/2 years of imports. The lowest ratio shown in the table is that of Germany in 1950; it was 7 per cent, which would have paid for only 26 days of imports. The second-lowest ratio is that for France in 1957, which was 10.5 per cent, or imports for 37 days.

Looking at the averages for 1961-1965, we see that Switzerland leads in the size of reserves relative to imports, with a ratio of 93.2 per cent, followed by the United States with a ratio of 90.6 per cent. The lowest ratio is that for the United Kingdom, 22.1 per cent, and next to it Sweden with 24.1 per cent. From Table A-I one can

181

FRITZ MACHLUP

see a further decline in the ratio maintained by the United Kingdom: in 1965 it was down to 18.6 per cent, or imports for 68 days.

England was not alone in the decline of its ratio of reserves to imports. Indeed, 12 of the 14 countries included in the survey "suffered" such a decline from 1961 to 1965, Austria and France being the only exceptions. This is shown in Table 2, which gives the ratios of reserves to imports for 1957, 1961 and 1965. The year 1957 is included in order to add another base year beside 1961. While in twelve countries the ratios were lower in 1965 than 1961, these ratios were above those of 1957 in eight countries. Consistent declines from 1957 to 1961 and to 1965 were registered only by Germany and the United States, which for Germany was entirely, and for the United States partly, due to large increases in imports.

TABLE 2

RATIOS OF RESERVES TO IMPORTS IN 14 INDUSTRIAL COUNTRIES:
for Selected Years, 1957, 1961, and 1965

	1957 %	1961 %	1965 %
Australia	68.9	56.3	42.0
Austria	46.4	56.9	62.4
Belgium-Luxembourg	33.3	42.9	34.8
Canada	31.1	36.7	34.7
France	10.5	56.9	61.3
Germany	68.9	65.4	42.5
Ireland	57.4	46.9	39.4
Italy	36.9	72.7	60.1
Japan	19.3	28.7	26.3
The Netherlands	24.6	38.5	32.4
Sweden	20.7	25.1	22.2
Switzerland	96.6	101.9	87.8
United Kingdom	21.0	27.0	18.6
United States	169.9	116.7	66.6

The computation of averages for all 14 countries together involves the problem of weighting. The different sizes of the countries obviously call for weighting, but the weights can be either by size of reserves or by size of imports. (The latter measure is identical

182

THE NEED FOR MONETARY RESERVES

with the ratio of aggregate reserves to aggregate imports.) More-over, since the reserve-currency countries present special problems, one may prefer to see separately the averages for the twelve countries exclusive of the United States and the United Kingdom. The results of these four computations for the five-year period 1961-1965 are shown in Table 3, which for the sake of simplicity omits the details of computing the weights. That the figures are higher for the 14 than for only 12 countries is due to the high ratio and large weights of the United States. That the ratios are higher if weighted by imports than if weighted by reserves is due to the fact that some countries with large shares in aggregate reserves have relatively low ratios of reserves to imports.

TABLE 3

AVERAGE RATIOS OF RESERVES TO IMPORTS, 1961-1965,
for 12 and 14 Countries, Weighted by Size of Reserves and by Size of Imports

Average Ratio of Reserves to Imports	for 14 countries	for 12 countries
Weighted by size of reserves	53.6%	48.5%
Weighted by size of imports	62.4%	53.7%

Is there any real significance in the ratios? If there is, I do not know any theory that would show and explain it. We might have taken different periods and would have obtained different average ratios, but I could not seriously propose any other numerical data with which the ratios or their changes might be meaningfully correlated or causally associated.

Looking again at Tables 1 and 2, especially at the ratios for individual countries in various years, we wonder whether one can detect any reasons why some countries should " need " reserves of 50 and more per cent of their imports, while others can do with 30 to 35 per cent, and again others with less than 25 per cent. We know no such reasons. One can perhaps explain why ratios of less than 20 per cent are regarded as " dangerously low ", but the reasons are more likely related to the possibility of *variations* in receipts and expenditures than to the *length of time* imports could be paid for if all receipts were stopped suddenly.

183

FRITZ MACHLUP

There have been some "amateur theories" linking reserves with imports, or rather with total foreign trade, by means of the conception of a need to "finance" trade. This is a naïve fallacy, for it confuses money, commercial-bank reserves, central-bank reserves, and the demand for credit. A trader (importer, exporter) who wants "finance" wants credit because his working capital is not adequate to tide him over the intervals between due dates of his payments and receipts. This has nothing to do with official reserves of either any individual country or all countries taken together.

Another theory links the size of imports with the probability of deficits in the balance of payments and the function of official reserves to finance such deficits. This theory will be discussed in another section dealing with the magnitudes of past deficits and the probabilities of future deficits. To associate the size of probable deficits with the volume of imports is to make several untenable assumptions. The most notable ones are 1) that significant changes in the net demand for foreign exchange depend on imports only and not at all on exports, capital movements, and unilateral payments; and 2) that the size of probable deficits would vary directly with the total value of imports.

We shall not go into details, but emphasize only one point. The assumption that clearing balances are likely to increase in direct proportion with total transactions is contrary to all experience. It has been shown that firms can do with relatively smaller cash balances when their total transactions increase. Assuming, though not admitting, that total international transactions are perfectly correlated with imports — so that one could safely disregard all transactions other than payments for imports — one may not disregard the fact that the magnitudes of probable deficits will rise absolutely but fall relatively with increasing imports. On these grounds one could expect declining ratios of "needed" or "wanted" reserves to total imports.

With some imagination one may conceive of a reason for holding, nevertheless, reserves in an undiminished ratio to imports: one might hold that the increase in world trade is a result of liberalized commercial policies and that exports, therefore, are more vulnerable to relapses into illiberal attitudes, which would justify reckoning with a greater risk of deficits. The fall in the need for reserves for "transactions purposes" would be offset by a rise in the desire for reserves to satisfy "precautionary" considerations.

184

THE NEED FOR MONETARY RESERVES

All this, I submit, is far from reasonable. As I see it, there is neither theoretical nor statistical support for attaching any real significance to the ratio of reserves to imports.

Reserves in Relation to Variations of the Trade Balance

In the previous section we mentioned that one might find a more plausible relation between the need for official reserves and *variations*, seasonal or cyclical, in the balance of trade. For example, if imports are evenly distributed over the year whereas exports are chiefly of a crop commodity and are bunched in the autumn, there will be trade deficits in three quarters of the year and a surplus in one. The ratio of reserves to foreign trade might in this case — if only in specific circumstances — be higher than if both exports and imports were evenly distributed over the year. Likewise if exports and imports are of very different sensitiveness to business fluctuations, one may expect cyclical variations in the trade balance, which could result in periodic accumulations and decumulations of reserves and a higher ratio of average reserves to trade than if exports and imports varied concurrently and equally.

However, movements of private capital could easily counteract any effects which such variations in the trade balance would have upon official operations in foreign exchange. Indeed, in the absence of governmental restrictions, hedging and speculation would operate to eliminate the expected succession of excess demand and excess supply in the market for foreign exchange. The net effects on official reserves would be nil.

In any case, in large industrial countries there is no indication of significant variations of this kind. They may play a role in developing countries with foreign-exchange controls, but precisely there, with the chronic and latent excess demand for foreign exchange, large accumulations of reserves are rare.

If there were any detectable effects of variations on the ratio of reserves to foreign trade, they would probably refer to comparisons among different countries rather than to the ratios of aggregates in the world at large. The whole theory, however, has not looked sufficiently promising to invite statistical tests. If any one is diligent enough to try, he will, I anticipate, find no confirmation of the theory.

185

FRITZ MACHLUP

Reserves in Relation to Imports and Capital Outflows

The theory that the need for foreign reserves is determined by the amounts paid for imports was rejected partly because it singled out one particular category of transactions and neglected all others. Just as the transactions of a household include payments for securities besides payments for consumer goods, the foreign transactions of a nation include capital outflow besides imports and commodities. Why not take all out-payments of a country into account?

That capital outflows can be of paramount significance in the payments position of a country has been well known in any number of instances of capital flight. But apart from " unusual circumstances ", the last 16 years of payments deficits of the United States testify to the importance of capital movements. Practically all these deficits were due to net outflows of capital and unilateral payments abroad in excess of net proceeds from export surpluses. Thus, if reserves were needed to finance deficits in the balance of payments, it must have been the capital outflows and transfer payments that played the determining role in the deterioration of the reserve position throughout these years.

Capital transactions are probably larger than payments for merchandise if they are counted on a gross rather than net basis. Total foreign transactions in the New York money market may be several hundred times as high as the change in net positions of foreign and domestic banks from the beginning to the end of the year. Of course, it is doubtful that large cash balances or official reserves are " needed " to support these transactions. Still, if one holds the theory that reserves are needed in some proportion to transactions, it is untenable to confine oneself to payments for imports and disregard all capital transactions.

Statistical tests of this extension of the theory are impossible because we have no data on international capital transactions, at least not in the two or three countries in which such transactions are likely to be a multiple of imports. I refer to the United States, Switzerland, and perhaps Germany. The reports collected for statistical purposes in the United States are all on the basis of net positions at a few dates per year, not on day-to-day transactions. One cannot infer the volume of transactions from changes in net positions at dates as far apart as a month or even a quarter of a year.

186

THE NEED FOR MONETARY RESERVES

We need not be particularly disturbed by the absence of statistical tests of a theory as weak as the one discussed. Imagine we had all the data required for the computation of ratios of reserves to the sum of imports and gross outflows on capital account. The results of such computations would probably show us ratios varying both from country to country and for each country from year to year. We would still lack any quantitative measure of the " need " for reserves in any meaningful sense.

Reserves in Relation to Past Deficits

A much more plausible theory is derived from the " most rational " assumption about the function of official reserves. This rational assumption — which, however, may be neither realistic nor relevant — takes it for granted that reserves have only one purpose: to be ready in a contingency. There is no other fully rational use.

The contingency in question is a deficit in the balance of payments. If reserves are held so that a country may be able to finance a payments deficit and not be compelled to take unpopular measures — such, as devaluation, deflation, or direct controls — it follows that the reserves have to be in some proportion to the size and duration of a potential deficit.

Here, then, is a theory of the need for reserves that satisfies the requirements specified earlier in this paper. It states the consequences to be expected from a lack or inadequacy of reserves, to wit, devaluation, deflation, or direct controls. The theory can explain how these consequences arise if reserves are lacking, and why they are regarded as " bad " and to be avoided if possible. And it may also help obtain an idea about the magnitude of the possible loss of reserves for which the authorities of a country think they ought to be prepared.

Contingencies are usually estimated on the basis of experience. In order to make a realistic estimate of a loss of reserves that may occur in the future, it is a reasonable procedure to take a look at the past. For certain kinds of contingency, to be sure, such a procedure would be unreasonable: I cannot judge from my largest damage or injury in a fire or accident in the past for what damages or injuries in the future I ought to prepare; still less can I conclude from the fact that I have never died before that I may safely dis-

187

regard the probability of my death in the future. For contingencies of this sort we must pool large numbers of people and calculate the actuarial probabilities. On the other hand, for such things as seasonal fluctuations, cyclical swings, and even irregular contingencies in the economic life of a nation, it is quite appropriate to look into its past experience for some indication of what one ought to be prepared for in the future.

I propose to examine the reserve-loss experience of our 14 industrial countries. For this purpose I have prepared statistical data for the three largest reserve losses which each of these countries has sustained between 1949 and 1965. These losses are then compared with the official reserves at three points of time, (a) at the peak before the deficit began, (b) at the trough reached when the deficit ended, and (c) at the end of 1965. Quarterly data are used and the duration of the deficit is defined as the interval from a peak in reserve holdings to the nearest trough that is not followed by another trough within one year. For example, if a country loses reserves for nine quarters in a row, then gains reserves for half a year (two quarters) but subsequently continues to lose reserves for another year (four quarters), reaching another low (which remains the low point for more than a year), the period of the deficit is measured to the second low point, that is, 15 quarters in all, and the total loss is measured by the difference between the reserve holdings at the beginning and at the end of the entire period extending over 15 quarters.

These data are presented in the Appendix in Table A-II. More detailed descriptions are supplied in the footnotes to the table. A short digest of the relation between each country's reserves at the end of 1965 to its largest reserve loss suffered since 1949 is furnished here in Table 4 for the convenience of the reader. The countries are arranged, not as before in alphabetic order, but in ascending order of the ratios. These ratios, incidentally, are not contained in Table A-II explicitly but only in the form of their reciprocals. It seems more appropriate there to show the proportion of the reserve losses to the reserves; after all, to say that a nation during a certain period lost one-half of its reserves sounds more plausible than to say that its reserves had been twice the loss suffered. In Table 4, however, which shows only the reserve holdings at the end of 1965, it is unobjectionable to state the ratios of reserves to the largest losses

188

THE NEED FOR MONETARY RESERVES

sustained. This way of expressing the relationship allows us to be consistent with our Tables 1, 2, and 3, and also with several more tables to follow.

TABLE 4

RATIOS OF RESERVES HELD IN 1965 BY 14 INDUSTRIAL COUNTRIES
TO THEIR LARGEST CUMULATIVE LOSS OF RESERVES BETWEEN 1949 AND 1965

United Kingdom	142 per cent
Australia	165 »
United States	255 »
Japan	417 »
Ireland	427 »
Germany	452 »
The Netherlands	473 »
France	477 »
Italy	506 »
Canada	660 »
Belgium-Luxembourg	922 »
Switzerland	981 »
Sweden	1262 »
Austria	1441 »

It is interesting to note that the two reserve-currency countries are among the three lowest reserve holders of the 14 industrial countries. The reserves held by the United Kingdom at the end of 1965 were only 142 per cent of the largest reserves loss that the country had sustained. The reserves held by the United States at the end of 1965 were 255 per cent of its largest reserve loss, but this will surely turn out to be a serious overstatement since the loss period had not ended in 1965 and reserves have continued to fall. Thus, the reserve-currency countries are poorly prepared for future deficits and, if their current official liabilities are taken into account — leaving at least the United Kingdom with negative net reserves — they can hardly be said to be prepared at all.

One may observe how many countries are in a middle category of preparedness for future deficits. Six of the 14 countries were holding reserves between 417 and 506 per cent of their largest past deficits. In other words, the reserves they held in December 1965 would finance deficits four or five times as large as the largest they had ever suffered. Their margin of safety is so wide that one may

189

FRITZ MACHLUP

assume that the authorities in charge have never appraised their position from this point of view.

This is even more so with regard to the countries with the highest ratios. Can anybody seriously contend that central banks hold reserves only for the purpose of meeting future deficits if these reserves are between 900 and 1,500 per cent of the largest deficits they have experienced? It would be ridiculous to entertain this thought. If Belgium and Switzerland are able to finance deficits nine or ten times as large as the largest in their experience, this is a leeway that cannot be consciously intended. This conclusion is well-nigh unavoidable with regard to Sweden and Austria, holding reserves 1,262 and 1,441 per cent of their largest past deficits. No central banker in his right mind would find it justifiable to carry such exorbitant over-insurance against the risk of deficits. He must have other reasons for carrying reserves in amounts he can never expect to " need " or use for their supposedly true purpose.

Reserves in Relation to Domestic Money Supply

There are other theories which may possibly explain why large reserves are held and are considered necessary. The oldest of all such theories relates reserves to the quantity of money; indeed, the phrase " reserve ratio " originally meant precisely the ratio of reserves to money, though " money " in this case meant in the first place money issued by the central bank.

In the sense of ratio of central-bank reserves to central-bank money, the reserve ratio was an outgrowth of an old banking tradition. For a long time, however, the difference between deposit liabilities and note issue was considered to crucial that in many countries the gold reserve was related to bank notes only. Where the maintenance of a minimum reserve ratio was made a legal requirement, reserves were, of course, needed — and some of the consequences of nonfulfillment of the requirement were spelled out in statutory law. As the volume of central-bank money issued increased, more reserves were needed to meet the requirement, and the managers of the bank had to gear their credit policies to the growth of reserves.

Some professors of central-banking theory, in the past more than in our time, were convinced of the economic rationale of a

190

THE NEED FOR MONETARY RESERVES

" gold backing " for domestic money, particularly for central-bank money. But regardless of the particular theory held — whether a certain gold backing was deemed necessary for the maintenance of the value of money, whether a reserve in a certain ratio to the money circulation was held necessary to meet the demand for foreign remittances that was likely to rise as the quantity of money was increased, or whether certain proportions kept in foreign liquid assets were regarded as needed to maintain a sound structure of the balance sheet — a " need " for increased reserves somehow in proportion to increased amounts of central-bank money has been taken for granted by most practitioners of central-bank management. One may regard all these theories and rules as primitive, naïve, obsolete, or what not, but nevertheless as fully effective in determining the monetary policies of many countries. This qualified acceptance of the need for reserves as actually guiding the central-bankers in their policies and as explaining the magnitudes of their official reserves must be withdrawn, however, if one sees the enormous variations in the reserve ratios from country to country. No theory indicates a need for reserves of over 90 per cent of central-bank money; yet such reserve ratios have existed in a few countries during the last 17 years.

Perhaps the limitation to central-bank money is inappropriate; most practitioners maybe have recognized, with the monetary theorists, that money issued by private financial institutions, especially by commercial banks, ought to be taken into account. They may well argue that the need for foreign reserves grows with the domestic supply of money. They could point to several theories in support of such an argument; for example, they might hold that effective demand and money incomes would rise roughly with the quantity of money in circulation, that — even with constant average propensities to import (and to invest abroad) — the volume of foreign trade (and other foreign transactions) is certain to increase, and that larger foreign reserves would be needed to finance occasional deficits in foreign payments. Let us see what the statistical data can tell us about the ratio of official reserves to the domestic money supply.

Views differ as to how inclusive the concept of money ought to be understood. Some insist that demand deposits in commercial banks are money, but time deposits are not. Others prefer to distinguish different kinds of time deposits and to include in the stock of money " certificates of deposits " and other highly liquid time deposits in commercial banks, but to exclude thrift deposits or " pass-

191

FRITZ MACHLUP

book savings accounts ". Institutions are different in different countries, and in some of them these distinctions cannot be made. It has become customary to speak of " near money " or " quasi-money ", but there is no agreement on exactly what should be included in this concept in particular countries. Are balances on current account in a postal-savings system to be regarded as money, as quasi-money, or as neither ? We shall not try to provide our own answers to such questions, but simply adopt the decisions made by the statisticians of the I.M.F. for their table published in *I.F.S.* They report for most (though not all) countries two figures, one for the money supply, another for quasi-money.

In the Appendix, Table A-III, the figures for official reserves, domestic money supply, and money plus quasi-money are presented for our 14 countries (for as many years as are available from *I.F.S.*) and reserve ratios are calculated. We have thus obtained a ratio of reserves to money and a ratio of reserves to money plus quasi-money. In view of some doubtful classifications, the comparability of the ratios may be somewhat impaired, but not sufficiently to make comparisons worthless. Where classifications have not changed in the course of the years, we can at least rely on the intertemporal comparability of the figures for the same country.

Again we present a digest for the convenience of the reader. Table 5 presents the highest and lowest ratios of official reserves to money supply and to money plus quasi-money that prevailed in our 14 countries between 1949 — or the first year for which statistical data are available — and 1965.

The table conveys a picture of almost incredible diversity in time and place. Looking only at the ratio of reserves to money, we find that the lowest of the lowest ratios was 3.8 per cent (France in 1957) and the highest of the highest ratios was 114.0 per cent (Ireland in 1950). The highest of the lowest ratios was 57.2 per cent (Ireland in 1965) and the lowest of the highest was 12.8 per cent (United Kingdom in 1960). The greatest change over time in the same country occured in Germany, with a low of 10.0 per cent (in 1951) and a high of 62.3 per cent (in 1960). Consistently low ratios prevailed in the United Kingdom, with a low of 7.0 per cent (in 1964) and a high of 12.8 per cent (in 1960). France too had rather low ratios: between 1949 and 1960 there were nine years with ratios below 9 per cent (and six years with ratios of 7 per cent or less), and the highest ratio in that period was 11.6 per cent. The

192

THE NEED FOR MONETARY RESERVES

TABLE 5

RATIOS OF RESERVES TO QUANTITY OF MONEY AND OF MONEY PLUS QUASI-MONEY IN 14 INDUSTRIAL COUNTRIES:
Highest and Lowest Ratios between 1949 and 1965, and Mean Ratios for 1961-1965

	Ratio of Reserves to Money Supply						Ratio of Reserves to Money plus Quasi-Money					
	Highest Ratio		Lowest Ratio		Mean Ratio		Highest Ratio		Lowest Ratio		Mean Ratio	
	Year	%	Year	%	Years	%	Year	%	Year	%	Years	%
Australia	1950	50.4	1960	22.4	1961-65	37.9	1950	27.8	1960	10.8	1961-65	15.3
Austria a	1953	73.4	1955	41.0	»	67.8	1953	52.3	1960	24.9	»	28.7
Belgium-Luxembourg b	1961	38.2	1950	25.2	»	36.0	1958	32.3	1950	23.2	»	29.3
Canada	1950	47.9	1960	32.2	»	36.2	1950	23.9	1960	14.8	»	17.5
France	1965	17.6	1957	3.8	»	16.6	1965	15.8	1957	3.6	»	15.0
Germany	1960	62.3	1951	10.0	»	47.5	1957	30.3	1951	7.0	»	19.7
Ireland	1950	114.0	1965	57.2	»	61.8	1950	40.8	1965	22.3	»	23.6
Italy a	1959	29.3	1953	12.6	»	21.6	1959	16.8	1953	8.6	»	12.3
Japan a	1956	17.9	1965	7.4	»	9.5	1953	8.2	1964	2.4	»	3.1
The Netherlands b	1960	62.6	1951	30.1	»	53.9	1953	48.0	1951	25.3	»	38.5
Sweden	1953	32.4	1959	21.0	»	27.6	1951	9.9	1959	5.3	»	7.3
Switzerland	1949	65.6	1964	47.6	»	49.8	1949	31.6	1965	17.8	»	19.8
United Kingdom c	1960	12.8	1964	7.0	»	9.4	—	—	—	—	—	—
United States	1949	23.7	1965	9.1	»	10.8	1949	18.0	1965	5.0	»	6.5

a Earliest data for 1953.   b Earliest data for 1950.   c Earliest data for 1951.

193

FRITZ MACHLUP

large increase in reserves after 1960 did not show up in especially high reserve ratios: the high was reached in 1965 with only 17.6 per cent. Consistently high ratios prevailed in Austria, with a low of 41.0 per cent and a high of 73.4 per cent, and in Switzerland with a low of 47.6 per cent and a high of 65.6 per cent.

The arithmetic averages of the reserve ratios in the five years 1961-1965 show again substantial differences among the 14 countries. United Kingdom, Japan, and the United States had the lowest average ratios with 9.4, 9.5, and 10.8 per cent, respectively. Austria had the highest ratio, 67.8 per cent, followed by Ireland with 61.8 per cent and the Netherlands with 53.9 per cent. Then came Switzerland with 49.8 per cent and Germany with 47.5 per cent.

The ratios of reserves to money inclusive of quasi-money are, of course, lower. The differences between the two ratios are large in countries where time deposits play a large role but are not considered " money proper ". Ireland leads in this respect: the average reserve ratios for 1961-1965 were 61.8 per cent for money and 23.6 per cent for money plus quasi-money. Other countries in which the former ratio is more than twice the latter are Australia, Austria, Canada, Germany, Japan, Sweden, and Switzerland. The difference is smallest in France; it is nil in the United Kingdom, where the category of quasi-money does not exist (at least not in *I.F.S.*).

Just for the purpose of helping us to judge which ratios may be regarded as high and which as low, I computed weighted averages of the ratios of reserves to money for the whole group of 14 industrial countries and also for the twelve countries excluding the two reserve-currency countries. For the period 1961-1965, the ratios of aggregate reserves to aggregate money stocks were 26.9 per cent for the 14 countries and 35.5 per cent for the twelve countries.

The enormous differences among countries compel rejection of any theory that would assert a needed or most desired ratio of foreign reserves to the quantity of domestic money, unless the theory included some parameter that would fit the ratio to particular circumstances. I am not aware of any such theory, but could imagine one. For example the needed or most desirable amount of foreign reserves might held to be a function of a country's marginal propensity to import (goods, services, and perhaps also securities) besides the stock of domestic money. This might be explained by referring to some intervening variables, especially changes in income; if the

194

THE NEED FOR MONETARY RESERVES

import propensity is high, a relatively small increase in the quantity of money might lead to a substantial increase in the demand for foreign exchange, for which the monetary authorities wish to be prepared.

I do not think that this theory holds much promise; at least I doubt that it describes the kind of reasoning that the managers of monetary policy in any of the countries in question seriously engage in. They might, however, be more impressed with their own balance sheets, and I shall turn to this possibility.

Reserves in Relation to Current Liabilities

It is in part a return to this notion, because we have previously mentioned that reserves might be considered as " needed " in relation to the amount of central-bank money outstanding. Central-bank money is largely the same as the current domestic liabilities of the central bank. Hence it is, in fact, a concern with a property of the balance sheet if liquid foreign assets (chiefly gold) are viewed in their " proper " relationship to current domestic liabilities.

The theory that it may be found desirable to maintain a certain ratio of liquid foreign assets (gold) to current domestic liabilities could be based only on one consideration: the probability that a certain portion of these liabilities may at any time be presented for conversion into foreign currency (gold). It is out of the question that the portion can ever come close to 100 per cent or even close to 50 per cent of the domestic liabilities, because the owners of these liabilities need them in their domestic business. The bank notes are needed for day-to-day transactions between households and the businesses catering to them, and deposit liabilities of the central bank are needed by commercial banks to meet legal or customary reserve requirements. At times, however, some of the holders of commercial-bank deposits may find that they have to make increasing remittances to foreign firms to pay for increased imports of goods, services, and securities from abroad, and, in the process, the commercial banks have to use some of their central-bank deposits to acquire foreign exchange (gold) from the central bank. If all commercial banks were always loaned-up, that is, without any excess reserves, and if the central bank were determined never to help them with loans, rediscounts, or open-market purchases, authorities

195

FRITZ MACHLUP

would be quite safe with a very small ratio of foreign reserves to current domestic liabilities. The greater the excess reserves of commercial banks and the greater the political responsibility accepted by the central bank for averting liquidity troubles on the part of commercial banks and industry, the larger have to be the foreign reserves in relation to the domestic liabilities of the central bank.

This is perhaps the most plausible of all theories thus far considered. For it not only explains a "need" for foreign reserves but also why this need is related to the size of current domestic liabilities and why the needed ratios may be very different from country to country. While one country may feel that it can do with a 10 per cent ratio, another may feel safe only with 30 per cent, another with 40 per cent. Ratios larger than this, however, can hardly be explained by this theory. What it does explain, on the other hand, is why countries will want to have their foreign reserves increase every year. Since in a growing economy the current domestic liabilities of the central bank have got to increase if declining wage and price levels are to be prevented, maintenance of the "safe" reserve ratio requires a steady increase in foreign reserves, approximately by the annual rate of economic growth.

We have thus far talked about the relation of reserves to current *domestic* liabilities only. Where all official reserves of all monetary authorities are gold, and no other "foreign assets" are held by any monetary authority, none of them could have foreign liabilities. Under the gold-exchange standard, however, where many countries hold foreign exchange among their reserve assets, the countries whose currencies are so held must have foreign liabilities. Do these countries or central banks "need" an extra reserve against their foreign liabilities? Is the probability of payment being demanded the same, or is it smaller or greater than in the case of domestic liabilities? No economic theory can be developed to answer these questions completely, because demands for conversion into gold are largely political decisions by the official claimants. Only to a small part is conversion explained by economic factors, namely, when countries that hold large portions of their foreign reserves in the form of foreign exchange develop payments deficits vis-à-vis countries that hold chiefly gold. The recipient central banks, in order to maintain their customary ratios between gold and foreign exchange, would convert their surplus holdings of exchange into

196

THE NEED FOR MONETARY RESERVES 357

gold. The probabilities of such occurrences are not easy to express in the form of numerical coefficients.

It is quite likely that the same countries have had at different times different attitudes concerning the need of foreign reserves against their foreign liabilities. In periods when foreign central banks were eager to build up their foreign-exchange reserves, the reserve-currency countries were probably quite unconcerned about demands for conversion into gold. Later, when the holders of currency reserves became apprehensive about further additions to their holdings, the issuers of these currencies became quite conscious of their inadequate preparedness to convert them into gold. In any case their holdings of gold and convertible foreign currencies will have to constitute reserves against *all* their current liabilities, foreign as well as domestic.

In order to see what ratios the major central banks have maintained over the years, I prepared again comprehensive statistics, based on the data published by *I.F.S.* Unfortunately, comparability is doubtful, probably because of different reporting practices in different countries. For the two reserve-currency countries, the United Kingdom and the United States, the data are really not usable for meaningful comparisons, particularly because of the " split personality " of their monetary authorities. The foreign reserves are held partly by the central bank, partly by agencies of the Treasury department; likewise the foreign liabilities are owed partly by the central bank, partly by the Treasury. These data will therefore be omitted and the tabulation confined to the twelve other countries. This has the additional advantage that we need not seriously concern ourselves with differences between total and domestic liabilities, since the foreign liabilities of these twelve central banks are negligible. Their total liabilities are virtually the same as their domestic liabilities.

Table 6 presents a digest, similar to those given in Tables 1, 4, and 5, of highest, lowest, and average ratios. The highest of the highest ratios of official reserves to total liabilities of the central banks of the 12 industrial, non-reserve-currency countries in the period from 1949 (or the earliest for which data are available) to 1964 is that of Switzerland with 103.1 per cent (in 1949). Next are the Netherlands with 98.9 per cent (in 1964), Canada with 88.3 per cent (in 1950), and Austria with 87.2 per cent (in 1953). The lowest of the lowest ratios is that of France with 7.1 pe cent (in 1957).

197

FRITZ MACHLUP

Next come Germany with 10.6 per cent (in 1951) and Japan with 22.3 per cent (in 1957).

The lowest of the highest ratios is that of France with 43.1 per cent (in 1964). And the highest of the lowest ratios is that of Switzerland with 87.4 per cent (in 1964). The average ratios for the four-year period 1961-1964 range from 39.5 per cent (France) to 94.7 per cent (The Netherlands).

TABLE 6

RATIOS OF RESERVES TO LIABILITIES OF THE CENTRAL BANKS
OF 12 INDUSTRIAL COUNTRIES

Highest and Lowest Ratios between 1949 and 1964, and Mean Ratios for 1961-1964

	Highest Ratio		Lowest Ratio		Mean Ratio	
	Year	%	Year	%	Years	%
Australia	1949	79.0	1960	37.5	1961-64	62.3
Austria a	1953	87.2	1955	46.9	»	73.7
Belgium-Luxembourg b	1964	64.5	1950	43.1	»	62.4
Canada	1950	88.3	1949	62.3	»	78.7
France	1964	43.1	1957	7.1	»	39.5
Germany c	1960	71.7	1951	10.6	»	63.0
Ireland f	—	—	—	—	—	—
Italy d	1961	72.0	1956	35.1	»	59.3
Japan e	1952	52.0	1957	22.3	»	26.3
The Netherlands b	1964	98.8	1951	34.0	»	94.7
Sweden	1964	47.1	1949	27.7	»	42.1
Switzerland	1949	103.1	1964	87.4	»	91.3

a Earliest data for 1953. b Earliest data for 1950. c Earliest data for 1951.
d Earliest data for 1955. f No data for liabilities.

As with all the previous reserve ratios, it is not possible to explain the differences in the ratios from year to year or from country to country by anything that could reasonably be called a " need for reserves ". If the Netherlands almost tripled their ratio of reserves to liabilities between 1951 to 1964, if France raised her ratios sixfold from 1957 to 1964, and if Germany's ratio in 1960 was seven times as high as in 1951, these enormous increases were the result of neither any need nor any desire for these high ratios. Indeed, at least two of these countries attempted to combat the inflow of

198

THE NEED FOR MONETARY RESERVES

reserves in that they appreciated their currencies in 1962, lowering thereby both the value of the reserves accumulated and the competitiveness of their industries in foreign trade.

Inconsistent Ratios

Some countries hold *large* reserves no matter how the relative size is measured, and others hold *low* reserves on all counts. In some instances, however, the picture is confusing, showing both high and low reserve ratios depending on the magnitudes with which the size of reserves is compared. Thus, a country may at the same time have a high reserve ratio in some respect and a low reserve ratio in other respects.

Take Sweden, with her low ratio of foreign reserves to imports — 22 per cent in 1965 — and high ratio of reserves to the largest deficit in the past — 1,262 per cent. Take France, with her low ratio of reserves to domestic money — 17,6 per cent in 1965 — and a high ratio to imports — 61.3 per cent. Such indices of reserve-holding practices appear inconsistent only if they are regarded as indications of particular preferences on the part of the national monetary authorities. I shall argue that they are not. Certain " structural relations ", such as those between domestic money supply, central-bank liabilities, and imports, are very different from country to country, and the men in charge may not even have made the comparisons to judge what proportions of reserves are desirable. I seriously doubt that the size of reserves is among the major targets or goals of economic policy, except where reserves are so *dangerously low* that a false step may bring the roof down or where reserves, though respectably high, show a *decline*.

An Analogy: My Wife's Wardrobe

Not long ago, when I had concluded that reserves were not needed for any of the purposes emphasized by either theorists or practitioners, I asked myself what really might be behind the commotion about their supposed inadequacy. I hit upon an analogy which I found helpful and, since it has been given wide currency in circles of specialists, I take the liberty of quoting my own statement.

199

FRITZ MACHLUP

" What then are foreign reserves needed for? They are not ' needed ' at all, strictly speaking. But monetary authorities make a fuss if they do not have all that they think they ought to have. Let me explain this by comparing the typical central banker with my wife, though this might be too flattering for most central bankers. How many dresses does my wife need? One, seven, 31, or 365? You may think that one dress is all she really needs — and even this is only because of our ' culture pattern '. I assure you, however, that she thinks she needs more. Whether she wants 25 or 52 depends on her upbringing and on the Joneses with whom she wishes to keep up. Perhaps she wants to maintain a fixed ratio of dresses to the family income. If that ratio declines, she will fuss and fret, and if I were to keep her from getting additional clothes, she would impose restrictions and controls affecting my home life and our external relations with friends and acquaintances. I conclude that the right amount of clothes owned by my wife is that which keeps her from fussing and fretting and spares me the danger of unpleasant restrictions. Before I leave this analogy between women and central bankers, let me point out that ' rights ' to borrow dresses from friends or from rental agencies would not take care of the matter in the least. Most women want to own their dresses, not to borrow them. I wish that my friends at the *I.M.F.* would take full cognizance of the psychological difference between owning and borrowing.

" Central bankers look not at their clothes closets but at their balance sheets, and they like to see among their assets foreign reserves far in excess of what they would need to cover their nudities; they would like to maintain certain ratios of foreign reserves to total liabilities. The ratio may be merely a matter of tradition or of fashion or, if you will, of religious doctrine. There is no point quarreling with such normative matters. The point is that most central bankers start fussing when the reserve ratio declines. Their liabilities have got to increase year after year, because notes and deposits, the domestic money supply, must increase if deflation is to be avoided. With labor force and productive facilities increasing continuously, and money wages refusing to go down, central bankers have to provide the additional money to avoid continuous deflation and increasing unemployment. Being used to certain traditional reserve ratios, they want their foreign reserves to increase roughly in proportion with their total liabilities. Not that they need it in

200

THE NEED FOR MONETARY RESERVES

any sense other than my wife needs more clothes. But if the central banks lose foreign reserves, and even if they find their reserve ratios declining, there will be demands for policies conducive to the inflow of reserves. I conclude that the ' need ' for reserves is determined by the ambitions of the monetary authorities. I submit we ought to see to it that they get foreign reserves in amounts sufficient to be happy and satisfied; in amounts, that is, that will keep them from urging or condoning policies restricting imports or capital movements " (2).

This idea has become known as " the Mrs. Machlup's Wardrobe Theory of Monetary Reserves ". I am not satisfied, however, with its first formulation and wish to propose an amendment.

A Revision: My Wife's Need for New Clothes

In the first formulation I mixed relevant with irrelevant points. Irrelevant is the emphasis upon the central bankers' ambition " to maintain certain ratios of foreign reserves to total liabilities ". Relevant is " that most central bankers start fussing when the reserve ratio declines ". Maintaining a certain reserve ratio would imply resistance to an increase as well as to a decrease. But it is only the political reaction to a *decrease* that matters.

The analogy of my wife's wardrobe was also not quite correctly phrased in that it stressed the number of dresses hanging in her clothes closets instead of the annual addition to her wardrobe. She does not really care so much whether she has 25 or 52 dresses, if only she gets a few new dresses each year. This ambition is the correct analogue of the central banker's ambition. He is not so much concerned whether his reserve ratio (to his liabilities or to the total money supply) is 47 or 74 per cent, if only his reserves increase, however modestly, and do not decrease.

With these amendments, my theory is probably correct. The " behavior equations " of my marital authority and our monetary authorities are sufficiently similar to make the analogy valid.

---

(2) Fritz Machlup, " International Monetary Systems and the Free Market Economy ", in *International Payments Problems: A Symposium* (Washington: American Enterprise Institute for Public Policy Research, 1966).

201

FRITZ MACHLUP
Not Need But Willingness to Accept

My theory, explaining only a need for additional reserves, cannot explain the sizes of reserves actually held. Since I have rejected all theories based on a need or desire for particular magnitudes of reserves, either for individual countries or for a group of countries, the question why the reserves are as high as they are is still open.

The search for an answer is not difficult if one is prepared to discard the idea that reserves are held for a purpose. The simplest explanation for the holding of " exorbitant " reserves is that all alternatives are considered undesirable. For, in order to reduce large foreign reserves, a country would have to pursue policies which it may want to avoid: appreciation of the currency, price and income inflation, or abolition of restrictions on imports. Currency appreciation is unpopular because it injures export industries (less able to compete in foreign markets) and industries competing with imports (becoming available at reduced prices); in addition, it reduces the values of gold and foreign assets held by the central bank (causing it a sometimes embarrassing capital loss). Domestic inflation is unpopular because of inequitable effects on income distribution and because of induced inefficiencies in the allocation of resources. The abolition of import restrictions is resisted by protected industries, their stockholders, workers and representatives in the legislature. If all policies designed to reduce foreign reserves and to avert further accumulations are " politically impossible ", the accumulation of reserves is allowed to continue, without much thought being given to the irrational allocation of national economic resources which is involved in accumulating assets that are not expected to be used, let alone needed.

In our discussion of the ratio of reserves to liabilities, we mentioned the huge increases in the reserve ratios of the Netherlands, France, and Germany, and of the attempts of two of these countries to combat the inflow of reserves by appreciating their currencies. In order to avoid the increase in the ratios of reserves to liabilities, they would have had to appreciate their currencies more drastically (not by only 5 per cent) or they would have had to create additional liabilities by expanding domestic credit much more than they did. Had they really wanted to keep the ratio of reserves to liabilities unchanged, the monetary authorities would have had to match the

202

THE NEED FOR MONETARY RESERVES

increase in foreign assets by the same percentage increase in domestic assets. Such an expansion of credit would have produced a rather serious inflation of incomes and prices. Unwilling to permit higher rates of inflation — they were already embarrassed by the rates they did permit — they put some restraint on the increase in domestic credit. In consequence, the ratio of foreign reserves to liabilities increased beyond anything the central banks wanted or could have needed for any purpose.

It should be clear by now that the volume of reserves, and their ratios to all sorts of magnitudes, are not determined by what the monetary authorities *want* to hold but rather by what they are offered and are *willing to accept* or, more correctly, unwilling to " fight off ". If we allow ourselves to use the terms " supply and demand " in this context, we may say that the demand for reserves is infinitely elastic and the amount taken and held is therefore determined by supply alone. The infinite elasticity of demand is implied in the resolution to maintain fixed exchange rates; a refusal to buy any amount of foreign exchange that may be offered to the authorities would result in a fall in the prices of foreign currencies, that is, in an appreciation of the currency of the country unwilling to accept more reserves. Rather than allow appreciation, most monetary authorities permit their reserves to increase to any level that is dictated by the supply of foreign exchange.

The Need for Additional Reserves

Let us repeat: it cannot be reasonably said of any particular amount of reserves, either in a particular country or in a group of countries, that it is needed or adequate, but it can be said convincingly that an *increase* in reserves will be needed or adequate to prevent restrictions on foreign trade and payments. Emphasis on the *size* of reserves is mistaken, emphasis on *additions* to reserves is justified.

The justification does not rest on biological or physical necessities, nor even on economic necessities; it is based on prevailing political attitudes. It is well known that in countries suffering losses in foreign reserves the authorities will sooner or later adopt policies to stop further outflows and that, of the alternative policies, they

203

FRITZ MACHLUP

are likely to choose restrictions on international trade and capital movements. Such restrictions are harmful to the performance of the economies of all countries affected. One way to avoid the restrictions is to avoid the causes (or pretexts) for their imposition, that is, deficits in the balances of international payments. The easiest way to avoid or reduce deficits is to provide for annual additions in official reserves. Hence, additional reserves are needed if restrictive policies are to be avoided.

The effect of the creation of new reserves upon the net surpluses in the balances of payments of all countries together is sometimes not fully understood. It may be explained most easily by comparing two situations, one in which the annual production of gold by South Africa is absorbed by private demand, the other where it is acquired by monetary authorities. Assume, for the sake of simplicity, that there are only ten countries besides South Africa. Assume further that South Africa uses all proceeds from exporting gold to purchase imports of goods, and the other ten countries purchase the gold in exchange for their exports to South Africa. If the gold is purchased by private parties, for industrial uses and for hoards, the trade balances of the ten countries taken together (as well as that of South Africa) will be completely balanced. Each of the ten countries may have a surplus or a deficit, but the sum of surpluses and deficits will be equal. (Incidentally, if some of the imports of nonmonetary gold were not recorded, the statistical balances would show a global export surplus offset by a negative balance on errors and omissions.) Alternatively, if the gold is purchased, not by private parties but, instead, by central banks of some of the ten countries, their composite balance of payments will show a net surplus. This net surplus of exports over imports will be offset by a net increase in monetary reserves. Some of the ten countries may be in surplus, some in deficit, but the sum of the surpluses will exceed the sum of the deficits exactly by the increase in monetary gold.

It is conceivable that either the number of countries in deficit will be the same or that the deficits of some countries will be the same in both situations; but the most likely result of the increase in monetary reserves will be that some countries will have smaller deficits and others will have surpluses instead of deficits. With smaller deficits and fewer countries in deficit, the pressures for restrictive policies will be reduced.

204

THE NEED FOR MONETARY RESERVES

If additional reserves are created, not through additions to the monetary gold stock, but through the creation and free distribution of fiduciary reserves, the effects are similar in that the sum of surpluses in payments balances will exceed the sum of deficits. Although this may look like an accounting trick, the balance-of-payments accountant would enter the deposit of his country's currency into the dormant account of the international reserve agency as an inflow of long-term capital (since it would not constitute a current liability) whereas the aquisition of the current claim against that agency would be shown below the line as an increase in the official reserve. Thus, the creation of a new reserve asset in the form designed by recent proposals would, like an increase in earned reserves, reduce the number of deficit countries and the sum of their combined deficits — assuming, however, that the statisticians make the proper distinction between dormant and active accounts.

How much of an increase in aggregate monetary reserves will be needed to reduce the size of the deficits and the number of deficit countries sufficiently to avert restrictions on trade and capital movements will depend on the distribution of the deficits and on the political propensities of various countries to impose restrictions. These propensities — to wit, how large and persistent a loss of reserve in a particular country will present a sufficient reason or pretext for the adoption of certain restrictive measures — are shaped by the beliefs of the men in charge of policy-making; and these beliefs, in turn, are derived from rational theories, irrational myths, and traditional principles or prejudices. Some countries may patiently put up with higher interest rates, some with effective wage stops, and some even with unemployment, when confronted with a deficit in their balance of payments. Other countries, however, may quickly, on the slightest provocation, turn to restrictions and controls on imports and payments. (For those with a taste for definitions, I may try to define the marginal propensity to restrict imports as the value of imports kept out by means of restrictions and direct controls in relation to a given loss of reserves suffered through a payments deficit.) Since one cannot foretell either which countries will suffer deficits of certain magnitudes or the propensities of the politicians in power, the determination of the " adequate " increase in total reserves can be only a matter of blunt, but still necessary, judgment.

205

FRITZ MACHLUP
Three Effects of Increases in Reserves

The increase in the monetary reserves of a country may have several effects which, though they are closely related, ought to be distinguished for the sake of clarity. We have just discussed the effect on the balance of payments and, as a probable reaction, on the countries' policies regarding foreign trade and capital movements.

A second effect is on the money supply. If reserves are earned through export surpluses or capital imports (other than borrowings by the monetary authorities), the purchase of the received foreign exchange by the central bank is financed by newly created domestic money. In the absence of offsetting policies, monetary circulation increases.

A third effect is on the reserve position and the resulting credit policy of the central bank. The improvement in the reserve position may make the monetary authorities bolder in their policies; they are likely to keep interest rates lower, to expand their portfolio of domestic loans and other assets, and to allow commercial banks to be more expansionary on their part.

There are certain differences to be noted between various forms of the increase in reserves. The first effect — on balances of payments and policies regarding foreign trade and capital movements — can be expected with greatest certainty from increases in monetary gold stocks, and with a degree of probability also from a distribution of gratis reserves (" reserve units ") by an international agency. The expansion of liabilities by reserve-currency countries in case of deficits in their foreign payments leads to an increase in gross reserves, not net reserves. However, as long as the reserve-currency countries are not worried about the deterioration of their position, the net effect on commercial policies is also liberalizing. The use of borrowing facilities extended by the I.M.F. may lead to an increase in earned reserves of the countries to whom the deficit countries pay the currencies drawn, but the net effects are not certain. If the accommodation extended to deficit countries is upon condition that they abstain from restrictive policies, then again the process is liberalizing.

The second effect — the direct effect on the money supply — is certain to arise in the case of increases in monetary gold stocks

206

THE NEED FOR MONETARY RESERVES

and currency reserves. This effect would not arise from the distribution of gratis reserves (" units ") by an international agency. This should be clear, since the central bank would not purchase these reserve units from domestic suppliers but would acquire them with its deposit into the dormant account of the agency, that is, with its non-circulating, non-current liability. The fact that this (rather revolutionary) form of creation of new reserves does not immediately increase the money supplies of the recipient countries commends it to those who, though seeking the first effect, are concerned about inflationary consequences of additions to reserves.

The third effect — on reserve positions and credit policies of the central banks — is probably associated with all forms of reserve creation. In can, of course, be counteracted by deliberate monetary policies if credit expansion is not wanted at the time.

Application to Present-Day Discussions

Our study, up to this point, has stayed within the confines of research and analysis, without explicit application to present-day problems and negotiations. Yet it should not be difficult to see the implications of our findings for the current discussions among official and academic experts trying to solve the problems of our time.

The most important findings, in terms of current controversies, are these:

1. There is no " need " for any particular sum of monetary reserves in the world.

2. There is no sense, therefore, in which it can be said that the world total of monetary reserves is inadequate.

3. Indeed, if the world total of reserves had not reached 70,000 million dollars but, say only 50,000 million dollars, there would still be no " shortage ".

4. Needed, however, is an annual increase in monetary reserves if policies restricting foreign trade and capital movements are to be averted.

5. The annual increase of total reserves should be of such a magnitude that the number of countries in deficit and the amounts

207

366   **FRITZ MACHLUP**

of their deficits are small enough to remove pressures toward restrictions on trade and capital movements.

6. Unless the large private absorptions of gold come to an end, the necessary annual increases in total reserves can be provided only by an international agency issuing new reserve assets.

7. Inflationary effects of the creation of new reserves can be counteracted by appropriate policies.

Princeton   FRITZ MACHLUP

THE NEED FOR MONETARY RESERVES
STATISTICAL APPENDIX

TABLE A-I

OFFICIAL RESERVES, IMPORTS, AND RATIOS OF RESERVES TO IMPORTS
FOR 14 INDUSTRIAL COUNTRIES, 1949-1965

(In millions of U.S. dollars)

Country	1949			1950			1951		
	Res.	Imp.	Res./Imp. %	Res.	Imp.	Res./Imp. %	Res.	Imp.	Res./Imp. %
Australia	1,123	1,590	70.6	1,492	1,620	92.1	1,134	2,420	46.9
Austria	92	592	15.5	91	477	19.1	106	653	16.2
Belgium-Luxemb. .	978	1,803	54.2	849	1,942	43.7	1.110	2,535	43.8
Canada	1,197	2,884	41.5	1,845	3,128	59.0	1.901	4,106	46.3
France	580	3,291	17.6	791	3,030	26.1	616	4,457	13.8
Germany	196	n.a.	n.a.	190	2,697	7.0	455	3,491	13.0
Ireland	342	481	71.1	391	446	87.7	331	573	57.8
Italy	n.a.	1,545	n.a.	602	1,488	40.5	774	2,167	35.7
Japan	n.a.	905	n.a.	n.a.	974	n.a.	n.a.	1,995	n.a.
Netherlands . . .	434	1,844	23.5	548	2,056	26.7	554	2,553	21.7
Sweden	269	1,171	23.0	289	1,182	24.5	520	1,776	29.3
Switzerland . . .	1,692	882	191.8	1,579	1,056	149.5	1,645	1,375	119.6
United Kingdom .	1,752	8,522	20.6	3,443	7,358	46.8	2,374	10,955	21.7
United States . .	26,024	7,544	345.0	24,265	9,631	251.9	24,299	11,922	203.8

TABLE A-I *cont'd*

Country	1952			1953			1954		
	Res.	Imp.	Res./Imp. %	Res.	Imp.	Res./Imp. %	Res.	Imp.	Res./Imp. %
Australia	1,032	1,979	52.1	1,362	1,470	92.6	1,133	1,870	60.6
Austria	152	652	23.3	325	546	59.5	425	653	65.1
Belgium-Luxemb. .	1,133	2,444	46.4	1,144	2,413	47.4	1,098	2,535	43.3
Canada	1,938	4,370	44.3	1,902	4,697	40.5	2,029	4,433	45.8
France	686	4,326	15.9	829	3,942	21.0	1,264	4,221	29.9
Germany	960	3,814	25.2	1,773	3,771	47.0	2,579	4,571	56.4
Ireland	317	482	65.8	335	511	65.6	364	504	72.2
Italy	696	2,336	29.8	768	2,420	31.7	927	2,439	38.0
Japan	1,101	2,028	54.3	892	2,410	37.0	930	2,399	38.8
Netherlands . .	944	2,224	42.4	1,232	2,376	51.9	1,278	2,858	44.7
Sweden	504	1,730	29.1	558	1,579	35.3	543	1,776	30.6
Switzerland . . .	1,667	1,208	138.0	1,768	1,176	150.3	1,837	1,300	141.3
United Kingdom .	1,958	9,802	20.0	2,670	9,314	28.7	3,034	9,405	32.3
United States . .	24,714	11,707	211.1	23,458	11,846	198.0	22,978	11,140	206.3

209

FRITZ MACHLUP

Country	1955			1956			1957		
	Res.	Imp.	Res./Imp. %	Res.	Imp.	Res./Imp. %	Res.	Imp.	Res./Imp. %
Australia	844	2,160	39.1	961	1,964	48.9	1,329	1,945	68.9
Austria	374	887	42.2	419	974	43.0	523	1,128	46.4
Belgium-Luxemb. .	1,203	2,830	42.5	1,219	3,288	37.1	1,148	3,444	33.3
Canada	1,985	5,020	39.5	2,035	6,110	33.3	1,926	6,188	31.1
France	1,975	4,739	41.7	1,311	5,558	23.6	645	6,175	10.5
Germany	3,018	5,793	52.1	4,202	6,617	63.5	5,197	7,542	68.9
Ireland	331	582	56.9	283	512	55.3	296	516	57.4
Italy	1,167	2,711	43.0	1,236	3,174	38.9	1,354	3,674	36.9
Japan	1,076	2,471	43.6	1,270	3,230	39.3	828	4,284	19.3
Netherlands . .	1,292	3,209	40.3	1,107	3,725	29.7	1,009	4,106	24.6
Sweden	522	1,997	26.1	535	2,209	24.2	501	2,428	20.7
Switzerland . .	1,847	1,489	124.0	1,882	1,766	106.6	1,898	1,964	96.6
United Kingdom .	2,392	10,809	22.1	2,276	10,812	21.1	2,374	11,322	21.0
United States . .	22,797	12,489	182.5	23,666	13,987	169.2	24,832	14,620	169.9

Country	1958			1959			1960		
	Res.	Imp.	Res./Imp. %	Res.	Imp.	Res./Imp. %	Res.	Imp.	Res./Imp. %
Australia	1,128	2,039	55.3	1,273	2,125	59.9	915	2,704	33.8
Austria	678	1,074	63.1	697	1,145	60.9	716	1,416	50.6
Belgium-Luxemb. .	1,553	3,129	49.6	1,306	3,442	37.9	1,506	3,969	37.9
Canada	2,038	5,638	36.1	2,029	6,242	32.5	1,989	6,150	32.3
France	1,050	5,609	18.7	1,736	5,088	34.1	2,272	6,281	36.2
Germany	5,879	7,576	77.6	4,790	8,482	56.5	7,032	10,107	69.6
Ireland	305	557	54.8	325	595	54.6	324	633	51.2
Italy	2,184	3,216	67.9	3,056	3,369	90.7	3,251	4,725	68.8
Japan	1,062	3,033	35.0	1,447	3,599	40.2	1,949	4,491	43.4
Netherlands . .	1,539	3,625	42.5	1,442	3,940	36.6	1,863	4,531	41.1
Sweden	516	2,368	21.8	478	2,414	19.8	528	2,901	18.2
Switzerland . .	2,063	1,706	120.9	2,063	1,923	107.3	2,324	2,243	103.6
United Kingdom .	3,105	10,493	29.6	2,801	11,153	25.1	3,719	12,714	29.3
United States . .	22,540	14,619	154.2	21,504	17,008	126.4	19,359	16,506	117.3

210

THE NEED FOR MONETARY RESERVES

TABLE A-I *cont'd*

Country	1961			1962			1963		
	Res.	Imp.	Res./Imp. %	Res.	Imp.	Res./Imp. %	Res.	Imp.	Res./Imp. %
Australia	1,348	2,394	56.3	1,387	2,551	54.4	1,880	2,776	67.7
Austria	845	1,485	56.9	1,081	1,552	69.7	1,229	1,675	73.4
Belgium-Luxemb. .	1,813	4,223	42.9	1,753	4,569	38.4	1,940	5,112	38.0
Canada	2,276	6,196	36.7	2,547	6,367	40.0	2,603	6,618	39.3
France	3,799	6,679	56.9	4,049	7,517	53.9	4,908	8,727	56.2
Germany	7,163	10,948	65.4	6,956	12,289	56.6	7,650	13,022	58.8
Ireland	343	732	46.9	359	766	46.9	406	858	47.3
Italy	3,799	5,223	72.7	3,818	6,075	62.9	3,406	7,590	44.9
Japan	1,666	5,811	28.7	2,022	5,637	35.9	2,058	6,737	30.6
Netherlands . . .	1,958	5,089	38.5	1,946	5,347	36.4	2,101	5,966	35.2
Sweden	736	2,929	25.1	801	3,123	25.7	758	3,393	22.3
Switzerland . . .	2,759	2,707	101.9	2,872	3,020	95.1	3,078	3,253	94.6
United Kingdom .	3,318	12,308	27.0	3,308	12,563	26.3	3,147	13,476	23.4
United States . .	18,753	16,071	116.7	17,220	17,764	96.9	16,843	18,590	90.6

TABLE A-I *cont'd*

Country	1964			1965		
	Res.	Imp.	Res./Imp. %	Res.	Imp.	Res./Imp. %
Australia	1,947	3,313	58.8	1,575	3,753	42.0
Austria	1,317	1,863	70.7	1,311	2,100	62.4
Belgium-Luxemb. .	2,192	5,901	37.2	2,304	6,326	34.8
Canada	2,881	7,556	38.1	3,027	8,715	34.7
France	5,724	10,070	56.8	6,343	10,341	61.3
Germany	7,882	14,618	53.9	7,429	17,482	42.5
Ireland	446	974	45.8	410	1,041	39.4
Italy	3,823	7,321	52.9	4,415	7,347	60.1
Japan	2,019	7,948	25.4	2,152	8,170	26.3
Netherlands . . .	2,349	7,055	33.3	2,416	7,463	32.4
Sweden	964	3,855	25.0	972	4,378	22.2
Switzerland . . .	3,123	3,610	86.5	3,247	3,697	87.8
United Kingdom .	2,316	15,438	15.0	3,004	16,138	18.6
United States . .	16,672	20,251	82.3	15,450	23,189	66.6

Notes: Reserves as well as imports are in millions of dollars. Reserves are as of the end of each year. Imports are at c.i.f. values. The letter n.a. mean «not available».

Sources: Data for 1949 to 1964 are from *International Financial Statistics*, 1965-66 Supplement. Data for 1965 are from the May 1966 issue.

211

FRITZ MACHLUP

TABLE A-II

THREE LARGEST LOSSES OF OFFICIAL RESERVES AND RATIOS OF LOSSES TO RESERVES
IN 14 INDUSTRIAL COUNTRIES BETWEEN 1949 (3rd QUARTER) AND DEC 1965

Country	Order of Loss	Period from	Period to	Reserves in millions of U.S. $ at peak	at trough	lost	Dec. 1965	Percentage of Loss to Reserves at peak	at trough	Dec. 1965
Australia	Largest loss	2nd Qu. 51	3rd Qu. 52	1,747	793	954	1,575	52.9	112.4	60.6
	2nd largest loss	1st » 54	1st » 56	1,375	751	624		45.4	83.2	39.6
	3rd » »	4th » 59	4th » 60	1,273	916	357		28.0	39.0	22.7
Austria	Largest loss	3rd Qu. 54	1st Qu. 56	453	362	91	1,311	20.1	25.1	6.9
	2nd largest loss	3rd » 59	1st » 61	754	675	79		10.5	11.7	6.0
	3rd » »	4th » 64	1st » 65	1,317	1,261	56		4.3	4.4	4.3
Belgium-Luxembourg	Largest loss	4th Qu. 58	3rd Qu. 60	1,553	1,303	250	2,304	16.1	19.2	10.9
	2nd largest loss	3rd » 49	4th » 50	1,033	849	184		17.8	21.7	8.0
	3rd » »	2nd » 52	2nd » 53	1,232	1,078	154		12.5	14.3	6.7
Canada	Largest loss	4th Qu. 61	2nd Qu. 62	2,276	1,817	459	3,027	20.2	25.3	15.2
	2nd largest loss	3rd » 50	3rd » 51	1,890	1,730	160		8.5	9.2	5.3
	3rd » »	4th » 52	2nd » 53	1,946	1,839	107		5.5	5.8	3.5
France	Largest loss	4th Qu. 55	4th Qu. 57	1,975	645	1,330	6,343	67.3	206.2	21.0
	2nd largest loss	3rd » 59	4th » 59	1,857	1,736	121		6.5	7.0	1.9
	3rd » »	1st » 53	3rd » 53	806	777	29		3.6	3.7	0.5
Germany	Largest loss	4th Qu. 58	3rd Qu. 59	5,879	4,234	1,645	7,429	28.0	38.9	22.1
	2nd largest loss	1st » 61	1st » 62	7,420	6,642	778		10.5	11.7	10.5
	3rd » »	4th » 64	4th » 65	7,882	7,429	453		5.8	6.1	6.1
Ireland	Largest loss	4th Qu. 50	2nd Qu. 52	246	150	96	410	24.6	32.5	23.4
	2nd largest loss	4th « 54	3rd » 56	364	274	90		24.7	32.8	22.0
	3rd » »	1st » 65	2nd » 65	451	400	51		11.3	12.8	12.4
Italy	Largest loss	4th Qu. 62	1st Qu. 64	3,818	2,946	872	4,415	22.8	29.6	19.8
	2nd largest loss	3rd » 50	1t » 51	648	490	158		24.4	32.2	3.6
	3rd » »	4th » 51	2nd » 53	775	627	148		19.1	23.6	3.4

THE NEED FOR MONETARY RESERVES

Japan	Largest loss	4th Qu. 56	3rd Qu. 57	1,270	754	516	2,152	38.5	62.6	24.0
	2nd largest loss	1st » 61	4th » 61	2,122	1,666	456		21.5	27.4	21.2
	3rd » »	2nd » 52	2nd » 53	1,242	980	262		21.1	26.7	12.2
Netherlands	Largest loss	1st Qu. 56	3rd Qu. 57	1,320	898	422	2,416	32.0	47.0	17.5
	2nd largest loss	4th » 58	2nd » 59	1,539	1,419	120		7.8	8.5	5.0
	3rd » »	2nd » 62	4th » 62	2,023	1,946	77		3.8	4.0	3.2
Sweden	Largest loss	3rd Qu. 59	1st Qu. 60	533	456	77	972	14.4	16.9	7.9
	2nd largest loss	3rd » 54	2nd » 55	561	492	69		12.3	14.0	7.1
	3rd » »	2nd » 52	1st » 53	533	485	48		9.0	9.9	4.9
Switzerland	Largest loss	4th Qu. 63	1st Qu. 64	3,078	2,747	331	3,247	10.8	12.1	10.2
	2nd largest loss	4th « 62	1st » 63	2,872	2,637	235		8.2	8.9	7.2
	3rd » »	3rd » 58	1st » 59	2,065	1,877	188		9.1	10.0	5.8
United Kingdom	Largest loss	2nd Qu. 51	2nd Qu. 52	3,906	1,797	2,109	3,004	54.0	117.4	70.2
	2nd largest loss	2nd » 54	3rd » 57	3,289	1,889	1,400		42.6	74.1	46.6
	3rd » »	3rd » 61	4th » 64	3,553	2,316	1,237		34.8	53.4	41.2
United States	Largest loss	4th Qu. 59	4th Qu. 64	21,504	15,450	6,054	15,450	28.1	39.2	39.2
	2nd largest loss	3rd » 49	2nd » 51	26,273	23,389	2,884		11.0	12.4	18.7
	3rd » »	2nd » 52	2nd » 55	25,012	22,783	2,229		8.8	9.7	14.3

Notes: Reserves are official holdings of gold and foreign exchange plus the gold-tranche position at the IMF.

End-of-quarter figures are used for the peaks and troughs in reserve holdings. Losses of reserves are calculated from a peak to the nearest trough that is not followed by a still lower one within a year. Absolute amounts, rather than percentage declines of reserves, are used in ordering the losses by size.

Where a loss period is listed as beginning in the third quarter of 1949 (or with the earliest available figure) it may in fact have begun earlier; where a loss period is listed as ending with the fourth quarter of 1965 it may in fact be continuing beyond that date. (Both these comments apply, among other countries, to the United States).

Sources: All data are taken or derived from *International Financial Statistics*. For 1957 to 1965, end-of-quarter figures are taken partly from the 1965-66 Supplement and partly from the October 1965 and May 1966 issues. For periods before 1957, year-end figures from various issues of the years 1952 to 1958 were used to derive end-of-quarter figures by linear interpolation.

For the following countries comparable series begin only later than the third quarter of 1949: Austria, first quarter of 1954; France and Germany, fourth quarter of 1952; and Japan, third quarter of 1951. The figures for Japan before the third quarter of 1959 were increased by $70 billion to make them comparable with the later series. (I acknowledge the help of Professor Yasukichi Yasuba and Mr. R. J. Suweeney.)

213

FRITZ MACHLUP

OFFICIAL RESERVES, MONEY SUPPLY, AND MONEY-PLUS-QUASI-MONEY,
WITH RATIOS OF RESERVES TO MONEY AND MONEY-PLUS-QUASI-MONEY
FOR 14 INDUSTRIAL COUNTRIES, 1949-1965

Country	1949				
	Billions of domestic money			Percentages	
	Res.	Money	M + QM	Res./M	Res./ M + QM
Australia	467.9 [a]	1,020 [a]	1,954 [a]	45.9	24.0
Austria	n.a.	11.01	n.a.	n.a.	n.a.
Belgium-Luxemb. .	48.90	n.a.	n.a.	n.a.	n.a.
Canada	1.32	3.96	8.05	33.4	16.4
France	2.03	27.12	27.5	7.5	7.4
Germany	0.82	n.a.	n.a.	n.a.	n.a.
Ireland	122.3 [b]	118.7 [b]	334.2 [b]	103.0	36.6
Italy	n.a.	n.a.	n.a.	n.a.	n.a.
Japan	n.a.	n.a.	n.a.	n.a.	n.a.
Netherlands . . .	1.65	n.a.	n.a.	n.a.	n.a.
Sweden	1.40	6.40	22.58	21.9	6.2
Switzerland . . .	7.28	11.10	23.02	65.6	31.6
United Kingdom .	625.9 [c]	n.a.	n.a.	n.a.	n.a.
United States. . .	26.0	109.9	144.8	23.7	18.0

TABLE A-III *continued*

Country	1950				
	Billions of domestic money			Percentages	
	Res.	Money	M + QM	Res./M	Res./ M + QM
Australia	621.7 [a]	1,233 [a]	2,236 [a]	50.4	27.8
Austria	n.a.	12.76	n.a.	n.a.	n.a.
Belgium-Luxemb. .	42.45	168.6	183.3	25.2	23.2
Canada	2.03	4.33	8.51	47.9	23.9
France	2.77	31.29	31.89	8.9	8.7
Germany	0.80	n.a.	n.a.	n.a.	n.a.
Ireland	139.6 [b]	122.5 [b]	342.5 [b]	114.0	40.8
Italy	376	n.a.	n.a.	n.a.	n.a.
Japan	n.a.	n.a.	n.a.	n.a.	n.a.
Netherlands . . .	2.80	6.85	7.76	40.9	36.1
Sweden	1.50	6.87	24.03	21.8	6.2
Switzerland . . .	6.79	11.43	23.89	59.4	28.4
United Kingdom .	1,230 [c]	n.a.	n.a.	n.a.	n.a.
United States . .	24.3	115.3	150.3	21.1	16.2

[a] Millions of Australian Pounds. [b] Millions of Irish Pounds. [c] Millions of Pounds Sterling.

214

THE NEED FOR MONETARY RESERVES

TABLE A-III *continued*

Country	1951				
	Billions of domestic money			Percentages	
	Res.	Money	M + QM	Res./M	Res./M + QM
Australia	493.0 [a]	1,434 [a]	2,521 [a]	34.4	19.6
Austria	n.a.	16.12	n.a.	n.a.	n.a.
Belgium-Luxemb. .	55.5	168.6	186.2	32.9	29.8
Canada	1.90	4.38	8.68	43.4	21.9
France	2.16	36.95	37.75	5.9	5.7
Germany	1.91	19.2	27.3	10.0	7.0
Ireland	118.2 [b]	131.6 [b]	360.2 [b]	89.8	32.8
Italy	483	n.a.	n.a.	n.a.	n.a.
Japan	n.a.	n.a.	n.a.	n.a.	n.a.
Netherlands . . .	2.11	7.02	8.34	30.1	25.3
Sweden	2.7	8.41	27.18	32.1	9.9
Switzerland . . .	7.07	11.92	25.19	59.3	28.1
United Kingdom .	848 [c]	8,213 [c]	n.a.	10.3	n.a.
United States . .	24.3	122.8	159.4	19.8	15.3

TABLE A-III *continued*

Country	1952				
	Billions of domestic money			Percentages	
	Res.	Money	M + QM	Res./M	Res./M + QM
Australia	448.7 [a]	1,382 [a]	2,506 [a]	32.5	17.9
Austria	n.a.	17.14	n.a.	n.a.	n.a.
Belgium-Luxemb. .	56.65	174.0	195.6	32.6	29.0
Canada	1.88	4.66	9.26	40.4	20.3
France	2.40	41.88	42.87	5.7	5.6
Germany	4.03	21.3	33.0	18.9	12.2
Ireland	113.2 [b]	137.4 [b]	370.9 [b]	82.4	30.5
Italy	435	n.a.	n.a.	n.a.	n.a.
Japan	398	n.a.	n.a.	n.a.	n.a.
Netherlands . . .	3.59	7.74	9.22	46.4	38.9
Sweden	2.62	8.58	28.12	30.5	9.3
Switzerland . . .	7.17	12.31	26.65	58.3	26.9
United Kingdom .	699 [c]	8,401 [c]	n.a.	8.3	n.a.
United States . .	24.7	129.2	168.7	19.1	14.6

[a] Millions of Australian Pounds. [b] Millions of Irish Pounds. [c] Millions of Pounds Sterling.

215

FRITZ MACHLUP

TABLE A-III *continued*

Country	1953 Billions of domestic money			1953 Percentages	
	Res.	Money	M + QM	Res./M	Res./ M + QM
Australia	592.2 [a]	1,553 [a]	2,759 [a]	38.1	21.5
Austria	14.25	19.52	27.33	73.4	52.3
Belgium-Luxemb. .	57.20	180.3	202.5	31.7	28.3
Canada	1.85	4.56	9.32	40.6	19.9
France	2.90	46.58	47.94	6.2	6.1
Germany	7.45	23.4	39.9	31.8	18.7
Ireland	119.6 [b]	145.2 [b]	395.4 [b]	82.4	30.3
Italy	480	3,817	5,596	12.6	8.6
Japan	322	1,937	3,952	16.6	8.2
Netherlands . .	4.68	8.27	9.75	57.1	18.0
Sweden	2.90	8.94	30.88	32.4	9.4
Switzerland . . .	7.60	12.84	28.71	59.2	26.5
United Kingdom .	954 [c]	8,755 [c]	n.a.	10.9	n.a.
United States . .	23.5	130.8	173.1	18.0	13.6

TABLE A-III *continued*

Country	1954 Billions of domestic money			1954 Percentages	
	Res.	Money	M + QM	Res./M	Res./ M + QM
Australia	492.6 [a]	1,593 [a]	2,892 [a]	31.0	17.1
Austria	11.09	24.02	35.39	46.2	31.3
Belgium-Luxemb. .	54.90	183.7	207.0	29.9	26.5
Canada	1.97	4.92	10.14	40.0	19.4
France	4.42	52.98	54.65	8.3	8.1
Germany	10.83	26.5	47.5	40.9	22.7
Ireland	130.0 [b]	152.3 [b]	413.1 [b]	85.4	31.5
Italy	579	4,134	6,253	14.0	9.3
Japan	336	2,013	4,556	16.7	7.4
Netherlands . .	4.86	8.83	10.53	55.0	46.2
Sweden	2.82	9.07	32.68	31.1	8.6
Switzerland . . .	7.90	13.2	30.05	59.9	26.3
United Kingdom .	1,083 [c]	9,108 [c]	n.a.	11.9	n.a.
United States . .	23.0	134.9	180.5	17.1	12.7

[a] Millions of Australian Pounds.   [b] Millions of Irish Pounds.   [c] Millions of Pounds Sterling.

216

THE NEED FOR MONETARY RESERVES

TABLE A-III *continued*

Country	1955 Billions of domestic money			1955 Percentages	
	Res.	Money	M + QM	Res./M	Res./ M + QM
Australia	367.0 [a]	1,630 [a]	2,963 [a]	22.5	12.4
Austria	9.76	23.83	38.07	41.0	25.6
Belgium-Luxemb. .	60.15	192.6	218.5	31.2	27.5
Canada	1.97	5.25	10.88	37.5	18.1
France	6.91	59.69	61.69	11.6	11.2
Germany	12.68	29.2	54.5	43.4	23.3
Ireland	118.2 [b]	154.7 [b]	419.4 [b]	76.4	28.2
Italy	729	4,519	7,014	16.1	10.4
Japan	388	2,331	5,395	16.6	7.2
Netherlands . . .	4.91	9.58	11.48	51.7	42.8
Sweden	2.71	9.16	33.75	29.6	8.0
Switzerland . . .	7.94	13.63	31.93	58.3	24.9
United Kingdom .	854 [c]	8,838 [c]	n.a.	9.7	n.a.
United States . .	22.8	138.0	185.0	16.5	12.3

TABLE A-III *continued*

Country	1956 Billions of domestic money			1956 Percentages	
	Res.	Money	M + QM	Res./M	Res./ M + QM
Australia	417.8 [a]	1,603 [a]	3,075 [a]	25.6	13.6
Austria	10.94	24.9	41.92	43.9	26.1
Belgium-Luxemb. .	60.95	198.2	223.7	30.8	27.3
Canada	1.95	5.18	11.19	37.7	17.4
France	4.59	65.85	68.17	7.0	6.7
Germany	17.65	31.3	61.1	56.4	28.9
Ireland	101.1 [b]	154.7 [b]	421.5 [b]	65.4	24.0
Italy	773	4,883	7,857	15.8	9.8
Japan	458	2,714	6,551	17.9	7.0
Netherlands . . .	4.21	9.23	11.21	45.6	37.6
Sweden	2.78	9.81	35.87	28.3	7.8
Switzerland . . .	8.09	14.61	34.06	55.4	23.8
United Kingdom .	813 [c]	8,978 [c]	n.a.	9.1	n.a.
United States . .	23.7	139.4	188.6	17.0	12.6

[a] Millions of Australian Pounds.   [b] Millions of Irish Pounds.   [c] Millions of Pounds Sterling.

217

FRITZ MACHLUP

TABLE A-III *continued*

Country	1957				
	Billions of domestic money			Percentages	
	Res.	Money	M + QM	Res./M	Res./ M + QM
Australia	577.8 [a]	1,710 [a]	3,267 [a]	33.8	17.7
Austria	13.65	26.55	48.44	51.5	28.2
Belgium-Luxemb. .	57.40	198.0	224.7	29.0	25.5
Canada	1.91	5.39	11.50	35.5	16.6
France	2.71	71.37	75.35	3.8	3.6
Germany	21.83	35.1	72.1	62.2	30.3
Ireland	105.7 [b]	165.5 [b]	441.4 [b]	63.9	23.8
Italy	846	5,131	8,588	16.5	9.9
Japan	298	2,824	7,591	10.5	3.9
Netherlands . . .	3.83	9.06	11.43	42.3	33.5
Sweden	2.60	10.05	38.67	25.9	6.7
Switzerland . . .	8.16	15.00	36.42	54.4	22.4
United Kingdom .	848 [c]	9,266 [c]	n.a.	9.2	n.a.
United States . .	24.8	138.2	192.9	18.0	12.9

TABLE A-III *continued*

Country	1958				
	Billions of domestic money			Percentages	
	Res.	Money	M + QM	Res./M	Res./ M + QM
Australia	490.4 [a]	1,668 [a]	3,315 [a]	29.4	14.8
Austria	17.63	29.44	57.88	59.9	30.5
Belgium-Luxemb. .	77.65	209.5	240.1	37.1	32.3
Canada	1.96	6.08	12.92	32.3	15.2
France	5.15	75.73	80.24	6.8	6.4
Germany	24.69	39.7	83.4	62.2	29.6
Ireland	108.9 [b]	164.7 [b]	450.7 [b]	66.1	24.2
Italy	1,363	5,681	10,017	24.0	13.6
Japan	382	3,185	9,055	12.0	4.2
Netherlands . . .	5.85	10.14	13.00	57.7	45.0
Sweden	2.68	10.20	41.93	26.3	6.4
Switzerland . . .	8.87	16.66	39.95	53.2	22.2
United Kingdom .	1,109 [c]	9,593 [c]	n.a.	11.6	n.a.
United States . .	22.5	143.9	205.6	15.6	10.9

[a] Millions of Australian Pounds. [b] Millions of Irish Pounds. [c] Millions of Pounds Sterling.

218

THE NEED FOR MONETARY RESERVES

TABLE A-III *continued*

Country	1959				
	Billions of domestic money			Percentages	
	Res.	Money	M + QM	Res./M	M + QM Res./
Australia	553.5 [a]	1,788 [a]	3,574 [a]	31.0	15.5
Austria	18.12	32.4	67.22	55.9	27.0
Belgium-Luxemb. .	65.30	216.3	252.7	30.2	25.8
Canada	1.93	5.89	12.79	32.8	15.1
France	8.51	83.92	90.20	10.1	9.4
Germany	20.12	44.4	97.0	45.3	20.7
Ireland	116.1 [b]	170.7 [b]	467.6 [b]	68.0	24.8
Italy	1,898	6,481	11,311	29.3	16.8
Japan	519	3,711	10,947	14.0	4.7
Netherlands . . .	5.48	10.59	14.2	51.7	38.6
Sweden	2.49	11.88	46.98	21.0	5.3
Switzerland . . .	8.87	17.46	42.45	50.8	20.9
United Kingdom .	1,000 [c]	10,138 [c]	n.a.	9.9	n.a.
United States . .	21.5	144.3	208.7	14.9	10.3

TABLE A-III *continued*

Country	1960				
	Billions of domestic money			Percentages	
	Res.	Money	M + QM	Res./M	Res./ M + QM
Australia	397.8 [a]	1,775 [a]	3,700 [a]	22.4	10.8
Austria	18.62	34.12	74.92	54.6	24.9
Belgium-Luxemb. .	75.30	220.6	262.7	34.1	28.7
Canada	1.99	6.19	13.41	32.2	14.8
France	11.13	95.79	104.80	11.6	10.6
Germany	29.54	47.4	107.8	62.3	27.4
Ireland	115.7 [b]	182.3 [b]	493.7 [b]	63.5	23.4
Italy	2,019	7,367	12,898	27.4	15.7
Japan	698	4,420	13,357	15.8	5.2
Netherlands . . .	7.08	11.31	15.76	62.6	44.9
Sweden	2.75	12.39	48.75	22.2	5.6
Switzerland . . .	9.99	19.26	47.47	51.9	21.0
United Kingdom .	1,328 [c]	10,376 [c]	n.a.	12.8	n.a.
United States . .	19.4	143.5	213.4	13.5	9.1

[a] Millions of Australian Pounds. [b] Millions of Irish Pounds. [c] Millions of Pounds Sterling.

219

FRITZ MACHLUP

TABLE A-III *continued*

Country	1 9 6 1				
	Billions of domestic money			Percentages	
	Res.	Money	M + QM	Res./M	Res./ M + QM
Australia	586.1 [a]	1,728 [a]	3,876 [a]	33.9	15.1
Austria	21.97	36.96	83.28	59.5	26.4
Belgium-Luxemb. .	90.65	237.4	289.0	38.2	31.4
Canada	.2.28	6.96	14.58	32.8	15.6
France	18.62	110.63	122.33	16.8	15.2
Germany	28.65	54.4	121.7	52.7	23.5
Ireland	122.5 [b]	193.6 [b]	526.5 [b]	63.3	23.3
Italy	2,359	8,523	15,011	27.7	15.7
Japan	603	5,258	16,353	11.5	3.7
Netherlands . . .	7.05	12.18	16.75	57.9	42.1
Sweden	3.83	13.57	51.52	28.2	7.4
Switzerland . . .	11.86	22.18	53.92	53.5	22.0
United Kingdom .	1,185 [c]	10,705 [c]	n.a.	11.1	n.a.
United States . .	18.8	148.7	227.6	12.6	8.3

TABLE A-III *continued*

Country	1 9 6 2				
	Billions of domestic money			Percentages	
	Res.	Money	M + QM	Res./M	Res./ M + QM
Australia	603.0 [a]	1,762 [a]	4,183 [a]	34.2	14.4
Austria	28.12	40.76	94.37	69.0	29.8
Belgium-Luxemb. .	87.65	254.5	310.4	34.4	28.2
Canada	2.80	7.19	15.12	38.9	18.5
France	19.84	130.70	144.58	15.2	13.7
Germany	27.82	58.0	134.6	48.0	20.7
Ireland	128.2 [b]	209.0 [b]	564.8 [b]	61.3	22.7
Italy	2,371	10,105	17,723	23.5	13.4
Japan	724	6,157	19,517	11.8	3.7
Netherlands . . .	7.01	13.10	18.28	53.5	38.3
Sweden	4.17	14.78	56.46	28.2	7.4
Switzerland . . .	12.35	24.66	60.08	50.1	20.6
United Kingdom .	1,181 [c]	11,172 [c]	n.a.	10.6	n..a
United States . .	17.2	151.6	245.6	11.3	7.0

[a] Millions of Australian Pounds.   [b] Millions of Irish Pounds.   [c] Millions of Pounds Sterling.

220

THE NEED FOR MONETARY RESERVES

Table A-III continued

Country	1963 Billions of domestic money			1963 Percentages	
	Res.	Money	M + QM	Res./M	Res./ M + QM
Australia	817.4 a	1,891 a	4,621 a	43.2	17.7
Austria	31.95	44.28	194.89	72.2	30.5
Belgium-Luxemb. .	97.00	279.0	343.1	34.8	28.3
Canada	2.86	7.71	16.15	37.1	17.7
France	24.05	149.76	164.33	16.1	14.6
Germany	30.6	62.2	150.8	49.2	20.3
Ireland	145.0 b	230.8 b	592.3 b	62.8	24.5
Italy	2,119	11,507	20,156	18.4	10.5
Japan	745	8,235	24,479	9.1	3.0
Netherlands . . .	7.56	14.31	20.03	52.9	37.7
Sweden	3.94	16.01	61.00	24.6	6.5
Switzerland . . .	13.24	26.46	66.42	50.0	19.9
United Kingdom .	1,124 c	11,210 c	n.a.	10.0	n.a.
United States . .	16.8	157.7	264.8	10.7	6.3

Table A-III continued

Country	1964 Billions of domestic money			1964 Percentages	
	Res.	Money	M + QM	Res./M	Res./ M + QM
Australia	846.5 a	1,995 a	5,156 a	42.4	16.4
Austria	34.24	47.36	118.39	72.3	28.9
Belgium-Luxemb. .	109.60	298.7	368.9	36.7	29.7
Canada	3.17	8.42	17.36	37.7	18.3
France	28.05	161.97	179.15	17.3	15.7
Germany	31.53	67.6	170.1	46.7	18.5
Ireland	159.3 b	247.6 b	630.7 b	64.3	25.3
Italy	2,389	12,415	21,936	19.2	10.9
Japan	723	9,412	28,428	7.7	2.4
Netherlands . . .	8.46	15.46	21.96	54.7	38.5
Sweden	5.01	17.34	66.16	28.9	7.6
Switzerland . . .	13.43	28.18	72.44	47.7	18.5
United Kingdom .	827 c	11,795 c	n.a.	7.0	n.a.
United States . .	16.7	164.2	283.9	10.2	5.9

a Millions of Australian Pounds.   b Millions of Irish Pounds.   c Millions of Pounds Sterling.

221

FRITZ MACHLUP

Country	1 9 6 5				
	Billions of domestic money			Percentages	
	Res.	Money	M + QM	Res./M	Res./M + QM
Australia	684.8 d	3,908 d	10,846 d	36.0	13.0
Austria	34.09	51.55	123.3	66.1	27.7
Belgium-Luxemb. .	115.2	320.0	401.8	36.0	28.7
Canada	3.33	9.62	19.31	34.6	17.2
France	31.08	176.82	197.0	17.6	15.8
Germany	29.72	72.7	192.5	40.9	15.4
Ireland	146.4 b	256.1 b	655.9 b	57.2	22.3
Italy	2,746	14,286	25,296	19.2	10.9
Japan	775	10,455	31,359	7.4	2.5
Netherlands . . .	8.70	17.16	24.30	50.7	35.8
Sweden	5.05	18.02	68.48	28.0	7.4
Switzerland . . .	13.96	29.27	78.26	46.6	17.8
United Kingdom .	1,073 c	12,704 c	n.a.	8.5	n.a.
United States . .	15.5	171.3	311.1	9.1	5.0

b Millions of Irish Pounds.   c Millions of Pounds Sterling.   d Millions of Australian Dollars (1965).

Notes: Reserves are as defined in Table A-II, but converted into domestic money at the official rates of the particular time. Where such conversion was not meaningful, the figure was regarded as not available (n.a.).

Money and Money-plus-Quasi-Money are in billions (milliards) of domestic money, except for Australia, Ireland, and the United Kingdom, where they are in millions.

Quasi-money includes:
in Australia: time and savings deposits in "deposit money banks" and in savings banks;
in Austria: time and savings deposits in deposits money banks;
in Belgium-Luxembourg: time and foreign-currency deposits in deposit money banks and "quasi-monetary liabilities" of the central bank;
in Canada: time deposits in deposit money banks;
in France: time deposits in deposit money banks;
in Germany: time deposits in deposit money banks;
in Ireland: time deposits in commercial banks and Post Office and Trustee Savings Bank deposits;
in Italy: time deposits and foreign-currency deposits in banks and savings banks;
in Japan: time deposits in commercial banks and in the Postal Savings System;
in the Netherlands: time, savings, and foreign-currency deposits;
in Sweden: time and savings deposits in commercial banks and savings deposits in savings banks;
in Switzerland: time and savings deposits and "bonds" in "large" banks, and in Cantonal, local, and savings banks;
in United Kingdom: nothing;
in the United States: time deposits in commercial banks.

Sources: for 1949 to 1964, *International Financial Statistics*, 1965-66 Supplement; for 1965, *I.F.S.*, May and June 1966 issues. (I am indebted to Mr. R. J. Sweeney for statistical work.)

222

[16]

THE
QUARTERLY JOURNAL
OF ECONOMICS

| Vol. LXXIX | August, 1965 | No. 3 |

THE CLOAKROOM RULE OF INTERNATIONAL RESERVES:
RESERVE CREATION AND RESOURCES TRANSFER

FRITZ MACHLUP

The cloakroom theory of commercial banking, 381.—The cloakroom rule for international reserves, 382.—The Bretton Woods Agreements, 383.—The cloakroom function of the IMF, 383.—Expanding the functions of the IMF, 384.—Three fundamental propositions, 385.—The "correct" rate of monetary expansion, 386.—Who gets the money first, 387.—Distributing the new international money, 388.—The first round of spending, 389.—The probability of an early turn-around, 390.—The transfer of real resources to developing countries, 392.—Summary and conclusion, 393.

THE CLOAKROOM THEORY OF COMMERCIAL BANKING

Older students of money and banking surely remember the cloakroom theory of commercial banking. It was a theory that gave bankers—shocked by the insinuation that the commercial banking system was able to "create" credit and thereby increase the supply of circulating media—new confidence and a confirmed belief in their own innocence. They were convinced of their incapacity to do anything as wicked, tricky, or magic as create credit, let alone money. After all, did not every banker know that he stood to lose reserves in amounts equal to those by which he extended his loans or investments? Did it not follow that banks could never lend more than they had been able to borrow from their depositors who, having confidence in the bankers' probity and liquidity, had put cash at their disposal? Was it not therefore clear that banks were similar to cloakrooms[1] in that they received deposits of their clients' paraphernalia and were obliged to return them on demand?

Present-day freshmen and sophomores in elementary courses in economics who, after some effort, have comprehended the theory of bank credit creation feel quite superior to the innocent bankers of past generations. These bankers had not grasped the difference between

1. The analogy was proposed by Edwin Cannan, "The Meaning of Bank Deposits," *Economica*, I (1921). The article is reproduced in Edwin Cannan, *An Economist's Protest* (London: King, 1927) under the title "The Difference Between a Bank and a Cloak-Room," pp. 256-66. The Difference, in Cannan's view, consisted only in the fact that "money is more homogenous than bags and their contents," so that depositors in a cloakroom insist on the *same* bag being returned whereas depositors in a bank are willing to accept other pieces of money in lieu of those they deposited. However, neither cloakrooms nor banks can create deposits. "The most abandoned cloakroom attendant cannot lend out more umbrellas or bicycles than have been entrusted to him, and the most reckless banker cannot lend out more money than he has of his own *plus* what he has of other people's" (pp. 258, 259).

storage and manufacture of money; in particular, they had not comprehended that the lending power of the commercial-banking system did not depend on money deposited with it but on the fact that the deposit liabilities of the banks had become money and could be increased by the act of lending.

Although one occasionally finds bankers who still believe the old cloakroom legend, the theory of commercial banking, in official as well as academic expositions, has safely freed itself of the stultifying effects of the old notion. Indeed, most countries, having understood the capacity of commercial banks to create money, have taken measures to control or limit the exercise of this power. These controls and limitations have generally been of a quantitative nature, usually in the form of requirements for banks to hold particular "reserve assets" in certain ratios to their deposit liabilities.

A requirement of 100 per cent reserves would have eliminated the banks' power of credit creation. But one can imagine other forms of limiting this power, say, by measures reducing the general acceptability of deposits as circulating media. For example, depositories could have been prohibited from promising payment on demand and from transferring deposit balances to other accounts or other financial institutions; or all legal protection against fraud by checks could have been withheld. Alternatively, financial intermediaries could have been forbidden to accept deposits altogether, and thus be confined to receiving funds by selling shares of equity capital or of participations in particular investments. (As a matter of fact, limitations of these types have been proposed or even adopted in some countries with regard to thrift deposits or savings institutions, with the intention of down-grading the moneyness of bank liabilities and, thereby, the capacity of banks to create credit.) Another, rather fantastic restriction could have reduced financial intermediaries to the status of mere "credit agents," neither borrowing nor lending, but receiving only the lenders' own cashier checks and passing them on to the borrowers.

These or other measures to hold commercial banks to a cloakroom function, to prevent them from graduating from warehouses of money to manufacturers of money, have not been adopted. According to the cloakroom theory commercial banks were unable to create credit; by a cloakroom rule they could be prevented from creating credit. No attempts have been made, however, since the cloakroom theory was exploded, to resort to a cloakroom rule of commercial banking. The authorities have been satisfied with quantitative limitations, controlling bank-credit creation but not preventing it.

THE CLOAKROOM RULE FOR INTERNATIONAL RESERVES

There has never been any serious doubt about the ability of national central banks to create national money. Regarding them, neither a cloakroom theory nor a cloakroom rule has been developed; their sight liabilities are money, without reservations. In order to limit the central banks' power of money creation many countries have adopted quantitative limitations, such as gold reserve requirements or minimum reserve ratios of gold and foreign-exchange holdings to bank note circulation or to both bank note and deposit liabilities. But countries have not tried to reduce the moneyness of such liabilities.

On the next higher level, however, in the case of international reserves, a cloakroom rule has been adopted for the foremost international monetary institutions. In full comprehension of the fact that an international money institution could be either a warehouse of existing money or a manufacturer of new international money, many or most central bankers of our time insist that an international institution such as the International Monetary Fund is and must be nothing but a warehouse and intermediary of currencies handed over to it; and they fight the idea that deposit liabilities of such an institution should be the accepted international reserve assets of national monetary authorities. The cloakroom rule for international reserves is strongly defended by a majority of practical experts and by many academic economists as well.

THE BRETTON WOODS AGREEMENTS

The experts preparing for the Bretton Woods Conference in 1944 carefully studied the Keynes Plan (April 1943) with its full recognition of the principle of credit creation. The proposed "International Clearing Union" was supposed to extend credit to countries in deficit and thereby create deposit liabilities accepted as international reserve by the central banks of member countries. This proposal was rejected by the United States, largely because of a fear that too much international money might be created and used to draw real resources from countries obliged to accept this fiat money in exchange for real goods and services demanded by over-spending nations.

The plan accepted in lieu of a credit-creating Clearing Union provided for a credit-transferring Monetary Fund. The IMF was to obtain national currencies by subscriptions from member countries and then to exchange limited amounts of such currencies against national currencies of countries in deficit. The "sale" of currencies of countries in surplus, out of the Fund's holding, against currencies of countries in deficit, with the obligation of the latter countries to "repurchase" their own currencies later with convertible currencies, is only a lending operation described in fancy terminology. In ordinary language, the Fund "lends" currencies it has held as assets to countries that want to borrow in order to finance their deficits. By insisting that international payments be made only in national currencies (of key currency countries) or in gold, but *not* in deposit liabilities of the IMF, the signers of the Bretton Woods Agreements made the Fund a warehouse and transfer agent of national moneys and guarded against the possibility of its becoming a factory of international money.

THE CLOAKROOM FUNCTION OF THE IMF

One may be tempted to resort to another analogy in order to emphasize the essential contrast between credit transfer and credit creation. Savings banks and building and loan associations in the United States can only transfer funds received from depositors; they receive check-deposit balances in (deposit liabilities of) commercial banks and lend them to borrowers (exchange them against the borrowers' promises to repay); they can lend only what they have received. Commercial banks, on the other hand, viewed as a group, do not lend anything they have received and lose no liquid assets in acquiring the borrowers' promises to pay; the borrowers or their payees receive deposit-liabilities of the commercial banks, deposits that are newly created in the process and constitute additions to the money supply.

Much of this contrast is analogous to that between an asset-lending IMF and a

339-40

liability-creating XIMF (if I may use Altman's code word for an "expanded" International Monetary Fund). But the analogy fails in one important respect: funds deposited with savings institutions ordinarily come from the active income stream; they constitute current saving by income recipients choosing to let someone else do the purchasing that they themselves forego. Most of the funds paid into the IMF, on the other hand, are newly created liabilities of national monetary authorities, not previously existing moneys in active circulation. The currencies held as assets by the IMF are therefore not the result of abstinence or saving by any person or nation; and when they are made available to countries in deficit for payments to other countries, these currencies become net additions to international reserves. The IMF thus does play a role in the creation of international reserves, though this role is confined to putting into circulation the currencies created by national monetary authorities.[2] It remains true that the IMF is a warehouse, transfer agent, and rental service for national currencies received from member countries.

The cloakroom function of the IMF is not the result of a theoretical misunderstanding on the part of the experts assembled at Bretton Woods. It is rather the result of a deliberate limitation on the prerogatives of the IMF. The United States and other founding countries did not want the Fund to become a credit-creating institution and, hence, they anxiously avoided what would have been a precondition to the creation of a new international currency, namely, the acceptability of the Fund's deposit liabilities in international payments among national monetary authorities.

EXPANDING THE FUNCTIONS OF THE IMF

For some fourteen years the world seemed well satisfied with the limitation on the Fund's functions to that of a rental service for currencies held in storage. This changed only when it was (slowly but increasingly) realized that the existing dual currency reserve and gold exchange system might not prove viable and that the continuous increase in dollar liabilities used as reserve assets of most of the nondollar world would cause trouble both if it went on and if it stopped. In the opinion of an increasing number of experts, the required reform or necessary evolution will take the form of extending the functions of the IMF and, especially, of allowing its liabilities to become reserve assets for national monetary authorities. The chief protagonist of this view has been Robert Triffin. The principle, however, of IMF deposits replacing or supplementing the present currency reserves is getting wide acceptance in academic circles and sporadic acceptance among official experts. In one form or another, the idea of IMF liabilities serving as reserve assets of national monetary authorities has been incorporated in the Stamp Plans, the Harrod Plans, the Day Plan, the Angell Plan, the Maudling Plan, one of the Bernstein Plans, to mention only the best-known proposals.[3]

The idea of shifting the source of the lending power of the IMF from the magnitude and composition of its *assets* to the acceptability of its *liabilities* is still resisted by many

2. Fritz Machlup, *Plans for Reform of the International Monetary System* (Revised edition; Princeton University, Department of Economics, International Finance Section, 1964), p. 11. Also *International Payments, Debts, and Gold* (New York: Scribners, 1964), p. 292.

3. For references see my study cited in the preceding footnote, pp. 39-61, and pp. 319-39, respectively.

341-42

central bankers and government experts. Some of the objections focus on possible impairments of the Fund's own "liquidity." The expansion of Fund liabilities is viewed as dependent upon the Fund's "resources" and as impinging on the Fund's ability to meet its obligations.

Even the officers and economists of the IMF are exceedingly cautious in discussing the possibilities of creating "unconditional liquidity on an international scale." Thus in considering purchases of "assets other than currencies," that is, investment by the Fund, they state that "Any acquisition of assets by investment would tend to put a strain on the Fund's resources. . . . Investment would be likely to require an extension of the Fund's own resources derived from subscriptions or of borrowing by the Fund beyond what would otherwise be necessary."[4]

This emphasis on the Funds' "resources" and on the composition of its assets calls for our critical attention.

THREE FUNDAMENTAL PROPOSITIONS

The essential points will be understood more readily if we go back to some more general relationships that hold on different levels of the monetary system and can be formulated in three fundamental propositions:

1. For payments among customers of the same (commercial) bank, the assets (amounts, quality, composition, liquidity) of that bank are irrelevant; they become relevant only for payments to customers of other banks, that is, for *interbank payments*.

2. For interbank payments in the same country, the assets (amounts, quality, composition, liquidity) of the national reserve bank are irrelvant; they become relevant only for payments to persons or banks in other countries, that is, for *international payments*.

3. For international payments in the same world, the assets (amounts, quality, composition, liquidity) of the international reserve bank (or an appropriately organized IMF) are irrelevant; they become relevant only for payments to persons, banks, or reserve banks on other planets, that is, for *interplanetary payments*.

Thus, as long as we are concerned only with international and not with interplanetary payments, there is no need to worry about the resources of an international reserve bank whose liabilities are accepted as reserve assets of national reserve banks. Some qualifications to this statement, however, are necessary. (And readers who are nervous lest the danger of inflation be disregarded may be reassured: this subject will be discussed presently.)

One qualification pertains to the first two propositions. They hold only if all payments are made by check or transfers from account to account. However, if there is also another kind of domestic money, say, coins or paper currency, some customers may wish to draw such money from their banks. The possible demand for nonbank currency is a factor to be taken into account. This demand may increase as the amount of bank money increases, because

---

4. International Monetary Fund, *Annual Report of the Executive Directors for the Fiscal Year Ended April 30, 1964* (Washington, D.C., 1964), pp. 38-39. The extension of the Fund's resources by "borrowing" is, of course, a correct legal description, since all deposit-liabilities are the logical legal correlative of "borrowing." From an economic point of view, however, it is the causal sequence that matters. Where certain liabilities enjoy acceptability as money and are transferred "from depositor to depositor," the acquisition of additional assets need not wait for any prior act of borrowing but, on the contrary, the liabilities arise as a consequence of the acquisition of assets.

342-43

there are some things that cannot conveniently be purchased and paid for by check (for example, purchases of street-car tickets and of goods sold by coin automats). A second source of demand for nonbank money may be the primitive peasant's distrust of banks; he may wish to check periodically whether the bank still has "his money," though he may leave it there once the teller produces enough currency from the till.

An analogous qualification is called for regarding the third proposition, which would be completely valid only if all international payments were made by transfers from account to account. However, if there is another kind of international money, say, gold bullion, some central banks may wish to add to their gold holdings. There is no increase in the demand for gold that can be explained by particular payments for which gold alone would be usable (as only coins can be used for automats). The sole source of demand for gold would be that of a distrustful national monetary authority wanting to check (like the primitive peasant) whether "its gold" was still there.

Our three fundamental propositions relate only to the problem of liquidity and ability to pay. They do not relate to the problems of the danger of price inflations and induced redistributions of real income. Yet, these problems are involved in the banks' decisions about acquisition of assets. Through their selection of assets, banks—commercial, national, and international—can affect absolute and relative prices, the allocation of productive services, and the distribution of products among persons and among nations. These problems, rather than that of the liquidity of the international reserve institution, require attention.

THE "CORRECT" RATE OF MONETARY EXPANSION

The first of these problems, the danger of inflation, has been discussed so often that brief reminders of generally accepted conclusions ought to suffice here. Let us remember that the fear of illiquidity on the part of individual commercial banks through deficits in interbank balances of payments acts as a brake in the speed of credit expansion by the commercial banking system, and that this expansion is also controlled by such things as (legal or traditional) reserve requirements and circumspection in the supply of commercial bank reserves (government money or central bank money) by the national monetary authorities. Let us further remember that the fear of illiquidity on the part of central banks through deficits in international balances of payments acts as a brake in the speed of credit expansion by central banks, and that this expansion is also controlled by such things as (legal or traditional) reserve ratios (gold and foreign-exchange-reserve requirements) and by scarcity of supply of central-bank reserves (new acquisitions of gold and convertible foreign exchange).

An analogous brake would not exist for an International Reserve Institution, say, an IRI or XIMF. It would not have to fear illiquidity through deficits in the interplanetary balance of payments, and consequently the expansion of its assets (loans and investments) and, therefore, of its deposit liabilities (the new reserve assets of national central banks) could go on without limit unless agreed institutional constraints are imposed on it. If one distrusts the intelligence, wisdom, and character of those who will (by international agreement) make the rules and regulations for the institution or of those who will determine its policies, then one is justified in fearing that the rate of expansion of international reserves would be excessive. An excessive rate of expansion of central-bank reserves would in all probability lead to an excessive rate of expansion in commercial-bank reserves, which in turn would be liable to lead

343-45

to an excessive rate of expansion in commercial-bank deposits.

On the other hand, there are those who believe that safe rules and regulations can be devised for the International Reserve Institution and that its management can be expected to pursue appropriate policies in determining the rate of expansion. They hold that the danger of inflation resulting from excessive creation of international reserves is greatly exaggerated. They hold that the annual increase of international reserves could be checked either by adherence to some rules of thumb or by discretion on the part of management correctly sizing up the total "need" of additional international reserves, that is, the rate of increase that would avoid serious inflationary or deflationary mistakes.[5]

For the sake of a clear exposition of the second problem—of the induced redistribution of world output through the chosen distribution of newly created international reserves—we shall assume that the annual rate of expansion can be controlled and that an appropriate rate can be "correctly" determined. This assumption, however, involves a serious complication for the amount depends on its distribution. If a larger portion of the new international reserves goes to national central banks with high propensities to expand credit in countries with high propensities to import, a given amount of new reserves will lead to a larger total of world demand and a stronger pull-up of prices and earning rates. If a larger portion of the new reserves goes to slowly expanding central banks in countries with low propensities to import, the effect of the reserve creation upon demand, incomes, and prices will be smaller. In addition, the effect will also depend on the form, terms, and conditions under which new reserves are obtained by central banks; that is to say, their marginal propensities to expand are likely to vary according to circumstances. It follows that a judgment of the "correct" amount of reserve creation presupposes separate estimates of a large number of variables.

Despite all these complications we shall proceed to a discussion of the distribution effects of the "correctly" determined, that is, noninflationary addition to international reserves.

WHO GETS THE MONEY FIRST

The new assets acquired by commercial banks may give an indication of who got the "new" money first when it was created. "Who gets the money first" may make a difference for various sectors of an economy. For if, with relatively full employment, the quantity of money increases over the years, the first spenders of the new money take real income away from others. This holds true whether productivity is constant or whether it increases. The first spenders of the new money obtain goods and services other members of the economy would have claimed; these others either suffer a net decline in "real intake" or fail to get their full share in the increase of the total product made available through the rise in productivity.

The new assets acquired by the central banks will not give the relevant information if the expansion of its credit is largely in the form of loans to commercial banks or of open market purchases of government securities at a time the government is not enlarging its debt. For, in

---

5. Even if one is pessimistic concerning judgment and backbone of prospective managers of a prospective world reserve bank, one must not compare their prospective errors and failures with an ideal. It would be difficult to believe that even the worst managers of an IRI or XIMF would have created nearly as much international reserve as was created under our present system from 1958 to 1963.

345-46

such instances, we do not know how the banks use the resulting increase in their lending power and how the sellers of securities (including banks) use their proceeds. The assets of the entire banking system would have to be examined to get some answer, however partial and ambiguous, to the question of the identity of the favored spenders. If business is the chief recipient of the new funds, a diagnosis of accelerated capital formation through "forced saving" may be justified, though only with qualifications. For it is possible that business firms finance an increase in consumer loans, in which case the borrowing consumers encroach on those who merely spend what they earn.

If increases in bank assets are matched by increases in government debt and government spending, the diagnosis may be of an increase in government services, or perhaps an increase in transfer payments (to the old, the sick, the unemployed) at the expense of individual consumers' real purchases. If the increase in government spending is for a public investment program, future generations may be the beneficiaries of the enforced abstinence of present consumers. Other government programs may involve intersectoral transfers of potential intake. There may be even a geographic redistribution of national output if the new money is first spent by or for the benefit of particular regions within the economy. The number of possible combinations is large. It may be worthwhile for some economist to work through various models of "redistribution through selection of first spenders of new money" and to search for operational indicators for the pertinence of particular models to particular situations.

On the international level the question is, in some ways, simpler because our interest is usually focused on the claims or drafts countries may make on one another's productive facilities. An international reserve institution, by providing new international money, enables the first spenders of this new money to obtain products from other countries. To the extent that the productive capacity of these other countries is fully utilized, involuntary abstinence is imposed on their nationals. Thus, we should not expect nations to be indifferent about the ways in which an international reserve institution uses its power to create international money and distributes it among various national monetary authorities. Power to create international money is power to take products from some countries and give them to others.

The case of underemployment in a country in which new international money is spent should be mentioned, chiefly because one may hold that such a country loses, to those that buy from it, little that it would have had without the additional foreign demand. On the other hand, such a country, had it been anxious to procure a higher level of employment, could have adopted internal policies to make sure that the output of the additional employment would go to its own nationals. Finally, the case of inflation in the exporting country deserves the comment that in this situation the international redistribution of output is combined with an intranational redistribution. In order to avoid complicating the problem, we shall assume that the increase in foreign demand does not imply price inflation. This assumption not only simplifies analysis; it also serves to drive home the fact that the problem of diverting a larger part of national output to the foreign spenders of the new international money is not merely an aspect of the phenomenon of price inflation.

DISTRIBUTING THE NEW INTERNATIONAL MONEY

Let us distinguish various ways in which the International Reserve Institution (IRI)

346-48

distributes, through its assets selection, its new deposit liabilities among different countries:

1. IRI gives loans to countries in deficit or to countries that wish to increase their reserves. Such loans might be of short, medium, or long term; they might be conditional or unconditional. They might be the result of an exercise of agreed borrowing rights or of discretionary decisions by the management.

2. IRI purchases from national monetary authorities currencies of other countries, within some limits, with or without commitments of the issuing countries to "repurchase" their currencies within short, medium, or long periods of time, and with gold-value or exchange-value guarantees.[6]

3. IRI purchases securities of IBRD, IDA, other international or national development aid institutions, or governments of developing countries.

4. IRI purchases gilt-edged securities (especially medium-term or long-term obligations of trusted governments of affluent countries, but perhaps also IBRD bonds) regularly traded in the world's largest capital markets. These purchases might be subject to prior consent, perhaps even upon invitation, by the governments concerned, and resales might also be subject to agreement, perhaps limited to maximum amounts per month or year or permissible only when certain conditions prevail, such as a surplus in the country's balance of payments.

5. IRI purchases national currencies (that is, obligations of national monetary authorities) in specified amounts and proportions fixed by some previously agreed formula. These currencies are not for resale or any use other than decorating the balance sheet of IRI (that is, they will stay there until IRI is liquidated or a member exercises a right to withdraw from the institution).[7]

THE FIRST ROUND OF SPENDING

What implications do the techniques of distributing the new reserves have for the speed with which the international buying power that they afford will actually be exercised? The reserves obtained by technique Number 1 are spent immediately ("today"), except in the case in which a country borrows only to show a larger gross reserve. The IRI deposits obtained by technique Number 2 may replace foreign-exchange reserves received "yesterday" for exports which, incidentally, the particular country might not have made had it not been assured of the exchangeability of the earned currency into IRI deposits. The IRI funds created by technique Number 3 and going—via IBRD, IDA, etc.—to less developed countries will probably be spent "tomorrow." Thus, these three techniques of reserve creation have in common that the new money is probably spent without delay.

6. There is no essential difference between the first and second technique, especially if the country that sells foreign exchange is not obligated in any respect. The possibility is listed here for only one reason: to disabuse readers of the belief that the surrender of "gold and foreign exchange" is different from the surrender of one's own currency, that is, from the sale of a bank's own liabilities. Assume that IRI was forbidden to purchase anything but "gold and foreign exchange"; if only country A had gold, and no other country had any foreign exchange to spare, A could sell its gold to B in exchange for B-currency, B could resell the gold to C in exchange for C-currency, and so on, with the result that any number of countries would have acquired foreign exchange, which they could sell to IRI.

7. The essential difference between the first two and the last of the five techniques described here lies in the "permanence" of the assets. Number 1 provides for repayment by the particular borrower (of course, not of all borrowers taken as a group, if world-wide deflation is to be avoided). Number 2 may provide for repayment, depending on the agreed terms. Number 5 provides for nonrepayable loans, with or without interest.

348-49

This is not so likely with regard to technique Number 4, which increases the reserves of countries where the sellers of the securities (acquired by IRI) spend or hold their proceeds. If the sellers are highly liquid financial intermediaries or commercial banks in countries in surplus, the new reserves may long remain unused. The increased lending power of the liquid financial institutions and of the liquid central bank may not be exercised for the time being and no excess demand for foreign exchange may develop. If, on the other hand, the sellers have sold the securities in order to make loans urgently demanded from them, or if they are in countries suffereing from balance-of-payments deficits, the reserves will not wait long before they are used for purchasing goods and services from abroad. In addition, the availability of these reserves may allow greater delays in the adoption of adjustment policies designed to remove the payments deficits of these countries. The probability that the new reserves will be spent quickly can be increased by selective open-market purchases, that is, if IRI makes its investments in deficit countries (or if it increases its holdings of IBRD bonds, assuming that IBRD has prompt uses for its funds).

It should be understood that "fast" and "slow" use of the additional funds refers in all cases to the first round of spending. Received by surplus countries in exchange for "real resources," the IRI deposits come to rest in the foreign reserves of these countries; they have changed their character from "unearned" to "earned" reserves.[8] A second round of spending will come along only when the balance of payments of these reserve-holders turns and they become deficit countries. Since the adjustment mechanism has been slowed down almost everywhere, the second round may be long in coming.

Even the first round will come later, on the average, for reserves distributed by technique Number 5. If the formula used in the distribution includes such variables as present reserve holdings, national income, foreign trade volume, or IMF quotas, a large part of the new IRI deposits will go to surplus countries. These have no current use for more reserves—if "use" means spending rather than holding (which may be poor semantics in the view of those who insist on reserves being what is held, not what is used up). If they are, moreover, conservative in their monetary policy—expanding domestic credit at a relatively slower pace than the fast-expanding and fast-spending countries—they will hold on to both earned and unearned reserves. It follows that only that part of the newly created IRI deposits that goes to deficit countries will have a quick first round of spending and will then come to rest in the reserves of the "thrifty."

THE PROBABILITY OF AN EARLY TURN-AROUND

Countries in deficit receive from countries in surplus real resources (or claims to real resources) and pay for these resources with the newly created IRI deposits. To be sure, the recipient countries hold their additional earned reserves as eventual counterclaims to real resources of other countries; but the actual return flow does not take place until the balance of payments turns, and this may be many years off; indeed the time may never come.

The probability of an early turn-around is highest if the new reserves are created through

---

8. Reserves are "unearned" if the nation obtained them without having to give up real resources, or claims to any of its real resources.

349-50

short-term loans to deficit countries with the condition that effective adjustment policies be pursued. If all countries pursue policies resulting in quick and short swings from deficit to surplus to deficit and again to surplus, the transfers of real resources will likewise be for short periods only; no country, then, can be regarded as a long-term beneficiary at the expense of others. However, in this case it will be doubtful if the creation of new IRI deposits will also serve the purpose of satisfying a growing world demand for international reserves, that is, for reserves to hold rather than to shuttle back and forth. If countries create domestic means of circulation at rates sufficient to avoid declining wage rates despite increasing labor force, and declining general price levels despite increasing outputs, they may want their foreign reserves to increase at approximately the same rates. Yet, a technique of reserve creation that regularly cancels most of any previous expansion will not achieve the desired continuous net growth. The erstwhile surplus countries, having now developed deficits, lose the reserves they have earned; and the erstwhile deficit countries, having now developed surpluses, repay their short-term loans to the international reserve institution. The reserves created by the loans are canceled as the loans are repaid.

Only if imbalances of payments increase over the years can the technique of short-term loans to deficit countries achieve a steady growth of international reserves. Assume that the first round of deficits is financed by loans of one billion dollars; if then the balance turns, the previous surplus countries swinging into deficit need not borrow except to the extent that their deficits are in excess of a billion. For example, if their deficits amounted to one-and-a-half billion dollars, a billion of IRI deposits is wiped out and only one-half of one billion remains as a net increase in total reserves. This is why some economists do not regard reserve creation through loan expansion for the finance of payments deficits as an adequate system to take care of a growing demand for reserves. (The offer of short-term loans to countries that may be willing to borrow more reserves to hold rather than to spend would probably not be taken advantage of in amounts sufficient to secure the growth needed to avoid deflationary pressures.)

Reserve creation through IRI investments in securities of development-finance institutions is different in that the probability of a return flow is slight. The first spending of the new funds by the beneficiaries, the less developed countries, draws real resources from developed countries. The IRI deposits are likely to come to rest as permanent reserves of the countries that earned them through their exports, though they may occasionally circulate among these countries as they take turns in getting into short-term deficits with one another. The point is that it is not likely that the developing countries will earn back the reserves of which they had been the first spenders.

Little can be said with any degree of confidence about the future career of reserves created through open-market policies. If the purchases of widely traded securities are undertaken at the initiative of the IRI, it should be possible for it to avoid a decline in its investment portfolio and hence in the volume of its corresponding deposit liabilities. But one cannot foretell whether these deposits would actively circulate among countries taking turns in swinging from deficit into surplus or whether they would stay inactive as owned reserves of countries with a steady (and steadily growing) demand for this "backing" behind their national money supply.

With regard to IRI deposit liabilities created and distributed by deposits of national currencies according to an agreed formula, we stated before that a large part of these unearned reserves would never be used in even a first round of spending. It would be moot to speculate

350-52

on the probability of an early second round for that portion which, through deficits of the first recipients, has been transformed from unearned into earned reserves.

THE TRANSFER OF REAL RESOURCES TO DEVELOPING COUNTRIES

The conclusion, undoubtedly, is that the creation of new international reserves can be instrumental in a transfer of real resources to countries in short-run deficit, to countries in long-lasting deficit, and to developing countries in perennial deficit. It is easy to understand the resulting conflicts of interest. Representatives of countries from which resources are withdrawn may object to the "involuntary" philanthropy involved in such schemes, especially in the relief for slow adjusters and in the aid to late developers. Spokesmen for the underdogs may point to the hardships usually associated with adjustment in deficit countries and to the crying need for resources on the part of less developed nations.

Leaving aside the controversy about the "proper" speed of adjusting imbalances of payments, let us examine the arguments for and against combining the creation of international reserves with the provision of aid to less developed countries. It should be understood from the outset: one may be genuinely impressed with the desirability of aiding poorer nations and with the desirability of providing for growing international reserves and may, nevertheless, resist schemes that try to do both these things in one process.

Any plan for reserve creation that is successful in avoiding deflationary pressures in developed countries will also benefit developing countries *indirectly* through its effects on the demand for primary commodities, supply of industrial products, and supply of capital. To insist on a "rider" for the provision of *direct* aid to developing countries may seem gratuitous. Built-in development aid—by handing the new reserves first to less developed countries and forcing the more developed countries to buy back, as it were, these reserves, that is, to earn them by surrendering real resources—may seem to some a scheme designed to conceal or confuse, perhaps as an arbitrary squeeze play. If a group of industrial countries, used to holding "tokens" for their financial settlements, want to increase their stocks of tokens because they want more to hold and more to hand back and forth among one another in settling temporary payments balances, why should they not be permitted to create such tokens for themselves without having to surrender real resources to poor countries? They may be willing to contribute most generously, they may even recognize a moral responsibility for aiding developing nations through liberal grants, loans, and investments—but they object to the arbitrary linking of matters that are inherently separate.

On the other hand, a very plausible argument can be made, on political as well as economic grounds, for combining development aid and reserve creation in one package deal. It may be politically difficult to obtain the appropriations for foreign aid that the governments may deem desirable; they may find it easier to get legislative approval for a plan establishing an international reserve institution whose investments will include securities of development-finance organizations. In political questions one cannot always insist on logical neatness and semantic clarity. The economic case for the package deal must rest largely on tradition: historically, international reserves have always been earned through the surrender of real resources and, to industrial countries, the cost of reserves under a plan of distributing new reserves first to less developed countries is not any higher than the cost of reserves under the gold standard.

352-53

The discovery that international money can be produced with cheap ink and paper, and need not be produced with hard work applied to metal dug out of the ground, affords a large saving. Should the holders of this cheap international money be the sole beneficiaries of the reduction in cost? If they are prepared to acquire additional gold reserves by surrendering real resources, one should think that they can pay the same price for a perfect substitute, for the deposits in the international reserve institution. The first spenders of the new deposits will be the beneficiaries of the technological progress in the production of international money, and these first spenders may "just as well" be the developing nations.

When gold is the only international reserve money, some Africans, Australians and Asians (and a few North Americans) must work in the mines to dig the stuff out of the ground. When credit entries in the books of an acceptable organization become substitutes for gold, work on highways, railroads, harbors, power plants, hospitals, and schools of developing countries can take the place of work in the gold mines[9]—provided the countries holding most of the international reserves are willing to pay for the "perfect substitute" the same price they used to pay and continue to pay for gold reserves. Equal prices for perfect substitutes are the rule, rather than the exception, in competitive markets. The savings in the production of the low-cost substitute must be distributed somehow, and if the producer, in this case the International Reserve Institution, holds a monopoly, the distribution is for the owners of the company to decide. If they are so inclined, they may well let the developing countries have the lion's share.

SUMMARY AND CONCLUSION

The cloakroom theory of banking contended that banks were unable to create means of circulation. A cloakroom rule is adopted if the banks' power to create money is recognized and deliberately suppressed. The International Monetary Fund was advisedly reduced to a cloakroom function because the nations were fearful of excessive creation of monetary reserves. The contracting governments confined the functions of the IMF to that of a warehouse and rental agent for a collection of currencies, and prohibited it from becoming a manufacturer of circulating deposit liabilities.

This limitation can no longer be maintained in a world determined to maintain fixed exchange rates, to employ monetary expansion to promote economic growth, and to adhere to the rule that the supply of money ought not to expand much faster than the monetary reserves. In such a world the stock of international reserves will have to be increased year after year. The future needs for international reserves can be met most cheaply and most efficiently by deposit creation of an international reserve institution. The danger of excessive reserve creation by such an institution can be averted by explicit constraints and responsible

---

9. The reader may wish to compare this thought with the famous Smithian remark about cheap paper currency being analogous to highways in the air. Here is the quotation: "The gold and silver money . . . may very properly be compared to a highway, which, while it circulates and carries to market all the grass and corn of the country, produces itself not a single pile of either. The judicious operations of banking, by providing, if I may be allowed so violent a metaphor, a sort of waggon-way through the air, enable the country to convert, as it were, a great part of its highways into good pastures and cornfields and thereby to increase very considerably the annual produce of its land and labour." Adam Smith, *An Inquiry into the Nature and Causes of the Wealth of Nations*, Book II, Chap. II (Routledge ed., p. 246; Modern Library ed., p. 305). The advantage of substituting paper for gold, by Smith considered from the point of view of one country, is regarded in the text as a saving to the world, with the benefit going to the less developed countries.

353-54

management; reserve creation would surely be more rational than under the present gold-exchange standard. But the question of induced transfers of real resources to the first spenders of the new reserves calls for political decisions. The acquisition of reserves under the gold standard involved the surrender of real resources. If additional reserves under the new system can be created at no cost, the saving will benefit someone and its distribution must needs be arbitrary. If developing countries were made the beneficiaries, the cost to reserve holders would be no greater than under a gold standard. This may be proposed as an argument in support of schemes linking the creation of international reserves with aid to developing countries. On the other hand, the industrial countries may object to clandestine aid schemes and claim that they, as the chief holders of reserves, should be allowed to create additional reserves without having to "earn" them through transfers of real resources to developing countries. Both arguments are persuasive and can be reasonably defended.

PRINCETON UNIVERSITY

355

[17]

Euro-Dollar Creation: A Mystery Story

This article will be about Euro-dollars and the "Euro-dollar market". We cannot intelligently talk about these matters before engaging in an extensive conceptual and theoretical preparation. There has been much confusion even among experts in the field, attributable probably to their courage, which led them to talk about the system before they had thought about it and to try to think before they had the necessary conceptual preparation.

The lack of conceptual clarity has contributed to serious differences in the experts' explanations of the fast growth of the Euro-dollar business and in their evaluation of it. Different writers have presented contradictory ideas about the sources and uses of the funds in question. One extreme position in this respect is that the bulk of Euro-dollar deposits are the result of multiple creation of credit by banks in a system of only fractional reserves; another extreme position is that all these deposits owe their existence to the decisions, on the part of owners and recipients of dollar balances, to deposit them with banks in Europe. Some writers see the source of most or all Euro-dollars in the deficit of the balance of payments of the United States; others have concluded that the growth of Euro-dollar deposits was not caused by, but has had certain effects upon the balance of payments of the United States. Most writers have judged the development and growth of the Euro-dollar market as healthy and beneficial for the economies concerned, others have pointed to considerable dangers, and a few have warned of an imminent collapse, of a "cataclysm" with catastrophic consequences. I shall not document any of these statements; their protagonists include some eminent economists.

If the present essay cannot reach definitive conclusions deciding all controversies on the subject, it will at least attempt to show why

219

FRITZ MACHLUP

some such conclusions cannot be obtained on the basis of the empirical evidence available at present and why certain conceptual obscurities have led us into blind alleys (1).

Flows and Stocks

The first thing to bear in mind is the fundamental distinction between *flow* concepts and *stock* concepts — flows per period and stocks at a moment of time. Production and consumption, imports and exports, sales and purchases, transactions and incomes are basic flow concepts. Inventories, capital, wealth, money stocks, claims and debts are basic stock concepts. Certain flow concepts have an implied reference to stocks; among the most essential of these are accumulation and depletion (of inventories, capital, etc.), profits and losses (considering differences in net asset values), creation and cancellation (of money), and turnover (of capital, money, etc.). And there are also a few ambiguous ones, which cause endless confusion; the chief culprits are loans and credit, either granted by period or outstanding at a moment, and deposit as an act, deposit as a claim, and deposit as a liability. Alas, loans, credit, and deposits are the chief subject matter of Euro-dollar talk.

The discussion of Euro-dollars and the Euro-dollar market involves several of the enumerated terms besides the three ambiguous ones. It is about transactions, turnover, debts and claims accumulations, money stocks, and even creation and cancellation of money. For, undoubtedly, many holders of claims vis-à-vis European banks that are denominated in dollars regard their holdings as perfectly liquid balances, which confers the quality of moneyness on these claims and which may make some of the growth of Euro-dollar deposits a creation of money.

---

(1) I do not claim to have come out of the dark and to see things clearly myself. I may indeed be as confused as most others, or even more so. From several patent errors and misunderstandings I have been saved by friendly criticisms of an earlier draft of this paper received from Stanley W. Black, Benjamin Jerry Cohen, Arthur B. Hersey, Fred H. Klopstock, Burton G. Malkiel, Helmut W. Mayer and Alexander K. Swoboda. I am sincerely grateful to them. They are of course not responsible for any errors or obscurities that have remained in my paper, especially where I have stubbornly resisted their efforts to enlighten and convert me.

220

EURO-DOLLAR CREATION

System and Market

The prevailing poverty of conceptualization in the current discussion shows itself in the thoughtless designation of the whole system of transactions, deposits, and so forth, as a *market*. A market is defined as a meeting (not necessarily a physical meeting) of people who offer something for sale, rent, or hire, with people who are interested in buying, renting, or hiring. There are, in fact, such market operations with regard to Euro-dollars; they are the new offers of, and bids for, credit in Euro-dollars, the new loans contracted during a market day, and the renegotiations of old loans. But there is very much more to the Euro-dollar system than a credit market: there are the loans outstanding, the assets held, the deposit liabilities owed, the creation, turnover, conversion, and cancellation of international money, a demand for working balances as well as precautionary and speculative balances of that money, and several other things that have little to do with a " market ". It may be misleading to speak of the whole system as a market, since the market aspects of it is *only a part of the picture.*

Take, for example, the statement, literally quoted, that " the Euro-dollar market's estimated net size at the end of June 1969 was about $37 billion... " and that " Euro-dollar market growth exceeded 35 per cent in 1968... ". How does one measure the "net size" and the " growth " of a market? For most markets total sales (rentals, hires) per period, or perhaps average sales per day over a period, would be an appropriate measure. Thus, new Euro-dollar loans contracted and old loans recontracted per day might be a measure of the size of the Euro-dollar market, just as the size of the stock market is measured by the turnover of shares of stock or by the value of shares sold. But the $37 billion at the end of June 1969 are not the amount involved in daily contracts. They are the sum of deposit liabilities (denominated in U.S. dollars) of banks and branches of banks operating in eight reporting European countries to nonbank depositors residing in the reporting area and to both banks and nonbank residents outside the reporting area.

The sum of deposit claims is a stock (or inventory) at a moment. Would anybody use the total value of shares of stock held by individuals and corporations as a measure of the size of the stock market? Would anybody use the sum of deposit claims against

221

FRITZ MACHLUP

American banks as the size of the American money market? Would anybody use the sum of foreign-currency balances held by individuals, corporations, and banks (and perhaps even central banks) on a certain day as a measure of the size of the foreign-exchange market? Would anybody, if I am permitted to add one more absurdity, use the total gold stock as a measure of the size of the gold market?

The ratios of sales per day to total stock are of course very different in the various systems and markets referred to in my rhetorical questions. I have to admit that the substitution of total loans outstanding for loans transacted per day is more acceptable than some of the palpably absurd hypothetical confusions would be. It is more acceptable because the amount of the new Euro-dollar loans contracted and old loans recontracted on a day may conceivably be closer to the total outstanding and because, as some of the Euro-dollar claims are in the nature of day-to-day loans, a decision *not* to call yesterday's loan may be regarded as a decision to grant a new loan. Moreover, there are a few other markets in which not the turnover but the total outstanding is used as the measure of their size. In the market for commercial paper, for example, and in the market for bankers' acceptances, the amounts of paper outstanding at a moment of time are taken as the relevant figures. There is, however, an essential difference between these credit markets and the Euro-dollar system: the analysis of the credit markets focuses on the particular credit instruments, whereas the analysis of the Euro-dollar system must comprise so much more: a large variety of dollar assets held by the European banks, and their dollar liabilities owed to various classes of creditors chiefly in the form of deposits. To take the total of these dollar liabilities as a measure of the size of the Euro-dollar *credit market* would be like taking the check-deposit balances which individuals and corporations hold in American banks ($208 billion in December 1969) as their "loans" to the banks (which in a legal sense they are), and like interpreting the decisions of the depositors not to withdraw their balances as decisions to grant (or renew) these "loans" every day. The deposit claims against American commercial banks were over $400 billions in December 1969, if both time and demand deposits, domestic and foreign (but not savings deposits) are counted; this figure is highly significant, but not as a measure of the size of the American money market.

222

EURO-DOLLAR CREATION

My point is that there is indeed a market aspect of the Euro-dollar system; it is especially conspicuous where banks in Europe compete for deposits as well as for earning assets denominated in U.S. dollars. The changing interest rates for Euro-dollars constantly remind us of the market aspect of the system, with the banks offering as "attractive" rates as they can afford to pay the suppliers of funds and charging only slightly higher rates to place the funds. This, however, is only a part of the whole picture and, I submit, not the most crucial part. Words guide the attention of the audience; the use of the word "market" may divert attention from the important nonmarket aspects of the Euro-dollar system.

Loans and Money

To hold money is to hold perfectly liquid claims against the issuer (2), claims that are accepted as media of exchange by sellers of goods, services, and securities. To hold such claims is usually, in a legal sense, to have made a "loan", and this implies that the legal debtor has "borrowed".

However, to regard all the people who own deposit balances with commercial banks as lenders and suppliers of funds to the banking system is no more helpful for economic analysis than to regard those who carry bank notes in their wallets as lenders and suppliers of funds to the central banks, and those who have coins or currency notes in their pockets or purses as lenders to the treasury.

Every sophomore in "Money and Banking" is taught how to resolve this paradox of *having lent but still holding* money: in an economic sense the holder of money is not to be regarded as a lender, since what he has really "lent out" he can no longer have in his possession, and what he still possesses as a cash balance he cannot have lent out. The paradox is more difficult to resolve from the point of view of the issuer, that is, for the deposit bank and its having "borrowed"; the customary device for resolving it is to

---

(2) Coins are the only common currency that is not a legal claim against the issuer. Special drawing rights are international money for national monetary authorities without being claims against the issuing agency. These are exceptions. Another exception is gold, an international money for monetary authorities, but it has no "issuer", unless one wishes to give this name to the producer or to the first bank that acquires and resells it.

223

FRITZ MACHLUP

take all banks together as a group of institutions whose liquid liabilities are money to the individuals and corporations holding the deposit claims.

This device is not always understood by bankers, who (fortunately) cannot forget that they have "borrowed" from their depositors, even if the depositors, especially the owners of check-deposit balances, do not think of themselves as lenders. The device seems particularly hard to apply to an international banking system in which any bank in any country may offer especially attractive terms to depositors, foreign and domestic, in order to "borrow" dollar funds from them. Yet, the economic fact is that a holder of money has a choice of holding it in various forms: currency notes, bank notes, bank deposits denominated in domestic currency, or bank deposits denominated in foreign currency. In all these cases he is a "creditor" of the issuing institution in the legal sense only. From the economic point of view, he has not lent his money but has it in his possession and can use it any time for making payments to others. Hence, for purposes of certain kinds of analysis, one will have to suppress the notion that the existence of dollar deposit liabilities of European banks necessarily indicates an act of "borrowing" by the international banking system.

This perspective on bank deposits — seeing them as money balances held, rather than as loans made, by the depositors — is appropriate as long as individuals and nonbank corporations own the balances. It is less appropriate if other banks own them, and downright inappropriate if these other banks are on the same "liquidity level" as the bank that owes them. If there is a vertical structure of the banking system, where the deposit liabilities of one layer of banks are "higher-powered money" serving as the reserve balances for the next layer of banks, the view of these deposits as money for their holders including the banks holding them as reserves is still appropriate. For example, the deposit liabilities of the Federal Reserve banks are the money and reserve balances of the member banks in the United States — not loans granted by member banks to the Federal Reserve banks. Likewise, the deposit liabilities of the member banks are money owned by individuals and nonbank corporations but also money and reserve balances of nonmember banks — not loans granted by individuals, corporations and nonmember banks to member banks. However, for interbank

224

EURO-DOLLAR CREATION

deposits among banks of the same level this conceptual framework is inadequate.

To give an illustration, if Member Bank A of New York makes a loans to Member Bank B of New York, it transfers some of its Federal Reserve balances to, and will hold a deposit claim against, Bank B. It would be theoretically messy if we were to regard this deposit claim as money, and it would be an unsound practice if the managers of Bank A regarded it as money and as part of its primary reserve. Certainly, they would not be permitted to count it among the money assets that satisfy its legal reserve requirements. And the deposit liability of Bank B to Bank A would likewise be excluded from the statistics of the money stock of the United States; interbank deposits of this sort are "netted out".

Applying these theoretically reasonable and practically sound principles to the structure of the Euro-dollar system, one should insist on strict distinctions between the holding of dollar assets of perfect moneyness and near-moneyness, on the one hand, and holding dollar claims (loans) and securities of lesser degrees of liquidity, on the other. Likewise, the dollar liabilities of European banks have to be neatly classified as to the degree of moneyness they have for their holders. The criterion of moneyness is immediate availability without loss for use in discharge of debt. (It should be noted that not only demand deposits but also several kinds of time deposits may qualify as money).

This criterion is undoubtedly met with respect to the Euro-dollar deposits owned by individuals and nonbank corporations. The viability and stability of the Euro-dollar system largely depends on the share of deposit balances held by individuals and nonbank corporations doing business for which these deposit balances are wanted or needed. The transactions demand for these dollar balances is the stable element; the investment or asset demand for deposit balances, which is a function of relative earnings of interest, and the speculative demand, which is largely a function of expectations regarding exchange-rate changes, are more volatile elements. In any case, there is a demand for Euro-dollar deposits which is a "demand for money to hold" — and not a "supply of Euro-dollar loans".

The figures reported for the size of the Euro-dollar market include deposit claims of banks against the banks in the eight reporting European countries. Only for the deposits owned by

225

FRITZ MACHLUP

residents of the " inside area ", that is, of the eight European countries, are separate figures available for the holdings by non-banks and banks. Thus the $37 billions which have been mentioned before, and the even larger figures reported for more recent dates, contain claims by banks as well as nonbanks. (And, as will be shown below, there may be some double counting in the statistics of bank claims). The inclusion of interbank deposits, if only of banks operating in the " outside area ", prevents us from knowing what part of Euro-dollar deposits should be regarded as loans and what part as money, from an economic, not legal, point of view. (This distinction may be judged as utterly foolish by many practical bankers, but I submit that it makes a significant difference whether the creditor thinks he has made a loan which he must collect before he can use his funds for making payments or whether he thinks he is holding cash).

Credit versus Money

This brings us to a distinction which most economists understand clearly when they talk about domestic credit creation. The main points are (1) that a credit from a nonbank lender to a nonbank borrower is not " credit creation ", because the resulting claim cannot be used as money but simply indicates that spending power has been transferred from one who refrains from using it to one who intends to use it; (2) that additional bank credit to a nonbank borrower constitutes credit creation because the borrower can use new spending power which no one has given up; (3) that the act of creation of bank credit on one day may create money virtually for eternity; and (4) that the supply of credit must not be confused with the supply of money, particularly since credit in this context is a flow concept while money is a stock concept.

If commercial banks, having unused lending capacity, are making new loans (more loans than are being repaid) on Monday, the banks are thereby increasing the supply (or the quantity supplied (3)) of credit — but only Monday, not necessarily also

---

(3) An increase in supply is represented by a shift in the supply function; an increase in the quantity supplied, by a movement along a given supply function. Thus, the "supply" is increased if, with given demand, new loans are taken only at terms more favorable to

EURO-DOLLAR CREATION

Tuesday or any subsequent day. If the funds so lent stay as additional balances on demand deposits with the banks of the system, the banks will have also increased the supply of money, not only for Monday but also for Tuesday, Wednesday, and all subsequent days, as long as demand deposits do not decline either as a result of a reduction in credit outstanding or because of an outflow from the system as a result of net payments to other countries.

How does this apply to the Euro-dollar system? If Euro-banks extend to nonbank borrowers new loans denominated in Euro-dollars, they increase the supply (or quantity supplied) of credit in the Euro-dollar market, but only on the day the loans are made. If the proceeds of the loans stay in the system in the form of Euro-dollar deposits (not of the borrowers, except perhaps for a fraction of their borrowing, but of some of their immediate, secondary, or subsequent payees), the supply (stock) of Euro-dollar deposits, an international money or near-money, will have increased for as long as it does not decline again. It may decline either as a result of a reduction of the loan portfolios of the Euro-banks or as a result of a net outflow from the Euro-dollar banking system to any of the national banking systems. (Such an outflow, if it is not to the United States, would imply conversion into other national currencies).

It can be reasonably said for any banking system, including the Euro-dollar banking system, that it increases the supply of *credit* on the day when it increases its combined loan portfolio (including securities, but excluding loans to other banks of the system). It increases the supply of *money* for that day and any day thereafter as long as its combined liquid deposit liabilities (excluding those to other banks of the system) stay at the volume enlarged through the extension of the loan portfolio and are treated as " cash on hand " or " cash assets " by those who hold them.

It will be advisable to keep these differences between the supply of credit as a flow and the supply of money as a stock firmly in mind and to question any statement about " supply " in the Euro-

---

borrowers. The " quantity supplied " is increased if new loans are actively sought by borrowers, that is, if the demand for loans is increased and, with given supply, is met at terms more favorable to lenders. It is largely a question of where the initiative lies: either lenders try to place more funds or borrowers seek to obtain more funds. In the first case, the supply of loans is increased spontaneously; in the second case, an increase in the amount of loans supplied is being induced by the increase in demand.

227

FRITZ MACHLUP

dollar market that is silent about exactly what is or was supplied. The economist's term "supply of money" is admittedly confusing in that it does not refer to the function (of one or more variables) that is usually denoted by the word "supply" but rather to the amount of money existing at the moment, the given stock of money. Even more reason, however, for being careful about keeping the supply of Euro-dollar *credit* and the supply (i.e. stock) of Euro-dollar *balances* strictly apart.

The analogous distinction is required also regarding the demand side. The demand for Euro-dollar *credit* is a demand for loans denominated in Euro-dollars, a new flow of funds to borrowers who seek these funds to pay them out (or, in some instances, to hold them as balances needed in their business) and who find them cheaper or easier to obtain than funds from alternative sources. The demand for Euro-dollar *deposit balances* is a demand for money or near-money to hold in this particular form because of a combination of advantages over holding cash in other forms. Interest earned on the deposits, savings in conversion-and-reconversion costs, and greater convenience in various respects are among the major advantages (4).

One of the snares in the analysis of the Euro-dollar system is that many writers identify the demand for Euro-dollar balances with the supply of Euro-dollar credit. The former, however, is a demand for *holding a stock of money*, whereas the latter is a supply

---

(4) The traditional terminology of monetary theory may be charged with inconsistency in its use of supply and demand for stocks of money. The *supply* of money is understood as a given stock without reference to the intentions which individual decision-makers are assumed to have with regard to supplying anything or supplying more of it or less. The *demand* for money, on the other hand, is understood as an aggregation of the amounts of cash balances which it is assumed the millions of households and firms would want to hold at various levels of prices of goods, services, and securities. The entire stock of money in existence is, of course, held by all individuals and firms together, but some of them may feel that they are holding as an average cash balance a little more (or a little less) than they would like to go on holding at given prices, transactions, incomes, and recurring expenditures. Thus, the aggregate amounts of money balances demanded may be larger (or smaller) than the amounts "supplied" (actually held) and this excess (or shortfall) would express itself in increased (or reduced) disbursements which would pull up (or depress) prices to higher (or lower) levels than those prevailing at the moment.

If there are alternative forms of holding cash — for example, bank notes, check-deposits or time deposits, in domestic banks or in foreign banks, denominated in domestic money or in foreign money — the demand for each particular money will be a more complicated function involving alternative benefits and opportunity costs. This is one of the difficulties surrounding the notion of the demand for Euro-dollar balances.

228

EURO-DOLLAR CREATION

of *credit* on a day, a *flow* of funds per period. This supply of credit does not originate from those who have a demand for money balances, as analysts seem to assume. Some of the statistical investigations of the " Euro-dollar market " look into the " sources " of funds by classifying the holders of Euro-dollars deposit claims. To be sure, the fact that there are people willing to hold deposit claims makes it possible for banks to supply loans which they could not supply otherwise; however, holders of the deposits need not have been the suppliers of the funds that have been or are being offered to borrowers. If banks find that they are able to extend Euro-dollar loans and if the borrowers use the funds obtained for payments that initiate chains of transactions leading to an increased demand for working balances in Euro-dollars, the eventual holders of the enlarged balances are surely not those who have supplied credit. Their deposits should, therefore, not be regarded as the " sources of funds lent out " in the Euro-dollar credit market (5).

These propositions need not apply to Euro-dollar deposit claims by banks. Bank claims against other banks may well be the result of the depositor bank having transferred existing funds to the bank that has borrowed.

Redepositing

For years I have been puzzled by the assertion that " redepositing " was playing a great role in the increase of Euro-dollar deposits. Some writers used this term in connection with the catchword " pyramiding of deposits ". Both these expressions call forth an association with the theory of multiple credit creation. This theory,

---

(5) The proposition that the holders of bank deposits need not have been the suppliers of funds offered to borrowers can be made plausible by a simple analogy. Assume that a gang of forgers of currency notes disposes of them by loans to all sorts of borrowers. The notes are spent by the borrowers and continue to circulate without anybody discovering the forgery. The notes will have become part of the cash balances held by individuals and corporations. These holders of the forged notes are surely not the same people as those who supplied initially the funds for the loans.

Sources-and-uses-of-funds analyses can be very enlightening for individual firms and individual banks, though even there the findings will differ according to the period chosen. For the economy as a whole or a large sector of it, over a period in which the money stock has increased, such analyses can be misleading if the words are given their literal meaning.

229

FRITZ MACHLUP

as the reader hardly needs to be reminded of, holds that drawings on check deposits will not reduce either the total of deposit liabilities of all banks taken together or the total of their reserves as long as the recipients of checks or cash currency *redeposit* with banks of the same group or system; as a result all banks in the system, moving approximately in step with one another, can extend additional loans without losing reserves. The " pyramid " was an analogy for the increasing extension of deposits " based " on a given foundation of reserves.

I have at last found out that this was not the notion of redepositing and pyramiding which the writers on Euro-dollars had in their minds. In what they meant to convey no pyramiding was involved at all, and the redepositing was neither by the depositors nor by their payees nor by any subsequent payees, but rather by the European banks which had received dollars and were placing them with other banks in other countries in Europe or Asia. To illustrate, let us assume that Mr. X of Kuwait has deposited U.S. dollars with a London bank, which has re-lent them to a bank in Milan, which in turn has re-lent them to a bank in Zurich, which in turn has lent them to a nonbank customer, Mr. Y, in Brazil, who has used them to buy Euro-bonds. The chain of relending will have left its trace in a statistics of dollar assets and liabilities: the London bank has a claim against the Italian bank and a deposit liability to the resident of the Middle East; the Italian bank has a claim against the Swiss bank and a deposit liability to the London bank; and the Swiss bank has a claim against its nonbank customer in Brazil and a deposit liability to the Italian bank. The three banks may be regarded as intermediaries between Messrs X and Y; the spread between the interest rate paid by Y and the rate received by X was divided among the three banks. From the point of view of economics the jump in Euro-dollar deposits as a result of the multiple intermediation is not a significant development; it is merely a matter of statistics, and of low relevance at that. Interbank deposits, even if the banks are in different countries, ought to be reported separately from deposit liabilities to nonbank customers.

The desirability of reporting Euro-dollar deposits net of interbank deposits was soon recognized. Interbank deposits were " netted out " not only within each country but, quite properly, also within the eight reporting European countries regarded as the " inside area "; but they are still counted in the statistics of the " Euro-

230

EURO-DOLLAR CREATION

currency market " if the deposit liabilities are to, and the deposit claims held by, banks in the " outside area ", that is, banks located in countries other than the eight reporting European countries (6).

Euro-Dollars and Federal Funds

One often hears that the Euro-dollar market is " like the Federal Funds market ". There are, of course, similarities, but also essential differences; the analogy may mislead more than help those who try to understand the Euro-dollar system.

The major similarity is that a New York bank seeking in a hurry to increase its reserve with the Fed (Federal Reserve Bank) may borrow from another bank either in the United States or in Europe. In either case the borrowing bank acquires reserves which another American bank loses. In one case the lending bank gives up some of its reserves because it has more than it needs at the moment. In the other case the bank losing reserves does not give them up intentionally but rather because it is drawn upon by a European bank which has an account with it and has lent dollars to the borrowing bank or to a European branch of the borrowing bank.

Another similarity is that both the Federal Funds market and the Euro-dollar market are highly competitive. The banks that wish to borrow in these markets have to offer competitive rates. This does not mean that the rates will be the same. That Federal Funds and Euro-dollars are substitutes for some larger American banks in need of reserves means only that a rise in the interest rate for Federal Funds may induce some of these banks, especially those with European branches, to tap the Euro-dollar market.

The dissimilarities between the two markets are quite significant. The Federal Funds market is exclusively national in that lenders as well as borrowers are residents of the United States (though this includes New York agencies of foreign banks); the Euro-dollar market is essentially international, with the contracting parties more often than not residing in different countries. The Federal Funds

---

(6) These are United Kingdom, France, Italy, Switzerland, Belgium, Western Germany, Netherlands, and Sweden, listed in the order of their banks' short-term liabilities denominated in dollars in December 1969.

231

FRITZ MACHLUP

market consists chiefly of American banks, both as lenders and as borrowers, but also of dealers in government securities and some Federal agencies; the parties in the Euro-dollar market include virtually all types of people and institutions: individuals, small businesses, large corporations (nonfinancial as well as financial), commercial banks, investment bankers, central banks, government agencies, insurance companies, mutual funds, international corporations, international organizations.

The typical maturities of the loans in the two markets are very different. In the Federal Funds market the largest part of the lending is over night, with only smaller portions of day-to-day or demand obligations and loans with specified maturities of less than 15 days and some also a little longer (chiefly to dealers in government securities). In the Euro-dollar market as much as three-fourths of the loans are on terms between several days and six months. Even interbank loans — for example, the liabilities of American banks to their foreign branches — are for longer periods than those prevailing in the Federal Funds market.

The most significant differences, however, concern the effects of the operations in the two markets, especially the effects on total reserves of American banks with the Fed, on required reserves with the Fed, and on total deposit liabilities of the banks lending or borrowing.

The Federal Reserve Banks can control the total of their liabilities by controlling the total of their assets. The largest part of their liabilities are the reserves of American banks. No amount of interbank borrowing in the Federal Funds market can affect the size of these reserves; they merely change hands. This holds in principle with regard to the Euro-dollar market, as long as the lending and borrowing is limited to nonofficial parties and no foreign central bank gets into the action. Borrowing by American banks from European banks merely transfers to the borrowing banks some of the reserves of those other American banks with which the lending European banks hold their American dollar balances. However, some of the lending banks or their debtors in Europe may meet their payments by buying from a European central bank dollars which the central bank has held with the Federal Reserve Bank of New York rather than (as more usual) with a commercial bank in New York. In this case, foreign official liabilities of the Fed are transformed into liabilities to domestic banks, and

232

EURO-DOLLAR CREATION

total bank reserves with the Fed are thus increased. It is well known that certain European central banks occasionally have placed in the Euro-dollar market substantial amounts out of their dollar holdings and have thereby financed some of the loans to American banks. Indeed, there have been times when central banks used the official swap arrangements — the " central-bank-swap network " — to borrow from the Federal Reserve the dollars with which they financed the outflow caused by the lending by European to American banks. In such instances, the American borrowing in the Euro-dollar market did, though indirectly, produce an increase of the banks' total reserves with the Fed.

The effects on required reserves may also be different. Lending and borrowing among American banks leave required reserves unchanged since any resulting interbank deposits are not subject to reserve requirements. When American banks, however, borrowed in the Euro-dollar market and the resulting debts took the form of nondeposit liabilities, especially to their own overseas branches, these liabilities were (before August 1969) not subject to reserve requirements; at the same time, the corresponding banks of the European lenders found their foreign deposit liabilities, and consequently their required reserves, reduced. The net effect was a reduction of total required reserves. The new reserve requirements, imposed in August 1969, on increases in liabilities to overseas branches changed this situation, which had prevailed throughout the period of rapid increase in American borrowing, 1966 to 1969.

The effects which the activities in the two markets have on total deposit liabilities are most unlike, unless considerations are confined to operations induced by American borrowing. The statements asserting that the Euro-dollar market is " like the Federal Funds market " were perhaps meant to refer only to loans taken by American banks. However, if they are understood to refer to the bulk of all operations, one must point out that the activities in the Euro-dollar market are likely to lead to large and lasting increases in total deposit liabilities of the banks involved, whereas activities in the Federal Funds market do not as a rule have this effect. The lending and borrowing of Euro-dollars has resulted in a growth of dollar deposit liabilities of European banks that has astounded most observers and alarmed many. No such growth of deposit liabilities of American banks can be attributed to the working

233

FRITZ MACHLUP

of the Federal Funds market (7). The difference is probably due to the fact that the Federal Funds market is a market, and only a market, whereas the Euro-dollar market is a part of a much more complex system. The lending and borrowing that has taken place in the Federal Funds market, say, in 1968 and 1969, has not resulted in any lasting increase in the stock of money or near-money held by anybody. The activities that have taken place in these years in the Euro-dollar market have had such results.

Euro-Dollars and Nonmember-Bank Deposits

Having found one proposed analogy rather unhelpful, I may propose an analogy that fits the Euro-dollar system much better, though by no means perfectly: The system of nonmember banks in the United States has certain rather important features in common with the Euro-dollar system.

One of the features they have in common is that the banks in both systems use deposit balances with member banks of the Federal Reserve System as primary reserves, without themselves being subject to control by the Fed. Both the Euro-dollar system and the American nonmember-bank system are, so to speak, additional layers in the "pyramid" of dollar deposits.

The "pyramid" metaphor has long been used in explaining the structure of the monetary system of the United States. Gold certificates and other obligations of the U.S. Government serve as reserves for the mutual settlements among the Federal Reserve Banks; deposit liabilities of the Federal Reserve Banks serve as reserves for the member banks; deposit liabilities of the member banks serve as primary cash reserves of nonmember banks; and deposit liabilities of nonmember banks are part of the money stock in circulation. (The simile of the inverted pyramid gives a poor description of this structure since its top floor is much narrower than the third floor). Now, like the American nonmember banks, the European banks that are active in the Euro-dollar business use deposit liabilities (and perhaps also nondeposit liabilities) of member

---

(7) A qualification is needed: as banks with relatively less opportunities to expand their loans lend some of their excess reserves to relatively more expansive banks, total creation of credit and deposit money is accelerated.

234

EURO-DOLLAR CREATION

banks as primary reserves against their own dollar liabilities. (To continue using the metaphor, the Euro-banks share the fourth floor with the American nonmember banks).

Deposit balances with the Federal Reserve Banks are often regarded as high-powered money, because they function as " basis " for the low-powered money issued by the member banks. To the extent that the latter becomes again a " basis " for liquid bank liabilities, it assumes the character of another layer of high-powered money. That is to say, in the hands of nonbanks, deposit balances with member banks are low-powered money; however, as cash reserves for American nonmember banks and for European banks engaging in Euro-dollar deposit banking, the deposit balances with member banks are high-powered money giving rise to additional supplies of deposit liabilities by the nonmember and Euro-banks.

This similarity between American and European nonmember banks may help demonstrate the capacity of the Euro-dollar system to increase the stock of dollars. No one doubts that the nonmember banks create additional dollars in the United States. Any payment from a depositor of a member bank to a depositor of a nonmember bank transforms the cash balance of the payor into a reserve balance of the payee's nonmember bank, which may serve as the basis for loans by the latter as long as the stream of payments is not reversed. Likewise, any payment from a depositor of an American bank to a depositor of a Euro-bank transforms the cash balance of the payor into a reserve balance of the payee's European bank, which may serve as the basis for dollar loans by the latter as long as the stream of payments is not reversed (8).

The deposit liabilities of the commercial nonmember banks in the United States are part of the U.S. money stock. The dollar deposit liabilities of the European banks, on the other hand, are not included in any statistics of the money stock of any country. Yet, if they are regarded as money assets by their holders, they probably

---

(8) One of my critical readers has offered the following interesting comment: " The analogy between American and European nonmember banks could be carried further: they both have interest-bearing time deposits, and the stream of payments that allows credit creation to go on includes payments from money holders to the banks to acquire interest-bearing deposits. The analogy breaks down on the matter of what proportion of total deposits are interest-bearing time deposits ".

Another of my critics has commented on differences in the ways in which checks of American and European nonmember banks are cleared. Such differences, I believe, would not destroy the heuristic value of the analogy.

235

FRITZ MACHLUP

should be included, though one would have to decide to which country's money stock they ought to be added: to that of the country in which the holder of the deposit claim resides, to that of the country in which the bank or bank branch is located, or to that of the country in whose currency the deposit balance is denominated. If dollar notes, issued by a Federal Reserve Bank, circulate abroad, they are still counted among the money stock of the United States. This is unavoidable because it is not known in what amounts and in which countries these bank notes are held. If dollar deposits are owed by foreign banks and owned by foreign residents, this is ascertainable and it seems obvious that they are not part of the money circulation of the United States. It would probably be most reasonable to count these balances among the money stock of the depositor's country. As it is, they are completely left out; as " stateless " money they escape national enumeration by the monetary census takers.

Primary and Derivative Deposits

The genesis of Euro-dollar deposits is as difficult to ascertain as that of deposits in commercial banks in general. For most of the 19th and the first third of the 20th century, bankers believed that deposits came into existence only by people depositing currency (bank notes and coins) and that the banks were able to make loans only thanks to the reserves received, which they had to pay out again to the borrowers or their payees. When an economist occasionally attempted to enlighten the bankers by pointing to the fact that the total of their deposit liabilities had grown to a multiple of currency in circulation, they replied that this had been due to a chain of acts of saving and depositing the currency by the people and of lending and paying it out again by the banks; they thought that all deposits had been " primary " and all lending had been possible only to the extent to which primary deposits had been received. I suspect that the stubborn rejection of the theory of money creation by commercial banks was overcome eventually thanks to the spread of university education. Those who learned the theory before they became practical bankers found it easier to grasp and accept. Today the power of the commercial banks as a group to create additional deposits by granting additional credit is no longer questioned.

236

EURO-DOLLAR CREATION

That this power should extend to the creation of credit and deposits denominated in foreign currency is a novel thought, which is again resisted by most practitioners. Just as most bankers fifty years ago indignantly rejected the insinuation that they were fabricating domestic money, most bankers in the Euro-dollar system today cannot bear the thought that they are able to fabricate, and are in fact fabricating, foreign money. How could one believe that honest bankers in London, Zurich, Frankfurt, and Milan were busy creating U.S. dollars? A preposterous idea close to malicious libel — except for those who have thought it through in a class room, rather than in the board room of a bank.

A few monetary theorists have been impressed by the denial of dollar creation on the part of respected members of the Euro-banking community. For several years academic commentators on the Euro-dollar system have been engaged in a controversy about the causes of the growth of Euro-dollar deposits, some attributing all or most of it to credit creation, others denying that any credit creation has been involved, and a third group in the middle accepting the hypothesis in principle but arguing that only a very small part of the growth has been the Euro-banks' own creation.

The old distinction between primary and derivative deposits has disappeared from most textbooks in monetary theory, perhaps because the process of credit creation is now more generally understood without the help of these concepts. The distinction should perhaps be revived now that the process of Euro-dollar creation is being questioned. A primary deposit is one that increases at the same time the total deposit liabilities and the total cash reserves of the group of banks under consideration. A derivative deposit is one that owes its existence to a simultaneous or preceding extension of the loan-and-securities portfolio of any banks in the group (country, region, or system); it increases the total deposit liabilities but not the total cash reserves of the group.

If a holder of a demand or time deposit in New York transfers it to a dollar account with a bank in Europe, or makes a payment to a holder of a dollar account with a bank in Europe, both the dollar deposit liabilities and the dollar cash reserves of the European banks will be increased. The increase is therefore regarded as due to a primary deposit. If the Euro-bank with its newly acquired dollar cash reserve extends a dollar loan, it is possible that the borrower and those to whom he pays, and those to whom they

237

FRITZ MACHLUP

pay, keep some or all of their receipts on dollar accounts with some banks in Europe. In this case some or all of the dollar cash reserves of the European banks as a group remain in their possession, and the net increase of their total dollar liabilities will have to be attributed to the dollar loan extended. This second increase in dollar deposit liabilities of European banks will be regarded as derivative.

It is unquestioned that a European bank, paying high interest rates on its dollar deposit liabilities, will not keep unnecessarily large amounts of dollar cash reserves on hand; it will want to use them to acquire assets earning higher yields, preferably short-term dollar claims. As long as the dollar cash reserves stay within the system as the borrowers and their subsequent payees prefer to keep dollar balances with European banks, additional Euro-dollar loans will be extended by each of the banks receiving the deposits derived from the loans made by other banks within the system. The process of additional credit creation may continue for several intra-system transfers of the cash reserve, or it may end after one or two banks, or it may not even get started. If the very first loan, granted by the bank that received the primary deposit, goes to a borrower outside the system, say, an American bank, there will not even be a " second " deposit. However, if it goes to a corporation doing business in both Europe and overseas, the chances are high that a sequence of additional Euro-dollar loans will be engendered.

Thus, it is possible that there has been a substantial amount of dollar creation by banks in Europe; but it is also possible that Euro-dollar creation by Euro-banks has been responsible for only a *small* portion of the growth of Euro-dollar deposit liabilities. Available statistics, unfortunately, cannot decide this controversial question, for reasons which will be explained later. Inquiries of bankers are useless, because bankers cannot know whether deposits received derive from the lending activities of other banks; after all, their depositors do not know whether the dollar checks they deposit have been received from payors who had obtained dollar loans from Europeans banks. Practically all deposits look to the banker like primary deposits, even when they are indirectly offshoots of his own loans to other customers. This extreme case, however, of a borrower making payments to other customers of the same bank need never occur: each borrower may make payments to firms keeping their deposit balances with other banks, and all banks may

238

EURO-DOLLAR CREATION

experience a growth in what they believe to be primary deposits but what in fact are deposits derived from loans by any of the banks in the group or system.

Statistical evidence could prove at best the complete negation of the hypothesis of dollar creation by European banks, namely, if all dollar assets held by these banks were in the form of perfectly liquid claims against New York banks and no dollar loans to European borrowers were outstanding, so that the dollar deposit liabilities of European banks would be covered 100 per cent by demand-deposit balances with New York. Since this is definitely not the case, a statistical disproof of the credit-creation hypothesis is excluded.

How large are in fact the dollar cash reserves which banks in Europe are keeping as a proportion of their dollar liabilities? We have been told of ratios as low as 3 per cent, but we do not know precisely what was compared with what. We know that the European branches of American banks hold what they consider "perfectly liquid" claims against their head offices in amounts between $12,000 million and $14,000 million; however, these are interest-bearing claims, largely in the nature of short-term or even call loans, not demand-deposit balances. Whether one may regard these dollar assets as cash reserves is not easy to decide.

No matter, however, whether the ratio of dollar cash reserves to dollar deposit liabilities of Euro-banks is high or low, the fact that the total of deposit liabilities is a multiple of the cash reserves is no positive proof of the hypothesis of credit creation. *Any* ratio may be consistent with the old cloak-room theory, according to which banks can never lend more than they have received as primary deposits. A statistical "reserve multiplier" is no evidence for a positive credit multiplier.

The Reserve Ratio as the Inverse of a Multiplier

The required or self-imposed reserve ratio of commercial banks — the ratio of cash reserves to deposit liabilities — determines the upper limit of bank-credit creation. With a reserve ratio of 20 per cent (or 1/5) of the banks' deposit liabilities, these liabilities can grow only to 5 times cash reserves; with a ratio of 3 per cent (or 1/33) of deposits, the growth limit is 33 times reserves. A naive

239

FRITZ MACHLUP

interpretation would suggest that the banks as a group can create additional deposits — additional to the primary ones — in amounts 4 times or 32 times, respectively, the deposits originally received, and that they have in fact done so when these reserve ratios actually obtain.

This potential creation of additional bank credit presupposes, however, that the banks as a group do not lose any of their combined cash reserves as a result of the extension of their loans. This would mean, in the Euro-dollar system, that all borrowers were using the borrowed funds for payments to persons who keep their accounts in dollars with banks of the same group and who in turn make payments to others who hold dollar deposit balances with the same group of banks. Any net payments to "outsiders" — to individuals or firms who hold their money balances in another form — encroach on the cash reserves of the group or system of Euro-banks. Yet, while such outflows will lower the growth limit of deposits created by loans, it need not reduce the statistical ratio of reserves to deposits. For it is an arithmetically trivial fact that the same ratio can be the outcome of an increase in deposits or of a decrease in reserves.

Assume that U.S. $100 million are received by banks in London (or any other European place) as primary deposits, perhaps from corporations that are transferring their own dollar balances from New York, or from some who have received dollars in payment for goods or securities sold in the United States, or from some who are converting other currencies into dollars. The banks obtaining these primary deposits will surely not keep a dollar cash reserve of 100 per cent against their dollar deposit liabilities and will, accordingly, proceed to make dollar loans. If the borrowers or their payees use the funds to make dollar payments to the United States or to convert the dollars into other currencies, the lending banks — not only individually but collectively as a group — will find their dollar cash reserves reduced by the amounts of these out-payments. Their loans, therefore, will not add to the dollar deposit liabilities of the Euro-dollar banking system but, instead, deplete their dollar cash balances with the New York banks. If the Euro-dollar loans are used entirely for out-payments of the sort mentioned, the dollar cash reserves may go down to $20, 10 or 3 million, depending on what fractional reserve is regarded as the minimum required. The eventually attained reserve ratio would be the inverse

240

EURO-DOLLAR CREATION

of a statistical multiplier, but not of a multiplier indicating a process of credit creation.

If every dollar loan by European banks or branches during the past ten years had been at the expense of dollar cash reserves, it would be difficult to explain the rapid increase in Euro-dollar deposits, but it would not be impossible. With some strain of the imagination, it is conceivable that all or most Euro-dollar balances have been primary deposits, and none or only insignificant amounts have been derived from the Euro-dollar loans extended by European banks. The available statistical evidence does not rule out this interpretation, but to make it plausible one would need some positive evidence that the net transfers of balances from American to European banks and other dollars supplied to European banks from certain items of the payments deficit of the United States in any particular year came close in magnitude to that year's increase in Euro-dollar deposits.

There is a question whether conversions of nondollar reserves and nondollar deposit liabilities into dollar reserves and dollar liabilities, respectively, should be regarded as increases in primary dollar deposits. The answer is affirmative at best regarding *existing* nondollar deposit liabilities: if their owners convert them into dollars so that both nondollar deposits and nondollar reserves are transformed into dollars by purchases from central banks, one can say that no dollar credit creation has taken place. However, if the conversion is initiated by banks, swapping some of their reserves in domestic money against dollars offered by the central bank, this transformation of cash reserves does not by itself create dollar deposit liabilities. Any subsequent increase in such liabilities can only be the result of dollar loans made by the banks as they utilize their increased dollar-lending capacity.

To some extent, even the strict cloak-room theory of bank lending cannot deny that the world supply of loans and the total amount of deposit balances are increased by the Euro-banks loaning-out most of the dollars received through primary deposits. If $1,000 million are transferred by depositors from banks in New York to banks in Europe, the former as a group will not lose any reserves and will have no change in total liabilities. (Before August 1969 their lending capacity may even have increased as a result of the transfer, because some of it may have been from deposit liabilities subject to reserve requirements to liabilities to their own branches

241

FRITZ MACHLUP

abroad, which until that time were not subject to reserve requirements). The European banks, receiving new dollar cash reserves of $1,000 million against an equal amount of deposit liabilities find their lending capacity increased even if they count on losing a dollar of cash for each dollar lent. (Whether they will loan out the full $1,000 million or only less will depend on the dollar cash-reserve ratio which they want to maintain. The maturities of their loans will depend on whether the new liabilities are on demand or time deposit. But the fact that they will supply additional short loans approaching the $1,000 received can hardly be denied). And all this without any of the additional credit creation assumed by some theorists and denied by most practitioners.

The Growing Preference for Euro-Dollars

No matter whether the bulk of Euro-dollars has been the European banks' own creation or has come from other sources, there must have been reasons for their owners to hold increasing amounts of them, and reasons for banks and nonbanks to place and seek Euro-dollar loans in preference to available alternatives. Many of the reasons derive from institutional practices, regulations, and restrictions.

As far as the holders of Euro-dollar deposits are concerned, the increase in their preference over holding either dollar balances (or dollar securities) in the United States or balances in their own currencies with their domestic banks is explainable chiefly by a combination of higher interest rates, lower transactions costs, greater convenience, and lower risks (exchange risks or risks of inconvertibility). Not all of these variables may have been operative all the time, and some may at times have had the opposite sign, reducing rather than increasing the attractiveness of holding Euro-dollars. That interest rates on dollar deposits in European banks have in recent years been higher than on dollar deposits in the United States and higher also than on domestic currency deposits in European banks is largely the result of regulations imposed by the authorities and of conventions agreed among the banks under cartel arrangements in several countries. Transactions costs, likewise, may be lower partly because certain regulations and conventions applying to residents' accounts do not apply to transactions by

242

EURO-DOLLAR CREATION

nonresidents and partly because conversion-and-reconversion costs between dollars and other currencies are kept high by official regulations and cartel arrangements among banks.

Among the reasons why some large American banks have preferred to accept funds through their European branches has long been the fact that their liabilities to their own foreign branches were free from the reserve requirements which they had to meet for deposit liabilities to individuals and corporations. (Reserve requirements work like a tax on deposit liabilities, since they imply holding a legal reserve that does not earn interest). An added reason for seeking loans through their European branches has been Regulation Q, which prevented American banks from paying competitive interest rates on time deposits (certificates of deposit) and thus caused them to lose large amounts of these deposits.

Among the reasons why some European banks prefer to seek funds denominated in dollars are their conventions and agreements with other banks in their countries designed to control and limit competition; the Euro-currency business is a clearly demarcated field in which competition can be allowed without leading to a breakdown of the cartel constraints on the rest of their banking business. Among the reasons why some European banks have preferred placing dollar loans have been, in several countries (especially Germany and Italy) attractive swap arrangements offered by their central banks which, by making dollars available in exchange for domestic bank reserves, reduced the banks' lending capacity in domestic money and increased their lending capacity in dollars. Limitations in some countries on interest rates charged on loans to residents have also increased the attractiveness of making loans in dollars or other foreign currencies.

It is probably an exaggeration to attribute the growing preference for dollar loans and dollar deposits in European banks *entirely* to interferences with free and unlimited competition and to the (sometimes very clumsy) attempts of monetary authorities to control the foreign-exchange and money markets. That the dollar has become the foremost international transactions currency, that the largest part of the rapidly expanding world trade is invoiced and paid for in dollars, that the capital and money markets of the United States are the largest in the world, and that the elasticities of supply and demand of dollars both in the exchange markets and in the money markets are much higher than those of any

243

FRITZ MACHLUP

other currency — these are facts that must weigh heavily in explanations of the growing use of the dollar in the banking business outside the United States.

It has been said that the dollar has become the most suitable currency for international transactions and thus the best money to hold by firms engaged in international transactions, and that the City of London has developed a system providing not only the lowest transactions cost but also payment of interest on all kinds of deposit balances. Thus, dollar transactions in London seem to be the ideal combination of currency and location — which may go a long way toward explaining why London banks, including the London branches of American banks, are the largest Euro-dollar depositories. These advantages may explain a more or less steady growth of Euro-dollar deposits along with the growth of world trade and international capital movements. However, they can hardly explain the explosive increase of Euro-dollar deposits at certain times, especially in the first half of 1969. The causes for an upsurge of this sort can probably be found in the artificial conditions which were produced by the control devices of the authorities and the conventions among the banks and became " acute " in particular situations.

A certain part of the 1969 explosion of Euro-dollar lending and borrowing — though it was not a large part — was the combined result of the low ceiling rate which American banks under Regulation Q could pay on time certificates of deposit (C/D's) and the high interest rates produced by the restrictive monetary policy of the Federal Reserve. When market rates of interest rose above the maximum 6-1/4 per cent which banks were allowed to pay on time deposits, some holders of C/D's let them run off and transferred their dollars to European banks (and indirectly to European branches of American banks), which were paying much higher rates, at times as much as twice the C/D rate in the United States. These transfers of dollar deposits gave the European banks demand deposits with New York banks, which they promptly " lent " to those of the American banks that were borrowing in the Euro-dollar market. The Euro-banks were paying competitive interest rates to their dollar depositors and charging competitive interest rates on their loans to American banks. The change in the position of the American banks was concentrated on the liability side of their balance sheets: a switch from deposit liabilities owed

244

EURO-DOLLAR CREATION

to nonbanks at low interest rates to liabilities owed to banks in Europe at high interest rates.

This call for a " change of partners " in a silly square dance was almost entirely a matter of regulation by the authorities. It involved decisions and actions by many thousands of people; it helped some of the largest cash holders to avoid losing the high yields earned on liquid funds; it deprived smaller cash holders of the chance of earning competitive rates on their holdings, since they could not avail themselves of the roundabout way of avoiding the effects of the regulation. Unnecessary transactions cost, unproductive uses of resources, and discrimination against owners of small bank deposits are among the consequences of the regulation of interest rates on bank deposits.

The Change of Partners

The case of " change of partners " is interesting because it illustrates several cause-and-effect relationships in what I have called a " square dance " and others have called a " merry-go-round " or " dollar round trip ". In actual fact the case was not very important quantitatively: according to the reported statistics, the withdrawals of time deposits from American banks and placements of these dollars with European banks was, in 1969, not much more than one-fourth of the dollars which American banks borrowed from European banks, chiefly from their own branches.

Moreover, instead of saying that the American banks borrowed dollars in Europe because they were losing dollars to depositors withdrawing their time deposits, one may with equal justification say that the American banks' borrowing in Europe were bidding up interest rates for Euro-dollars so much that owners of time deposits with American banks found the temptation of the higher earnings irresistable and tansferred their dollars to Europe. In other words, the round-trip did not always start with the eastbound voyage, but often with the westbound one.

Finally, most of these voyages are made by telecommunication rather than air transportation, so that the return trip may be simultaneous with the outward journey. The trouble with observation of rapid movements is that the observer gets a blurred picture. Only a slow-motion sketch can help him to see and analyse the

245

FRITZ MACHLUP

process — and many of those who have watched the "real" show will protest that the slow sequence with intervals between single steps is unrealistic. Just as a slow-motion film can show a hurdler stop motionless in mid-air, a slow-motion sequence will make a banker hold a non-earning demand deposit much longer than any real banker ever would.

Let us then trace, in slow-motion technique and in bookkeeper's language, the steps in an eastbound transfer of dollars hitherto kept on time deposit with banks in New York, and then the steps in a westbound transfer of Euro-dollar lent to banks in New York; whereby we make the stipulation that neither the Federal Reserve Banks nor any central banks in Europe get into the act. (We shall later make different stipulations in order to see different effects).

Holders (residents or nonresidents) of time deposits in New York, letting their certificates of deposit run off, deposit the proceeds with banks in Europe. The latter will now have demand-deposit balances in New York. An imaginary consolidated balance sheet of the American banks will show a reduction of their time-deposit liabilities to private nonbank residents and nonresidents and an increase of demand-deposit liabilities to foreign banks; hence, no change in assets and only a change in the composition of liabilities. An imaginary consolidated balance sheet of the European banks will show an increase in dollar demand-deposit claims against New York banks and an equal increase in dollar time-deposit liabilities to nonbank nonresidents.

The European banks with their increased dollar cash reserves on deposit with their correspondent banks in New York will be eager to place them in the loans market. Some American banks will have lost reserve balances with the Fed to those other American banks which have the accounts of the European banks. The reserve losers could, in the Federal Funds market, borrow directly from the reserve gainers; or they could obtain the needed reserve balances by selling securities; or they could take the Euro-dollar loans offered by the European banks and thus, indirectly, get back the reserve balances which the New York correspondents of the European banks have gained from them. If this last alternative is chosen, the situation will look as follows: The American banks will have no change whatsoever in their assets and only a change in the composition of their liabilities, in that what originally were time-deposit liabilities to nonbank residents and nonresidents (and then,

246

EURO-DOLLAR CREATION

for a moment, were demand-deposit liabilities to foreign banks) are now nondeposit liabilities to foreign banks, including their own branches. The foreign banks will have maintained the increased amount of their dollar time-deposit liabilities to nonbank non-residents but will have transformed their momentary holdings of demand-deposit claims into short-term nondeposit claims against American banks. (The consolidated balance sheets have, of course, netted-out all interbank deposits).

The end-results of the complete round trip are, for the American banks, only the change of partners together with a change in the maturities of obligations; for the European banks, an increase in dollar assets — their loans to American banks — and an increase in dollar liabilities. Noteworthy, however, is that this increase is the result of the capital movement from the United States to Europe, and *not* of the return trip of the dollars, *not* of the Euro-dollar borrowing by American banks.

And what are the effects upon the balance of payments of the United States? The outflow of private capital of resident owners of deposits from the United States is a deficit item on capital account, financed by an increase in liquid liabilities to foreign banks; hence, a deficit on " liquidity basis ". This deficit is neither increased nor reduced by the American borrowing in the Euro-dollar market. To the extent that nonresidents withdrew time-deposit balances from American banks, the transactions were entered " below the line " as reductions in liquid liabilities to nonofficial foreigners, just like the offsetting increases in liquid liabilities to the foreign banks which received their deposits; hence, neither the withdrawal by nonresident depositors nor the subsequent borrowing by American from European banks affected the balance of payments of the United States.

Central Banks Joining the Act

The stipulation in the foregoing sketch was that no central bank gets into the act. This was not a severe restriction on the generality of the results, because under the circumstances assumed there was no reason for any intervention by any central bank. The Federal Reserve evidently did not want to increase the reserve balances of the member banks; and the European central banks were not faced

247

FRITZ MACHLUP

with either an excess supply of dollars or an excess demand in the foreign-exchange market. However, we now want to see the effects of central-bank intervention. In order to make it sensible, we assume that American banks, with domestic lending opportunities exceeding their lending capacity, want to borrow from European banks, including their own branches, more dollars than are being withdrawn from their time-deposit liabilities to nonbank residents and nonresidents. In other words, the westbound traffic is much heavier than it would be if only dollars with return tickets were going home.

European central banks may have various reasons for supplying dollars out of their reserves to the Euro-dollar market. For example, they may not like the interest rate for Euro-dollars to rise too high under the impact of the American demand for loans; they may not want to see the exchange rate of the dollar rise, as it might if banks or private owners of domestic currencies were seeking dollars to take advantage of the higher interest rates; they may have accumulated large amounts of dollars which they would be glad to dispose of, to place with more attractive yields, or perhaps to " hide " by swapping them out of their portfolio into the portfolios of commercial banks; or they may want to mop up some excessive domestic liquidity, which their previous purchases of dollars may have created. Any one of the reasons may induce them to sell dollars outright or temporarily through swaps with commercial banks (sales with repurchase agreements).

The immediate effects on the balance sheets of the European banks are reductions of cash reserves in domestic currency and increases in demand-deposit claims against American banks. The effects on the balance sheets of the American banks depend on the form in which the central banks have been holding the dollars. If the dollars have been deposit claims against commercial banks in the United States, we see a simple switch from American deposit liabilities to official foreign holders to deposit liabilities to foreign banks. If the dollars in the reserves of the central banks have been claims against the Federal Reserve Bank of New York, the American banks will now be the holders of these claims, that is, they will have obtained increased reserve balances with the Fed (not, however, through their borrowing in Europe but as a result of the sales by central banks to commercial banks in Europe). If the dollars held by the central banks have been U.S. Treasury notes or bills which they liquidate when they intervene in the market, we must ask who

248

EURO-DOLLAR CREATION

has bought the Treasury securities; if the Fed bought them, the member banks obtained additional reserve balances as in the case just mentioned; if American nonbank residents bought them, the member banks' deposit liabilities to residents are reduced by the same amount by which their deposit liabilities to foreign banks are increased. (We need not consider the case of the member banks buying the Treasury securities, because we have assumed that the banks were seeking additional liquidity and thus not prepared to buy securities).

In our slow-motion sketch of the process we have stopped the sequence with the sale of dollars by central banks to commercial banks in Europe, and have not yet come to the Euro-dollar lending to American banks. We may hold this position a little longer to consider the effects these dollar sales have on the balance of payments of the United States. In all four cases, liquid liabilities (assuming that the Treasury securities had maturities of one year or less) to official foreign holders were transformed into liquid liabilities to foreign banks. Hence, the liquidity balance of payments was unchanged, and the official-settlements balance was improved as a result of the sale of dollars out of official reserves to commercial banks (including branches of American banks) in Europe.

Now at last we allow the sketch to proceed to the next step: European banks lend to American banks the dollars they have acquired from their central banks. This merely transforms dollar demand-deposit claims of European banks into nondeposit claims against American banks; or, from the American point of view, demand-deposit liabilities into nondeposit liabilities to European banks. Thus, the actual borrowing by the American banks in Europe causes no change in their reserve balances or any other assets, and only a change in the composition and maturity of their liabilities; furthermore, it causes no further change in the balance of payments of the United States, either on liquidity basis or on official-settlements basis; and finally, it causes no increase and no decrease in Euro-dollar deposits in European banks (including the branches of American banks) provided interbank deposits are netted out and only balances owed to nonbank holders are counted.

The results of this analysis are different from those reported by the most experienced Dollar-Eurologists in the profession. If I may assume that my analysis is correct, what can have caused the

249

differences in our findings? I submit that most analysts have looked at too many things at the same time instead of isolating each process from all the other processes going on simultaneously. They have wanted to see everything at once and have thereby failed to sort things out neatly in clean and sterilized mental operations.

Cash Assets and Loans: An Information Gap

One of the most troublesome questions in Euro-dollar lending to American banks concerns the liquidity of these loans. The compilers of Euro-dollar statistics have provided no judgments regarding the liquidity of the dollar assets which banks and bank branches hold in the form of claims against American banks; the data do not separate demand-deposit claims, time-deposit claims, and non-deposit claims. Moreover, it ought to be made clear to what extent the transformation of dollar demand-deposit claims into dollar loans to large American banks involves a reduction in the liquidity position of the lending banks. When a bank in Europe makes a seven-day loan to the Chase or the First National City Bank, does it feel less liquid than if it had kept all its funds on demand deposit with its permanent correspondent bank in New York? When a large American bank takes a call loan from one of its European branches, will the latter treat this as a perfectly liquid claim, perhaps even a part of its cash reserve? This blurring of the borderline between cash assets and loans clouds both the statistical and the theoretical picture.

The application of monetary theory in statistical analysis of developments in banking in the United States is greatly helped by the availability of operational definitions of "legal" reserves of commercial banks. Years ago these reserves consisted only of deposit balances with the Federal Reserve; now U.S. currency is also included. Nothing else, not even demand-deposit balances with other American banks, can be counted as legal reserve. While a bank in a smaller city will perhaps treat its current-account balance with its correspondent banks in New York and Chicago as cash, and while any bank that has lent out some of its excess reserve over night in the Federal Funds market will for internal deliberations include this claim in its cash position, monetary analysts take their statistical data from the reports of the Federal Reserve Board, and

250

EURO-DOLLAR CREATION

these data are not affected by what any banks may regard as cash. The legal reserves, as reported in the official statistics on member banks of the Federal Reserve System, contain no deposit claims other than those against the Federal Reserve Banks and no loans whatsoever, however liquid.

The statistical data about the dollar assets of banks in Europe are not that pure. In some countries even the central bank lacks the information that would be needed for a clear analysis of the cash position of the commercial banks in the country. (I was told that the Swiss National Bank does not get all the data required for such an analysis — and Switzerland has been the largest net lender of dollars on short term among the eight countries in the Euro-currency system). For most countries we know at best total dollar assets, or short-term dollar assets, unclassified with respect to liquidity or maturity (9). If demand-deposit claims of Swiss banks against New York banks, call loans to banks in London, seven-day loans to banks in Milan, and 90-day loans to large corporations in Belgium are lumped together as short-term dollar claims against nonresidents, it becomes impossible to separate cash reserves and loans. The data compiled by the United States for its balance of payments allow statisticians to make somewhat finer distinctions than would be possible from the reports of the European banks, but a clear separation of the European banks' holdings of New York balances payable on demand from those other dollar claims into which these cash balances are transformed through the banks' loans and investments seems difficult, if not impossible, on the basis of available information (10).

What would be needed for a clean analysis are detailed reports classifying the dollar assets of European banks by country, and for each country by category of debtor (central government, provincial governments, central bank, commercial banks, other banks, other financial institutions, nonbank corporations, etc.) as well as by maturity (demand, over-night, weekend, seven days, and so forth).

---

(9) The *Bank of England Quarterly Bulletin*, Vol. 10 (No. 1, March 1970), pp. 31-49, contains a detailed breakdown of liabilities and claims in nonsterling currencies of banks in the United Kingdom, with the classifications asked for in the text.

(10) One authority on the subject wrote to me that the dollar assets reported by European banks included at best 1 per cent in the form of demand deposits with American banks; another, however, was willing to confer upon the claims of American bank branches in Europe against their head offices the designation of perfectly liquid dollar assets.

251

FRITZ MACHLUP

Similar classifications would be needed for dollar liabilities: by country, by category of creditor, and by maturity. Yet, even the most detailed breakdown by objective criteria would be insufficient for a full interpretation of the " moneyness " of the banks' liabilities in the eyes of their holders. This deficiency has long been known from American experience with gradual, but sometimes rapid, switches between time and demand deposits. Some theorists have long held out against the inclusion of certain more liquid types of time-deposit balances in the stock of money or near-money. The same resistance exists now with respect to the moneyness of Euro-dollar time deposits. Perhaps the resistance to their inclusion in the money supply is justified, but this is difficult to know. In order to find out, one would have to learn the motivations and expectations of the holders of these balances. Survey research could possibly provide answers, though any answer would be good only for the time of the inquiry and might be inapplicable a few months later.

In addition or in lieu of survey research of samples of depositors, we should have sample studies of dollar accounts held with several large banks in London and other European centers. We could find out what share of total dollar balances is on current account of more or less permanent customers showing considerable turnover and relatively stable or increasing maximum, minimum, and average balances; what share is in the nature of time deposits of stable groups of customers showing little turnover; and what share is on merely temporary deposits of transient customers. Other categories of deposit balances may also prove significant.

These types of information would be needed also for an educated estimate regarding the extent to which the Euro-dollar deposits now in existence may have been derived from credits extended by European banks. Only if there is a demand for Euro-dollar deposits to hold as money or near-money — for transactions, precautionary, or speculative purposes — can it be expected that Euro-dollars received in payment or obtained through loans or through conversion of other currencies will continue to be held as liquid balances. For only in this case can European banks create additional dollars through their own lending operations.

252

EURO-DOLLAR CREATION

Theoretical Propositions

No amount of data, however, can provide a conclusive answer to the question of the genesis of the growing amounts of Euro-dollar deposits unless we get a better theoretical understanding regarding the effects of various kinds of actions and transactions. Those who deny that there has been a good deal of multiple credit creation through the lending activities of the European banks must offer plausible alternative hypotheses and hints pointing to the sources of all those primary deposits that could have added up to the recorded total volume of existing Euro-dollar deposits. This presupposes that we are agreed on which kinds of transaction can and which cannot produce dollar deposit balances with European banks. Some analysts, however, who deny that bank credit creation has contributed much to the growth of Euro-dollar deposits deny also the quantitative importance of the very transactions that could have produced primary dollar deposits with European banks; and the transactions to which they attach great importance could not, as I see the working of the system, have produced any primary dollar deposits.

Several of the types of transactions in question are closely associated with effects on the reserve balances of American banks and on the balance of payments of the United States. I therefore propose to formulate a few propositions about the effects which various types of transactions have on all these scores. Some of my statements contradict the views of several of my fellow analysts. These statements should provide clear targets for their criticism, so that we may soon be able to straighten things out and disentangle some of the nests of confusion, theirs, mine, or ours. The propositions will refer to entire banking systems, not to individual banks; thus, when I say "European banks", I mean all of them taken as a group, and when I say "American banks" I likewise mean all of them combined in a consolidated balance sheet.

Proposition 1: Dollar deposit liabilities of European banks to nonbank depositors increase when the latter are credited on their dollar accounts for U.S. dollars deposited, which they may have (a) received in payment for exports of goods and services sold to residents of the United States, (b) received in payment for securities

253

FRITZ MACHLUP

sold to residents of the United States, or (c) withdrawn from their deposit balances with American banks. In all these cases the European banks receive dollar cash reserves, which they will try to use for acquiring earning assets (loans or securities) but which they must hold at least momentarily. Again in all three cases — except if the depositors are nonresidents of the United States who have withdrawn from American banks time deposits payable in less than one year — the increase in American liquid liabilities to nonofficial foreigners is financing deficit items on (a) current account, (b) long-term capital account, and (c) short-term capital account in the balance of payments of the United States. The American banks will have no reduction in their total reserve balances but only a redistribution of balances among individual banks, and no change in their total deposit liabilities but only changes in their composition (as foreign banks have taken the place of domestic or foreign individuals and corporations).

Proposition 2: Dollar deposit liabilities of European banks to nonbank depositors may or may not increase beyond the level reached as a result of the transactions described in Proposition 1. They will *not* increase further if American banks borrow from the European banks just the amounts of dollar cash reserves which the latter had obtained from the described transactions. These loans transform the dollar cash reserves of the European banks into interest-earning short-term nondeposit claims against American banks. They do *not* change total reserve balances of American banks, though they redistribute them again; they do *not* change the balance of payments of the United States either on liquidity basis or on official-settlements basis; and they do *not* change the total of Euro-dollar deposits of nonbank holders, though there may be much interbank lending with consequent increases in interbank deposits.

Proposition 3: Euro-dollar deposits of nonbank holders will be further increased, without any associated increase or reduction in total dollar cash reserves of Euro-banks, if these banks make dollar loans to nonbank residents of countries other than the United States who use them for payments to firms or persons keeping dollar deposits with banks or branches of banks within the eight European countries. As long as no payments are made to residents of countries

254

EURO-DOLLAR CREATION

other than this inside area, and the dollar balances are not converted into other currencies, and no loans are made to American banks, the dollar cash reserves continue to be held by a succession of different European banks (11).

Proposition 4: Dollar deposit liabilities of European banks to nonbank depositors will also increase when holders of nondollar balances convert them into dollars. The banks may execute such conversion by purchasing dollars from central banks, especially if they find lending dollars more attractive than loans in domestic currency. The switch of dollars from official to nonofficial holders leaves the balance of payments of the United States unchanged on liquidity basis but improves it on official-settlements basis. However, the conversion of nondollars into dollar balances on deposit with European banks need not be associated with purchases of dollars from central banks. In order to remove the short position in dollars created by the conversion of liabilities, the banks may gradually, in the process of renegotiations and renewals of loans, change their denomination from European currencies to dollars. Thus, it is possible that assets as well as liabilities are converted into dollars without anything changing in the positions of either European or American banks or in the balances of payments of any of the countries concerned.

Proposition 5: Most residents of the eight European countries receiving U.S. dollars in payment for (a) exports of goods and services to residents of the United States, (b) sales of securities to residents of the United States, and perhaps also (c) withdrawals from deposits held with American banks, sell their dollar proceeds for domestic currency. Some of the banks purchasing these dollars may find that they have better uses for dollars than for domestic reserve balances. If so, they will not resell the surplus of dollars acquired over dollars sold, as they normally would, to the central bank. The effects upon the balance of payments of the United States are exactly the same as stated in Proposition 1. Although the European banks are now ready to offer dollar loans, there is

---

(11) To illustrate: Euro-dollar loans may be made to purchasers of Euro-dollar bonds issued by large corporations which keep the proceeds from the bonds on interest-paying dollar accounts with European banks until they use them for payments for direct investments to payees who again hold dollar balances with European banks.

255

FRITZ MACHLUP

as yet no increase in Euro-dollar deposit liabilities to nonbank holders. Such an increase will not come about if all the dollar loans are made to American banks; it will come about if dollar loans are made to nonbank residents of the Euro-dollar countries, as described in Proposition 3.

Proposition 6: Euro-dollar deposits may also increase, together with dollar cash reserves of European banks, as a result of payments or of loans received from residents of countries other than the United States and the eight European countries. The payments may be for goods and services or for securities bought from residents of the Euro-banking area; alternatively, they may be liquid funds from residents in the outside area placed with the Euro-banks. These funds may come in various currencies to be converted into dollars in the foreign-exchange market of the inside area or they may arrive already as U.S. dollars. In the latter case the European banks merely take the place of residents of the outside area in holding dollar claims against Americans; if these residents of the outside area have been holders of less than perfectly liquid assets in U.S. dollars, their act of liquidating and depositing them with European banks constitutes an outflow of private short-term capital from the United States which is financed by an increase in liquid liabilities to nonofficial foreigners and is, therefore, a deficit item in the balance of payments on liquidity basis, but not on official-settlements basis. If the residents of the outside area have been holding dollars through banks located in their area, the liquid liabilities of the United States are merely moved into another geographic category and the balance of payments on any definition is not affected. If, however, the depositors from the outside area convert other currencies into dollars, it makes a difference whether the dollars are acquired from a central bank — which evidently acquired them in the process of financing a payments deficit of the United States some time in the *past* — or from private suppliers in the foreign-exchange market disposing of dollars received as part of the *current* payments deficit. In the first case the records will show no change on liquidity basis but an improvement on official-settlements basis; in the second case the depositing of the dollars with European banks, leading to an increase in liquid liabilities to nonofficial foreigners, will be the first record of the financing of the present payments deficit of the United States. One may say, however, that the purchase

256

EURO-DOLLAR CREATION

of these dollars for deposit with Euro-banks makes it unnecessary for the central bank to purchase them, and, hence, that it prevents the deterioration of the official settlements balance that would otherwise occur.

Creation of Euro-Dollars

Some of the propositions, which I offered for criticism and amendment by analysts with more insight, may be found to be false and others perhaps irrelevant. Assuming, however, that they are relevant and correct, we may ask whether they can help us to obtain an impression about the extent to which the growth of Euro-dollar deposits has been a result of multiple credit creation.

Propositions 1, 4, and 6 describe transactions resulting in an increase of Euro-dollar deposits that cannot be attributed to the dollar-lending activities of European banks and bank branches. This is perhaps a good way of distinguishing (in pure theorizing, not in statistical operations) between primary and derivative bank deposits: primary deposits would have come about also if no bank had been making any loans or investments. All other deposit balances are derivative, the result of the banks' "autonomous" decisions to acquire earning assets. The first task in estimating the magnitude of the Euro-dollar growth that has been due to bank credit creation would therefore be to obtain estimates of the primary deposits. Of course, our enumeration of transactions resulting in primary deposits may have been incomplete. Any empirical analysis would first have to make sure that *all* the sources of primary Euro-dollar deposits have been "covered".

It may be instructive to look for a moment at the increase of dollar deposits with commercial banks within the United States and to ask how that increase is explained by monetary analysts. From the end of 1966 to the end of 1969, demand deposits (exclusive of interbank deposits) increased by $40,000 million, time deposits by $33,900 million, and nondeposit borrowings by $12,900 million, together $86,800 million. Adding the increase in interbank deposits and in the capital accounts of the banks, we find that the total liabilities and capital accounts of commercial banks in the United States increased over the three years by about $100,000 million. In the same period total loans outstanding of these banks increased

257

FRITZ MACHLUP

by $75,900 million, securities holdings by $20,300 million, and Federal Reserve balances by $3,500 million, which also adds up to about $100,000 million. An accountant or statistician might conclude that the various depositors and lenders (plus, to some small extent, the owners of the banks' equity) had supplied the funds which the commercial banks used to make all these loans, to purchase the securities, and to increase their balances with the Fed. Now, I ask, would any economic analyst make such a statement?

I doubt that we can find many naive souls who would take the accounting figures of the American bank statements as information about the "suppliers" of the funds "lent" to the banks and "used" by them to make all these loans and investments. The official analysts in the Federal Reserve Banks and of the Board of Governors would certainly not try to explain the growth of bank deposits in this fashion. In their reports they leave no doubt that the increase in the reserve balances was *not* due to the commercial banks' decisions to "use" funds "received from their depositors" for "making deposits" with Federal Reserve Banks but, on the contrary, that the increase was due to actions of the Federal Reserve Banks creating claims against themselves chiefly by purchasing securities in the open market. They do not question, furthermore, that the commercial banks by making loans and purchasing securities created claims against themselves, claims which individuals and corporations now hold in the form of demand and time deposits.

This explanation does not rule out the possibility that now and then a few primary deposits of treasury currency have contributed for a few weeks to the growth of total deposits. In the longer run, however, the amounts deposited were smaller than the amounts of currency which depositors drew from the banks, lowering thereby their deposit claims. It is, for the American banking system, more plausible to state that *virtually all* deposits in the commercial banks (taken as a group) have been created by the activities of the banks and not by any spontaneous actions of depositors.

To what extent does this explanation of the growth of deposit liabilities of commercial banks apply to the European banking system and, in particular, to the growth of its dollar liabilities? If we were to take all commercial banks of the financially developed world together — America, Europe, and the "outside area" — and all their business in any currency — U.S. dollars, Euro-dollars, and any other currencies — it would be sensible to regard their aggregate

258

EURO-DOLLAR CREATION

deposit liabilities to nonbank holders as the result of their own credit-creating activities. However, if we cut up the world into various segments and look separately at the commercial banks in selected countries of Europe and at their deposit liabilities denominated in U.S. dollars, "inflows" from the other segments must be given a special place in the explanation of the observed growth. But to explain the entire growth by inflows from other segments would be just as wrong as to explain it entirely as the result of the Euro-dollar lending by the Euro-banks.

The differences between complete aggregation, partial aggregation, and complete disaggregation can be made quite clear to students of the American banking system if one reminds them of the difference between the individual bank and the system as a whole. What the individual bank sees as balances received from its depositors, the analyst of the system as a whole sees as balances created by the Federal Reserve Banks and the commercial banks themselves. If we invite the analyst to look at only one district, rather than at the whole country, he will have to accept an intermediate position: he will have to explain the growth of the deposit liabilities of the banks of that particular district as the combined result of inflows from the outside and creation by the banks inside. Of course, "inflows" will at times be negative, that is, there will be net outflows to other districts. This fact constitutes perhaps a significant difference between the banks in a district in the United States and the Euro-dollar business of the Euro-banks. For it seems that during the last ten years there have been no net outflows and only net inflows of funds into the Euro-dollar system; at least this is the impression one receives from reading the reports of the organizations that have kept track of what they call the Euro-currency "market".

The impression may be a wrong one, largely because the reports are couched entirely in terms of inflows of funds, without any mention being made of the possibility of endogenous creation of Euro-dollar credit, let alone, any attempt to measure the relative magnitudes of such creation. Since it is highly probable that inflows vary considerably over time, and by no means improbable that at times they are negative, the view that endogenous creation must have been very significant at least during certain periods has strong support from general monetary theory.

259

FRITZ MACHLUP

Other Euro-Currencies

The exposition in this article has been in terms of Euro-dollars rather than Euro-currencies. This narrowness of scope will, I hope, be forgiven, especially in view of the fact that the magnitudes of deposit liabilities denominated in other Euro-currencies are so much smaller. We have statistics of six Euro-currencies besides the Euro-dollar: the German mark, the Swiss franc, the pound sterling, the Dutch guilder, the French franc, and the Italian lira. That is to say, banks in European countries other than the homes of these currencies have deposit liabilities denominated in these currencies. But in the six currencies together the deposit liabilities were, in December 1969, only 18 per cent of total Euro-currency deposits; the largest of the six was the German mark, with Euro-mark deposits amounting to 8.3 per cent of the total, and Euro-sterling, Euro-guilders, Euro-French francs, and Euro-lire together amounting to 2.6 per cent of the total. In view of the relative size and in view of the associated problems of American borrowing and the payments deficit of the United States, the restriction of the discussion to the Euro-dollar system will, I trust, be understood.

FRITZ MACHLUP

Princeton

Stab. Aristide Staderini - Roma - Via Baccina, 45

260

PART FIVE

ECONOMICS OF KNOWLEDGE
AND TECHNICAL CHANGE

[18]

The Supply of Inventors and Inventions

By

Professor Dr. Dr. h. c. **Fritz Machlup**

Princeton, N.J.

Contents: I. The Supply of Inventive Labor: 1. Why Inventors Invent; 2. Extra Effort and Overtime; 3. Quality Differences and New Recruitment; 4. The Short-Run Supply; 5. The Long-Run Supply; 6. Research Workers' Rent and Marginal Cost; 7. The Social Cost of Additional Labor in Industrial Research. — II. The Production of Inventions: 1. The Quantity of Inventions: Problems of Definition, Identification, and Counting; 2. The Quantity of Inventions: Problems of Weighting their Importance and Difficulty; 3. The "Invention Industry;" 4. Increasing or Diminishing Returns in the Individual Firm; 5. The Rate of Inventive Output in the Economy as a Whole; 6. The Laws of Returns and the Technology of Producing Technology; 7. Diminishing Returns; 8. Problem-Raising Problem-Solutions; 9. Inventions Selected or Rejected for Use; 10. Ten Reasons for an Increasing Rejection Ratio. — III. The Effective Supply and Cost of Inventions: The Four Shrinkages.

The word "supply" is customarily used in two different meanings: it means either a quantity actually made available or a schedule of quantities hypothetically made available as a function of one or more independent variables, particularly as a function of the price offered for the good or service in question while other conditions are assumed to be unchanged. In the following discussion of the supply of inventions, supply is understood in the second sense: it refers to the hypothetical variations of the flow of new inventions becoming available for eventual industrial application as in response to variations in the compensation society offers to those who undertake the production of inventions.

Lest we expect from this analysis more than it can yield, we shall note that even the best clues it may afford concerning the flow of inventions would help us towards only a very partial understanding of the determinants of realized technical progress. For, ordinarily, the tempo of effective advance in the productivity of resources will be determined by other

Remark: A paper presented to the Conference on the Economic and Social Factors Determining the Rate and Direction of Inventive Activity, Minneapolis, May 1960, sponsored by the Universities-National Bureau Committee for Economic Research.

things besides the supply of new inventions; in particular, by the rate of *actual innovation*, which does not depend solely on the rate of invention, and by the rate of the *general adoption or imitation* of improved technologies, which may be the most decisive variable involved. However, awareness of the fact that answers to many questions are needed does not make any one of them superfluous.

The analysis of the supply of inventions divides itself logically into three sections: (1) the supply of inventive labor, — the chief input for the production of inventions; (2) the input-output relationship, — the technical "production function" describing the transformation of inventive labor into useful inventions; and (3) the supply and cost of useful inventions, — the output obtained from the use of inventive labor. All this, of course, follows the pattern in which the supply of any economic good is analyzed in modern economic theory.

I. The Supply of Inventive Labor

No unambiguous numerical estimates of the elasticities of supply of inventive talent and effort over substantial ranges can be derived from any data now available or likely to become available in the foreseeable future. Very general statements will have to do for our present purposes. What is needed here are educated guesses, intelligent judgments about whether the supply of qualified personnel is relatively scarce, and what are the possibilities of new recruitment and of increased efforts supplied by a given work force. The judgment about the ease or difficulty of recruitment to the inventive labor force will call for some clarification with regard to differential qualifications of the recruits, the speed with which the additions to the force are to be secured, and the size of the force from which one starts.

The last of these three questions is equivalent to the question, in economic parlance, of different elasticities at different points of a supply curve. It means, in simple language, that it makes a difference whether a nation seeks to increase its inventive personnel from 4,000 men to 4,400, from 8,000 to 8,800, or from 80,000 to 88,000, — though it is a ten percent increase in each case. A very modest "bait" may achieve the first increase in staff; a rather stiff raise in compensation may be needed for the second; and no raise whatsoever may be able to accomplish the third. Most of us, when asked about an elasticity of supply, are inclined first to think of the elasticity at the point of present employment. In many problems, however, the elasticity at points of smaller or larger employment is relevant. For this and other reasons a few preliminary questions have to be asked.

1. Why Inventors Invent

Why inventors invent; what non-pecuniary motivations they may have; whether pecuniary returns may be necessary to secure inventive effort beyond a point; whether the size of these returns significantly influences the amount of effort devoted to inventive activity; whether increased lucrativeness of inventing attracts proportionately increased personnel; whether increased personnel and increased efforts are likely to yield proportionately increased inventive capacity; these are some of the questions to be examined.

Inventions are sometimes made by accident, not as a result of special purposive efforts. But since even an accidental invention calls for some work — at least for its formulation or description — we may regard inventing **as** a special effort of labor, capital, and enterprise, and ask for the motivations behind the expenditure of this effort.

Without trying to present an exhaustive list, we distinguish (1) inventing for fun, (2) inventing for fame, (3) inventing for serving mankind, and (4) inventing for money. Perhaps we should add (5) inventing as an expression of the "instinct of workmanship"[1] or of the "instinct of contrivance"[2].

There are those who would not see much difference between exertion "for the fun of it" — motive (1) — and exertion for the sake of "getting the job done" — motive (5). From a psychological and sociological point of view the difference is perhaps significant. But from the point of view relevant to this analysis, the inventor who enjoys every minute of his activities — as a game or sport, as it were — and the inventor who takes pains toiling and sweating over the problems which his instinct of workmanship dictates him to solve, have in common that they ask nothing in return for their efforts.

The only return expected by him who exerts himself inventing in order to serve humanity — motive (3) — is the successful completion of his projects and the feeling that this will contribute to social progress and to the happiness of man. The return expected by the fame-seeking inventor — motive (2) — does not cost society much, because the recognition which it can show for the valuable inventions, the honors which it can bestow upon the great inventor, do not absorb any part of its productive capacity or of its national product, no matter how much productivity may increase

---

[1] Thorstein Veblen, "The Instinct of Workmanship and the Irksomeness of Labor", *The American Journal of Sociology*, Vol. IV, Chicago, 1898/99, pp. 187sqq. – *Idem, The Instinct of Workmanship and the State of the Industrial Arts*, New York, 1914.

[2] F. W. Taussig, *Inventors and Money-Makers*, Lectures on Some Relations Between Economics and Psychology Delivered at Brown University in Connection with the Celebration of the 150th Anniversary of the Foundation of the University, New York, 1915, p. 17.

as a result of the new inventions. (There will of course be a social cost consisting in the alternative uses of the inventors' time and effort. But we are discussing here the compensations received by the inventors.)

The inventors who do their work as amateur sportsmen, workman-like professionals, applause-seeking stars, or high-minded public servants require no money rewards, — though they may be willing or even anxious to accept pecuniary advantages if such are given to other inventors under the institutional arrangements adopted by society. Any income they derive from their inventive activity is, therefore, in the nature of pure economic rent, that is, of a payment not needed to call forth their efforts. What part of all inventive activity undertaken in our society is actually of these types is anybody's guess. It may be only an insignificant fraction of the total inventive effort or it may be a substantial portion, at least of the labor effort of the highest qualities of inventive personnel. Certainly it cannot be the whole, simply because, if for no other reason, most people could not afford to spend much of their time on inventive work if it did not pay. Thus, undoubtedly some part of the labor devoted to the production of new inventions is supplied only in consideration of the pecuniary compensation that is held out for such labor[1].

Merely in order to avoid misleading associations in our minds, let us make sure that absence or presence of pecuniary compensations for inventive labor is not the same thing as absence or presence of a patent system. The existence of a patent system may be thought of as an important factor in the effective *demand* for such labor. (In view of the profits expected from patent protection, firms are perhaps more inclined to hire research staffs. In the case of the self-employed inventor, the patent system may be said to stimulate his demand for his own labor for inventive purposes.) We are, at the moment, not concerned with the demand for, but with the *supply* of inventive labor (as a prerequisite of the supply of inventions). And if we have concluded from the considerations put forth in the preceding paragraphs that certain amounts of inventive labor would be supplied even in the absence of pecuniary compensation, this implies that a supply curve of such labor would for a certain length follow the quantity-axis, the supply prices in terms of money being zero.

Beyond a certain amount the supply of inventive effort will depend on the offer (or hope) of pecuniary compensation. Thus, the supply curve

---

[1] Polled by questionnaire, 710 individual inventors reported on their motivation; 193 of them listed "love of inventing," 189 listed "desire to improve;" as against these 382 amateurs, sportsmen, and idealists, only 167 answered that "financial gain" had been their motive. But, in answer to a different question, 265 of the 710 inventors, or 38.2 percent, reported that they were earning their livelihood by inventing. Joseph Rossman, "The Motives of Inventors", *The Quarterly Journal of Economics*, Vol. XLV, Cambridge, Mass., 1930/31, pp. 522, 526.

will start rising. Will this rise be gentle or abrupt? How elastic will the supply of inventive labor be once it becomes a function of pay? A judicious answer will first require that we distinguish between labor force, labor time, labor energy, labor quality, and labor effectiveness.

2. Extra Effort and Overtime

The distinction between *labor time* and *labor energy* is relevant where account must be taken of the fact that people sometimes "loaf on the job," that many work without straining themselves, that some work hard most of the time, and that a few exert themselves much more than others would ever be able or willing to do; and of the possibility that a change in pecuniary stimuli will produce responses in the form of increases in the amount of energy expended per labour hour. The probability of consistent responses of this sort does not seem to be great, however, in the case of inventive activities, and we need not make matters more complicated. Thus, without endangering the relevance of our argument, we may assume that the labor energy expended per hour will not be affected by the amount of compensation.

The distinction between *labor force* and *labor time* is relevant because there may be some elasticity in the supply of inventive labor merely through changes in the number of hours worked per man. This would be socially significant because an increase in inventive labor, to the extent that it is only at the expense of people's leisure, would not encroach upon alternative productive activities. Persons with a bent for tinkering and inventing, busy with other jobs during their regular hours, may be willing to devote more of their free evenings and week-ends to inventive activity. Scientists and engineers, employed in research and development, may be willing to work overtime. But, however important this possibility might be in times of emergency for the implementation of "crash programs" in research and development, long-run programs, designed for "progress in general," cannot successfully be based on the continuous and continual supply of overtime labor. The other source of supply of extra labour hours — the spare time of amateur researchers and tinkerers — can possibly be drawn upon regularly. (To have mobilized these "individual inventors" is perhaps one of the achievements of the patent system in times past.) But it is a very limited source of supply, probably fully exhausted in the earliest phase of the rising supply curve of inventive labor. (Moreover, the role of the "evenings-and-Sunday inventors" has become less significant in our age of organized research and development.) We may conclude that the possible sacrifice of leisure cannot be counted on to provide substantial amounts of labor for additional inventive activity; and it will therefore be no serious mistake to think of new recruitments to the inventive labor force, diverting labor from other occupations, as the only significant element in the elasticity of supply of inventive labor.

Thus, when we speak of the supply of inventive labor, we shall not stop to differentiate between the size of the inventive labor *force* and the amounts of *time* and *energy* per man, but shall simply think of the total amount of inventive labor as some number of men (or man-hours); indeed we shall, for the sake of simpler expression, use the term "inventive labor force" as equivalent to the "total effort devoted to the search for inventions."

3. Quality Differences and New Recruitment

We must not, however, neglect differences in labor quality; they are particularly important in the case of researchers and inventors. It would seem that the blend of training, experience, originality, tenacity, and perhaps genius which makes a man a potentially successful inventor is too "special" to permit the economic theorist to make his customary assumption of "homogeneity of productive resources" — unless he has very good excuses. Whether his trick of translating different qualities into one standard quality ("efficiency units" or "corrected natural units") can serve here a good purpose, will have to be examined. Off hand, a statement such as that five hours of Mr. Doakes were the equivalent of one hour of Mr. Edison or of two hours of Mr. Bessemer would sound preposterous. But if such "misplaced concreteness" is avoided, the device may prove helpful in abstract arguments.

Inasmuch as the problem of differences in the quality of inventive talent concerns us chiefly in connection with new recruits to the inventive labor force, the speed with which the recruitment is to be accomplished will be an important consideration. The time element is always significant in elasticity problems; it is particularly so regarding entry into an occupation such as "inventing," for which training and experience are essential.

A distinction between the short run and the long run is the customary device for focusing attention on important differences in the length of time allowed for certain reactions to given changes. Present membership in the labor force may be made the criterion for the distinction between short-run and long-run supply of inventive labor. The short-run supply curve would then depict the rates of compensation necessary to secure an expansion of the inventive work force through transfers from other fields and occupations; the long-run supply curve would depict the rates at which an expansion can be secured through both transfers of persons already in the labor force and recruitment of persons entering the labor force for the first time[1].

The short-run supply function of inventive labor expresses the ease or difficulty of drawing on trained, though probably less experienced, personnel; for the most part, these will be persons now engaged in teaching or fundamental research who can be induced to switch to applied research and development work. The long-run supply function must include considerations of the teaching capacity of the universities and institutes of technology, and of the pool or flow of potentially qualified students. Obviously, the elasticity of the long-run supply is greater than that of the short-run supply; it will be largely a matter of letting public knowledge of job openings and of differential earnings potentials steer young students into the natural science and engineering departments of the institutions of higher education. The question is whether, in both the long run and the short, additions to a given amount of inventive labor — additions in response to higher pay — are apt to be of lower quality.

4. The Short-Run Supply

Some of the clues that come to mind when one reflects on the question of quality differences in connection with the short-run supply of inventive labor seem to be contradictory. There is the case of the academic scientist who, bribed into industrial research, out-invents the most seasoned inventors. The success stories of former university professors as salaried inventors employed in industrial research and development work may be presented as evidence in support of an argument that the quality of the new members of the inventive labor force need not be below the previous average, and may even be above it, — at least as long as there are still enough professors that can be lured from their academic posts. (This reservation is significant; it shows again that much depends on where one "starts" adding to the force already employed, that is, on how many more researchers can be obtained in further raids on college and university faculties.) The validity of the evidence, however, may be questioned on several grounds: that the cases cited were exceptions to the rule; that many of the new members of industrial research staffs had previously

---

[1] It is convenient to think of the new entrants into the labor force as equal in number to those leaving the labor force through death or retirement. This simplification is designed to separate the problem of allocation from the problem of population growth. This does not mean that a long-run supply curve of this sort will be less relevant in an analysis of the allocation problem of a growing total labor force; but the supply curve of any particular kind of labor would have to be in terms of percentage shares of the growing labor force. For the sake of simpler expression it is customary to discuss resource allocation under the assumption of a given labor force, even for the long-run.

been engaged in inventive work of a more fundamental nature and that their transfer from academic to industrial positions was in fact not a net addition to the inventive work force; that many of these transfers were made in response, not to the lure of money, but to appeals to undertake tasks of immediate usefulness in a national emergency.

The opposite contention can also be defended: that as a rule the qualifications of new transfers to the inventive work force will be inferior to those of persons who have entered it earlier for less pay. Such an argument may be based on rather broad generalizations about "typical" human attitudes: that, ordinarily, people prefer to do things they are good at; that he who likes it better to teach or write, and will only by much higher rates of compensation be attracted to the engineer's draft-board or the industrial laboratory, is probably less qualified for inventive work than the "tinkers and contrivers" who follow an almost irresistible drive to find and try new devices. No matter whether more weight is given to deductions from such speculative assumptions or to inductive generalizations from individual observations, one will have to yield to the common-sense judgment that a point must exist beyond which further transfers to the research and development work force cannot possibly be of the same quality. The number of trained people in the labor force is limited and if research and development staffs are to be expanded close to that limit or beyond it, less qualified persons will have to be included.

5. The Long-Run Supply

Regarding the long-run supply of inventive labor, is there any presumption that those who are attracted only by higher rates of pay are less qualified than those willing to work for less? Youngsters, at the time when they choose their professional training, may not yet have developed preferences consistent with their aptitudes. They may have a preference for one thing, but superior aptitude for another. Better earnings prospects might then bring into a field young people not less qualified than those who would have chosen it also with poorer earnings prospects. If this should be a valid argument in speculating about the long-run supply of inventive labor, it certainly cannot be valid for unlimited amounts of labor. For the potential supply of inventive labor, innate ability counts undoubtedly as much as training, if not much more. The popular hero-worship for inventors may have been a gross exaggeration of the scarcity of inventive genius, but to suppose that mere training could produce any desired amounts of inventive capacity is a worse exaggeration in the opposite direction. One may, of course, steer more young people toward inventive work; but one must not expect always to obtain equally qualified ones[1].

If additional personnel is attracted to the inventive labor force only by higher rates of compensation and, by and large, is less qualified than those who are willing to work for less, the elasticity of "effective supply" of inventive labor is held down by both factors, preference and aptitude. If the supply of inventive labor, expressed merely in terms of natural units (man-hours), is not very elastic, it will certainly be still less elastic if expressed in terms of units corrected for differential qualification[2].

Higher rates of pay (or expected pay) might, at some point, call forth hardly any more "inventors" at all, but merely more "associate inventors" and "assistant inventors," that is, talents not apt to produce independently, but only to assist the leading men, taking off their shoulders some of the work that can be assigned, and thus releasing some of their time and thought for the really creative tasks. The aggregate capacity to produce new inventions can thus be increased through additions to the inventive labor force, regardless of whether the additional men are working independently of or in collaboration with those previously at work[3]. But the

---

[1] To some extent it may be possible to make good researchers out of people who are not naturally research-minded. A Research Co-ordinator of the Standard Oil Company of Indiana made this statement: "We ... find the self-directed individual being largely replaced by highly organized team attack in which we employ many people who, if left entirely to their own devices, might not really be research minded. In other words, we *hire* people to be curious as a group ... we are undertaking to *create* research capability by the sheer pressure of money." Daniel P. Barnard, in: *Proceedings of the Ninth Annual Conference on the Administration of Research*, September 7—9, 1955, Northwestern University Technological Institute, Evanston, Ill., New York, 1956, p. 26. On the other hand, even if motivation can be "created," the mental equipment must be there to start with. The scarcity of intellectual capacity was shown by the relative decline in the proportion of first-class honors degrees when the number of students increased in British universities: "The number of full-time students at British universities is some 60 per cent greater than before the war ... But the numbers obtaining *first*-class honors degrees have risen by only about 25 per cent. This is a small gain from a large improvement in methods of selection; if university examinations are accepted as consistent evidence of quality, it strongly suggests that a further scraping of the barrel will not yield many more first-class minds." Charles F. Carter and B. R. Williams, *Industry and Technical Progress: Factors Governing the Speed of Applicatiou of Science*, London, 1957, pp. 90sq.

[2] The technique of "corrected natural units" is used here only as an analogy, not as a measuring device. A supply curve in terms of "corrected natural units" is not only less elastic than the supply curve in natural units but also smaller (to the left of it) over at least a part of its course.

[3] In a sense, another errand boy hired for an industrial research laboratory would be an addition to the inventive labor force inasmuch as he may enable the staff to work with fewer interruptions. However, if we went that far in expanding the concept of "inventive labor," some of our earlier generalizations concerning its supply in terms of natural units would lose validity. It is preferable to confine the concept to the professional personnel.

addition of thousands of hours of work of assisting specialists (engineers, researchers, etc.) may mean merely hundreds of hours added to really inventive activity or capacity[1], and the latter can therefore be had only at a very much increased money cost.

This does not say anything about the prospect that increased amounts of inventive talent put to work will actually produce new inventions in proportionately increased amounts. The supply we have been discussing was merely that of talent and effort ready to be put to work — the input — not that of the actual product of this talent and effort — the output in the form of workable inventions.

6. Research Workers' Rent and Marginal Cost

Two kinds of supply curves can be used to describe the availability of inventive labor: one depicting the amounts of labor in man-years or man-hours regardless of quality differences, the other showing these units corrected for quality differences. While such corrections should be rejected if actual measurements are intended, they are admissible where only broad tendencies are referred to and quantitative statements are merely in the nature of "more" or "less," attempting an approximate ordering or ranking.

Speaking first of the long-run supply of inventive labor in terms of uncorrected (natural) units, we may say that beyond the amount of work which inventors would do for the love of it — that is, without pecuniary compensation — the supply curve will be rising, because offers or promises of increasingly attractive rates of pay will be necessary to steer additional labor away from other gainful or interesting pursuits (and, in the early ranges of the curve, away from leisure). Speaking only of the rising part of the curve, the elasticity of supply begins — since some labor is available at a zero price — at zero and may never rise as high as unity[2].

The rising supply curve — indicating rising rates of compensation paid for larger amounts of inventive labor — induces two phenomena:

[1] "The real moving spirits are few and the rest pedestrian, although of course useful, supporters. Quantity cannot make up for quality and little purpose is served in lamenting the absence of what are in fact unattainable levels of intellectual coordination when there are always too few minds of the highest calibre and there is a limit to the help that can be afforded them in their original thinking." John Jewkes, David Sawers, and Richard Stillerman, *The Sources of Invention*, London and New York, 1958, p. 162.

[2] Where the curve first leaves the ground — the quantity axis — the elasticity is zero by mathematical necessity (because the price increase from zero is by an infinite percentage). For the elasticity of supply to become as high as unity, the curve would have to flatten out sufficiently to have its tangent go through the origin of the coordinates; and the elasticity can be above unity only when the tangent intersects the price axis, rather than the quantity axis, which is the less likely to happen the larger the quantity of labor offered without pay.

the marginal cost of such labor will be in excess of the actual rate paid[1], and there will be a "research workers' surplus," a rent income received by research workers who would be willing to work for less money. An elasticity of supply below unity implies that, of the additional outlay required to obtain additional quantities of inventive labor, the bigger portion will be research workers' rent, going to those who would have worked for less, and only the smaller portion will go to those who have newly entered the inventive force.

An arithmetical illustration may be helpful in demonstrating these points. Assume that 150,000 scientists and engineers have been engaged in research and development, at an average salary of $ 10,000 per year. A ten percent increase of this inventive labor force is now desired; in the process of attracting the wanted 15,000 scientists and engineers, the whole salary scale, of the old staff members as well as the new, is raised by twenty percent — the elasticity of supply being 0.5 —, bringing the annual average to $ 12,000. The total amount paid for the research and development force is thus raised from $ 1,500,000,000 to $ 1,980,000,000, or by 32 percent. The addition of 15,000 men requires therefore an additional outlay of $ 480,000,000 (or $ 32,000 per man added), of which the new entrants collect $ 180,000,000 (i.e., $ 12,000 per man) while the other $ 300,000,000 will go as an additional rent income to the "old" staff. If the 15,000 newly employed are of the same quality as the old, $ 480,000,000 are spent annually for an amount of labor that at the previous rates of pay would have been worth no more than $ 150,000,000.

In summary, adding the new men to the inventive work force, by raising the average rate of compensation by $ 2,000, increases marginal cost to $ 32,000 per man, of which $ 12,000 is the new average salary and $ 20,000 is the average per new man of the increase in research workers' rent collected by the old work force[2].

The supply curve in terms of men-years corrected for differences in quality must rise more steeply than the curve in terms of uncorrected

---

[1] Marginal cost from the point of view of the "invention industry" as a whole, not necessarily from the point of view of every firm employing inventive labor.

[2] The figure pictures these relationships. The supply curve runs from O to K horizontally and then rises toward S. An addition to the research work force from OK to OL will be achieved through securing a rate of compensation of OP. Of the total cost, OLAP, the bulk, OKAP, will be rent and only the trifle, KLA, constitutes the payment of opportunity costs. Putting it differently, OKBP will have to be paid to those who would have worked for nothing, while only KLAB will go to the new members of the force. For an increase in the force from OM (= 150,000) to ON (= 165,000) an amount of MNDE (15,000 × 12,000 = 180,000,000) will have to be paid to the new men and RCES (150,000 × 2,000 = 300,000,000) to the incumbents. This slice RCES converted into the equal area DEFG (15,000 × 20,000 = 300,000,000) on top of the pay to the new men, MNDE, will show the big bar MNGF

men-years if additional personnel is less qualified. In such a curve, inferior labor is counted as the equivalent of a smaller quantity of labor of the average quality employed thus far. The corrected supply curve will show the effects of both the increase in the average rate of compensation paid per man-year and the reduction in average qualification. Any addition to the personnel working on inventions will mean a less than proportional addition to the capacity to work on inventions, with the result that a given dollar amount paid for the additional personnel will buy only an acutely reduced "worth" of new working capacity in terms of the previously prevailing cost.

Starting from the same arithmetic illustration as before, we shall now assume that the average quality of the 150,000 scientists and engineers working on research and development cannot be matched by that of newly obtained personnel. If a ten percent increase of the working capacity of the inventive force is desired, 15,000 men cannot achieve it; supposing that one new research worker is on the average only as good as three-fourths of one of the present average quality, 20,000 new men will be

(15,000 × 32,000 = 480,000,000) representing the whole increment to total cost due to the addition of 15,000 men to the work force.

Figure — *Supply of Labor for Research Work; Average Rates of Compensation, Rents, and Marginal Cost*

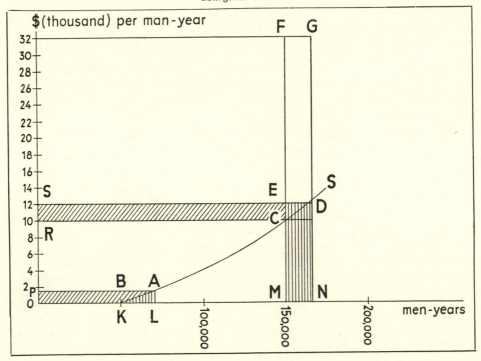

needed to do the job that 15,000 of the present caliber would be able to do. In the process of attracting 20,000 scientists and engineers the salary scale will again be bid up[1]. By how much? The elasticity of supply in uncorrected units — men-years regardless of quality — was assumed to be 0.5, and may be assumed to be a little smaller over the larger arc of the curve (i.e., for 20,000 men instead of 15,000). The 20,000 men represent a 13.3 percent increase in the work force; hence, they should command a salary more than 26.6 percent above $ 10,000, say, $ 13,000. The better men, however, will be paid still more, because, even if they were generous enough not to resent being underpaid relative to their inferior new colleagues, competition among employers bidding for the relatively cheaper men of superior ability will tend to establish salary differentials more nearly commensurate with quality differentials. Thus, if the new, less qualified men are paid $ 13,000 a year, the average salary for the men of standard quality will tend to rise to $ 17,333. There would then be 150,000 men receiving $ 17,333 each, or $ 2,600,000,000, and 20,000 men receiving $ 13,000 each, or $ 260,000,000; the total salary bill would amount to $ 2,860,000,000, that is $ 1,360,000,000, or 90.7 percent, above the previous total paid.

This additional outlay due to the addition of 20,000 less qualified men is for the most part additional rent income going to the old staff: $ 1,100,000,000 (i.e., 150,000 men getting an average raise of $ 7,333) is of this nature, while only $ 260,000,000 is paid *to* the new personnel. The sum of $ 1,360,000,000 is spent *for* the new personnel, that is, to obtain an amount of labor capacity which at the previous rates of pay would have been worth no more than $ 150,000,000 (i.e., 15,000 men at $ 10,000).

In brief, the increase in the inventive work force by ten percent, or by 15,000 men of standard quality or 20,000 men of available quality, raises the average rate of compensation by $ 7,333 for research workers of standard quality, and increases their marginal cost to $ 90,667 (i. e., the additional outlay, $ 1,360,000,000 divided by 15,000, the number of additional men-years of standard quality). Of the $ 90,667 only $ 13,000, on the average, goes to each of the new members of the staff, or rather $ 17,333 if each of them is counted only as three-fourth of a research worker of standard quality; the rest, $ 73,333, is what the "invention industry" has to pay, for each of the 15,000 additional standard men-years, in the form of salary increases to members of the old work force.

---

[1] The newly attracted scientists and engineers are assumed to be less qualified for inventive work only, but not for alternative uses of their skills. For example, in production engineering, quality control, computing work, basic research, teaching, writing, etc., they may be as good as their colleagues or even better. Hence, their salaries, before their transfer, would not be below the salaries of those in inventive work.

These are truly staggering figures, showing, perhaps hyperbolically, the effects which an increase in research and development may have upon the cost per man-year employed. The chief factor in this cost inflation was the drastic quality deterioration assumed for the additional research personnel. Smaller differences in qualifications would of course have shown somewhat less spectacular figures for marginal cost[1]. But the principle would not be altered. Any scarcity in research personnel, reflected in increasing rates of compensation and decreasing research capacity per man, will result in raising the marginal cost of inventive labor above the average rates paid.

7. The Social Cost of the Additional Labor in Industrial Research

The additional money outlay required to secure a small addition to the inventive labor force is no fair indication of the social cost involved. The money outlay includes the research workers' surplus, or rent, accruing to inventive personnel who would have been willing to work for less than the rate of compensation that is actually paid in order to attract more people to research and development work. These rent payments do not themselves signify a use of more resources; and only the use of resources, that is, the sacrificing of alternative uses of resources, constitutes a social cost. The increased rent payments are merely transfers of income from one part of society to another; they are losses to "society exclusive of inventive personnel," and gains for the members of the "inventive labor force" (who are of course part of "society as a whole").

These questions will be taken up elsewhere and treated in detail when the social cost of inventions is analyzed, because the cost of output, the inventions, cannot be less than the cost of the required input. (More correctly, the cost of any sort of output is determined by the value of the most valuable alternative output that could be produced with the same input.) But it should be mentioned at this point that the prices paid for any sort of input will reflect the social value of its potential output only where the resources are acquired in competitive markets and where the market prices of all alternative outputs reflect their full contributions to economic welfare. It is very doubtful that these conditions are met in the

---

[1] Assume, for example, that the difference in quality is only ten percent, so that not 20,000 but only 16,500 are needed to do the job which 15,000 men of standard quality could be expected to do. The addition of 11 percent to the personnel might lift the salary by 23 percent to $ 12,300 for the new men, and by another 10 percent to $ 13,530 for the old. Total outlay would be $ 2,232,450,000, an increase of $ 732,450,000 over the former total. The marginal cost per man (of standard quality) would be $ 48,830.

case of the resources required for the production and development of inventions and with regard to the alternative uses of the resources, chiefly basic research and higher education. The social benefits resulting from basic research and higher education are far above any private benefits conferred on their "buyers;" and the market prices of education and basic research, and the compensations paid to scholars, are no more commensurate with the social value of their services than the market prices of inventions, and the compensations paid to inventors, with the social value of inventions. Thus, the compensations needed to attract additional labor into the business of inventing do not reflect the social values of education and basic research that are forgone by the transfer of personnel. These issues will be dealt with and elaborated elsewhere[1].

II. The Production of Inventions

To regard a study of the supply of inventive labor as a prerequisite of a study of the cost and supply of inventions is to assume that there is a quantitative relationship between the input of labor and the output of inventions; in other words, that inventions are "produced," that the volume of production can be measured or at least "sized up" to the extent necessary to make it meaningful to speak of an increase and a decrease in the flow of new inventions, and that changes in output depend on changes in input, at least partially. These assumptions should not be made without attempting to justify them.

One might take the position, and defend it on good grounds, that one cannot even define "invention," let alone identify, count, or weight inventions for purposes of measuring the quantity produced by the inventive effort. And if it is meaningless to quantify the output, it must be meaningless to assert or posit the existence of a quantitative relationship between input and output. Or, one might take a less negative position and grant the possibility of quantifying the inputs and outputs, at least roughly or merely for purposes of constructional reasoning, but at the same time hold that the incidence of accidents in making inventions is too great to legitimize, even provisionally, the assumption of a "production function," a functional relationship between input and output.

---

[1] For a preliminary discussion of the alternative costs of education, basic research, and industrial research, all competing for the same productive resources, see my article "Can There Be Too Much Research?", *Science*, Vol. CXXVIII, Washington, D.C., 1958, pp. 1320sqq. – A more detailed treatment, including relevant statistical information, will be found in *The Allocation of Scientific Personnel*, a doctoral dissertation by Vladimir Stoikov, submitted to the Johns Hopkins University (May 1960).

1. The Quantity of Inventions: Problems of Definition, Identification, and Counting

The literature on patent law and patent litigation is full of controversial discussions about the definition and identification of "invention." Patent offices disagree with patent attorneys, courts disagree with patent offices, appeals courts disagree with lower courts, experts of all sorts disagree with the appeals courts, and legislators cry out about the absence of firm standards for deciding what constitutes invention. If this uncertainty, about just what makes an idea an invention, irks the engineers, the businessmen, and the lawyers, there is little hope that economists should find the touchstone to resolve the inherent perplexities.

Economists are perhaps even more than others disturbed about the arbitrariness of singling out as separate inventions particular fragments from what appears to them as "an indivisible moving stream" of new or improved technological knowledge[1]. But the theory of the "continuous social growth" of technological knowledge, though it contradicts perhaps the claim that particular inventors can be correctly identified, does not exclude the possibility of identifying or sizing up the growth of knowledge that has occurred in society over a certain period of time. There is no use denying the desirability of a generally accepted definition of "invention;" yet the fact that none of the many definitions proposed has been generally accepted does not seriously hamper our present task: almost any definition, applied with reasonable consistency, would do for our present purposes — to theorize about relative changes in the amount of invention per

---

[1] "What is an invention? Technical progress is an indivisible moving stream from which it seems impossible, except in an arbitrary fashion, to isolate one fragment for independent examination." Jewkes, Sawers, and Stillerman, *op. cit.*, p. 12. — "I believe the [patent] law is essentially deficient, because it aims at a purpose which cannot be rationally achieved. It tries to parcel up a stream of creative thought into a series of distinct claims, each of which is to constitute the basis of a separately owned monopoly. But the growth of human knowledge cannot be divided up into such sharply circumscribed phases. Ideas usually develop gradually by shades of emphasis, and even when, from time to time, sparks of discovery flare up and suddenly reveal a new understanding, it usually appears on closer scrutiny that the new idea had been at least partly foreshadowed in previous speculations. Moreover, discovery and invention do not progress only along one sequence of thought, which perhaps could somehow be divided up into consecutive segments. Mental progress interacts at every stage with the whole network of human knowledge and draws at every moment on the most varied and dispersed stimuli. Invention, and particularly modern invention which relies more and more on a systematic process of trial and error, is a drama enacted on a crowded stage. It may be possible to analyze its various scenes and acts, and to ascribe different degrees of merit to the participants; but it is not possible, in general, to attribute to any of them one decisive self-contained mental operation which can be formulated in a definite claim." Michael Polanyi, "Patent Reform", *The Review of Economic Studies*, Vol. XI, Cambridge, 1943/44, pp. 70 sq.

year — because the results would surely not be radically different if different definitions were used[1].

One may readily admit that there is neither a unit of invention in any but a very arbitrary sense nor a reasonable degree of comparability which would permit us to reduce the heterogeneous mass of invention to a quasi-homogeneous aggregate of definite magnitude. Yet, one need not for that reason deny that it makes good sense to speak of a rapid or slow flow of new inventions, or to compare the rates of invention in different periods. There are many things in life, and even in idealized models of economic life, which *cannot* be quantified in any strict sense, but *must* be and *are* quantified in a makeshift way for purposes of description and analysis. One may modestly insist that no "measurement" is intended, or one may merely disclaim its "exactness," but then one goes ahead and measures anyhow[2] or at least engages in "roughly sizing up" the non-measurables.

The problem of the unit of invention has been of very practical concern to the patent offices and patent lawyers all over the world. Frequently what one patent lawyer prefers to regard as two different inventions another may claim to be integral parts of only one invention. And what an applicant for a patent may describe as one invention the examiner in the patent office may regard as two or more separate inventions, and he may order a division of the application. Improvements which under most patent laws are considered as new and separate inventions may by others be viewed as parts of the original invention. Amendments of or additions to the claims of a pending patent application, permissible in many countries, may by some be held to be in fact new inventions. These are only a few examples indicating the difficulty of counting the number of patented inventions. But this difficulty is resolved in actual practice and it need not bar the economic analyst from speaking of the number of inventions made per year — as long as they are patented.

An undetermined number of inventions remain unpatented, either because they are not patentable or because the inventors choose not to patent them. To the extent that non-patented inventions are published — publication can secure for inventors all that many patentees try to

---

[1] "There can be no doubt that an over rigid insistence upon definition would immediately bring all discussion of invention ... to a dead stop. The choice must be between discussing these matters with concepts that are necessarily somewhat vague and not discussing them at all." Jewkes, Sawers, and Stillerman, *op. cit.*, p. 13.

[2] Compare Frank H. Knight, who says that Lord Kelvin's famous dictum on the need for measurement largely means in practice: "'if you cannot measure, measure anyhow!'" ("'What is Truth' in Economics?" *The Journal of Political Economy*, Vol. XLVIII, Chicago, Ill., 1940, p. 18, footnote 10.) Of course, the quantification relevant to the discussion in the text above is merely an imaginary quantification for purposes of theoretical analysis.

achieve, namely, protection against patent suits for using their own inventions — it should be possible for experts to examine and identify them and to count them just as patent offices count patented inventions. But to the extent that inventions remain unpublished — perhaps because inventors try to keep them secret — enumeration is not practically possible.

Empirical studies are seriously hampered by our inability to count, or even to estimate reliably, the number of unpatented inventions. Even with regard to patented inventions, intertemporal and international comparisons may be encumbered or vitiated by changes in patent-office practices over time and by differences between countries. But more serious is the obstacle which changes in the inventors' propensity to apply for patents put in the way of reliable estimates of the number of inventions. Attempts to overcome this obstacle have not thus far succeeded, though our specialists on the statistics of patents and inventions keep trying.

This gap in our empirical knowledge is due to a practical difficulty, not a conceptual impossibility. It would be conceivable that a reliable census of the number of inventions per year, patented and unpatented, be made by analysts gaining the confidence of the inventors or their employers; and rough estimates of the number of unpatented inventions could in actual practice become obtainable through sample surveys of cooperating business firms in the major industries. (It may not be worth the effort and money needed to develop this information.) In any case, for purposes of purely theoretical analysis, the *numbers* of inventions produced may be assumed to be ascertainable information.

2. The Quantity of Inventions:
Problems of Weighting their Importance and Difficulty

Much more embarrassing for our purposes is the fact that inventions are so different from one another that we must question whether it makes sense to count the numbers and then speak of changes in the amount of invention per year if we know only unweighted quantities. Inventions are by definition heterogeneous: for only a novel idea, sufficiently different from all "prior art," can be regarded as an invention.

The differences are of three kinds: in socio-economic importance, in commercial value, and in technical difficulty. The contributions which different inventions make to the total welfare of society (or to national income), the contributions they make to business profits, and the time and effort it takes to make different kinds of inventions — all these are too different to let us forget about possibilities of weighting.

The invention of the diesel engine or the radio tube is undoubtedly of a different order of economic and social importance than the invention of the bobby pin and the electric shaver. Moreover, a distinction ought to be made between basic inventions and improvement inventions, since *one* invention of a most fundamental sort may be followed by *scores* of inventions embodying minor improvements[1]. Can we find any practicable method of comparing the importance of different inventions? It has been said — in oral discussion, if not in print — that experts could probably agree on the relative importance of inventions and on ranking them in the order of importance. Others have doubted this[2]. In any case, mere ranking would not suffice and would not solve the problem of weighting. One will probably have to admit the practical impossibility of assigning to particular inventions relative weights or values objectively established.

In pure theory only, one may conceive of a hypothetical computation of the welfare contribution made by each invention, and of the determination of weights accordingly. These weights would express the money equivalents of the increments in real national income (measuring economic satisfaction) attributable to the changes in production and consumption that are due to each invention. (The presence of complementary and substitutable inventions in the same bundle would require that they be valued together, rather than separately.) Such a hypothetical procedure is of course abstract theory of a practically non-operational type, but it may give meaning to a conception of a theoretical "amount" of invention in terms of social value, not in terms of a mere count of numbers. On such a basis one may hold that the concept of an annual rate of invention, or amount of invention per year, in the sense of a properly weighted magnitude is "conceivably operational" — and therefore not meaningless by the standards of neo-positivistic logic — even if one would not dare to propose practical methods of determining the proper weights.

The commercial value of inventions does not reflect their social value; indeed, if an invention is fully utilized and its social value therefore maximized, so that the price of the final product covers only the marginal

---

[1] "For example, in the incandescent lamp, the early patents of Edison and Swan on different types of electrodes represented a major advance. So also did Langmuir's patent on the gas-filled lamp. But such minor later improvements as the 'tipless' lamp, 'inside frosting,' and other comparable advances gave rise to a greater number of patents." W. Rupert Maclaurin, "The Sequence from Invention to Innovation and Its Relation to Economic Growth", *The Quarterly Journal of Economics*, Vol. LXVII, 1953, p. 103.

[2] "What is an *important* invention? Anyone seeking to generalize about inventions from case histories must confine himself to the salient novelties. There is no way of measuring the totality of invention; only its sporadic dominating features can be picked out. Yet there are no economic principles to which to appeal to determine whether one invention is more 'important' than another." Jewkes, Sawers, and Stillerman, *op. cit.*, p. 13.

cost of producing it, the commercial value of the invention is necessarily zero. An invention has commercial value to the extent that its utilization is monopolistically restricted. Thus, patent rights may have commercial value in that they are rights to exclude competitors from the use of inventions. The commercial values of the exclusive rights to given inventions will be different depending on the time extension, space extension, scope, and enforceability of monopoly protection. For all these reasons, the market values of patents cannot be of any use in assigning weights for the purpose of measuring the flow of new inventions.

The third kind of heterogeneity of inventions lies in the wide differences in the difficulty of making them. Some inventions are relatively easy to make, others require the expenditure of huge efforts. And, incidentally, these differences need not be the same *ex ante* and *ex post*. Experts may agree in their estimates of how manymen-years of research may be needed for this or that project, but in their execution the projects may turn out to be much easier or much harder than had been expected.

On first blush one might suspect that some relationship exists between the commercial "value" and the private "cost" of inventions. If business decisions are sensible, there should be a rough relation between the anticipated commercial value of patentable inventions and the anticipated difficulty — in terms of dollar expenses — of making them; but this would apply only to inventive activity financed exclusively by profit-seeking enterprise. In actual fact, much of the inventive activity nowadays is subsidized or contracted for by the government. Besides, whatever relationship could be established between anticipated cost and commercial value of patentable inventions, it would supply no clues to the problem of weighting inventions either with regard to their socio-economic importance or with regard to the technical difficulty of making them.

In pure theory again, one may conceive of a hypothetical estimation of "weights of difficulty," expressing the relative (man-year) efforts or (dollar) expenses required, under given conditions, to solve the various technical problems at hand. Some device of this sort is needed since some technological problems are easy to solve while others are tough, and the *number* of solutions to an unknown mix of easy and hard problems does not measure the achievement of the problem solvers. Of course, one would have to be careful to avoid reducing in this fashion the quantities of "output" to quantities of input needed to produce the output. It would be all too easy, by trying to "homogenize" the output (inventions) with respect to the "necessary input" (inventive effort), actually to "tautologize" the whole business and express output in terms of input. The idea of an input-output function would then have fallen through a logical trap door[1]. An *ex post* measure of the amount of invention corrected for the quantity of inventive effort actually required would be nothing but the quantity of input. For reflections on input-output ratios and their variations, either over time or as a function of the volume of inventive activity, one needs a different kind of correction for differences in the difficulty of the problems handed to the inventors.

The problem of heterogeneity of output from both points of view — production cost and utility — exists of course with respect to many products, but it is probably most intractable in the production of inventions. In the case of *physical goods* of great heterogeneity (say, houses of different size and quality) there is usually a practical way of reducing output to homogeneous units (say, floor space or cubic space of some standard type). In the case of specific *personal services* (doctors', lawyers', musicians') it is frequently impossible to quantify physical output (separately from physical input) but the market value may be an acceptable substitute for measured output. In the case of inventions neither of these devices are of avail: there seems to be no way of reducing different units of output (the number of inventions, the number of patent claims, etc.) to physically comparable units, and no way of accepting market values as a measure of output.

The most feasible expedient to overcome the weighting problem in the quantification of the output of inventive activity is to *assume* that large numbers of inventions will include similar mixtures of solutions to easy and hard problems and similar mixtures of more important and less important findings. In large numbers of inventions the distribution of "degrees of importance" and of "degrees of difficulty" may actually not vary too seriously. Different bundles of 1,000 inventions each are likely to be much more homogeneous, in difficulty as well as in importance, than bundles of only 100 inventions each would be. Therefore, in some theoretical speculations involving large numbers of inventions, the assumption of an approximately homogeneous degree of average importance and average difficulty can be condoned. (The adoption of this "homogenizing device" may be misleading when long stretches of time with drastically changing states of scientific knowledge are taken into consideration; but it may be permissible for the hypothetical quantification of hypothetical outputs of inventive activity at a given time.)

At the moment we are concerned only with some general relationships between broadly defined variables in purely theoretical analysis, and we

---

[1] The reverse kind of logical trap was once visited by Mrs. Robinson, when she wanted to demonstrate laws of return but construed "efficiency units" of input, where efficiency was measured in terms of output. See Joan Robinson, *The Economics of Imperfect Competition*, London, 1933, Appendix, p. 332.

shall proceed under the unrealistic assumption that the problem of quantification has been solved — or at least successfully suppressed.

3. The "Invention Industry"

If it makes sense to quantify the input — inventive labor plus equipment and whatever else is needed — as well as the output — new technical inventions —, will a model that assumes a functional relation between input and output be relevant in an interpretation of the "real facts" concerning the flow of inventions?

An affirmative answer — at least to the extent that an increase in input will, as a rule, produce an increase in output — is implied in the theory that invention can be "stimulated" by patent systems or subsidization. Even more than that is implied in the familiar arguments about the need or desirability of increased industrial research and development: they implicitly deny, on the one hand, that a very small increase in research will suffice to produce a vast increase in inventions, and, on the other, that a huge increase in research will produce but a trivial increase in inventions. Thus there has always been an implicit acceptance of a sort of "production function" affirming a positive correlation between input and output and expressing certain restraints which exclude extreme values of the input-output ratio.

These restraints have long been thought to apply only to the "invention industry" as a whole. For individual producers of inventions no functional dependence of output upon input seemed to hold: a most extravagant increase in input might yield no inventions whatsoever, and a reduction in inventive effort might by a fluke result in the output that had in vain been sought with great expense. As in a lottery, individuals would still make plans involving high stakes on the basis of a probability calculus that applied only to the whole population of gamblers, rather than to any single one. The making of inventions would be a lucky accident, nothing the individual firm could count on. The inventive process, however, has become more methodical[1] than it used to be in earlier times, more systematic, mechanized, routinized, — until it now seems that the probability calculus applies to individual producers of inventions, even to medium- and small-scale establishments[2]. All of the large firms and a good many

---

[1] "The greatest invention of the nineteenth century was the invention of the method of invention." Alfred North Whitehead, *Science and the Modern World*, London, 1925, p. 120.

[2] "In the larger firms of today, the flow of new ideas for product and process innovation results, not from the chance inspiration of exceptional individuals, but from a deliberate decision by management to spend money on research and development. There is still a great need for the inspiration of genius, but much routine discovery and improvement waits simply for the investment of sufficient resources." Carter and Williams, *op. cit.*, p. 108.

smaller ones, in the industries in which technology has been advancing rapidly, regularly allocate funds for research and development, and one could hardly assume that they do so as a sheer gamble, without rational and reasonable expectations of a satisfactory return. They have learnt that research expenditures can be profitable[1], and this implies that they expect inputs of inventive labor and complementary resources to produce workable new inventions[2].

All production functions involve probability distributions of some sort, with more or less wide deviations from the norm resulting from such things as variations in the performance (speed, accuracy) of human operations, differences in the quality (purity, strength, consistence) of materials, unevenness in the operation (speed, accuracy) of tools and machines, fluctuations in the supply (quantity, pressure, tension) of energy, changes in weather (precipitation, humidity, sunshine, winds), etc. The deviations are notoriously great in agricultural production, with its dependence on weather (rainfall, frosts), insects, fungi, etc. This does not prevent anybody from basing theoretical as well as practical considerations upon production functions for agricultural products. Both the individual farmer and the government adviser on farm policy assume for their plans — the former for his private production plan, the latter for some national program — that the use of more land, more seed, more fertilizer, more labor would increase output by certain quantities. Perhaps there is less uncertainty in the production plans for an entire region or country than there is for an individual farm, because of the likelihood that positive and negative deviations cancel out in the larger "population."

---

[1] "Technological research was becoming an industry ... The industry of discovery is one of the most rapidly growing industries in the country ... it has become possible to find a large number of problems or areas of investigation on which money may be spent with a reasonable expectation that the outlay will produce enough useful information and understanding to justify the expense ... Of course, there can be no guarantee that a particular inquiry will produce the required knowledge within the estimated time and cost. When economic calculations are applied to research, the application has to be made in a somewhat different way from the application of economic calculations to the use of known and tried methods of production. Economists as yet do not understand the process by which highly uncertain costs are balanced against highly uncertain returns. But the evidence that some sort of calculus is being applied is found in the enormous growth of research budgets. Industry is not throwing its money away; it is spending on research and development because it has good reason to think that the outlays will prove profitable." Sumner H. Slichter, "The Passing of Keynesian Economics", *The Atlantic Monthly*, Vol. CC, Concord and Boston, 1957, No. 5, p. 143.

[2] "We have now reached a stage in many fields where inventions are almost made to order, and where there *can* be a definite correlation between the numbers of applied scientists employed (and the funds at their disposal) and the inventive results." Maclaurin, *op. cit.*, p. 104.

That chance, luck, accident play an unusually great role in the "invention industry" need not preclude the existence of sufficient regularities in the production of inventions to permit expressing the relationships in the form of production functions. What does, however, complicate matters in the invention industry is the extreme heterogeneity of the product as well as of the producing units. May one assume much similarity in the input-output relations that are relevant for "individual inventors" (self-employed freelancers), small teams of experts specializing in research and consultation work in particular fields, large independent or cooperative research laboratories, scientific or engineering departments of universities, governmental research agencies, research and development divisions of large industrial concerns? Is it reasonable to expect much similarity in the input-output relations in the inventive work in aeronautics, electronics, nuclear physics, chemical engineering, automotive mechanics, etc.? Can one justify the assumption that there is some reasonably stable ratio of successful to unsuccessful tries in the mass of all inventive work of uncertain composition?

To ask these questions is to suggest negative answers. Contrary to other industries, where the "probable errors" are larger for the individual producers than for the industry as a whole, the "invention industry" is apt to present smaller dispersions in the probability distribution for the individual producer. The individual firm undertaking inventive work in a certain field and attempting to solve some problems related to more or less circumscribed objectives is quite capable of setting out with fixed budgets, appropriations, and time schedules, that is, with a specification of the inputs believed necessary to achieve the goal, to produce the inventions wanted. This is true for the small independent research outfit (producing nothing but inventions) as well as for one integrated with a firm that also produces other products, particularly the kind of product for which the wanted inventions would be most useful. But to develop a production function for "inventions in general" for the "invention industry as a whole" seems an impossible task, especially if nothing is said about what kinds of inventions are sought.

Such a disappointingly negative conclusion, however, implies an excessively literal interpretation of the term "production function." One need only remember the universally accepted proposition that "agriculture operates under diminishing returns" to realize that no definite, numerically specifiable production function for agricultural output is referred to in the context; obviously, there cannot be one definite aggregate production function for a variable composite of barley, wheat, rye, corn, rice, cotton, tobacco, potatoes, carrots, spinach, and all the rest, produced on land of all grades and locations, by farms of all sizes. Yet, a statement concerning constant or diminishing returns in agriculture of a certain country at a certain time makes perfectly good sense. The unit of output would be some "homogenized bushel of produce" and the shape of the production function would merely illuminate the general nature of such quantitative relationships as are regarded as relevant to the problem at hand. It is in this sense that one may speak of the "invention industry" and of its "output," which evidently cannot be "homogeneous" but which can be "homogenized" for the sake of reasoning and discussing. To repeat it, the "production function" of "inventions in general" in the "invention industry as a whole" is only an abstract construction designed to characterize some quantitative relationships which are regarded as empirically relevant.

The production of inventions is in the range of increasing returns as long as an increase in the quantity of inventive labor employed would bring forth a more than proportionate increase in the amount of invention; and is in the range of diminishing returns when an increase in the quantity of inventive labor employed would bring forth a less than proportionate increase in the amount of invention. But before we deal with the production possibilities in the invention industry, we should say a word or two about the conditions facing an individual producer.

4. Increasing or Diminishing Returns in the Individual Firm

The existence of an initial range of increasing returns in the inventive work of the individual firm has often been mentioned as the reason why small firms cannot ordinarily afford to maintain their own research staff. (The limited divisibility of human resources is sometimes overcome by a small industrial firm retaining a research scientist or consulting engineer for one day a week or even less. But the efficiency of such an arrangement is probably small, that is, the work is apt to be in the range of increasing returns.) The usual explanation is that part-time inventive work is less productive than full-time work, that in many areas of research the pooling of different kinds of specialized knowledge and experience is necessary, that collaboration is urgently indicated not only because of the advantages of division of labor but also because of the mutual stimulation ("cross-fertilization") afforded by discussion among different experts[1].

---

[1] "A laboratory designed to increase the flow of new ideas represents an attempt to *organize* research for three obvious purposes: first, to gather together more of the resources incidental to research, to provide the research worker with the best aids, devices and working conditions; second, to encourage co-operation between different minds, and third, to try to give some guidance about the kind of inventions which would be most useful to the firm." Jewkes, Sawers, and Stillerman, *op. cit.*, p. 132. — "It has become generally established

The possibility of diminishing returns in the inventive work of the individual firm is due in part to the existence of internal diseconomies of large scale operation, — sometimes held to be avoidable by improved managerial techniques, but often said to be inevitable[1]. It is also due to the limitation in the stock of problems in the solution of which the firm is interested. This point will become clear later, when we discuss the technology of the production of inventions.

What is the significance of inquiring into the question of increasing and diminishing returns in the inventive work of the firm, of analyzing the "optimum size" of an individual research laboratory? Such inquiries may be relevant to a number of problems, such as

(1) the problem of efficient organization within a particular firm or institution;

(2) the problem of "big business" versus "small business," because the former can have integrated or affiliated research divisions whereas the latter may have to depend on cooperative or public research organizations, or on independent research enterprises;

(3) the problem of public policy with regard to technological research, especially concerning the maintenance of governmental research agencies and concerning governmental support or protection of independent inventors. (With respect to the latter question it has been said that independent inventors remain important as a source of radically novel inventions while the integrated indus-

---

that scientific progress is the result of well-organized research teams. The day of the garret scientist, working alone in a near-bare loft by the flickering light of an oil lamp is almost past. For the scope of knowledge in any one field is so vast that few individuals can fully master it. In addition, an individual effort is dwarfed by the large scale attack on the frontiers of our technical knowledge by incalculable numbers of scientific workers in many great laboratories with unlimited facilities. Even in purely theoretical contributions, the facilities available in these million dollar laboratories are almost indispensable to original work; in experimental investigations the facilities of large laboratories are even more essential." Abraham Coblenz and Harry L. Owens, *Transistors: Theory and Applications*, New York, 1955, p. 1.

[1] "There is much to be said for the small group. It can work quite efficiently. Efficiency does not increase proportionately with numbers. A large group creates complicated administrative problems, and much effort is spent in organisation." Laura Fermi, *Atoms in the Family: My Life with Enrico Fermi*, Chicago, 1954, p. 185. — "The great laboratory may do many important things, at its best, but at its worst it is a morass which engulfs the abilities of the leaders as much as those of the followers." Norbert Wiener, *I am a Mathematician*, Garden City, N.Y., 1956, p. 364.

trial research laboratories are the more efficient producers of the mass of routine inventions[1].)

The main concern of this study is not, however, with problems of the individual research organization but rather with the efficiency of technological research in the economy as a whole.

5. The Rate of Inventive Output in the Economy as a Whole

Are there ranges of increasing and diminishing returns in the production of inventions in the economy as a whole? Is there an optimum point or range in the resource allocation to the "invention industry?" Is the total inventive effort in the economy more likely to be of such dimensions that it would be more efficient if it were expanded or if it were cut down? Not that efficiency in the production of inventions — that is, the smallest possible number of researchers and developers per invention — should be regarded as an end in itself; if society were getting as many inventions per year as it wanted, it would be foolish to push for more just because this would raise the average output per inventive worker; and if the flow of inventions were inadequate and society wanted to increase it, it would be foolish to hold back just because the increase would lower the average per inventive worker. But, even if the possibility of improving the input-output ratio in the production of inventions (by expanding it under increasing returns or curtailing it under diminishing returns) cannot be a decisive factor in society's decision concerning the desired flow of inventions, it is nevertheless something to be taken into account.

Superficially it might appear that the question of increasing or decreasing returns to inventive effort in the economy as a whole is the same as, or related to, the frequently discussed question of the acceleration or retardation of the rate of invention in the course of time. There have been two schools of thought on the subject of the effect of the flow of inventions upon the ease of making further inventions. According to the "acceleration school," the more there is invented the easier it becomes

---

[1] Cf. the testimony of Dr. Frank B. Jewett, President of the Bell Telephone Laboratories, Inc., New York City: "I think it is inevitable that the great bulk of what you might call the run-of-the-mine patents in an industry like ours will inevitably come from your own people ... I think it is equally the case that those few fundamental patents, the things which really mark big changes in the art, are more likely to come from the outside than from the inside. ... there are certain sectors where the independent inventor cannot operate ...There are certain sectors ... where ... the chances are 10 to 1 that they [the fundamental ideas] are going to come from outside big laboratories simply because of the nature of the things." *Investigation of Concentration of Economic Power*, Hearings Before the Temporary National Economic Committee, Seventy-Sixth Congress, First Session, Part 3, Washington, 1939, pp. 971, 976.

to invent still more. This is deduced from the assumption that every new invention furnishes a new idea for potential combination with vast numbers of existing ideas; and from the mathematical proposition that the number of possible combinations increases geometrically with the number of elements. According to the "retardation school," the more there is invented, the harder it becomes to invent still more. This is deduced from the assumption that there are limits to the improvement of technology. In its extreme form, this thesis states that the more there has been invented the less there is left to be invented.

Although this issue concerning the historical — past or future — change in the potential rate of technological progress will presently be shown not to be relevant to the question of the potential returns to inventive effort at any particular time, it is worth while reflecting about it. There is no *a priori* reason why the possibilities of technological development should be either narrowly limited or virtually limitless. Nor is there any legitimate basis for inductive inferences from the relatively brief periods in which accelerated or retarded rates of inventive accomplishment were observed.

In periods of depression the voices of prophets of technological stagnation were usually listened to with greater attention, and repeatedly over the last hundred years persons recognized as authorities at the time told the world that all important inventions had already been made and no further inventions of great import could be expected. Such pessimistic predictions of the future of technological exploration look particularly comical to a reader who has the advantage of hindsight: for they were made before the automotive, electrical, radio-magnetic, and nuclear revolutions of technology had occurred. Thus the predictions were surely wrong at the time they were made. There is little inclination to accept such predictions as correct at the present.

Predictions of an ever-increasing flow of inventions have also been disappointed. Even if patent statistics (which show a drastic decline in patenting relative to the manpower employed in research and development) are rejected as a yardstick for the flow of inventions, no evidence has been presented to support the thesis that the rate of inventive accomplishment has been increasing relative to the size of the population, the labor force, or the inventive work force. There are indications that inventing is becoming increasingly expensive in terms of man-hours. But this need not be taken as counter-evidence to the assertion that inventing becomes easier over time; it may merely be the effect of overly intensive efforts to achieve too much in a short time. And this brings us back to the question of increasing and decreasing returns to inventive activity at a given time.

16*

These are two essentially different issues: one refers to the *shape* of the production function (in the invention industry) at a certain time; the other refers to the *shift* of the production function in the course of time. In other words, increasing or diminishing returns relate to the production possibilities existing at a certain time; accelerating or retarding rates of invention relate to changes of the production possibilities over time. In the former relationship the accomplishment per man is a function of the number of men employed while "time," with all environmental conditions, is unchanged; in the latter the accomplishment per man is a function of time while the number of men employed (in the invention industry) is unchanged (absolutely or relatively to the labor force).

6. The Laws of Returns and the Technology of Producing Technology

Increasing returns in the inventive work of a nation can prevail if the national scale of research is too small to permit sufficient division of labor among specialists and enough cross-fertilization between experts in different fields of knowledge. There may be such a thing as "balanced growth of knowledge" that can be achieved only if the total amount of research is large enough for simultaneous work in many areas. If some of the "frontiers of knowledge" are not manned with sufficiently large forces, the progress of work along other sectors may be retarded. An increase in total work force may then bring about a more than proportional increase in the rate of invention. This range of increasing returns is of course limited: as soon as the required minimum numbers of research workers are allocated to all areas of scientific and technological knowledge, further additions to the inventive work force can at best produce proportional increases in inventions.

As from time to time fundamental discoveries open up entirely new areas of research, development, and experimentation, the opportunities to produce new inventions may be radically improved and an inventive work force which had been large enough to extend far beyond the range of increasing returns may suddenly be too small to take advantage of the new opportunities. In other words, the new (or shifted) production function for inventions may be such that a given amount of inventive labor, previously operating under constant or diminishing returns, would be back in the range of increasing returns.

The possibility of diminishing returns in the invention industry may seem puzzling on first thought. The phenomenon of diminishing returns is always attributable to the presence of one or more "fixed factors,"

factors necessary in the production but not present in increased quantities when the input of "variable factors" is increased. The variable factors, in the case before us, are inventive labor plus the required facilities for research and experimentation (laboratory space, instruments and machines, materials, energy, administrative and clerical help). What are "fixed factors" in the production of inventions?

In order to answer this we must inquire a little into the technology of the production of technological inventions. It is a rather peculiar, bewildering business: in general, technology is the art of transforming certain materials into certain products, usually with the aid of certain kinds of equipment; in the production of inventions, however, technology is also the chief "raw material" and "equipment," and technology is also the "product" to boot. The inventor starts with technology, applies technology, and ends up with technology.

The process of inventing may be schematized as follows. First, the inventor is confronted with a problem, that is, with the dissatisfaction about the ways certain things are done, coupled with a feeling that there are better ways of doing them. Second, he tries to think of similar problems that have been solved before, which either are familiar to him or which he proceeds to study. This usually gives him clues for possible plans to be followed in the solution of his problem. Third, he carries out these plans, several of which may not work but may in their failure suggest other clues. Finally, he finds a solution[1]. If this scheme describes the "technology" of problem-solving and inventing, it also makes clear that in the earlier steps "technology," the existing stock of scientific knowledge and of the industrial arts, enters as raw material and equipment, while in the end "technology," an advance in the technical arts, emerges as the product of the inventive process.

Once the multiple role of technology in the inventive process is understood, it will not appear paradoxical if the existing stock of scientific knowledge and of the industrial arts at any moment of time is named as a fixed factor in the process of producing new inventions. The amount of problems to be solved (the stock of known problems) is another factor fixed at any moment of time. If increasing amounts of variable factors — inventive labor effort with all the required facilities — are applied to a given amount of known problems and a given equipment of known technology, the increase in the amount of product in the form of technological advances will, beyond a point, be less than proportional.

---

[1] Cf. G. Polya, *How to Solve It*, Princeton, 1948, *passim.* From this schematic description it ought to become obvious that a separation of the cost of failures from the cost of successful tries cannot reasonably be attempted.

7. Diminishing Returns

Increased amounts of inventive talent devoted to the search for solutions to *given problems*, and drawing on the *given stock of knowledge*, will bring forth novel solutions in increased amounts but, after some point, the increase in output — solutions, inventions — will not be in proportion to the increase in input. The addition of more research men working on the production of new knowledge would of course always be technically possible (in contrast to those kinds of production where the fixed factor is a tangible thing, such as land or machinery, and where men, beyond some number, would get in one another's way or could physically not get near the fixed factor). But the addition of more re-searchers, beyond some number, would imply duplication of work done by others, resulting not in more new solutions to open problems, but in more frequent instances of simultaneous or nearly simultaneous arrivals by several inventors at similar solutions to the identical problems. The output of new inventions might not be much increased.

Merely in order to guard against misunderstandings, it should be remembered (1) that diminishing returns in the production of inventions prevail not from the start, that is, not for small amounts of input of effort, but only after input has reached a certain point; and (2) that the point where diminishing returns set in is apt to be pushed up as the stock of existing knowledge grows, because the number of problems on which work may fruitfully be done is likely to increase with that growth.

Some economists with an exaggerated opinion of "dynamic theory" and an inadequate understanding of "static reasoning" might hold that the entire conception of diminishing returns is out of place in an area as "intrinsically dynamic" as the production of knowledge. Since any new discovery or invention changes the stock of knowledge as well as the stock of problems to be solved, what sense is there in assuming that knowledge and problems are fixed?

If some seem to have such a hard time seeing the sense of such an assumption, an explanation must be provided even if it schould insult the intelligence of those to whom the point is obvious. The point is that an allocation of research personnel that will fit the research agenda of next year need not fit the agenda today. If the list of problems to be solved is apt to grow from today to next month, and still more to next year, this does not mean that it would serve any good purpose now to employ a research staff too large for the present tasks. It may of course be wise to provide for a gradual increase in the research staff commensurate to the increase in the stock of problems to be solved. At any moment, however, the number of men used for inventive work may be such that the amount of duplication is moderate, substantial, or enormous. At any moment, in other words, the production of inventions may have been pushed far into the range of diminishing returns, conceivably even into the range where marginal returns to inventive input are zero. If the manpower so lavishly employed is kept unchanged for some time, it is possible for the research agenda to grow eventually into the oversized research outfit. This would not make the original overallocation of resources any more justifiable than it would be in any other industry: the expectation of growth, and therefore of growing manpower needs, does not warrant the employment of more labor than can be efficiently used at the time being.

Comprehension of this point is perhaps made more difficult by the realization that the technological horizon may rather suddenly be expanded by a fundamental discovery, shifting the production function for technical inventions most drastically. In view of this peculiar way in which the dynamic aspects of the growth of knowledge impinge on the relevance of static theorizing, it may be desirable to deal once more with the effects which discoveries and inventions may have upon the production of inventions.

8. Problem-Raising Problem-Solutions

Invention is the solution of a technological problem; but it is possible that in the course of solving a problem or as a result of solving it new problems are raised. Thus, an invention may fulfill a task and at the same time create more tasks. To be sure, not all inventions are of this sort. The solution of an old problem may leave less to be done, one item of the agenda having been checked off as completed. We may call such a solution an "agenda-reducing" invention. If the solution, by raising new problems, leaves more to be done than there had been before, we may call it an "agenda-increasing" invention or discovery.

Fundamental discoveries and basic inventions, by definition, open up new vistas and create new opportunities for further invention. Thus, one might be tempted to generalize and state that basic research will yield agenda-increasing discoveries while applied research will yield agenda-reducing inventions. This would, however, be an exaggeration. Industrial research of a definitely "applied" kind may result in inventions of considerable complementarity with solutions to new technical problems. Indeed, a relatively narrow invention may point to some previously unnoticed gap in basic knowledge and thus raise problems for fundamental research. And, more often, an invention of the "mere gadget" type may unexpectedly create the opportunity — nay, the necessity — for scores of additional inventions in the sequel.

Several writers have distinguished between two kinds of invention: fundamental (basic, major, revolutionary, break-through, key) inventions and accessory (adaptive, minor, perfecting, improvement) inventions. Every fundamental invention creates the opportunity for making many accessory inventions. Hence, the emergence of a fundamental invention is apt to change the input-output ratio of inventive effort, that is, the productivity of a given size, and the productivity of a given increase, of the inventive labor force. But the dichotomy is not the same as that between agenda-increasing and agenda-reducing inventions. Merely perfecting inventions, improvement inventions, may likewise suggest possible combinations with other technological elements or possible applications to entirely different kinds of products, and may thus be of the agenda-increasing type, leaving more, not less, to be done in times to come.

The predictions of acceleration or of retardation in the rate of invention, which we have mentioned above, reflect to some extent judgments about the relative frequencies of agenda-increasing and agenda-reducing inventions. But the conflict of recorded opinion is probably less serious than one may think. For it seems that several writers assuming a prevalence of agenda-reducing inventions, and predicting therefore a retardation in the rate of inventive achievements, have been thinking of particular industries or particular areas of technology. Those, on the other hand, who assumed a prevalence of agenda-increasing inventions, and consequently predicted an acceleration of invention, appear to have been thinking of the entire domain of technology. Retardation of invention in particular industries would be perfectly compatible with acceleration of invention in the economy as a whole.

For the economy as a whole, or for the entire domain of technology, the assumption of a prevalence of agenda-increasing inventions is probably more plausible[1]. This does not, however, imply that the production

---

[1] "If there were, in fact, a finite stock of possible inventions and if it could be assumed that the easiest would be made first, then each invention would render the next step more complex and costly and less certain. Or again, if inventive progress is conceived of as a series of 'master' inventions, each giving rise to a limited family of smaller 'improvement' inventions, then ultimately the fecundity of the master invention would become exhausted. It is difficult to draw much support from past experiences for these fundamentally pessimistic assumptions. The conception of a fixed stock of inventive possibilities implies the existence of some ultimate barrier to knowledge. And even if the progeny of each major invention were limited, the number of master inventions, providing the jumping off point for still further inventions, might remain unrestricted.

It is a more realistic hypothesis to suppose that each new invention multiplies the possible combinations of existing ideas and thereby widens the scope for originality. A new invention may at one stroke give fresh value to older ideas up to then unutilised because of some unsurmountable obstacle. A vast accumulation of imperfect ideas is always lying dormant, lacking only some element which can bring them to life. 'Inventions that come before their

function will necessarily shift *upwards* in the sense that a given number of inventors will produce more inventions per unit of time. The continuing increase in the stock of technological problems to be solved, which is implied in the assumption of a prevalence of agenda-increasing inventions, will extend both the ranges of increasing and of diminishing returns to inventive personnel and, thus, will allow a larger inventive work force to be employed without excessively wasteful duplication. But the enlargement of the agenda, the increase in the number of problems on which work can be done, need not increase productivity per research worker. Most of the new problems may be "tougher" than the older problems used to be. The increase in opportunities to invent need not mean that inventions become easier to make; on the contrary, they may become harder to make. In this case, there could be a retardation of invention despite the prevalence of agenda-increasing inventions and despite the continuing increase in "inventive possibilities."

This hypothesis of the increasing difficulties of the new technological problems would force abandonment of the "homogenizing device" proposed in the discussion of the quantification of invention (see above pp. 230 and 234). It may be permissible to speak of an output of inventions of "average difficulty" as long as one deals with the potential solutions of *given* technological problems worked upon by varying numbers of inventive personnel. But if one has to deal with the "dynamic" problem of changes, from period to period, in the state of knowledge and in the stock of problems to be solved, then the "homogenizing" of the output of inventions becomes useless and even misleading.

---

time' must often await some further new idea, perhaps having a usefulness in itself but also acting as a fertilising agent in bringing older ideas to fruition. ... Inventions, each having an importance in its own right, may be combined together to produce a third invention. ... One invention may create a demand for a complementary one. If an invention speeds up only a part of a process, the unimproved part becomes a drag on output and points to a new need. ... Many new inventions create the need for progress in ancillary manufacturing equipment. ...

The discovery of a material with novel physical qualities may be tantamount to a reshuffling of all the technical cards in the pack. If, for example, a metal should be discovered lighter for a given strength than anything known, it might make practicable many devices hitherto frustrated by gravity, and it would have widespread influence upon the design of machines, the relative advantage of hand and natural power and of different types of natural power. ... A new material may lead to a widespread search for possible uses and then success ... the possibilities in the future seem to be limited only by the generality, energy and ingenuity put into search.

The opportunity for invention therefore continually proliferates; what is discovered is a minute fraction of what is discoverable. A sudden mutation, a master invention, opens up new fields both through its cross fertilisation with older ideas and through its possible crop of improvement inventions, and it further clears the ground for other possible major innovations." Jewkes, Sawers, and Stillerman, *op. cit.*, pp. 121sqq.

If the separability of the "static" problem from the "dynamic" problem is conceded, if it is understood that the shift of the production function for inventions is one thing and its shape is another, and if the implications of that shape for problems of resource allocation are realized, then the previously stated conclusion will no longer be questioned; it is possible for society to devote so large amounts of productive resources to the production of inventions that additional inputs will lead to less than proportional increases in output. Whether at any given moment the inventive labor force employed is actually working under diminishing returns or has not been expanded that far, is a question for practical expert judgment.

In any event, even if we knew for certain that society had pushed its inventive efforts far into the phase of diminishing returns, one could not infer that it had gone too far; nor would the most certain knowledge that we are still far away from that phase provide by itself a reason for society to go more heavily into the business of inventing. After all, the evaluation of the *physical* cost of inventing is only a small part of the task of evaluating the economic or social net benefit of inventive work. But it is by no means irrelevant or unimportant to know that the cost of inventions in terms of physical inputs may, depending on the circumstances, be diminishing, constant, or increasing, and also to know under what circumstances one might have to take account of the possibility that the cost is increasing at a forbidding rate.

9. Inventions Selected or Rejected for Use

Not all new inventions turn out to be workable; not all that seem technically workable turn out to be commercially usable; and not all that might be commercially usable are actually used, many being rejected in favor of others that look more promising. As a matter of fact, the percentage of all new inventions actually put to practical use is very small indeed[1].

---

[1] "Invention is necessarily wasteful. When everything feasible has been done to plan research coherently, the uncertainty of the outcome, even of the less revolutionary inventions, is bound to mean much failure and disappointment. Thus Carter and Williams report that: 'It is not possible to get useful statistics for the proportion of good ideas that are rejected after applied research — in industrial laboratories that we have visited it varies between 50 and 90 per cent. — but certainly the proportion is high.' Even the ideas that pass this technical test may fail to pass the economic test and may very properly be rejected at this stage." Thomas Wilson, "Science and Industry", *Lloyds Bank Review*, London, October, 1957, p. 37. — It has been estimated that between 80 and 90 percent of all patented inventions remain unused for technical or economic reasons. Cf. Peter Meinhardt, *Inventions, Patents, and Monopoly*, 2nd Ed., London, 1950, p. 256. Other estimates are even more pessimistic:

Should only the inventions selected for use or also the rejected ones be counted in the quantity of inventions produced? One may wish to follow the practice of other industries in reporting total output, and ask whether "rejects" — "units" or "lots" discarded as substandard — are commonly included in or excluded from "total output." It happens that conventions are not uniform. In a large number of industries, anything that is rejected as inferior, defective, or below standard before it is shipped or sold is not regarded as produced, whereas waste or discard in processing plants or in distributing establishments is included in total output. (For example, in fruit crops, the quantities not approved for sale are excluded, but the quantities spoiled in transport or at the distributors are included; the steel output excludes defective lots which the steel mill regards as scrap, but includes the waste and scrap at the fabricators; total paper production excludes the socalled "broke" in paper manufacturing mills, but includes the waste in paper converting mills.) Thus, it usually depends on where the quality control takes place and who does the rejecting. But, no matter whether this or any other terminological convention is followed, it should always be possible to distinguish "gross" and "net" production and to ascertain the "net output" — quantity produced net of all rejected or discarded portions — or the "effective supply" — the schedule of quantities supplied after deducting rejected quantities. If the ratio of "rejects" to gross output is in any way related to changes in the latter, it will be highly significant not to stop the analysis with the gross output. This seems to be an important consideration with regard to inventions: for there are several strong reasons for expecting that the share of rejected inventions increases as the total output of inventions, selected plus rejected ones, increases.

The rejection of an invention may be either implicit in the failure to consider its application or explicit after hasty or thorough consideration. Such rejection may occur at many different points; the invention may

"Perhaps 95 per cent of all patents have no commercial value at all." Jewkes, Sawers, and Stillerman, *op. cit.*, p. 106. — The failure of patentees to renew their patents, in countries charging renewal fees, throws some light on this question. In Germany before 1920, 80 percent of all patents had been allowed to lapse after six years and more than 96 percent had been allowed to lapse earlier than after 15 years, their maximum duration. See Robolski and Lutter, "Patentrecht", *Handwörterbuch der Staatswissenschaften*, 4., gänzlich umgearb. Aufl., Bd. VI, Jena, 1925, p. 826. On the other hand a recent study of "patent use" comes to a surprisingly high ratio of patented inventions actually used by the patentee or his assignee; but it was based on a questionnaire method, which is not usually satisfactory evidence. Barkev S. Sanders, Joseph Rossman, and L. James Harris, "The Non-Use of Patented Inventions", *The Patent, Trademark, and Copyright Journal of Research and Education*, Vol. II, Washington, D. C., 1958, pp. 1sqq.

not be accepted as a project for applied research and development[1]; it may be so accepted but dropped later at some stage during the development phase[2]; it may be fully developed but still require large-scale testing in pioneer plants, regarded as too costly and too risky[3]; it may technically be all ready for practical application except that it has yet to pass a market test judged to be too risky by the sales department; it may be given a market test, but fail; it may have passed all technical and market tests, and still fail to be adopted in competition with other ventures looking more promising to a busy management which cannot get around to doing all the things that might look good. At almost every one of these points in the career of an invention toward its application the ratio of rejections is likely to increase as the flow of invention, in the sense of the "gross total" of inventions produced, is enlarged.

10. Ten Reasons for an Increasing Rejection Ratio

The following reasons for the increasing rejection ratio deserve emphasis:

(1) Some inventions are alternative solutions of the same or similar production problems and provide new methods of production which are

---

[1] There is not "any simple or uniform percentage of research results that go into development. That varies very largely from firm to firm with the origin of their research or development projects and with the ways in which potential projects are evaluated. Nevertheless many research results are not taken further, either because it seems fairly clear that it would be unprofitable to develop them, or because some must be excluded on cost grounds. The greater the cost of development, the greater the importance of exclusion. The less the attention of the research staff to the commercial significance of their projects, the greater the chance that research with great potentialities in industrial application will be excluded, if only because a man who is preoccupied with research as such will not be anxious to follow his idea on to the development staff." Carter and Williams, *op. cit.*, p. 58.

[2] "Development is a term which is loosely used in general discussion to cover a wide range of activities and purposes, but all these activities seem to satisfy three conditions. One, development is the stage at which known technical methods are applied to a new problem which, in wider or narrower terms, has been defined by the original invention. Of course, it may happen that in the course of development a blockage occurs, existing technology may provide no answers, and then, what is strictly another invention, is called for to set the ball rolling once more. Two, and consequentially, development is the stage at which the task to be performed is more precisely defined, the aim more exactly set, the search more specific, the chances of final success more susceptible to measurement than is true at the stage of invention. Invention is the stage at which the scent is first picked up, development the stage at which the hunt is in full cry. . . . Three, development is the phase in which commercial considerations can be, and indeed must be, more systematically examined, the limits of feasibility imposed by the market are narrowed down." Jewkes, Sawers, and Stillerman, *op. cit.*, pp. 18 sq.

[3] "Sometimes development consists of finding ways of producing on a large scale the same thing — or broadly the same thing — as has been produced already on a small scale . . ." *Ibid.*, p. 199.

substitutable for each other. Naturally, only the best will be used. The ratio of inventions of technologically substitutable processes to the total number of inventions is likely to be greater if the total is greater[1].

(2) Some inventions usually refer to new products which appear to be so strongly substitutable for each other that only the most promising ones are exploited. Again, the number of inventions of new "inferior substitutes" is likely to be a greater part of all inventions made within a period if the total number of inventions is greater[2].

(3) Some inventions of improved processes for producing or fabricating known products may never be used if these products are displaced by new products developed at the same time on the basis of other inventions. In other words, the annual crop of inventions may contain some that make obsolete, not older inventions, but also inventions which are part of the same crop. The greater the number of inventions, the greater probably will be the ratio of inventions of new processes applicable only to products which are on the way out.

(4) Limits in the size or growth of the research and development departments of industrial firms may make it impossible to increase the number of inventions accepted for development work at the same rate as the gross output of inventions increases. Often the same personnel is charged with both inventive and developmental work, and the stepping up of the former, if it has not encroached on the latter, may not have permitted it to grow proportionately[3]. In this case, the decision to undertake the development of new inventions will be merely a choice among

---

[1] The increased ratio of substitute process inventions is due to the same condition that causes an increased ratio of multiple inventions, namely, the fact that every age presents its researchers and inventors with certain technical problems and, as the number of people engaged in inventive activities increases, the number of those working on the same problems will increase. It is inevitable that an increasing percentage of the solutions will overlap. In the case of "multiple" inventions only the first-finished is patentable and the duplicate, the triplicates, etc., are not counted even among the "gross total;" "substitute" inventions, however, are recognized as different inventions and are therefore counted among the gross output — though they probably remain unused.

[2] What was said, in the preceding footnote, about substitute-process inventions applies fully to substitute-product inventions.

[3] "The limit to the rate of growth in research departments in any one period ... is set by finance — for the use of the research department to increase turnover is often a precondition of an increase in research expenditure; it is set by the efficient rate of growth in the research team itself — newcomers must become familiar with the problems of the firm and new graduates with the ways of industrial research, projects must be formulated and planned, research leaders must be recruited and trained; it is set by the capacity of the production departments to absorb change, and this capacity is often dependent on draining scientists and technologists away from the research department itself." Carter and Williams, *op. cit.*, p. 57.

alternative projects, a more discriminating selection from an increased supply of "raw inventions." Thus, the ratio of inventions not accepted for further development may increase with the flow of inventions.

(5) Some inventions require not only enormous development work but also large-scale testing in pilot plants[1]. The amount of investment in pilot plants and the amount of time management can devote to such undertakings within a certain period are limited and may not be expansible at the same rate at which the flow of inventions is enlarged. Unless the ratio of inventions that need large-scale testing is reduced, the ratio of inventions that remain unused for lack of testing is apt to increase with the total number of inventions.

(6) Inventions of new products may present serious problems of consumer acceptance, especially if only mass production of these products would be economical. But there is a limit to the number of market tests which the selling department of a firm may be able and willing to undertake at the same time; and surely a limit to the number of new products for which sales campaigns can be conducted simultaneously with good chances of success. Thus, unless the ratio of inventions of new products for which markets have to be tested or created is reduced, the ratio of inventions remaining unused because of uncertain marketability will probably increase when the number of inventions increases.

(7) The exploitation of certain inventions depends on the availability of adequate supplies of particular factors of production and may become impossible if these factors become too dear. It may happen that many of the new inventions would require the use of the same factors — specific types of labor, material — and that increased prices of these factors will make the exploitation of some of the inventions commercially impossible. The occurrence of such instances will be more likely the larger the total number of inventions.

(8) Resources regularly required for the exploitation of inventions are capital funds. Even so-called capital-saving inventions may in the short run increase the demand for investment funds. Limitations in the availability of increased funds will ordinarily imply limitations in the rate of exploitation of new inventions. A larger number of new inventions, therefore, may merely enlarge the scope of the *choice* of inventions for practical utilization but not the *number* of inventions actually utilized. The scarcity of investible funds makes it almost inevitable that the share

---

[1] "The task of producing on a large scale may be different in kind or highly different in degree from that of producing on a small. In the chemical industry especially the manufacture in quantity of what has already successfully been produced in a test tube in a laboratory may confront the developers even with different chemical reactions arising out of the scale of operation." Jewkes, Sawers, and Stillerman, *op. cit.*, p. 19.

of unexploited inventions will be greater the larger the total number of new inventions made per unit of time.

(9) Entrepreneurial energy and managerial effort are indispensable for the execution of innovations. But there is a limit to the amount of innovative work that management can undertake within a period[1]. When there are more projects that look attractive, potential innovations that appear promising, this may merely force management to be more selective in their decisions to innovate. Thus, the ratio of inventions remaining unused because of limitations of innovative enterprise is apt to increase with the flow of inventions in search of innovators.

(10) The utilization of inventions of improved processes and superior equipment is often postponed until the full cost of the new production is clearly below the prime cost of production with the old equipment. For only in such cases will the premature scrapping of old equipment appear economical. It stands to reason that the relative share of inventions the exploitation of which is "temporarily postponed" (and in the meantime completely superseded by later inventions) will be greater as the number of inventions increases[2].

There may be several other reasons, besides those enumerated here, why the ratio of "new inventions put to use" to "new inventions made" will be smaller the faster the rate of invention. It is probably safe to predict that an increase in the number of "raw" inventions generated under the inducement of increased rates of compensation will ordinarily be associated with a smaller than proportional increase in the number of inventions actually put to work.

III. The Effective Supply and Cost of Inventions

We have now reached a convenient point to bring together the major results of our analyses of the supply of inventive labor, the production of inventions, and their selection for use.

---

[1] "... there is plainly a *physical* maximum to the number of things any individual or group of individuals can do ..." Edith Tilton Penrose, *The Theory of the Growth of the Firm*, Oxford, 1959, p. 45.

[2] It may be worth remarking that only the last of the ten listed reasons for non-use of inventions may be related to what is often decried as "suppression of patents" by monopolistic interests attempting to slow down the obsolescence of capital equipment. But the motive alone (to avoid "premature" obsolescence) is not acceptable as a criterion in a test of "suppression" since the continued use of old equipment, and non-use of superior equipment and processes, may be consistent with the "economic principle" and the "competitive norm."

The Four Shrinkages

First, we discussed the supply of inventive labor, regardless of quality, and found it to be subject to increasing supply prices. Second, we looked into the supply of inventive labor capacity and were impressed with the possibility that additions to the inventive personnel are of inferior quality. Third, we analyzed the supply of new (raw) inventions and concluded that, beyond a point, the law of diminishing returns will be operative. And fourth, we inquired into the supply of inventions selected for actual use and discovered a tendency toward a diminishing ratio of exploitation.

These findings may be formulated in the following four propositions:

(I) As the total amount of compensation for inventive work increases, the amount of inventive labor is likely to increase less than proportionately.

(II) As the total amount of employment of inventive labor increases, the size of inventive labor capacity (the amount of inventive labor corrected for quality) is likely to increase less than proportionately.

(III) As the total amount of inventive labor capacity (the input of inventive labor of standard quality) increases, the amount of new inventions made (the output in the form of workable technological ideas) may increase less than proportionately.

(IV) As the total amount of new inventions increases, the amount of "effective" new inventions (inventions developed and actually put to work) is likely to increase less than proportionately.

The cumulative loss in the efficiency of incremental compensation for inventive work may be very serious. We shall show elsewhere that the four "transmission-losses" in the transformation of social energy need not exhaust the list of possible cost items in the accelerated procurement of workable inventions.

These relationships can be expressed in the form of four supply functions — namely, the supply of (i) inventive personnel, (ii) inventive capacity, (iii) new "raw" inventions, and (iv) effective ("worked") inventions — in terms of the prices or compensations offered, that is, as functions of the compensation paid (i) per inventive worker, (ii) per unit of inventive labor of standard quality, (iii) per invention of standard importance, and (iv) per utilized invention of standard importance. Put in this form, one may state that

(I) the supply of inventive labor is unlikely to be infinitely elastic and quite likely to be relatively inelastic,

(II) the supply of inventive labor capacity is probably even less elastic than the supply of inventive labor,

(III) the supply of new raw inventions may, in certain circumstances, be even less elastic than the supply of inventive labor capacity, and

(IV) the supply of effective (worked) inventions is likely to be even less elastic than the supply of raw inventions.

Of course, it is *conceivable* that all four supply functions are infinitely elastic: additional inventive labor may be available at the same rate of pay and of the same quality, and new raw inventions may be produceable under constant returns and found to be eligible for application at an undiminished rate. In this case a given percentage increase in the outlay for inventive work will yield an equal percentage increase in the number of inventions selected for application. But there are four potential "shrinkages" of the percentage increase in yield: higher rates of pay, lower quality of the personnel, smaller output of raw inventions per input of inventive capacity, and a higher rate of rejection in the selection of inventions for use. These shrinkages are independent of one another; but they may add up with a vengeance.

* * *

Zusammenfassung: Das Angebot von Erfindern und Erfindungen. — Die Analyse des Angebots von Erfindungen kann logisch in drei Teile gegliedert werden: 1. in das Angebot von Erfinderarbeit — der Hauptfaktor für die Produktion von Erfindungen; 2. in die Einsatz-Ausstoß-Beziehung (input-output relationship) — die technische »Produktionsfunktion«, die die Umformung von Erfinderarbeit in nützliche Erfindungen beschreibt, und 3. in das Angebot und die Kosten nützlicher Erfindungen — das Ergebnis der beiden eben genannten Funktionen.

Das Angebot von Erfinderarbeit ist auf kurze Sicht relativ unelastisch und auch auf lange Sicht nicht sehr elastisch. Zusätzliche Forscher können nur durch höhere Gehälter angelockt werden und mögen weniger qualifiziert sein. Daher dürften die Grenzkosten der Erfinderarbeit außerordentlich schnell steigen.

Eine Produktionsfunktion von Erfindungen ist theoretisch sinnvoll, selbst wenn sie weder rechnerisch noch sonstwie empirisch erfaßt werden können. Wie hoch ist das Grenzprodukt bei Erfinderarbeit? Es ist durchaus möglich, daß abnehmende Erträge vorwiegen werden: zu viele Erfinder mögen an einer gegebenen Zahl von Problemen arbeiten. Es gibt jedoch Problemlösungen, die ihrerseits wieder neue Probleme aufwerfen, wodurch die Produktionsfunktion verschoben wird, so daß sich ein gegenwärtig übermäßiger Aufwand für Forschung und Entwicklungsarbeiten in der Zukunft nicht als übertrieben erweisen könnte. Die Annahme einer Beschleunigung der Rate der Erfindungen mag, obwohl es zweifelhaft ist, nicht unvereinbar mit abnehmenden Erträgen sein; die letzten beziehen sich auf einen Zeitpunkt, die erste auf eine lange Periode.

Nur ein Bruchteil aller Erfindungen wird tatsächlich in der Produktion verwendet, und dieser Bruchteil nimmt noch ab, wenn mehr Erfindungen gemacht werden. Das ist aus verschiedenen Gründen so, vor allem wegen der Grenzen, die durch das jeweilige Kapitalangebot, die Leistungsfähigkeit des unternehmerischen Leistungsapparats und die Größe des mit der Weiterentwicklung der »Roh«-Erfindungen betrauten Stabs gesetzt werden. Dazu kommt noch die Tatsache, daß der Prozentsatz der untereinander substituierbaren Erfindungen mit der Zahl der Erfindungen, die in der Zeiteinheit gemacht werden, zunimmt.

Die Wirksamkeit von wachsenden Zuwendungen finanzieller Mittel für die Erfindertätigkeit wird so durch vier Faktoren verringert: durch höhere Gehälter, eine niedrigere Qualität der Arbeitskräfte, einen kleineren Ausstoß von »Roh«-Erfindungen je eingesetzter Einheit von Erfinderkapazität und eine höhere Rate von Zurückweisungen bei der Auswahl von Erfindungen für die praktische Verwendung.

*

Résumé: L'offre d'inventeurs et d'inventions. — L'analyse de l'offre d'inventions se divise logiquement en trois parties: 1. l'offre du travail d'invention — le facteur le plus important pour la production d'inventions; 2. la relation entre *input* et *output* — la fonction productrice technique, qui décrit la transformation du travail d'invention en inventions utiles; 3. l'offre et les coûts d'inventions utiles — le résultat des deux fonctions susmentionnées.

L'offre de travail inventif est relativement inélastique à court terme; elle n'est pas très élastique à long terme non plus. Un travail de recherche additionnel ne s'obtient qu'au moyen de salaires plus élevés, et les nouveaux rechercheurs pourraient être moins bien qualifiés. C'est pourquoi le coût marginal du travail inventif montera très rapidement.

La fonction productrice des inventions est bien d'un intérêt théorique, même si leur valeur ne peut être calculée ni même déterminée empiriquement. Quel sera le produit marginal du travail d'invention? Il est bien possible, que les rendements diminuants seront de règle. Il se peut qu'un nombre trop grand de rechercheurs travaille à un nombre donné de problèmes. Toutefois, il y a des problèmes, dont la solution crée de nouveaux problèmes, ce qui déplacera la fonction productrice, de sorte que les dépenses pour travaux de recherche et de développement, qui paraissent excessives pour le moment, soient justifiées plus tard. L'idée d'une accélération de la production d'inventions, bien que douteuse, n'est pas incompatible avec un rendement diminuant. Ce dernier se rapporte à un instant, tandis que l'accélération se rapporte à une longue période.

Ce n'est qu'une partie de toutes les inventions qui est utilisée dans la production, et cette partie diminuera encore, dès que les inventions augmenteront. Et cela pour plusieurs raisons; surtout à cause des limitations générales imposées par l'offre de capital, la capacité d'entreprise et le nombre de personnes engagées dans le développement des inventions «brutes». A part tout cela, le pourcentage des inventions mutuellement substituables augmente avec le nombre d'inventions faites dans l'unité de temps.

L'efficacité de l'augmentation des ressources financières allouées à l'activité inventive est donc diminuée par quatre facteurs: l'augmentation des salaires, qualification moindre du personnel, diminution de l'*output* d'inventions «brutes» par unité d'*input*, et rejet d'un plus grand nombre d'inventions à la sélection pour l'utilisation pratique.

Resumen: La oferta de inventores y de invenciones. — El análisis de la oferta de invenciones se divide lógicamente en tres partes: 1. la oferta del trabajo inventivo — el factor principal para la producción de invenciones. 2. la relación entre entradas y salidas («input-output relationship») — la «función de producción» técnica que describe la transformación del trabajo inventivo en invenciones útiles; 3. la oferta y el coste de invenciones útiles — el resultado de las dos funciones mencionadas.

La oferta de trabajo inventivo es relativamente rígida a plazo corto, y a plazo largo tampoco es muy elástica. Investigaciones adicionales se obtienen solamente por salarios más elevados y los nuevos inventores pueden ser menos calificados. Es por eso que el coste marginal del trabajo inventivo subirá muy de prisa.

Una función productiva de invenciones es teóricamente de gran alcance, aunque no pueda ser calculada ni determinada empíricamente. ¿ Qué será el producto marginal del trabajo inventivo ? Es muy posible que rendimientos decrecientes prevalezcan. Puede presentarse el caso que un grupo demasiado grande de inventores trabaja en un número dado de problemas. Pero hay problemas, la solución de los cuales crea nuevos problemas, lo que desplazará la función productiva, de manera que los gastos para trabajos de investigación y de desarrollo, según parece excesivos por el momento, podrían mostrarse justificados más tarde. La noción de una aceleración en la producción de invenciones, aunque sea dudosa, no es incompatible con un rendimiento decreciente. El último se refiere a un instante, mientras que la aceleración se refiere a un período largo.

Solamente una parte de todas las invenciones es utilizada en la producción y esta parte disminuirá todavía, luego que las invenciones aumentarán. Y eso por varias razones. Las más importantes son las limitaciones generales provenientes de la oferta de capital, la capacidad emprendedora y el número de personas que trabajan al desarollo de invenciones «brutas». Además el porcentaje de las invenciones mutuamente sustituíbles aumenta con la cantidad de las invenciones hechas en la unidad de tiempo.

La eficacia del uso creciente de medios financieros para la actividad inventiva es reducida así por cuatro factores: el aumento de los salarios, la calidad inferior del personal, la diminución de la salida (output) de invenciones «brutas» por unidad de entrada y el aumento de rechazos en la selección de invenciones para el uso práctico.

*

Riassunto: L'offerta di inventori e di invenzioni. — L'analisi dell'offerta di invenzioni è logicamente divisa in tre parti: 1. l'offerta del lavoro inventivo — il fattore principale per la produzione di invenzioni, 2. la relazione fra immissione ed erogazione («input-output relationship») — la «funzione di produzione» tecnica che descrive la trasformazione del lavoro inventivo in invenzioni utili. 3. l'offerta ed i costi di invenzioni utili — risultato delle due funzioni menzionate.

L'offerta di lavoro inventivo è relativamente rigida a corto termine ed anche a lungo termine non è molto elastica. Ricerche addizionali sono ottenute soltanto per mezzo di salari più alti e i nuovi inventori possono mostrarsi meno qualificati. Da ciò deriva che i costi marginali del lavoro inventivo aumenteranno con gran velocità.

Una funzione produttiva delle invenzioni è teoricamente significativa, benchè non si possa calcolarla nè determinarla empiricamente. Quale sarà il prodotto marginale del lavoro inventivo ? Può essere che rendimenti decrescenti saranno prevalenti. Può accadere che un gruppo troppo grande di inventori lavora in un numero dato di problemi. Però vi sono problemi che con la loro soluzione creano nuovi problemi e per questo la funzione produttiva sarà spostata, cosicchè le spese per lavori di ricerca e di sviluppo, a quanto pare eccessive per il momento, potrebbero mostrarsi giustificate più tardi. La nozione di un'accelerazione nella produzione di invenzioni, benchè

17*

dubbiosa, non è incompatibile con un rendimento decrescente. L'ultimo si riferisce a un istante, mentre che l'accelerazione si riferisce a un lungo periodo.

Soltanto una parte di tutte le invenzioni è utilizzata nella produzione e questa parte diminuirà ancora, appena che le invenzioni aumenteranno. E cioè per varie ragioni, soprattutto a causa delle limitazioni generali che sono imposte per l'offerta di capitale, la capacità imprenditora ed il numero di persone que lavoran allo sviluppo delle invenzioni «brute». Oltre ciò la percentuale delle invenzioni mutuamente sostituibili aumenta con la quantità delle invenzioni fatte nell'unità di tempo.

L'efficacia dell'uso crescente di mezzi finanziari per l'attività inventiva è ridotta così per quattro fattori: l'aumento dei salari, la qualità inferiore del personale, la diminuzione dell'erogazione (output) di invenzioni «brute» per unità di immissione e l'aumento dei rifiuti nella selezione di invenzioni per l'uso pratico.

[19]

The Optimum Lag of Imitation Behind Innovation

By FRITZ MACHLUP

Prefatorial note: The following essay was contributed to a volume in honor of Fredrik Zeuthen.

Defining »innovation« as the first application of a new idea in the production of goods and services, and calling any of its subsequent applications by other producers »imitation«, we may say that technical progress, or the increase in the productivity of given quantities of productive resources, will depend on both innovation and imitation. If, for example, only one agricultural producer introduces an improved technique while all the others continue to use the old techniques, the realized productivity increase will be negligible as far as the economy as a whole is concerned. If one industrial producer introduces a new process while his competitors go on using less efficient methods of production, the economies made possible by the technological advance will be confined to the part of the output produced by the innovator (and consumers may hardly benefit at all). If a manufacturer introduces a novel product, but produces it only in quantities far below those saleable at a price that would cover long-run marginal costs, and if no other producer takes up this production, the realized increase in productivity may be substantially below the potential increase.[1]

The Rate of Innovation and the Rate of Imitation

It is perhaps not too trite a tautology to spell out that in a »world of monopolies«, in which the entire world output of any one commodity is produced by a single firm, and in which new technologies apply to

---

[1] Where technological progress consists in the availability of new products the resulting increase in productivity (and national product) is not measured by customary social-accounting methods.

one product only, imitation would play no role, and the rate of innovation alone would determine the effective growth of productivity. In a world of multi-firm industries, on the other hand, where no firm produces a large portion of the industry's total output and where new technologies would apply to many other firms and perhaps also to other industries, the rate of imitation would be of paramount importance in the determination of the effective growth of productivity. It is less tautological, and may sound even slightly paradoxical, if we add that the profit-oriented incentive to innovate is likely to be largest in an economy that approaches neither a world of monopolies nor a world of diminutive units in densely populated industries: in the former, the incentive may be small because of the absence of actual or anticipated competitive pressure, in the latter it may be small because of the fear of swift competitive imitation squelching the hopes for high profits from innovation. If the lag of competitive imitation behind innovation were zero, profits would be zero and business firms could not afford to invest in innovation; if the lag were infinite, everybody enjoying a permanent monopoly, profits would be »comfortable« without innovation, and firms would not be under pressure to innovate. This suggests that, in an enterprise economy, competitive imitation with a time lag greater than zero and less than infinity is important for the growth of productivity in two respects: it functions as a spur to the *first* application and it assures the *general* application of new technical ideas. In other words, competitive imitation after some, not too extended, interval not only is the vehicle by which technological advance becomes effective as a general increase in productivity, but it is also a spur to innovation and thus helps towards there being more to imitate.

The present essay will not deal with all relationships involved here, but primarily with the fear that unrestrained competitive imitation is too rapid for an adequate rate of innovation; with the consequent belief that measures, by business and government, to increase the lag of imitation behind innovation will always increase the rate of innovation; with the possibility that the lag may actually be too great and thus retard the growth of productivity without accelerating innovation to any significant degree; and with the notion of an »optimum lag« of imitation behind innovation. Before we embark on this discussion, comments on two concepts customarily employed in such discourses would be helpful: the concepts of »changes in the production function« and »perfect competition«. But we shall dispense with this digression.

Innovators' Sunk Costs and Quasi-Rents

Our main task is to examine the relationship between the incentive to innovate and the length of the time lag of competitive imitation behind innovation. It is almost self-evident that the size of the sunk cost of innovation, the size of the quasi-rents attributable to the innovation, the rate of interest, and the discount for the uncertainty of future net in-comes will be among the chief variables in any model built for the analysis of this problem. Such a model can be made more »realistic« by adding additional variables and making »life-like« assumptions concerning all variables, but as a general rule such realism would be at the expense not only of convenience but also of relevance.

We shall attempt to avoid cumbersome or irrelevant realism by the following stipulations: The »*sunk cost of innovations*« include all such outlays for research, development, experimentation, and implementation of the novel piece of technology, as need not be incurred by any subsequent imitators. The »*innovator's quasi-rents*« are all those parts of their gross revenues that can be attributed to the innovation (that is, that would not have accrued but for the innovation) and will be eliminated when imitators in sufficient number take up the business and depress selling prices to the competitive level.[2] Under realistic assumptions, an innovator's quasi-rent would rise and fall gradually; it may not begin to flow until some time after the innovation is completed; its rise may be checked by a price policy designed not to attract competitive imitators; it may not start falling for some time after the first competitive imitators have entered the field; and it may decline little by little as the number of imitators increases and selling prices are depressed towards the level of imitators' marginal cost. In counterfactual simplification of our model we shall assume that the quasi-rent begins to flow immediately after the innovated production is started; that it remains unchanged at the level consistent with the most sensible price policy of a seller not expecting his policy to affect the appearance

---

[2] The term »quasi-rents« is used in preference to »monopoly-profits« because the period before the entry of the imitators need not be artificially lengthened by »monopolistic« devices.

16

242   FRITZ MACHLUP

of competitive imitators and the disappearance of his quasi-rent; that these imitators come upon the scene all at the same time and slash selling prices at one stroke; in brief, that the annual quasi-rent remains constant from the beginning to its sudden end. The »*rate of interest*« is the opportunity cost of the financial resources used by the innovator to defray the sunk cost of innovation, and also the rate at which future quasi-rents are capitalized; it will be assumed to be uniform for all innovators and to include the rate of discount for the uncertainty with which such future quasi-rents are expected. »More realistic« rates of discount for uncertainty would be neither uniform nor independent of the futurity of the expected incomes; uncertainty surely increases with the time-distance, and the rates of discount would therefore be greater for quasi-rents of a more distant future. This, undoubtedly, is highly relevant but may yet be disregarded in »first approximations« to the problem, because it merely reinforces the effect of time distance and would unduly complicate the algebraic form of our model.[3]

Perhaps the least legitimate feature of this model is its failure to make the imitation lag a function of the size of the innovator's quasi-rent (relative to the current cost and the capital requirements of imitative production). The innovator has some discretion in setting his selling prices and thus in determining the size of his quasi-rents; he may thus affect the strength of the inducement to others to imitate him. The less moderate the innovator is in his policies concerning prices and profits, the shorter may be the imitation lag. This dependence is disregarded here for reasons of analytical convenience.

An innovation will pay for itself if the quasi-rents received over the years of the imitation lag will fully cover the sunk cost of innovation. Assuming that innovations will be undertaken only when they are expected to pay for themselves, the expected quasi-rents during the years of the expected imitation lag, capitalized at the rate of discount

---

[3] For the algebraic form of the model we shall use the following notations: S .... the sunk cost of innovation; Q ... the quasi-rents per year before imitators invade the field and depress prices; t ... the time-lag of imitation behind innovation, i.e., the number of years in which Q is received; i ... the rate of discount for both futurity and uncertainty of expected rents. S, Q, and t refer to *actual* magnitudes, known to an omniscient being; *expected* magnitudes are denoted by the same symbols, marked with a dot: thus, expected sunk costs are $\dot{S}$, expected quasi-rents, $\dot{Q}$, and the expected lag is $\dot{t}$.

for futurity and uncertainty, must be at least equal to the expected sunk cost.[4] If the discount rate were zero, and the expected imitation lag (i. e., the life of the quasi-rent) were ten years, the expected sunk cost ought not to be larger than ten times the expected annual quasi-rent (that is, the quasi-rent must not be smaller than one-tenth the sunk cost). If the discount rate is positive, so that future incomes are discounted, quasi-rents required for a project to be attractive must be relatively higher in order to make up for the discount. For example, if the rate of discount is ten per cent per annum and the expected imitation lag is ten years, the expected sunk cost ought not to be larger than six and one-third times the expected annual quasi-rent (that is, the quasi-rent must not be much smaller than one-sixth the sunk cost).[5]

The Imitation Lag and the Incentive to Innovate

Let us now inquire into the »adequacy« of the imitation lag when the sunk costs of innovation and the annual quasi-rents of the innovator are assumed to be given.

The relationships are easily seen especially if, for a moment only, we imagine the discount rate to be zero.[6] Where the sunk costs are relatively small, or the quasi-rents relatively large, a short imitation lag will suffice for the rents to cover the costs. In such instances the expectation of merely the »natural headstart« of the innovator – due to the simple fact that all human action takes time, even where there are no deliberate delays – may be adequate to induce innovation.

Where the sunk costs are relatively large, or the quasi-rents relatively

---

[4] A decision to innovate will be made when

$$\frac{1}{i}(1 - e^{-ii})\dot{Q} \gtreqless \dot{S},$$

where e is the base of the natural logarithm, conveniently used for finding the present value of an annuity with continuous compounding. If $i = 0$, the above formula reduces to

$$i\dot{Q} \gtreqless \dot{S}.$$

[5] If $i = 10$ and $i = 0.10$, $\frac{1}{i}(1 - e^{-ii}) = 10(1 - \frac{1}{e}) = 10 - \frac{10}{2.7\ldots} = 6.3\ldots$

[6] If $i = 0$, an innovation will look commercially sound when $i \geq \frac{\dot{S}}{\dot{Q}}$.

16*

small, only a long imitation lag can make it possible for the rents to cover the costs. Such a long imitation lag can often be secured through government measures delaying imitation beyond the natural lag. Patent systems, without broad provisions for compulsory licensing, attempt to create such a delay by conferring temporary monopolies in the commercial use of inventions; but the patent monopoly will often fail to prolong the life of the innovator's quasi-rent. For in lieu of close imitation, which alone can be barred by the patent law, the development of substitute techniques or substitute products may evoke the competition that effects the crucial price reductions and the elimination of the innovator's rent. As a result, innovators cannot count on the interval before the advent of effective competition to extend over the entire period of patent protection for their invention. This is an awkward quandary: for, while patent protection cannot protect the innovator from competitive circum-invention and while the innovator will therefore be inclined to reckon with a lag shorter than the term of the patent monopoly, he may actually succeed by all sorts of devices (including improvement patents, trademark, goodwill) in securing a monopoly position for a period exceeding the duration of the patent. In such cases the *actual* lag would exceed the patent term, while the *expected* lag would fall short of it. Yet it is the expected lag that is supposed to encourage innovation.

Because circum-invention can take the place of direct imitation in terminating the innovator's quasi-rents, and because innovators are well aware of this fact, patent terms of 16 or 17 years are probably no more effective in stimulating innovation than terms of only 12 or 14 years would be; furthermore, subsidization of innovation through direct contributions to the sunk cost (e. g., government-financed research[7]) or through contributions to the innovator's rents, is apt to be more effective and less wasteful than the indirect subsidization through attempts to prolong by means of patents the period for which innovators can count on receiving quasi-rents – if they are lucky enough to receive any at all.

[7] In the United States as well as in the United Kingdom more than 50 per cent of all outlays for research and development have in recent years been financed by the government. This, of course, has been a part of the defense efforts and would probably not have evolved in the absence of the cold war.

This argument – that the incentive to innovate created by a longer patent term would hardly be much greater than that created by a shorter term – is reinforced when one assumes that the rate of interest is positive. Incomes expected to accrue in a distant future are »shrunk« to very small present values if the discount rate is high. (For example, one dollar collected 17 years from now has a present value of only 8 cents or 3 cents if the internal interest rate is 15 or 20 per cent, respectively. A 20 per cent rate for internal profitability calculations is by no means unusual). The argument becomes still stronger if one introduces a rate of discount for uncertainty that increases with the time-distance, that is, if incomes expected in a more remote future are discounted at a higher rate than incomes expected sooner. Three facts thus explain why the extension of patent protection over more years is apt to become worthless as an additional incentive for innovation: (a) the increasing probability of obsolescence through circum-invention and other sorts of substitution before the expiration of the patent; (b) the increasingly reduced present values of incomes expected in a more distant future; and (c) the increasing degree of uncertainty with which incomes of a more distant future may be expected.[8]

Besides competivite imitation after expiration of the patent, and competitive circum-invention and substitution before its expiration, there is also the possibility of authorized imitation by a licensed competitor; this has been disregarded in our model. However, as long as licensing is not so general that anybody who wants a license can get it, the results deduced from a model that abstracts from licensed imitation would not be seriously altered. It is true that a patentee may be able to ward off circum-invention by competitors when he is willing to license them

---

[8] For an algebraic solution of the problem of the »adequate« duration of innovators' rents, it will be much simpler to operate with a uniform and constant rate of discount for both futurity and uncertainty. If $i > 0$, an innovation will look sound when $i \geqq -\frac{1}{i} \log_e (1 - \frac{i\dot{S}}{Q})$. (Since $\frac{i\dot{S}}{Q}$ will always be positive and the natural logarithm of numbers smaller than 1 is negative, the entire product will again be positive. An alternative way of writing the condition would be $i \geqq \log_e (1 - \frac{i\dot{S}}{Q})^{-\frac{1}{i}}$). If the rate of discount is itself a function of time, because of the increased uncertainty, we should have to say that $i = i(\dot{t})$, and this would make it quite cumbersome to solve the equation (or inequality) for i.

to use his patented inventions; but this does not mean that a firm considering a decision to innovate will at that time count on its ability to avoid circum-invention simply by promising to license all competitors at a reasonable fee; and it will never be able to count on its ability to avert other forms of substitution that would make its novel processes or products prematurely obsolete.

Variable Patent Terms to Fit Each Case

Some innovations pay off in two or three years, others cannot pay off in as many as twenty or thirty years. Any uniform period of protection fixed for all kinds of projects must needs be too long for some and too short for others. It is obviously wasteful for an economy to delay imitation for many years when a short lag would suffice to secure the profitability of the particular innovation; and it may be too bad if an economy must forego the benefits of a useful innovation that would be undertaken only if protection could defer imitation a few years longer than is possible through patents with fixed terms. Thus, the idea of patents with terms adjustable to the requirements of each particular situation suggests itself.[9] The duration of each patent might be made to »fit«, for each particular project, the relationship between sunk cost, interest rate, and the expected innovator's rent, so that the protection granted in each instance would be just adequate to induce the innovation.

In order to simplify examining this idea let us assume (1) that patent protection is fully effective in eliminating competition during the entire term of the patent, i. e., that neither circum-invention nor any other kind of substitution will prematurely reduce or destroy the innovator's rents; (2) that the government is equipped with all the foresight needed to estimate »correctly« the sunk cost of innovation and the innovator's rent (as well as the interest rate) for each project, so that an »adequate« patent term could be stipulated in each case; and (3) that the innovators not only make the same »correct« estimates of costs and

---

[9] In Australia, a patent's duration is fixed by a court, within specified legal limits, as may be appropriate to permit the patentee to make a reasonable profit from his invention. See Corwin D. Edwards, *Varieties of Patent Legislation* (Mimeographed report), pp. 16—17.

rents (and interest rate) but also correctly anticipate that the patent term will secure them their rents for the full duration, i. e., that they neither overestimate nor underestimate the length of time for which they are protected from competition.[10]

Could under these assumptions every project, however costly, that promises any quasi-rent at all, however small, be made attractive by the device of adjusting the patent terms to the situation? With a zero rate of interest this could be done. There would always be some period of rent protection just long enough to compensate for high innovation cost. If, for example, one million dollars had to be sunk into a particular project that promised a quasi-rent of only one thousand dollars a year, a patent protecting this rent for a thousand years would make the innovation pay for itself. Where people are imaginative and can »think up« such wild projects, or even less wild ones, the demand for innovative talent would become unlimited. With competitive bidding for a limited supply of research and engineering personnel, the cost of innovation would be driven higher and higher, but the ever-rising costs would always have to be compensated for by ever-lengthened terms of patent protection. The race would be *ad infinitum,* and the whole idea of making the patent term fit every possible case would be reduced *ad absurdum* — were it not absurd from the outset because of the assumption of a zero rate of interest.

A positive rate of interest would set a practical limit far short of infinity, indeed, short of the period of a human generation. Let us recall that at a rate of interest of 12 per cent one dollar collectable thirty years from now has a present value of only three cents; at 15 per cent, only one cent; and at 20 per cent, less than one-quarter of one cent; that at a 20 per cent interest rate one dollar collectable twenty or twenty-five years from now has a present value of only two or one cent, respectively. Let us add that any stimulation of investment which a lengthening of the patent term might tend to bring about would increase the demand

---

[10] If t is the *actual* period of »freedom from competition«, or length of life of the innovator's rent, and τ is the duration of the *patent*, and $\dot{t}$ is the life of the innovator's rent expected by the innovator, the first of the above assumptions states that $t = \tau$, the second that $\tau = -\dfrac{1}{i} \log_e (1 - \dfrac{iS}{Q})$, and the third that $\dot{S} = S$, $\dot{Q} = Q$, and $\tau = \dot{t}$. Hence, $t = \tau = \dot{t}$.

for investible funds and raise the (explicit or implicit) interest rate; that the discount for uncertainty that would be applied to incomes of a more distant future would rapidly approach 100 per cent of the incomes; and that on both counts the effectiveness of increased periods of rent protection would decline quickly. Beyond some period – probably not much over twenty years – an increase in the duration of rent protection would add nothing – certainly nothing substantial – to the present value of the innovator's rent, which is supposed to cover his sunk cost.[11]

Thus the notion of patent terms adjustable to any and all kinds of innovation project is made impractical by the operation of the rate of discount; if the supply of investment funds were unlimited, an inflationary spiral between patent terms and research and development cost would »explode« the scheme; and if the supply of research and development personnel were unlimited – in a world in which everybody were qualified and could be recruited for innovative work by hiring him away from current production – something else would have to stop the foolishness of trying to make everybody work on innovations and nobody on providing for our daily needs. We definitely do not want the government to encourage *all* innovations people can think of. Yet, if only some innovations ought to be encouraged, where should the line be drawn? If a patent, or innovator's rent protection, of zero duration is felt to be inadequate, and if a »perfectly adjustable« patent term, giving sufficient protection to all innovating enterprise, is evidently too much, what then is the »optimum« term of protection?

There are alternative interpretations of what may constitute an »optimum« duration of innovator's protection or »optimum« lag of imitation behind innovation. It may refer to the time lag adequate (1) to evoke a maximum amount of innovators' outlay, or (2) to evoke such an amount of innovators' outlay as appears appropriate at a particular time in the light of the supply of innovative resources (human, mate-

---

[11] As t is increased beyond all bounds, the present value of future rents, $\frac{1}{i}(1 - e^{-ti})Q$ approaches $\frac{Q}{i}$. Hence, regardless of the length of rent protection, no innovation can be made attractive unless $\frac{Q}{i} \geqq \dot{S}$.

rial, and capital) and of all competing demands for them, or (3) to maximize the rate of effective growth of productivity, which would imply an optimum combination of innovation and imitation, because the highest possible speed of imitation would not be compatible with the highest possible rate of innovation. The first of these three meanings must be rejected, and nobody who knows the first principles of economics will have to be told why. The relationships between the other two are too complex to be analyzed here (especially because fastest growth might be attainable only if too much current consumption is sacrificed). But we shall briefly examine some of the implications of the second conception, the notion of a term of patent protection designed to secure a desired amount of innovator's outlay.

Fixed Patent Term to Induce Optimum Outlay on Innovation

The optimum amount for society to sink into research, development, and other innovative investment will vary with the supply of resources – scientists, engineers, capital – and with the competing demands for these resources – for education, construction, current production. We cannot expect this amount to remain the same, absolutely or relatively, from year to year. Nor can the amount of innovators' outlay in the economy as a whole be expected to be an unchanging function of the duration of patent protection, independent of general economic and political conditions. It would be no less than a miracle if changes in the relationship between patent duration and total innovative outlay and changes in the outlay that would be best for society were to offset each other so perfectly that a fixed patent term would always secure the desired outlay. But, disregarding changes in the outlay desired by society and changes in the outlay induced by a given term of patent protection, we may inquire into the problem of fixing the »correct« term to induce a chosen amount of outlay, under given and unchanging conditions.

Let us temporarily assume that »society« has made a sound decision on what would be the »optimum« outlay on innovation; that patent protection is fully effective in eliminating competition during the entire term of the patent; and that the government has sufficient foresight to make a tabulation of the required sunk costs of innovation and the obtainable quasi-rents (as well as interest rates) for all potential innovative projects. How would the government fix the uniform patent term to encourage just the desired amount of total outlay for innovation?

The problem is soluble as long as one can make the additional assumptions that innovators have the same foresight as the government concerning sunk costs, interest rates, and quasi-rents, and that they correctly estimate the period of rent protection they will enjoy. But even if the government can find the »right« patent duration that will evoke the desired amount of innovators' outlay, it may be questionable whether this objective could not be secured in a less wasteful way. Every extension of the duration of innovators' rent protection, though it may produce a desired increase in innovators' outlay, causes completely unnecessary additional delays in the imitation of new technologies that would be undertaken also with shorter imitation lags. These delays are costly to society in that they postpone the general introduction of improvements which may be essential for the realization of increases in productivity.[12]

Supposing, however, that society is willing to bear this cost of inducing, through increased imitation lags, the amount of innovators' outlay that it has determined to be desirable; how will the problem of fixing the »right« patent duration be affected by innovators' optimistic or pessimistic attitudes? Let us assume that innovators, while estimating sunk costs and obtainable rents correctly and without bias, are either unduly optimistic or unduly pessimistic in their expectations concerning the period of effective rent protection. They may be optimistic in anticipating that their monopoly power first secured by patents will survive the patents by several years, owing to entrenched market positions.[13] They may be pessimistic in anticipating that their monopolies will be destroyed by circum-inventions and other forms of substitution before

---

[12] One may find it necessary to complicate the problem by recognizing that the optimum outlay for innovation is not independent of expectations of future increases in income, which are of course influenced by the speed of imitation of novel techniques; and that, therefore, the »optimum« outlay for innovation would be different depending on the methods by which it is brought forth. We choose to disregard this complication.

[13] While $t = \tau$, $i > \tau$.

the termination of their patents.[14] What would follow from these distorted expectations, provided the government is not omniscient and cannot know and correctly offset such biases?

Undue optimism on the part of innovators would cause them to increase their outlays beyond the »socially desirable« amount, and to employ more capital funds, scientists, technicians, etc., than society »wants« to have allocated in this way. As a result, other sectors of the economy would be deprived of the use of these resources. Innovators as a group would lose some money over the years, having overestimated the period of rent protection. This loss would not be balanced by an equal gain of »consumers« in general. The transfer of income would be to suppliers of resources needed in research and development, while other consumer groups could be worse off, depending on which sectors of the economy suffer most by the shift of resources away from education, construction, and various fields of production.

Undue pessimism on the part of innovators would cause them to spend less on innovative activity than »society« has decided to be desirable. Less capital and less scientific and technical personnel employed for research, development, and actual innovation means that more of these resources remain available to other sectors of the economy. While this might be a short-run gain to consumers, it is, by assumption, contrary to »what society wants.« On the other hand, innovators' quasirents would now continue to be collected beyond their expectations. These rents are in excess of what would be needed to pay for the innovations actually undertaken and, as we have emphasized above, they indicate a maldistribution of productive resources during the excess period in question.

Society as a whole thus stands to lose in either case. In both cases innovation will be different from what is »wanted«; if society knows what is best for itself, any deviation from the »optimum« must be a Bad Thing. In the case of innovators' pessimism, there is the additional waste due to the unnecessary delay in imitation, the prolonged misallocation of resources.

There is one constellation of circumstances in which the consequences of wrong expectations by innovators can become beneficial to society:

---

[14] While $t = \tau$, $i < \tau$.

when innovators tend to be over-optimistic, and the government knows it and fixes an accordingly shorter patent term that will still induce the desired amount of innovators' outlay. In this case, innovation is not bought at an undue cost in terms of delayed imitation. This is the possibility described in an earlier analysis by the present author:

> »For the pessimistic monopolist we can plausibly generalize that open avenues of technological advance will remain untried. Investment in industrial research, development, and innovation will not appear promising in view of the supposedly imminent advent of competition. Inventions will be suppressed if the time for the amortization of the required new investments seems too short.

> ». . . we may point to the possibility of the opposite error, the over-optimistic entrepreneur who underestimates the actual degree of pliopoly [i.e., newcomers' competition] and over-estimates the safe period. He need not be an actual monopolist, nor even imagine that he is one; it suffices that he believes it will take his competitors —imitators or makers of substitutes—longer than it actually does to start competing with him. This optimism is the best promotor of technical progress. Progress calls for both innovation and imitation. If firms anticipate rapid imitation, they will not risk expensive innovations. But if imitation is rapid while the firms expect it to be slow, society will get the benefit of innovation as well as of rapid imitation.

> »To buy innovation by paying with unnecessarily long delays of imitation is a poor bargain for society to make. Imitation always and necessarily lags behind innovation. It will be the best deal from the point of view of society if innovators optimistically overestimate this lag. If they expect the lag to be longer than it actually is, innovation will be enhanced and imitation will not be delayed. That it may create this socially wholesome illusion on the part of innovators is the strongest justification for a well-designed patent system.«[15]

Without this illusion the patent system is not likely to function as an effective and economical spur to the growth of productivity.

---

[15] *Fritz Machlup*, The Economics of Sellers' Competition (Baltimore: John Hopkins Press, 1952), pp. 555—56.

Patent Terms and Innovators' Expectations

Let us assume an omniscient government knowing not only the future but also all the accurate and erroneous expectations entertained by the citizens concerning the future; and on the basis of this knowledge trying to fix a uniform patent duration designed to call forth just the amount of innovators' outlay considered optimum for society. The resulting problem holds fascinating complexities for the economic theorist.

The knotty-point is the interpendence between patent duration and innovators' expectations of the effective periods of rent protection. The government is supposed to fix the patent term taking full account of innovators' expectations, while innovators' expectations may be very different depending on the patent terms fixed by the government. In other words, the »omniscience« of the government must extend, beyond the entrepreneurial expectations actually in the minds of potential innovators, to the hypothetical expectations which they might hold if the patent terms were different from what they are.[16]

What potential innovators expect concerning the length of time they will be able to earn quasi-rents probably depends to some extent on experience, their own and that of others, with innovation of the particular or similar type in the particular or similar industry. Such experience, as well as the expectations based on it, can be represented by a frequency distribution of the durations of quasi-rent earnings attributable to a number of comparable innovations. Assume the patent term has been fixed at 16 years; effective rent protection has been, and is expected to be, much less in most of the instances, the mode being, say, ten years. The modal period falls short of the fixed patent term because of the frequency of circum-invention and the development of substitute processes and products.[17] But there may be a wide dispersion: there may be instances in which rents die in their infancy, so to speak, not because of imitation, but because of the almost simultaneous inven-

---

[16] Algebraically speaking, $i = f(\tau)$.

[17] We assume all along that circum-invention and substitution terminate the innovator's rent at one stroke. In reality, oligopolistic competition may emerge and permit the innovator's rents to continue at a reduced level. Our counterfactua assumption simplifies the model without destroying its relevance.

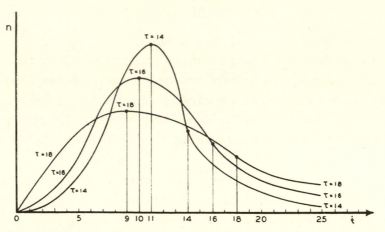

Imaginary frequency distributions of innovators' quasi-rent terminations
with patent protection for 14, 16, and 18 years.

tion of a good substitute process or product; and, at the other end, there
may be instances in which rents survive the termination of the respective patents, thanks to the ability of the innovator to entrench himself
firmly in a favorable market position.

If the mode alone, and not the entire shape of the frequency distribution, were to determine innovators' decisions, the problem would be
less complicated. Indeed, it might conceivably be argued that variations
in the patent term, say between 12 and 20 years, would not materially
affect the mode since it is substitution, and not direct imitation, which
essentially determines the mode at an earlier point (10 years, as we
have assumed). Such an argument should be countered by pointing to
the fact, or probability, that the incentive to invent around a patent will
be stronger the longer the term of patent protection. In consequence,
an extension of patent protection from 16 to 18 years might lead to
more and earlier circum-invention–shifting the mode to, say, 9 years–
whereas a shortening of the patent term to 14 years might reduce and
retard circum-invention–shifting the mode to, say, 11 years. But such
speculations about the shift of the mode will not suffice since the rest
of the frequency distribution will surely have some bearing on innovators' decisions. The relative probabilities of very short and very long
periods of innovators' rent receipts must have an influence apart from

the location of the mode, that is, apart from the fact that the »most probable« period is, say, 10 years.

Can anything, however speculative, be said about the comparative frequency distributions of innovators' quasi-rent periods if the patent term is fixed at different lengths? Let us compare the frequency distributions that may be visualized for three different patent terms, 14, 16, and 18 years. The most probable quasi-rent periods would, according to the preceding argument, be 11, 10, and 9 years, respectively; these modal periods were thought to be shorter the longer the patent terms were, because the incentive to invent around a patent would become stronger under longer patent terms. For the same reason, however, the frequencies of earlier rent termination—earlier than the mode—would be greater for longer patent terms: the increased incentive for circum-invention and substitution would result in increased mortality rates for the quasi-rents in their earlier lives. (See Fig. 1, where curves are drawn to depict hypothetical rent mortality under patents of 14, 16, and 18 years duration). On the other hand, the frequencies of longer rent periods may also be greater for longer patent terms: the protected innovator's opportunities of getting entrenched in the market will increase with the duration of patent protection. Thus, if our speculation is valid, the frequency distributions of innovator's quasi-rent periods are apt to yield flatter curves for longer-term patent protection, and greater concentration around the mode for shorter-term patent protection.

The implications of these (highly speculative) findings are rather subtle and should be regarded as highly tentative hypotheses. If an extension of the patent term from 14 to 16 and to 18 years is apt to increase the probabilities of earlier as well as of later quasi-rent terminations, the effect on the mean may be quite small. But if the mean of the expected rent periods is of determining influence upon potential innovators' decisions, longer patent terms will be woefully ineffectual in stimulating innovation, and terribly wasteful to boot. The increased frequencies of earlier rent termination will not be the result of costless imitation but largely of expensive inventing-around (requiring the extra cost of pseudo-innovation); the increased frequencies of later rent termination will be indicative of unnecessarily delayed imitation, with uneconomic resource allocation in the meantime. It is hard to imagine a poorer bargain for society to make, even if it could be assumed that the government is omniscient and can fix the patent term in full consider-ation of the hypothetical expectation functions of the potential inno-vators. If the government, lacking omniscience, should fix a 16 or 18 year term for patent protection although on the basis of the innovators' rent expectations a shorter patent term would secure a closer approx-imation to the desired total outlay for innovation, the loss to society would be still greater.

The Optimum Lag and the Patent System

While numerous arguments have been presented here which strongly suggest that »longer« imitation lags are uneconomical and lags shorter than the present ones would be socially more desirable, no reliable clue has turned up as to the length of the »optimum lag«. Perhaps an attempt at tying together the various strains of thought advanced here will yield an approach to the theoretical solution of this problem. This does not mean that we are now restrained from stating our general impression of the practical implications of our provisional analysis.

It is obvious that a »zero« lag would be undesirable–but of this there is no danger since there is always the innovator's natural headstart. One must suspect that governmental intervention to delay imitation for periods of 16 years or longer is an ineffectual and wasteful way of promoting innovation. And it is the impression of the present analyst that the optimum lag of imitation behind innovation is closer to the length of the natural headstart than to the length of the patent protec-tion now afforded to innovators in most countries.

PART SIX

ECONOMIC AND POLITICAL PHILOSOPHY

[20]

Liberalism and the Choice of Freedoms
Fritz Machlup

Prefatorial note: The first version of this essay was presented in 1955 as one in a series of addresses initiated by Professor Hayek at Claremont Men's College. In the years since then, I have given this paper at numerous convocations in various colleges and universities and have extended it on several issues in response to questions and comments from my audiences. I have saved publication for a suitable occasion; surely none could be more suitable than this anniversary volume for Professor Hayek, with whom I have been bound in friendship for 45 years and to whom my thinking owes more than I can say.

It would be easy to present a collection of statements on 'liberals' and 'liberalism' so contradictory of one another that it would be evident on first inspection either that the authors did not know what they were talking about or had decided to talk about very different men and ideas. The meanings of liberalism have varied over time but differ chiefly among countries. The differences are most pronounced for continental Europe, on the one hand, and the United States of America, on the other.

A Regional Survey

A quick survey will bear this out. Take a look at Swiss papers and journals, for example, the *Zürcher Zeitung* and the *Schweizerische Monatshefte* and you will find that 'liberals' oppose socialism in all forms and are critical of anything that smacks of government intervention in business. Read some German papers and periodicals of any persuasion from the left to the right, and you will confirm that 'liberals' have detested and finally abolished price and production controls. Dr. Ludwig Erhard, German Minister of Economic Affairs for many years and later Chancellor, is called a liberal by his

117

FRITZ MACHLUP

friends as well as his foes because he believes in an uncontrolled economy and has battled against any kind of governmental economic planning and against all sorts of control measures favored by socialists and bureaucrats.

Turn to the north of Europe, to Norway, a country which until recently has had a socialist government, strict price controls, investment controls, and all the rest. The 'liberals' were in the opposition, furiously barking at the majority and claiming that only a free-enterprise economy, free from well-meant but ill-conceived government interventions, could save the nation from ruin. A glance into the 'liberal' weekly *Farmand* or into the socialist papers of Norway, will remove any doubt that the 'liberal' is anti-socialist and the socialist is anti-liberal. It is almost the same story in France, only that none of the numerous political parties there has a 'liberal' program and liberalism is regarded as a largely impractical ideal. Some industrialists support the 'liberal' cause, because the liberal is against strong trade unionism, against high taxes, and against socialism.

The situation is not quite so clear in England, chiefly because there is a Liberal Party and hence a confusion between a Liberal as a member of this party and a liberal in the anti-socialist and anti-interventionist sense. The Liberal Party, though opposed to the Labour Party, has not been anti-interventionist in the twentieth century. Nevertheless, if someone in England is called 'liberal' there is a good chance that he is somehow in favor of more *laissez faire* than there exists in his country.

Turning now to the United States, we find a completely different picture, and a more confusing one at that. Until a generation ago everybody, no matter what his views were, wanted to be regarded as a liberal. But what had long been an honorific has become an epithet designed to arouse suspicion. 'Liberal', in the United States, is now widely used as a name for a political color somewhere between pink and red. Many use it as a synonym for 'communist fellow traveler'. And if some editorial writers want to be particularly derogatory of anybody, they call him a 'liberal-intellectual'. This used to be an everyday occurrence in the *Baltimore Sun*.

But even in the nineteen-thirties and forties, an American was called liberal when he was a New Dealer, an advocate of economic policies to support the underprivileged, to strengthen trade unions, to maintain price and rent controls. In short, the American liberal

118

is just the man whom the European liberal is opposing with all his might. A liberal in America would be an anti-liberal in continental Europe, and a liberal in Europe would be an anti-liberal in the States.

Some people have tried to explain this terminological paradox by literary isolationism, by unfamiliarity with foreign literature. This is an oversimplification. We can find other explanations, historical and semantic. We shall see presently that the history of liberalism reveals some intrinsic contradictions that have given rise to developments in diametrically opposite directions.

A Historical Survey

The term 'liberal' originated in Spain, where in 1812 the conservatives used *vosotros liberales* referring to the constitutional party. The idea, however, was older; John Locke has been called the founding father of the political, economic, and social principles that came to constitute nineteenth-century liberalism.[1]

There can be no doubt that liberalism first stressed freedom from government interference.[2] Liberalism was individualism, emphasizing the removal of coercive restraints by which the state had restricted the individual's freedom in many activities and had thereby reduced his self-reliance, self-responsibility, self-respect, and self-realization.

A major split developed when after the imposing success of 'individualistic liberalism' a so-called 'organic liberalism' began to be expounded. The former had stressed the freedoms of individuals as individuals, the latter stressed the freedom of groups of organized individuals, especially labor organizations. The former – especially the 'Manchester liberals', Cobden and Bright – had fought chiefly for free trade, free markets, free enterprise. The latter – led by writers such as Thomas Hill Green and L. T. Hobhouse – fought chiefly for free coalition of workers. Individualist liberals sometimes

1 Goetz Briefs, 'Staat und Wirtschaft im Zeitalter der Interessenverbände', in *Laisser-Faire Pluralismus*, Berlin 1966, p. 19.
2 One of the best historians of liberalism defined liberalism as opposition to all 'coercive interference, whether in the moral, the religious, the intellectual, the social, the economic, or the political sphere'. And he stated that 'At an early stage of its development . . . the forces of liberalism concentrated on the crucial problem of limiting the interference of the state . . .' Guido de Ruggiero, 'Liberalism' in *Encyclopaedia of the Social Sciences*, New York 1933, Vol. IX.

119

FRITZ MACHLUP

describe the development of 'organic liberalism' as an attempt of collectivists and egalitarians to steal the attractive banner of 'liberalism' as a front for their objectives.

But there was still widespread recognition of the fact that a harmonious linking of liberty with equality was only possible as long as equality referred to the treatment of people before the law, not to income or wealth. In other words, liberty and equality were regarded as partly complementary, partly antithetical. Even a socialist like Harold Laski refrained from expanding the concept of liberalism to include the idea of income equality, which most of the time may have been closer to his heart than was individual freedom. He once said that in a state of 'distressing inequality . . . freedom is not worth having.' But he kept the two ideas apart, even if he did not see or show a conflict between the two as social goals.[3]

To join the two ideals in one's political program without making it clear that they may conflict with each other, and without deciding which one is to have priority in case of conflict, is bad enough. It is worse if the two are conceptually merged, as it was done by many European socialists and American liberals who changed the concept of freedom from that of non-interference to that of 'effective power'. It started with a French political philosopher, Paul Janet, 1878, became accepted doctrine among many socialists, and was given American philosophical blessing by John Dewey, who stated that 'liberty is the effective power to do specific things'. This fusion of the idea of non-interference with the idea of effective power (which often means buying power) could not but spread confusion. We shall have to say more about it; at this point we merely state that this was one of the chief points from which American and European liberals moved in different directions. To illustrate, I quote Justice

3 See Laski's description of the development of English liberalism from its earlier emphasis on the 'antithesis of individual and state' to its recent acceptance or advocacy of the social welfare state. According to Laski, 'the body of ideas we call liberalism emphasized the undesirability of restraint . . .', and the idea of 'liberty was divorced from the ideas of both equality and justice.' This changed only after most of the aims of liberalism had been attained in England. 'Democratic agitation, which from 1600 to about 1870 had been occupied with the removal of barriers upon individual action, after 1870 began to press for the deliberate creation of equalitarian conditions.' Thus, 'the liberal state of the nineteenth century was gradually replaced by the social service state of the twentieth. This may be described by saying that it again joins the ideal of liberty to that of equality, and this in the name of social justice'. Harold Laski, 'Liberty' in *Encyclopaedia of the Social Sciences*, New York 1933, Vol. IX, p. 443.

120

LIBERALISM AND THE CHOICE OF FREEDOMS

William O. Douglas, stating in *An Almanac of Liberty*, (1954, p. vi), that he 'ranks freedom to eat with freedom to speak.'

There are still other elements in the historical development of the liberalist movement that may explain the present terminological paradoxes. I refer chiefly to the identification of the liberal in the nineteenth century with the reformer, the progressive. A liberal was one who favored institutional changes. In the words of John Stuart Mill (1865), 'A Liberal is he who looks forward for his principles of government: a Tory looks backward.'

Surely, Mill did not mean this to be a definition of a liberal. Not every change or reform increases the freedoms of the people, and a liberal must certainly not be favorable to illiberal reforms. In an illiberal society the liberal must be a reformer in order to obtain freedom, in a liberal society he must be a conservative in order to maintain freedom. In the great days of classical liberalism the 'radical reformers' fought for the removal of illiberal restraints and interferences. The idea of the liberal as a perennial radical reformer was strong and has probably contributed to the notion, so widespread in America, that all radical reformers are liberals.

Finally, good liberals respect the thinking of others, and are tolerant of other views; more than that, they have usually come to the defense of anybody who was threatened by state or society because of his non-conformance. A good defense attorney often develops sympathy with his defendant. Thus, the tolerance and defense of socialist and other illiberal views may have made many a good liberal sympathetic with these views and may have blinded him to the incompatibility of the position defended with the position he originally stood for.

'Fuzzy Liberalism'

Thus, we can trace the present-day confusion about the meaning of liberalism to several developments:

1. The liberal demand for freedom of coalition has been extended to the demand for unlimited freedom for groups and unions even where such collective freedom is in conflict with the freedom of the individual; this is the *collectivist* streak in fuzzy liberalism.

2. The liberal demand for equality before the law has been

121

FRITZ MACHLUP

extended to equality of income even where measures to that effect are in conflict with the freedom of the individual; this is the *egalitarian* streak in fuzzy liberalism.

3. The liberal demand for individual freedom has been extended from the mere absence of coercive interference to positive measures to increase and equalize the individuals' effective power to do or get what they want even where such measures are in conflict with the freedom of the individual; this is another *redistributive* streak in fuzzy liberalism.

4. The liberal demand for progressive and radical reforms designed to increase the welfare of society by releasing forces previously restrained has been extended to reforms to increase collective welfare even when in conflict with the freedom of the individual: this is the *radical-interventionist* streak in fuzzy liberalism.

5. The liberal demand for tolerance of dissenting opinions and for the defense of the disseminators of these ideas and their right to advocate communism or anything they like has been extended to the actual support of socialist ideas which are basically in conflict with the freedom of the individual: this is the *fellow-travelling* streak in fuzzy liberalism.

These explanations for the perversion of the original liberal position to what most Americans now call liberalism is not inconsistent with the simple explanation that most of those who sound off – *pro* or *con* – about 'liberalism' are unfamiliar with the classical writings. I do not wish to deny anybody the right to be ignorant. But I believe it is fair to state that, despite all its historical developments and inherent contradictions, American liberalism could not have become quite so fuzzy if the so-called intellectuals had really been intellectuals in the sense of people who read books, including foreign literature. They would have learnt that the collectivist, egalitarian, radical-interventionist and fellow-traveling streaks in American 'liberalism' are incompatible with liberalism in the classical, individualistic sense.

Two Fundamental Errors

Fuzzy thinking about liberalism is fostered by some esoteric concepts of freedom and aggravated by errors of reasoning. The esoteric

122

LIBERALISM AND THE CHOICE OF FREEDOMS

concepts of freedom shall be relegated to the honored place of a footnote.[4] The more worldly confusions – some merely grammatical and semantic – shall be reviewed here in the simplest possible form.

A relatively simple confusion is that between being '*free to*' and '*free from*'. It is most manifest in the pronouncement of the 'four essential human freedoms' by President Franklin D. Roosevelt. These are four admirable principles; no well-meaning person in our time will ever oppose freedom of speech, freedom of worship, freedom from want, and freedom from fear. The trouble is only that many people see in these principles the foundations of liberalism, each expressing an important freedom or liberty. In fact, only the first two are liberties, the others are not. Freedom of speech and of religion give people the rights to speak, express themselves, and worship in any way they like; these freedoms mean that state and society should not coerce or restrain individuals in the realms of thought expression and religion. Freedom from want and from fear are of an entirely different nature: they express the hope that governments will take measures designed to abolish poverty and war. To be free from want is to be 'rid' of destitution; to be free from fear is to be safe from war and aggression; just as to be free from disease is to be healthy, perhaps thanks to having found effective vaccines. Measures designed to abolish poverty and war are most desirable, but they do not give people any rights 'to do or not to do, as they please'. They do not call for the proscription of public restraints on actions of the individual, but require positive prescription for action by the government.

President Lyndon B. Johnson, in January 1968, added a 'fifth freedom' to the 'aspirations' of the nation, and it is again chiefly designed to make people 'free from', not 'free to': he proclaimed the 'freedom from ignorance', to be secured by better educational

---

4 Mortimer J. Adler, in his work *The Idea of Freedom*, New York 1958–61, proposed three fundamentally different concepts: the freedoms of 'self-perfection', 'self-realization', and 'self-determination'. The first is an inner freedom beyond the reach of outward circumstances, a capacity to order one's will in accordance with wisdom and goodness; it includes the 'inner freedom' of the slave and the prisoner. The second is the ability to carry out one's intention without outward obstacles, without shackles, threats, or social disapproval. The third is 'free will' in contrast to determinism of one's motives; it means that man's will is not the effect of certain knowable causes and not constrained by outer forces. Only the second of these concepts, the freedom of self-realization, corresponds to the mundane notion of freedom, though it does not sufficiently distinguish the source of the outward obstacles: are they always man-made or can they be natural?

123

FRITZ MACHLUP

facilities for all. Perhaps, though, in this case, with the history of unequal access to schools, there is a blending of the two ideas, provision of additional services by the government and abolition of legal and illegal restraints that keep individuals from partaking of what is available. To the extent that government is called upon to provide additional educational services, the nation may become better educated and eventually 'free from ignorance'. To the extent that individual children will not be coerced into bad schools and not intimidated from going to better schools, they will be 'free to attend' the latter. Yet, even where the two meanings of 'free' seem to converge in practice, to be 'free from' something is different from being 'free to do' something.

Of course, one may say that we are free to do as we please only if we are free from external coercion and restraint. Thus we could formulate freedom of speech as freedom from restraints on speech and expression; and we could formulate freedom of worship as freedom from restraints on religious or irreligious pursuits. In these cases, the absence of coercion and intimidation secures freedom. On the other hand, in order to make people 'free from' want or ignorance, positive efforts are required, for which, in President Johnson's words, 'Americans have always stood ready to pay the cost in energy and treasure' and which the nation can afford only as it becomes 'wealthier'. Please note that no wealth is needed to secure the freedoms of speech and of worship.

A second fundamental, though related, error may be referred to as the confusion between '*I may*' and '*I can*'. It bears again on the previously mentioned confusion between freedom as non-interference with an individual's actions and his effective power to act. Capacity to act, having the power and the means to do something, is surely not the same thing as having the freedom to do it. The fusion of the idea of effective power with the idea of freedom was obviously proposed by those who held that freedom in the sense of non-interference was of no practical value to those who lacked the power, chiefly the buying power. The sentiment behind this proposition may be illustrated by the grumbling declaration 'I do not care if I *may* do what I *cannot* do. Why should anybody be free to do things which I cannot afford?'

I must admit that the freedom to buy a Rolls-Royce and a luxury yacht has little practical relevance to those who have no money to buy them. But this does not mean that we should expand the

124

LIBERALISM AND THE CHOICE OF FREEDOMS

concept of 'freedom' to include 'capacity to buy'. I *can* buy illegal drugs if I have enough money, but I *may* not lawfully do so. I *may*, under present law and moral norms, buy the most expensive diamond for my dear wife but, alas, I *cannot* do so within my income. Just as I can understand that many poor people find it uninteresting that they are free to buy what they are unable to buy, I can also understand that many uneducated people find it ridiculous that so much fuss is being made about freedom to teach and inquire, things they cannot do anyhow. Apart from the few who comprehend that they and their children may be indirectly affected, to the masses freedom of scientific inquiry is of little interest. However, would it not be silly to extend the concept of freedom of scientific research so that it includes the capacity for it? Would it not be preposterous if some ultra-pragmatists were to say that Professor X lacks freedom of inquiry since, although no one limits his research activities, his reasoning powers are limited?

I find it difficult to understand what may have compelled learned men and eminent thinkers to take three different ideas – (1) 'I am physically and mentally capable of doing it', (2) 'I have enough money to afford it', and (3) 'I shall not be prevented from doing nor punished for having done it', – and to throw all three into one pot and scramble them into an omelette, which they call 'freedom' or, synonymously 'effective power'. This omelette may be all right for some practical purposes and thus appeal to the pragmatist philosopher. But surely for other purposes, equally practical, we ought to keep the three ideas apart, and this means to use words that help maintain the separation. Unfortunately, too many writers prefer the omelette. D. G. Ingle, a physiologist, wrote this: 'We know many physical and biological limitations on freedom. Man is not free to live without oxygen, water, and food. He cannot jump as much as eight feet into the air or lift a house or become young after once being old. Freedom is extended by the use of tools and knowledge . . . Freedoms are limited by the nature of inborn drives, likes and dislikes . . . The burned child is no longer free to seek the fire . . .'[5]

As an example of the mixing of the second and third of the three ideas, I have earlier quoted Justice Douglas, pronouncing an equivalence of freedom to eat and freedom to speak. In an equally strong pronouncement, Sidney and Beatrice Webb once contended

5 D.G.I.: 'Editorial: The Biology of Freedom', *Perspectives in Biology and Medicine*, VII (Winter, 1964) p. 141.

125

FRITZ MACHLUP

that 'Personal freedom means, in effect, the power of the individual to buy sufficient food, shelter, and clothing.' This confusion between buying power and personal freedom can perhaps be illucidated by the reminder that there may be religious, moral, or legal prohibitions of using existing buying power in particular ways. Even affluent Brahmins may not feel free to eat meat, nor affluent orthodox Jews and Muslims to eat pork. If religious taboos are not sufficiently impressive to drive home my point, let me allude to legal restraints and switch from the 'freedom to eat' to the 'freedom to drink'. The difference between *having the means* to buy gin and whiskey and *being free* to buy such drinks became quite clear to all Americans (or to all drinking Americans, to stay within the confines of pragmatism) when the prohibition laws were enacted. Having money neither gives nor implies freedom; it merely enables you to exercise more of the existing freedoms.

As another example of the mixing of the first and third ideas, let me once more contrast physical incapacity and legal prohibition. If we were to put the physiological incapacity of a mute person and the authoritarian restraint on an advocate of subversion into the same category and declared that neither of the two was 'free' to speak, we would be guilty of badly confusing the issue. The one is unable to speak, say, because of a congenital defect, a disease, an accident; the other is punished if he speaks out and advocates subversion. To include both in the concept of freedom of speech is nonsense.

A definition of freedom which negates the difference between non-interference and effective power (or welfare or want satisfaction) destroys the essential meaning of the word 'freedom'. If it is defined as the capacity or opportunity to get what one wants, we are barred from analyzing the important question whether the development of this capacity or opportunity is better served by restrictionism or by non-interference, by collective control or by individual freedom.

Five Other Errors

Besides the 'fundamental' errors just reviewed, a few other errors concerning freedom and restraints on freedom ought to be mentioned. They are neither grammatical nor semantic, but refer to

126

questions of political theory. Like all questions of theory, these 'corrections of errors' should be presented with reservations and admissions of uncertain knowledge. In the concise formulations attempted here, my statements may sound more apodictic than they are intended. On the other hand, I do not think that my contentions will be terribly controversial. After the two errors discussed, we may continue the enumeration of the next five.

The third error lies in the assumption that the coercive restraints, the presence of which means *negations of freedom, are always effected by the state*, the government, the 'magistrate' (to use the classical term). In actual fact, while the state is usually the most effective negator of freedom, certain coercive restraints may come from all sorts of people or groups in society. At all times have mob violence, clique action and pressure-group manoeuvres been operating to infringe, restrict, or completely eliminate freedoms in several spheres of activity.

A fourth error lies in the belief that *only the state, the government, can effectively uphold freedom* and protect individuals from coercive restraints. Certain types of restraint cannot be restrained by legal prohibition and coercion, but only by moral code and by a strong feeling for tact and manners slowly developed and perpetuated by the upbringing of the young.

A fifth error lies in the belief that freedom implies the *absence of coercion of any sort*. This overlooks that coercion may be required to enforce guarantees of freedom and to protect individuals from certain coercive restraints imposed by other individuals or groups. Of course, all coercive power must be vested in government and must be exercised strictly under the 'rule of law'. This means that all laws apply with equal force to everybody without discrimination and are of such general nature that they can be applied without arbitrary discretion. Under the 'rule of law' no one has a right that is denied to others. But equality before the law involves enforcement of the law, and enforcement involves the use of coercive power by the state.

A sixth error lies in the *identification of liberalism with* laissez-faire. There is a strong presumption for Thomas Jefferson's rule that 'the best government is the one that governs least', but this does not means that individual freedoms are always most securely guarded where government is confined to the prevention of violence, theft, and fraud. The preservation of a maximum of freedom may

127

FRITZ MACHLUP

call for government measures to maintain competition, which private contracts might restrict, to provide services which private enterprise cannot supply, and to prevent misery which private charity cannot cope with.

This error of making liberalism equal to *laissez-faire* was forcefully criticized by one whom careless readers have sometimes accused of having committed it, namely Professor Hayek in his *Road to Serfdom* (London 1944, p. 13). This is what he wrote:

> There is nothing in the basic principles of Liberalism to make it a stationary creed, there are no hard-and-fast rules fixed once and for all. The fundamental principle that in the ordering of our affairs we should make as much use as possible of the spontaneous forces of society, and resort as little as possible to coercion, is capable of an infinite variety of applications. There is, in particular, all the difference between deliberately creating a system within which competition will work as beneficially as possible, and passively accepting institutions as they are. Probably nothing has done so much harm to the liberal cause as the wooden insistence of some liberals on certain rough rules of thumb, above all the principle of *laissez-faire*. Yet in a sense this was necessary and unavoidable. Against the innumerable interests who could show that particular measures would confer immediate and obvious benefits on some, while the harm they caused was much more indirect and difficult to see, nothing short of some hard-and-fast rule would have been effective. And since a strong presumption in favour of industrial liberty had undoubtedly been established, the temptation to present it as a rule which knew no exceptions was too strong always to be resisted.

A seventh error lies in believing that '*freedom is indivisible*'. This is a beautiful and well-meant slogan, but it just is not so. There is not one indivisible freedom, but there are many freedoms, many kinds of human activity to which the principle of non-interference may or may not be applied. Some of these freedoms may be independent of each other, others complementary or competing in the sense that more of one may permit either more or less of another. That is to say, greater freedom in one realm of human action may make it either easier or harder to achieve freedom in another realm of action. Some freedoms support one another, others impair one

128

another; and where there is such a conflict of freedoms it is important to know it and to analyse their comparative value for the pursuit of happiness, present or future.

The hierarchy of freedoms in our systems of value may be highly complicated and uncertain. Depending on our moral and social philosophy, we may regard some freedoms as absolute or ultimate values, others only as instrumental or intermediate values. Moreover, one and the same freedom may be valued both as an end in itself and as a means to other ends. For example, freedom of enterprise may be a means to more material progress and abundance, a means to the preservation of other liberties and, at least for some of its advocates, an end in itself. The same may be said about the freedom of teaching: a means to faster progress, to greater happiness, to the more secure attainment of other freedoms, and an end in itself. At the same time these freedoms may conflict with other goals of society. To close our eyes to these complications would be rather irresponsible. These interrelationships between different freedoms have to be examined in greater detail, but we have several tasks to do before we are ready for it.

Opportunity and Freedom

If, in the discussion of the pragmatists' identification of freedom with effective power, I succeeded in establishing a forward position in the opponents' territory, I must not leave it unprotected from counterattacks. Too often have I seen that, after an initial retreat, the forces proclaiming that freedom requires power came up resurging with new strength and compelled me to resume the battle. Previous arguments had to be repeated and new ones adduced to reinforce the previous. I have realized that the pragmatists' conception of freedom is too firmly ingrained in the thinking on these issues to be uprooted in one try.

I have sometimes resorted to quoting Frank H. Knight as an ally, but found it to be of questionable help. His pronouncement on the central issue is so ambiguous that it may just as easily be used against my position as in its support. Here it is:

Freedom, correctly conceived, *implies* opportunity, unobstructed

129

FRITZ MACHLUP

opportunity, to use power, which must be possessed, to give content to freedom, or make it effective. It is a common fallacy to demand power under the name of freedom, and usage badly needs the expression 'effective freedom' to take account of power and of knowledge and other dimensions in the scope of voluntary action.[6]

I believe Knight means virtually the same that I am trying to say – especially when he offers the expression 'effective freedom' as a substitute for the pragmatists' 'effective power.' However, his statement may easily be misinterpreted – especially where it says that freedom implies power already possessed. This formulation disregards the great fertility of freedom even where the power to take advantage of freedom does not yet exist and the acquisition of such power through special efforts, often in the search for new knowledge, is made attractive precisely because the freedom is still unused or in Knight's phrase 'ineffective'. In other words, certain freedoms may be of great importance for individuals and for society when no knowledge, no opportunity, and no power exist as yet to make use of presumably 'empty' freedoms. Their importance lies in the aspirations and ambitions which they arouse and which may lead to the search for the knowledge, opportunity, and power that are required to exercise the previously unused freedoms. In short, 'ineffective' freedoms can be highly effective.

As a strong believer in the persuasiveness of primitive examples, I propose to offer one that can both expose the fallacy inherent in the notion of freedom as effective power and exhibit the usefulness of the notion of effective 'ineffective freedom' without power. Suppose an automobile capable of doing 100 miles an hour is restricted to a maximum speed of 25 m.p.h. owing to a speed-limit enforced by the police. Suppose further that I, on my bicycle on the same roads, cannot pedal more than about 20 m.p.h. owing to my physical limitations. Does it make much sense to insist on a concept of freedom that makes my freedom 20 m.p.h. and the automobilist's 25 m.p.h.? Is it not more reasonable to admit that our physical powers are different (his 100 m.p.h. against my 20 m.p.h.) whereas our freedom is restricted to the same limit (25 m.p.h.)? And would it not be sensible to hold that an increase

6 Frank H. Knight, 'Laissez-Faire: Pro and Con', *Journal of Political Economy*, 75 (December, 1967), p. 790.

130

or abolition of the legal speed-limit would increase my desire to take advantage of the unused freedom – and acquire a faster vehicle?

The point should be easy to see. As long as the law restricts all traffic on the roads to 25 m.p.h., I can certainly gain no more than 5 m.p.h. by acquiring a car and I do not find it worth while to work harder to earn the money to buy the car. If the speed limit is increased or abolished, that is, if I am free to go much faster, or as fast as I can and wish, then I will make the effort that will eventually enable me to exercise my freedom. In the particular example, the freedom to go fast precedes my 'opportunity' or 'capacity' to go fast. Actual capacity and opportunity are created only after the freedom is established and a potential is made into a reality.

The relationship between actual and potential opportunity, on the one hand, and freedom, on the other, becomes very complicated in the context of the social objective of 'equality of opportunities'. It is a hopeless task to analyze this notion successfully unless distinctions are made with regard to the origin of the opportunities in question. We must distinguish (1) opportunities offered by society, in particular by the government, such as access to facilities (schools, hospitals, police protection) or to jobs or markets, (2) opportunities offered as gifts of nature such as the people's physical and mental endowments, and (3) opportunities offered by the environment into which we were born, including the situation of the parents to whom we were born. Realizing that all three types of opportunity can be very unequal, we ought to contemplate the implications which any attempts to equalize opportunities would have for freedom.

(1) Equalizing the opportunities provided by the state, or society in general, can be a requirement of several freedoms, for example, freedom of access to employment, freedom of entry into trades, or freedom of consumer choice. (2) Opportunities offered as gifts of nature cannot be equalized at all, but can at best be compensated for by deliberate imposition of social handicaps upon persons favored by nature; attempts of this sort constitute reductions of individual freedoms. (3) Inequalities of the third type can be removed only by society providing special assistance to the disfavored. If the cost of this assistance is heavy and is borne chiefly by those favored by their lucky choice of parents or environment, the implied redistribution of income may again amount to a system of assigning handicaps to the more fortunate. But even if the cost is small and the benefits to the assisted are great, the provision of the assistance is

131

FRITZ MACHLUP

not a 'freedom'. Some may see it as an act of 'social justice'; it may serve a widely desired social objective; but it has nothing to do with liberty.

Action designed to provide 'equality of opportunities' has thus three very different relationships to freedom. It may enhance freedom, it may reduce freedom, or it may have no connection with freedom. It depends on the origin of the opportunities that are unequal and about which intervention by the government is proposed.

Limitations by Nature and Restrictions by Man

In the distinctions between types of opportunity the same theme recurred that I previously developed in my criticism of the confusion between 'I can' and 'I may': the difference between limitations by nature and restrictions by man. Perhaps one should not dispute about semantic tastes and linguistic preferences, but I regard it as an obfuscation of thought and a diseconomy of words to expand the meaning of freedom so much that it requires the absence not only of acts of oppression and measures of restriction committed by men but also of limitations of human capacities or opportunities by 'nature'.

There is a gray area between black and white, where it may be possible to differ in judging whether certain limitations are entirely dictated by laws of nature or perhaps to some extent chargeable to human action or failures to act. Limitations on men's opportunities that have not been caused by human action but could with some good will be removed by human effort, at no large cost to anybody, can perhaps, without undue strain, be included, along with the restrictions imposed by men upon fellow-men, among infringements of freedom.

Foremost among the limitations that are neither completely natural nor consciously designed by man are self-grown social institutions possibly leading to results that some groups in society do not recognize as independent of human will. If such recognition or non-recognition is merely a matter of ideology, not subject to evidence and logical argument, the conflict whether a limitation of freedom is involved cannot be resolved objectively. Yet, even if the

132

LIBERALISM AND THE CHOICE OF FREEDOMS

conflict cannot be resolved without resort to fundamental postulates of social philosophy, it is often possible to engage in immanent criticism and to show the extent to which contentions and convictions bear on the conclusions.

The generalities of the preceding paragraph, however good they sound, will remain empty phrases if we do not offer illustrations of the type of issue in question. I shall try. What effects upon real incomes of industrial labor and agricultural labor can be attributed to (a) all land being owned by the state or community, (b) all land being privately owned but distributed very unequally, most of it being held by large owners, or (c) all land being broadly distributed in only small holdings? The point of the argument is, of course, that many do not accept the given historical situation as a result of an immutable law of nature, even if no man alive had had anything to do with its evolution. There are, however, objective ways of separating the marginal productivities of labor and of land, and of showing that pure labor incomes are independent of the distribution of land property. What is really involved is who gets the rent of land. In the case of public ownership of land, the government may use the rent collected from the producers in any way it likes; it may, in one form or another, use it for the benefit of industrial labor, agricultural labor, or any group in society. Most of the *ideologues* confuse the question of property in land with the question of monopoly in the sale of the produce of land. If such monopolies exist, they can have strong effects upon the incomes of labor as well as of other groups. Such monopolies, moreover, are clearly the result of conscious and deliberate interventions enforced or condoned by the present government and have, therefore, the character of man-made restrictions upon people's freedom of choice.

Another illustration from the gray area: While the laws of nature are independent of human will, knowledge of these laws and the use of that knowledge can surely be influenced by human action. Conceivably, government can restrict the freedom of scientific research and thus reduce the production of new knowledge; it can restrict the freedom of teaching and thus reduce the dissemination of existing knowledge; it can restrict the freedom of applying existing knowledge and thus reduce the use of knowledge in production. These would be examples of infringements of freedoms. The government may also take positive actions to promote scientific research,

133

FRITZ MACHLUP

to promote education (that is, the transmission of knowledge), and to promote practical application of technology (for example, through agricultural field service). While these 'positive' influences on people's choices may extend the scope of producers' and consumers' choices, I see no advantage in characterizing these influences as enlargements of freedom. I see no point in using the findings of economic welfare analysis – that is, findings of whether the increase of material welfare is accelerated or retarded by certain interventions in the allocation of resources – for judgments of whether 'freedom' is being enhanced or restricted. To be free is one thing, to be well off is another, as I am going to argue presently.

My insistence on separating the origins of any limitations on human choices and on regarding as limitations of freedom only those that are the result of restrictions and restraints which man imposes upon man is by no means a position outside the main stream in the history of ideas. I have some rather strange precursors in expressing this position and I am taking the risk of quoting the anarchist Mikhail Bakunin as an ally on this issue. In his *Dieu et l'Etat* (posthumously published in 1876), Bakunin wrote this: 'The liberty of man consists solely in this, that he obeys the laws of Nature because he has himself recognized them as such and not because they have been imposed upon him externally by any foreign will whatever, be it divine, collective, or individual.'

Let me put this in my own way, to express my own point of view. If certain constraints on my actions are suspected by me not to have originated from impartial 'nature' but to have been imposed upon me by some evil power, by a foreign will, by man, then I will feel these constraints as encroachments on my freedom. As long as I cannot blame anybody for the constraints, my freedom is not infringed.

The concept of freedom, I submit, is logically correlated with the concept of suppression, that is with the threat of man being suppressed, restrained, or punished by fellow man. *Actual* existence of freedom presupposes *potential* suppression, for it means that there need not be fear of this suppression actually to occur. To be fully comprehended, the meaning of freedom requires a specification of both the potentially suppressed and the potential suppressors and in addition a specification of the activities of the former which the latter may be inclined to restrain or punish. Hence, there can be no freedom that is not the freedom of a person to do specified things

134

LIBERALISM AND THE CHOICE OF FREEDOMS

– which he may or may not be capable of doing – without fear of restraint or punishment by one or more other persons.

Welfare and Freedom

The great protest of the opponents of this concept of freedom is that it is merely *negative*: the absence of restriction, coercion and suppression, and the absence of justified fear of restriction, coercion or punishment. The pragmatist wants a more *positive* concept of freedom, such as that of the effective power to do things. If nature denies me the capacity to do certain things or society refuses me the buying power I would need to afford them, then I am not really 'free' to do what I want – so argues the pragmatist. I have rejected this merger of separate ideas as a violation of good analytic practice.

At one point in the preceding section I objected also to the widespread notion that an increase in one's economic welfare would enhance one's 'freedom'. Some of those who protest against the 'merely negative' concept of freedom as nonrestriction and nonsuppression want to make it 'positive' by having it comprise all the goodies that life provides, the entire bundle of goods and services that make up our economic welfare. Economists will find this a strange case of logical intransitivity. For they are used to a concept of total welfare that includes not only economic welfare but also such nice and satisfying things as being left alone: freedom. Thus, for the economist freedom is included in total welfare; yet, for the pragmatic philosopher welfare is included in freedom. Since formal logic tells us that if A includes B, B cannot include A, we had better start agreeing which is the A and which is the B in our universe of discourse. We need not in the process sacrifice our theories about the possibly mutual effects of freedom as non-restraint upon economic welfare (or upon freedom as effective power). The decision in the Court of Logic, however, must be unanimous: if freedom is a part of welfare, welfare cannot be a part of freedom.

Since even dogs may have strong views about the relative satisfactions derived, on the one hand, from being free to bark and not being kept on a leash and, on the other hand, from being served good and plentiful foods enriched with meat and bones, the dogs surely will take my side: freedom is a part of welfare and its

135

FRITZ MACHLUP

significance is not reduced by being 'merely' negative. In a dog's life the non-punishment for barking and the non-restraint by the leash may be of such utility that he may consider these negatives a fair trade-off for the positive contents of his food tray – apart from the fact that the unleashing may allow him to find some extra tidbits not provided for in his master's plan.

A Catalogue of Freedom

In the discussion of the 'seventh' error of the assertion that 'freedom is indivisible', I advanced the thesis of the multiplicity of freedoms, some of which are reinforcing one another, others conflicting with one another, some are regarded as instrumental values, others as ultimate values.

As an aid in the examination of the relationship among the many separate freedoms, I have prepared a catalogue of freedoms. This catalogue is incomplete in several respects. Apart from my inability to give it adequate comprehensiveness, there must be omissions in the sense that the grant of certain freedoms is out of the question, because they would conflict with other more important freedoms, not only beyond some point, but from the very outset. To give the most obvious examples, a freedom to kill would be incompatible with other people's freedom to live; a freedom to take what belongs to others would be incompatible with the freedom to have property. Or to give an example where we stay within the same kind of activity, a freedom to continue to drive while the traffic light is red would interfere with other people's freedom to drive while they have the green light, and it might even restrict people's freedom to stay whole and alive.

As Herbert Spencer put it, liberalism claims the right of each to the maximum freedom compatible with equal freedom for all others. But since these freedoms may relate to different kinds of human activity, this postulate presupposes a rough quantification of the values of freedoms and sometimes a weighing and balancing of different freedoms of different people.

My catalogue contains two dozens of freedoms, some of them overlapping. All are freedoms 'to do or not to do'; not all exist in our society, and some exist only to a limited extent. We may divide

136

LIBERALISM AND THE CHOICE OF FREEDOMS

A catalogue of some important freedoms – to do or not to do as we please – which may exist in various spheres of activity

Freedom of	would mean that everybody is free, without restraint, to
Work	work in any kind of occupation, or not to work at all
Enterprise	apply any kind of resources to any kind of business in any field of production
Trade	transport, import, or export any kind and quantity of commodities
Travel	travel abroad and everywhere in the country
Migration	move and make his residence abroad or everywhere in the country
Contract	make any sort of binding contract with anyone, except under duress, or with deceit or fraud
Markets	buy or sell any quantity at any price agreeable to him and to the other party
Competition and entry	enter any industry, trade, or market and compete in any way except with use of violence, deceit, or fraud
Choice of consumption	use his buying power for any goods or services he chooses, with prices reflecting the demand for them and the supply of resources required for their production
Choice of occupation	use his labor power and skills in any occupation he chooses, with wages reflecting the supply of the labor in question and the demand for the products to which it contributes
Coalition and association	combine with anybody for any purpose not involving harm to others
Assembly	convene or attend gatherings for discussion and deliberation of any subject whatsoever
Vote	cast his vote in free and secret balloting in periodic elections and referenda
Revolution	overthrow a government that denies essential freedoms
Thought and expression	think, write, and express in art, music or any other way
Speech	speak privately and publicly on any subject and in any vein whatsoever
Press	Print and publish anything and distribute it in any way
Privacy	work, play, rest, converse, and correspond unexposed to the view or knowledge by any uninvited
Nonconformance and eccentricity	be different in appearance, habits and ways of life, however foolish, perverse or wrong it may look to others
Teaching	teach any subject, facts, ideas, or methods
Research	investigate any subject by any method
Learning	study or attend lectures on any subject
Religion	worship in any way or not at all, if he so wishes
Conscience	refuse to do things against his conscience

Left margin labels: ECONOMICS · POLITICAL · INTELLECTUAL AND MORAL

137

FRITZ MACHLUP

them roughly into three groups, again partly overlapping: economic freedoms, political freedoms, and intellectual and moral (or cultural) freedoms.

I cannot take the space to comment on every item on the list. One could spend several hours, perhaps an entire academic term, discussing the interrelationships between the various freedoms. I can select only a few points for discussion here.

Economic Freedoms

Free choice of consumption and occupation, two of the economic freedoms listed, may be understood either in a merely formal way, as a mere absence of rationing restrictions, of prohibitions and other barriers, or in a comprehensive way, as the operation of a price mechanism that assures perfect realization of the law of supply and demand under competition in every market. If the two freedoms of choice were only formal, they would be consistent with the most thorough central planning of the economy by a dictator. Assume the dictator decides on the basis of his judgment what is good for the nation, and how much of each commodity ought to be produced. He can carry out this decision either by coercion or by using the price mechanism: he may set wages so that he attracts no more and no fewer workers than are required in each industry to produce the planned output and he may set prices so that he attracts no more and no fewer consumers than he can serve out of his planned output. The dictator will then find that there are high profits and serious losses in various industries, but he can take care of that through taxes and subsidies. Neither the worker nor the consumer needs to know that he is barred from following his own free choice; yet *we* know that under such a system the consumption and occupation patterns would express only the wish of the dictatorial planner and not the preferences of the consumers and workers. Only when all wage rates and prices are consistent in the sense that they reflect the supply of labor in each occupation and the demand for products in each industry can we say that there is really full freedom of choice. In this case, however, the freedoms of choice of occupation and consumption are so comprehensive in their scope that they include or presuppose several of the other economic freedoms in our catalogue.

138

LIBERALISM AND THE CHOICE OF FREEDOMS

Another case of overlapping or even duplication is free enterprise and free competition if the latter is understood in the sense of unrestricted entry into the industry (and has no connotation of absence of power or domination over markets, supplies, and prices).

On the other hand, there are some serious conflicts of freedoms within the economic sphere. The freedoms of coalition and of contract may be used to restrict the freedoms of work and enterprise, and thereby the freedoms of choice of consumption and occupation. We know of many instances where workers' or businessmen's combinations have created monopolistic positions restricting entry into occupations or industries.

Mere freedom of coalition could not have created all the strong labor monopolies of our days; active government interventions and failure to suppress private coercive activities have helped in this process. But once labor unions have attained great power, they can maintain it and exercise it (to restrict the freedom to work and freedom to enter the occupation of one's choice) by the mere use of the freedom of combination and contract. Hence, some limitations have been made in the freedom of contract between unions and employers in the hope to increase the freedoms that have been encroached upon. But who can say that the laws to this effect have been successful? Many trade unions use the freedoms of coalition and of contract in ways badly restricting the freedom to work. And no practical solution of this problem is in sight.

The use by businessmen of the freedom of contract, together with a host of governmental restrictions of trade and entry, have resulted in restrictions of free enterprise. Freeing trade and entry by removing the restrictions which governments through tariffs, quotas, licenses, and many other measures have imposed on foreign and domestic competition might solve the problem to a large extent. Without government support, businessmen would probably not be able to use their freedom of contract to restrict very seriously the freedom of enterprise and competition. But there is no sign that governments are ready to do anything in the indicated direction, and thus the conflict of freedoms remains.

Political Freedoms

There is less conflict among the various freedoms in the political

139

FRITZ MACHLUP

sphere; but some of these freedoms have been reduced or abolished even in the United States. The freedom to revolt, to which the founding fathers appealed when they successfully subverted the previous government, was often cited and glorified in the early years of the republic. Several of the state constitutions included the freedom to revolt among the fundamental rights of the people; and Abraham Lincoln, in his First Inaugural Address (1861) reconfirmed this principle in ringing words: 'Whenever the people shall grow weary of the existing government, they can exercise their constitutional right of amending it or their revolutionary right to dismember or overthrow it'.

A 'freedom of revolution' to overthrow a government of which people have 'grown weary' is an odd idea. What percentage of the people must have become dissatisfied? Would the state ever grant to a disenchanted minority a legal right to use violence to remove a lawfully elected government? Could one reasonably expect a government not to attempt to suppress such violence? I suppose what the founding fathers, and later Lincoln, meant by the 'freedom to revolt' and the 'revolutionary right' of the people was a *moral* right to revolt against oppression when all legal means of bringing about change – that is, an end to the denial by the government of essential freedoms – had failed. A freedom to change by violence the form of a lawfully elected and freedom-respecting government cannot be supported by reasonable men. However, since peaceful change should remain possible, insistence on a freedom to *advocate* a change of the government and of the form of government remains a valid position. Such a freedom is, of course, closely linked with the freedom of speech, freedom of the press, and freedom of teaching. And I am inclined to go further and include in these freedoms the right to advocate violent revolution, as long as there is no clear and present danger that the advocacy will be followed by the immediate use of deadly weapons. Advocacy of a violent uprising where there is time for reasoned argument and for countering advocacy of acquiescence, patience, or peaceful procedures of bringing about reforms is among the freedoms which under a truly democratic form of government are granted to the citizens.

My catalogue is woefully incomplete in the area of political freedoms. The freedom of possession of firearms is now much debated in the United States. In early times this was regarded as an important right of the citizen in a democracy; in recent times the

140

LIBERALISM AND THE CHOICE OF FREEDOMS

possession of firearms by criminal or insane persons has reduced other people's freedom to live, to work, to retain their properties, and so forth. An evaluation of the relative importance of unlimited possession of firearms presupposes estimates of their misuse and of the damage caused. Personal habits, local customs, love of sport, and a few other things will bear on the comparative evaluation of the importance of some people giving up their arms and other people giving up their lives. A compromise between these conflicting values seems imperative and some restrictions on the possession of firearms seem strongly indicated.

Much ought to be said, though little can be said here, about the freedom to vote. My definition makes it a right to cast a vote in free and secret balloting in periodic elections. Secrecy of the ballot is an integral part of the right if it is not to be a fake. But there are serious questions about limitations concerning age, sanity, permanent residence, and literacy. Regarding the last of these, one may on first thought insist on literacy as a condition for the right to vote. But if access to schools has been limited or restricted with the result that large sectors of the population have remained illiterate, should they forever be deprived of the freedom to vote?

In view of the many nations that have recently become independent after decades of foreign rule, the question of individual political freedom and democratic elections for people with limited political experience and a low rate of literacy is of sometimes tragic complexity. Maybe, democracy works only for informed people who can distinguish between deceptive promises and realistic programs. It may also be true that political intelligence can be acquired by practice, and only by practice, so that a costly learning process has to be accepted.

One thought, far too seldom considered, is the possible conflict between collective (national) freedom and individual freedom. Liberation from colonial rule is often associated with severe restrictions on personal liberty. Examples from the New Africa come to mind, where national independence sooner or later led to restrictions on political and intellectual freedoms. If the new 'freedom' for the nation means less freedom for its citizens, it may almost be named the government's freedom to suppress its people. Clean semantic analysis would use the words 'independence' or 'autonomy' for the collective, and reserve the word 'freedom' for the individual. It would then be more clearly understood that national 'liberation' in

141

FRITZ MACHLUP

the sense of achieving independence from some foreign power can lead to 'illiberation' of the people.

I may have given the impression of a serious bias on these questions. May I admit that I really am of two minds? Let me recall Mill's dictum that there can be no liberty for 'savages'. Replace this harsh word by 'politically and intellectually immature people' and reflect on the proposition that full democracy may not be the most suitable system of government for such people; that, for example, the unlimited right to vote and elect the men who will govern the country may lead to the destruction of many other freedoms and also of any real chance for economic development. Communist, socialist, and capitalist countries have resorted to denials of political freedom in order to permit the execution of development programs. Now I am probably giving the impression of the opposite bias. This is intentional, for we must see the difficult choices and the almost inevitable conflicts between different freedoms and between freedoms and other social objectives.

In recent years one of the most fundamental political (and also moral) freedoms, the right to privacy, has been invaded in many ways. Telephone wires have been tapped, mail has been intercepted, pressure has been brought on people to testify on matters they would have chosen to keep secret, and citizens were questioned on their political beliefs, which should be nobody's business where freedom of privacy is respected.

Moral and Intellectual Freedoms

In the moral sphere, the freedom of nonconformance and eccentricity has never been respected to any high degree. John Stuart Mill, more than a hundred years ago complained that the English, who had gone further than most other nations in securing individual liberties, had not seen fit to grant their nonconformers the freedom to be different without being embarrassed or harassed. We have not matured on this score; nonconformance is subject to public disapproval, to social ostracism, and in many instances to legal punishment.

The next three freedoms in my catalogue, the freedoms of teaching, research, and learning are usually discussed under the

142

LIBERALISM AND THE CHOICE OF FREEDOMS

combined designation of academic freedom. This is a topic on which I published an essay in 1955 (in the *Bulletin* of the American Association of University Professors) and have undertaken to write a comprehensive article (in the forthcoming *Encyclopedia of Education*). It is amazing how much the academic scene has changed in this short period. In 1955, I discussed the major mis-understandings of academic freedom on the part of those who, alarmed by the danger of communist subversion, felt insecure under a system of full freedom to teach. In 1969, the greatest threat to academic freedom is not from conservative trustees and sub-servient administrators, but from exuberant and militant students suspicious of the 'establishment' and intolerant of academic tradi-tion. Rather than expatiate here on these issues, I may refer the reader to the two publications in which I deal exclusively with the subject of academic freedom.

Perhaps I should say just a word about freedom of conscience. There were times when our society was willing to respect it to a greater extent than it has since the early 1950s. In the McCarthy (Joseph, not Eugene) period in the United States, the refusal of some people to bear arms, to salute the flag, to inform on former friends, and to do other things which the government may require but which their own conscience forbids, subjected many of these conscientious objectors to severe penalties, social and economic as well as legal.

The Choice of Freedoms

I have emphasized the interrelationships among different freedoms: they may conflict with one another or reinforce one another. The conflicts will compel the liberal to choose among liberties or at least among various degrees to which he wants conflicting liberties to be realized. But apart from these 'interlibertarian' conflicts there are the conflicts between various freedoms and other social goals. For example, the objectives of greater income equality, social security, and national security cannot be pursued without sacrificing some of the liberties to some extent. These conflicts compel the liberal to choose between certain liberties, or high degrees of them, and other objectives. The extreme libertarians are not willing to pay much for

143

FRITZ MACHLUP

the attainments of competing social objectives; the American 'liberal' (in the usual sense, described at the beginning of this essay) is prepared to give up most of the economic freedoms in order to get more income equality and social security; some timid liberals are ready to sacrifice economic, political and intellectual freedoms for the sake of national security; and some economic liberals are inclined to restrict intellectual freedoms if these might through political action endanger economic freedoms.

Under these circumstances it is not surprising that we find the adherents of liberalism split in several directions. Perhaps one might say that timidity and liberalism are not compatible and, thus, that those who in the absence of a clear and present danger sacrifice freedoms for increased national security are no liberals at heart. Perhaps one might say that egalitarianism and liberalism are largely contradictory and, thus, that those who sacrifice freedoms for more economic equality and social security are no liberals at heart. But even if one takes such points of view, enough conflicts remain to prevent even the purest liberals or libertarians from agreeing on the 'proper' choice and balance of freedoms.

The most deplorable split, in my opinion, is between those intellectual liberals who have little respect for economic liberties and those economic liberals who have little concern for intellectual liberties. Indeed there are some intellectual liberals who are anxious to restrict, if not altogether strangle, free enterprise and free markets and who wish to introduce more and more central 'planning' in the supply of goods and services to consumers. On the other side, there are some economic liberals who would not mind silencing a teacher of opposite persuasion and who are inclined to see a strong dose of 'planning' introduced in the supply of ideas to university students.

While these illiberal liberals, or demi-liberals, despise each other and call each other such names as 'fascist' and 'communist', their positions can be rationalized by plausible argument. The economic liberal is convinced that economic freedoms provide the most efficient organization not only for creating welfare but also for maintaining political freedoms. I share this conviction. In the long run, a society without a large scope for economic freedom is not likely to retain the political liberties treasured by all liberals. However, from this the pre-eminently economic liberal goes on to argue that the teaching of antiliberal economics will lead to an increasing

144

LIBERALISM AND THE CHOICE OF FREEDOMS

flow of socialist interventions and to the emergence of central economic planning that can be carried through only when the planners restrict political freedoms. He concludes that in order to prevent such developments it is imperative to suppress what he regards as 'subversive' teaching.

The intellectual liberal is convinced that the existence of abject poverty in the midst of plenty is intolerable for humanitarian reasons and, moreover, will provide a fertile breeding ground for revolutionary movements. I share this conviction. A society that tolerates the existence of misery which it economically could afford to mitigate may not be able to resist movements to overthrow the whole system. However, from this the pre-eminently intellectual liberal goes on to argue that the free-enterprise system is incapable of producing welfare for all and must therefore provoke a hostility that will kill political freedom in order to get rid of economic 'injustice'. He concludes that measures to restrict economic freedoms are imperative for the sake of social justice as well as political freedom.

I submit that both these demi-liberalisms suffer from a lack of faith in liberty. Economic liberals who distrust intellectual freedom and intellectual liberals who distrust economic freedom are equally deficient in their understanding of the fundamental idea of liberty. To be sure, every liberal position must imply some compromise because of the inevitable conflict of competing freedoms. Even the best liberal may recognize a hierarchy of freedoms, attaching, for example, highest importance to civil liberties and giving other liberties a less exalted place in his system of values. But he will never disregard, disparage, distrust, or discard any of the freedoms valued by others.

Does this leave us with a definition of a liberal – a pure, all-round liberal? Not really. Perhaps though we may say that a liberal is one who values liberty above all other social goals and who will never consent to the restriction of any freedom, economic, political, or intellectual, except as the price to be paid for the fuller realization of other freedoms. He must demonstrate that this price is worth paying; he must always be ready to re-examine his and other positions; and he must not place material welfare above liberty.

I do not say that anybody ought to be a liberal; I do not say that one ought to love or promote liberty above material welfare; nor do I say that one ought to neglect promotion of security or welfare for

FRITZ MACHLUP

the poor. I only say one ought not to declare oneself a 'liberal' as one promotes such programs. Food is not liberty, and liberty is not food. Medical care is not liberty, and liberty is not medical care. It is admirable to provide food and medical care for the poor – but let us not misuse the term 'liberalism' in advocating these policies.

146

BIBLIOGRAPHY
of
Fritz Machlup

A. Books, Sole Authorship

B. Books, Joint Authorship

C. Essays, Papers, and Chapters in Collective Works

D. Articles and Notes in Major Periodicals

E. Articles and Notes in Minor Journals

F. Discussions, Abstracts, Reports, Corrections, Prefaces

G. Official Reports, Memoranda, Testimonies in Public Documents

H. Book Reviews (excluding Review Articles)

Note: Omitted from this bibliography are 178 articles and columns in daily papers; translations of such articles published in foreign-language journals; and articles on nonprofessional subjects.

BIBLIOGRAPHY

A. BOOKS, SOLE AUTHORSHIP

1   *Die Goldkernwährung* (Halberstadt: Meyer, 1925), xv and 203 pages.

    REPRODUCTIONS
    Partial reproduction of the Appendix under the title *Vorschläge für eine wirt-schaftliche und sichere Währung* von David Ricardo (Halberstadt: Meyer, 1927), 29 pages.

2   *Die neuen Währungen in Europa*. Finanz-und Volkswirtschaftliche Zeitfragen, No. 92 (Stuttgart: Enke, 1927), 83 pages.

3   *Börsenkredit, Industriekredit und Kapitalbildung* (Wien: Springer, 1931), xi and 220 pages.

    TRANSLATIONS
    English translation of an enlarged edition under the title *The Stock Market, Credit and Capital Formation* (London: Hodge, and New York: Macmillan, 1940), xii and 416 pages.
    Japanese translation, *Kabushikisijyo Sinyo Oyobi Sihon-Keisei* (Tokyo: Chikura Shobo, 1970), 17 and 296 and 41 and 13 pages.

4   *Führer durch die Krisenpolitik* (Wien: Springer, 1934), xi and 232 pages.

    TRANSLATIONS
    French translation, *Guide à travers les panacées économiques* (Paris: Librairie de Médicis, 1939), 331 pages.

5   *International Trade and the National Income Multiplier* (Philadelphia: Blakiston, 1943), xvi and 237 pages. (Second printing, Philadelphia, 1950. Third printing, New York: Augustus M. Kelley, 1961.)

    REPRODUCTIONS
    Partial reproduction of parts of Chapters VIII and IX under the titles "The Transfer Problem: Income Effects and Price Effects" and "Capital Movements and Trade Balance," in Fritz Machlup, *International Payments, Debts, and Gold* (New

York: Scribners, 1964), pp. 425-432 and 447-464; also in second, enlarged edition (New York University Press, 1976): also in Fritz Machlup, *International Monetary Economics* (London: Allen & Unwin, 1966), pp. 425-432 and 447-464.

TRANSLATIONS

Serbocroatian translation, *Medunarodna Trgovina i Multiplikator Nacionalnog Dohotka* (Sarajevo: Svjetlost, Izdavacko Preduzece, 1973), 191 pages.

6 *The Basing-Point System* (Philadelphia: Blakiston, 1949), vii and 275 pages.

7 *The Political Economy of Monopoly* (Baltimore: Johns Hopkins Press, 1952), xvi and 544 pages. (Fourth printing, Baltimore, 1967.)

REPRODUCTIONS

Partial reproduction of Chapter 7 under the title "Taxation and Monopoly Power," in Randall B. Ripley, ed., *Public Policies and their Politics* (New York: W. W. Norton, 1966), pp. 161-172.

TRANSLATIONS

Italian translation, *La concorrenza ed il monopolio* (Torino: Unione Tipografico-Editrice Torinese, 1956), xv and 660 pages.

8 *The Economics of Sellers' Competition* (Baltimore: Johns Hopkins Press, 1952), xx and 582 pages. (Fifth printing, Baltimore, 1969.)

TRANSLATIONS

Japanese translation, *Urite Kyoso-no Keizai Gaku* (Tokyo: Chikura-Shobo, 1965), 612 and lxxii pages.

German translation, *Wettbewerb im Verkauf: Modellanalyse des Anbieterverhaltens* (Göttingen: Vandenhoeck & Ruprecht, 1966), xviii and 568 pages.

Partial reproduction of German translation of Chapter 13 under the title "Die Formen und Grade der Kollusion," in Hans-Heinrich Barnikel, ed., *Theorie und Praxis der Kartelle* (Darmstadt: Wissenschaftliche Buchgesellschaft, 1972), pp. 295-316.

9 *An Economic Review of the Patent System*. Study of the Subcommittee on Patents, Trademarks, and Copyrights of the Committee on the Judiciary, U.S. Senate (Washington: Government Printing Office, 1958), vi and 89 pages.

TRANSLATIONS

Partial German translations, "Die wirtschaftlichen Grundlagen des Patentrechts," *Gewerblicher Rechtsschutz und Urheberrecht: Auslands-und Internationaler Teil*, 1961.

1. Teil (August/September), pp. 373-390; translation of pp. 2-5, 19-44.

2. Teil (Oktober), pp. 473-482; translation of pp. 44-58.

3. Teil (November), pp. 524-537; translation of pp. 58-80.

German translation, *Die wirtschaftlichen Grundlagen des Patentrechts* (Weinheim: Verlag Chemie, 1962), 141 pages.

Japanese translation, *Tokkyoseido no Keizaigaku* (Tokyo: Nihon Keizai Shimbun, 1975), 214 pp.

10 *Der Wettstreit zwischen Mikro- und Makrotheorien in der Nationalökonomie.* Walter Eucken Institut, Vorträge und Aufsätze, No. 4 (Tübingen: Mohr-Siebeck, 1960), 55 pages.

TRANSLATIONS

English translation under the title "Micro- and Macro-Economics: Contested Boundaries and Claims of Superiority," in Fritz Machlup, *Essays in Economic Semantics* (Englewood Cliffs, N.J.: Prentice-Hall, 1963; Second printing, New York: W. W. Norton, 1967; Third printing, New York: New York University Press, 1975), pp. 97-144.

French translation under the title "Théories micro-économique et macro-économique: Leurs frontières et leur place respective," in Fritz Machlup, *Essais de sémantique économique* (Paris: Calmann-Levy, 1971), pp. 47-99.

Spanish translation under the title "Micro y macroeconomia: Fronteras disputadas y pretensiones de superioridad," in Fritz Machlup, *Semántica Económica* (Mexico: Siglo Vientiuno Editores, 1974), pp. 101-147.

11 *Die Pläne zur Reform des internationalen Geldwesens.* Kieler Vorträge, Neue Folge, No. 23. (Kiel: Universität Kiel, 1962), 65 pages.

TRANSLATIONS

English translation, *Plans for Reform of the International Monetary System* (Special Papers in International Economics, No. 3. Princeton: International Finance Section, 1962), 70 pages.

Revised English edition, *Plans for Reform of the International Monetary System* (Special Paper in International Economics, Princeton: International Finance Section, 1964), 93 pages.

Italian translation, "Progetti di riforma del sistema monetario internazionale," *Bancaria*, Vol. 1962. Parte I (Agosto), pp. 879-900; Parte II (Settembre), pp. 1007-1020.

Partial Italian translation, "Piani di riforma del sistema monetario internazionale," in Fabrizio Onida, ed., *Problemi di teoria monetaria internazionale* (Milano: Etas Kompass, 1971), Ch. 11, pp. 307-327.

Japanese translation, "Kokusai tsuka seido no kaikaku" (Jo) ["Reforms of the International Monetary System," Part I], *Chosa Geppo* [Monthly Bulletin of Research, Research Department, Ministry of Finance] Vol. 52, No. 2 (February 1963), pp. 110-121. "Kokusai tsuka seido kaikaku-an ni tsuite" (Ge) ["Plans for Reform of the International Monetary System," Part II], *Chosa Geppo*, Vol. 52, No. 4 (April 1963), pp. 139-168.

Russian translation, *Plany perestroiki mezhdunarodnoi valutnoi sistemy* (Moscow: Progress, 1966), 159 pages.

REPRODUCTIONS OF THE REVISED ENGLISH EDITION

Full reproduction under the same title in Fritz Machlup, *International Payments, Debts, and Gold* (New York: Scribner's, 1964), pp. 282-366; also in second, enlarged edition (New York: New York University Press, 1976); also in Fritz Machlup, *International Monetary Economics* (London: Allen & Unwin, 1966), pp. 282-366.

Partial reproduction under the title "Plans for Reform of the International Monetary System—Charges against the System," in James A. Crutchfield, Charles N. Henning, and William Pigott, eds., *Money, Financial Institutions, and the Economy* (Englewood Cliffs, N.J.: Prentice Hall, 1965), Selection 45, pp. 432-439.

12 *The Production and Distribution of Knowledge in the United States* (Princeton: Princeton University Press, 1962), xix and 416 pages; (Fourth printing, 1971.)

EDITIONS

The Production and Distribution of Knowledge in the United States (Princeton, N.J.: Princeton University Press, paperback edition, 1972), xix and 416 pages.

REPRODUCTIONS

Partial reproduction of Chapter IX under the title "Knowledge Production Grows Faster than GNP—A Sign of Real Economic Growth," in *Congressional Record— Appendix,* Extension of Remarks of Hon. Thomas B. Curtis, of Missouri, in the House of Representatives, June 4, 1963, pp. A3551-A3554.

Partial reproduction of Chapter I under the same title in Ian Burton and Robert W. Kates, eds., *Readings in Resource Management and Conservation* (Chicago: University of Chicago Press, 1965), Ch. 7, pp. 445-449.

Partial reproduction of Chapter IV under the title "Acceleration of Intellectual Growth," in *Crisis in School Finance*, Southern California Research Council, Report No. 14 (Los Angeles: Occidental College, 1966), pp. 51-55.

Partial reproduction from Chapters VI and IX under the title "The Media of Communication," in Mary Virginia Gaver, ed., *Background Readings in Building Library Collections* (Metuchen, N.J.: Scarecrow Press, 1969), Vol. II, pp. 844-869.

Reproductions of Chapters I and III under the title "The Knowledge Industry," in Natsuo Shamut, ed., *Readings Now* (Tokyo: Kenkyusho, 1970), Ch. 9, pp. 249-271.

TRANSLATIONS

Russian translation, *Proizvodstvo i rasprostranenie zani v SShA* (Moscow: Progress, 1966), 462 pages.

Japanese translation, *Chishiki Sangyō* (Tokyo: Sangyō Nohritsu Tanki Daigaku, 1969), 35 and 477 and 16 pages.

German translation of part of Chapter V, under the title "Patente und der Aufwand für Forschung und Entwicklung," in Jens Naumann, ed., *Forschungsökonomie und Forschungspolitik* (Stuttgart: Klett, 1970) pp. 161-172.

13 *Essays on Economic Semantics* (Englewood Cliffs, N.J.: Prentice-Hall, 1963), xxxii and 304 pages.

EDITIONS

Essays in Economic Semantics (New York: W. W. Norton; Paperback edition, with corrections and new preface, 1967), xiv and 304 pages. (New printing, New York: New York University Press, 1975, paperback and hard cover.)

TRANSLATIONS

Spanish translation of three chapters, *Ensayos de Semántica Económica*. Colleción Metodológica, No. 1, (Bahia Blanca, Argentina: Universidad Nacional de Sur, 1962), 128 pages.

French translation, *Essais de Sémantique Économique* (Paris: Calmann-Lévy, 1971), iv and 342 pages.

French translation of two sections from a chapter, "Texte N° 17" and "N° 18," in Henri Guitton & Michel Bessis, *Analyse micro-économique*(Paris:Sirey, 1971) pp. 45-49.

Spanish translation, *Semántica Económica* (Mexico: Siglo Veintiuno Editores, 1974), viii and 306 pages.

14 *International Payments, Debts, and Gold* (New York: Scribners, 1964), viii and 472 pages.

EDITIONS

International Monetary Economics (London: George Allen & Unwin Ltd., 1966), viii and 472 pages.

International Payments, Debts, and Gold (New York: New York University Press, second, enlarged edition, 1976), viii and 515 pages

REPRODUCTIONS

Full reproduction of Chapters XII and XIII under the title "Liquidity, International and Domestic: A Study of the Demand for Foreign Reserves," *Archeion*, *Oikonomikon kai Koinonikon Epistemon*, Vol. 44 (1964), pp. 29-58; also *Anakoinoseis, 1962-1963* (Athens: Bibliopoleion tes Estias, 1963), pp. 29-58.

Reproduction of Chapter XI under the title "A Proposal to Reduce the Price of Gold," in *Guidelines for International Monetary Reform*, Hearings before the Subcommittee on International Exchange and Payments of the Joint Economic Committee, Congress of the United States, 89th Congress, 1st Session (Washington: 1965), pp. 571-575.

TRANSLATIONS

Japanese translation, *Kokusai Kinyu no Riron* (Tokyo: Diamondo, 1973), 17 and 327 pages.

15 *Involuntary Foreign Lending* (Stockholm: Almquist & Wiksell, 1965), 129 pages.

16 *Remaking the International Monetary System: The Rio Agreement and Beyond* (Baltimore: Johns Hopkins Press, for the Committee for Economic Development, 1968), x and 161 pages. (Second printing, 1971.)

TRANSLATIONS

Swedish translation, *Kris i Valutasystemet: Är Pappersguldet Lösningen*(Stockholm: Studieförbundet Näringsliv och Samhälle, 1970), 204 pages.

17 *Education and Economic Growth* (Lincoln: University of Nebraska Press, 1970), ix and 106 pages. (Second printing, New York: New York University Press, 1975, paperback and hard cover.)

TRANSLATIONS

Dutch translation, *Inleiding tot de onderwijs-economie* (Rotterdam: Universitaire Pers, 1971). ix and 59 pages.

18 *Chishiki Sangyō no Kōzō* [The Structure of the Knowledge Industry], collected by the Institute for General Telecommunication Research (Tokyo: Diamondo, 1971), xxiv and 188 pages.

19 *Gendai Keizaigaku no Tembo* [Views on Selected Topics in Modern Economics], (Tokyo: Nihon Keizai Shimbun Sha, 1971), 199 pages.

20 *The Book Value of Monetary Gold* (Princeton, N.J.: International Finance Section, 1971), 24 pages.

REPRODUCTIONS

Full reproduction under the same title *Banca Nazionale del Lavoro Quarterly Review*, Vol. XXIV (December 1971), pp. 299-315.

Full reproduction under the same title, *Banc Ceannais na h Éireann Faisnéis Ráithiúil* [*Central Bank of Ireland Quarterly Bulletin*] (Spring 1972), pp. 80-96.

Partial reproduction under the same title in Robert E. Baldwin and J. David Richardson, eds., *International Trade and Finance: Readings* (Boston: Little, Brown and Co., 1974). pp. 386-398.

ABSTRACTS

Abstract under the same title, *Journal of Economic Literature*, Vol. X (September 1972), p. 1095.

21 *The Alignment of Foreign Exchange Rates* (New York: Praeger Publishers, 1972), xi and 95 pages. (New distributor, New York: New York University Press, 1976).

22 *Hochschulbildung für jedermann: Eine Auseinandersetzung mit einem Gleichheitsideal* (Zurich: Schulthess Polygraphischer Verlag, 1973), 43 pages.

23 *Der Aussenwert des Dollars: Zum Problem der Unterbewertung und Überbewertung einer Währung auf den Devisenmärkten.* Kieler Vorträge, Neue Folge No. 79 (Tübingen: Mohr—Siebeck, 1974), 54 pages.

24 *International Monetary Systems* (Morristown: N.J.,: General Learning Press, 1975), 60 pages.

B. BOOKS, JOINT AUTHORSHIP

1 *Financing American Prosperity*, Paul T. Homan and Fritz Machlup, eds. (New York: Twentieth Century Fund, 1945), xi and 508 pages, esp. pp. 394-496. (Fourth printing, New York, 1949).

2 *A Cartel Policy for the United Nations*, Corwin D. Edwards, ed. (New York: Columbia University Press, 1945), vi and 124 pages, esp. pp. 1-24.

3 *International Monetary Arrangements: The Problem of Choice*, Report on the Deliberations of an International Group of 32 Economists, Fritz Machlup and Burton G. Malkiel, eds. (Princeton, N.J.: International Finance Section, 1964), 121 pages.

   TRANSLATIONS

   Spanish translation, *Planes de Reforma del Sistema Monetario Internacional* (Mexico: Centro de Estudios Monetarios Latinoamericanos, 1965), 251 pp.

4 *Maintaining and Restoring Balance in International Payments* [with William Fellner, Robert Triffin, and eleven others] (Princeton, N.J.: Princeton University Press, 1966), xii and 259 pages, esp. pp. vii-ix, 3-8, 33-84, 167-170, 243-254.

   TRANSLATIONS

   Spanish translation, *Mantenimiento y Restauración de la Balanza de los Pagos Internacionales* (Barcelona: Gustavo Gili, 1969), xiv and 306 pages.

5 *Economic Means and Social Ends: Essays in Political Economics* [with Adolf Lowe *et. al.]*, Robert L. Heilbroner, ed. (Englewood Cliffs, N.J.: Prentice-Hall, 1969, ix and 240 pages, esp. pp. 99-129.

6 *Roads to Freedom: Essays in Honor of Friedrich A. von Hayek* [with Erich Streissler *et al.*], Erich Streissler, Gottfried Haberler, Friedrich A. Lutz, Fritz Machlup, eds. (London: Routledge & Kegan Paul, 1969), xix and 315 pages, esp. pp. 117-146.

7 *Approaches to Greater Flexibility of Exchange Rates: The Bürgenstock Papers* [with C. Fred Bergsten, George N. Halm, Robert V. Roosa *et al.*], George N. Halm, ed. (Princeton, N.J.: Princeton University Press, 1970), xi and 436 pages, esp. pp. 31-47, 297-306, 309, 320-321.

8 *Reshaping the International Economic Order*: *A Tripartite Report* by Twelve Economists [with C. Fred Bergsten *et al.*], (Washington, D.C.: Brookings Institution, January 1972), 23 pages, esp. pp. 6-11.

9 *International Monetary Problems* [with Armin Gutowski and Friedrich A. Lutz] (Washington: American Enterprise Institute for Public Policy Research, 1972), 136 pages, esp. pp. 3-36, 55-57.

10 *International Mobility and Movement of Capital*, Fritz Machlup, Walter Salant, and Lorie Tarshis, eds. (New York: National Bureau of Economic Research—Columbia University Press, 1972),xi and 708 pages, esp. pp. 1-24.

11 *Optimum Social Welfare and Productivity* [with Jan Tinbergen, Abram Bergson, and Oskar Morgenstern]. (New York: New York University Press, 1972), 175 pages, esp. pp. 153-165.

C. ESSAYS, PAPERS, AND CHAPTERS IN COLLECTIVE WORKS

1 "Inflation and Decreasing Costs of Production," in H. Parker Willis and John M. Chapman, eds. *The Economics of Inflation* (New York: Columbia University Press, 1935), pp. 280-287.

2 "On the Meaning of the Marginal Product," *Explorations in Economics, in Honor of F.W. Taussig* (New York: McGraw-Hill, 1937), pp. 250-263

REPRODUCTIONS

Full reproduction under the same title in William Fellner and Bernard F. Haley, eds., *Readings in the Theory of Income Distribution* (Philadelphia: Blakiston, 1946), Ch. 8, pp. 158-174.

Full reproduction under the same title in Fritz Machlup, *Essays in Economic Semantics* (Englewood Cliffs, N.J.: Prentice-Hall, 1963; Second printing, New York: W.W. Norton, 1967; Third printing, New York: New York University Press, 1975), pp.191-210.

3 "Can We Control the Boom?" *Can We Control the Boom? A Symposium* (Minneapolis: University of Minnesota Press, 1937), pp. 11-18.

4 "Programs to Maintain Employment," *Social Security in America,* National Conference on Social Security (Washington: Chamber of Commerce of the United States, 1944), pp. 14-23.

5 "Monopolistic Wage Determination as a Part of the General Problem of Monopoly," *Wage Determination and the Economics of Liberalism*. Economic Institute (Washington: Chamber of Commerce of the United States, 1947), pp. 49-82.

REPRODUCTIONS

Full reproduction under the same title in *Social Sciences 3: Syllabus and Selected Readings* (Chicago: University of Chicago Press, 15th ed., 1950), Ch. 62, pp. 433-466.

Full reproduction under the same title in Joseph Shister, ed., *Readings in Labor Economics and Industrial Relations* (Philadelphia: Lippincott, 1951), pp. 383-392; also 2nd ed., (1956), pp. 434-443.

Partial reproduction under the title "Monopolistic Wage Determination," in Paul A. Samuelson, Robert L. Bishop, and John R. Coleman, eds., *Readings in Economics* (New York: McGraw-Hill, 1952), Ch. 36, pp. 290-297; also 2nd ed. (1955); 3rd ed. (1958), pp. 271-277.

Partial reproduction under the title "Monopolistic Wage Determination," in George P. Schultz and John R. Coleman, eds., *Labor Problems: Cases and Readings* (New York: McGraw-Hill, 1953), Ch. 44, pp. 342-348; also 2nd ed., (1959), Ch. 47, pp. 409-415.

TRANSLATIONS

German translation of Chapter VI under the title "Der Lohn," in Alfred Kruse, ed., *Nationalökonomie: Ausgewählte Texte zur Geschichte einer Wissenschaft* (Stuttgart: Koehler, 1960), pp. 165-174.

6 "What's Best for the Competitive Enterprise System?" *Delivered Pricing and the Future of American Business*. Economic Institute (Washington: Chamber of Commerce of the United States, 1948), pp. 193-199.

7 "Monopoly and the Problem of Economic Stability," in Edward H. Chamberlin, ed., for the International Economic Association, *Monopoly and Competition and their Regulation* (London: Macmillan, 1954), pp. 385-397.

8 "Characteristics and Types of Price Discrimination," in George Stigler, ed., for the Universities—National Bureau Committee for Economic Research, *Business Concentration* and *Price Policies* (Princeton: Princeton University Press, 1955). pp. 397-440.

REPRODUCTIONS

Full reproduction under the same title, in George H. Brown, John E. Jeuck, and Peter G. Peterson, eds., *Marketing: Readings in Market Organization and Price Policies* (Chicago: University of Chicago Press, 1952), pp. 253-298.

Full reproduction under the same title, in Werner Sichel, ed., *Industrial Organization and Public Policy: Selected Readings* (Boston: Houghton Mifflin, 1967), Ch. 30, pp. 349-377.

9 "The Inferiority Complex of the Social Sciences," in Mary Sennholz, ed., *On Freedom*

and Free Enterprise: Essays in Honor of Ludwig von Mises (Princeton, N.J.: D.Van Nostrand Company, 1956), pp. 161-172.

10 "The Optimum Lag of Imitation Behind Innovation," *Til Frederik Zeuthen, 9 September 1958* (Copenhagen: Nationalokonomisk Forening, 1958), pp. 239-256.

11 "Does Economic Development Require Central Planning?" in Kenneth E. Boulding *et al. Segments of the Economy, 1956* (Cleveland: Allen, 1957), pp. 218-231.

12 "Why Not Hahnism?" *Eine Freundesgabe für Albert Hahn* (Frankfurt a. Main: Fritz Knapp Verlag, 1959), pp. 50-53.

13 "Erfindung und technische Forschung," *Handwörterbuch der Sozialwissenschaften* (Stuttgart: Fischer; Tübinger: Mohr-Siebeck; Göttingen: Vandenhoeck & Ruprecht, 1960), Vol. 3, pp. 280-291.

TRANSLATIONS
   French translation, "Invention et recherche technique," *Economie Appliquée*, Vol. XIV (1961), pp. 275-296.

14 "Monopol," *Handwörterbuch der Sozialwissenschaften* (Stuttgart: Fischer; Tübingen: Mohr-Siebeck; Göttingen: Vandenhoeck & Ruprecht, 1960), Vol. 7, pp. 427-452.

15 "Oligopol," *Handwörterbuch der Sozialwissenschaften* (Stuttgart: Fischer; Tübingen: Mohr-Siebeck; Göttingen:Vandenhoeck & Ruprecht, 1961), Vol. 8, pp. 82-94.

16 "Wettbewerb (III): Wirtschaftstheoretische Betrachtung," *Handwörterbuch der Sozialwissenschaften* (Stuttgart: Fischer; Tübingen: Mohr-Siebeck; Göttingen: Vandenhoeck & Ruprecht, 1962), Vol. 12, pp. 36-49.

17 "Patentwesen (1):Geschichtlicher Überblick," *Handwörterbuch der Sozialwissenschaften* (Stuttgart: Fischer; Tübingen: Mohr-Siebeck; Göttingen: Vandenhoeck & Ruprecht, 1962), Vol. 8, pp. 231-240.

18 "Patentwesen (II): Wirtschaftstheoretische Betrachtung," *Handwörterbuch der Sozialwissenschaften* (Stuttgart: Fischer; Tübingen: Mohr-Siebeck; Göttingen: Vandenhoeck & Ruprecht, 1962), Vol. 8, pp. 240-252.

19 "Polypol," *Handwörterbuch der Sozialwissenschaften* (Stuttgart: Fischer; Tübingen: Mohr-Siebeck; Göttingen: Vandenhoeck & Ruprecht, 1963), Vol. 8, pp. 407-421.

20 "Die Produktivität der naturwissenschaftlichen und technischen Forschung und Entwicklung," *Arbeitsgemeinschaft für Forschung des Landes Nordrhein-Westfalen*, Heft 122 (Köln und Opladen: Westdeutscher Verlag, 1963), pp. 37-64, 68-70.

21 "International Economic Co-operation," in Edgar O. Edwards, *The Nation's Economic Objectives* (Chicago: University of Chicago Press, 1964), pp. 73-105.

22 "Strategies in the War on Poverty," in Margaret S. Gordon, ed., *Poverty in America* (San Francisco: Chandler, 1965), pp. 445-465.

REPRODUCTIONS

Full reproduction under the same title, in J. Alan Winter, Jerome Rabow, and Mark Chesler, eds., *Vital Problems for American Society* (New York: Random House, 1968), Ch. VI, pp. 352-369.

"International Aspects," in Richard A. Musgrave, ed., *The Economic Report of January 1965: An Evaluation* (Princeton: Woodrow Wilson School of Public and International Affairs, 1965), pp. 51-57.

24 "Adjustment, Compensatory Correction, and Financing of Imbalances in International Payments," in Robert E. Baldwin *et al.*, *Trade, Growth, and the Balance of Payments: Essays in Honor of Gottfried Haberler* (Chicago: Rand McNally, and Amsterdam: North-Holland Publ. Co., 1965), pp. 185-213.

TRANSLATIONS

Spanish translation, "Ajuste real, correcciones compensatorias y financiamento externo de los disneveles en los pagos internacionales," in *Comercio Internacional Balanza de Pagos y Politicas y Sistemas Cambiarios*, Vol. I (Mexico, D.F.: Centro de Estudios Monetarios Latinoamericanos, 1969), pp. 119-153.

25 "International Monetary Systems and the Free Market Economy," in *International Payments Problems*, Symposium sponsored by the American Enterprise Institute for Public Policy Research (Washington: 1966), pp. 153-176, 193-194.

REPRODUCTIONS

Full reproduction under the same title, "International Monetary Systems and the Free Market Economy," in S. Mittra, ed., *Dimensions of Macroeconomics* (New York: Random House, 1971), pp. 452-471.

TRANSLATIONS

German translation, "Internationale Währungssysteme und die freie Marktwirtschaft," *Die Aussprache*, 16. Jahrgang (May-June 1966), pp. 118-124, 127-131.

26 "Operationalism and Pure Theory in Economics," in Sherman Roy Krupp, ed., *The Structure of Economic Science* (Englewood Cliffs, N.J.: Prentice-Hall, 1966), pp. 53-67.

TRANSLATIONS

Italian translation, "Operazionalismo e teoria pura nella scienza economica," *L'Industria*, (No. 1, March 1967), pp. 3-18.

27 "Freiheit und Planung in der Marktwirtschaft," *Die Wirtschaft in der Politischen Verantwortung*, Wirtschaftstag der CDU/CSU, Bonn, Januar 1967, pp. 38-52.

28 "L'homo oeconomicus et ses collègues," in Jacques Rueff, *Les Fondements Philosophiques des Systèmes Economiques* (Paris: Payot, 1967), pp. 117-130.

29 "Allgemeine Überlegungen zur Frage grösserer oder kleinerer Wirtschaftsräume," *Euroforum 68: Europa in der Welt von Morgen*, Protokolle, Wirtschaftsrat der CDU, Bonn, Januar 1968, pp. 124-130, 149, 157.

TRANSLATIONS

English translation, "Larger or Smaller Market Areas: General Considerations," *Euroforum 68: Europe in the World of Tomorrow*, Proceedings, Economic Council of the CDU, Bonn, January 1968, pp. 112-117, 134, 141-142.

French translations, "Considérations générales sur la question des espaces économiques plus grands ou plus petits," *Euroforum 68: L'Europe dans le monde de domain*, Procèsverbaux, Conseil Economique de la CDU, Bonn, Janvier 1968, pp. 122-128, 147, 155-156.

Italian translation, "Considerazioni generali in merito alla questione delle dimensioni delle aree economiche," *Euroforum 68: L'Europa nel mondo di domani*, Verbali, Consiglio Economico della CDU, Bonn, Gennaio 1968, pp. 116-122, 139-140, 147-148.

30 "Patents," in David L. Sills, ed., *International Encyclopedia of the Social Sciences*, Vol. 11 (New York: Macmillan & Free Press, 1968), pp. 461-472.

31 "Summary Report on the Round Tables relating to Professor Tibor Scitovsky's Paper," in Paul A. Samuelson, ed., *International Economic Relations, Proceedings of the Third Congress of the International Economic Association* (London: Macmillan, 1969), pp. 270-276.

TRANSLATIONS

Italian translation, "Resoconto riassuntivo delle Tavole Rotonde riguardanti la relazione del Prof. Scitovsky," *Economia Internazionale*, Vol. XXIII (May-August 1970), pp. 351-358; also in *Il Futuro degli Scambi Internazionali* (Genova: Istituto di Economia Internazionale, 1970), pp. 351-358.

Franch translation, "Compte rendu des travaux des tables rondes sur le rapport du Pr. Tibor Scitovsky," in Paul A. Samuelson, ed., *L'Avenir des Relations Economiques Internationales* (Paris: Calmann-Lévy, 1971), pp. 348-356.

32 "If Matter Could Talk," in Sidney Morgenbesser, Patrick Suppes, and Morton White, eds., *Philosophy, Science, and Method* (New York: St. Martin's Press, 1969), pp. 286-305.

33 "Theoretical Problems: The Phillips Curve," in *On Incomes Policy: Papers and Proceedings from a Conference in Honour of Erik Lundberg* (Stockholm: Studieförbundet Näringsliv och Samhälle, 1969), pp. 49-53.

34 "Homo Oeconomicus and His Class Mates," in Maurice Natanson, ed., *Phenomenology and Social Reality: Essays in Memory of Alfred Schutz* (The Hague: Nijhoff, 1970), pp. 122-139.

35 "International Adjustment: Issues and Options"; "Choices in Exchange-Rate Policy"; and "Concluding Observations," in Randall Hinshaw, ed., *The Economics of International Adjustment* (Baltimore: Johns Hopkins Press, 1971), pp. 10-15, 89, 92-93, and 143-155.

36 "Longer Education: Thinner, Broader, or Higher," in *Proceedings of the 1970 Invitational Conference on Testing Problems* (Princeton, N.J.: Educational Testing Service, 1971), 3-13.

REPRODUCTIONS

Full reproduction under the title "Are We Overselling College?" *Princeton Alumni Weekly*, Vol. 72, No. 3 (October 12, 1971), pp. 6-8, 15.

Partial reproduction under the title "Reserve Higher Education for the Intellectually Elite," *The National Observer* (January 8, 1972), p. 11.

37 "European Universities as Partisans," in *Neutrality or Partisanship: A Dilemma of Academic Institutions* (New York: Carnegie Foundation, 1971), pp. 7-30.

38 "The Faculty: A Body without Mind or Voice," in *Neutrality or Partisanship: A Dilemma of Academic Institutions* (New York: Carnegie Foundation, 1971), pp. 31-37.

39 "Financing, Correcting, and Adjustment: Three Ways to Deal with an Imbalance of Payments," in *Toward Liberty: Essays in Honor of Ludwig von Mises* (Menlo Park, Cal.: Institute for Humane Studies, 1971), Vol. II, pp. 220-238.

40 "Academic Freedom," in *Encyclopedia of Education* (New York: Crowell Collier and Macmillan, 1971), pp. 6-24.

41 "College Teaching: Tenure in Colleges and Universities," in *Encyclopedia of Education* (New York: Crowell Collier and Macmillan, 1971), Vol. 2, pp. 257-264.

42 "Changes in the International Monetary System and the Effects on Banks," in *Banking in a Changing World* (Rome: Associazione Bancaria Italiana, 1971), pp. 153-184.

TRANSLATIONS

Italian translation, "Evoluzione del sistema monetario internazionale ed effetti sulle banche," *Bancaria*, Anno XXVII (July 1971), pp. 847-859.

REPRODUCTIONS

Full reproduction of Italian translation under the same title in *La banca in un mondo che si evolve* (Rome: Associazione Bancaria Italiana, 1971), pp. 205-250.

43 "Comment on Monetary Theory and Controlled Flexibility," in Emil Claassen and Pascal Salin, eds., *Stabilization Policies in Interdependent Economies* (Amsterdam: North-Holland Publishing Company, 1972), pp. 33-40.

44 "World Inflation," in Emil Claassen and Pascal Salin, eds., *Stabilization Policies in Interdependent Economies* (Amsterdam: North-Holland Publishing Co., 1972), pp. 299-303, 306,310,313,314,316,318,323,324.

45 "Nationalism, Provincialism, Fixed Exchange Rates, and Monetary Union," in Wolfgang Schmitz, ed., *Convertibility, Multilateralism and Freedom* (Wien-New York: Springer-Verlag, 1972), pp. 265-273.

REPRODUCTIONS

Partial reproduction under the title "European Union: Present Central Banks Must Go," *The Money Manager*, Vol. 2, No. 7 (New York, July 10, 1972), pp. 3, 14-15.

TRANSLATIONS

German translation, "Wechselkurse und Währungsunion im Spiel von Nationalismus und Partikularismus," in Wolfgang Schmitz, ed., *Freiheit und Kooperation in Wirtschaft und Währung* (Wien: Molden, 1972), pp. 177-190.

46 "Matters of Measure," in Logan Wilson, ed., *Universal Higher Education: Costs, Benefits, Options* (Washington: American Council on Education, 1972), pp. 78-84.

47 "The Universal Bogey," in Maurice Peston and Bernard Corry, eds., *Essays in Honour of Lord Robbins* (London: Weidenfeld & Nicolson, 1972), pp. 99-117.

48 "Chishiko Sangyō," ["The Knowledge Industry"], in *Gendai Sekai Hyakka Dai Ji Ten* [Modern World Encyclopedia] (Tokyo: Kodansha, 1972), Vol. 2, pp. 740-741.

49 "World Inflation: Factual Background" (Ch. IV); "Eurodollars: The Role of 'Stateless Money' in World Inflation" (Ch. VI); "Options in Therapy: Incomes Policy as a Remedy for Cost-Push Inflation" (Ch. VII); "Options in Therapy: The Role of Fiscal Policy and Monetary Policy" (Ch. VIII); in Randall Hinshaw, ed., *Inflation as a Global Problem* (Baltimore: Johns Hopkins Press, 1972), pp. 26-38, 75-76, 86-91, 107-109, and 118-119.

50 "Learning More About Knowledge," in *Seventh Annual Report, National Endowment for the Humanities* (Washington: National Endowment for the Humanities, 1973), pp. 10-19.

51 "Stateless Money," in C. Fred Bergsten and William G. Tyler, eds., *Leading Issues in International Economic Policy: Essays in Honor of George N. Halm* (Lexington, Mass.: Lexington Books, 1973), pp. 115-122.

52 "Perspectives on the Benefits of Postsecondary Education," in Lewis C. Solmon and Paul J. Taubman, eds., *Does College Matter?* (New York: Academic Press, 1973), pp. 353-363.

53 "The Expanded Role of SDRs and the Possibilities of an SDR Standard," in Alexander K. Swoboda, ed., *Europe and the Evolution of the International monetary System* (Leiden: A.W. Sijthoff, 1973), pp. 25-34.

54 "Internationale Liquidität," in *Zur Neuordnung des internationalen Währungssystems*, Heft 20, Beihefte der Konjunkturpolitik (Berlin: Duncker & Humblot, 1973), pp. 66-72.

55 "Adresse des Präsidenten der International Economic Association," in Hans K. Schneider and Christian Watrin, eds., *Macht und ökonomisches Gesetz*, Schriften des Vereins fur Socialpolitik, Neue Folge, Band 74/1 (Berlin: Duncker & Humblot, 1973), pp. 16-23.

56 "The Illusion of Universal Higher Education" and "A Reply to My Critics," in Sidney Hook, Paul Kurtz, and Miro Todorovich, eds., *The Idea of a Modern University* (Buffalo, N.Y.: Prometheus Books, 1974), pp. 3-19, and 53-57.

57 "Integrationshemmende Integrationspolitik," in Herbert Giersch, ed., *Berhard-Harms-Vorlesungen 5/6* (Kiel: Institut für Weltwirtschaft, 1974), pp. 37-60.

58 Comments on "Exchange-Rate Issues," (Ch. IV); "The Designs of Reform," (Ch. V); "Other Views," (Ch. VI); "The Problem of Capital Movements" (Ch. VIII); in Randall Hinshaw, ed., *Key Issues in International Monetary Reform* (New York: Marcel Dekker, 1975), pp. 51-53, 57, 61, 89, 107-108, 109-110, 111, 113, 114-115, 140-141, 142, 143, 144, 148, 152, 156, and 157.

59 "Effects of Innovation on the Demand for and Earnings of Productive Factors" (with George Bitros and Kenneth W. Leeson), in H.R. Clauser, ed., *Progress in Assessing Technological Innovation: 1974*, Summary Reports of National R&D Assessment Program Projects, National Science Foundation (Westport, Conn.: Technomic Publishing Co., 1975), pp. 65-69.

60 "Between Outline and Outcome the Reform Was Lost," in Edward M. Bernstein *et al.*, *Reflections on Jamaica*, Essays in International Finance, No. 115 (Princeton, N.J.: International Finance Section, April 1976), pp. 30-38.

61 "Opening Remarks: Mises, Keynes, and the Question of Influence," and "Closing Remarks," in Lawrence S. Moss, ed., *The Economics of Ludwig von Mises: Toward a Critical Reappraisal* (Kansas City, Missouri: Sheed and Ward, 1976), pp. 9-12 and 11-116.

D. ARTICLES AND NOTES IN MAJOR PERIODICALS

1 ''Währung und Auslandsverschuldung,'' *Mitteilungen des Verbandes österreichischer Banken und Bankiers*, Vol. X (1928), pp. 194-209.

TRANSLATIONS

    English translation under the title ''Foreign Debts, Reparations, and the Transfer Problem,'' in Fritz Machlup, *International Payments, Debts, and Gold* (New York: Scribners, 1964), pp. 396-416; also in second, enlarged edition (New York: New York University Press, 1976);

    also in Fritz Machlup *International Monetary Economics* (London: Allen & Unwin, 1966), pp. 396-416.

2 ''Geldtheorie und Konjunkturtheorie,'' *Mitteilungen des Verbandes österreichischer Banken und Bankiers*, Vol. XI (1929), pp. 166-174.

3 ''Transfer und Preisbewegung,'' *Zeitschrift für Nationalökonomie*, Vol. I (1930), pp. 555-560.

TRANSLATIONS

    English translation under the title ''Transfer and Price Effects,'' in Fritz Machlup, *International Payments, Debts, and Gold* (New York: Scribners, 1964), pp. 417-424; also in second, enlarged edition (New York University Press, 1976);

    also in Fritz Machlup, *International Monetary Economics* (London: Allen & Unwin, 1966), pp. 417-424.

4 ''Begriffliches und Terminologisches zur Kapitalstheorie,'' *Zeitschrift für Nationalökonomie*, Vol. II (1931), pp. 632-639.

5 ''The Liquidity of Short-Term Capital,'' *Economica*, Vol. XII (1932), pp. 27-284.

6 ''Die Theorie der Kapitalflucht,'' *Weltwirtschaftliches Archiv*, Vol. XXXVI (1932), pp. 512-529.

7 ''Industrialisierung, Autarkisierung und Arbeitslosigkeit,'' *Mitteilungen des Verbandes österreichischer Banken und Bankiers*, Vol. XIV (1932), pp. 278-286.

8 ''Zur Frage der Ankurbelung durch Kreditpolitik,'' *Zeitschrift für Nationalökonomie*, Vol. IV (1933), pp. 398-404.

9 ''Die Währungs-und Kreditkrise,'' *Schmollers Jahrbuch*, Vol. LVII (1933), pp. 373-388.

10 ''A Note on Fixed Costs,'' *Quarterly Journal of Economics*, Vol. XLVIII (1934), pp. 559-564.

11 ''The Consumption of Capital in Austria,'' *Review of Economic Statistics*, Vol. XVII (1935), pp. 13-19.

12 "The Commonsense of the Elasticity of Substitution," *Review of Economic Studies*, Vol. II (1935), pp. 202-213.

13 "The Rate of Interest as Cost Factor and as Capitalization Factor," *American Economic Review*, Vol. XXV (1935), pp. 459-465.

14 "Professor Knight and the Period of Production," *Journal of Political Economy*, Vol. XLIII (1935), pp. 577-624.

15 "Why Bother with Methodology?" *Economica*, New Series, Vol. III (1936), pp. 39-45.

16 "Further Notes on the Elasticity of Substitution: Reply," *Review of Economic Studies*, Vol. III (1936), pp. 151-152.

17 "Monopoly and Competition: A Classification of Market Positions," *American Economic Review*, Vol. XXVII (1937), pp. 445-451.

REPRODUCTIONS

Full reproduction under the same title in David R. Kamerschen, ed., *Readings in Microeconomics* (Cleveland and New York: The World Publishing Co., 1967; second printing, New York: Wiley, 1969), Ch. 21, pp. 299-306.

TRANSLATIONS

German translation, "Monopol und Konkurrenz: Eine Klassifikation der Markt-formen," in Alfred Eugen Ott, ed., *Preistheorie* (Köln: Kiepenheuer & Witsch, 1965), pp. 270-279.

18 "Evaluation of the Practical Significance of the Theory of Monopolistic Competition," *American Economic Review*, Vol. XXIX (1939), pp. 227-236.

19 "Period Analysis and Multiplier Theory," *Quarterly Journal of Economics*, Vol. LIV (1939), pp. 1-27.

REPRODUCTIONS

Full reproduction under the same title in Gottfried Haberler, ed., *Readings on Business Cycle Theory* (Philadelphia: Blakiston, 1944), Ch. 10, pp. 203-234.

TRANSLATIONS

Spanish translation, "El Análisis del Tiempo y la Teoria del Multiplicador," in Gottfried Haberler, ed., *Ensayos sobre el Ciclo Económico* (México: Fondo de Cultura Económica, 1946), Ch. 10, pp. 207-238.

German translation, "Periodenanalyse und Multiplikatortheorie," in Wilhelm Weber und Hubert Neiss, eds., *Konjunktur- und Beschäftigungstheorie* (Köln & Berlin: Kiepenheuer & Witsch, 1967), pp. 143-169.

20 "The Theory of Foreign Exchange," Part I-*Economica*, New Series Vol. VI (1939), pp. 375-397; Part II-*Economica*, New Series Vol. VII (1940), pp. 23-49.

REPRODUCTIONS

Full reproduction under the same title in Howard S. Ellis and Lloyd A. Metzler, eds., *Readings in the Theory of International Trade* (Philadelphia: Blakiston, 1949), Ch. 5, pp. 104-158.

TRANSLATIONS

Spanish translation, "La teoria del cambio extranjero," in *Ensayos sobre Teoria del Comercio Internacional* (Mexico-Buenos Aires: Fondo de Cultura Económica, 1953), Ch. 5, pp. 93-139.

German translation, "Die Theorie des Devisenmarktes," in Klaus Rose, ed., *Theorie der internationalen Wirtschaftsbeziehungen* (Köln: Kiepenheuer & Witsch, 1965), pp. 169-213.

Full reproduction under the same title in Fritz Machlup, *International Payments, Debts, and Gold* (New York: Scribners, 1964), pp. 7-50; also in second, enlarged edition (New York: New York University Press, 1976);

also in Fritz Machlup, *International Monetary Economics* (London: Allen & Unwin, 1966), pp. 7-50.

21 "Professor Hicks' Statics," *Quarterly Journal of Economics*, Vol. LIV (1940), pp. 277-297.

22 "Bank Deposits and the Stock Market in the Cycle," *American Economic Review, Papers and Proceedings*, Vol. XXX (1940), pp. 83-91.

23 "Eight Questions on Gold," *American Economic Review, Papers and Proceedings*, Vol. XXX (1941), pp. 30-37.

REPRODUCTIONS

Extended reproduction under the same title in Fritz Machlup, *International Payments, Debts, and Gold* (New York: Scribners, 1964), pp. 228-238; also in second, enlarged edition (New York: New York University Press, 1976); also in Fritz Machlup, *International Monetary Economics* (London: Allen & Unwin, 1966), pp. 228-238.

Full extended reproduction under the same title in Deane Carson, ed., *Money and Finance* (New York: John Wiley, 1966), pp. 32-43.

24 "Tipi di concorrenza nella vendita," *Giornale degli Economisti e Annali di Economia*, New Series Vol. III (1941), pp. 5-26.

25 "Competition, Pliopoly and Profit," *Economica*, New Series Vol. IX (1942), Part I, pp. 1-23, Part II, pp. 153-173.

26 "Forced or Induced Saving: An Exploration into Its Synonyms and Homonyms," *Review of Economic Statistics*, Vol. XXV (1943), pp. 26-39.

REPRODUCTIONS

Full reproduction under the same title in Fritz Machlup, *Essays in Economic Semantics* (Englewood Cliffs, N.J.: Prentice-Hall, 1963; Second printing, New

York: W.W. Norton, 1967; Third printing, New York: New York University Press, 1975), pp. 213-240.

27 "The Division of Labor between Government and Private Enterprise," *American Economic Review, Papers and Proceedings*, Vol. XXXIII (1943), pp. 87-104.

28 "Capitalism and Its Future Appraised by Two Liberal Economists," *American Economic Review*, Vol. XXXIII (1943), pp. 301-320.

29 "Marginal Analysis and Empirical Research," *American Economic Review*, Vol. XXX-VI (1946), pp. 519-554.

REPRODUCTIONS

Full reproduction under the same title in *Readings in Price and Income* (Stanford, Cal.: Department of Economics, Stanford University, 1949), Ch. 6, pp. 65-94.

Full reproduction under the same title in Richard V. Clemence, ed., *Readings in Economic Analysis*, Vol. 2 (Cambridge, Mass.: Addison-Wesley Press, 1950), Ch. 7, pp. 124-159.

Partial reproduction under the title "Marginal Analysis," in Arleigh P. Hess, Robert E. Gallman, John P. Rice, and Carl Stern, eds., *Outside Readings in Economics* (New York: Crowell, 1951), Ch. 19, pp. 152-166.

Partial reproduction under the title "Marginal Analysis and the Full-Cost Principle," in Jules Backman, *Price Practices and Price Policies* (New York: Ronald Press, 1953), pp. 132-135.

Partial reproduction under the same title in Richard Perlman, ed., *Wage Determination: Market or Power Forces?* (Boston: D.C. Heath & Co., 1964), pp. 30-53.

Full reproduction under the same title in Fritz Machlup, *Essays in Economic Semantics* (Englewood Cliffs, N.J.: Prentice-Hall, 1963; Second printing, New York: W.W. Norton, 1967; Third printing, New York: New York University Press, 1975), pp. 147-190.

Partial reproduction under the same title in B.J. McCormick and E. Owen Smith, eds., *The Labour Market* (Harmondsworth, England: Penguin Books, 1968), Ch. 2, pp. 37-45.

Partial reproduction under the title "Marginal Analysis," in Robert P. Vichas and W. Glenn Moore, eds., *Coeval Economics* (Berkeley, Cal.: McCutchan, 1970), pp. 203-213.

TRANSLATIONS

German translation, "Marginalanalyse und empirische Forschung," in Reimut Jochimsen und Helmut Knobel, eds., *Gegenstand und Methoden der Nationalökonomie* (Köln: Kiepenheuer & Witsch, 1971), pp. 297-320.

30 "Rejoinder to an Antimarginalist," *American Economic Review*, Vol. XXXVII, (1947), pp. 148-154.

REPRODUCTIONS

Full reproduction under the same title in Richard V. Clemence, ed., *Readings in Economic Analysis*, Vol. 2 (Cambridge, Mass.: Addison-Wesley Press, 1950), Ch. 9, pp. 173-179.

31 "The Webb-Pomerene Law: A Consensus Report" [with E.S. Mason, A.R. Burns, and M.W. Watkins], *American Economic Review*, Vol. XXXVII (1947), pp. 848-863.

32 "Misconceptions about the Current Inflation," *The Review of Economics and Statistics*, Vol. XXX (1948), pp. 17-22.

33 "The Teaching of Money and Banking," *The Journal of Finance*, Vol. IV (1949), pp. 227-230.

34 "Elasticity Pessimism in International Trade," *Economia Internazionale*, Vol. III (1950), pp. 118-141.

REPRODUCTIONS

Full reproduction under the same title in Fritz Machlup, *International Payments, Debts, and Gold* (New York: Scribners, 1964), pp. 51-68; also in second, revised edition (New York: New York University Press, 1976);
also in Fritz Machlup, *International Monetary Economics* (London: Allen & Unwin, 1966), pp. 51-68.

35 "Three Concepts of the Balance of Payments and the So-called Dollar Shortage," *The Economic Journal*, Vol. LX (1950), pp. 46-68.

REPRODUCTIONS

Extended reproduction under the same title in William R. Allen and Clark Lee Allen, eds., *Foreign Trade and Finance* (New York: Macmillan, 1959), Ch. 5, pp. 97-123.
Full extended reproduction under the same title in Fritz Machlup, *International Payments, Debts, and Gold* (New York: Scribners, 1964), pp. 69-92; also in second revised edition (New York: New York University Press, 1976);
also in Fritz Machlup, *International Monetary Economics* (London: Allen & Unwin, 1966), pp. 69-92.

TRANSLATIONS

Japanese translation under the title "Kokusaishushi no Mittsu no Gainen to iwayuru Dorafusoku ni tsuite" ["Three Concepts of the Balance of Payments and the So-called Dollar Shortage"], *Chōsa Geppō* [Monthly Bulletin of Research Department], Ministry of Finance, Vol. 42, No. 11 (Year 28, November 1953), pp. 115-129.

36 "The Patent Controversy in the Nineteenth Century" [with Edith Penrose], *The Journal of Economic History*, Vol. X (1950), pp. 1-29.

37 "Schumpeter's Economic Methodology," *The Review of Economics and Statistics*, Vol. XXXIII (1951), pp. 145-155.

REPRODUCTIONS

Full reproduction under the same title in Seymour E. Harris, ed., *Schumpeter, Social Scientist* (Cambridge, Mass.: Harvard University Press, 1951), pp. 95-101.

TRANSLATIONS

Japanese translation, "Schumpeter no Keizaigaku Hohoron" ["Schumpeter's Economic Methodology"] in S.E. Harris, ed., *Shakai-Kagakusha Schumpeter*

[Social Scientist Schumpeter], Nakayama and Tohata, eds., (Tokyo: Oriental Economist, 1955), pp. 261-280.

38 "The American Antitrust Laws—Success or Failure?" *Schweizerische Zeitschrift für Volkswirtschaft und Statistik*, Vol. LXXXVII (1951), pp. 513-520.

39 "Oligopolistic Indeterminacy," *Weltwirtschaftliches Archiv*, Vol. LXVIII (1952), pp. 1-19.

40 "The Characteristics and Classifications of Oligopoly," *Kyklos*, Vol. V (1952), pp. 145-163.

41 "Volkswirtschaftliche Scheinverluste beim Zustrom neuer Wettbewerber," *Ordo*, Vol. V (1952), pp. 115-133.

TRANSLATIONS

Spanish translation, "Pérdidas económicas aparentes en case de entrada de nuevos competidores en el mercado," in Walter Eucken, . . . Fritz Machlup *et. al.*, *La economía de mercado*, Tomo I (Madrid: Sociedad de Estudios y Publicaciones, 1963), pp. 233-262.

42 "Do Economists Know Anything?" *The American Scholar*, Vol. XXII (1953), pp. 167-182.

43 "Dollar Shortage and Disparities in the Growth of Productivity," *Scottish Journal of Political Economy*, Vol. I (1954), pp. 250-267.

REPRODUCTIONS

Full reproduction under the same title in Fritz Machlup, *International Payments, Debts, and Gold* (New York: Scribners, 1964), pp. 93-109; also in second, enlarged edition (New York: New York University Press, 1976);
also in Fritz Machlup, *International Monetary Economics* (London: Allen & Unwin, 1966); pp. 93-109.

TRANSLATIONS

Japanese translation, "Dorafusoku to Seisanryoku Hatten niokeru Fukinto" ["Dollar Shortage and Disparities in the Growth of Productivity"] Chōsa Geppō [Monthly Bulletin of Research], Research Department, Ministry of Finance, Vol. 44, No. 6 (June 1955), pp. 127-137.
Portuguese translation, "A Escassez de Dólares e as Disparidades na Elevacao de Produtividade," in *Revista de Ciéncias Economicas*, No. 73 (São Paulo, June-September 1955), pp. 3-22.

44 "Relative Prices and Aggregate Spending in the Analysis of Devaluation," *American Economic Review*, Vol. XLV (1955), pp. 255-278.

REPRODUCTIONS

Full reproduction under the same title in Fritz Machlup, *International Payments,*

Debts, and Gold (New York: Scribners, 1964), pp. 171-194; also in second, enlarged edition (New York: New York University Press, 1976);

also in Fritz Machlup, *International Monetary Economics* (London: Allen & Unwin, 1966), pp. 171-194.

TRANSLATIONS

Japanese translation, "Heika-Kirisage no Bunseki niokeru sotai-Kakaku to soshishutsu" ["Relative Prices and Aggregate Spending in the Analysis of Devaluation"], Chōsa Geppō [Monthly Bulletin of Research], Research Department, Ministry of Finance, Vol. 44, No. 10 (October 1955), pp. 60-74.

Italian translation, "Prezzi relativi e spesa aggregata nell'analisi della svalutazione," in Fabrizio Onida, ed., *Problemi di teoria monetaria internazionale* (Milano: Etas Kompass, 1971), Ch. 2, pp. 85-114.

45 "The Problem of Verification in Economics," *The Southern Economic Journal*, Vol. XXII (1955), pp. 1-21.

TRANSLATIONS

Italian translation, "Il problema della verifica in economia," *L'Industria* (1958, No. 3), pp. 336-363.

Spanish translation, "El problema de la verificación en la economía," *Revista de Economía Política*, Vol. IX (1958), pp. 398-432.

Italian translation, *La verifica delle leggi economiche* [with T.W. Hutchison, E. Grunberg] (Milano: Editrice L'Industria, 1959), 79 pages, esp. pp. 7-35, 49-62.

Spanish translation, "El Problema de la verificacion en economia," in J. Hortala Arau, *Lecturas sobre teoría económica*, Vol. 1 (Barcelona: Departamento de Teoría Económica, 1969), pp. 101-121.

46 "Reply to Professor Takata," *Osaka Economic Papers*, Vol. IV (1955), pp. 13-16.

REPRODUCTIONS

Full reproduction under the same title in Fritz Machlup, *Essays in Economic Semantics* (Englewood Cliffs, N.J.: Prentice-Hall, 1963; Second printing, New York: W.W. Norton, 1967; Third printing, New York: New York University Press, 1975), pp. 207-210.

47 "Shihonshugi to Marukusu-Keizaigaku" ("Capitalism and Marxian Economics," translated by Hideo Aoyama), *Kezai Hyoron*, Vol. IV (1955), pp. 118-135.

48 "On Some Misconceptions Concerning Academic Freedom," *American Association of University Professors Bulletin*, Vol. 41 (1955), pp. 753-784.

REPRODUCTIONS

Full reproduction under the same title in Louis Joughin, ed., *Academic Freedom and Tenure* (Madison: University of Wisconsin Press, 1967), Appendix B, pp. 177-209.

49 "Rejoinder to a Reluctant Ultra-Empiricist," *Southern Economic Journal*, Vol. XXII (1956), pp. 483-493.

TRANSLATIONS

Italian translation, "Replica a un ultra empirico riluttante," *L'Industria* (1958, No. 3), pp. 375-387.

Spanish translation, "Contrarréplica a un recalcitrante ultra-empirista," *Revista de Economía Política*, Vol. IX (1958), pp. 446-461.

50 "The Finance of Development in Poor Countries: Foreign Capital and Domestic Inflation," *Economic Studies Quarterly (Kikan Riron Keizaigaku)*, Vol. VI (1956), pp. 112-123.

TRANSLATIONS

Japanese translation, "Hinkyu Shokoku no Kaihatsu Yushi: Gaikoku-shihonto Kokunai-infure," *Kikan Riron Keizaigaku* [*Economic Studies Quarterly*], Vol. VI, No. 1-2 (1956), pp. 103-111.

51 "The Terms-of-Trade Effects of Devaluation upon Real Income and the Balance of Trade," *Kyklos*, Vol. IX (1956), pp. 417-452.

REPRODUCTIONS

Full reproduction under the title "The Terms-of-Trade Effects of Devaluation upon Trade Balance and Real Income," in Boulding *et al.*, *Segments of the Economy*, 1956 (Cleveland: Allen, 1957), pp. 232-258.

Full reproduction under the original title in Fritz Machlup, *International Payments, Debts, and Gold* (New York: Scribners, 1964), pp. 195-222; also in second, enlarged edition (New York: New York University Press, 1976);

also in Fritz Machlup, *International Monetary Economics* (London: Allen & Unwin, 1966), pp. 195-222.

52 "Professor Hicks' Revision of Demand Theory," *American Economic Review*, Vol. XLVII (1957), pp. 119-135.

REPRODUCTIONS

Full reproduction under the same title in William Breit and Harold M. Hochman, eds., *Readings in Microeconomics* (New York: Holt, Rinehart, and Winston, 1968), Ch. 6, pp. 89-103, Second edition, 1971, Ch. 5, pp. 77-91.

53 "Disputes, Paradoxes, and Dilemmas Concerning Economic Development," *Rivista Internazionale di Scienze Economiche e Commerciali*, Vol. IV (1957), pp. 801-833.

REPRODUCTIONS

Full reproduction under the same title in Boulding *et al.*, *Segments of the Economy, 1956* (Cleveland: Allen, 1957), pp. 191-217.

Full reproduction under the same title in Fritz Machlup, *Essays in Economic Semantics* (Englewood Cliffs, N.J.: Prentice-Hall, 1963; Second printing. New York: W.W. Norton, 1967; Third printing, New York: New York University Press, 1975), pp. 269-301.

TRANSLATIONS

Japanese summary, "Kezai Hatten Nikansuru Ronso Mujun Oyobi Jilemma," *Keizai*

Keikaku no Sho Keitai [Annal of Japan Economic Policy Association], No. 7 (1959), pp. 182-189.

54 "Equilibrium and Disequilibrium: Misplaced Concreteness and Disguised Politics," *The Economic Journal*, Vol. LXVIII (1958), pp. 1-24.

REPRODUCTIONS

Full reproduction under the same title in Fritz Machlup, *Essays in Economic Semantics* (Englewood Cliffs, N.J.: Prentice-Hall, 1963; Second printing, New York: W.W. Norton, 1967; Third printing, New York: New York University Press, 1975), pp. 43-72.

Full reproduction under the same title in Fritz Machlup, *International Payments, Debts, and Gold* (New York: Scribners, 1964), pp. 110-135; also in second, enlarged edition (New York: New York University Press, 1976);

also in Fritz Machlup, *International Monetary Economics* (London: Allen & Unwin, 1966), pp. 110-135.

Partial reproduction under the same title in N.J. Demerath III and Richard A. Peterson, eds., *System, Change and Conflict* (New York: The Free Press, 1967), Ch. 26, pp. 445-454.

55 "Grading of Academic Salary Scales," *American Association of University Professors Bulletin*, Vol. 44 (1958), pp. 219-236.

56 "Can There Be Too Much Research?" *Science*, Vol. 128, (November 28, 1958), pp. 1320-1325.

REPRODUCTIONS

Full reproduction under the same title in Edmund S. Phelps, ed., *The Goal of Economic Growth* (New York: W.W. Norton, 1962), pp. 141-152.

57 "Structure and Structural Change: Weaselwords and Jargon," *Zeitschrift für Nationalökonomie*, Vol. XVIII (1958), pp. 280-298.

REPRODUCTIONS

Full reproduction under the same title in Fritz Machlup, *Essays in Economic Semantics* (Englewood Cliffs, N.J.: Prentice-Hall, 1963; Second printing, New York: W.W. Norton, 1967; Third printing, New York: New York University Press, 1975), pp. 73-96.

58 "Academic Salaries, 1958-1959: Report of Committee Z on the Economic Status of the Profession," *American Association of University Professors Bulletin*, Vol. 45 (1959), pp. 157-176.

59 "Statics and Dynamics: Kaleidoscopic Words," *The Southern Economic Journal*, Vol. XXVI (1959), pp. 91-110.

REPRODUCTIONS

Full reproduction under the same title in Fritz Machlup, *Essays in Economic Semantics* (Englewood Cliffs, N.J.: Prentice-Hall, 1963; Second printing, New York:

W.W. Norton, 1967; Third printing, New York: New York University Press, 1975), pp. 9-42.

TRANSLATIONS

Spanish translation, under the title "Estática y dinámica: palabras caleidoscópicas," *Revista de Economía Política*, Vol. X (1959), pp. 465-511.

Japanese translation, "Seigaku to Dogaku: Henka Kiuamarinai Kotoba," under the title *Americana: Jimbun Shakai Shisen*, Vol. VI (1960), pp. 1-32.

60 "Die Finanzierung des technischen Fortschritts," *Ordo*, Vol. XI (1959), pp. 117-131.

TRANSLATIONS

Spanish translation, "La financiación del progreso técnico," in F.A. Hayek, . . . Fritz Machlup *et al., La economía de mercado*, Tomo II (Madrid: Sociedad de Estudios y Publicaciones, 1963), pp. 195-219.

61 "Another View of Cost-Push and Demand-Pull Inflation," *Review of Economics and Statistics*, Vol. XLII (1960), pp. 125-139.

REPRODUCTIONS

Full reproduction under the same title in Richard Perlman, ed., *Inflation: Demand-Pull or Cost Push?* (Boston: D. C. Heath, 1959), pp. 64-91.

Full reproduction under the same title in Fritz Machlup, *Essays in Economic Semantics* (Englewood Cliffs, N.J.: Prentice-Hall, 1963; Second printing, New York: W.W. Norton, 1967; Third Printing, New York: New York University Press, 1975), pp. 241-268.

Full reproduction under the same title in Donald Grunewald and Henry L. Bass, eds., *Public Policy and the Modern Corporation* (New York: Appleton-Century-Crofts, 1966), Ch. 6, pp. 96-119.

Full reproduction under the title "Another View of Cost-Push and Demand-Pull Inflation," in John Lindauer, ed., *Macroeconomic Readings* (New York: The Free Press, 1968), Ch. 23, pp. 207-220.

Full reproduction under the title "Cost Push and Demand Pull," in R.J. Ball and Peter Doyle, eds., *Inflation* (Harmondsworth, England: Penguin Books, 1969), Ch. 9, pp. 149-176.

Full reproduction under the title "Another View of Cost-Push and Demand-Pull Inflation," in Edward Shapiro, ed., *Macroeconomics: Selected Readings* (New York: Harcourt, Brace & World, 1970), Ch. 24, pp. 344-367.

TRANSLATIONS

Dutch translation of two parts, "Loonronden en Produktiviteit," *Burgerrecht, National Weekblad* (Amsterdam), Vol. 16 (November 25, 1961), p. 21; and "Prijsverlagingen en economische stabiliteit," *Burgerrecht, National Weekblad* (Amsterdam), Vol. 16 (December 30, 1961), p. 18.

Spanish translation, "Otro punto de vista con respecto a la inflación por empuje de los costos y tracción de la demanda," in *Proceso Inflacionario y el Caso de America Latina*, Vol. II (Mexico, D.F.: Centro de Estudios Monetarios Latinoamericanos 1971), pp. 111-140.

Italian translation, "Spinta dei costi e trazione della domanda," in R.J. Ball and Peter Doyle, eds., *Inflazione* (Milan: Franco Angeli Editore, 1972), pp.

62 "Bilateral Monopoly, Successive Monopoly and Vertical Integration," (with Martha Taber), *Economica*, New Series, Vol. XXVII (1960), pp. 101-119.

REPRODUCTIONS

Full reproduction under the same title in *The Journal of Reprints for Antitrust Law and Economics*, Vol. II (Summer 1970), pp. 171-189.

Full reproduction under the same title in Basil S. Yamey, ed., *Economics of Industrial Structure* (Harmondsworth, England: Penguin Education, 1973), pp. 271-290.

63 "The Economic Status of the Profession, 1959-60: Annual Report of Committee Z," *American Association of University Professors Bulletin*, Vol. 46 (1960), pp. 156-193.

64 "Operational Concepts and Mental Constructs in Model and Theory Formation," *Giornale degli Economisti*, Vol. XIX [Nuova Serie] (1960), pp. 553-582.

REPRODUCTIONS

Full reproduction under the same title in Universitá Commerciale Luigi Bocconi, Milano, ed., *Studi di Economia, Finanza e Statistica in Onore di Gustavo del Vecchio* (Padova: Cedam, 1963), pp. 467-496.

65 "The Supply of Inventors and Inventions," *Weltwirtschaftliches Archiv*, Band 85 (1960), pp. 210-254.

REPRODUCTIONS

Partial reproduction under the same title in *the Rate and Direction of Inventive Activity: Economic and Social Factors*. Universities-National Bureau Committee for Economic Research (Princeton: Princeton University Press, 1962), pp. 143-167.

Full reproduction under the same title in Marvin J. Cetron and Joel B. Goldhar, eds., *The Science of Managing Organized Technology* (New York: Gordon and Breach, 1970), Vol. 2, pp. 695-718.

TRANSLATIONS

French translation, "L'offre d'inventeurs et d'inventions," *Economie Appliquée*, Vol. XIV (1961), pp. 225-274.

66 "Are the Social Sciences Really Inferior?" *The Southern Economic Journal*, Vol. XXVII (1961), pp. 173-184.

REPRODUCTIONS

Full reproduction under the same title in Maurice Natanson, ed., *Philosophy of the Social Sciences* (New York: Random House, 1963), pp. 158-180.

Full reproduction under the same title in Gloria B. Levitas, ed., *Culture and Consciousness: Perspectives in the Social Sciences* (New York: Braziller, 1967), pp. 194-215.

Full reproduction under the title "On the Alleged Inferiority of the Social Sciences," in Leonard I. Krimerman, ed., *The Nature and Scope of Social Science* (New York: Appleton-Century-Crofts, 1969), Ch. 15, pp. 168-180.

TRANSLATIONS

Italian translation, "Le scienze sociali sono davvero inferiori?" *L'Industria* (No. 4, 1961), pp. 483-504.

New Italian translation, "Le scienze sociali sono davvero inferiori?" in Ellen B. Hill, ed., *Alcuni aspetti delle scienze sociali oggi, Centro Sociale*, Vol. XI, No. 55-56 (1964), pp. 10-29.

67 "Idealtypus, Wirklichkeit und Konstruktion," *Ordo*, Vol. XII (1961), pp. 21-57.

REPRODUCTIONS

Full reproduction under the same title in Reimut Jochimsen und Helmut Knobel, eds., *Gegenstand und Methoden der Nationalökonomie* (Köln: Kiepenheuer & Witsch, 1971), pp. 226-254.

68 "Patents and Inventive Effort," *Science*, Vol. 133 (May 12, 1961), pp. 1463-1466.

69 "Comments on the 'Balance of Payments' and a Proposal to Reduce the Price of Gold," *Journal of Finance*, Vol. XVI (1961), pp. 186-193.

REPRODUCTIONS

Full reproduction of the "Comments on 'the Balance of Payments' " in Chapter VI and of "A Proposal to Reduce the Price of Gold" in Chapter XI in Fritz Machlup, *International Payments, Debts, and Gold* (New York: Scribners, 1964), pp. 136-139 and 239-244; also in second, enlarged edition (New York: New York University Press, 1976);

also in Fritz Machlup, *International Monetary Economics* (London: Allen & Unwin, 1966), pp. 136-139 and 239-244.

70 "Produzione di conoscenza e struttura dell'occupazione negli Stati Uniti," *Rivista Internazionale di Scienze Economiche e Commerciali*, Vol. VIII (1961), pp. 901-924.

71 "Liquidité internationale et nationale," *Bulletin d'Information et de Documentation*, Banque Nationale de Belgique, XXXVIIme année (Fevrier 1962), pp. 105-116.

TRANSLATIONS

Flemish translation, "Internationale en binnenlandse liquiditeit," *Tijdschrift voor Documentatie en Voorlichting*, Nationale Bank von Belgie, XXXVIIe jaargang (February 1962), pp. 105-116.

English translation of an enlarged version under the titles "The Fuzzy Concepts of Liquidity, International and Domestic" and "Further Reflections on the Demand for Foreign Reserves" in Fritz Machlup, *International Payments, Debts, and Gold* (New York: Scribners, 1944), pp. 245-276; also in second, enlarged edition (New York: New York University Press, 1976);

also in Fritz Machlup, *International Monetary Economics* (London: Allen & Unwin, 1966), pp. 245-276.

72 "Das Transferproblem: Thema und vier Variationen," *Ordo*, Vol. XIV (1963), pp. 139-167.

TRANSLATIONS

English translation under the title "The Transfer Problem: Theme and Four Variations," in Fritz Machlup, *International Payments, Debts, and Gold* (New York: Scribners, 1964), pp. 374-395; also in second, enlarged edition (New York: New York University Press, 1976);

also in Fritz Machlup, *International Monetary Economics* (London: Allen & Unwin, 1966), pp. 374-395.

73 "In Defense of Academic Tenure," *American Association of University Professors Bulletin*, Vol. 50 (June 1964), pp. 112-124.

REPRODUCTIONS

Full reproduction under the same title in Louis Joughin, ed., *Academic Freedom and Tenure* (Madison: University of Wisconsin Press, 1967), Appendix G, pp. 306-338.

Partial reproduction under the same title in *AGB Reports* (Association of Governing Boards of Universities and Colleges), Vol. 11, No. 7 (March 1969), pp. 3-20.

74 "Teaching Social Sciences in Colleges and Universities," *American Association of University Professors Bulletin*, Vol. 50 (September 1964), pp. 271-272.

REPRODUCTIONS

Full reproduction under the title "On Deciding to Teach a Social Science," *University, A Princeton Quarterly*, Number 25 (Summer 1965), p. 1.

75 "Professor Samuelson on Theory and Realism," *American Economic Review*, Vol. LIV (September 1964), pp. 733-736.

76 "Why Economists Disagree," *Proceedings of the American Philosophical Society*, Vol. 109 (February 1965), pp. 1-7.

77 "The Fascination of Gold. Comment on the Article 'Gold' by Zay Jeffries," *Proceedings of the American Philosophical Society*, Vol. 109 (April 1965), pp. 105-107.

78 "The Report of the Nongovernment Economists' Study Group," *American Economic Review, Papers and Proceedings*, Vol. LV (1965), pp. 166-177.

79 "The Cloakroom Rule of International Reserves: Reserve Creation and Resources Transfer," *Quarterly Journal of Economics*, Vol. LXXIX (August 1965), pp. 337-355.

REPRODUCTIONS

Full reproduction under the same title in Richard N. Cooper, ed., *International Finance* (Harmondsworth, England: Penguin Books, 1969), Ch. 15, pp. 337-357.

ABSTRACTS

Abstract under the title "The Cloakroom Rule of International Reserves," *The Journal of Economic Abstracts*, Vol. III (October 1965), pp. 567-568.

TRANSLATIONS

Italian translation, "La regola del 'guardaroba' per il governo della liquidita internazionale: creazione di riserve e trasferimento di risorse," in Fabrizio Onida, ed., *Problemi di teoria monetaria internazionale* (Milano: Etas Kompass, 1971), Ch. 14, pp. 361-381.

Spanish translation, "La 'regla de la consigna' de las reservas internacionales: creación de reservas y transferencia de recursos," in Richard N. Cooper, ed., *Financiación internacional: textos escogidos* (Madrid: Editorial Tecnos, 1974), Ch. 15, pp. 291-308.

80 "World Monetary Debate—Bases for Agreement," *The Banker*, Vol. 116 (September 1966), pp. 598-611.

81 "The Need for Monetary Reserves," *Banca Nazionale del Lavoro Quarterly Review*, No. 78 (September 1966), pp. 175-222.

REPRODUCTIONS

Partial reproduction under the same title in *The Oriental Economist*, Vol. 35 (December 1967), pp. 757-765.

TRANSLATIONS

Italian translation, "Il bisogno di riserve monetarie," Banca Nazionale del Lavoro; *Moneta e Credito*, Vol. XX (March 1967), pp. 3-50.

Partial Japanese translation, "Gaika-junbi wa Yokubo no Kansu" ["The Need for Foreign Reserves"], *Shukan Toyo-Keizai* [The Weekly Oriental Economist], Supplementary Issue on the International Balance of Payments (December 5, 1967).

82 "Theories of the Firm: Marginalist, Behavioral, Managerial," *American Economic Review*, Vol. LVII (March 1967), pp. 1-33.

REPRODUCTIONS

Full reproduction under the same title in Douglas Needham, ed., *Readings in the Economics of Industrial Organization* (New York: Holt, Rinehart, and Winston, 1970), Ch. 1, pp. 3-31.

Partial reproduction under the same title in Edwin Mansfield, ed., *Microeconomics: Selected Readings* (New York: W.W. Norton, 1971), pp. 99-114.

Full reproduction under the same title in Michael Schiff and Arie Y. Lewin, eds., *Behavioral Aspects of Accounting* (Englewood Cliffs, N.J.: Prentice-Hall, 1974), Ch. 1, pp. 15-41.

ABSTRACTS

Abstract under the same title in *The Journal of Economic Abstracts*, Vol. V (June 1967), pp. 280-282.

TRANSLATIONS

Spanish translation, "Teorias de la empresa: teoria marginalista, teoria del comportamiento y teoria de la dirección y gestión de empresas," *De Economia*, Ano XXIII, No. 115 (Madrid, October 1970), pp. 799-835.

83 "Credit Facilities or Reserve Allotments?" *Banca Nazionale del Lavoro Quarterly Review*, No. 81 (June 1967), pp. 135-156.

TRANSLATIONS

Italian translation, "Concessioni creditizie o assegnazioni di riserve?" *Moneta e Credito*, Vol. XX (June 1967), pp. 3-50.

84 "Oligopoly and the Free Society," *Antitrust Law and Economics Review*, Vol. I (July-August 1967), pp. 11-34.

REPRODUCTIONS

Full reproduction under the same title in *Il Politico*, Vol. XXXII (1967), pp. 253-273.

Full reproduction under the same title in Pasquale Scaramozzino, ed., *Problemi Economici del Mondo Contemporaneo* (Milano: Dott. A. Giuffre, 1968), pp. 69-88.

TRANSLATIONS

German translation, "Oligopol und Freiheit," *Ordo*, Vol. XVIII (1967), pp. 35-64.

85 "From Dormant Liabilities to Dormant Assets," *The Banker*, Vol. 117 (September 1967), pp. 788-797.

86 "Corporate Management, National Interest, and Behavioral Theory," *Journal of Political Economy*, Vol. 75 (October 1967), pp. 772-774.

TRANSLATIONS

Norwegian translation, "Aerede Styremedlemmer . . .," *Farmand*, Vol. 73, No. 50 (December 12, 1968), pp. 109-115.

87 "College and University Government: St. John's University (N.Y.)" [with John A. Christie, Valerie A. Earle, and Jacob D. Hyman], *American Association of University Professors Bulletin*, Vol. 54 (September 1968), pp. 325-361.

88 "The Price of Gold," *The Banker*, Vol. 118 (September 1968), pp. 782-791.

TRANSLATIONS

Spanish translation, "El precio del oro," *Información Comercial Española*, Num. 434 (October 1969), pp. 121-128.

89 "The Transfer Gap of the United States," *Banca Nazionale del Lavoro Quarterly Review*, No. 86 (September 1968), pp. 195-238.

TRANSLATIONS

Italian translation, "Il 'transfer gap' degli Stati Uniti," *Moneta e Credito*, Vol. XXII (June 1969), pp. 149-193.

90 "Speculations on Gold Speculation," *American Economic Review, Papers and Proceedings*, Vol. LIX (May 1969), pp. 332-343.

TRANSLATIONS

Spanish translation, "Especulaciones sobre la especulación del oro," *Información Comercial Española*, Num. 434 (October 1969), pp. 111-119.

91   "Round Table on Exchange Rate Policy," *American Economic Review, Papers and Proceedings*, Vol. LIX (May 1969), pp. 366-369.

REPRODUCTIONS

Full reproduction under the same title in Lee Charles Nehrt, ed., *International Finance for Multinational Business*, 2nd ed. (Scranton, Pa.: Intext Educational Publishers, 1972), pp. 228-234.

Partial reproduction under the same title in Robert E. Baldwin and J. David Richardson, eds., *International Trade and Finance: Readings* (Boston: Little, Brown and Co., 1974), pp. 344-347.

TRANSLATIONS

Spanish translation, "Mesa redonda sobre el tipo de cambio," *Información Comercial Española*, Num. 434 (October 1969), pp. 165-167.

92   "Aspects of Education and Economic Growth," *Il Politico*, Vol. XXXIV (1969, No. 3), pp. 393-406.

TRANSLATIONS

German translation, "Ausbildung und Wirtschaftswachstum", *IBB-Bulletin, Bildungsforschung, Entwicklungshilfe* No. 6 (December 1970), pp. 24-34.

93   "On Terms, Concepts, Theories, and Strategies in the Discussion of Greater Flexibility of Exchange Rates," *Banca Nazionale del Lavoro Quarterly Review*, No. 92 (March 1970), pp. 3-22.

ABSTRACTS

Abstract under the same title in *Journal of Economic Literature*, Vol. IX (March 1971), p. 352.

TRANSLATIONS

Italian translation, "Sul problema di una maggiore flessibilitá dei cambi: definizioni, teorie, strategie," *Moneta e Credito*, Vol. XXIII (March 1970), pp. 3-22.

94   "Euro-Dollar Creation: A Mystery Story," *Banca Nazionale del Lavoro Quarterly Review*, No. 94 (September 1970), pp. 219-260.

ABSTRACTS

Abstract under the same title in *Journal of Economic Literature*, Vol. IX (June 1971), p. 744.

TRANSLATIONS

Spanish translation, "La creación de eurodólares: un cuento de misterio," *Cemla Boletín Mensual*, Vol. XVII, Part I (April 1971), pp. 131-141; Part II (May 1971), pp. 187-197.

Full reproduction of this Spanish translation in *Analisis sobre el mercado de Eurodolares* (Mexico: Centro de Estudios Monetarios Latinoamericanos, 1971), viii and 100 pages.

Italian translation, "La creazione di eurodollari: una storia misteriosa," *Moneta e Credito*, Vol. XXIV, No. 95 (September 1971), pp. 249-288.

"International Money: The Way Forward Now," *The Banker*, Vol. 122, No. 553 (March 1972), pp. 287-296.

96 "Il dollaro convertibile . . . in che cosa?" *Bancaria*, Vol. XXVIII, No. 1, (January 1972), pp. 13-15.

ABSTRACTS

Abstract under the same title in *Journal of Economic Literature*, Vol. XI (March 1973), p. 424.

97 "What the World Thought of Jacob Viner," *Journal of Political Economy*, Vol. 80, No. 1 (January-February 1972), pp. 1-4.

98 "What Was Left on Viner's Desk," *Journal of Political Economy*, Vol. 80, No. 2 (March-April 1972), pp. 353-364.

99 "Universal Higher Education: Promise or Illusion?" *The Humanist*, Vol. XXXII, No. 3 (May/June 1972), pp. 17-23.

ABSTRACTS

Abstract under the same title in *The Philosophic Index*, Vol. VI (Summer 1972), p. 423.

100 "Euro-Dollars, Once Again," *Banca Nazionale del Lavoro Quarterly Review*, No. 101 (June 1972), pp. 119-137.

ABSTRACTS

Abstract under the same title in *Journal of Economic Literature*, Vol. XI (March 1973), p. 424.

TRANSLATIONS

Italian translation, "Ancora sull' eurodollaro," *Moneta e Credito*, Vol. XXV, No. 98 (June 1972), pp. 136-165.

101 "Five Errors about the Eurodollar System," *Euromoney* (July 1972), pp. 8-10, 12, 14.

102 "Less Rigidity Is Not Enough," *Euromoney* (March 1973), pp. 37-41.

103 "Exchange-Rate Flexibility," *Banca Nazionale del Lavoro Quarterly Review*, No. 106 (September 1973), pp. 183-205.

REPRODUCTIONS

Full reproduction with some expansion under the title "Exchange-Rate Flexibility: A Variety of Choices," in G. C. Wiegand, ed., *Toward a New World Monetary System* (New York: Engineering and Mining Journal, 1973), pp. 110-126.

ABSTRACTS

Abstract under the same title in *Journal of Economic Literature*, Vol. XII (June 1974), pp. 809-810.

TRANSLATIONS
Italian translation, "La scelta di un sistema di cambi flessibili," *Moneta e Credito*, Vol. XXVI, No. 103 (September 1973), pp. 139-161.

104 "The Official SDR Standard and Private SDR Money," *Euromoney* (November 1973), pp. 29-33.

105 "Situational Determinism in Economics," *British Journal for the Philosophy of Science*, Vol. 25 (Septembert 1974), pp. 271-284.
ABSTRACTS
Abstract under the same title in *The Philosopher's Index*, Vol. 9 (Spring 1975), p. 59.

106 "Friedrich von Hayek's Contribution to Economics," *The Swedish Journal of Economics*, Vol. 76 (December 1974), pp. 498-531.
REPRODUCTIONS
Enlarged reproduction under the title "Hayek's Contribution to Economics," in Fritz Machlup, ed., *Essays on Hayek* (New York: New York University Press, 1976), pp. 13-58.

107 "How Inflation Is Transmitted and Imported," *Euromoney* (September 1975), pp. 58-63.

108 "Workers Who Produce Knowledge: A Steady Growth, 1900-1970" (with Trude Kronwinkler), *Weltwirtschaftliches Archiv*, Vol. 111, No. 4, (1975), pp. 752-759.

E. ARTICLES AND NOTES IN MINOR JOURNALS

1 "Auslandskredite und Währung," *Oesterreichische Revue für Finanzpolitik und Volkswirtschaft*, Vol. II (June 30, 1924), No. 40.

2 "Lohnsenkung durch Zollpolitik und Währungspolitik," *Der Oesterreichische Volkswirt*, Vol. XXIV (October 17, 1931), No. 3, pp. 63-64.

3 "Zinsfuss und Lagerhaltung—Eine Glosse," *Der Oesterreichische Volkswirt*, Vol. XXIV (October 31, 1931), No. 5, p. 108.

4 "Die Zahlungsbilanz," *Allgemeiner Tarif-Anzeiger*, Vol. L (December 12, 1931), No. 50.

5 "Die Papierbranche in der Wirtschaftskrise," *Papier-und Schreibwarenzeitung*, Vol. XXXIX (April 23, 1932), pp. 1-3.

REPRODUCTIONS

Full reproduction under the title "Fehler der Wirtschaftspolitik," *Der Handel* (Vienna, April 30, 1932).

Full reproduction under the original title in *Zentralblatt für die Papierindustrie*, Vol. L (Vienna, May 1, 1932), pp. 134-139.

6 "Zwangswirtschaft oder Wirtschaftsfreiheit?" *Wiener Wirtschafts-Woche*, Vol. I (October 12, 1932).

7 "Grosse oder kleine Einfuhrkontingente?" *Der Oesterreichische Volkswirt*, Vol. XXV (November 26, 1932), No. 9, pp. 208-210.

8 "Handelspolitik und Handelsbilanz," *Wiener Wirtschafts-Woche*, Vol. I (November 30, 1932).

9 "Kostensenkung oder Kreditausweitung?" *Der Oesterreichische Volkswirt*, Vol. XXV (May 13, 1933), No. 33, pp. 780-782.

10 "Indexwährung," *Der Oesterreichische Volkswirt*, Vol. XXV (July 15, 1933), No. 42, pp. 1011-1014.

11 "Nochmals Indexwährung," *Der Oesterreichische Volkswirt*, Vol. XXV (July 29, 1933), No. 44, pp. 1058-1061.

12 "Diagnose des Falls Amerika," *Der Oesterreichische Volkswirt*, Vol. XXVI (December 23, 1933), No. 13-14, pp. 314-318.

13 "Stop Inflation," *The Buffalo Banker*, Vol. VII (May 1937), No. 3, pp. 1-2.

14 "The Health of the U.S. Economy," *Keizai-jin [Homo Economicus]*, Vol. IX (August 1955), pp. 6-10.
    TRANSLATIONS
    Japanese translation under the title, "Beikoku Keizai Shindan: Marukisuto no Shit-subō" ["Diagnosis of the U.S. Economy: A Disappointment for Marxists"] *Keizai-jin [Homo Economicus]*, Vol. IX (August 1955), pp. 67-80.

15 "Economics as a Profession in Business and Government," *Keizai-jin [Homo Economicus]*, Vol. IX (September 1955), pp. 11-16.
    TRANSLATIONS
    Japanese translation under the title, "Kigyo oyobi Seifu niokeru Keisaisenmonka" [Economic Specialists in Business and Government], *Keizai-jin [Homo Economicus]*, Vol. IX (September 1955), pp. 81-84.

16 "Where Do We Go from Here? Reforming the International Monetary System" (with Desprès, Triffin, and Wallich), *Challenge, The Magazine of Economic Affairs* (November-December 1965), pp. 17-23, and 48.

17 "Readings in Methodology of the Social Sciences," *The American Economist*, Vol. IX (Summer 1965), pp. 58-62.

18 "Disagreements among the Like-minded," in *Farmand* (Anniversary Issue, February 1966), pp. 112-120.

19 "Soll die Bandbreite des DM-Wechselkurses verbreitert werden?" *Der Volkswirt*, Vol. 22, No. 26 (June 28, 1968), p. 24.

"International Monetary Arrangements: Weighting Priorities and Alternatives," *Financial Analysts Journal*, Vol. 24 (July-August 1968), pp. 25-30.

21 "Die Zukunft der internationalen Währungsordnung," *Alpbach Korrespondenz*, No. 29-30 (February 1970), pp. 49-52.

22 "Chishiki Sangyō no Mirai" [The Future of the Knowledge Industry], *Shukan Diamondo* (June 15, 1970), pp. 48-51

23 "Praktische Erfahrung und Theoretische Einsicht in Fragen der Währungspolitik," *Sparkasse*, 87 Jg. (June 1970), pp. 165-168.

24 "Kanzen Yunyū Jyūka ka En-Kiriage ga Hitsuyō" [Need for Complete Import Liberalization or Upvaluation of the Yen?] (Translated by Yasukichi Yasuba), *Nihon Keizai Kenkyu Centah Kaiho*, No. 130 (June 15, 1970), pp. 18-32.

25 "Zōdai Suru Kyōikuhi" [The Growth of Educational Costs] (Translated by Chiaki Nishiyama), Nihon Keizai Kenkyu Centah Kaiho, No. 132 (July 15, 1970), pp. 3-13.

26 "Chishiki Sangyō Jidai no Kadai" [Tasks in the Era of the Knowledge Industry], *Economisto* (July 14, 1970), pp. 72-81.

27 "Chishiki Sangyō ni Kansuru Mitsu no Shitsumon" [Three Questions Concerning the Knowledge Industry], *Manejimento Gaido* (August 1970), pp. 129-144.

28 "Readings in International Economics," *The American Economist*, Vol. XIV (Fall 1970), pp. 101-108.

29 " 'Higher' Education Is Not for Everyone, Says Princeton's Machlup," *The Chronicle of Higher Education*, Vol. V (November 16, 1970), p. 4.

30 "The Magicians and Their Rabbits," *The Morgan Guaranty Survey*, (May 1971), pp. 3-13.

REPRODUCTIONS

Full reproduction under the same title in *Essays in Honour of Giuseppe Ugo Papi* (Padova: Cedam, 1973), pp. 245-260.

TRANSLATIONS

Spanish translation under the title, "Los prestidigitadores y sus conejos," *Cemla Boletín Mensual*, Vol. XVII (July 1971), pp. 263-271.

Partial French translation, "Les magiciens et leurs lapins," *Banque*, No. 298 (July-August 1971), pp. 711-715.

Partial German translation, "Euro-Dollar Markt: Die Zauberkünstler und ihre Kaninchen," *Wirtschaftswoche, Der Volkswirt*, 25. Jahrgang, No. 39 (September 24, 1971), pp. 33-36.

31 "Rückkehr zur alten Parität hiesse für die Bundesrepublik Wiederanschluss an die Weltinflation," *Wirtschaftswoche, Der Volkswirt*, 25. Jahrgang, No. 30 (July 31, 1971), pp. 23-26.

32 "L'inflation mondiale," *Banque*, No. 302 (December 1971), pp. 1055-1070.

33 "Is Greater Flexibility of Exchange Rates a Handicap to Foreign Trade and Investment?" *Note Economiche del Monte dei Paschi di Siena*, Vol. IV, No. 6 (December 1971), pp. 7-14.

REPRODUCTIONS

"Is Greater Flexibility of Exchange Rates a Handicap to Foreign Trade and Investment?" *Economic Notes of Monte dei Paschi di Siena*, Vol. 1 (January-April 1972), pp. 40-45.

"Is Greater Flexibility of Exchange Rates a Handicap to Foreign Trade and Investment?" *SAIS Review*, Vol. 17, No. 3 (Spring 1973), pp. 3-7.

34 "The International Monetary System—Where Do We Go From Here?" *Looking Ahead*, Vol. 20, No. 1 (February 1972), pp. 1-4.

35 "The Role of Gold in the International Monetary System," *Economic Notes* (Monte dei Paschi di Siena), Vol. I, No. 2-3 (1972), pp. 7-18.

36 "Reform des Weltwährungssystems—ungelöste Probleme," *West-Ost Journal*, No. 1, 6. Jahrgang (March 1973), p. 3.

37 "Expériences Récentes de Changes Flottants," *Banque*, No. 334 (November 1974), pp. 1021-1022.

38 "Y aura-t-il une autre grande dépression?" *Bulletin de l'Institut Economique de Paris* (February 1975), pp. 1-4.

39 "Letters: On Myrdal and Hayek," *Challenge*, Vol. 18, No. 1 (March-April 1975), pp. 63-64.

40 "The Production and Distribution of Scientific and Technical Information," Association of Research Libraries, *Minutes of the Eighty-Sixth Meeting* (May 8-9, 1975), pp. 18-26: "Discussion," pp. 30, 31, 34.

41 "Why Initials Instead of First Names in ISI's Indexes?" *Current Contents*, Vol. 7, No. 32 (August 11, 1975), p. 5.

42 "They Don't Know They Are Sick," *Publishers Weekly*, Vol. 208, No. 13 (September 29, 1975), pp. 24-25.

43 "The Sick and the Healthy: Rejoinder to Mr. Rolo," *Publishers Weekly*, Vol. 208, No. 14 (October 4, 1975), p. 39.

44 "Will Gold Be Remonetized?" *Boletín Internacional* (Bilbao: Banco de Vizcaya), No. 1 (March 1975), pp. 2-7.

TRANSLATIONS

Spanish translation, "Va a ser 'remonetizado' el oro?" *Boletín Internacional* (Bilbao: Banco de Vizcaya), No. 1 (March 1976), pp. 2-8.

F. DISCUSSIONS, ABSTRACTS, REPORTS, CORRECTIONS, PREFACES

1 "The Period of Production: A Further Word," *Journal of Political Economy*, Vol. XLIII (1935), p. 608.

2 Abstract of Paper on "Security Regulation," *American Economic Review, Papers and Proceedings*, Vol. XXVIII (1958), p. 79.

3 Abstract of Paper on "The Practical Significance of the Theory of Monopolistic Competition," *American Economic Review, Papers and Proceedings*, Vol. XXIX (1939), pp. 100-101.

4 Discussion of "Differential Pricing," *Journal of Marketing*, Vol. VI (1942), pp. 184-185.

5 "Report of the Acting Managing Editor of the American Economic Review," *American Economic Review, Papers and Proceedings*, Vol. XXXV (1945), pp. 469-471.

6 Discussion of "International Cartels," *American Economic Review, Papers and Proceedings*, Vol. XXXVI (1946), pp. 770-774.

7 "Correction," *Review of Economics and Statistics*, Vol. XXX (1948), p. 230.

Discussion of "The Economics of Preparedness for War," *American Economic Review, Papers and Proceedings*, Vol. XXXIX (1949), pp. 379-383.

9 Comments on "The Inflationary Process," *Review of Economics and Statistics*, Vol. XXXI (1949), pp. 210-212.

TRANSLATIONS

French translation, "A Propos de la Hausse des Prix," *Economie Contemporaine* (March 1948), pp. 5-8.

10 Report on Grant No. 995 (1947) for "An Analysis of the Economics of the Patent System," American Philosophical Society, *Year Book 1948* (Philadelphia: 1949), pp. 180-182.

11 Report on Grant No. 1085 (1948) for "An Analysis of the Economics of Patents and Copyrights," American Philosophical Society, *Year Book 1949* (Philadelphia: 1950), pp. 199-200.

12 Abstract of Discussion of "Import Elasticities," *Econometrica*, Vol. XVIII (1950), p. 284.

13 Foreword to *The Economics of the International Patent System* by Edith Tilton Penrose (Baltimore, 1951), pp. vii-ix.

14 Introductory Remarks and Discussion of "Issues in Methodology," *American Economic Review, Papers and Proceedings*, Vol. XLII (1952), pp. 34, 69-73.

    REPRODUCTIONS

        Full reproduction under the title "Discussion" [of Issues in Methodology], in Paul A. Samuelson, "Economic Theory and Mathematics—An Appraisal," *Cowles Commission Papers*, New Series, No. 61 (1952).

15 Abstract of Discussion of "Issues in Methodology," *Econometrica*, Vol. XX (1952), pp. 485-486.

16 "An Obvious Error," *The American Scholar*, Vol. XXII (1953), p. 383.

17 Discussion of "Concepts of Competition and Monopoly," *American Economic Review, Papers and Proceedings*, Vol. XLV (1055), pp. 480-483.

    REPRODUCTIONS

        Partial reproduction under the title "Discussion of Competition: Static Models and Dynamic Aspects," in *Readings in Industrial Organization and Public Policy* (Homewood, Ill.' Irwin, 1958), Ch. 14, pp. 256-258.

18 "Comment" on [E. M. Bernstein's] "Strategic Factors in Balance of Payments Adjustment," *The Review of Economics and Statistics*, Vol. XL (1958), No. 1, Part 2, pp. 137-140.

19 "Report of the Committee on Academic Freedom and Civil Liberties," *American Economic Review, Papers and Proceedings*, Vol. XLVIII (1958), pp. 651-653.

20 "Report of the Committee on Academic Freedom and Civil Liberties," *American Economic Review, Papers and Proceedings*, Vol. XLIX (1959), pp. 649-650.

21 "Progress Report on the Salary Grading Program," *American Association of University Professors Bulletin*, Vol. 45 (1959), pp. 493-495.

22 "Medical School Salaries, 1958-59: A Report of Committee Z on the Economic Status of the Profession," *American Association of University Professors Bulletin*, Vol. 45 (1959), pp. 496-501.

23 "Can a Liberal Defend Government Interventions to Restrict the Freedom of Business to Restrict Business?" *The Mont Pélerin Quarterly*, Vol. I (1960), No. 4, pp. 9-17.

    TRANSLATIONS

        German translation, "Beschränkung der Freiheit oder der Wirtschaft," *Die Aussprache*, Vol. X (1960), pp. 229-235.

24 "Revision of Salary Grading Tables: An Announcement by Committee Z on the Economic Status of the Profession," *American Association of University Professors Bulletin*, Vol. 46 (1960), p. 18.

Discussion of "Relations between Economic Theory and Economic Policy," *American Economic Review, Papers and Proceedings*, Vol. L (1960), pp. 49-52.

26 "Report of the Committee on Academic Freedom and Civil Liberties," *American Economic Review, Papers and Proceedings*, Vol. L (1960), pp. 713-714.

27 "Revised Salary Grading Tables for 1960-61," *American Association of University Professors Bulletin*, Vol. 46 (1960), pp. 194-197.

28 "Letters: Patent System" [Reply to Hinkley, Fleming, Linnell, and Robertson], *Science*, Vol. 134 (September 8, 1961), p. 639.

29 "Niet hinken op twee gedachten. Antwoord van prof. dr. Fritz Machlup," *Burgerrecht, National Weekblad* (Amsterdam), Vol. 16 (September 23, 1961), p. 6.

30 "Some Economic Aspects of the United States Patent System," and "Discussion," in *The Role of Patents in Research*, Part II, *Proceedings* of a Symposium (Washington: National Academy of Sciences-National Research Council, 1962), pp. 30-31, 56-69, 74, 85-88, 103-107, 111-115, 158, 190, 196-203, 211-216.

31 "Problems of Methodology: Introductory Remarks," *American Economic Review, Papers and Proceedings*, Vol. LIII (1963), p. 204.

32 "The Francis A. Walker Award: Citation, December 27, on the Occasion of Conferring the Medal on Jacob Viner," *American Economic Review, Papers and Proceedings*, Vol. LIII (1963), p. 686.

33 "An Educated Guess," [Letters to Fortune], *Fortune*, Vol. LXXI (January 1965), p. 108.

34 "Comments" on "Preventing High School Dropouts," in Robert Dorfman, ed., *Measuring Benefits of Government Investments* (Washington: Brookings Institution, 1965), pp. 149-157.

35 "Discussion," in E.A.G. Robinson, ed., *Problems in Economic Development*, Proceedings of a Conference held by the International Economic Association (London: Macmillan, 1965), pp. 107-108.

36 "A Comprehensive Examination in Microeconomic Theory for Graduate Students," Appendix to C.E. Ferguson, *Microeconomic Theory* (Homewood, Ill.: Irwin, 1966), pp. 399-427. Second edition, 1969; third edition, 1972; fourth edition by C.E. Ferguson and J.P. Gould (Homewood, Ill.: Irwin, 1975), pp.485-518.

37 "Program of the Seventy-Eighth Annual Meeting of the American Economic Association," *American Economic Review, Papers and Proceedings*, Vol. LVI (1966), pp. ix-xii.

38 "Dicsussions," in E.A.G. Robinson and J.E. Vaizey, eds., *The Economics of Education*, Proceedings of a Conference held by the International Economic Association (London: Macmillan, 1966), pp. 609-611, 613, 615-616, 659, 693-695, 721, 745-746.

39 "Representation of Economic Interests: Dissenting Statement" (with Professor Robert Bierstedt), *American Association of University Professors Bulletin*, Vol. 52 (June 1966), pp. 232-233.

40 "Free Market Economy—Today and Tomorrow" (with I. Nakayama and G. Haberler), *The Oriental Economist*, Vol. XXXIV (October 1966), pp. 612-619.

TRANSLATIONS

Japanese translation under the title "Jiyu-shijo Keizai no Kyo to Asu" [The Free Market Economy, Today and Tomorrow] (with G. Haberler and I. Nakayama), *Shukan Toyo-Keizai*, Special Issue, September 27, 1966, pp. 4-13.

41 "Report of Representative to the International Economic Association," *American Economic Review, Papers and Proceedings*, Vol. LCIII (May 1968), p. 728.

42 "Report of Representative to the International Economic Association," *American Economic Review, Papers and Proceedings*, Vol. LIX (May 1969), p. 604.

43 "Ludwig von Mises: Distinguished Fellow, 1969," [Citation on the Occasion of Conferring the Award] *American Economic Review*, Vol. LIX (September 1969), frontispiece.

44 "Report of Representative to the International Economic Association," *American Economic Review, Papers and Proceedings*, Vol. LX (May 1970), p. 523.

45 "Alexander Gerschenkron: Distinguished Fellow, 1970," [Citation on the Occasion of Conferring the Award], *American Economic Review*, Vol. LX (June 1970), frontispiece.

46 "Report of Representative to the International Economic Association," *American Economic Review, Papers and Proceedings*, Vol. LXI (May 1971), p. 511.

47 "Geleitwort," in Gerhard Prosi, *Ökonomische Theorie des Buches* (Düsseldorf: Bertelsmann, 1971), pp. 9-12.

48 "International Monetary Problems," in *The International Economic Association 1968-1971, Three Years Report* (Paris: 1971), pp. 21-22.

49 "Diskussion" des Referats von T.W. Hutchison, *Zeitschrift für Nationalökonomie*, Vol. 32 (No. 1, 1972), pp. 117-119.

50 "Report of Representative to the International Economic Association," *American Economic Review, Papers and Proceedings*, Vol. LXIII (May 1972), pp. 510-511.

51 "Conversations: Challenge and Change" [with John Coleman *et al.*], in Harvey T. Stephens, ed. (Philadelphia: Ara-Slater Services, 1972), pp. 1-28.

52 "Foreword" to The German Council of Economic Experts, *Toward a New Basis for International Monetary Policy*, Princeton Studies in International Finance No. 31 (Princeton: International Finance Section, 1972), pp. v-viii.

53 Discussion of J.O.N. Perkins' paper on "Balance of Payments Effects of Direct Investment in the Pacific Area," in Peter Drysdale, ed., *Direct Foreign Investment in Asia and the Pacific* (Canberra: Australian National University Press, 1972), Ch. 13, pp. 308-311.

54 Answers to Questionnaire, in *Project on 'Welfare and Inflation'* (Tokyo: Tokyo Colloquium, December 1972), pp. 3, 6, 9, 12, 14, 17, 20, and 22.

55 "Euro-Dollars, Once Again: A Correction," *Banca Nazionale del Lavoro Quarterly Review*, No. 103 (December 1972), p. 440.

56 "Let Us Forget Gold" [An interview], *Acta Oeconomica* (Akadémiai Kiadó, Budapest), Vol. 9 (2) (1972), pp. 195-198.

57 "Report of Representative to the International Economic Association," *American Economic Review, Papers and Proceedings*, Vol. LXIII (May 1973), pp. 516-517.

58 "Discussion of the Paper by Professor Sen," in B.R. Williams, ed., *Science and Technology in Economic Growth* (London: Macmillan, 1973), pp. 405-408, 413-414.

59 "Comments by Fritz Machlup" [on the paper by Walter Salant], in Lawrence B. Krause and Walter S. Salant, eds., *European Monetary Unification and Its Meaning for the United States* (Washington: Brookings Institution, 1973), pp. 247-249.

60 "Diskussionsbeiträge," in *Zur Neuordnung des internationalen Währungssystems*, Heft 20, Beihefte der Konjunkturpolitik (Berlin: Duncker & Humblot, 1973), pp. 31, 33, 37, 44-50, 54, 56, 84, 88-93, 96, 112, 113, 137.

61 "Währungsreform—Welt der Illusionen" [Interview], *Wirtschaftsdienst*, 54. Jahrgang, No. 2 (February 1974), pp. 70-72.

TRANSLATIONS

English translation, "Currency Reform—A Scenario of Illusions" [An Interview], *Intereconomics*, No. 2 (Hamburg: February 1974), pp. 38-40.

62 "Would the Nation Be Better Off If Fewer People Went to College?" (with Colette Manoil, Paul Kurtz *et al.*), *The Advocates* (WGBH, Boston, Jan. 3, 1974), pp. 3-8.

63 "Report of Representative to the International Economic Association," *American Economic Review, Papers and Proceedings*, Vol. LXIV (May 1974), pp. 516-517.

64 "In Memoriam: Ludwig von Mises, 1881-1973," *American Economic Review*, Vol. LXIV (June 1974), p. 518.

65 "Proxies and Dummies" [Miscellany], *Journal of Political Economy*, Vol. 82 (July-August 1974), p. 892.

66 "Discussion of the Paper by H. Uzawa," in J. Rothenberg and Ian G. Heggie, eds., *The Management of Water Quality and the Environment*, Proceedings of a Conference held by the IEA at Lyngby, Denmark (London: Macmillan, 1974), pp. 18-19.

67 "Report of Representative to the International Economic Association," *American Economic Review, Papers and Proceedings*, Vol. 65 (May 1975), pp. 509-510.

68 "His Work Lives," in Arthur Shenfield and Joaquin Reig, eds., *Tribute to Mises* (London: Mont Pelerin Society, 1975), pp. 10-16.

TRANSLATIONS
German translation under the title, "Erinnerungen an Ludwig von Mises," *Monatshefte für freiheitliche Wirtschaftspolitik*, Vol. 21 (November-December 1975), pp. 413-416.

69 "General Discussion" of "The Political Economy of Franchise in the Welfare State" and of "Corporate Altruism and Individualistic Methodology," in Richard T. Seldon, ed., *Capitalism and Freedom: Problems and Prospects*, Proceedings of a Conference in Honor of Milton Friedman (Charlottesville: University Press of Virginia, 1975), pp. 67-88, 147-148, 154-155.

70 Answers to Questionnaire, in Kinhide Mushakoji, ed., *The Views on a New International Order* (Tokyo: The Tokyo Colloquium, September 1975), pp. 15-16, 34, 54, 69, 88, 103, 114, and 130.

71 "Discussion of the Paper by Professor Malinvaud"; "Discussion of the Paper by Professor Aganbegyan"; "Discussion of the Paper by Professor Stojanović"; "Discussion of the Papers by Professor Mansfield and M. Aujac"; "Discussion of the Papers by Dr. Grove and Mr. Horimoto"; in Tigran S. Khachaturov, ed., *Methods of Long-Term Planning and Forecasting*, Proceedings of a Conference held by the International Economic Association at Moscow (London: Macmillan, 1976), pp. 41, 44, 85-86, 168-169, 331-332, 362, and 454.

TRANSLATIONS
Russian translation in T.S. Khachaturov, ed., *Dolgospotchnoye Planirovanyie i Prognosirovanyie* (Moscow: Progress, 1975), pp. 351, 367, 371, 385, 430, 471, 477, 509, and 515.

72 "Discussion of the Paper by . . . Professor Stone," in Ansley J. Coale, ed., *Economic Factors in Population Growth*, Proceedings of a Conference held by the International Economic Association at Valescure, France (London: Macmillan, 1976), pp. 582-585.

73 "Report of Representative to the International Economic Association," *American Economic Review, Papers and Proceedings*, Vol. 66 (May 1976), pp. 520-521.

74 "Report of the Committee on U.S.-Soviet Exchanges," *American Economic Review, Papers and Proceedings*, Vol. 66 (May 1976), pp. 524-528.

G. OFFICIAL REPORTS, MEMORANDA, TESTIMONIES IN PUBLIC DOCUMENTS

1 "La Crise Monétaire et Financière," Societé des Nations, Comité Economique, Hors Serie 51, June 2, 1932.

2 "Réglementation des Devises en Autriche," Societé des Nations, F/Tres./(1932).

3 *Annual Report*, Fiscal Year Ending June 30, 1944, *Office of Alien Property Custodian* (Washington: 1945) [with reserach staff].

4 "Statement of the Honorable James E. Markham, Alien Property Custodian," *Elimination of German Resources for War*, Hearings before a Subcommittee of the Committee on Military Affairs, U.S. Senate, 79th Congress, First Session, Part 4 (Washington: 1945), pp. 580-614 [with research staff].

5 "Answers Submitted by the Alien Property Custodian to Questions of Subcommittee on War Mobilization," *Elimination of German Resources for War*, Hearings before a Subcommittee of the Committee on Military Affairs, U.S. Senate, 79th Congress, First Session, Part 5 (Washington: 1945), pp. 887-896 [with research staff].

6 "Statements of Francis J. McNamara, Deputy Alien Property Custodian; . . . and F. Machlup, Chief, Division of Research and Statistics." *National War Agencies Appropriation Bill for 1946*, Hearings before a Subcommittee of the Committee on Appropriations, United States Senate, 79th Contress, First Session (Washington: 1945), pp. 198-215.

7 "Statements of James E. Markham, Alien Property Custodian, . . . F. Machlup, Chief, Division of Research and Statistics," *First Supplemental Surplus Appropriation*

Rescission Bill, 1946, Hearings before the Subcommittee of the Committee on Appropriations, United States Senate, 79th Congress, First Session (Washington: 1945), pp. 293-311.

8 "Statements of James E. Markham, Custodian; . . . F. Machlup, Chief, Division of Research and Statistics . . . ." *First Deficiency Appropriation Bill for 1946*, Hearings before the Subcommittee of the Committee on Appropriations, House of Representatives, 79th Congress, First Session (Washington: 1945), pp. 589-603.

9 *Annual Report*, Fiscal Year Ending June 30, 1945, *Office of Alien Property Custodian* (Washington: 1946) [with research staff].

10 "Statements of James E. Markham, Alien Property Custodian; . . . Fritz Machlup, Chief of Division of Research and Statistics . . .," *Third Deficiency Appropriation Bill for 1946*, Hearings before the Subcommittee of the Committee on Appropriations, House of Representatives, 79th Congress, Second Session (Washington: 1946), pp. 113-134.

11 "Statement of Dr. Fritz Machlup, Professor of Political Economy, The Johns Hopkins University," *Small Business Objections on Basing Point Legislation, Particularly S. 1008*, Hearings before the Select Committee on Small Business, House of Representatives, 81st Congress, First Session (Washington: 1949), pp. 212-213.

12 "Statement of Fritz Machlup, Professor of Political Economy of the Johns Hopkins University," *Study of Monopoly Power*, Hearings before Subcommittee on Study of Monopoly Power of the Committee on the Judiciary, House of Representatives, 31st Congress, First Session [Serial No. 14, Part 2-A] (Washington: 1950), pp. 500-522.

13 "Replies by Economists" to Questions for the Use of the Subcommittee on General Credit Control and Debt Management, *Monetary Policy and the Management of the Public Debt*, Joint Committee on the Economic Report, Part 2 (Washington: 1952), pp. 1025-1026, 1053, 1072, 1086, 1095, 1106.

14 "Statement of Fritz Machlup, Professor of Political Economy, Johns Hopkins University" on Fair Trade Practices, *Discount-House Operations*, Hearings before a Subcommittee of the Select Committee on Small Business, United States Senate, 85th Congress, Second Session (Washington: 1958), pp. 170-186.

REPRODUCTIONS

Partial reproduction under the title "Resale Price Maintenance," in S. George Walters, Max D. Snider, and Morris L. Sweet, eds., *Readings in Marketing* (Cincinnati: South-Western Publishing Co., 1962), Ch. 29, pp. 309-319.

Partial reproduction under the title "Resale Price Maintenance," in Raymond E. Glos and Harold A. Baker, eds., *Student Supplement for Introduction to Business*, 5th ed. (Cincinnati: South-Western Publishing Co., 1963), pp. 44-48.

Partial reproduction under the title "Resale Price Maintenance," in J. H. Westing and Gerald Albaum, eds., *Modern Marketing Thought* (New York: Macmillan, 1964), Ch. 27, pp. 136-143.

Partial reproduction under the title "Resale Price Maintenance," in S. George Walters, Morris L. Sweet, and Max D. Snider, eds., *Marketing Management Viewpoints*, 2nd ed. (Cincinnati: South-Western Publishing Co., 1970), Ch. 6, pp. 57-67.

15 "Statement of Fritz Machlup, Professor of Political Economy, The Johns Hopkins University," *Fair Trade*, Hearings before a Subcommittee of the Committee on Interstate and Foreign Commerce, House of Representatives, 85th Congress, Second Session, on H.R. 10527 and other Bills to Amend the Federal Trade Commission Act, so as to equalize rights in the distribution of identified merchandise (Washington: 1958), pp. 669-672.

16 "Testimony of Fritz Machlup, Professor of Political Economy, The Johns Hopkins University," *Fair Trade*, Hearings before the Committee on Interstate and Foreign Commerce, United States Senate, 85th Congress, Second Session (Washington: 1958), pp. 63-68, 92-98.

17 "Statement of Fritz Machlup, Professor of Political Economy, Johns Hopkins University," *Administered Prices*, Hearings before the Subcommittee on Antitrust and Monopoly of the Committee on the Judiciary, United States Senate, 86th Congress, First Session, Part 10, (Washington:1959), pp. 4950-4973.

18 "Statement of Fritz Machlup, The Johns Hopkins University," *Employment, Growth, and Price Levels*, Hearings before the Joint Economic Committee, Congress of the United States, 86th Congress, First Session, Part 9A, (Washington: 1959), pp. 2819-2861.

REPRODUCTIONS

Full reproduction under the title "Employment, Growth, and a Stable Price Level," in Lawrence S. Ritter, ed., *Money and Economic Activity* (Boston: Houghton Mifflin, 1961), Ch. 52, pp. 375-388.

19 "Statement of Dr. Fritz Machlup, Professor of Economics, Princeton University," *Drug Industry Antitrust Act*, Hearings before the Subcommittee on Antitrust and Monopoly of the Committee on the Judiciary, United States Senate, 37th Congress, First Session, Part 3, Patent Provisions (Washington: 1962), pp. 1361-1390.

20 "Proposals for Reform of the International Monetary System," in *Factors Affecting the United States Balance of Payments*, materials prepared for the Subcommittee on International Exchange and Payments of the Joint Economic Committee, Congress of the United States, 87th Congress, 2nd Session, Part 3, The International Monetary System: Defects and Remedies (Washington: 1962), pp. 209-237.

21 "Statement of Dr. Fritz Machlup, Professor of Economics and Finance and Director of the International Finance Section, Princeton University," *Outlook for United States*

Balance of Payments, Hearings before the Subcommittee on International Exchange and Payments of the Joint Economic Committee, Congress of the United States, 87th Congress, 2nd Session, December 12, 13, and 14, 1962 (Washington: 1963), pp. 198-205, 227-230, 232, 234, 237-238.

REPRODUCTIONS

Partial reproduction under the title "Reform of the International Monetary System," in Herbert G. Grubel, ed., *World Monetary Reform* (Stanford, Cal.: Stanford University Press, 1963), Ch. 13, pp. 253-260.

Partial reproduction under the title "Three Experts on the Reform Plans," in Herbert G. Grubel, ed., *World Monetary Reform* (Stanford, Cal.: Stanford University Press, 1963), Ch. 22, pp. 394-396, 398, 401-403.

22 "Statement by Fritz Machlup," in *The United States Balance of Payments*, Statements on The Brookings Institution Study, "The United States Balance of Payments in 1968," materials submitted to the Joint Economic Committee, Congress of the United States, 88th Congress, 1st Session (Washington: 1963), pp. 301-308.

23 "Statement of Dr. Fritz Machlup," in *Balance of Payments—1965*, Hearings before a Subcommittee of the Committee on Banking and Currency, United States Senate, 89th Congress, 1st Session (Washington: 1965), pp. 340-360.

REPRODUCTIONS

Full reproduction under the title "Professor Machlup Attacks Administration's Program to Curb Capital Outflows," *Congressional Record, House*, Extension of Remarks of Mr. Curtis in the House of Representatives, April 6, 1965, pp. 6931-6934.

24 "Fritz Machlup, Princeton University," Camera dei Deputati, *Atti della Commissione Parlamentare di Inchiesta sui Limiti Posti alla Concorrenza nel Campo Economico*, Vol. IX. Opinioni di Esperti Stranieri sui Problemi della Concorrenza (Roma: 1965), pp. 84-86.

25 "International Agreements and Unilateral Actions: Statement by Fritz Machlup," in *Contingency Planning for U.S. International Monetary Policy*, Statements by Private Economists Submitted to the Subcommittee on International Exchange and Payments of the Joint Economic Committee, Congress of the United States, 89th Congress, 2nd Session (Washington: 1966), pp. 73-82.

TRANSLATIONS

Italian translation under the title "La riforma del sistema monetario internationale: accordi multilaterali e iniziative unilaterali," *Bancaria*, Vol. XXIII (July 1967), pp. 803-810.

26 "Statement of Fritz Machlup, Walker Professor of Economics and International Finance, Princeton University," in *The 1968 Economic Report of the President*, Hearings before the Joint Economic Committee, Congress of the United States, 90th Congress, 2nd Session (Washington: 1968), pp. 394-416, 432-434, 437, 442, 447-451, 453-454, 458-463.

REPRODUCTIONS
>   Partial reproduction under the title "The Need for Confidence," *Princeton Business Today* (Spring 1968), pp. 19-24.
>   Partial reproduction under the title "The Adjustment Problem and the Balance of Payments Policy of the United States," in Lawrence H. Officer and Thomas D. Willett, eds., *The International Monetary System* (Englewood Cliffs, N.J.: Prentice-Hall, 1969), pp. 92-106.

27   "Statement of Fritz Machlup, Professor of Economics, Princeton University," in *Next Steps in International Monetary Reform*, Hearings before the Subcommittee on International Exchange and Payments of the Joint Economic Committee, Congress of the United States, 90th Congress, 2nd Session (Washington: 1968), pp. 56-91, 125-128, 136-138.

28   "Statement of Fritz Machlup, Professor, Princeton University," in *The Proposed IMF Quota Increase and Its Implications for the Two-Tier Gold Market*, Hearings before the Subcommittee on International Exchange and Payments of the Joint Economic Committee, Congress of the United States, 91st Congress, 1st Session (Washington: 1970), pp. 19, 21-22, 24, 25-27, 28-31, 33, 36, 51-54.

29   *Effects of Innovation on Demand for and Earnings of Productive Factors* [with George Bitros and Kenneth W. Leeson], Vol. 1, Executive Summary and Analytical Report, vi and 123 pages; Vol. II, Abstracts and Indexing Systems, 307 pages (Washington: National Technical Information Service, U.S. Department of Commerce, 1974).

30   "Statement of Fritz Machlup, Professor of Economics, New York University," in *The IMF Gold Agreement*, Hearing before the Subcommittee on International Economics of the Joint Economic Committee, Congress of the United States, 94th Congress, 1st Session (Washington: 1976), pp. 30-41, 54-58, 60, 63-64.

H. BOOK REVIEWS (excl. review articles)

1 Dierschke und Möller, *Die Notenbanken der Welt* (Berlin, 1926), Vol. I: xii and 588 pages, Vol. II: vii and 652 pages; in *Mitteilungen des Verbandes österreichischer Banken und Bankiers*, Vol. IX (1927), p. 29.

2 Wilhelm Andreae, *Bausteine zu einer universalistischen Steuerlehre* (Jena, 1927), 140 pages; in *Der Oesterreichische Volkswirt*, Vol. II (1927), p. 273.

3 Ludwig von Mises, *Geldwertstabilisierung und Konjunkturpolitik* (Jena, 1928), 84 pages; in *Münchner Telegramm Zeitung* (July 30, 1928, No. 145).

4 R. Kuczynski, *Deutsche Anleihen im Ausland 1924 bis 1927* (Berlin, 1928), 65 pages; in *Mitteilungen des Verbandes österreichischer Banken und Bankiers*, Vol. XI (1929), p. 29.

5 Richard Kerschagl, ed., *Die österreichischen Währungs- und Notenbankgesetze* (Wien, 1929), xviii and 315 pages; in *Zentralblatt für die Juristische Praxis*, Vol. XLVII (1929), p. 697.

6 Erich Egner, *Versuch einer autonomen Lehre der Währungspolitik* (Leipzig, 1928), vii and 232 pages; in *Zeitschrift für Nationalökonomie*, Vol. I (1929), pp. 475-478.

7 Henry Behnsen und Werner Genzmer, *Unzureichende Abschreibungen, Scheingewinne und Substanzverluste* (Leipzig, 1929), vii and 87 pages; in *Zeitschrift für Nationalökonomie*, Vol. I (1930), p. 637.

8 H. Oswalt, *Grundzüge der Geldtheorie* (Jena, 1929), 78 pages; in *Mitteilungen des Verbandes österreichischer Banken und Bankiers*, Vol. XII (1930), pp. 161-162.

9 Martha Stephanie Braun, *Theorie der staatlichen Wirtschaftspolitik* (Leipzig und Wien, 1929), ix and 234 pages; in *Mitteilungen des Verbandes österreichischer Banken und Bankiers*, Vol. XII (1930), pp. 162-163.

10 Carl Landauer, *Das Wesen der Wirtschaft* (Berlin, 1928), 121 pages; in *Zeitschrift für Nationalökonomie*, Vol. II (1930), pp. 134-139.

11 Gustav W. Silverstolpe, *Nationalökonomie für Alle* (Leipzig, 1929), 200 pages; in *Zeitschrift für Nationalökonomie*, Vol. II (1930), pp. 134-139.

12 Lisel Enderlen, *Versuch einer Synthese zwischen Metallismus und Nominalismus* (Berlin and Leipzig, 1929), 138 pages; in *Zeitschrift für Nationalökonomie*, Vol. II (1930), p. 288.

13 Julius Domany, *Die Golddevisen-Währung* (Berlin, 1931), 36 pages; in *Zeitschrift für Nationalökonomie*, Vol. II (1931), pp. 823-824.

14 Heinrich Göppert, *Börse und Publikum* (Berlin, 1930), 31 pages; in *Zeitschrift für Nationalökonomie*, Vol. II (1931), p. 850.

15 Fritz Spohn, *Abschreibungsnachweis an den Anlagewerten* (Wien, 1930), 25 pages; in *Zeitschrift für Nationalökonomie*, Vol. III (1931), pp. 155-156.

16 Erich Welter, *Die Ursache des Kapitalmangels in Deutschland* (Tübingen, 1931), xi and 221 pages; in *Der Oesterreichische Volkswirt*, Vol. XXIV (1931), No. 11.

17 Dennis H. Robertson, *Economic Fragments* (London, 1931), viii and 267 pages; in *Zeitschrift für Nationalökonomie*, Vol. III (1931), pp. 272-275.

18 W. Prion, *Die Preisbildung an der Wertpapierbörse* (München and Leipzig, 1929), xi and 250 pages; in *Zeitschrift für Nationalökonomie*, Vol. III (1932), pp. 469-472.

19 Karl Meithner, *Die Preisbildung an der Effektenbörse* (Wien, 1930), vi and 158 pages; in *Zeitschrift für Nationalökonomie*, Vol. III (1932), pp. 469-472.

20 Franz Gutmann, *Auslandskredite und Auslandsverschuldung* (Berlin, 1930), 45 pages; in *Zeitschrift für Nationalökonomie*, Vol. III (1932), p. 642.

21 John Maynard Keynes, *A Treatise on Money* (London, 1930), Vol. I:363 pp.; Vol. II:424 pp; German edition *Vom Gelde* (München and Leipzig, 1932), xx and 635 pages; in *Der Oesterreichische Volkswirt*, Vol. XXIV (1932), No. 40, pp. 967-970.

22 Wilhelm Hagemann, *Das Verhältnis der deutschen Grossbanken zur Industrie* (Berlin, 1931), 200 pages; in *Archiv für Sozialwissenschaft und Sozialpolitik*, Vol. LXVIII (1932), pp. 242-243.

23 Junichi Ohno, *Sozialökonomische Theorie des Geldes* (Leipzig, 1931), ix and 130 pages; in *Zeitschrift für Nationalökonomie*, Vol. IV (1932), pp. 133-135.

24 Jakob Conrad, *Die Selbstfinanzierung der Unternehmung* (Berlin and Wien, 1931), 62 pages; in *Archiv für Sozialwissenschaft und Sozialpolitik*, Vol. LXVIII (1933), pp. 504-505.

25 Elemer Hantos, *Die Kooperation der Notenbanken als Mittel zur Rationalisierung der Weltwirtschaft* (Tübingen, 1951), viii and 116 pages; in *Zeitschrift für Nationalökonomie*, Vol. IV (1933), p. 232.

26 Xenophon Zolotas, *L'étalon-or en théorie et en pratique* (Paris, 1933), 266 Pages: in *Mitteilungen des Verbandes österreichischer Banken und Bankiers*, Vol. XV (1933), pp. 111-112.

27 Alfred Tismer, *Grenzen der Diskontpolitik* (München and Leipzig, 1932), 160 pages; in *Archiv für Sozialwissenschaft und Sozialpolitik*, Vol. LXIX (1933), pp. 243-250.

28 William T. Foster and Waddill Catchings, *Progress and Plenty* (Boston and New York, 1930), xiii and 214 pages; in *Zeitschrift für Nationalökonomie*, Vol. IV (1933), pp. 537-538.

29 Bernhard Harms, ed., *Kapital und Kapitalismus* (Berlin, 1931), Vol. I, viii and 513 pages; Vol. II, viii and 511 pages; in *Archiv für Sozialwissenschaft und Sozialpolitik*, Vol. LXIX (1933), pp. 745-748.

30 Paul Mori, *Das Geld* (Bern-Berlin, 1930), 117 pages; in *Zeitschrift für Nationalökonomie*, Vol. V (1934), p. 253.

31 Alfred Müller-Armack, *Entwicklungsgesetze des Kapitalismus* (Berlin, 1932), vi and 218 pages; in *Deutsche Literaturzeitung*, 1934, No. 39, pp. 1861-1866.

32 Werner Brylewski, *Die verschiedenen Vorstellungsinhalte des Begriffes Kapital* (Stuttgart and Berlin, 1933), 203 pages; in *The Journal of Political Economy*, Vol. XLIII (1935), p. 141.

33 R. F. Fowler, *The Depreciation of Capital* (London, 1934), xii and 143 pages; in *Economica*, New Series, Vol. II (1935), pp. 106-109.

34 Hans Busse, *Die Golddevisenwährung* (Berlin, 1932), 134 pages; in *Zeitschrift für Nationalökonomie*, Vol. VI (1935), pp. 108-111.

35 Julius Domany, *Die Zukunft der Goldwährung* (Berlin, 1932), 32 pages; in *Zeitschrift für Nationalökonomie*, Vol. VI (1935), pp. 108-111.

36 Karl Muhs, *Die Entthronung des Goldes* (Berlin, 1932), 52 pages; in *Zeitschrift für Nationalökonomie*, Vol. VI (1935), pp. 108-111.

37 Howard S. Ellis, *German Monetary Theory, 1905-1933* (Cambridge, Mass., 1934), xv and 462 pages; in *The Journal of Political Economy*, Vol. XLIII (1935), pp. 392-396.

38 Richard von Strigl, *Kapital und Produktion* (Wien, 1934), x and 247 pages; in *Economica*, New Series, Vol. II (1935), pp. 332-336.

39 Walter Eucken, *Kapitaltheoretische Untersuchungen* (Jena, 1934), vi and 194 pages; in *Economica*, New Series, Vol. II (1935), pp. 332-336.

40 Adolph A. Berle, Jr., and Victoria J. Pederson, *Liquid Claims and National Wealth* (New York, 1934), xvi and 248 pages; in *Zeitschrift für Nationalökonomie*, Vol. VIII (1937), pp. 671-673.

41 Richard von Strigl, *Einführung in die Grundlagen der Nationalökonomie* (Wien, 1937), viii and 223 pages; in *American Economic Review*, Vol. XXVIII (1938), pp. 325-326.

42 Alvin H. Hansen, *Full Recovery or Stagnation?* (New York, 1938), 350 pages; in *Journal of the American Statistical Association,* Vol. XXXIV (1939), pp. 186-188.

43 Valentin F. Wagner, *Geschichte der Kredittheorien* (Wien, 1937), xvi and 521 pages; in *American Economic Review*, Vol. XXIX (1939), pp. 808-810.

44 E. A. G. Robinson, *Monopoly* (London, 1941), xvi and 298 pages; in *Economica*, New Series, Vol. IX (1942), pp. 207-211.

45 George E. Folk, *Patents and Industrial Progress* (New York, 1942), xiii and 393 pages; in *American Economic Review*, Vol. XXXII (1942), p. 907.

46 George J. Stigler, *The Theory of Competitive Price* (New York, 1942), vii and 197 pages; in *The Journal of Political Economy*, Vol. LI (1942), pp. 263-265.

47 *Economic Research and the Development of Economic Science and Public Policy.* National Bureau of Economic Research (New York, 1946), ix and 198 pages; in *The Journal of Political Economy,* Vol. LVI (1948), pp. 263-265.

48 Harold G. Fox, *Monopolies and Patents: A Study of the History and Future of the Patent Monopoly* (Toronto, 1947), xxv and 388 pages; in *The Journal of Economic History*, Vol. VIII (1948), pp. 215-217.

49 Heinrich von Stackelberg, *Grundlagen der Theoretischen Volkswirtschaftslehre* (Bern, 1948), xvi and 368 pages; in *The Southern Economic Journal*, Vol. XV (1949), pp. 341-342.

50 Erich Schneider, *Einführung in die Wirtschaftstheorie, I. Teil: Theorie des Wirtschaftskreislaufs* (Tübingen, 1947), vi and 82 pages; in *American Economic Review*, Vol. XXXIX (1949), pp. 989-991.

51 Erich Schneider, *Einführung in die Wirtschaftstheorie, II. Teil: Wirtschaftspläne und wirtschaftliches Gleichgewicht in der Verkehrswirtschaft* (Tübingen, 1949), vii and 334 pages; in *American Economic Review*, Vol. XL (1950), pp. 656-658.

52 Andreas Paulsen, *Neue Wirtschaftslehre* (Berlin and Frankfurt, 1952), ix and 272 pages; in *The Southern Economic Journal*, Vol. XIX (1952), pp. 254-255.

53 Erich Schneider, *Einführung in die Wirtschaftstheorie, III. Teil: Geld, Kredit, Volkseinkommen und Beschäftigung* (Tübingen, 1952), vi and 220 pages; in *American Economic Review*, Vol. XLIII (1953), pp. 398-401.

54 Joseph A. Schumpeter, *Aufsätze zur ökonomischen Theorie* (Tübingen, 1952), 608 pages; in *Econometrica*, Vol. XXI (1956), pp. 498-500.

55 Roy F. Harrod, *Economic Essays* (London, 1952), xiii and 301 pages; in *Kyklos* Vol. VI (1953), pp. 174-175.

56 Ludwig von Mises, *The Theory of Money and Credit*. Revised (New Haven, 1953), 493 pages; in *Econometrica*, Vol. XXII (1954), pp. 401-402.

57 Arthur F. Burns, *The Frontiers of Economic Knowledge* (published for the National Bureau of Economic Research. Princeton, 1954), ix and 367 pages; in *The Southern Economic Journal*, Vol. XXI (1954), pp. 208-210.

58 John Madge, *The Tools of Social Science* (New York, 1953), x and 308 pages; in *American Economic Review*, Vol. XLV (1955), pp. 394-395.

59 Arnold M. Rose, *Theory and Method in the Social Sciences* (Minneapolis, 1954), xii and 351 pages; in *American Economic Review*, Vol. XLV (1955), pp. 395.

60 Hans L. Zetterberg, *On Theory and Verification in Sociology* (New York, 1954), 78 pages; in *American Economic Review*, Vol. XLV (1955), pp. 395-396.

61 Gunnar Myrdal, *The Political Element in the Development of Economic Theory*, translated by Paul Streeten, (Cambridge, 1954), xvii and 248 pages; in *American Economic Review*, Vol. XLV (1955), pp. 948-952.

62 John Neville Keynes, *The Scope and Method of Political Economy* (Reprint of 4th ed., New York, 1955), xiv and 382 pages; in *The Southern Economic Journal*, Vol. XXIII (1957), pp. 330-332.

63 Gottfried Bombach, ed., *Stabile Preise in wachsender Wirtschaft: Das Inflationsproblem. Erich Schneider zum 60. Geburtstag* (Tübingen, 1960), x and 274 pages; in *American Economic Review*, Vol. LI (1961), pp. 1058-1062.

64 Johan Åkerman, *Theory of Industrialism—Causal Analysis and Economic Plans* (Lund, 1960), 332 pages; in *Zeitschrift für Nationalökonomie*, Vol. XXII (1963), pp. 420-423.

65 Herbert G. Grubel, ed., *World Monetary Reform: Plans and Issues* (Stanford, 1963), xiii and 446 pages; in *American Economic Review*, Vol. LIV (1964), pp. 828-829.

Index